The Globe

The School

S0-BNA-658

WITHDRAWN

THE MAGIC CURTAIN

THE AUTHOR.

The
MAGIC
CURTAIN

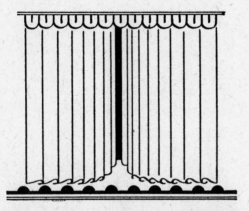

THE STORY OF A LIFE IN TWO
FIELDS, THEATRE AND INVENTION
BY THE FOUNDER OF THE THEATRE GUILD

Lawrence Langner

E · P · DUTTON & COMPANY, INC., NEW YORK · 1951
A STORY PRESS BOOK

272041

COPYRIGHT, 1951
BY LAWRENCE LANGNER

All rights reserved

PRINTED IN THE U.S.A.

FIRST EDITION

No part of this book may be reproduced in any form without permission in writing from the publisher, except by a reviewer who wishes to quote brief passages in connection with a review written for inclusion in magazine or newspaper or radio broadcast.

For photo credits see List of Illustrations, pages ix and x.

Parts of Chapter XXXI of this book have already been published in *The New York Times,* and part of Chapter XVI in *The Saturday Review of Literature.*

PN
2295
T5
L3

AMERICAN BOOK—KNICKERBOCKER PRESS, INC., NEW YORK

To

ARMINA

Contents

	List of Illustrations	ix
	Preface	xi
I.	Childhood	1
II.	Boyhood	12
III.	I Go to Work	18
IV.	The Technical Assistant	28
V.	Prelude to Departure	34
VI.	A New World	42
VII.	Prelude to Independence	56
VIII.	Lower Broadway and Greenwich Village	65
IX.	Chicago, Berlin and World War I	80
X.	The Washington Square Players	90
XI.	A Village Wooing and Other Matters	105
XII.	A Theatre Is Born	114
XIII.	Shaw and *Back to Methuselah*	130
XIV.	I Visit the Playwrights	142
XV.	The Theatre Guild Grows	157
XVI.	Shaw, *Saint Joan* and Stresa	174
XVII.	Art and the Prohibition Era	192

XVIII. The Guild Theatre and The Acting Company   211

XIX. O'Neill and *Strange Interlude*   228

XX. Trouble Ahead   243

XXI. Inner Tensions and Contact with Youth   264

XXII. O'Neill, *Ah, Wilderness!* and *Days Without End*   275

XXIII. Shaw and His American Visit   288

XXIV. The Westport Country Playhouse   296

XXV. The New Regime   316

XXVI. Double Life   342

XXVII. The National Inventors Council   353

XXVIII. *Oklahoma!*   368

XXIX. Tallulah, *Carousel* and the Lunts   384

XXX. O'Neill and *The Iceman Cometh*   397

XXXI. Shaw, the Latter Days   410

XXXII. Widening Horizons   425

XXXIII. Summation   439

Appendices

I. The Washington Square Players   451

II. *Geneva* Correspondence with Bernard Shaw   454

III. Westport Country Playhouse   459

IV. Plays by the Author   463

V. National Inventors Council   466

VI. American Shakespeare Festival Theatre   468

VII. Plays in Which Alfred Lunt and Lynn Fontanne Have Appeared   472

VIII. List of Theatre Guild Plays   473

Index   481

List of Illustrations

(with photo credits)

Lawrence Langner *(Parry Studio), frontispiece*

(between pages 18 and 19)

The author, at the age of seven

Ellen Terry as Portia *(Window & Grove)*

Lunt and Fontanne in *The Taming of the Shrew*, 1935 *(Vandamm)*

Helen Hayes in *Twelfth Night*, 1940 *(Bob Golby)*

Helen Hayes and the author, 1941

Jessie Royce Landis and Florence Reed in *The Winter's Tale*, 1946 *(Vandamm)*

Armina Marshall and Romney Brent in *As You Like It* at the Westport Country Playhouse, 1932 *(E. T. Monroe)*

Charles Coburn in *The Merry Wives of Windsor*, 1946 *(Vandamm)*

Maurice Evans in *Twelfth Night*, 1940 *(Bob Golby)*

Katharine Hepburn in *As You Like It*, 1949 *(Vandamm)*

(between pages 114 and 115)

Helen Westley and Jose Ruben in *Another Way Out*, 1916 *(White Studios)*

George Cram Cook and Katharine Cornell

Susan Glaspell and Edward Goodman

The Board of Managers of the Theatre Guild, 1923

Helen Freeman, Augustin Duncan, and Helen Westley in *John Ferguson*, 1919

Richard Bennett and Margalo Gillmore in *He Who Gets Slapped*, 1922 *(Francis Bruguiere)*

Richard Bennett, Sidney Howard, Pauline Lord, and Glenn Anders rehearsing *They Knew What They Wanted*, 1924 *(Vandamm)*

St. John Ervine *(Berington)*, Franz Werfel, A. A. Milne, Ferenc Molnar

Joseph Schildkraut, Eva LeGallienne, Alice Brady, Arnold Daly

(between pages 178 and 179)

Erskine Sanford, Elizabeth Risdon, Ralph Roeder, Fred Eric, Lucille Watson, and Albert Perry in *Heartbreak House*, 1920 *(Ira Schwarz)*

George Gaul, Eleanor Woodruff, Ernita Lascelles and Albert Brunning in *Back to Methuselah*, 1922 *(Bruguiere)*

Winifred Lenihan in *Saint Joan*, 1923

Lynn Fontanne in *Pygmalion*, 1926 *(Vandamm)*

Romney Brent and Alla Nazimova in *The Simpleton of the Unexpected Isle*, 1935 *(Vandamm)*

Alfred Lunt in *The Doctor's Dilemma*, 1927 *(Vandamm)*

Beatrice Lillie and Hope Williams in *Too True to Be Good*, 1932 *(Vandamm)*

G.B.S. at Stresa, 1929

G.B.S. and Armina Marshall at Stresa, 1929

Bernard Shaw posing for statue by Prince Paul Troubetzkoy, Stresa, 1929

Shaw at Stresa, 1929

Shaw at Stresa, 1929

(between pages 226 and 227)

Glenn Anders, Lynn Fontanne, Tom Powers, and Earle Larimore in *Strange Interlude*, 1928 *(Vandamm)*

Alla Nazimova and Alice Brady in *Mourning Becomes Electra*, 1931 *(Vandamm)*

Eugene O'Neill in his twenties

Eugene O'Neill at his home at Spithead, Bermuda, 1927

Gene Lockhart and George M. Cohan in *Ah, Wilderness!*, 1941 *(Vandamm)*

A rehearsal of *The Iceman Cometh*, 1946 *(Pix, Inc.)*

ix

Lawrence Langner at the age of Thirty-five (*Nickolas Muray*)

(between pages 306 and 307)

The Westport Country Playhouse (*Russell O. Kuhner*)

Rollo Peters, Armina Marshall, Knowles Entrekin, Dorothy Gish, and Romney Brent at Westport

Peggy Conklin and Tonio Selwart in *The Pursuit of Happiness*, 1933 (*White Studios*)

The author, Armina Marshall, and John C. Wilson, Directors of the Westport Playhouse

Ruth Gordon in *The Country Wife*, 1933 (*Vandamm*)

Violet Hemming in *Lady Godiva*, 1933 (*Manugian*)

Jose Ferrer in *The Silver Whistle*, 1948 (*Kuhner*)

Thornton Wilder, Betty Field, and Armina Marshall in *The Skin of Our Teeth*, 1949

Langnerlane Farm (*Ray Long*)

Oval swimming pool

Leo Godowsky and the author, 1930

Olivia DeHavilland and Marcus Goodrich, 1946

Philip Langner, the author's son, at Westport, 1950 (*Ted Reed*)

Luigi Pirandello and the author, 1935

Tallulah and her lion cub

(between pages 338 and 339)

The Garrick Gaieties, 1925 (*Ira Schwarz, Drix Duryea and Cosmo-Sileo*)

Ina Claire in *Biography*, 1932 (*Vandamm*)

Michael Bartlett, Osgood Perkins, and June Walker in *The School for Husbands*, 1933 (*Vandamm*)

Helen Hayes and Philip Merivale in *Mary of Scotland*, 1933

Alexander Woollcott in *Wine of Choice*, 1938 (*Vandamm*)

William Saroyan, Eddie Dowling, and Gene Kelly in Saroyan's *The Time of Your Life*, 1939 (*Vandamm*)

Katharine Hepburn in *The Philadelphia Story*, 1939 (*Vandamm*)

(between pages 370 and 371)

Mayor LaGuardia presents an award to Rodgers and Hammerstein for *Oklahoma!*

Fourth anniversary party for *Oklahoma!* (*Cosmo-Sileo*)

The finale of the original *Oklahoma!* (*Vandamm*)

The original can-can girls of *Oklahoma!* (*Vandamm*)

The Theatre Guild production of *Carousel*, 1945 (*Vandamm*)

(between pages 386 and 387)

Lunt and Fontanne in *The Guardsman*, 1924

Lunt and Fontanne in *Elizabeth, The Queen*, 1930 (*Vandamm*)

Alfred Lunt, Lynn Fontanne, and Henry Travers in *Reunion in Vienna*, 1931 (*Vandamm*)

Lunt and Fontanne in *The Pirate*, 1942 (*Vandamm*)

Alfred Lunt and chorus in *Idiot's Delight*, 1936

Lunt and Fontanne in *Idiot's Delight* (*Vandamm*)

Lunt and Fontanne in *Amphitryon 38*, 1937 (*Vandamm*)

Lunt and Fontanne in *I Know My Love*, 1949 (*Vandamm*)

(between pages 418 and 419)

Pictures posed especially for this book by Bernard Shaw, Ayot St. Lawrence, 1948

Charles F. Kettering demonstrating the first Delco self-starter, 1912 (*G. M. Photo*)

The first meeting of the National Inventors Council, 1940

The N.I.C. visits the Willow Run Plant

Meeting of the Council at Wright Field

Theresa Helburn (*Winifred Gail*)

Armina Marshall (*Winifred Gail*)

Lawrence Langner and Armina Marshall at the Westport Playhouse, 1935 (*Ben Pinchot*)

Rehearsal interlude from *Carousel*, Boston, 1945

The author at rest, Weston, Connecticut

The author in Wyoming

Armina Marshall

Preface

This is the story of my life, spent in two fields of endeavor, art and invention, both of them creative, and not as unrelated as one might think. It is the story, in part, of some notable plays and figures of the theatre and of some notable inventions of this era.

I do not know of any way to divide my story in outright compartments of art and the practical life. I have tried to do so in living my life, but I have failed. And if my narrative should, as a consequence, lack the ideal unity of narration, it is because my life itself has lacked unity in living in an era which was one of the most turbulent in recorded history, yet the most creative in invention and one of the most creative in the theatre.

As I look back upon the years of my activity in theatrical, industrial and scientific enterprise, I find myself far from satisfied; I can think of many things which I, along with others, might have ordered more wisely, and the thought is sometimes distressing. Yet I, along with many others of my generation, was motivated by an ambition to achieve progress in both fields of endeavor, and, whatever our shortcomings, they were not due to a lack of effort.

This book would not have been possible without the help of my colleagues of the Washington Square Players and the Theatre Guild, and especially Theresa Helburn and Armina Marshall, and of my partners in the firm of Langner, Parry, Card and Langner, and especially John Parry and my brother, Herbert Langner. To them go my heartfelt thanks and gratitude. And I should also like to add my thanks to Whit Burnett whose idea it was that I should write this book, and who has edited it, and to my friend, John Gassner, who has helped me to keep my story within bounds.

I also wish to thank Nickolas Muray and Florence Vandamm who have supplied most of the photographs used to illustrate this book.

LAWRENCE LANGNER

June 1951

THE MAGIC CURTAIN

CHAPTER I

Childhood

I WAS born in the town of Swansea in South Wales on May 30, 1890. Swansea was, at the time, a small manufacturing town, and I am grateful that I was thus able to spend my childhood in an environment in which the ugliness of the industrial world was contrasted with the beautiful countryside and a background of Celtic mysticism and imagination. I was actually brought into the world in a little stone house which looked exactly like every other little stone house on a terrace which looked exactly like a dozen other terraces on a hillside overlooking the town.

Swansea itself, with its business district and docks, lay sprawling along the margin of Swansea Bay on the Bristol Channel, which was said to resemble and to rival the Bay of Naples. Later on in life I saw the Bay of Naples and can report that the resemblance is superficial. When Vesuvius is in eruption, the Bay of Naples is obscured by dense smoke clouds. But Vesuvius erupts only rarely, whereas the smelters, collieries, factories and chemical works around Swansea Bay were in eruption most of the time and continually belched forth smoke and grime. Added to this, at Landore, an outlying neighborhood, a mountain of coal dust caught on fire internally in the early eighties and was smoldering all through my childhood. For all I know, it is still smoldering, having stubbornly resisted every method known to man to put out the conflagration. But if all the houses on Eaton Crescent were outwardly the same, the lives lived in them were strangely different, and none perhaps so strange and different as those lived in No. 23, where my father and mother made their home.

My father, a tall, slender, intellectual-looking man with a high fore-

1

head and a dark mustache, was regarded by his friends as an eccentric, for he was erratic, moody and possessed of a violent temper. He also had a keen interest in music, art, literature and science, which alone would have aroused the suspicions of his more provincial neighbors. Inheriting a successful jewelry business from his father, he dabbled in many other pursuits, including a brickfield, a building enterprise, a furniture business and a cinema, in all of which he lost considerable money. He was also a Town Councilor, and each year was elected for his district, much to the delight of his children, since he was regularly brought home after each election balanced precariously on a chair carried on the shoulders of four stalwart coal miners. Invariably, too, he made a speech from the balcony outside the second-floor bedroom window which always ended in three cheers and the singing of "God Save the Queen."

My father's interest in science took the form of buying every gadget or invention which appeared on the market; he was the proud possessor of the first snapshot camera, the first automatic player piano, the first two-wheel bicycle, the first gramophone, and the first rubber-tired dogcart in town. My father also had the first aluminum bicycle with a celluloid gear cover, which was so highly inflammable that it caught on fire while he was riding it. He thought that if he pedaled hard enough, the rush of air would put out the flames, and it was not until his trouser legs had been singed off that he decided to dismount and pay attention to his own injuries, instead of to the bicycle's.

His musical interest went far beyond the owning of an automatic player piano and a gramophone; he not only attended all the concerts in the local Albert Hall, but he also played a variety of musical instruments, and was constantly purchasing new ones, learning them and trying them out on the family. One of his ambitions was to have each of his children play a different instrument, as well as the piano, and since there were soon six of us in the family, a small orchestra was in the making. My elder brother played the violin and piano, while to my lot fell the 'cello and the piano. Neither of us, however, appreciated the necessity for practicing a full hour each day, and our interest was somewhat less than enthusiastic. After trying the expedient of locking us in our rooms for our practice periods, my father, incensed by the strange squeaks and squeals my brother was producing on his violin, lost his temper, threw the violin on the floor and trampled it violently underfoot. I remember envying my brother his good luck, and wishing my father would wreak equal violence on the grand piano and the 'cello with which I was struggling.

My first and most significant early memory is of the day when, for my birthday, my father bought me a present consisting of hundreds of lead soldiers and mule-borne mountain artillery with guns which fired, all calculated to cause the heart of a small boy to leap with joy. Then my father placed all of us children on chairs on one side of the table, while from the other side he set up the soldiers and carried on a miniature battle for our benefit, enjoying himself so hugely that he did not notice the look of envy on the face of one small child—myself—who vowed that one day *he* would be putting the show on the stage and that others would be watching it!

My mother was a handsome and talented Londoner, with dark-brown hair and eyes which puckered up underneath whenever she smiled, which was often. She was an omnivorous reader and matched my father's interests with her own. They had in common a love of music, for my mother had been trained as a pianist and had intended to make a professional career of her playing; all this was abandoned in favor of my father, to whom she presented a child each year with a regularity which was conspicuous because in all else she was entirely irregular. Lighthearted, gay, and endowed with a zest for life which continued to a late age (during World War II, at seventy-eight, she returned to London from the country because, as she put it, she'd "rather be bombed to death than bored to death"), she found living in Swansea a dull affair. She spent a good deal of her time running back and forth to London, returning with the latest songs and music, accompanied by my father with the latest inventions. My mother was a devotee of Gilbert and Sullivan, and so each evening before going to bed we would be grouped around the piano while she taught us "Tit Willow" or "A Wandering Minstrel I." My father adored her, and on Sundays, when we all sat perched on our chairs around the dining-room table, six faces turned toward the roast beef and Yorkshire pudding, he would remark, "Who is the most beautiful woman in the world?" to which a chorus of thin treble voices would reply enthusiastically, "Mother!" Then my mother would tell my father to behave himself and not act so foolishly in front of the children, and he would carve the roast beef with comical dexterity while the six children watched him hungrily.

I was the second of the children to arrive in the world, and I was called Lawrence in honor of an old sweetheart of my mother's, a partner in the firm of Saqui and Lawrence, the London silversmiths. I was told that he had been my mother's fiancé, and but for the fact that he had unfortunately taken a dose of poison by mistake for medicine and come to an untimely end, my mother would have married him, and not my father. I never arrived at the truth of this romantic story, however, for when my mother was a widow of seventy, Mr. Lawrence—unless it was his ghost—suddenly appeared in London and spent the rest of his life escorting my mother to restaurants and the theatres, for all the world as though he had been her resurrected husband.

The burden of bearing so many children made it impossible for my mother to spend much time raising us. Had she done so, we would undoubtedly have been brought up on novels by Ouida, Mrs. Humphrey Ward and Frank Danby, musical comedies of "The Geisha" variety, and fed nothing but cakes and ale; for she was no housekeeper or housewife, but a girl made for parties and a mother more by accident than by temperament. She loved us as a child loves her dolls, but for the more serious duties of life there were nurses and a governess—indeed a succession of governesses, for none of them stayed longer than a few months, with the notable exception of a Miss Gwenyth Jones, a beautiful clear-eyed brunette who had a classic forehead and finely chiseled nose and mouth. She was the daughter of a Welsh denominational clergyman who lived in Sketty, a nearby village, and we children loved her with deep devotion. She was pure Welsh, with the mystical Celtic imagination, and a born storyteller. She knew all the old fairy tales and poured them out to us by the hour while we listened spellbound. Going for a walk with Miss Jones was sheer delight. She knew stories about the wayside flowers and the birds, and in the spring, on a long walk in the country, we would sit on a fallen log in a woods carpeted with bluebells and primroses while she told us stories of Merlin and Prince Arthur, and we listened enchanted until she brought her tale to an end with a brisk, "Come along, children, we *must* get home in time for supper!"

Almost every woman in whom I have since had a romantic interest has somehow reminded me of her. When I finally realized this preconditioning of my emotions, I referred to it as my "governess complex." It made me especially susceptible to the charms of independent young women, and resulted in my marrying, on separate occasions, two extremely attractive ex-school teachers.

In the neighborhood of Swansea was a Druid monument known as King Arthur's Stone, and we were often taken there in the family dogcart with pneumatic tires (another of my father's gadgets) driven by our coachman Charlie, and we would picnic on a large monolith which made a natural dining table at the foot of King Arthur's Stone. On those occasions Arthur and Guinevere seemed almost neighbors, and had they dropped in for a sandwich, I doubt if I should have been greatly surprised. We were fortunate that on one side of Swansea was the peninsula of Gower, one of the most beautiful sections of South Wales. Here, but a few miles away from the coal yards, smelters, tramp steamers at the docks, and the mining villages of the Rhondda Valley, was a peaceful countryside abounding in rich farms, woods with rushing streams, and miles of wild "commons" yellow with gorse, and bordering the cliffs which frowned upon the Bristol Channel across which, on a clear day, one could see Ilfracombe in Devonshire. That Welsh countryside is indelibly imprinted in my childhood recollections and after all these years I am still moved with emotion remembering its dramatic beauty, the great dark cliffs of its coast line against which the ocean shatters itself eternally, its old Roman castles, its mysterious caves which, with other boys, I explored by the light of candles, its good salt sea smell, the rocks covered with blue-green mussels at Caswell Bay, the sturdy stone lighthouse at the Mumbles Head, and here and there, piercing the green shrubbery of a lovely hillside, an abandoned coal shaft writing a black smudge upon the verdant landscape.

My childhood life, however, was not all nature and Guinevere, nor all Gilbert and Sullivan and gadgets. I had a foretaste of my future at the solemn age of six when a touring company gave a Christmas pantomime entitled *Little Bo Peep* at the old Wine Street Theatre, remembered by most English actors and actresses as one of the worst in the world. English Christmas pantomimes were resplendent with tinsel, fairy queens, ballets, low comedians and the so-called Principal Boy, who belied her name by conspicuously displaying her bust and hips in the most femininely audacious of bodices and tights. After the performance, I was taken backstage by my father and introduced to some of the bespangled beauties and eventually to the Principal Boy herself. My downfall was complete. Even to this day I cannot witness a ballet without immediately deciding that it is high time for the Theatre Guild to stop the serious nonsense of producing plays, and get down to the real business of the theatre, which is to produce ballets. Indeed, on one occasion, in Moliere's *The School for Husbands,* I succeeded in smuggling into the production a full-sized Ballet-Interlude with Doris Humphrey and Charles Weidman, and this with no visible ill effect other than to deplete the Guild's shrinking bank balance, a mishap which was later compensated for by my suggesting Agnes De Mille as the choreographer for the ballets of *Oklahoma!*

Our summers were usually spent at Mrs. William Williams' farm at

Killay, a village about ten miles outside Swansea, where the white-washed farmhouse with thatched roof housed our six children, as well as the numerous progeny of the Williams family. Mrs. William Williams ruled the farm by day and at night retired to bed with her elderly husband in a large closet in the kitchen wall, the door of which they closed on retiring. In these unhealthy surroundings Mrs. Williams, a massive apple-cheeked old darling, had reached the age of seventy-two, and was as strong as a horse, while her husband was well over eighty, and with a little fresh air at night, might have lived to be a thousand. At four in the morning, Mrs. Williams would rise from her closet, hitch her horse to the milk wagon and drive to Swansea to deliver milk to her customers. I often accompanied her on these trips. At the door of each house a jug had been left outside the night before, and my duty was to carry this jug to the milk wagon, where Mrs. Williams filled it with clean white milk; then I carefully carried it back and deposited it outside the door. This was the first useful work I performed in the world, work which in an age of sterilization can no longer be done by small boys of seven or thereabouts.

Mysteriously, however, our idyllic life came to a sudden end. One day my father and mother returned from London where they had witnessed Queen Victoria's Diamond Jubilee. There seemed to be a strain between them, and the former atmosphere of gaiety and happiness which existed in our home was changed to one of somberness and suspicion, followed by whisperings among the servants, discussions which came to an abrupt end on my entering a room, and all those signs by which a child can guess that something is wrong without knowing just what it is. Finally the storm broke with brutal abruptness. My father, who had been away on business for a few days, came home as we children were having dinner with our mother. We were ordered out of the room, but my father's loud accusations and my mother's paroxysms of tears brought us all running back again, and we clung like frightened babes to our mother's skirts. Our father was behaving exactly like a third-rate actor in a Victorian melodrama. Everything he said sounded as though it had been written expressly for the stage, and indeed was probably remembered from just such a scene in the theatre. Stanislavsky once told me that when men come to a crisis in their lives and do not know how to meet it, they usually fall back on the theatre. He instanced a case he had witnessed when a dying man, not knowing just what to do, played his death scene exactly like an actor in the death scene of a play currently running in a Moscow theatre. My father played the role of the outraged husband with great vigor. "Leave this house," he cried in stentorian tones. "It's my house, and I'll break every stick of furniture in it if I want to!" The outraged wife protested her innocence in vain.

My poor mother, to the accompaniment of howls from five of her heartbroken children, went upstairs to where the sixth and youngest was sleeping, and like the heroine of the selfsame melodrama, she wrapped the baby in a shawl, carried it downstairs and went out weeping into the night. The only thing missing from this grim theatrical scene, which shattered our lives with the suddenness of an earthquake, was the usual snowstorm and slow violin music. But if my father's and mother's separation can be seen through the years in terms of a Victorian melodrama, it was sheer tragedy at the time to the children who witnessed the performance. Our household disbanded. We were taken to London. My brothers and I were sent to a horrible boarding school at Eastbourne while the divorce action was pending. There were meetings with our mother in a solicitor's office in London—weepings and partings mingled with the excitement of being in London which, seen for the first time under these circumstances, was an occasion for frightened bewilderment. Finally the case came up for trial, and the divorce took place, which enabled my mother to marry again with happy results, while our father nursed a broken heart and disliked himself thoroughly for inflicting so much punishment on himself, his six small children, and his innocent wife.

After the divorce, what was left of our family was reinstated in a small villa which our father bought in the village of Westcross, a few miles outside Swansea. It was reached by the famous Mumbles train, the first railway in the world to use metal rails, and the ancient cars of which had double-decks, on the upper one of which any mild lunatic could sit and imbibe the fresh sea air mingled with clouds of jet-black smoke, soot and grime from the engine smokestack. Our house, which faced the Bristol Channel, was presided over by Miss Byrne, a new governess from Dublin, who, in an unbelievably hard brogue, informed us that the best English spoken in the world was Dublin English and endeavored to make us all speak like little Dubliners.

I was an irritating pupil at school, generally well up in my studies but always in trouble because I was in the habit of asking the teachers questions they found difficult to answer and thought I had asked merely to demonstrate their ignorance to the rest of the boys. As there was a certain modicum of truth in this, I was not at all popular, and was deservedly punished by what was known as "P.D.," meaning punishment drill. With about two dozen other youthful miscreants I was drilled by a retired army sergeant for an hour after school each day, the net result of which was to make me regard exercise as a form of punishment which I have carefully avoided ever since. Another time my father punished me for using bad language by the ingenious method of making me wear a small placard on which was written "This boy swears." The effect was magical and kept my language, if not my thoughts, pure for thirty years, until I told a psychoanalyst the story, whereupon he suggested that I lock myself in a bathroom every day for a month and shout all the four-letter words I knew at the top of my voice until I could say them without shuddering inwardly. In this way I was ultimately successful in overcoming the effect of the placard, and can now use four-letter words with the best of them when the occasion demands.

Going to school, playing on the beach, fishing, robbing apple orchards and exploring the caves (in one of them we found a Roman dagger and a bronze coin) formed the background of my life at Westcross. But I had a special interest not shared by the rest of my family, a large toy theatre, a present from my father, and a set of scenery and actors of the "penny plain and two-pence colored" variety. This kind of children's toy, so far as I know, does not exist in the United States. It consisted of a highly colored Victorian proscenium mounted on a wooden box, with red-and-gold curtains, wings, drops, transformations, and the actors themselves, all printed bravely on sheets of cardboard. The embryo manager cut these out with scissors or penknife, painted them himself if his pocket did not run to the "two-pence colored" sheets, and with the use of candles for lighting effects, wires to manipulate the cardboard actors, and a book of the dialogue, it was possible to give effective performances of *The Corsican Brothers, The Sleeping Beauty, Box and Cox* and other theatre pieces of the Mid-Victorian era. I became so absorbed in this theatre that my aunt, who was visiting us at the time, sailed into the parlor one day to request me to stop the performance, since my father was seriously ill on the next floor and was being disturbed by the loudness of the play. Nor was this due to callousness on my part. I knew that my father would probably not recover, and I found in my theatre an escape from the intolerable reality of his oncoming death. This occurred in 1900 when I was ten.

During the illness which brought his life to a close, I spent many long hours with my father as he lay in bed. In order to encourage my taste in literature, he had purchased for me a small library known as

Sir John Lubbock's Hundred Best Books, the English equivalent of Professor Eliot's Five Foot Book Shelf in the United States. Since this collection included all the time-honored Victorians it is surprising that my enjoyment of literature survived these heavy masterpieces, but I read avidly and was soon as familiar with *The Last Days of Pompeii* and *Plutarch's Lives* as I was with *Don Quixote* or *Origin of Species.* My father and I read many of these books together. I remember that he selected Carlyle's *History of the French Revolution* which I would read aloud, while he would explain the meaning when I came to a word or passage I did not understand. My admiration for my father's tastes was unbounded. I devoured all I could learn from him with an increasing appetite; and to him I owe mostly my interest in books, the theatre and inventions. The last few years of my father's life were as unhappy for him as they were for his children, and he died a relatively young man at the age of thirty-seven, just as the Twentieth Century dawned upon a world which welcomed it with the pealing of church bells and special editions of the newspapers printed in golden type.

The day after my father's death, I rose and stole into his bedroom in the early morning while no one was about, and stood looking at his pale features and wasted body which seemed so thin as to be barely discernible beneath the bedcovers. My eyes filled with tears as I reflected on how much affection he had bestowed on me, and how he had been cheated by life, to have died so young, and to have had so much unhappiness. This picture of my father wrote itself so deeply into my memory that I unconsciously decided to crowd everything I possibly could into my own life before reaching the age of thirty-seven, and under no circumstances ever to be divorced! From then on, I was always in a hurry to get on with my life, a condition which did not leave me until I passed the age of thirty-seven, when the tension was miraculously relieved.

My father's long illness had depleted the small family fortune. His businesses were sold for what they could bring, and with no other inheritance than his gold chiming watch and platinum watch chain, we were left as orphans to the good graces of our relatives. Our mother, who had remarried, came to our rescue, and for a time my brothers and I lived as boarders in the home of a family in Swansea, while our sisters went to live with my father's sister in Manchester.

A few weeks after my father's death, I read in the local newspaper that our family belongings would be sold at Public Auction. Knowing nothing of such proceedings, but being curious to learn what would happen, I attended the sale in a shabby auction room, unbeknown to any of our relatives. Standing unnoticed in the back, I saw our father's beloved possessions, the prints and pictures he had treasured, the Georgian furniture of which he was so proud, the automatic player piano and gramophone with earpieces which he was the first to bring to Swansea, and then the very bed in which he had died—all were forlornly heaped together on one side of the auction room while each article was discussed and appraised, sometimes jokingly, sometimes critically, by the auctioneer who, one time when a paltry price was offered remarked, "Come, come, gentlemen, remember there are six little children." This remark, which suggested that we were objects of public charity, made the experience unbearable, and I left hurriedly, wishing I had never come. I took away with me from that auction room a burning desire to be independent, as well as a picture of the ephemeral nature of possessions, which I hope I shall never lose.

Together with my brothers, I was sent by my cousin Michael, who had been appointed our guardian, to the Swansea Intermediate School, one of the best schools in Wales, and we were as happy in our new surroundings as could be reasonably expected. We were now no longer sheltered under the wings of a nurse and governess, but could play in the streets with other boys and stay up as late as we pleased. Moreover, trips could be taken to quarters formerly forbidden, such as the docks, where cargo ships were arriving from and departing to ports all over the world. These visits to the docks opened up a vista of the great world beyond the small corner of Wales in which we lived, and I filled in what I learned from the sailors with stories by Robert Louis Stevenson, G. A. Henty, Fenimore Cooper and a hundred other novels of adventure in strange lands.

From time to time political figures of national importance came to Swansea and lectured at the Albert Hall. My natural curiosity led me to attend many of these lectures, two of which made a great impression on me. One was by Lord Rosebury, the most eloquent of all English speakers at the time. He spoke on hobbies. His thesis was that Englishmen differed from men of all other nationalities by their interest in hobbies, which enabled them to perform their everyday work with a sense of humor and perspective lacking in men who devoted all their efforts to their business alone. This philosophy so impressed me that I made it my own, and later on in life always separated in my own mind my vocation and my avocation with the least possible mental conflict. Another lecture I attended was given by David Lloyd George, then a young member of Parliament from the neighboring

Rhondda Valley. He was a pro-Boer at the time, and had recently been mobbed while speaking in Birmingham so that he had to be smuggled out of the hall disguised as a policeman. In Swansea he spoke passionately against the wrongs of British Imperialism. The slim, vivid, emotional figure impressed me with his Welsh eloquence and courage, for here too he was howled down by the audience and finally had to leave the Hall by the rear to escape the angry crowd.

I continued to make good progress at school, especially in literature and English composition, much to the apparent disgust of my teacher in those subjects, a Welshman of part Belgian extraction named Etienne Morgan. His dislike for me was due to an old quarrel with my father, already dead for over a year, but which this vindictive individual now visited upon me as the second generation with truly Biblical vengeance. To some slighting remark to me about my father one day in the presence of the other boys in the class room, I retorted angrily. I was reported by Morgan to the Supervisor, who called me into his study and without any discussion of the rights or wrongs of the case, took out a heavy rattan cane from a cupboard and thrashed me until I collapsed to the floor. I returned home and was put to bed, the doctor was called and over a dozen heavy weals across the fleshy part of my legs were medically treated. My cousin Michael called on the school and demanded an explanation. A minor scandal broke, which resulted in a change in the local practice of caning boys in this brutal fashion. Years later, my cousin Michael wrote me from Swansea that Morgan had been sent to prison for two years for stabbing his wife.

This brutal beating had a dramatic consequence in my life. My mother, learning of it, discussed the situation with my stepfather, and it was decided that we boys should come to live with them in London. My two sisters followed us later. Thus through Etienne Morgan, who wished me no good, came my start along the road which was to lead me first from Swansea to London, and later from London to New York and to my greatest happiness.

CHAPTER II

Boyhood

M Y BROTHERS and I arrived in London in the spring of 1901, to live in the home of our mother and stepfather. Driving from St. Pancras station to Woburn Square near the British museum, where my mother lived with her new husband, was for a boy of eleven a journey full of terrors. What would my mother look like? What kind of man was our stepfather? How would they greet us? Would we be welcome or unwelcome, or even packed off to an orphan asylum? Arrived at our destination, we found our mother waiting for us at the front door of No. 8, a spacious house adjoining the charming Georgian church, and after a brief moment of embarrassment, she was hugging and kissing us all. We had not seen her, nor she us, for nearly five years, and she appeared to be warm and pretty, and indeed the epitome of everything a small boy would want in his mother.

When our stepfather returned from his solicitors' office a few hours later and scrutinized his new family, our fears began to rise again. He was a strange-looking little man, sprucely dressed in a gray morning-coat suit. He had keen deep-set eyes under a close-cropped head of brown hair and a sharp pointed Vandyke beard which gave him an air of distinction. His atttude toward us was most kindly but enigmatic at the time, and I doubt that he had entirely recovered from the shock of acquiring this new full-fledged family of six children in addition to two of his own. If you can imagine the feelings of a young cuckoo when he realizes that he is an interloper in another family's nest, you will have some idea of the acutely uncomfortable feeling we children had in living in our stepfather's home. No matter how welcome he made us (and he did his best, poor man) we felt our position keenly. We were all extremely happy at the thought of living with our mother, but we soon realized that in these new circumstances, we owed it to our stepfather to show our gratitude by behaving like little angels rather than normal children. This was quite a strain, especially for me.

We were duly enrolled in the London Polytechnic, an imposing-looking school on Regent Street, to which we walked every day from our home, enjoying the sights on the way, as country boys would. Arriving late for school one day, as usual, I was stopped at the school entrance by a handsome elderly gentleman who caught me running in, held me in his arms, and reprimanded me in the kindliest manner. He was Quentin Hogg, the leading spirit of the institution, whose work for British boys has since become legend, while his son Quentin Hogg, Jr., M.P., has recently become known in this country as one of the main supporters of the Beveridge Plan. Thanks to Mr. Hogg, I began to pay attention to such important matters as punctuality, but I was not a very successful child, either at school or at home. I was lazy, untidy, dreamy and entirely unco-operative. My mother, who continued to be a delightfully irresponsible housekeeper, would invariably neglect her household duties for more interesting activities, such as going to the theatre or reading a good novel. She was apt at the last moment to dispatch any one of her four sons to Mudie's Lending Library to change her book, or to send him on shopping errands with the admonition that, as the supplies were needed in time for dinner, they must be brought back immediately. Thus, my brothers and I were constantly running to the grocer, the dairy or the chemist, and, more often than not, on returning from one of these errands, we had to return again immediately because Mater or cook had forgotten to order something else the first time. There soon developed a legend that it was no use sending me on errands, because I either forgot what I was sent for, or I omitted to return home until hours later. This was largely because I spent the greater part of my spare time reading, and as I was invariably asked to run on an errand when I was at a most interesting part of my book, I usually took it with me and trudged along the London streets reading as I walked.

Not unnaturally, I was a source of continual annoyance to my stepfather, for I appeared to lack appreciation for the many kindnesses which he bestowed upon me. I tried hard to conform, but I seemed molded for rebellion. I soon developed a scorn for my mother's lack of organizing ability, and even had the temerity to lecture her on her shortcomings as a housewife. After putting up with me with incredible patience for over a year, during which I attended the London Polytechnic on Regent Street, my stepfather finally decided that a few terms at boarding school would be a good thing for me, and even better for him; so along with my younger brother, Herbert, I found myself enrolled as a pupil at the Margate Grammar School.

This high-sounding institution of learning was at that time a collection of small houses grouped around the main building on a hilltop overlooking Margate, an English seaside resort which was deserted in winter but was a mecca for trippers and excursionists from London in the summer. The school was presided over by a fussy but efficient little Scotch-English pedagogue with beady black eyes and a receding chin, who belonged to the peculiar sect known as the Plymouth Brethren. He applied himself equally to religion, learning and association football with a zest which can be found only among the inhabitants of the British Isles. There, on a diet consisting largely of thick bread and butter, which the boys termed "doorsteps," and weak tea, known as "slops," I spent two happy years, for if the food was uninteresting, there were many compensations. Chief among these was the opportunity for uninterrupted reading. I was soon made School Librarian, and also edited the school magazine, a typewritten affair which was tacked up from time to time on the classroom Bulletin Board. My literary interests attracted the attention of the Headmaster's wife, a kindly bespectacled lady who towered almost a foot above her diminutive husband, so that the boys irreverently called them "the long and short of it."

One day I was sent for by the dominie. A request to visit him in his study, especially in my case, was usually ominous, for it was here that he caned the boys who merited punishment. Wondering what I was now in for, I entered, and was greeted with the friendliest of smiles by the little man. His wife, sitting stiffly at his side and towering above him, was also smiling, a rather disturbing proceeding, for her front teeth projected precariously, as though they might drop out at any moment. I looked apprehensively from one to the other, the smiles having failed to reassure me. "Lawrence," said he, "we are going to put on a play for the school, and we want you to act in it." "But I've never acted," I replied, adding hastily, "though of course I know how." "Of course, dear," said his wife, nodding her head without moving her shoulders, for all the world like a china mandarin, "and we've decided that you should play the part of the *girl.*" My heart sank. To appear before all the other boys dressed as a girl—this was far worse than any caning or other punishment. I doubted whether I should ever be able to live it down. My expression must have denoted my inner fears, but it was misunderstood. "Don't worry, old chap," said the dominie, with as much geniality as he could command, "you'll make a wonderful girl!" "Nobody at school could do better," said the smiling teeth, nodding in approval. I was trapped—caught between my desire to act and my fear of being ridiculous. But there was nothing to do but acquiesce, so I played the part of Polly in the school play, an experience which produced so many inhibitions in me that never from that day to this have I desired to act again.

On the opening night, I was pushed and pulled into a whalebone corset, which laced both up the back and front after the fashion of those days. This completed, I was examined closely, but obviously *not* with approval by the Headmaster's wife, for she rushed out of the dressing room, returning a few moments later with what appeared to be a pair of round pincushions connected together by tapes. These she pushed hastily into the gaping spaces of the corset where Polly's bust should have been but wasn't, and said, turning crimson—"There, child, now you'll look all right, but don't tell anybody I loaned you those. They're mine." The little Headmaster then walked briskly into the dressing room shouting, "Hurry up, everybody!", came over to me, put his arm around my waist, hugged me energetically, and remarked to all present, "My, what a pretty girl!" This put the finishing touches to my humiliation. One often hears the statement that most playwrights, stage directors and managers are frustrated actors. My own frustration came early.

At boarding school I learned an invaluable lesson about audience reactions. Not receiving any regular pocket money from home, I was usually bribed by the other boys who slept in my dormitory, by gifts of sweets or other favors, to tell them stories at night after "lights out." It was not long before I realized that the reasons the boys wanted me to tell these stories was almost entirely because of their soporific effect. As I would proceed, one by one the boys would doze pleasantly off to sleep. It ultimately became a point of vanity with me to keep them awake as long as possible. I then invented the technique of talking very much louder from time to time, which had the effect of waking up the dozers who stayed to listen again. A little noise and excitement at ten-thirty in any play helps the audience to stay awake at the time when they are sleepiest.

My two years of boarding school came to an end, and at thirteen I was turned out into the world to earn my own living with a half-baked education which included a smattering of French, a fair knowledge of English history, more especially from the reign of Henry VIII to Queen Anne, geography, and large masses of undigested English literature from William Shakespeare to Anthony Hope. However, I experienced no misgivings about my educational shortcomings. In fact, I was convinced that no subject existed which I could not master, given the time and the inclination to do so. It was therefore in no desperate mood that I returned to London to start out on the first rung of the ladder. It was all an adventure in which, through "luck" and the failure of the family fortunes, I was making an earlier start than most other boys. Scanning the London newspapers each day for advertisements of situations vacant, I soon discovered that boys of my age could find positions only as Office Boys or Junior Clerks. The latter appellation caught my fancy. To a boy of thirteen there was something *infra dig* about being an Office Boy, so I considered it definitely settled that I was to be a Junior Clerk. My attention was attracted by two advertisements in the *Daily Telegraph*, the first of which read as follows:

JUNIOR CLERK WANTED—excellent opportunity for ambitious young man, apply Jays', Oxford Circus.

There was something heartwarming about this advertisement. It suggested (a) that I was a young man, and (b) that within a very short time I would undoubtedly rise to be the head of one of the largest department stores in London. The other advertisement was not nearly so arresting. It merely read:

JUNIOR CLERK WANTED: Theatrical business. Apply in person. J. Bannister Howard, 3 Bedford Street, Strand.

But for the magical words "theatrical business" this advertisement would have passed unnoticed by me. I showed both advertisements to my mother, who advised that I call at Jays' first, and if unsuccessful in demonstrating that I was the ambitious young man they were looking for, I should then go on to the theatrical business, which, while of dubious import, was nevertheless better than nothing.

Face scrubbed, hair brushed and wearing a clean collar, neat tie, and a new suit in place of the Etons I had worn at school, I set out to call first on Messrs. Jays, and then on Mr. J. Bannister Howard. Arrived at Jays', I was directed to the ladies' stocking department where a tall, elegant, middle-aged lady told me I was just the "office boy" they were looking for, and would I come back in a day or so after they had examined my references. My dignity was doubly wounded; first to be called an office boy, and then to work in a ladies' stocking department. Heaven forbid! I resolved *not* to tell my mother of my ill-starred success and I continued on to No. 3 Bedford Street, Strand, where the theatrical business and all it implied was awaiting me.

CHAPTER III

I Go to Work

BEDFORD STREET, Strand, where Mr. Bannister Howard's office was situated, was at that time in the center of the London theatrical district, which ran through Maiden Lane to Covent Garden. No. 3 Bedford Street, a dark red brick building, housed one of the most famous public houses of the district, The Bodega, where for over half a century thousands of actors had consumed millions of Scotches while reading their notices to one another and exchanging stories of "the good old days." Across the entrance of No. 3 hung a large sign bearing the legend, "THE BEN GREET ACADEMY OF ACTING, Frederick Topham, Director," and on a brass plate at the side of the door was displayed in even larger type the name, "J. BANNISTER HOWARD." I entered the dark hall, my heart beating with excitement, and breathed in the pleasant odor of old port, whisky and beer which was wafted along with me from The Bodega as I mounted the stone stairs that led to Mr. Howard's office.

I knocked timidly on the door; it was opened by a kindly, motherly-looking woman who invited me in. "My name is Miss Matthews. You're no doubt the young man who answered our advertisement," she said, leading me into her office where she did her best to make me feel at home. I glanced around at the theatrical photographs and posters which lined the walls. "And now tell me about your previous experience," she said, interrupting my examination of the room. "I'm afraid I have had none," I answered, apprehensively. "That's not necessary," said this angel from heaven, "provided you can learn. Do you think you'd like the theatrical business?" I glanced at the photographs and posters again, and thought of the Christmas pantomimes at the Swan-

The author, *center*, at the age of seven, with his brothers, Herbert, *above*, and Julian, *right*. The lady in the boater is Miss Jones.

Ellen Terry as Portia. Her influence on the author resulted in the
Theatre Guild Shakespearean productions, pictures of which follow.

Lunt and Fontanne in the Theatre Guild production
of Shakespeare's *The Taming of the Shrew*, 1935.

Above: Helen Hayes and the author at a party given in her honor on Twelfth Night, January, 1941.

Helen Hayes in the Theatre Guild's production of Shakespeare's *Twelfth Night*, 1940.

Jessie Royce Landis and Florence Reed in the Theatre
Guild's production of Shakespeare's *The Winter's Tale*, 1946.

Westport Country Playhouse production of *As You Like It* with Armina Marshall as Rosalind and Romney Brent as Touchstone, 1932.

Above: Charles Coburn as Falstaff in the Theatre Guild production of *The Merry Wives of Windsor*, 1946. *Below:* Maurice Evans as Malvolio in the Theatre Guild production of *Twelfth Night*, 1940.

Katharine Hepburn in the Theatre Guild production of Shakespeare's *As You Like It*, 1949.

sea theatre. "Oh, I know I will," I answered, eagerly. "Very well," she smiled. "The salary will be eight shillings a week. When can you start to work?" "Oh, *at once!*" I replied. "And what about references?" she asked. "Oh, dear!" My heart sank again. "I have none, but you can telephone my mother." Miss Matthews rose. "Very well," she said. "Come back tomorrow."

Later on I met my employer, Mr. J. Bannister Howard, a huge man dressed elegantly in a tail-coat suit of voluminous proportions and a shiny silk hat, whose habit it was to rush in and out of the office two or three times a day like an elephant gone berserk, scarcely deigning to cast a glance at the new boy who was seated at the desk in the waiting room. Here it was my duty to meet the actors and actresses who were looking for jobs, for Mr. Howard was what we call a "road manager" in the United States, since he operated provincial theatres and touring companies. He shared his suite of offices with other theatrical managers, one of whom was a Mr. William Courtney, manager for Ellen Terry and also London representative for the Ben Greet Shakespearean Company which at that time was at the peak of its success in the United States, with Ben Greet and Edith Wynn Mathison touring from coast to coast.

I soon felt at home in the waiting room which was my special domain, and enjoyed chatting with the actors and actresses who were seated around me, waiting to be shown in to Miss Matthews. Between times I explored the dark building in which we were housed, and unraveled its fascinating mysteries. Chief of these was the Ben Greet Academy of Acting which was situated on the floor above, and included a large rehearsal room. At one end was a small platform, while the other end contained the interesting collection of props, gilded furniture, ancient weapons and lighting equipment which usually accumulates in a theatrical office. Here were numerous similar plaster busts which belonged to a play by Hall Caine called *The Eternal City*, the plot of which required the smashing of a bust each night by the leading actor, who struck it savagely with a mallet. As this play was touring, it was my duty to send the necessary busts to each theatre on the road, so that there would always be a bust available for that big scene. I had been solemnly warned by Miss Matthews that on no account must I miss sending them, for on one occasion my predecessor had failed to do so and the touring company had had to borrow a marble statue in a remote city which refused to break when struck by the actor and consequently ruined the climax of the play.

Mr. Frederick Topham, who presided over the Ben Greet Academy of Acting, was a neatly dressed little man, who wore a gray cutaway suit and a monocle which raised his right eyebrow and gave him a perpetually astonished expression. This, I thought, was partly due to the fact that the Academy appeared to have no pupils, and was mainly used as a rehearsal room by the various theatrical companies in the neighborhood. This was fortunate for me, for when there were no errands to run, and especially when J. Bannister Howard was visiting one of his provincial theatres, I could creep up the dark stairs and sit on a Shakespearean throne in the rehearsal room, while the actors were out to lunch, eating some sandwiches I had brought from home.

One day the activity at the office increased. It was noised about by the mysterious grapevine which always exists in the theatre that Ellen Terry was going to revive *The Merchant of Venice*. Undoubtedly she had told an actor to hold himself in readiness for a role in the play, but to keep it an absolute secret; he in turn had told another actor the same story, and within twenty-four hours everyone on Maiden Lane knew about it. Shakespearean actors by the scores stormed the outer office until I grew weary showing them in to Mr. William Courtney, who was in charge of this particular enterprise.

Photographs and posters of Miss Terry began to arrive, showing her dressed in the round red velvet cap and robes of Portia, probably one of the most glamorous portraits ever seen in the theatre. Soon rehearsals began, and the reasons why I should leave the outer office and run upstairs to the rehearsal room multiplied. For example, there was the mail. By spreading this over the best part of the morning I could deliver it personally to each actor at rehearsal and make at least a dozen trips upstairs. I began with Miss Terry's mail. Which of these ladies was Miss Terry? Surely I would recognize her from the photographs. She would be beautiful, queenly, humorous, altogether enthralling.

"Miss Terry's over there," said one of the supernumeraries pointing towards a handsome gray-haired middle-aged woman of matronly proportions, wearing glasses and bustling about with all the efficiency of a country schoolmarm. I gasped, so unexpected was her appearance, but I delivered the letters to her in my most precise junior-clerk manner. She smiled her wonderful smile as she thanked me, and I saw for a fleeting moment the photograph of Portia again; but she went right back to business, for in addition to acting in the play she was also directing it. In my frequent trips to the rehearsal room I saw her showing each actor how to play his or her part, a bustling businesslike figure of a woman, energetic and authoritative, giving the precise read-

ings and intonations learned from her years of experience in the play.
It had been one of the most successful in her repertoire with Sir Henry
Irving, from whom she was now separated.

One day in the hall I met Mr. Courtney, and this charming man,
who always had a kind word for me, asked if I would like to see Miss
Terry play when *The Merchant of Venice* opened, and he placed a
pair of tickets in my name at the Camden Town Theatre (the equivalent of a suburban theatre in New York), from which neighborhood
theatre the revival was to set out on tour. The night of the performance arrived, and when I saw Ellen Terry for the first time on the
stage as Portia, I saw her as the beautiful, humorous, witty, feminine
young creature with the blonde hair and the divinely musical voice
which made all men fall in love with her. She was no longer the bustling businesslike matron who but a week before had been rehearsing
her actors like a schoolmistress lecturing a group of pupils. Enchanted
by the transformation, I surrendered completely to the performance.
Here was a Portia who was all heroine, who fought evil and destroyed
it with her wit and grace. Her "quality of mercy" speech lifted the
audience from the shabby, tumble-down old Camden Town Theatre
to a realm where beauty, poetry and nobility of thought held sway,
and when the curtain fell at last it was as though a glimpse into a
brighter, lovelier world had come to an untimely end.

In less than three brief hours I learned to love the Shakespearean
theatre with an undying affection and thereafter attended every Shakespearean production in London; but more than that, I appreciated
what great roles can do for great actors and actresses. This is a knowledge which I have passed on from time to time to our own great actors
and actresses at critical points in their careers—for there will always
come a time when each important actor must either play Shakespeare
successfully or fail to reach the top of his profession.

The lasting impression made on me by Ellen Terry in my boyhood
had its effect on my entire life. Many years later, I wrote an article
for *Stage Magazine* urging Katharine Cornell, who had just appeared
in Obey's *The Rape of Lucrece* to try her hand at the real Shakespeare
instead of pseudo-Shakespeare. Soon after, she invited me to supper
and told me she had decided to play the part of Juliet. Then again,
on another memorable evening, Helen Westley and I called on Alfred
Lunt and Lynn Fontanne to obtain their agreement to appear in *The
Taming of the Shrew* for the Guild. And some years later I was to
lunch with Helen Hayes and to suggest that she play Hermione in
The Winter's Tale, which she transformed to the more suitable role of

Viola in *Twelfth Night*. I also suggested to Judith Anderson that she leave her home in Hollywood to appear as Lady Macbeth with Maurice Evans. And I finally induced Katharine Hepburn to essay the role of Rosalind in *As You Like It*. Thus the seeds sown that evening in Camden Town came to ultimate fruition in the American Theatre. "Whenever an actor plays Shakespeare," Louis Calvert, one of the greatest actors of our time, once told me, "he gains something in stature which he never loses. If you have once played a Shakespearean king, you can play the role of a king written by a lesser author but something of the Shakespearean kingliness will cling to you like an invisible mantle, and sustain and enhance your performance in the lesser role."

Many times during the matinees of the Theatre Guild's production of *Twelfth Night* I was surrounded by school children. Watching the enraptured expressions on their upturned faces as they sat enchanted by the performance of Helen Hayes and her company, I knew that every child present would grow into a more sensitive, more complete human being, because of this experience; for when children are touched by beauty and imagination, something is enkindled in them which never wholly leaves them.

After Ellen Terry and her company had gone on tour, all was quiet again at 3 Bedford Street until Ben Greet arrived from the United States. Then there were numerous errands to be performed for him, letters to be delivered backstage which enabled me to peep into the rehearsals of other managements, so that before long I was familiar with the mysterious underground passages and tortuous alleyways behind the scenes of the London theatres. On the day of his leave-taking for New York, Ben Greet thanked me warmly for the little services I had performed, but—humiliation of humiliations—forced a five-shilling piece into my hand. I flushed crimson—the very idea of "tipping" a junior clerk! I refused the money, but he was adamant, no doubt regarding me as a quaint young imbecile. No boy suffered more from loss of dignity than I did that day. I could think of only one way to appease my wounded pride, which was to purchase a coveted foreign postage stamp for my stamp album with the five-shilling piece and to regard it as a gift from the famous actor.

Soon after this, a musical comedy went into rehearsal, and the front office, crowded with attractive young chorus girls, comedians and dancers seeking parts, now became a scene of gaiety, bustle and intrigue. I was importuned on all sides to tell Miss Matthews, who first interviewed the applicants, that this beauty or that wished to see her; and since there were usually dozens of attractive young people seated around the office, it began to take on the appearance and atmosphere of a jolly social gathering. Seated at my desk a short distance away from where the actors and actresses congregated, I was at a disadvantage in taking part in the general goings on, because my chair was too low for me, and being still a relatively small boy, only the upper part of my shoulders emerged above the desk. Lunching one day upstairs among the busts, however, I ran across a wooden box about twelve inches high on which was painted the word "Dynamite." It was evidently a prop from some old farce, and just the thing to sit on and be head and shoulders taller than I was. Alas, this small box, among other things, was to bring about my ultimate undoing, for one eventful morning my mother dropped into the office at a time when J. Bannister Howard was out-of-town, and the high jinks were at their highest. She saw me literally sitting on dynamite, surrounded by a bevy of chorus girls, and evidently a popular favorite with them; largely, I hasten to add, because of my willingness to arrange casting interviews for them with the amiable Miss Matthews. Seated on my table, and making a very pretty display of stockinged ankles, was a particularly attractive girl who, at the moment, was using all her feminine blandishments on me in order to ascertain when Mr. Howard would be back in town, and could she see him? My mother surveyed the scene and situation sternly. She was no Puritan, but was this atmosphere the best for a boy just turned thirteen? She decided that it was not, and my fate was sealed.

At the small private hotel in Bloomsbury where my family lived at the time, my mother had made friends with a group of young men who used to foregather in the evening and sit around the piano as she played Gilbert and Sullivan or the latest popular songs. Among these were Francis MacMillan, the American violinist, and his brother Charles. Others in the group were Arthur Tidman, a man of distinguished literary tastes who had recently returned from teaching school in Australia, and Wallace Cranston Fairweather, a redheaded, redfaced Scotsman from Glasgow with an accent so full of burrs that it called for the services of an interpreter. But if Wallace Cranston was incomprehensible in speech, he had a mind as keen as a buzz saw. Having lately been dispatched by his firm to forage among the Sassenachs, he had opened a branch office in Chancery Lane for the Chartered Patent Agency which his father had conducted for many years in Glasgow under the name of Cruikshank and Fairweather, and by his brilliance and erudition he had built it to great success. It was in the lap of this strangely assorted coterie that my mother placed the problem of her son and his career in the theatre. Wallace Cranston solved it simply by saying that he'd take "the little divil" into his office and teach him the profession. "Of cour'r'se there'll be er'r'rands to r'run," he added, and then he launched into a long harangue upon the advantages of being a Chartered Patent Agent. I gathered that it was an "uncrowded" profession, that I would have to study at night school, and that the financial prospects were, to say the least, very rosy indeed since I was to begin at a salary of ten shillings a week. He made a sufficient impression on my mother for her to throw the weight of her influence against my continuing at No. 3 Bedford Street, and so I reluctantly turned my back on the theatre, Mr. J. Bannister Howard and Miss Matthews, and all that they implied.

Despite the attraction which the theatre held for me, I did not, at thirteen, feel that I had a special bent for it in contrast with other forms of aristic work. Indeed, I had been encouraged by Arthur Tidman to write short stories, and had a number of these under way, and I was also interested in drawing and painting. All of these interests were kept in a separate part of my personality labeled "Art," while earning a living was confined to another compartment labeled "Business." This separation of myself into two parts was not uncommon under the circumstances, for the idea that writers starved in garrets was prevalent in those days before the talking pictures, which have since made the successful novelist and dramatist among the best-paid professional men on earth. Inventions had always interested me, and I hoped that by working industriously at my new profession I would ultimately earn enough leisure to apply myself solely to writing. The plan, made so early in my life, I carried through to fruition in later years; and it was also this separation of myself into two compartments, so to speak, which led me later to help found the Washington Square Players and the Theatre Guild with no thought of personal financial gain.

No. 33 Chancery Lane, the London office of the firm of Cruikshank and Fairweather, was a bleak stone building unfit for human habitation in the year 1903, and now thoroughly bombed out of existence. My duties there were to copy the letters, address and mail them, and run back and forth with documents to the British Patent Office. Wallace Cranston, true to his promise, began to teach me. "Do you know German, Lawrence?" he asked me. "No," I replied, warily. "Well, here's the specification of an invention which is supposed to be in

English, but the translation's hellish. However, here's the original German and here's a dictionary, now put it into good English." I read over the document. The invention purported to be a device for spraying lawns; it could also be used to spray gravy over joints. I wondered how. Thus I was introduced to the mysteries of patent specifications, and soon by the aid of a few dictionaries began to pick up technical German and French words which almost completely ruined my ability to converse freely in those languages, so apt was I to use a technical expression instead of the colloquial one. Years later, I was to hear a continental patent attorney attempt to explain that he and his good wife often took a walk in the evening, by saying, "Each night my wife and I make a little movement together!"

The wars which, later on, were to boil with fury over the face of the entire world, were vaguely in the air in 1903, and it was my destiny to work on many of the inventions which were to write a chapter of horrors unequaled in any period since man rose to a little higher level than the ape. My first experience came at fourteen when a heavy-set mild-mannered Connecticut Yankee, with keen eyes, bushy eyebrows and a cigar projecting aggressively from the corner of his mouth, visited us at the office. He was Simon Lake, the inventor of the modern submarine, and he was on his way to Russia to build a fleet of these submarines for the Czar to use against the Japanese. I was delegated to act as his guide and to show him around the business section of London, which I did with all the enthusiasm of a pup leading around the hero of Jules Verne's *Twenty Thousand Leagues Under the Sea.* Little did I think, as I piloted this gentle individual to the British Admiralty and the Russian Embassy, that forty years later I would be arranging for an interview between this same Simon Lake and a Board of twelve American admirals who heard with amazement his plans for new long-range cargo submarines and other undersea marvels which are still deep naval secrets. Unable to obtain a serious hearing until after Pearl Harbor, Simon Lake was almost blind and so poor that he could not even afford a typewriter to describe his latest ideas. It was, nevertheless, unfortunate for the world that when I acted as Simon Lake's guide in London, I did not lose him somewhere in the tortuous passages of the Underground, for after leaving London, he visited Germany. Here he met Admiral von Tirpitz, who, so the story goes, after talking to Lake, conceived the idea of total submarine warfare which cost the world so terrible a toll in lives and ships.

Life in Chancery Lane was always exciting, thanks to the vagaries of the brilliant and volatile young Wallace Cranston Fairweather. Soon after I was installed in the office, he fell in love with a charming American girl, and hell broke loose as a result. Each morning he would rush through all the work of the day so that he could be free as early as possible to write to her in the afternoon. By two-thirty he was raging around the office in a passion, and bedeviling us for any delays which might have occurred. Then, at the stroke of three, and in a state of tearing temper, he locked himself in his private office, took the telephone off the hook, and began to write a long love letter to his American sweetheart. The two clerks and I would sink back in our chairs in the outer office in a state of exhaustion, and a great quiet would descend over the premises. But not for long. The door of Wallace Cranston's office would open and his face, looking very pink, would appear. "Lawrence, what's the name of the Goddess of Music? Ach, hell, you wouldn't know! Look it up in the *Encyclopaedia Britannica!*" This letter finished, he behaved angelically for the rest of the day.

Wallace Cranston's marriage finally resulted in his having to leave London for Glasgow. This was a tragedy for me, for I admired him greatly. He was keenly interested in modern literature and thought, and was an enthusiast for the plays of Shaw and the books of H. G. Wells and G. K. Chesterton. My own interests followed similar lines. I became a devout follower of Ruskin. I studied the paintings in the National and Tate Galleries and took sides in the ancient quarrel over the relative merits of Turner and Poussin. I haunted the British Museum on Saturday afternoons and Sundays, and learned all I could of Greek art and philosophy. My social instincts were awakened by the repellent poverty of the London slums. I talked this over with Arthur Tidman, who introduced me to the works of Bernard Shaw, and later on I heard him lecture at the Fabian Society. I became sympathetic to social reform and felt it was my duty to leave the world a better place than it had been before I came into it. I was never happier than during this formative period. Only one circumstance cast a shadow, the fact that I did not get along with my stepfather, which made me want to leave home as soon as possible. I saw an opportunity for this in Wallace Cranston's leaving London for Glasgow, so I asked him to take me along with him. He agreed on one condition—that I learn shorthand, so that I could be his secretary. I was not very cordial to this suggestion until my stepfather convincingly pointed out that secretarial work was the Royal Road to Success and that many prominent men had begun their careers as secretaries.

One fateful day Wallace Cranston arrived from Glasgow, and called me into his office. I entered expectantly. He addressed me in a torrent of the purest Scottish dialect into which he had relapsed since his return to Scotland. Harry Lauder spoke drawing-room English by comparison. I gathered that he would test me with a letter. I brought in my shorthand notebook, and Wallace Cranston began to dictate, pacing back and forth while I clutched my pencil and raced it madly over the paper. "That's all, Lawrence, an' dinna fash yousel' too much orrrrit!" (This, translated into English, meant that I was not to worry myself too much over it.) I answered with a confident smile. "I'll type it and bring it back right away." I stepped over to a typewriter in the outer office, placed the paper in the machine, and began to read my notes. My heart sank. Not one word could I decipher except the first "Dear Sir."

A few weeks later Wallace Cranston gave me another chance, and I failed just as badly. But I consoled myself with the thought that the special Providence which was in charge of my destiny did not intend me to be either a stenographer or a secretary. Years later I spent a day in Glasgow. It was cold, dark, foggy and raining cats and dogs. As I left this dismal scene on a brightly lighted train mercifully bound for London, and which seemed to be as happy over leaving Glasgow as I was, I muttered to myself, "Thank the Lord I lost my way on the Royal Road to Success!" I had only one regret, that I thus parted from the company of Wallace Cranston Fairweather, who had taken the trouble to teach me the difficult profession in which I labored so many years of my life, and whose endearing good humor, kindness and friendship have made me everlastingly grateful to him.

CHAPTER IV

The Technical Assistant

SOON after I had failed a second time in my effort to go to Glasgow, I learned of a vacancy in the technical staff of Haseltine Lake and Co., a large firm of Chartered Patent Agents, also located in Southampton Buildings, Chancery Lane. By this time I was nearly seventeen and had acquired a considerable knowledge of patent practice. With what Wallace Cranston Fairweather had taught me, added to what I had picked up during my three years in his office and the smattering of engineering and chemistry I had learned in evening classes at the London Polytechnic and County Council Schools, I felt qualified for a more important position. The British Parliament had obligingly passed a new patent law, the Act of 1907, which made young men like myself in considerable demand. After being pleasantly interviewed by a sharp-eyed clerical-looking gentleman named Alfred White (who years later became my London partner), I was promptly engaged as a "technical assistant" at the handsome stipend of one pound per week, for which I was to prosecute patent applications, most of which came from America, before the British Patent Office.

My desk, along with some thirty others, was in a large, shabbily furnished room, a portion of which also served as the waiting room, the intention being (so it was said) to give the office the appearance of an ancient and hence reliable English bank. Had the intention also been to make it as difficult as possible for us to work on our cases without constant disturbance, the arrangement could be regarded as perfect. As it was, we would try to read and understand the descriptions and drawings of complicated inventions, interrupted by the constant comings and goings of the clerks and clients, while every afternoon after lunch a German band outside the corner public house, playing some lachrymose melody such as "It's Only a Beautiful Picture in a Beautiful Golden Frame," would add its ump-tum-tum, ump-tum-tum to the clicking of the typewriters and the general buzz of conversation. Constantly working under these conditions gave me powers of concentration of great value later. But this has also been the source of the greatest irritation to my family and such friends as I have been able to keep, for guns can go off within earshot if I am reading or otherwise concentrating, and the best method of attracting my attention under these conditions is to shake me violently. (I hasten to add that, soon after, the firm moved into a suite of sumptuous offices in the Birkbeck Bank Building, and has remained throughout all these years, one of the most outstanding British firms of Chartered Patent Agents.)

Seated in this large room were a number of clerks and technical assistants ranging from office boys of fifteen to an old-maidish gentleman of sixty named Jepson, to whom all inventions relating to corsets, as well as those appertaining to the more intimate feminine functions, were referred as a standing office joke. Indeed, the spectacle of this prim, elderly gentleman, embarrassed and blushing, so far as his pale ivory skin would permit him to blush, while a shameless lady inventor would ruthlessly initiate him into the mysteries of some new form of brassiere or girdle, would send the rest of the office staff into stitches.

In a section walled off like an enclosure in a zoological garden for the rarer specimens, sat Mr. White and his flock of assistants of the Foreign Department, in which, by reason of my ability to use the dictionaries, I was duly installed. There I met two young men, John Parry and William Card, who became my bosom friends and later my partners in America. John Parry was a Welshman from Aberystwith, slender, with dark curly hair and the keenest of black eyes, argumentative, emotional and the best engineer on the staff. William Card was tall, athletic and handsome. He divided his interests between raising large carnations in his father's flower garden in Clapham Junction and developing his bicep muscles, for which purpose he carried in his pockets a pair of spring handgrips which he opened and closed in rhythmic succession as he walked to and from the office.

The three of us were in the habit of lunching together at Noon's, an old restaurant in Holborn, where, for a shilling one could eat a three-course lunch and read American magazines such as *The Saturday Evening Post*, which, although spotted with gravy from the plates of previous diners, were nevertheless one of the prime attractions of the place. John, Bill and I amused ourselves by commenting in a patronizing way on the quaintness of American slang, and these old magazines played an important part in arousing our interest in America. In the Foreign Department we were of course constantly dealing with American inventions, corresponding with American lawyers, and during the summer receiving visits from American clients.

The inventions from America were sheer joy to work on, and since they were beautifully described and illustrated, they continuously aroused my curiosity as to the kind of people who turned them out. At times we would have distinguished American visitors. One of them was a Mr. Gillette, a tall gentleman from Boston with sideburns who had invented a safety razor with "a thin flexible blade." The inventions from the continent of Europe gave more trouble. They were usually badly prepared and translated; and while most of the American inventions were for purposes of peace, many of the European inventions were wicked-looking guns and armaments coming from the Creusot-Schneider works in France and Skoda in Bohemia, for my employers handled the patents for the so-called European armament ring, and from time to time the sinister figure of the great Zaharoff himself, the mysterious Greek munitions king of Europe, was to be seen in the waiting room.

One day when the general din had died down in the office, because almost everyone except myself had gone to lunch, the main door opened and a strange figure entered—a thick-set little man wearing a long frock coat and silk hat, and a goatee which made him look like an abbreviated edition of Uncle Sam. I looked up from my work and was angrily addressed by this gentleman in nasal Yankee accents. "Hi, you, tell Mr. Jackson I'm here, and look sma't about it!" I rose with great dignity. Didn't this man realize I was a technical assistant and not a mere clerk to be ordered about in this way? Towering above him I asked icily, "Who shall I say it is?" The great man drew himself up at least an inch taller. "Wa'al, boy, at home they call me Sir Hiram Maxim! Haven't you ever heard of me?" "No," I replied, untruthfully. "Never heard of you, Sir Hiram—but come along, I'm sure Mr. Jackson will see you," with which I led the famous inventor of the automatic machine gun into the presence of the head of the firm, who, later on, lectured me severely on my lack of tact.

My life was now a crowded kaleidoscope of inventions, law lectures, science classes, theatres, writing stories, politics and falling in love, although how I found time for this last pursuit now baffles me. My first love was an actress who worked for Mr. George Alexander—a matinee idol at that time—who paid not the slightest attention to me. I promptly transferred my affections to her sister, who was studying to be a dancer. She, too, seemed indifferent, and I finally wound up in love with the third sister, a young art student named Pamela who was studying at Slade's, and whose daily journey to the Underground coincided with my own to the office. Pamela reciprocated my feelings to a mild degree, and my affections remained reasonably stable for several years. Since Pamela's father happened to be the leading representative of the Conservative Party in the neighborhood, I violently attacked this gentleman, much to the annoyance of Pamela, but finally ended up by supporting the party on its program of Tariff Reform. With one of my friends, George Taylor, who had a penchant for politics, I attended meetings in Hyde Park on Sundays and heckled the Atheists and Anarchists who harangued the crowds until a shower of rain would cause their arguments and their listeners alike to disappear rapidly into thin air.

George Taylor introduced me to a parliamentary debating society known as the West London Parliament which was organized on a party basis and carried out its debates as an exact counterpart to those of the House of Commons. The debating society met each Monday at the Marylebone Town Hall, where we used the main Council Chamber which imparted considerable dignity to our proceedings. A body known as the Fabian Nursery was in command of the Socialist benches, led by a brilliant lynx-eyed young man named Herman Schlosser, who later in life became Solicitor General of England and finally a Judge. My friend George Taylor, for no good reason, was Whip to the Socialist Party, while I, for no better reason, was Minister of Agriculture and Fisheries in the Conservative Party. George confided in me one day that the reason he liked the Socialists better than the others was because they all had reasonably bad habits, but, unlike the Conservatives and Liberals, were not hypocrites. There was one old gentleman, a leader of the Conservative Party, a red-faced white-bearded old fellow with a long red nose and goggly silver spectacles, who publicly assured us that this world was but the waiting room in a station on the railroad to Heaven, and those who traveled with any but the Conservative Party would miss the last train home. This did not deter him, however, from privately drinking himself under the table when some of the younger men took him out "pub-crawling" in Leicester Square and Piccadilly Circus once the official debates were over.

Indeed, our official debates were dull and tame affairs compared with those which took place over tables in the pubs and restaurants after our sessions. Here our vital young members would be accosted by ladies of easy virtue who sat at our tables and imbibed Scotch or beer while discussion ranged from religion to evolution, taking in politics and economics en route, and usually ending up heavily on the subject of sex, about which we talked a great deal, but so far as I could observe, did very little; and I fear that the professional ladies who drank with us gained nothing from our company but a smattering of education diluted with alcohol.

As Minister of Agriculture for the Conservative Party, I was requested to prepare a Bill known as the Small Holdings Act, based on the theory that everyone could live in reasonable comfort and happiness on three acres and a cow. The Bill was prepared and duly printed when I was approached by my Prime Minister, an aggressive young chap by the name of Harding, and told that the fate of the entire Conservative Party was bound up in my Bill and hung in the balance, for the reason that Lord Robert Cecil was to be the guest of honor at the next Annual Dinner, and there was a plot on the part of the Liberals and Socialists to combine together to defeat the Bill, and so throw us out of office. As a result, the Liberals would be in control of the Annual Dinner and all the fun of speech making, introducing the Guest of Honor, allotment of seats, and so forth, would go to them, instead of to us. In due course my Bill came up for action, and was greeted with the utmost contempt by the Opposition benches. Judge my surprise when a thin blond-haired young man rose from the Socialist benches and, with a dry North Irish accent, spoke in favor of the Bill. But in supporting it, he not only attacked me violently but he also attacked the Liberals and Socialists and all the other Irish members as well. "Who is this man?" I asked, as the verbal bombardment subsided. "He seems to be against everybody!" "He's St. John Ervine," I was told, "the member from Belfast. He's a holy terror!" St. John pleaded for the passage of my Bill so eloquently that it was carried by a narrow majority, and we had the dubious honor of being hosts to Lord Robert, who sat with his head bowed almost to his plate all through dinner. He finally delivered a speech on "Banking and Credit" which was no credit to England's greatest family of legislators, and sent us all to sleep until he finished. After this our little crowd of cronies departed to the West End, where we argued long into the night on the subject of heredity and the House of Lords, one group holding that Lord Robert was so erudite that we were unable to understand him, while the other alleged that they understood him only too well.

St. John Ervine, having supported my Bill and partaken of some liquid refreshment with me after meetings, dropped out of my life, only to return into it many years later as the successful author of *John Ferguson*.

My boon companion at this time was the aforesaid young man with the plain name of George Taylor, but George's name was the only thing connected with him which was plain. Tall, blond, and with eyes which were gray-green and smiled on the least provocation, George was the embodiment to me of all that was smart and sophisticated. George's particular charm was to be gay and lighthearted in all matters where I was serious and moralistic. He was, so to speak, a piccolo virtuoso, to whom I played a 'cello accompaniment in a minor key. I lived to some extent in a reflection of his life, and since he was most attractive to women, he had the experiences, while I profited by them, as I was too fastidious to follow his example and too cautious not to learn from his mistakes.

During this period, and indeed until I reached the age of twenty-three, my ideas on the subject of love were, to say the least, naive, and were derived largely from literature rather than life. I believed firmly in what Stendhal called "the love of crystallization." When the bough of a tree is dipped in water containing a crystalline solution, the crystals will be deposited on the bough and outline it in glamorous beauty. Seen through the eyes of a lover, wrote Stendhal, the beloved is similarly transformed beyond reality. Like Werther and his Charlotte, I mooned and mooned over Pamela. These were pre-Havelock Ellis days and many adolescent young people like myself were in a state of inner conflict. My feelings were sublimated in a starry-eyed belief in the love of Dante for Beatrice, in the infinite purity of the Burne-Jones pre-Raphaelite angels, and in my worship of Pamela. She became for me a symbol on a pedestal from which she obligingly descended at times to go roller-skating with me at a new American rink or for tea at Rumpelmeyer's or the Vienna Café, where in a most unsymbolic manner she devoured quantities of Vienna pastries washed down with copious draughts of Vienna coffee. But love for me was still "a thing apart," and did nothing to hinder the plans I was making for my future.

CHAPTER V

Prelude to Departure

THROUGHOUT my life in London my family was friendly with an elderly gentleman and his wife who lived in my step-father's house in Woburn Square. He was a large white-bearded Viennese with twinkling blue eyes and an infectious laugh who brought an air of jollity with him on all occasions, and was known to us and to all his friends as "old Hartl." He was a retired business man who had lived in Paris where he had amassed a modest fortune. He now lived on his income and indulged himself in his hobby, which was the grand opera. His home was always thronged with the artists from Covent Garden while the season was on, and since an opera singer had the same effect on old Hartl as good champagne, he lived in a state of high excitement the moment the opera season opened. As a young man in Paris he had spent his days in business and his evenings at the opera as a supernumerary, where his experiences, which he recounted to me, were vivid and various. Once a large chorine attired as an angel became unhooked from the wire by which she was suspended, fell on top of him and almost broke his neck. Another time he was a "super" in the first performance of *Lohengrin* which took place in Paris after the Franco-Prussian War of 1870. The audience listened in angry silence until Hartl appeared leading two large dogs, whereupon there was an outburst of applause and cries of *"Bravo les chiens!"* which brought the house down.

In addition to recounting these stories out of the past, old Hartl invited us to meet many of the opera singers who attended his receptions, and they in turn were lavish in turning over free tickets to us when Covent Garden Opera House needed "papering." As a result, I

34

and my brothers attended most of the unpopular operas in London, and even some of the popular ones when "business" was poor. I managed in four years of opera-going to hear all the leading singers of those days, including Caruso, Melba, Tetrazini, Scotti and Emmy Destinn, and to become acutely critical of opera as a form of the theatre, since the best voices seemed to belong to the worst actors, and *vice versa.* I was particularly disappointed in the barrel-like figure of Caruso who, for all his golden voice, stubbornly refused to fit into any of the romantic roles he was called upon to play, and I could not help feeling that to enjoy his performances fully, the audiences should have been blindfolded.

In my boyhood, private theatricals, amateur reciters and musical performers were rampant. My mother's brother was an amateur musician, as addicted to his hobby as a drug fiend to cocaine, and with results not unsimilar, for he would play absent-mindedly at the piano for hours until he had his entire family in hysterics. "Can't somebody stop your father playing?" was my Aunt Janey's constant complaint to her children. The children, consisting of my cousin Lillian, who was a singer, and her brothers Basil and D'Arcy, both of whom were excellent musicians, maintained a strictly profesional attitude, and every Sunday evening they held a musicale at their home. These affairs were conducted with great solemnity, and through them I became acquainted with the songs of Schubert, Schumann and the French Bergerette songs sung delightfully by Lillian, which I used many years later in the theatre.

To an elderly lady named Emily Soldene I owe my interest in operetta. At the height of her career, Emily Soldene was England's operetta queen, and she created the leading roles of some of Offenbach's works in London; but the operetta for which she was most famous was *Geneviève de Brabant,* which she sang both in England and the United States. Nearly six feet tall, attired in white tights, and singing the famous "Voici le Sabre de Mon Père!" from *La Grande Duchesse* with a verve which no longer exists in the mustical theatre of today, it is small wonder that the portly Prince of Wales, who was later to become Edward the Seventh, fell a victim to her ample charms. He remained her devoted admirer until, upon the last of her many retirements from the stage, she wrote her reminiscences,[1] which threw the whole of London society into an uproar and caused Queen Victoria to

---

[1] Emily Soldene, *My Theatrical and Musical Recollections,* Downey & Co., Ltd., London, 1897.

send for her erring son and reprimand him severely for setting so bad an example to his admiring fellow countrymen.

Emily Soldene visited our home often, for she lived near us in a down-at-heel "private hotel," by which appellation superior Bloomsbury boarding houses unsuccessfully attempted to disguise themselves. One evening we gave a party in her honor for some of her old admirers, and at their insistence, she sang the old songs, and the old men sitting in the drawing room listening to her, were moved to tears by the magic of music and old memories. She died in obscurity a few years later, but her reminiscences remain one of the finest pictures of the English and American theatre of the seventies and eighties.

While my interest in the arts was thus developing, I was continuing my studies in engineering at night school, in order the better to fit myself for my work at the office. However, I was not popular with the partners of the firm of Chartered Patent Agents where I worked, chiefly because I was both bumptious and argumentative. Indeed, I felt so cocksure of myself, that any doubts my superiors might have had of me were discounted by my own good opinion of myself. My unpopularity spread to the British Patent Office where the government examiners, put off guard by my youth, found that I could argue the hind leg off a donkey. Attired in a tail coat, and a shiny silk hat which belonged to the office and was worn by all the younger members of the staff in turn when they visited the Patent Office, I attended Hearings before the British Comptroller General and, to the irritation of my opponents, I often won my cases because I was better prepared than they were. One principal examiner, an Irishman named Rutherford, was so angered by the continued successes of this young whippersnapper, that he called on the head of our firm and warned him that I was doing our clients no good by stirring up so much official resentment. I was sent for by the head and severely reprimanded. "If you want to win your cases," he said, not unreasonably, "you've just got to do it without upsetting the examiners." It was a good lesson for me, though it seemed unfair at the time.

The international nature of the firm's business was calculated to interest me in international affairs, which coincided with the international character of my family on my mother's side. Her relatives were scattered from Paris to Bombay, and from Montreal to Buenos Aires. During my childhood our foreign relatives visited London and kept in touch with the English branch, so that my first, second, third and fourth cousins from the United States, Canada, Argentina or France formed a background for my youthful years, and gave me a vista of a world far larger than the London in which I lived. My mother's family was held together more by family pride than affection, the pride stemming from the fact that she was a descendant of the de Solas, one of the oldest Spanish-Jewish families, which was said to include among its ancestors a Viceroy of Navarre, as well as one of the Seven Sages of Castile.

My life was considerably influenced, when I was about seventeen, by the arrival in England of my Uncle Leopold, Aunt Jenny and their four children from Buenos Aires. Leopold Orsay, a tall, handsome middle-aged Frenchman with a military bearing imparted to him by some years in the French army, was an imposing figure with fierce upstanding mustaches which gave him an air of imminent piracy. As a boy, he had slept with a cavalry sword in his bed during the capture of Paris by the Germans in 1870, and he never lost his hatred of *les sales Boches*. He had married my mother's sister and embarked for the Argentine some twenty-odd years earlier, where his children Pedro, Marghareta, Stella and Dolly were born. They were very Latin in type, and the girls were given to giggling over everything English, much of which language they professed to find improper; indeed, my cousin Marghareta one day asked me with great curiosity what was this crime so often committed by Englishmen called in the newspapers "man's laughter" and seemed quite disappointed when I explained that there was nothing either esoteric or erotic about it. My cousin Pedro, who was dark and dashing, was far more mature than the average English boy of his age, and became my constant friend. Together we purchased bicycles, and spent our week ends with George Taylor, a happy trio touring over the pleasant high roads leading out of London. Uncle Leopold, who had conducted various enterprises in Buenos Aires, ended up the wealthy owner of a gold mine, and promptly invested his money in Paris *rentes*. He lived at this time at the Hotel Cecil, and amused himself by giving large family parties, where the Argentine relatives met cousins from Paris, Montreal, New York, Capetown, the Midlands, and a large assortment of Londoners who spent a good deal of their time admiring their ancestors.

Chief objects for the family ancestor worship were my mother's great-grandfather, the Reverend Raphael Meldola, who headed the Spanish-Jewish congregation in England in the time of George III, and his more famous son-in-law, the Reverend D. A. de Sola, who succeeded him and fathered five sons and seven daughters, known familiarly to the congregation at Bevis Marks, according to my mother, as the Seven Ugly Sisters, one of whom was my grandmother. My mother's first cousins included the Reverend Meldola de Sola of Montreal, Dr. Pereria Mendes and Dr. de Sola Mendes of New York, and Dr. D. de Sola Pool of London and later of New York. So affected was I by having all these ministers in the family, that I rebelled against any form of religious orthodoxy at an early age, and began to write a book to prove that all religions were fundamentally the same, in doing which I became for a short time a devout follower of Ingersoll.

I was, however, greatly impressed by my Uncle Leopold's career. Here, I thought, was the complete pattern for my own life. I shall leave England some day, make my fortune in the New World, and then retire at an early age, but unlike Uncle Leopold, I shall devote myself to writing.

My friend John Parry and I decided that we would sit for the examination of the British Chartered Institute of Patent Agents, the passing of which would qualify us to practice our profession. This was a difficult undertaking. Not only was it necessary to know the patent and trade-mark laws of the world; we were also required to be scientifically proficient and to be able to pass examinations in such varied subjects as chemistry, electricity, mechanical drawing and manufacturing, in which latter subject one was supposed to be able to describe how anything was made, from a silk hat to a steel cable. We studied together evenings steadfastly for three years, were six days under examination, and came out of the ordeal at the end two spindly palefaced youths looking badly in need of fresh air. We proceeded for a vacation to Brighton, where my Uncle Leopold was staying, and he promptly invited me to join him and his family in Paris, where one of our French cousins, Elise Tucker, was marrying a Canadian, who, for some unaccountable reason, was the Paris Manager of Savon Cadum, a firm of French soap manufacturers. Their advertisements showing a picture of a baby were plastered all over France, and indeed must have portrayed more children than actually existed in that country with its declining birth rate.

The wedding of my cousin Elise was set for the summer, and I joined the Orsays at their hotel near the Banque de France. Here Pedro and I spent many a happy evening together, chaperoned by Uncle Leopold, who would leave his wife and daughters at the hotel with the observation that since Pedro and I were no longer boys, it was better for us to see Paris night life under his guidance than to go out alone. So the three of us would set off to Montmartre or the Folies Bergère with its spectacles of sad-looking naked women, where we were thoroughly disturbed by all that we saw, which was not very much. For our wise old uncle took good care not to take us anywhere except the most superficially improper places, such as the side shows in the Music Halls where unhappy ladies in Moorish costumes moved their tummies rhythmically to the accompaniment of insistent tom-toms.

I soon realized that our excursions were merely Uncle Leopold's excuse for trotting off in the evening unencumbered by a wife and three daughters. He was delightful company, adored by all the women who met him, and like all wealthy Argentinians, was welcome every-where. "Nevaire be stingy with ze girls," he would say to Pedro and myself, paying for several rounds of drinks and distributing bills to groups of gaily attired females who gathered around him, vainly try-ing to engage our deeper and more lucrative interests. And by twelve or twelve-thirty he would say, "Boys, it's time to be home." And off the three of us would go, having inspected "vice" without tasting it.

In due time cousins, uncles and aunts arrived from the four corners of the earth for Elise's wedding. Her husband hailed from Montreal and was the brother of the Canadian opera singer Donalda, the pro-tégée of Sir Donald Strathcona, then Premier of Canada, from whose name she had concocted her own. Naturally, Canadian relatives were there in quantities. There were also two handsome American girls, Alice and Claire Raphael, distantly related to the Canadian relatives, who were traveling in Europe with their mother. Alice had just writ-ten a novel called *Fulfillment* which impressed me enormously, while Claire could play Bach on the piano by the hour. I realized with a shock that these American girls, unlike so many bespectacled Amer-ican schoolteachers who swarmed over Europe during the summer, were not only beautiful, but were intelligent and well-educated as well. This surprised and interested me, and I asked them a great many questions about America, and especially about the schoolteachers. "All American women," said Alice, "are not schoolteachers, although most of them could be if they wanted to." "Yes," said Claire, tossing her dark curls, "women can be anything they want to be in America." Some years later, as Mrs. Arthur Reis, she founded the League of Composers in New York which has done so much for modern music and musicians in America, while Alice also achieved fame with her version of Goethe's *Faust*. These two sisters made a vivid impression on me, and awakened my interest in the United States far more than did my American cousins who periodically visited London. After the wedding was over, and the aunts, uncles and cousins had dispersed all over the globe, I took my leave of Alice and Claire, telling them I was going to come to New York to see them again which, of course, neither of them believed. Nor, to be truthful, did I.

On my return to London from Paris, I learned that John Parry and I had passed the Chartered Institute Examination, both with extremely high marks. I called on the head of the firm and gave him the good news, adding that I would like to join the New York office, which was then doing rather badly. Since I was informed that high marks were not the slightest indication of ability, I settled down to my normal work. But a few weeks later I was sent for by the head of the firm. "Mr. Langner," he said, "we've thought over your proposal and we've decided to send you to New York!" I was to be the technical assistant at the New York office, which was in the charge of an efficient American lady who had once been his secretary. My salary was to be eighteen dollars per week. My heart leaped, for compared with the paltry thirty shillings I was earning at the time, this sum was a fortune. I meditated on how wonderfully I had impressed the head of the firm to cause him to change his mind so quickly. I learned later that our principal competitors, another large British firm, had just opened a New York office, and I was being sent there as a pawn in the competitive battle being waged between these two large concerns. So I owed my departure to America, not to my own efforts, but to those of our firm's leading competitors.

The next month was spent in a whirl of preparation and leave-takings. My main regret was in parting from my beloved Pamela, by this time a mature young lady of nineteen, with large blue eyes, a turned-up nose, and a large bow in her soft brown hair. The day before I sailed, I took Pamela, who was on her way to becoming an accomplished painter, to lunch at the Holborn Restaurant, ordered a bottle of champagne and informed her that I intended to make my fortune in America. While I was not quite ready to offer marriage on a salary of eighteen dollars a week, I would find out as soon as I arrived how far this sum would go, and if it turned out to be sufficient, I would send for her immediately. Under the influence of the champagne, Pamela assented, but with her fingers crossed. No adventurer setting forth for the Klondike in search of gold at the risk of his life sounded braver than I did as I talked of my journey to New York and what I would accomplish there. No heroine sounded nobler than Pamela as she told me she would be painting and waiting, and waiting and painting, until I sent for her. Like most young English people of those days, our ideas of America were largely gained from "Western" silent pictures, and the novels of J. Fenimore Cooper.

"I suppose you'll be carrying a six-shooter in your hip pocket," Pamela said quite simply. "Yes, I guess everybody does in New York," I replied carelessly. "Do take care of yourself, Law'ence," she said. (She had no "r's" in her voice, due, she told me, to having been educated in Belgium.) I mentally determined to avoid all conflict with the cowboys or desperadoes in the countryside around New York in order that I might keep myself intact for Pamela's sweet sake, if not for my own. We took a cab, and said good-by tenderly. I kissed her for the first time and felt extremely devilish. She said, "W'ite to me, Law'ence," and fled, and I was left sitting slightly intoxicated, but enormously elated, in the cavernous depths of the cab. "Nature," I reflected, "is definitely wonderful." A day later, December 28, 1910, I embarked on the S. S. *Minnehaha* for New York City, full of expectancy for the future, and with a raging toothache.

In my steamer trunk I carried three heavy knitted woolen sweaters, and a dozen pairs of thick woolen combination union suits with long sleeves and legs, which hugged me in a stifling embrace all the way from my wrists to my ankles. My stepfather in a sudden fit of generosity had given me his fur-lined overcoat with a heavy beaver collar, then a faithful relic some sixteen years old. No explorer setting out for the North Pole could have been better outfitted than I was. Only one thing was missing, but I firmly resolved that on arriving in New York I would rectify this omission by purchasing a small Browning automatic for my hip pocket, to protect myself against the Indians who I felt certain would lie in wait to ambush me at the region where Broadway converges into the prairies.

CHAPTER VI

A New World

I ARRIVED in New York City January 8, 1910, at the age of twenty. Thousands of immigrants have described their emotions on first seeing the New York skyline, but very few have had a violent toothache at the time. My feeling of exhilaration on arriving in the New World was heightened by the certain knowledge that somewhere lurking behind the delicate silhouettes of the magical skyscrapers was an American dentist who would soon put me out of my misery.

I was met by my mother's cousin, Rosie Belais, a kindly lady a year or so older than my mother, who embraced me and literally took me to her heart, and from then on treated me more as a son than a mere second cousin. We drove in a taxi along the cobble-paved streets of the waterfront, until I was delivered at a boarding house on West Seventy-sixth Street, just across the street from my cousin Rosie's apartment. Behind the tall buildings I found other tall buildings, much to my surprise, for I was firmly convinced before I arrived that while the main streets of New York might contain skyscrapers and large hotels, on the back streets would be the wooden shacks one found in the frontier towns which I had seen so often in the cinema. The boarding house was an old-fashioned brownstone building, furnished with atrocious Victorian furniture. The landlady and the other guests obviously belonged to the same period. At the dining table I was introduced to these old-fashioned ladies and gentlemen, and was asked on all sides how I liked America, a question which was difficult to answer, as I had arrived only that morning. I was also busy taking in my new surroundings and at the same time wrestling with the dinner itself, an extremely puzzling affair. The meat course was served on a single large plate surrounded by a constellation of small dishes each filled with a smattering of vegetables which called for far more attention on my part than I had ever given to a meal before.

I was promptly visited by the younger generation of my American cousins, these being Raymond and Stella Mendes, and their younger brother, Henry, a beguiling young man who took pity on my innocence and made it his business to show me the town. They all insisted that I live as their neighbor on West Ninety-second Street, and so in a so-called railroad tenement at the corner of this street and Amsterdam Avenue, for the sum of two dollars a week, I became the tenant of a hall bedroom. It was just large enough to contain a bed, a dresser and a chair, but I lived as happily as a lark on the other sixteen dollars of my salary.

As soon as I was able, I introduced myself to the manageress of the New York office of my firm, which was located in the Wall Street district. I was made to feel welcome and important by this extraordinary lady who had faithfully devoted over twenty years of her life to the interests of her British employers, but who, because she was a woman, was the butt of many of the men in the London office. Soon it became evident that the rival British concern was being extremely successful, and together she and I planned to circumvent their inroads into our practice by making personal contacts with the clients. I made the very best appearance I could upon my slender salary, but I found that my heavy underwear and fur-lined coat were such impediments that I rapidly discarded them. Everywhere I went I was met with the utmost kindness, my opinion of America being almost invariably asked for, while opinions of England were almost always volunteered in return.

One day I called upon Park Benjamin, one of the most famous patent lawyers in the country at the time, whose daughter Dorothy later married Enrico Caruso. Park Benjamin was a white-haired, irascible old gentleman and a genius in his field. He greeted me by telling me he was damned glad the firm had sent me to America, and then proceeded to insult me, the firm and everything British for thirty minutes. I apologized for myself and the firm, but took a strong stand about the British. He relented, and proceeded to inform me that the British were the finest people in the world, that he had sixteen *Mayflower* ancestors, and that he was damned glad to meet me.

The railroad apartment in which I was a lodger was appropriately occupied by a retired Irish-American railroad engineer, his wife and three pretty daughters, all of whom shared breakfast with me. I was carefree and happy in my new life, and especially because I was no longer under the restraints imposed upon me by living at home with my stepfather.

In due course, I called upon my friends Alice and Claire Raphael, who lived on Central Park in a spacious apartment, each girl having her own sitting room, which impressed me enormously. They were the center of an attractive group of young people and included among their friends many young men and women who, later on in life, became my associates in the theatre. Among these were Theresa Helburn, then a wild-looking, highly educated young woman with a high forehead, who had recently come to New York from Boston; Edward Goodman, a dramatic-looking young man who reminded me vaguely of Edgar Allan Poe, and who later became the director of the Washington Square Players; and Philip Moeller, a gay, witty and attractive young man, who was to make a brilliant career in the theatre as a playwright and stage director. Others whom I met were Walter Lippmann, the political writer, then nicknamed "The Boy Buddha," who looked like a young Sir Oracle, and his inseparable friend, Alfred Kuttner; Waldo Frank, the novelist, with a basso personality and a treble voice; and J. Russell Herts, who at that time was the editor of a magazine of mysterious political import called *Moods International*, and which seemed to attack everyone except its own editors. I was also especially friendly with Walter Binger, who later became a construction engineer and Commissioner of Sanitation in New York City.

On my twenty-first birthday, Alice and Claire gave a party for me to which Walter Lippmann and Waldo Frank were invited. I was taken afterward to Coney Island in order to amuse the rest of the company with the effect of this madhouse on an impressionable young Englishman. In the company of this strange quartet, I was conducted through the roller coasters, shooting galleries, hot-dog stands and side shows. Whether they were sufficiently rewarded for their efforts, I do not know, for I was more impressed by the extraordinary people who were with me than by the extraordinary sights which they showed me. Lippmann, then a radical, ultimately became the most conservative of writers, while Waldo Frank, who struck me then as a conservative, was later to become quite radical.

I was introduced by Philip Moeller to his cousin, Josephine A. Meyer, who became a deep and moving influence in my life. A frail-looking girl, with grave gray eyes spaced wide apart, and hair which was usually awry, a smile always lurked on the corners of her generous mouth, and in her eyes was a keen, lovable expression of friendship and eager interest in her friends and what they were doing. One could not talk with her more than a few moments without becoming aware of her physical delicacy and also of her tremendous spiritual strength. She was concerned with every expression of art, wrote well, drew well and was also a first-rate actress. For her the world of the imagination had more reality than anything concrete or material. She was the spiritual leader of these young people, and her idealistic attitude toward art animated all of us when we were both discovering and creating a new spirit in the American theatre. At her home, and at the homes of Edward Goodman and Philip Moeller, this group met evenings to read plays aloud, and I was invited to join. The American theatre then was in the throes of the struggle between the Shuberts and Klaw and Erlanger. The so-called artistic play, by which we meant the plays of Ibsen, Chekhov, Shaw and others, had been given scant houseroom, and American playwriting had not yet emerged from the era of which Clyde Fitch was the best exemplar. My first assignment with this playreading group was to appear in a private performance of Bernard Shaw's one-act play entitled *Press Cuttings* in which I played a Shavian love scene with Theresa Helburn, who portrayed Egeria. This group took itself very seriously indeed, which was fortunate, since no one else did. Indeed, their friends regarded them as arty dilettantes who talked much but accomplished nothing. As time went on, however, Edward Goodman and Philip Moeller joined an organization known as "The Socialist Press Club" and took over its dramatic activities by producing one-act plays.

The artistic groups living in New York at this time were divided into the "up-towners" who lived on the West Side, and the "down-towners" who lived in Gramercy Park and Greenwich Village. There was, however, a kind of common meeting place at a basement restaurant known as Petitpas's, on West Twenty-ninth Street, run by the three Petitpas sisters from Normandy. The oldest sister was matronly and stern, the youngest, dark, slender and gracious, while the middle sister partook of the good qualities of both. Here, for an unbelievably low price, one could eat an unbelievably good French table d'hôte dinner with red wine, and meet some of the most interesting of New York's writers and painters seated around a long table at the head of which sat the tall, white-bearded old painter and philosopher Jack Yeats, the father of the great Irish poet and playwright, William Butler Yeats. As you dined, the Petitpas sisters bounced back and forth from the kitchen, banging plates on the table with extreme enthusiasm and rushing from guest to guest to serve heaped-up dishes of deliciously cooked *poulet au vin* or *boeuf à la mode*.

Jack Yeats, who looked like the Ancient Mariner, was a witty and wise conversationalist, and the habitués of the restaurant, including such celebrities as the painter Robert Henri, Fred King, then Editor of the *Literary Digest*, John Sloan and Van Wyck Brooks, gathered around to enjoy good food and good conversation with him. From time to time, crackpot poets and amateur littérateurs irritated the old gentleman by sitting next to him and boring him with their inept remarks. On one occasion when I was present, a daffy young poetess, who was constantly bothering him to read her poetry, piped up in a lisping voice and asked Yeats what he thought of nudism, a subject which was being discussed *ad nauseum* at the time. "My dear young woman," he said, with a painter's bluntness, "nothing is less esthetic than a woman's naked body. Besides," said the old gentleman, who was nearly eighty at the time, his blue eyes peering at her through his silver-rimmed glasses, "would you deprive us men of the privilege of undressing you, before we—?" He paused dramatically, and the poetess, who was a timid soul, blushed and fled from the table, never to return.

I had long given up any idea of sending for Pamela and marrying her on my salary of eighteen dollars a week, which barely paid for my necessities. Indeed, had it not been for numerous invitations to dinners from my friends and relatives, I doubt whether I could have managed on this sum. I maintained a one-sided correspondence with Pamela in London, the ratio being about four to one; that is, I would write her four letters to which I would receive one reply. I was therefore neither surprised nor grieved at receiving a letter from her telling me she had married an altogether charming young man who was both wealthy and contiguous. Under these circumstances I should have mustered up a broken heart, but I could not raise even a semblance of one, for I was caught up in the excitement of my new life in the New World. This was partly because the times themselves were exciting, the young people whom I had the good fortune to know being engaged in the rebellion against Victorianism in which I was deeply involved. Also I was no longer in a subordinate position in the office and constantly being repressed by older people, as had been customary in England. America seemed to me to be not only the land of opportunity, but also a land of youth and happiness. I eagerly applied for my first naturalization papers, and as soon as possible thereafter, I became a citizen. I took a keen interest in the controversial issues of the times, one of which was woman suffrage. Alice and Claire wished to march in the famous Suffrage Parade; their mother, a handsome hard-headed Scotswoman from Edinburgh, regarded woman suffrage as so much nonsense, and positively forbade the two girls to march, but Walter Binger and I encouraged them to rebel against their mother, and they marched!

As my circle of friends grew larger, my hall bedroom seemed to grow smaller, so I moved to larger quarters in the neighborhood. There my brother Herbert joined me, having decided to leave England and my stepfather's law office for a more glamorous future in America.

In the fall of 1912, Walter Binger suggested that we spend a week end at Chestnut Hill Farm near Haverhill, Massachusetts, where some of the more liberally inclined young men at Harvard were in the habit of visiting as the guests of its owner, Hazel Albertson. We planned to meet Walter's brother, Carl Binger, then studying to be a doctor, who was staying with Hazel at the time. We took a train to Haverhill, and drove over to the farm, a group of white New England buildings standing between the gentle Merrimac River, beloved of Thoreau, and a stand of handsome chestnuts on top of a small hill which gave the farm its name. Here I was introduced to Hazel Albertson, our hostess, a flaxen-blond young woman with the bluest of blue eyes, broad generous smiling mouth and a healthy pink complexion which always looked as though it had just been scrubbed with soap and water. She was dressed in a white middy blouse and white bloomers, which latter struck me as odd, for this was long before the days when women habitually wore shorts and slacks, and her attire stamped her at once as unconventional. It also made her look very pretty and feminine, which is more than can be said for some of her sisters of today. She greeted us graciously and introduced us to the family, which consisted of her stepdaughters, Fay and Phyllis Albertson, both handsome girls with blue eyes and pink faces; her chubby children ranging in age from two to twelve; and her sister Florence, a taller, thinner edition of herself. The entire family wore white, were dressed in white bloomers, had the same pink-and-white appearance as Hazel, and were a living testimonial to the advantages of soap and water over rouge and lipstick.

There were also some young men present. One of them, George Cronin (who I learned later was a poet), was nursing a broken leg caused by wrestling with the embryo medical doctor Carl Binger a day or so earlier, and Carl was busily engaged in having it mended, thereby gaining valuable clinical experience. There was also present a tall, lean, emaciated-looking young man with long bony hands and arms, who was introduced as "Bobby" and was described as Robert Edmond Jones, an assistant art instructor at Harvard, who was later to become our most important scenic artist and costume designer.

That evening, after a simple supper at the conclusion of which we all trooped into the kitchen and washed the dishes, we were entertained by Florence Albertson who played the violin, and was dressed in a peculiar Grecian-like evening robe made by Jones out of a few pieces of colored silks pinned together. And I learned later that Florence played the violin at a picture theatre in a nearby town, and since she could not afford a different evening dress for each performance, Jones was in the habit of rearranging the pieces of silk and pinning them together again, so that one evening they became a period costume, another evening a Spanish gypsy costume, and again a modern evening dress, the only drawback being that, at any moment, the pieces might fall apart and reveal the handsome Florence playing her fiddle in her underwear.

Life at the Albertson Farm was physically exhausting but mentally stimulating. Hazel was adored by all the young men, and it was easy to see why. She was their spiritual mother, and while I believe that most of them were unconsciously in love with her, I am sure they would have regarded it as a sacrilege even to admit this to themselves. She was what Jung calls "the Anima figure" to the group of young men and women who made a weekly or monthly pilgrimage to her farm. She somehow managed to find time to walk or talk with each of her visitors in turn, and to impart to all of them her enthusiasm for what they felt to be their mission in life. Gay, discerning and wise, she was always interested in these young people's problems, and the boys and girls poured out their hearts to her, and gained from her a clarification of their inner conflicts; and talking with her, they were purged of their more materialistic desires, for Hazel cared little for wealth or its accumulation. So far as her own personal fortunes were concerned, she was always at her wits' end to pay the farm bills, for neither the vegetables nor the crops were remunerative in this fertile intellectual soil. Indeed the finest produce of the farm were Hazel's babies, who grew up into stalwart young men and women, happily unaffected by the neuroses of the artists who surrounded them in their childhood.

Hazel maintained an ambiguous relationship with her husband, Ralph Albertson, a rosy-cheeked ex-clergyman, who had left the pulpit in Seattle for an executive position with Butler's store in Boston, for which concern he worked with far more successful results than he had ever accomplished for the Almighty.

Many men and women who later on contributed worthily to American life and letters were visitors at the farm and owe much to Hazel's understanding and friendship. Among those I met there, in addition to those I have already mentioned, were Arthur Garfield Hays, one of our most prominent liberal lawyers, who courageously defended the Communist Georgi Dimitrov in the Reichstag Fire trial in Berlin; Kenneth Macgowan, erstwhile dramatic critic, producer at Twentieth Century Fox, now head of the dramatic department of University of California, Los Angeles; Hiram Motherwell, author of many books on the theatre; Samuel Eliot, grandson of President Eliot of Harvard, and sometime Professor of English at Smith College; and two young crusaders from New Jersey named Albert and Charles Boni, who later entered the publishing field with considerable success. For a number of years I was a frequent visitor to the farm, and stopped going there only when, like many others of my generation, I lost contact with Hazel because of my absorption in my own family. Notwithstanding the lapse of years, the Albertson farm still flourishes, and Hazel, now many times a grandmother, and looking as pink and white as ever, is surrounded by a new generation of boys and girls, who, stimulated by her enthusiasm, will no doubt also sally forth and try to make a better world.

While many of my evenings were given to my new-found friends, in the daytime I gave all my enthusiasm to rebuilding the practice of the firm which had sent me to America. I found myself welcomed by the American patent attorneys who were glad to secure firsthand information regarding European patent practice, and were able to consult with me instead of writing letters to London. The practice thrived, for I quickly learned that my youth did not deter the clients. A few months after my arrival, a telegram was received from Pittsburgh, requesting the firm to send its representative to that city to take over the foreign patents of the United States Steel Corporation. I cabled the information to London, feeling that so important an assignment might well warrant a trip by one of the English partners. A cable was received in reply requesting me to go to Pittsburgh and to handle the matter to the best of my ability. As I was just over twenty-one at the time, I feared that United States Steel would have none of me, and would rush immediately to our competitors. I therefore arrived at Pittsburgh trying to appear as old as possible, and called upon the Pittsburgh patent lawyer of the company, a deep-voiced handsome man of about forty named Richard Little, who received me tolerantly in his office in the Oliver Building, which was filled with the fumes of long Pittsburgh stogies which he smoked incessantly. "Won't you have one, Mr. Langner?" he asked, producing one of these villainous-looking black cigars. "I never smoke in the morning," I answered evasively. I felt I was impressing him rather well, and we settled down to the business in hand.

Later, Mr. Little took me to lunch at McCreery's and when the coffee arrived, he again offered me one of his Pittsburgh stogies. By this time I felt I was doing so well that I could carry off practically anything including the cigar. So I accepted it, lit it, and smoked it with the most nonchalant air I could muster. Suddenly my head swam, and I rushed away from the lunch table, fearing that I was not only losing my dignity, but also my lunch, and along with it, the patent work of the United States Steel Corporation. Shaken and white, I returned with Mr. Little to his office, greatly relieved by his telling me that Pittsburgh stogies had a way of creeping up on people who were not used to smoking them.

With nothing but kindness in his heart, this gentleman then invited me to visit the Homestead Steel Mills the following day, and to witness the operation of a new process for casting steel railroad wheels. I drove out to the Homestead works, and at the entrance a bespectacled young man produced a printed document which I was asked to sign, stating that in the event of loss of life or limb during my visit, the company was not to be held in any way responsible. I was told to fill in my name and address, so that they would know where to send my body. I was also told my destination was about a mile and a half within the plant.

I proceeded to stagger through an industrial no man's land in which I dodged shrieking locomotives hauling flatcars loaded with red-hot ingots, cranes carrying long chains with hooks at the ends which swung at me, while every so often blasts of steam and jets of chemicals narrowly missed drenching me. Happily I fell in with a kindly workman who knew his way around this inferno, and he was good enough to show me the building where the process was being tried out. I entered the shop, a dark, cavernous structure in which stood a huge machine. The engineer in charge greeted me and then turned on an electric switch. Suddenly the entire building was filled with pieces of steel hurtling in every direction. I ducked, as did the engineer, who jammed off the switch and explained that a careless mechanic had been repairing the machine and had evidently left a number of metal parts on it, which became so many projectiles when the huge wheels began to spin. That night, with considerable relief, I journeyed back to New York safe and sound in life and limb and with the business of the United States Steel Corporation snugly reposing in the firm's portfolio.

I was introduced one day by a mutual friend, William Bohleber, to a brilliant young attorney named John B. Hayward, who was in his early thirties, but had already reached considerable eminence in his profession as patent counsel of the National Cash Register Company of Dayton, Ohio. A Bostonian and the son of a Unitarian minister, John Hayward, a slight aristocratic young man, with a mind as fast as a whippet, soon became my ideal, and I learned as much as I could from his example. He was known to his friends in Dayton as "Drawing Room John," a nickname he had earned because he spent a great deal of his time traveling back and forth in drawing rooms between Dayton and New York, in which latter city he was a member of the important patent-law firm of Kerr, Page, Cooper and Hayward. He was also an accomplished musician and a collector of paintings, and between us grew up a friendship which has lasted all our lives.

About two years had now elapsed from the time when I had left England, and the head of the British firm arrived in New York to discuss my future. He stated that his English partners were pleased with the way I had developed their practice, and we began to negotiate a contract which would have given me a permanent position as an employee in their office. However, their lawyers and mine disagreed so violently over the conditions that it was impossible for us to get together. Under these circumstances, there was nothing for me to do but sever my connection with the British firm, and I duly gave them my notice. I also talked over the situation with John Hayward, who invited me to visit him at Dayton, to discuss the possibility of being employed by one of his clients.

A new company had been formed in Dayton to manufacture the Delco electric self-starter for automobiles which was intended to do away with the cranking of the engine by hand, and to light the car by electricity, instead of by the acetylene gas then in vogue. I arrived at Dayton with Mr. Hayward, and put up at the old Algonquin, then the fashionable hotel. The next morning, wearing my best English clothes and beaver hat which I had purchased in London just before leaving for America, wing collar, bow tie, brown spats and a handsome malacca cane, I set forth to find the Delco factory. On Main Street I accosted a newsboy, and in my most polite manner asked, "Excuse me, could you direct me to the Delco factory?" "Yes," said the newsboy, looking me over contemptuously, and taking in my British accent and attire, "Three blocks down, dear."

The factory was a newly built concrete structure humming with activity. John Hayward met me at the street entrance and told me to sit in the front seat of a Cadillac car which was standing at the curb. He joined me and pressed his foot on a pedal, and then a miracle occurred. There was a slight grinding of gear teeth and the "chug-chug-chug" of the electric cranking motor, until the ignition took hold and the engine started, breaking out into the quickening vibrations with which everyone is now familiar, but which, on that particular day, were new to the whole world, and sounded in my ears almost as exciting as a Beethoven symphony. John Hayward then conducted me through the various floors of the factory until I reached the top, where I was introduced to the inventor of the Delco starter, Charles F. Kettering, and to his financial backer, Edward A. Deeds.

"Ket," or "Boss Kettering," as Mr. Kettering was affectionately referred to by his collaborators at the plant, has since become one of the greatest of American inventors, and while he has made no single invention as spectacular as Edison's electric lamp or talking machine, nevertheless to his genius, directly or indirectly, can be attributed many of the most spectacular improvements in our time. To Kettering the modern world owes thanks not merely for the starting and lighting of automobiles by electricity, but also for the modern ignition systems on these cars. He pioneered in electrical farm lighting with the Delco-Light equipment; he took over a decrepit refrigeration device and from it developed the Frigidaire refrigerator, and he developed the General Motors Diesel Locomotive which pulls our fastest passenger trains from San Francisco to Chicago. He employed the services of Tom Midgely, Jr., of whom more later, for the research which led to the invention of Ethyl gasoline, which alone has produced more horsepower than fifty Boulder Dams, and with the collaboration of Midgely, who participated in the invention of the non-poisonous refrigerant known as "Freon," he is largely responsible for modern air-conditioning in trains and buildings. He also developed the Duco types of lacquer and the famous "Fever Machine" which is now so successfully curing many diseases. We are also indebted to him for the guidance and subsidy of the basic research which is being conducted by Antioch University on the extraction of energy from the sun, and along with

Alfred Sloan, for the Sloan Kettering Cancer Foundation. Finally, for the war he developed the first successful remote-controlled aerial torpedo, and with Admiral Harold G. Bowen of the Navy and George Codrington of Cleveland, he is responsible for the high-powered Diesel engines which have made our submarines the fastest in the world. He also served as the Director of the General Motors Research Laboratory, and Chairman of the National Inventors Council, of which I am the Secretary, this being the official body to which inventions sent by civilian inventors to the Army and Navy are referred for evaluation and distribution.

At the time I first met Mr. Kettering, most of those inventions were in the future. He was then a tall, rawboned man in his thirties, as lean as a bean pole, and with a forehead which seemed almost as high as a house. He reminded me of no one so much as the young Abraham Lincoln, for he was genial, wise and convivial, with a fund of homely stories which made him one of the most brilliant speakers in the country in his later years. He greeted me warmly, and together with Mr. Deeds, who was to become one of the leading industrialists of the Middle West and president of the National Cash Register Company, we discussed the possibilities of the automobile self-starter in Europe. Mr. Deeds, a distinguished-looking gentleman with a quiet voice and cultured manners, whose pioneering spirit and enthusiasm for new inventions had caused him to invest all his available funds in Kettering's new self-starter, talked over the business aspects. They felt their inventions should be protected thoroughly in the leading countries of Europe, and discussed the possibility of my going over there for them for six or eight months. At the same time they would send one of their engineers, John Hunt, to discuss a European manufacturing contract with Mr. Kurt Rathenau, nephew of the great Walter Rathenau, founder of the German General Electric Company and later Prime Minister under the Weimar Republic.

I found, on close acquaintance with Mr. Kettering, that he combined the keenest observation with a delightful sense of humor, and that there were practically no limits to his enthusiasm and interest in his work. There was a bedroom on the top floor of the factory, and when "Ket" was working on a problem connected with the self-starter, he often did not go home for days on end, working late into the night and snatching a few hours' sleep. Mrs. Kettering, his handsome and admiring wife, who was also an accomplished musician, was fortunately possessed of a philosophic disposition which she applied to her brilliant husband's eccentricities. This carried her through many a lonely evening while her husband continued working at the factory. Once she said to me, "If I didn't buy Charlie a new suit every so often, he would be wearing the same clothes for years."

The day following my attendance at the Delco factory, I visited the factory of the National Cash Register Company, then considered to be the most modern in the world, and was introduced to Mr. Patterson and his Sales Manager, Thomas J. Watson, later the head of the great International Business Machines Company. Mr. Patterson was one of the first employers in America to adopt a humane attitude toward his workmen, and to build a clean, attractive factory surrounded by trees and gardens. In the factory itself, all the fumes and dust were sucked out of the rooms by high-powered vacuum pumps. He also fathered entertainment clubs, welfare associations and group activities for his workers, all of which went well until he tried to turn his employees into vegetarians. On the walls of the factory were placards on which were printed in bold type such legends as "Think" and "Plan Your Work and Work Your Plan," while over the main entrance was engraved in stone the words, "It is Degrading for a Human Being to Do the Work Which a Machine Can Perform." This legend made a great impression on me, for it asked me this question to which I have not yet found the answer: "If the machines do all the work, what kind of work will human beings do?"—for if it is degrading for them to do the work of a machine, it is even more degrading to do nothing.

At my next interview with Mr. Deeds and Mr. Hayward, the question of my going to Europe was discussed in full detail, as well as my remuneration. "We will pay your expenses in Europe," said Mr. Hayward, "and we want you to visit London, Paris, Berlin, Vienna and Budapest, where you will work on securing the patents. A month or so later we will send Mr. Hunt to Berlin where you will meet him to conclude the arrangements for manufacturing the Delco self-starter in Germany. In addition to your expenses, we propose to pay you a salary of $250 a week, and when you return to New York we will pay you a retainer of $300 a month for one week of your time each month. And if we need more of your time, we will pay for it at the same rate." This offer, which virtually took my breath away, was accepted on the spot, and we discussed rather casually the time of my departure.

In the meanwhile a tragic happening in Paris unexpectedly wrote itself into this chapter of my life. Isadora Duncan, illustrious pioneer of the dance, and crusader for the freedom of women from the Victorian restraints which caused them to be ashamed of their bodies, had undoubtedly pushed the pendulum too far in the opposite direction. Rebelling against marriage and the conventional attitude toward bringing children into the world, she had planned to have a child by each of a number of illustrious fathers. Two of these children, who were the living symbols of her courageous spirit, were in Paris at the time, and one unhappy day they were seated in an automobile near the banks of the river Seine. The chauffeur stepped out of the car to turn the handle to crank the engine, but unfortunately he had not disconnected it from the wheels, with the horrible result that the car lurched forward, knocking him down and plunging into the river and drowning both the children. Twenty years later I was at Antibes, lunching with Isadora, Bernadine Szold and their friend, Glenway Westcott, and we spent the afternoon together on the beach. Two days later, the newspapers carried the story of her death. She was riding through Nice in an automobile wearing a gay scarf which floated in the breeze. At a tragic moment, the scarf caught in the wheels of the car and strangled her. Isadora, modern symbol of Greek civilization, hated the machine age, and the machines hated Isadora. In the end they murdered Isadora as well as her children.

I was back in New York awaiting final instructions from Dayton, when the news of the accident to Isadora's children spread all over Europe and America. Articles were written in the newspapers of two continents on the dangers of cranking cars by hand. A cable from Berlin arrived in Dayton reading, "Most important we start manufacturing self-starter in Europe for European automobiles soonest possible date." A cryptic cable was sent in reply—"Lawrence Langner sailing for Europe immediately. Our engineer John Hunt will follow later."

CHAPTER VII

Prelude to Independence

ARLY in 1913 I sailed for England, highly elated over my future prospects and determined that every motorcar in Europe would shortly be cranked by electricity. My main destination was Berlin, but I stayed in London long enough to arrange with my old friend A. E. White, then in patent practice for himself, to carry on the Delco patent work in England. Climbing up the stone stairs of a cheerless old building in Chancery Lane to his office, I descended upon him like an avalanche, and buried him under the numerous British patent applications which covered these Kettering inventions. White, a man with sharp features, white hair and dignified clerical appearance which belied a Falstaffian wit, was one of the most brilliant patent practitioners in England, and was noted for his scathing sarcasm which won him many a legal battle. I was fortunate in always finding myself on the right side of his tongue, and when I broached the subject, he readily assented to becoming my London representative.

I then set out for Berlin. This was my first visit to that city, which I found then and later to be cold and heartless to strangers. I was struck by the great prosperity of the town, the affluence of its citizens and the frequent mingling of uniforms with civilian garb on the streets. Berlin was far happier and more elegant in the European sense in that year of 1913 than it has ever been since or will be in our time. But the writing on the wall had already begun. I often had to wait on a Berlin street corner for half an hour while a small army marched by, and on the Unter den Linden one day, with the street lined with soldiers, I saw the Kaiser, accompanied by several of his stalwart

Hohenzollern sons, all marching in a row at the head of a Prussian regiment of Death's Head Hussars.

My first duty on arriving in Berlin was to call on Kurt Rathenau of the Harat Export Company, who was to become the licensee under the Kettering German patents. My second was to appoint a German Patent Attorney to represent the Delco patent applications before the German Patent Office. Rathenau was a charming man who spoke excellent English, and he placed me in touch with a number of German patent attorneys, none of whom impressed me. I was invited by one of these attorneys to attend a luncheon meeting of the Verband der Deutsche Patentanwalte (Association of German Patent Attorneys) and was amazed to note with what gusto these voracious gentlemen put away a six-course lunch, washed down with huge seidels of beer. I ate lightly and returned to my host's office, where he had the greatest difficulty in keeping awake as we conversed. After this experience I vowed I would entrust Mr. Kettering's patent applications only to a thin underfed man. A day or so later I was introduced to a Dr. George Benjamin, a young man a few years older than myself, but who, like Cassius, wore a lean and hungry look. We became friends, and in addition to handling the Delco patent work for me, Dr. Benjamin undertook to give me lessons in the German patent practice, one of the most difficult in the world, which stood me in good stead later.

Realizing that I would have to spend several months in Berlin, I moved from the Hotel Adlon to a pension in a large apartment in the Kurfürstendamm section, which was presided over by a beaming lady of ample proportions named Frau Heym. Here, while awaiting the arrival of Mr. Hunt, the Delco engineer, I lived for several weeks, spending my time during the day on patent and business matters, and in the evenings going to the theatres or sitting in the cafés on the Kurfürstendamm listening to the orchestras. My interest in the stage, which had lain dormant, was aroused again by the Berlin theatres which I now visited not only for amusement but to study their new methods of stagecraft. Max Reinhardt was making theatrical history at the Deutsches Theater by presenting the most satisfying productions to be seen anywhere in the world at the time, with the possible exception of Stanislavsky's Moscow Art Theatre. Reinhardt was then a relatively young man, and not yet afflicted with the elephantiasis of the imagination which later led him into producing the monstrosities of the Grosse Schauspielhaus. He was sincere and sufficiently unspoiled to be simple, and his productions of *Faust* and *Hamlet,* in both of which the famous actor Alexander Moissi appeared, were the finest I had seen or envisaged in the theatre. Moissi was at once darkly fascinating to the eye, moved as gracefully as a dancer, and had a voice which could miraculously make the German language sound like a caress. This astonishing young man was of Italian origin, and had Jewish but no German blood. With young Moissi acting and young Reinhardt directing, I saw the world's most thrilling presentation of *Hamlet* while even Goethe's *Faust* became palatable to an audience under their ministrations.

I also visited the famous Volksbühne Theater, then under the direction of Emmanuel Reicher, father of Frank and Hedwig Reicher, now of Hollywood. This theatre, with its fifty thousand subscribers, made a strong impression on me which I utilized later on.

Finally John Hunt arrived in Berlin from Dayton to teach the Germans how to make Delco self-starters. He was a tall, handsome young scientist who had once taught physics at Ohio State University, and hence was nicknamed "Professor" by the "boys" at Delco. He went through Berlin like a breeze, and his caustic comments on the "Heinies," as he called the Germans, kept us both in gales of laughter. What amused him most of all were the methods by which the Germans were attempting to design the first European self-starters. "These Heinies try to get it all correct on paper before they spend a nickel building a model," he said. "We work just the opposite way. We build the model first, and keep changing it until it works, and then we put it on paper!" German thoroughness made the German engineers ten times slower than our American engineers, and they spent months making blueprints of the electric starter which, when the model was finally made, was still full of defects. It is this quality of venturesomeness in our American engineers which enabled us to outbuild and outinvent the Germans in the last war, and I predicted that this would be so, long before the war broke out. I make the same prediction as regards Russia.

Through the long arm of coincidence which is seldom permitted to appear on the stage, but which reaches into life all the time, a mutual friend introduced me to a young American woman who was in Berlin on a visit to study the German theatre. Her name was not Celeste, but for the purpose of this history, it will do as well as any other. Celeste was neither fair nor dark, though her light-brown hair, blue eyes and transparent skin made one remember her as a blond rather than a brunette. She was a creature of great enthusiasms, and had a habit of growing so excited over them that she often choked up and became both breathless and speechless, and would have to let her eyes and facial expression finish her sentences for her. She was a few years older than I, but we were the same age in our enthusiasm over the theatre and Bernard Shaw, and she was even younger when it came to discussing politics and Victorian morality, against which she was in even greater revolt than I was.

One evening in May we attended a performance of Tolstoy's *The Living Corpse* at the Deutsches Theater where, under Reinhardt's superb direction, Moissi had given one of the finest performances of his career. The poignant story of the Russian husband whose sensitivity made it impossible for him to go through the divorce courts for some peculiarly Russian reasons, coupled with the beauty of the production and its unforgettable scene among the gypsies, to say nothing of the Russian gypsy music, cast a spell on both of us, and we decided to walk to Celeste's hotel through the Tiergarten, instead of taking a cab. We passed through the Kaiser Wilhelm Allee with its stilted statues of Teutonic kings looking out among the trees like so many symmetrically arranged ghosts, until we reached a quieter part of the park where not even the statues disturbed our privacy. The moonlight shone brightly on the old trees and they cast transparent shadows on the grassy lawns which faced us. Celeste and I stood still, wrapped in the beauty of the scene, then turned to each other. At that moment it was clear to her, though not to me, that we were falling in love. But I was still full of theories and inhibitions, and I murmured something vaguely about how much I liked her, and enjoyed being with her, and could this be platonic love about which I had heard so much? She thought that it might be, so I kissed her gently on the forehead and then, after exchanging a few tender sentences, I accompanied her to her hotel, and left her reluctantly at the door. I returned to my pension with the feeling that platonic love, if this be it, was wonderful, but should be pursued to some sort of conclusion, platonic or otherwise.

My patent work in Berlin was now about at an end, and it was necessary for me to visit Vienna and Budapest to complete my arrangements for handling the Delco patents for Austria and Hungary prior to returning to London. Celeste saw me to the train and we exchanged farewells, as full of affection as devotees to platonic love can bestow upon one another without slipping. She would be in Berlin on my return, and might possibly visit London as well, no doubt to study the British theatre with me.

I arrived in Vienna in the early summer and saw it before two devastating wars had transformed this fairest of all European capitals into a shabby patchwork of its former brilliant self. I transacted my business by day, and at night visited the theatres and night clubs. In one, in particular, the name of which I have forgotten, under the soft glow of the lights from crystal chandeliers, distinguished men and high officers of the Army and Navy in colorful uniforms danced with tall, beautifully gowned women, to the music of Strauss waltzes, recalling vividly the scene at the end of the second act of *Fledermaus*, which I never witness in the theatre without remembering this same evening in the Vienna of Franz Josef.

But in spite of all the pleasurable sensations I was experiencing, I was alone and lonely, and my thoughts constantly reverted to Celeste in Berlin. I therefore pushed on to Budapest, where I stayed at the Ritz Hotel, a hostelry so modern that I could hardly believe I was not in New York City, instead of halfway across Europe. Here again I attended to my business during the days, but felt even lonelier than in Vienna, notwithstanding the hospitality of the firm of Hungarian patent attorneys to whom I had entrusted my patent work, and the solicitations of buxom Hungarian wenches at cafés who offered, for a consideration, to share their beds with me. I spent Sunday at St. Margaret's Isle, an island in the Danube which was a pleasure park, with restaurants, swings, lawns on which the children played, and all the happy trappings which enabled the poorer people to enjoy a breath of fresh air without leaving the city. The jolly young fathers and mothers with their babes, the old Magyar grandfathers with handle-bar mustachios and old-fashioned clothes, the wrinkled grandmothers who sat nodding patiently at their sides, the boys and girls flirting or playing games and trying to look as American as possible (it was then the goal of almost every young Hungarian to emigrate to the United States), made a happy picture in the warm summer sun, and produced in me an intense nostalgic longing to return to Celeste. I rushed through my business the next day, and having accomplished my purpose, took the fastest train back to Berlin.

I learned from Celeste, on my arrival, that she had missed me, while I, to be exact, had to confess that neither the diversions of Vienna nor Budapest had consoled me for the lack of her company. We decided to take the afternoon off, have dinner in the country and talk over our plans, before I returned to London, where I intended to stay for a few days before sailing back to the States. The day was cloudy, and Celeste took her umbrella along, a dainty little affair made more for appearance than utility. We selected a little village near Potsdam as our destination, and there we walked in the pine woods, happy to be together again, and feeling more than ever that the joys of platonic love such as ours were not sufficiently appreciated in this wicked old world of the flesh. Providence must have smiled cynically over this, for as we passed through the woods, a heavy shower started to fall, and we decided to sit on the carpet of pine needles, and shelter ourselves under the umbrella. But so small was this particular umbrella that we were not nearly close enough together to avoid the downpour. There was nothing for me to do but put my arm around Celeste's waist, and draw her to me, while the rain beat an astonished tattoo on the taut covering over our heads.

The feelings which now swept over me were not platonic at all, but I felt I should not take unfair advantage of the situation, so I held onto Celeste and the umbrella with equal intensity, while we talked of the possibility of spending a vacation together before leaving for London. Soon, with her head on my shoulder, she looked up at me and said, "Let's not philander—let's be honest and direct, and live together!" We thereupon analyzed our feelings for one another with all the intellectual honesty of two disciples of Bernard Shaw, while the rain wet us to our skins without our noticing or caring. Marriage for us, we agreed, was out of the question until we knew from living together that we were suited to one another. A two weeks' summer vacation was due me, so we planned a walking trip through the Bavarian Alps below Munich, where we arranged to meet a few days later.

We met at Munich, staying at different hotels, for Celeste had planned that our life together should not begin until we had reached the summit of a high mountain which she had selected from her *Baedeker,* and on the peak of which was a small *Gasthaus* to which she had wired for accommodations. "Thus," said Celeste, "we will start living together where Nature is most majestic, so that in the solitude of great heights and distances, we can feel our relation to infinity as well as to one another." The prospect of a honeymoon under such conditions was inspiring, although I was less enthusiastic than she was on the subject of mountain tops, which seemed to involve a good deal of hard exercise.

The next day we met at the railroad station, and soon our train was chugging up the slopes of the Alps. A few hours later we reached our destination, and descended at Walchensee, our rucksacks on our backs, and set out for the small Bavarian hotel which was our destination for the night. Here we shared a clean primly whitewashed room, with two enormous beds chastely separated on opposite sides of the window, and since we were still in the valley while the mountain lay ahead of us, we each slept in our separate bed, waiting like young acolytes for the dawn of the momentous tomorrow. Waking in the night, I saw Celeste standing by the window at the side of my bed. Rising and going to her, I followed her gaze over the lake which lay in the moonlight like a sheet of shimmering silver. On one side of it stood the high mountain which reached far into the starlit heavens, and on the top of it tiny pink lights blinked occasionally as though to apprise us that some humans had the temerity to live high above the valley where ordinary mortals dwell.

Where the mountain had seemed near by moonlight, in the cold accurate light of the early morning sun it was obviously miles away, and even more obviously, to me at least, it was going to be a devil of a climb for us to reach the top. We strode along the footpath with a springy gait, our rucksacks throwing our shoulders back and our chins tilted upwardly, which gave us momentarily the illusion of far greater athletic prowess than we actually possessed. At noon we unpacked our luncheon and rested in the shade of a giant pine. This was a mistake, for we grew sleepy and tarried too long. With each step upward, our rucksacks now grew heavier, and the fathers, mothers and children of the master race, whom we had passed with such superiority earlier in the day, now began to overtake us. This was an indignity which neither of us could support, so we spurted up toward the *Gasthaus* which now seemed at least twenty miles above us, and we reached it only long after evening had fallen. When we ultimately arrived, exhausted and weary, our feet blistered and our backs bent, we were far too late to see the magnificent view which Celeste had promised us in the exuberance of our early morning start.

The *Gasthaus* itself was a modern wooden structure, utterly lacking in charm or romance, and we were shown into our bedroom, which was a mere cubicle separated from the rooms on either side of it by the thinnest of wooden partitions. We exchanged unhappy glances, but resolved to make the best of it, and being as hungry as the proverbial hunter, we adjourned to the dining room which was filled with a crowd of bourgeois Germans, conversing in loud aggressive voices, and filling the room with an atmosphere of stale tobacco smoke, beer and perspiration. "Nature," I reflected, "on this particular mountain top is not nearly as majestic as Celeste has led me to believe." Partaking of a hasty meal, Celeste and I walked away from the hotel and looked down the mountain to the lake below. In the distance, it looked like a mirror of moonlight bounded by mysterious shadows.

After a while we retired, arm in arm, to our cubicle. On one side of us we heard the sounds of heavy snoring; on the other, a man and his wife were quarreling in guttural snatches. Every sound could be heard through the thin walls, and we had the uncomfortable feeling that we were about to sleep together in public. Our natural embarrassment, accentuated by our weariness and the distracting noises which peopled our cubicle with the presence of all the surrounding guests, worked on our imaginations to such an extent that there was nothing for us to do but retire to sleep as best we could in our separate beds, angry, humiliated and unfulfilled.

The next morning we were up at dawn and descended from the mountain top where, in the solitude of great heights and distances, we had so hopefully expected to experience our relation to infinity as well as to one another. I took the matter firmly in hand. As to infinity, I felt our relationship was mediocre indeed, but as to one another, I was certain that on a lower level, in the valley and beside the lake, it could be greatly improved upon. So back to the neat little hotel we went, and under less pretentious but more private auspices, we began our new life together. That night I looked out of our window over the lake again. There was no moon, but the lights on top of the mountain winked at me. I winked back at them.

One morning in Oberammergau, looking through our window, Celeste called to me laughingly, "Come quickly and see who are in the garden, drinking wine!" I looked out and saw Anton Lang, who had portrayed the character of Christ for many years in the Passion Play, sitting at a table in the hotel yard drinking and chatting in the sunlight with another Biblical character, who, from his beetled brows and villainous countenance, was undoubtedly Judas. Lang rose and left Judas to pay the bill as somewhere in the distance the church bells pealed with mocking laughter.

For the next two weeks we tramped through the countryside, and as we walked, with the mountains on either side of us and the cool fresh wind blowing against our foreheads, we talked of America and of what each of us planned to do there on our return. Celeste, like myself, had become infatuated with the productions at the Deutsches Theater, and wanted to see plays presented in this new way in the American theatre. From the time she had been a young girl, she had fallen in love with the theatre, and also with a famous romantic actor who, however, had not shown the slightest interest in her. Her purpose in visiting Germany was to learn modern play production, which knowledge she intended to put to good purpose by starting a theatre of her own in America, her father being quite wealthy and willing to finance her in the venture. I was excited about her plans, but did not wish to participate in them for I was too deeply involved in my own career, which I saw first in terms of establishing my office in New York, and then, when this was accomplished successfully, launching into the theatre with a venture of my own. It was Celeste, in those long walks in the Bavarian Alps, who gave substance to my vision of a theatre in America in which I would ultimately participate.

CHAPTER VIII

Lower Broadway and Greenwich Village

OUR vacation came rapidly to an end, and Celeste and I returned to Berlin where I finished up my business with the German Patent Office. While there, we began to plan our careers in the States on our return there. Though Celeste and I had many interests in common, yet, as we planned our futures, we never talked of working together in the theatre. We were both equally individualistic, and neither of us was willing to give an inch to the other, so that when, later on, she actually produced some plays with considerable success a few months before I plunged into the Washington Square Players, there was a feeling of strong rivalry between us; and when we discussed marrying, we were both reluctant to take the step, because, although we were happy together, neither of us was willing to make concessions to the other. Our marriage, we conceded, if it came at all, would be dependent on how well we got along together, and we left it at that. On my part, there was considerable reluctance to marry a girl as wealthy as Celeste, for I wished to preserve my personal independence which I felt instinctively would be threatened if I became her husband.

At the end of June, Celeste returned to the States, while I rejoined Professor Hunt in London, where he was making some headway in establishing the Delco starter. While I attended at the Patent Office, Mr. Hunt called on the British motorcar manufacturers, and I sometimes accompanied him. On one of these visits, he explained the Delco self-starter to an extremely elegant gentleman who, from his appearance, should have been a member of the House of Lords rather than the Managing Director of a mere firm of motorcar manufacturers. He

65

hemmed, hawed and drawled as Mr. Hunt explained the advantages of the electric self-starter and how convenient it was, when the owner drove, to crank the engine by pushing a pedal.

"But the gentlemen who own *our* cars *never* drive them," said the elegant gentleman. "They employ chauffeurs."

"Ah," said Mr. Hunt, quick as a trivet, "but our self-starter avoids hand cranking, which often results in breaking the chauffeur's arm when there is a backfire."

"But the gentlemen who own our cars always carry insurance for their chauffeurs," said the elegant gentleman, "so why pay extra for a self-starter?"

Mr. Hunt was baffled but not yet beaten.

"Why, sir, if you place this self-starter on your cars, it will double your sales, because women will be able to drive them, as well as men."

The elegant gentleman responded as though he had been shot. "What!" said he, "Women drive! God forbid!"

A few days later I sailed for New York, looking forward to meeting Celeste there, and setting up in international patent practice for myself. My brother Herbert was awaiting me and had already found a suitable office building, and on August 1, 1913, we opened our New York office, consisting of two rooms on the twelfth floor of the Singer Building on lower Broadway. From these small beginnings, the firm expanded and now conducts offices in Chicago and London, as well as in New York, with legal associates in all those countries which are still left in a diminishing world. The firm's expansion was due not only to my own efforts, but to those of my brother Herbert, my partner, John Parry, and my other able partners and associates, who were (and still are) at all times put to the embarrassment of explaining to hard-boiled American industrialists that, despite my personal interest in the arts, the firm which bears my name is both reputable and expert in its field. The original staff consisted of my brother Herbert, who has since become one of the leading authorities on international trade-marks, and Valerie Beletti, a diminutive blond Italian-American of some seventeen summers, who remained with us for many years, but ultimately left for California on account of her health, where she became the secretary of the motion-picture producer, Samuel Goldwyn, whose letters, I have since learned, took on a surprising literary quality while she was with him.

My brother and I rented a small apartment on Charles Street, Greenwich Village, over a thriving Chinese laundry, and here, for the first time in our lives, we tasted the full liberty of living in our own home, which was delightful in spite of the smell of wet steam from the laundry which usually pervaded the atmosphere. We had chosen the Village because the Boni brothers and some of our other friends lived in the neighborhood. Besides, rents were low and it was the residential district closest to our office. Greenwich Village was New York's *Quartier Latin* at this time, which was years before the advent of commercialized bohemianism. Groups of writers, poets and painters were moving into New York from all over the country, and settled in the neighborhood of Washington Square, where living was cheap and the buildings picturesque, while the basement restaurants purveyed indifferent food at reasonable prices, mixed with good companionship and exciting discussions of art, literature, sex and psychology. When a member of these groups struck a windfall, he and his friends patronized the old Brevoort Hotel on lower Fifth Avenue or the Lafayette on University Place, where the food was heavenly but the prices were considerably higher.

I was taken by an acquaintance to an apartment in the Gramercy Square neighborhood where the Liberal Club had been recently opened by a group of Villagers. Tea was served, and I was informed that the membership was torn by internal strife over the question of whether Negroes should be admitted. The pro-Negro element won, and the Club split up. The winning faction moved downtown to MacDougal Street just off Washington Square, where, in spite of this victory, Negroes apparently showed not the slightest interest in joining. The Liberal Club soon became the center of social life in Greenwich Village, and from it sprang two important theatre groups which, in the space of twenty-five years, changed the entire character of the American theatre—the Washington Square Players, progenitors of the Theatre Guild, and the Provincetown Players which contributed mainly to the development of playwriting, and first presented the works of Eugene O'Neill, Susan Glaspell, and other important American dramatists.

The Liberal Club was located on MacDougal Street, next door to what was later the Provincetown Playhouse, in a brownstone residence owned by Mrs. Bellardi, a handsome dark-eyed Italian woman who wore a habitually worried expression, due to earning a precarious livelihood by renting rooms and floors to the impecunious artists and writers who lived in the neighborhood. The Club itself occupied the two large parlors and a sunroom on the first floor, with high ceilings, open fireplaces and magnificent mahogany portals. The rooms were sparsely furnished, the walls covered with paintings of the "art moderne" type, and the current interest in ragtime, which was just being spoken of as a new American art, was represented by an old weather-beaten electric piano that was made to hammer out the popular music of the day whenever the assembled male and female club members felt like publicly hugging one another in what was then known as "modern dancing." The interest displayed by the boys and girls of the group in one another, as demonstrated by the intimacy of their rhyth-mic embraces, belied the Club's somewhat ostentatious motto, which appeared in quotations on all its literature, that it was "A Meeting Place for Those Interested in New Ideas."

But even in this new dancing there was, so to speak, a spirit of re-volt against the older more formal dances, such as the Boston and the old-fashioned waltz, in which the women, incased in stiff corsets, were held away at arm's length by the men, as though to avoid moral con-tamination by bodily contact. As you clutched your feminine partner and led her through the crowded dance floor at the Club, you felt you were doing something for the progress of humanity, as well as for yourself and, in some cases, for her. Indeed, despite the freedom of thought and the removal of the barriers between the sexes which marked this particular period of our social history, the morals of the young people were stricter than those of thousands who attend coun-try clubs and dance halls throughout the country today. The attitude of the young people toward sex was in the nature of a crusade, and when a young man and young woman decided to live together with-out benefit of clergy it was then called "free love," and books and essays and plays were written about it. In fact, free love soon became so respectable, that no "modern" young man would go out with a girl who was living with another man, with the result that free lovers were usually thrown on each other's company to such an extent that they became bored to distraction with one another and ultimately got mar-ried just in order to have a little more freedom. In this way the Lib-eral Club, in retrospect, became singularly successful in promoting matches, and many a happy couple now celebrating their silver wed-dings were led into marriage by the very vehemence of their denial of its value as an institution.

When the Club moved to MacDougal Street I joined it, and was in-troduced to its president, Ernest Holcombe, a blond bearded Lohen-grin-like giant who was an engineer in the service of the City of New York, and his wife, Grace Potter, a distinguished social worker who later became a psychoanalyst. This genial couple, happily serious, pre-sided over the Club like a kindly father and mother, and its initial success was largely due to them, for they attracted members of all persuasions and professions.

If your tastes ran to poetry, and you were a member of the Club, you could discuss this topic with a thin, rather emaciated-looking, bespectacled youth named Alfred Kreymborg, or a robust, ruddy-faced young Kansan, Harry Kemp, who was always thumping his chest and starting new religions which never quite hatched; or you might listen to Vachel Lindsay, on one of his visits to New York, chanting his poem "The Congo" while banging the table to emphasize the rhythm; or on rare occasions you might spend an evening hearing reminiscences of Walt Whitman told by his friend, Horace Traubel, a white-haired old man who was brought to the Club by Albert Boni. Later on, too, the club rooms became brighter for the presence of an exquisitely delicate, elfin-like girl, who shed a radiance all around her. She was Edna St. Vincent Millay, just recently arrived from Maine via Vassar, from which college, still later, came another beautiful poetess, Ruth Pickering, whose girlish poems shocked the campus out of a year's growth of daisy chains. And one could tease another attractive poetess, Mary Carolyn Davies, who in theory was very wild and Western but in fact very naive and shockable.

If sociology was your dish, the Club had plenty of members in that line, and they usually wrote novels and poetry for good measure. Upton Sinclair, then recently crowned with laurels for his exposé of the Chicago meat packers in *The Jungle*, was often there, as well as Max Eastman, tall, handsome and beloved of all the ladies, who was editor of *The Masses* and one of the white hopes of the Socialists. Other "Liberals" were Simeon Strunsky, rotund and smiling, and a host of other Strunskys, including Anna, married to William English Walling, another Socialist white hope who lent respectability to the movement. There was also John Reed, then known as a writer of stories and playlets, who was later to crusade for Villa and Lenin, and whose remains now repose in a well-advertised grave in the Kremlin. Hutchins Hapgood and his wife, Neith Boyce, both distinguished writers of fiction and social subjects, were there, too. Also, Nickolas Muray, the Greenwich Village photographer, many of whose pictures appear in this book, and who devoted his time to photographing his penurious friends and winning every contest in sight for fencing and sabre-duelling; and Bobby Edwards, tall and cadaverous, who was the Village troubadour and composed its songs and sang them to his guitar accompaniment. And there were those times when the Club was excited by the visit of some allegedly dangerous political personage such as Alexander Berkman, the anarchist, a subdued, frail-looking man with a troubled expression on his face, who always spoke in a low voice as though afraid of being overheard. Another alleged revolutionary was a gentle, chubby round-headed little man with horn-rimmed glasses and a shock of bushy curls, named Hippolyte Havel, who earned his living washing the dishes in Polly's restaurant and was said to have been imprisoned as an anarchist in Austria, and who became the basis of one of the characters in Eugene O'Neill's play, *The Iceman Cometh*. There was also Maurice Parmalee, a thin, bearded wisp of a man who seemed far more interested in sociology than in women, but wrote a book on nudism which caused him, thirty years later, to be bounced from an important government position through the activities of Congressman Dies. And, if you were in the mood, you could always have an argument at the drop of a hat with a red-haired, rawboned engineer named Howard Scott, who specialized in puncturing the economic fallacies of others and substituting fallacies of his own, which were later hailed by his bewildered fellow countrymen in the depths of the depression of the thirties under the beguiling title of "Technocracy."

Of novelists and story writers the Club boasted a round dozen or more. One of the most popular was Mary Heaton Vorse, who was always in a dither over a new husband or a new child, and kept the railroad tracks busy between the Village and Provincetown, running from one to the other. Floyd Dell, a recent arrival from Chicago, a blond young man who emanated a sense of the importance of literature, became one of the Club's most active members. Another member was Sinclair Lewis, known as "Red" Lewis, a gaunt-looking refugee from Minnesota, who satirized the Village later in a play called *Hobohemia*, now mercifuly forgotten. Still another was Louise Bryant, a handsome vivacious Irish girl from Oregon, who claimed kinship to Oscar Wilde, and married, in turn, John Reed and William Bullitt. Theodore Dreiser, big and dour, whose moods and movements resembled his novels, for he was large and ponderous, walked about and talked like an enduring monument. Then there was Susan Glaspell, a delicate woman with sad eyes and a sweet smile who seemed as fragile as old lace, until you talked with her and glimpsed the steel lining beneath the tender surface. One could meet also her journalistic friend, Lucy Huffaker, pretty and prematurely gray, with a cigarette always held in a little metal holder in her hand; Inez Haynes Gillmore, stately and beautiful, who crusaded with novels for woman's suffrage, and her sister, Daisy, pretty and petite, who married Paul Thompson, dean of newspaper photographers.

The graphic arts were represented at the Club by genial Art Young, the Socialist caricaturist, looking for all the world like a country squire living happily under capitalism; by Marsden Hartley, a pale, hawk-faced man, whose appearance was as abstract as some of his paintings; and by Charles Demuth, whom I observed later portraying a yellow sand dune at Provincetown by industriously painting what appeared to be large pink and blue worms on his white canvas. Among other artists were a handsome, delicate youth named Robert Locker, who designed and illustrated in the best K. Neilsen tradition, and from time to time, a young man with a high forehead and a long black beard named Jo Davidson would look in at the Club mysteriously and frighten everybody.

There was also a smattering of lawyers, newspapermen and publishers, who lived in the Village and made the Club their headquarters. Among these was Lincoln Steffens, a short-bearded man wearing a squashed-in hat and flowing tie, who spoke glibly of European politics and seemed like a traveler from another world, Augustus B. Meyers, author of the *History of Tammany Hall*, Justus Sheffield, lawyer and bibliophile, and Harry Weinberger, doughty crusader for liberty and Eugene O'Neill's confidant and attorney. Also present was Harry Scherman, then a quiet, whimsical young man with an interest in literature and economics. He had an enterprising turn of mind which led him successively to marry Bernardine Kielty, a handsome brunette who was one of our Club's most attractive members, and, later to found the Book-of-the-Month Club, both ventures turning out successfully. Among others, I recall Gilbert Seldes, an argumentative young esthete with a time sense which led him in easy stages from literature to television, Frank Shay, a breezy giant who lived in Provincetown and published collections of plays, and Harold Stearns, a popular young writer and editor of the *Dial*, who was expatriated by Prohibition, and on his return to this country wrote two excellent books about America.

I was especially friendly with the members of the Club who were interested in theatricals; among these, in addition to Susan Glaspell, was her husband, George Cram Cook, who with Eugene O'Neill was later to found and direct the Provincetown Players. He was a big, white-haired, pink-faced man with a hearty manner and the appearance of a Roman senator. His secret desire was to dwell on Mount Olympus like an ancient Greek philosopher, and this ambition he was able to achieve in his later years. He died there and was buried on its slopes by the humble shepherds among whom he lived. At the Club I also met Helen Westley, a woman of vivid dark beauty, imagination and charm, one of the Village celebrities, who was said to be an actress but to earn her living by selling subscriptions to magazines; as no one ever actually saw her sell anything during her entire lifetime, I believe this can be regarded as a myth. There was also Teddy Ballantine, painter and Provincetown actor, whose wife, Stella, dramatic and dominant, was one of the Village's more attractive hostesses. Her brother, Saxe Commins, a dentist from Rochester, and a frequent visitor at the Club, took care of Eugene O'Neill's dental difficulties with such success that when, under his ministrations, 'Gene's teeth became practically perfect, Saxe gave up dentistry for literature and became O'Neill's literary adviser. He is now Editor in Chief for Bennett Cerf, the engaging publisher of Random House.

Each week a lecture by a celebrity was given at the Club. One was the late Professor Jacques Loeb, who both thrilled and mystified the membership by reciting his discoveries of sex determination by chromosomes. Another was Big Bill Haywood, leader of the I.W.W.'s or "Wobblies," who died in Russia, and to whom we listened with the feeling that we were doing something extremely dangerous and radical. A third was the gallant Christabel Pankhurst, the English Suffrage leader, whom I had secretly admired ever since the days when I had listened to her handling mobs of jeering hecklers at Hyde Park, London, who yelled derisively at her, "Down with the trousers and up with the skirts!" I was assigned the task of taking her back to her hotel after the lecture, and in a cozy taxi we discussed her topic, "Love and the Modern Woman." "How do you have any time for love, with all your other activities?" I asked. She looked at me coolly with her clear eyes. "How do you?" she replied.

It may be imagined that when the membership of this Club foregathered, foreheads literally steamed with discussions of the arts and the changing social order. This was not the case, however, for the Club was primarily a social meeting place, and very few heated discussions survived the onslaught of the electric piano. There was a ferment in the air, however, and the Club served as a focal point where all the young men and women who were interested in what was new and modern in the arts and economics mixed and mutually stimulated one another. I found in this atmosphere a welcome antidote to the activities in which I was plunged during the day, and evenings usually consisted of dinner in the basement of "Polly's" and then dropping in at the Club for the remainder of the evening.

Viewed in retrospect, the Liberal Club was a dividing point in the lives of most of its members. A minority led by John Reed turned to the extreme Left, others passed over to the Right, but the majority remained Liberals and contributed in all fields to our country's greatness. My association with the Liberal Club taught me to be tolerant of all forms of opinion, and in my theatre work, to regard the stage as a forum for any point of view, whether I subscribed to it or not, so long as it was embodied in a play which was primarily a work of art and not merely a work of propaganda.

My life in the Village was periodically interrupted by my life with Celeste, which turned out to be a series of railroad jumps broken by journeys to many of the mountainous sections of the United States, where she indulged her passion for seeing what was on the other side of the range. Celeste lived in four homes, all inconveniently situated several hundred miles apart, and we seemed to meet mostly in Chicago. She developed an unfortunate determination to have me visit all of her homes in turn, which made earning a livelihood impractical. I did my best to induce her to settle in New York, but was unsuccessful, for Celeste felt cramped by its buildings, and bewildered by its vibrations. She gasped for spiritual air, and regarded my Village friends with suspicion. Our mutual interest had the effect of separating us instead of bringing us closer together. She wished to begin her career in the theatre by producing a long play for children, which seemed incredibly stupid to me, since children, in my opinion, should go to bed in the evenings and do their theatre going at matinees. This line of reasoning did not impress Celeste, however, so she went ahead blithely on her own and produced her children's play, and proved that the American public felt exactly as she did, and not as I did, which was most irritating to my vanity.

As time rolled by, discussions with Celeste began to take on the aspect of a prolonged battle as to whose views on matters theatrical should prevail. In this atmosphere of workaday reality we began to be estranged, and Celeste's visits to New York became less and less frequent.

The patent practice to which I was devoting the greater part of my time began to flourish at the Singer Building, and soon we had to add rooms and to take on a larger staff. A few months after we opened our office, I was flattered by a visit from Sir George Croyden Marks, the senior partner of the British concern whose competition had originally caused my departure for America. He offered me a position in his firm, which I respectfully declined.

One of the first tasks entrusted to my office was to register the trade-marks, "American Biograph" and "AB" for silent motion pictures all over the world, these being trade-marks of the company which employed Mary Pickford and John Bunny, who then shared with Charles Chaplin the comedic leadership of the screen. I was to meet Mary Pickford some months later at the Beechhurst Yacht Club, situated at Beechhurst on Long Island Sound, where resided not only Miss Pickford and her husband Owen Moore, but also such vaudeville and theatrical celebrities as Eva Tanguay, Belle Baker and Joseph Schenk, who, with their week end guests, enlivened the gay Saturday night dances at the Club.

On the "wrong" side of the railroad track from Beechhurst was a so-called Raines Law hotel, situated at Whitestone Landing, and here Bill Card, who had left his former employers and joined up with us, my brother Herbert and I decided to live for the summer. The hotel, in reality a large public house facing the water front, was operated by a handsome politician named Dewar, and his charming wife; and the rooms, though cheaply furnished, were kept immaculately clean. Under the Raines Law, long since forgotten, liquor could be sold on Sundays in New York State only at *bona fide* hotels, and by residing there, we imparted this status to what would have otherwise been merely a lowly longshore saloon. Our bedrooms were situated above the bar, and we were extremely comfortable, except when occasionally some overconvivial guest would place a nickel in the electric piano after we had gone to sleep. Since we were serving a useful purpose in changing the premises from a saloon to a hotel, the rates were extremely cheap, and we were allowed all the beer we could consume "free."

During the weekdays, the saloon was peaceful, and we spent our evenings reading, or in company with the longshoremen, policemen and local politicians who made the bar their headquarters. On Sundays, however, great was the change. At nine in the morning, tugboats began to scream, and hundreds of excursionists, male and female, wearing white yachting caps, poured off the docks into the Picnic Grounds, Baseball Park and Dance Hall operated by the Dewars. Throughout the day the hotel and its purlieus were thronged by a mob of drunken Democrats or inebriated Republicans, as the case might be, for the Dewars were impartial to both political machines, and served good beer and steaks as copiously to one as to the other. These out-ings, so-called, were paid for by the local saloonkeepers in New York City, each of whom was required to deliver a given quota of votes for the party to which he owed allegiance. The recipients of these favors, after a thoroughly good time in the open air, would repair with their wives and sweethearts to the Dance Hall, where, to the syncopated rhythm of the tugboat band, they would stagger through the steps of the Bunny Hug or Turkey Trot, locked in each other's arms in bacchic embrace. "Do you *allow* this kind of dancing?" I asked in a shocked voice of a policeman who was watching a particularly orgiastic display. "Sure," said the cop, "go as far as you like."

In this delicate atmosphere, we three young Englishmen thrived for two summers, and since the Dewars encouraged us to bring week-end guests by giving them the same favorable rates as we ourselves enjoyed, our hotel soon became a resort for our Greenwich Village friends from the Liberal Club. There, walking on the beach with Albert and Charles Boni, then just beginning in their publishing careers which ultimately brought the "Modern Library" books and the publishing firm of Boni and Liveright into existence, I expounded the theory that books should not be sold in the same manner as shoes or other commodities, but should be displayed under the most inviting conditions and disposed of by literate clerks who should be lovers of literature rather than salesmen. The Boni brothers responded to this impractical suggestion with enthusiasm, and backed by myself and Walter Binger's brother Robert, we opened the Washington Square Book Shop next door to the Liberal Club. This bookshop is still in existence on Eighth Street, New York, its longevity being probably due to the fact that Albert, Charles and I long ago severed our connections with it.

The Washington Square Book Shop blossomed into being the following fall. A passageway was knocked through the wall between the bookshop and the Liberal Club, so that members of the Club who, in accordance with its motto, were "interested in new ideas" could enter the bookshop and browse around among the books. Our intention was to make the place as homelike and comfortable as possible, and we succeeded only too well. The two large rooms with open fireplaces were lined with books like a library, and potential book buyers and club members made themselves thoroughly at home there, sitting in the comfortable chairs before the open fire and reading most of the books and buying very few of them. Indeed, the uncommercial atmosphere of the bookshop was so persuasive that a well-known but impecunious minor poet habitually helped himself to books while no one was looking, and such was our sympathy with his plight that we habitually turned a blind eye to his peculations. Under these circumstances, it was not surprising that the bookshop soon ran into debt, and was kept alive only by our putting in more capital periodically.

To attract prospective book purchasers to the shop, lectures on literature and the arts were arranged there. On one historic occasion Norman Wilkinson, designer of Granville Barker's production of *Midsummer Night's Dream* (in which for some unaccountable reason the fairies were portrayed by girls with gilded faces), lectured on the theatre, and he attracted a goodly number of our friends who were interested in the stage. Among these were Sam Eliot and Robert Edmond Jones, and legend has it that during the evening, using the portiere which divided the two rooms as a proscenium arch, these enthusiastic amateurs gave a performance of Lord Dunsany's *Gods of the Mountain* from which was allegedly born the Washington Square Players. That such a performance took place is true, but that from it sprang the Washington Square Players is incorrect. Indeed, an onlooker informed me later that the acting was of a character to end a theatre rather than to begin one.

The bookshop was managed by the charming Boni brothers. Albert, the elder of the two who had long dark lashes shading flashing black eyes, was the imaginatively practical member of the family, while Charles, equally handsome but less ebullient, was deeper and probably the saner. Their assistant was a studious young literary man named Cuthbert Wright, for whom they deservedly had a great admiration. Numerous articles from his pen had appeared in that exciting New Testament of the Liberals, *The New Republic*, which had recently come into existence, with Walter Lippmann and Philip Littell prominently associated with its Editorial Board. Since very few customers ever darkened the doors of the bookshop, while those who did usually sat quietly reading as in a public library, Cuthbert drew up a small table each day in front of the fire and proceeded to work on his articles, his peaceful pursuits being rarely disturbed by prospective customers.

When, finally, one or two friends who actually wanted to buy books complained to me that they hated to disturb an assistant engaged in work of such an absorbing and erudite character, I brought the matter to Albert's attention. He pointed out, quite correctly, that the shop was so quiet that Cuthbert could work far better in this bookish atmosphere than in his own uncomfortable lodging. I agreed, but remarked that we were losing so heavily that we could no longer afford to pay for Cuthbert's services. Albert hesitantly decided to break the sad news to Cuthbert. Visiting the bookshop a week later, I was surprised to find Cuthbert still cozily seated before the fire, surrounded by papers and books, and busily engaged in writing for *The New Republic*. I asked Albert what had happened. "Well," he replied, pathetically, "I told Cuthbert we couldn't afford to keep him on, and he said he quite understands, and from now on he'll work for nothing."

The bookshop, notwithstanding all the care which was lavished on it, ultimately became a burden to us. Moreover, in its magical back room, plans were being hatched for new theatres and other enterprises (the prospectus for the Washington Square Players was sent out from there) which made the selling of books, even though done in a new and ineffectual way, a minor enterprise. The shop was sold to Frank Shay who in turn sold it to Renée La Coste, a handsome Frenchwoman, who in turn sold it to Egmont Arens, now a successful industrial designer who was, in his younger days, one of the most enterprising of the Greenwich Village entrepreneurs, being responsible for the Pagan Rout dances at Webster Hall and many other gay divertissements of the period. He gave the bookshop as a parting gift to his first wife, Josephine Bell, who still operates it on Eighth Street. Since Egmont was somewhat deaf and I was in the habit of raising my voice when talking to him, I never enter the bookshop to this day, some thirty odd years later, without shouting at the top of my voice to Josephine, who regards me with kindly pity, as one would an agreeable lunatic.

While my evenings were filled with activities in the Village, my days at the office were no less busy. My arrangements with Mr. Deeds and Mr. Kettering of Delco called for my spending one week out of every four in Dayton where, owing to Mr. Kettering's many inventions, the patent work was growing rapidly. One day Mr. Kettering showed me a small gasoline engine operating an electric generator. "This," he said, "will be a farm-lighting plant to be called 'Delco-Light,' which will enable the farmer and his wife to do many of their chores by electricity," and he explained that his desire to reduce the hard labor of women on farms sprang from his own childhood experiences with his mother. I took care of the foreign patents on the many inventions involved, and found that the only similar devices which existed in Europe were large expensive installations for lighting the country houses of the landed gentry and nobility. This made me realize how greatly responsible are our democratic ideals and attitude toward women for the spread of American inventions throughout the world, for had it not been for Mr. Kettering's appreciation of the problems of the farm wife, and his desire to supply an inexpensive plant which would light the farmhouse, run a washing machine, a butter churn, a vacuum cleaner, and other utensils and implements, the contemporary small farmhouse electrical power plant would not have come into being. In the rest of the world, women on farms were still regarded as so many domestic drudges.

During one of my trips to Dayton, Mr. Kettering conducted me and an Englishman who was visiting there over his new house at Moraine, which was then in process of building. It seemed as though we would never be able to proceed further than the basement, which was full of household machinery which Mr. Kettering demonstrated with a wealth of detail. After spending an hour in these mechanistic surroundings, I begged to be allowed to go upstairs to see the rest of the house. The "Boss" reluctantly assented, and conducted us immediately to the roof, on which he had installed an elaborately equipped observatory. "How many rooms are there in the house?" asked the Englishman, as he was being rushed downstairs to the basement again. "I haven't the slightest idea," said Ket, "but if Mrs. Kettering doesn't fill them full of furniture, the house will be all right to live in."

I did not appreciate the significance of this remark until some years later when I dined with the Ketterings and followed them into the drawing room for coffee. On the grand piano was a piece of complicated electrical equipment, other portions of which were scattered on the antique chairs and tabarets, and electric wires ran from one device to another like the strands of a gigantic spider's web. "Excuse me, I am running a 24-hour test on this," said Mr. Kettering apologetically, as we tried to enter the room. Mrs. Kettering smiled indulgently as he carefully removed a number of the contraptions from the chairs and placed them on the floor, so that we could sit down amid the tangle of wires and drink our after-dinner coffee without disturbing the test.

In line with the paternalism which was rampant in Dayton at the time, it was decided that all the Delco company executives should live together during the summer at a glorified summer camp outside Dayton which was called Delco Dell. The Ketterings and Deeds, having built their own homes, did not live there themselves, but the rest of the Delco executives were duly installed in summer bungalows throughout the estate, and the wives were relieved of all but light housekeeping by means of a Community Restaurant at which they all met for dinner. This communal effort was intended to be productive of good fellowship among the residents of the community, but so far as I could see when I visited them, it worked exactly the opposite way.

The wives of some of the executives, not all of whom were exactly enamored of one another, were able to devote a considerable portion of their time to gossip and to the discussion of the relative importance of the work contributed by their respective husbands to the success of Delco. Consternation broke loose when this gossip began to affect some of the executives. Fortunately for the company, the Delco Dell community ultimately broke up, and the executives went back to leading less idealistic but more practical lives as private rather than collective individuals.

In providing recreation for their employees, the Delco executives were far more successful. Mr. Deeds and Mr. Kettering presented their workmen with a charming site which was unattractively named Triangle Park, and my friend Forrest McNab, the patent attorney of the company, who was one of the most lovable of men, was given full play for his talents in providing outdoor entertainment, such as boxing matches for the factory employees. McNab was equally adept at writing a patent application and promoting a battle royal in which a dozen good-natured blindfolded Negroes slugged hammer blows at each other until only one of them, bruised and bloody, remained standing in the ring.

This crude form of entertainment, brutally exciting and sadistic, seemed to me, nevertheless, more alive than the commercial New York theatre at the time. With but a few exceptions, the Broadway plays were meretricious and cheap. The best plays were importations from England, mostly drawing-room comedies, which had little relation to American life. Musical shows abounded, and one was told that the purpose of the theatre was to entertain the tired business man, who seemed to be very tired indeed. I nursed a thoroughgoing contempt for Broadway. I was eager to work for a better theatre, and the success of my patent practice during the first years seemed to assure me of the ultimate leisure for creative writing to which I had looked forward. One evening I sat in my room with a pad of paper before me, and with a pencil I wrote on it the words "Licensed, a Social Comedy, by Lawrence Langner." On second thought, I struck out the name of the author. The play was on the subject of birth control, and showed somewhat melodramatically the sad results of ignoring the teachings of Margaret Sanger. Surely I would be arrested for writing such a play, which, by advocating birth control, was against the law! I thought of the effect on my clients, who would doubtless be horrified to learn that their foreign patent solicitor had been jailed. Changing the name of the author to "Basil Lawrence," I started to write my first serious play.

CHAPTER IX

Chicago, Berlin and World War I

A FEW months after I had opened my office in New York, John Hayward introduced me to his friend Frank Parker Davis of Chicago, who was in charge of the patent work of the leading adding machine company of the country. Since it was apparent that a good deal of foreign patent work would come to us from Chicago, I blithely decided to open an office in that city. I secured the services of a British technical assistant, and hung out my shingle in the Monadnock Building, then owned by Arthur Aldis, who with his wife Mary Aldis, was a leading patron of the arts. Our small Chicago staff was soon inundated with work, as other clients began to entrust their foreign patent matters to our care.

My first impressions of Chicago were most unfavorable, for it was not then the handsome city of wide boulevards and fine homes and hotels of today. The town was noisy and dirty, and many of the people who haunted the streets seemed to have faces which had not been entirely completed by their Creator. The main hotels were the Auditorium and the Annex, with its Pompeian Room and a circular fishpond into which drunken revelers were reputed to fall on New Year's Eve parties. There was also the Blackstone, then, as now, dignified and individual, where I liked to stay when I could afford to.

I knew hardly anyone in the city on my first visits, and on returning to New York, I told Floyd Dell of having opened my Chicago office. He suggested that on my next trip, I call upon his former wife, Margery Currey, a newspaper woman who lived in Jackson Park. He dropped her a line, and she invited me to spend an evening with her at her home. Arriving at the address, I found it to be one of a group of small one-story stores facing the park, which had been converted into apartments by the simple expedient of hanging curtains over the plate-glass windows. I rang the bell, but as there was no answer, I walked in. I heard the sound of groans proceeding from an inner room, which I entered. Lying on a couch was an attractive little woman, with dark intelligent eyes, now pain-stricken, who turned out to be Margery Currey. I thought she was probably dying, so introducing myself to her between groans, I suggested that I call a doctor. She insisted, however, that all she needed was bicarbonate of soda, which she might have obtained for herself, had she not waited for my appearance. I repaired at once to a nearby druggist, and on returning, gave her a generous dose which at once restored her to normal.

Meeting in this strange manner, we became good friends, and she decided to give me a "party," in order that I might meet a group of the writers and artists who formed the counterpart of Greenwich Village in Chicago. A few evenings later, I attended Margery's party which, like those of a similar character in New York, began with indiscriminate admixtures of greetings, cocktails and food, and ended with discussions of books, plays, music, pictures and sculpture, all of which were undergoing a thoroughgoing revolution, and over which people were apt to grow just as excited in those days as they did later on in discussions over Communism and the like. Among the guests was a slim young reporter named Ben Hecht, who pressed me for news of his friends who had migrated to Greenwich Village. Another guest was Sherwood Anderson, a middle-aged, ruddy-faced man with piercing black eyes which belied his easygoing manner. He informed me that he was engaged in the printing business. Later, in a talk together, he expressed his admiration for Charles Dickens and the English Victorian novelists whom, he stated, it was his intention to emulate when he could find time for writing. But the person who made the most vivid impression on me was a strikingly handsome girl, tall, blue-eyed and bubbling with enthusiasm, named Margaret Anderson, who was introduced to me as the editor of *The Little Review,* a magazine devoted to the arts but especially to poetry and literature. It was the first to introduce to America the works of James Joyce, T. S. Eliot, "H.D.," Ben Hecht and Richard Aldington. To this impressive list I modestly add my own name, since my own play, *Licensed,* first saw the light of day between the covers of Margaret's magazine.

As compared with their New York prototypes, the Chicago writers I met at Margery's parties seemed to me to be considerably more rugged, radical and real. Chicago was a city of brutal contrasts, and considerably closer to the pioneer life of America than New York, and this in turn made the artists stronger and tougher. Indeed, they had to be tough to survive in the center of America's most strenuous industries, and so violent was their protest on behalf of beauty that there were two magazines published in Chicago devoted to poetry, these being the aforesaid *Little Review* and *Poetry Magazine* edited by Harriet Monroe, while New York had none. After the Chicago artists succeeded in attracting attention, they unfortunately migrated to New York, where they became tamed and somehow lost the quality which was their best stock in trade.

Among the writers who maintained their Midwestern quality, however, were Sherwood Anderson and Edgar Lee Masters, who came to Margery's parties when he was in Chicago. At the time Masters practiced law in a little country town nearby and was engaged in writing the famous *Spoon River Anthology*. Other talented poets I met at Margery's parties were Eunice Tietjens, a buxom lady with delicate features and hair which was usually awry, her poet husband, Cloyd Head, whose hair was equally untidy, and the Boston poetess, Amy Lowell.

Amy Lowell, probably the largest poetess who ever wielded a delicate pen, was a frequent visitor to the Chicago poetry circles, and on one occasion I traveled with her to New York. She wore a flowing heliotrope gown which gave her the appearance of dawn on a mountainside. Seated on the larger part of one side of her drawing room, she lit a big cigar and proceeded with great wit and nimble dexterity to carve the Chicago poets into little pieces, a proceeding in which I was unable to join her since I possessed no personal Olympian heights from which I could look down on them.

I met at Margery's first party, an Englishman named Maurice Browne, who with his American wife, Ellen van Volkenburg, produced and acted in the plays of Shaw, Strindberg and Schnitzler at the Chicago Little Theatre, on a stage not much larger than a large dining-room table. This small theatre was situated in the Fine Arts Building on Michigan Boulevard along with the two poetry magazines, the Cliff Dwellers Club, the Baldwin Piano Company and a baker's dozen of art schools and singing studios. The theatre auditorium held less than one hundred people, and was decorated like a small Greek temple. Maurice Browne and Ellen van Volkenburg were in actual fact, the progenitors of the entire "Little Theatre" movement in America, a movement which has since become a very important part of the fabric of American cultural life, although at one time the

"Little Theatre" was in danger of becoming so microscopic as to disappear altogether.

As a reaction against the large theatres which were built throughout the country in the Victorian era, and stimulated by Winthrop Ames who built the Little Theatre in New York, theatres in America grew smaller and smaller until the actors and actresses almost sat in the laps of the audiences. This enabled amateur actors, largely lacking in powers of projection, to give what appeared to be excellent acting performances to a handful of audience. This, however, was fortunate in one respect, since it opened the door to a new group of inaudible actors and actresses, who were later to become famous when they learned to speak louder. The Little Theatre movement also led to a school of naturalistic acting in which the actor could be seldom heard beyond the fifth row, a tradition which is still persisted in by some members of the profession, and is more largely responsible for ticket speculation than almost any other factor, since patrons of the theatre will always prefer to hear what they are seeing, even if they have to pay higher than the box office price to do so.

Maurice Browne and his wife bloomed in the Chicago of those days like two orchids in a cultural desert. They underwent the severest financial vicissitudes, but kept their chins up with true British fortitude. After years of trying to dent the indifference of the Chicagoans without making any real impression on them, Maurice returned to England where he produced *Journey's End,* one of the finest war plays written in our time, and then just to show what ten years in Chicago could do for a man, collaborated with the poet Robert Nichols and wrote another magnificent play, *Wings Over Europe,* which prophesied the atomic bomb and was later produced with considerable success in New York by the Theatre Guild.

The fact that Maurice Browne was able to exist at all in Chicago made a great impression upon me, and I wrote to Celeste telling her that if an Art Theatre of this kind was possible in Chicago, it would be even more possible in New York. Celeste, who never permitted anyone else to do her thinking for her, decided exactly the opposite, and immediately rushed to Chicago and she opened her first play there, presumably on the theory that two art theatres could starve as easily as one. The play was a success artistically, though not financially, and later on she brought it to New York where it succeeded sufficiently to encourage her to pursue her theatre ambitions still further. She was restless, however, and decided to move some three thousand miles farther away to Los Angeles, to which city in whirlwind fashion she journeyed back and forth, picking up en route in Detroit, the young theatre genius Norman Bel Geddes, and in Chicago a rising architect named Frank Lloyd Wright, engaging him to design her a theatre which she never built.

During one of Celeste's hasty visits to Chicago, I introduced her to Margaret Anderson, whom she admired breathlessly. In return, Margaret admired her with equal breathlessness. Later on, Celeste picked up *The Little Review* lock, stock and barrel, and carted it and its editors out to the Pacific Coast, along with Emma Goldman, a voluble, didactic and motherly middle-aged lady of the utmost respectability, whose stock in trade was to lecture on Philosophic Anarchy to the younger generation, which generation felt extremely devilish as it listened to her extraordinarily illogical political views. In this way she was able to earn sufficient money to support a burly, six-foot doctor who, as a running accompaniment to her tirades on personal liberty, was in the habit of knocking her downstairs periodically and then using his medical knowledge to mend her bruises.

On one of my visits to Chicago, Margaret Anderson invited me to spend the week end at her camp on the beach of Lake Forest, adding that Emma Goldman was staying with her, and greatly enjoying the freedom from restraint inherent in living a carefree open-air life—the closest approach to Anarchy in the State of Illinois.

I arrived at the camp at noon and found the surroundings somewhat less than Utopian. Cooking utensils, furniture, newspapers and books littered the beach, while seated on a kitchen chair outside a tent sat the dignified matronly Emma Goldman, wearing a heavy black gown and looking like a disgruntled tragedy queen dispossessed from her rightful throne. "I don't know what I'm doing out here," she remarked to me, savagely killing a mosquito which had settled on the back of her neck, "I have a nice cool comfortable hotel room in Chicago, and I let Margaret drag me away for the week end." "But don't you feel free here?" said Margaret, looking like Ariadne in a baby-blue bathing suit. "Why don't you take off some of your clothes?" "The flies and mosquitoes are eating me alive," grumbled Emma. "I need more clothes, not less." A curly headed delicatessen dealer from Syracuse, who had accompanied Emma to the camp, was standing nearby dressed in bathing trunks, eating a large pickle. "Why Emma, I'm ashamed of you," he said. "Here you are free. You are free to take off your clothes. You can take off everything!" I began to feel alarmed. He turned to me, menacingly. "What right has the Government to insist that we should wear clothes, when we don't want to wear clothes?" I tactfully evaded the issue. "Under Anarchy," he continued, "if we want to go naked, we will go naked without a policeman interfering!" "Put on your clothes and come back to Chicago," said Emma, whose face grew redder by the minute. "I've had about all I can stand of this; I'm going right back to my hotel." "Poor Emma," said Margaret to me later, in explanation of the incident. "You see, she's a city Anarchist, and not used to real freedom—besides, she only recently converted the delicatessen dealer and he's running rampant and getting on her nerves!"

Emma Goldman was a brilliant critic of society, but on the constructive side her ideas were incredibly naive. She lectured intelligently on Ibsen, Shaw and the other dramatists of the period, but invariably tried to produce a social rabbit from every hat, a fault which I fear has permeated much dramatic criticism for the past twenty years.

Since Margaret had printed my first play *Licensed* in *The Little Review*, when I sold some time later another one-act comedy entitled *Another Way Out* to *Vanity Fair Magazine*, in a burst of gratitude I turned the funds over to her. She used the money to bring her magazine to New York, where it led a sporadic existence for several years, ultimately ending its days as an expatriate in Paris.

During the next few years, in my round trips between Dayton, Chicago and New York, I served as a liaison between the artistic colony of Chicago, and that of Greenwich Village. Sherwood Anderson, in his autobiography, refers to my visits in the following terms:

All this desire for revelation I found among the new acquaintances in the little converted retail storeroom at 57th & Stoney Island Ave. In Chicago— Floyd Dell, Arthur Davidson Ficke, Lawrence Langner, a patent lawyer interested in the theatre, coming now and then from N.Y. to give us a feast with drinks, speak to us of the new figures, Eugene O'Neill, Jig Cook and others coming to the front in the East, Ben Hecht, Alexander Kaun, occasional young professors from the University, talk and more talk.[1]

Yes, it was "talk and more talk," and the talk was good. One of the best talkers was Ben Hecht, whom I visited at his home on the North Shore, where he spent the evening discussing a series of horrible murder cases which he was covering as a reporter with Charles MacArthur. He expressed his intention of devoting his life entirely to pure literature, as evidenced by certain coruscating stories he had contributed to *The Little Review*. These, he said, would win him immortality, though he would undoubtedly die penniless in an attic.

---

[1] *Sherwood Anderson's Memoirs*, copyright 1942 by Harcourt, Brace & Co., Inc.

Years later I pondered over the evanescent nature of human intentions, as he informed me, with considerable bitterness, that he was then the highest-paid writer in Hollywood.

On one of my visits to Chicago, I called on Margaret Anderson, who greeted me with great excitement. "We have just discovered a new poet," said she, breathlessly, "probably one of the greatest in America, and now Harriet Monroe is trying to print one of his poems in *Poetry Magazine* so as to claim credit for his discovery before we publish him in *The Little Review*." As she spoke, her eyes darted flames of indignation, and she explained that she was forced to bring out her magazine a week or so early, in order to beat Harriet Monroe to the gun. I learned that the name of this new phenomenon was Maxwell Bodenheim, and I was invited to meet him the next day. Coming out of Margaret's office, I ran into Harriet Monroe, a strange, birdlike little woman, who told me as she hopped along at my side that she, too, had just discovered a new genius in American poetry named Maxwell Bodenheim. Calling at Margaret's office the next day, I was introduced to a clumsy, pink-and-white young man with a strong lisp, who informed me proudly that he had just been discharged from the U.S. Army, and then proceeded to recite a poem which was to appear in Margaret's magazine. His rendering, however, was so excruciating that only after reading it later was I able to decide it was actually much better than it sounded. Bodenheim, after being successfully launched by these ladies, came to New York later, and the last time I met him was at a party given by Horace Liveright, who was his publisher. At about two in the morning I heard a loud crash in the hall. I inquired timidly as to what it was. "That," said Horace, glumly, "is Maxwell Bodenheim falling downstairs."

Lest my portrayal of the humorous side of *The Little Review* be misunderstood, I hasten to add that I wish we had today in America a dozen magazines animated by the same pathfinding spirit—the spirit which led Margaret Anderson, for example, to publish the first novels of James Joyce. The appreciation of serious writing and poetry to which *The Little Review* was dedicated, ultimately spread far beyond the covers of the little magazine itself, and became a definite factor in the culture of Americans of my generation.

It was decided in the summer of 1914 that I should again visit Europe, and help form a British and French company which would manufacture the Delco self-starters in their respective countries. In London I visited Mr. C. A. Vandervell, a charming Englishman who looked more like a poet than a manufacturer of electrical equipment, and having received his proposition for forming the English company, I left for Berlin.

As I paced the platform while the train waited a few minutes in Hanover, a newspaper boy called an extra edition announcing the assassination of the Crown Prince Francis Ferdinand at Sarajevo. By the time I arrived in Berlin, the crowds which thronged the cafés were in a ferment of excitement, and frightening rumors spread from table to table. A German naval officer at the table next to mine informed me arrogantly that if war had to come, the German Navy was never better prepared for it than at that moment. Dr. Rathenau, the Delco licensee, was hopeful for peace, but he told me sadly that if Russia mobilized, war was inevitable. A day or so passed; we talked half-heartedly about the business in hand, when the news broke that Russia was mobilizing.

The following day, which was Wednesday, I dined with Herbert Wertheimer, a patent attorney who was associated with Dr. Benjamin. We discussed the question of whether I would be able to leave Berlin in good time in case Germany mobilized. "Don't worry about that," said Wertheimer. "On the day of mobilization the Army takes over the railroads. You simply get on your train and say you are going to join your regiment, and you can travel to the frontier at the expense of the German High Command." He smiled encouragingly, and to prove his point, showed me his mobilization papers which he carried with him, and which instructed him to go to a certain hotel on the second day of mobilization and to sit at Seat No. 5 of Table No. 273, and there to await further orders. "So don't worry," said Wertheimer. "Salute everybody and keep saying, 'I'm going to join my regiment.'" I thanked him for the advice, but decided not to follow it. I left the next evening, Thursday, on the last train to leave Berlin for Paris before war broke out. As hundreds of other British, American and French refugees had the same bright idea, I traveled most of the way standing up.

I arrived in Paris on Friday, where everything was at sixes and sevens. The waiters at restaurants refused to accept my paper money; men, women and children rushed through the streets to the railroad stations; and here and there I saw a young man and his wife or sweetheart parting in the street, the one waving good-by and the other weeping. In the Place de la Concorde I met "old man" Schwab, a venerable gray-bearded, old-fashioned German-American, the father of Charles Schwab of the Bethlehem Steel Company, and together with a young lawyer, we repaired to the Paris office of Raymond

Pynchon & Co. to hear what the stock tickers had to say. "Stock Exchange closed in London . . . in New York . . . in Paris . . . in Berlin." These words seemed more fraught with real drama than anything I had yet encountered; they seemed to punctuate what was happening with a deadly finality. I returned to my hotel dazed and distracted. The world seemed to be collapsing around my ears, and my own little personal world along with it.

The next morning war was declared between the Central Powers and Russia and France, and sitting at a street café, I saw a ragged throng of young men and boys carrying the Tricolor, followed by the British, Russian and American flags, marching through the boulevard singing the Marseillaise. The Parisians, old and young alike, rose to their feet, stood on chairs, tables and pavements, and cheered and cried and cheered again. I watched the people leaving the city, and in a few days, along with hundreds of other Americans and British, I crossed the channel for England. Arrived in London, I noted an unnatural calm. Placards reading "Business as Usual" were placed outside the leading stores. I rejoined my family. My Uncle Bertie was in his home poring excitedly over a large map of Europe, exclaiming, "They'll be massacred! They won't last three weeks! The French artillery is the finest in the world! Wait until the Cossacks get them! There won't be a German left to tell the tale!" I walked over to Downing Street that evening. Belgium had just been invaded, and a crowd of anxious men and women stood patiently outside the Prime Minister's house while the Cabinet met within. I stood there with the crowd as it shuffled uneasily through its long vigil. The front door opened and some of the Cabinet ministers and staff came out; the buzz of excitement developed into a hearty cheer when along with Viscount Grey the careworn features and trim figure of Lloyd George appeared, that same Lloyd George whom I had heard fifteen years before in Swansea denouncing the government. The next day the newspapers told us what we already knew was to happen. The Cabinet had decided to join the Allies, and the somber orchestra of World War I broke into its martial opening chords.

I stayed a few days in London awaiting developments, but meanwhile cables from New York and Dayton called me to return without further delay. I took a boat to Canada, and traveled through the submarine zone in the company of a large group of American surgeons who had been attending a Medical Convention in Paris. My brother Herbert met me at Quebec, and I learned, as I had expected, that our patent practice had vanished into thin air, at a time when I had many more employees and commitments than could be taken care of by my retainer from Delco.

Happily, the lucky star which seemed to be guiding my fortunes at this time, did not desert me. Many years before, an Irish-American named David Kenny was standing in a Pullman car having his coat brushed with a whiskbroom by a Negro porter, who raised such a dust that Kenny sneezed violently. That sneeze set Kenny thinking, and as a result he invented the modern vacuum cleaner. Dozens of manufacturers imitated his invention and he was engaged in heavy patent litigation which was in the hands of my attorney friends, Thomas Ewing and Frank Cole. Frank Cole, learning of our dilemma, put our entire staff at work making abstracts of the testimony, which kept us busy for the next six months, Bill Card and I spending alternate days dictating to Frank's secretary, Miss McPhail, before a cheerful coal fire in Mr. Ewing's old-fashioned Wall Street office, Mr. Ewing himself having left to fill the post of Commissioner of Patents at Washington.

The war accelerated in violence, and the filing of foreign patents and trade-marks entrusted to our firm were few and far between. Later on, we began to be flooded with war inventions, with the result that our dreaded bankruptcy was headed off, and we weathered the storm which threatened to engulf us.

CHAPTER X

The Washington Square Players

DESPITE World War I, during the winter of 1914 the interest of young people in the theatre in New York was growing rapidly, stimuated by the imaginative productions of Granville Barker and by the tour of Diaghilev's Ballet Russe with Nijinsky in his most famous roles, with costumes and scenery by Leon Bakst and other European masters. This tour, sponsored by the late Otto Kahn (who told me he incurred a loss of over $250,000 in presenting this magnificent company to an America which was still too undeveloped culturally to appreciate it) had a profound influence on the young American Theatre, and undoubtedly also began that interest in the ballet which has since spread throughout the country. But the general public of those days was indifferent to new art forms in the theatre, and the attitude of the great mass of Americans toward the ballet can best be illustrated by the reaction of an engineer friend of mine from Dayton, Ohio, whom I took to the Century Theatre to see Nijinsky in a superb program which included *L'Apres Midi d'un Faune*. "Gee, Lawrence," he said angrily, turning to me as Nijinsky leaped miraculously through the air, "how I'd like to take a sock at that guy! Why doesn't he *work* for a living?"

I mention this to show what we who pioneered in the theatre had to meet and overcome in the philistine attitude of the American public toward the arts, an attitude which was generally prevalent except for a small handful of people in the larger cities who were looked upon as cranks, eccentrics or "sissies" by their fellow rugged individualists.

One evening at the Liberal Club, Floyd Dell, the novelist, informed me that the Club had decided to form a dramatic branch to produce plays, and that the governing body wanted me to be its secretary. He also told me that he had written a one-act play for the new venture, about a young Spanish grandee and his gypsy sweetheart, and that he would like me to play the part of this young man. He added (somewhat too hastily, I thought) that he had offered me this part on account of my black mustache and Spanish appearance. I accepted the proposal with suspicion, and agreed to attend a trial rehearsal at the apartment of Theodore Dreiser in Greenwich Village, where Kirah Markham, an attractive dark-eyed young woman who had recently arrived from Chicago, was to rehearse opposite me. As she was to play the part of the gypsy, I suspect that she, too, had been cast to type. While Dreiser sat and watched us with ponderous amusement, Floyd directed the play, and during the rehearsal he criticized my faltering efforts on the ground that my diction was too British, and I was introducing a disconcerting nationalistic complication into the play. "This," he said, "is the way I want these lines read"—whereupon he declaimed his precious words in harsh Middle-Western accents which set my teeth on edge. "If that's the way you want the part acted," said I, sarcastically, "hadn't you better play it yourself?" "Perhaps I will," said Floyd. "I'll think it over." The next morning he called me on the phone and said, "I have decided to accept your resignation and to play the part myself." "Well," thought I, "if he wants to ruin his own play, that's his affair." The performance was given at the Liberal Club some weeks later, and Floyd was greeted with rounds of applause as the curtain fell.

Seated near me at the performance was an attractive, dark-haired woman, also with a touch of gypsy in her, named Ida Rauh, who was married at the time to Max Eastman, then editor of *The Masses*. "Lawrence," said Ida, when the play was over, "I could certainly play that gypsy better than Kirah Markham." "Yes," I replied, "and I could certainly play the Spanish grandee better than Floyd Dell, with his Iowa accent. Besides," I added, "one of my ancestors was a Viceroy of Navarre, so the part would have fitted me like a glove." "I, too, have Spanish blood," said Ida, looking at me with some personal interest for the first time. "I used to be in the theatre before I married Max, and now I'm determined to return to the theatre and act!" When a woman of Ida Rauh's character and will power is determined to act, she can move mountains—and she did.

A week later I met Albert Boni walking dreamily along the south side of Washington Square. "I have been talking to Ida Rauh," he said, "and she thinks the dramatic branch of the Liberal Club is absurd."

"So do I," I replied. "We ought to start a theatre of our own. Maurice Browne has done it in Chicago," and I described the Chicago theatre to him. Albert, who loved starting things just as much as I did, suggested that we spend an evening with Ida to talk over the possibility of opening our own theatre.

I spent the next evening at Max Eastman's home on West Thirteenth Street, where Albert, Ida and I planned to bring together different groups of our friends who were interested in the theatre. Albert agreed to invite the theatrically inclined members of the Albertson farm group, including Robert Edmond Jones and Sam Eliot, to join the organization. I agreed to discuss the matter with Edward Goodman, Philip Moeller and Josephine A. Meyer, who belonged to the uptown New York group associated with the Socialist Press Club, and we also added the names of George Cram Cook and Susan Glaspell, along with their friend, Lucy Huffaker, from the Chicago group which had recently moved to New York; and Helen Westley, Ralph Roeder, Daisy Thompson and Dudley Tucker of the Greenwich Village group, were also included. Thus, in the formation of this new theatre, which almost immediately took the name of the Washington Square Players, there were representatives of all the artistic groups with which I had come in contact during my four years of traveling around the country.[1]

We decided that an old cellar on MacDougal Street, which smelled most appetizingly of old wine, and later became the Provincetown Playhouse, was too small, and Florence Enright suggested that we take the little Bandbox Theatre on Fifty-seventh Street, just off Third Avenue. With a capital of a few hundred dollars, mostly contributed by Dudley Tucker and myself, and with a handful of subscribers, we embarked on our new theatrical venture.

As soon as word spread around among the younger generation that we were going to start a theatre, many of the young writers in the Village began to turn out plays. As none of us had the experience or patience to get further along than one act, we limited our efforts in the beginning to one-act plays, which was wise, for we were not sufficiently experienced to write longer plays, and our actors were equally unable to sustain them. Philip Moeller had already written a play for the Socialist Press Club, and started on another. Susan Glaspell and George Cram Cook wrote a one-act play called *Suppressed Desires*, which was the last word in modernity since it satirized Freud. Edward Goodman wrote a playlet called *Eugenically Speaking*, while

---

[1] See Appendix for list of original members of the Washington Square Players.

I put the finishing touches to *Licensed.* Other authors who sent in plays were Murdock Pemberton, John Reed, and a sylphlike lassie from St. Louis named Zoë Akins. Because of his experience with the Socialist Press Club, Edward Goodman was selected to be our Director, while Albert Boni and I were the business managers, which, in a practical sense, meant that he and I were dedicated to the difficult task of raising the money needed to launch the enterprise.

It was decided, in a burst of misplaced idealism, to operate the Washington Square Players on a strictly democratic basis, and this meant that everyone in the group, including the actors and the clerical force, right down to the office boy, had a vote on the selection and casting of plays, with results which were frequently fantastic. After weeks of arguing, democracy got the worst of it, and a committee was set up which limited the decisions to a group of five persons who were thick-skinned enough to disagree continuously without losing their respect for one another. Philip Moeller, Helen Westley and I succeeded in surviving this experience, and imported the committee system bodily into the Theatre Guild some years later under the title of "The Board of Managers."

When the would-be actors of the Liberal Club Dramatic Group learned that we intended to produce real plays on a real stage, they rallied to our banner, and before long we had enrolled more prospective thespians than we could possibly use. Among these was Helen Westley, then a tall, beautiful, dark-haired woman who spent a great deal of her time with Cuthbert Wright, our assistant in the bookshop, of whom she was said to be enamoured, and with whom she quarreled incessantly. Helen spent most of her time browsing around secondhand bookstores, and her apartment was lined with thousands of secondhand books, which overflowed into the kitchen and even into the bathtub. The theatre was quite up Helen's alley, for she had been a professional actress in her own right, and had also married a well-known actor, Jack Westley, from whom she was then separated. Thus, there came to be associated with us, and later with the Theatre Guild, this remarkable woman who was one of the most refreshing personalities in the theatre, as well as one of its most talented character actresses. But what made Helen Westley invaluable to the Washington Square Players, and later to the Theatre Guild, was her simple, direct enthusiasm for the greatest plays, her incisive mind which cut through any meretricious work like a surgeon's scalpel, her disregard for appearances, her dislike of mediocrity, and her unwillingness to sacrifice art for money, of which latter commodity she was not unduly scornful but never to the extent of letting it interfere with her integrity in selecting plays for the Players or for the Guild.

Helen placed all her earnings, which were considerable in her later years, in the savings banks, and carried her bankbooks at all times on her person. "Good Heavens, Helen!" said Edna Ferber one evening at my home, when Helen was sitting in a comfortable easy chair, wearing a bilious green batik dress, and low-heeled shoes. "What are those large lumps on your legs?" "My saving bankbooks," said Helen, "I keep them in my stockings." "But why?" asked Edna. "They're worth about seventy thousand dollars," replied Helen. "I couldn't possibly leave them anywhere else." During her membership on the Theatre Guild Board, when she was frustrated by a contrary vote, Helen would often remark, "I'll outlive all of you, and then I'll run the Guild alone, and produce only the greatest plays in the world!" Alas, she was the first of our group to pass away.

To set forth the purposes of the Players, Edward Goodman, Philip Moeller and I prepared the following Manifesto:

THE WASHINGTON SQUARE PLAYERS

Its Aims and Organization

The Washington Square Players, Inc.—an organization which takes its name from the district where it originated—is composed of individuals who believe in the future of the theatre in America, and includes playwrights, actors and producers, working with a common end in view. The fact that the Drama League can recommend at the present time, as worthy of the attention of its members, only three plays running in New York City (of which two are by foreign authors, while two productions are by English and part-English companies) is an incisive comment upon the present condition of the American drama. The Washington Square Players believe that a higher standard can be reached only as the outcome of experiment and initiative. Just as the finished productions of Mr. Granville Barker—which are now delighting New York audiences at Wallack's Theatre—are the culmination of a growth of some years in the development of new methods of acting and production in English drama, so we believe that hard work and perseverance, coupled with ability and the absence of purely commercial considerations, may result in the birth and healthy growth of an artistic theatre in this country. Your wholehearted support—a sympathetic appreciation of the possibilities of our experiment—will encourage us to greater efforts.

We have only one policy in regard to the plays which we will produce—they must have artistic merit. Preference will be given to American plays, but we shall also include in our repertory the works of well-known European authors which have been ignored by the commercial managers.

Though not organized for purposes of profit, we are not endowed. Money alone has never produced an artistic theatre. We are going to defray the expenses of our productions by the sale of tickets and subscriptions. Believing in democracy in the theatre, we have fixed the charge for admission at 50 cents. If we can secure sufficient support by the purchase of individual tickets, or subscriptions for ten tickets (two for each of our monthly performances) at the cost of $5.00, we shall be able to continue our work.

If you are in sympathy with our aims, we shall welcome you in our organization. You may be able to help us in a number of ways, whether you be playwright, actor, producer, or capable of assisting us in some executive capacity.

Our ultimate success depends upon our ability to accomplish our purpose AND your interest.

If this wording in the light of today sounds somewhat grandiose, it nevertheless indicated our serious purpose in bringing intelligence, an interest in social matters, and a serious critique of life into the theatre.

On the eventful night of February 19, 1915, the Washington Square Players gave their first performance at the Bandbox Theatre. The opening bill began with my one-act play *Licensed,* which showed a young girl whose fiancé had died a few minutes before her marriage was to take place. Her mother having called in the clergyman who was to perform the marriage, the girl confesses that she is about to have a child. The mother begs the clergyman to fill out the marriage certificate as though the marriage had taken place before her fiancé's death, to make the child legitimate. The play ends with a long propaganda speech by the unmarried bride on the subject of birth control, which, in retrospect, has had little effect in reducing the number of unwanted children in the United States. Ida Rauh, who played the part of the bride, suffered considerably as an actress from having once been told that she resembled Sarah Bernhardt, wore her hair in a manner to emphasize the resemblance, and dressed in a flowing white wedding dress which underlined her somewhat matronly form; and since she was already, at the time, the mother of an eight-year-old boy, she did not look quite as virginal as I wished her to.

However, the performance, to my surprise, was well received by the audience, made up, I may add, of our friends and relatives who could not, under such circumstances, be expected to respond very differently.

The next play was a naughty piece of impudence by Edward Goodman, *Eugenically Speaking,* in which Florence Enright and Karl Karsten played the leading roles, and the plot of which was amusingly described by George Jean Nathan in the *New York American* the next day as follows:

. . . A young girl, who has run across a magazine article by Shaw in which the latter expresses a characteristic idea or two on the subject of mating, is so impressed by Bernard's philosophy that she picks up a massive street-car conductor and totes him to her home. Once there, she proposes that he marry her. The conductor informs her that he is sorry, but he already has a wife. The girl is downcast and cries out her woe upon the bosom of her flabbergasted father. Whereupon the conductor, in passing out, tells the girl that Shaw was all right as far as he went in the article, but why stop there? And, as the curtain comes down, the girl's face lights up with a relevant idea (the censor interferes with a more concrete exposition).

This was followed by Maeterlinck's poetic *Interior*, after which came a divertissement entitled *Another Interior* in which the *mise-en-scene* represented the inside of a man's stomach, into which various foods portrayed by the actors, passed through the esophagus. In this unforgettable episode, Helen Westley, attired in a flowing gray robe, played the part of an oyster, while Philip Moeller, who had been known in his college days as Columbia University's best toe dancer, appeared last on the scene in the role of an irresistible liqueur. His advent caused all the other food on the stage to sway with a sickly, bilious rhythm, and finally rush out of the stomach. This pantomime, strange as it may appear, did not send the audience reeling out of the theatre for the same reason but, on the contrary, was heartily applauded.

Much to our surprise, the following morning the dramatic critics praised the performance highly. Here is what some of them said:

. . . every indication of fully realizing their aim, which is to present unusual pieces in an unpretentious and yet effective way in the hope of adding impetus to the artistic movement in the New York theatre, which of late has assumed proportions worthy of recognition.

If the Players can keep up their present pace they will make the Bandbox an institution.

New York Times

New Company Gives $2 Drama for Fifty Cents. Washington Square Players Open Their Season and Make a Big Hit.

New York Herald

. . . If the American stage is ever to extend its exhibitions beyond the "tired business man" type of music show and the farces and melodramas which have been such money makers in the last couple of seasons, it will be by reason of the competition of such organizations as the Washington Square Players.

New York Tribune

... The appeal is distinctly to the "highbrow" of revolutionary tendencies. That it will ever win an audience outside of the spiritual frontiers of Greenwich Village is not probable. ...

New York Evening Post

The casting of my play *Licensed* did not proceed without considerable argument. I wanted Theresa Helburn, who had been the theatrical white hope of Bryn Mawr College, to play the part of the mother, and she first agreed to do so. She started to rehearse, but shamefacedly sent in her regrets later, stating as the reason that her family regarded the play as immoral and did not wish her to take up acting. Not to be downed by her family, she then sat down and wrote a one-act play called *Enter the Hero* which the Washington Square Players put into rehearsal with Edna St. Vincent Millay in the feminine lead, but the results were not good. The play was withdrawn, and since has become one of the most popular one-acters in the amateur theatre.

In the action of my play *Licensed,* when the curtain rises, the body of the dead fiancé is discovered on a couch. My friend Otto Liveright was selected to play the part of the corpse, which was not very onerous, since it merely required him to lie still on the sofa covered by a white sheet. Otto, one of our best comedians, did his part exceedingly well on the opening night; but on the second night, perhaps overconfident after reading the newspaper notices, he was in a sitting-up position when the curtain rose. With a frightened look at the audience, he threw himself down on the couch and covered his head with the sheet. The audience roared with laughter, and Ida Rauh, backstage, refused to go on with the play.

The curtain was rung down, and a debate took place between Ida and the Committee which lasted for twenty minutes, during which Ida told them the story of the man whose beard fell off while playing King Lear, and how, every time he opened his mouth thereafter the audience roared. "That's just what'll happen to me if I go on now," said Ida. She was adamant until Eddie Goodman exerted his authority as director, and insisted that she go on stage, which she did, the audience by this time having waited so long as to consider it no longer a joke.

So great was our initial success that we immediately put on a second bill, consisting of *Love of One's Neighbor* by Andreyev; *Moondown* by John Reed; *My Lady's Honor* by Murdock Pemberton; *Two Blind Beggars and One Less Blind* by Philip Moeller; and *The*

Shepherd in the Distance, a pantomime in black and white by Holland Hudson.

After the second bill, some professional actors joined the Players, including Roland Young, a recent arrival from England, who treated us all with extreme superciliousness, which had the desired result of making us feel that he knew far more about the theatre than the rest of us, which was then undoubtedly true; Frank Conroy, another Englishman, who made up in backstage charm for Roland's lack of it; and Frank's handsome friend, Harold Meltzer, son of Charles Meltzer, the dramatic critic. With these good actors added to our company, we proceeded to finish our season, which was generally considered to have been a great success.

Our first bill of the second season included a play entitled *The Antick* by Percy Mackaye about a group of French Canadians, in which Lydia Lopokova, the famous Russian ballerina, appeared along with a large white odoriferous goat, which, according to Otto Liveright, made its presence felt so strongly to the occupants of the first ten rows of the orchestra, that these became the least desirable seats in the house.

The same bill of one-act plays also included a brilliant one-act comedy by Philip Moeller, *Helena's Husband,* which won great praise from the critics.

Each evening after the performance, we visited the back room of a saloon at Fifty-sixth Street and Third Avenue, where a long table was set up, and the actors and actresses and our friends foregathered for sandwiches and beer. This back room soon became a favorite meeting place for the town's *literati,* and the circle of friends who gathered there included a number of the younger dramatic critics, such as Alexander Woollcott, Heywood Broun and George Kaufman.

After the opening night of the Canuck play, *The Antick,* some of the critics joined the Players' table at the saloon, and Lucy Huffaker introduced Heywood Broun to Lydia Lopokova. Broun, big, gauche and unmarried, was obviously smitten with Lydia, and stood smiling shyly, towering above her like an embarrassed young elephant. Soon they were seated together, and became noticeably engrossed in one another. The next day Broun wrote the following notice which appeared in the *New York Tribune:*

. . . After watching Lydia Lopokova romp through Percy Mackaye's "The Antick" we felt a glowing enthusiasm for all the world. . . . All words denoting, connoting or appertaining in any way to charm we would bestow on Lydia Lopokova.

As Julie Bonheur, a Canuck girl, she is a mite mighty in enticement. Never have we— But, no; we'll set no time limit on our opinion, for Julie herself complains: "These Yankees, they say only that: I love you always, forever! Why not they say: I love you—all this week?"

And so, until Tuesday, October 12, we will continue to maintain that Lydia Lopokova is the most charming young person who has trod the stage in New York this season. But she did not tread. She did not even walk. She skipped, she danced, she pranced, and as like as not, she never touched the stage. Or so it seemed. . . . For our part, we would rather see Lydia Lopokova rise to her full four-feet-seven inches on extended toes than watch two hundred chorus girls climb to the roof of the Hippodrome on their rope ladders of electric lights.

How young and wonderful the world was when dramatic critics could write so ecstatically of their admiration for an actress! Later the *Tribune* carried the following in Broun's column:

"What the *Tribune* said about me Wednesday was nice," remarked Miss Lopokova, "but I do not think I was so good as the story said."
Lydia Lopokova, you may see, is a remarkable actress.

Not unexpectedly, a few weeks later, Broun's engagement to Lydia was announced, and can you wonder? The romance, alas, did not materialize; and soon after, Heywood married Ruth Hale, a brilliant and exciting lady of pronounced feminist views, while Lydia went to England and married John Maynard Keynes, the noted British economist.

The success of *The Antick* encouraged me to write a pantomime, in collaboration with Jo Meyer, for Lydia Lopokova called *The Red Cloak,* Lydia, however, had to leave us for a dancing engagement, and her part was played by Florence Enright with a cast which was notable for the fact that it included Glenn Hunter, Roland Young and a young actor named Harold Freedman, who appeared in medieval doublet and hose which so embarrassed him that I do not believe he ever played any other part, and thereafter devoted his talents to becoming the most successful play agent in America, if not in the entire world.

After the second bill, Ida Rauh resigned from the Washington Square Players, not caring for the parts that were offered to her. She spent the summer at Provincetown in the company of George Cram Cook, Susan Glaspell and Eugene O'Neill, an unknown young man who had written some one-act plays which had been published and were attracting considerable attention. With them, she helped found the Provincetown Players.

Encouraged by the audiences which stormed the Bandbox Theatre when we were not playing Chekhov (we had disastrous results with the *Sea-Gull* because, like most amateurs, we played it in semi-darkness), we decided after our second season to move to the Comedy Theatre on West Thirty-eighth Street, a deserted playhouse which was leased to us by the Shuberts on unusually reasonable terms. We rented an empty loft building across the street, with a large number of rooms for our offices. This building ultimately resulted in our financial downfall, for we all began to engage assistants and sub-assistants to fill these rooms, which gave us the appearance of great prosperity while contributing to our impoverishment.

It was my duty, as business manager, to arrange for a lease of the Comedy Theatre with the Shuberts. Having made so many insulting remarks in our publicity about "the commercial theatre," I was apprehensive of the reception I would receive on being told that Mr. Lee Shubert wanted to see me to discuss our proposition. My fears were not allayed when, along with Eddie Goodman, I called at the Shubert offices and passed through a series of ominous coffin-shaped doors into the small inner sanctum. There we were met by Mr. Lee Shubert, a small neatly attired keen-looking man with piercing eyes, who at that time vaguely resembled a young Indian chieftain without the head feathers. He put us at our ease and discussed the matter with great intelligence and kindness, quickly making the necessary business arrangements. It did not take me long to realize that Mr. Lee was enamoured of the theatre, and that he was ready to gamble with any newcomers whose talents he felt would be productive, a kindly trait which has continued right down to the present day.

Having leased the Comedy Theatre, we continued our policy of producing one-act plays with occasional longer ones. One of our most ambitious undertakings at the Comedy Theatre was Andreyev's play *The Life of Man.* The play begins with a father pacing anxiously in one room, while his baby is being born in the next room, to the accompaniment of the agonized screams of the off-stage mother, thus indicating to the audience the obvious fact that Man is born in pain. The various actresses attached to the Players were tested for the quality of their screams, especially those who were mothers. Strange to relate, the actresses who had actually had babies, as though to demonstrate how simple it all was, could barely be heard beyond the third row of the orchestra. Finally, a young girl recently introduced to the company was tested. She let out the most bloodcurdling shrieks imaginable, though she was neither wife nor mother. The task was assigned to her, and when the curtain went up, so horrific were the screams which came from off stage, that two frightened old ladies who were sitting in the front rows of the orchestra rose from their seats, rushed up the aisle and fled the theatre. The name of the young woman whose imagination prompted her to let out these blood-curdling yells was Katharine Cornell, a novice who had been taught Shakespeare at the Merrill School in New Rochelle by Theresa Helburn, who played Sir Tony Belch to her Malvolio in the school play, and had been recommended by our director, Edward Goodman, as a promising actress.

Earlier, we presented a Japanese one-act play entitled *Bushido*, in which the leading part was played by José Ruben. At the end of the play, the mother, Shusai, walked across the stage, dressed in a ceremonial kimono of white satin, saying the words, "My son! My Son!", and he reached out his arms to her as the curtain descended. Katharine said, "I nearly died of joy the morning I learned I had the part," which was the first she played in the professional theatre; and although she did no more than walk across the stage and say these words, she made so vivid an impression on me and others that I foresaw a striking future for her. She appeared in speaking parts in other one-act plays with the Washington Square Players, the principal one being *Plots and Playwrights* by Edward Massey, in which she showed marked ability.

Later on, when we formed the Theatre Guild, I endeavored to secure her interest in the new organization. She attended the first Guild meetings at my home on Eleventh Street, where she met a pale, frail young man named Guthrie McClintic, who made a far greater impression on her than I did. Meeting her again later in Detroit, he became interested in her both artistically and matrimonially, with excellent and lasting results in both fields of endeavor.

On the same bill as *Bushido*, which introduced Katharine Cornell into the theatre, was another one-act play of which I was the author, *Another Way Out*, based on my observation of the prevalent Greenwich Village cult of free love. *Another Way Out* achieved the longest run of any one-act play in New York, and is still sporadically presented by venturesome amateur groups.

I spent all my spare time and energies left over from my patent practice writing plays for the Washington Square Players, and finally persuaded my colleagues to present my first long play, *The Family Exit*. I had been writing only one-act plays up to this time, with the result that my first three-act play consisted of three one-act plays strung together. This play resulted in my receiving the only good notice I ever had from the pen of George Jean Nathan, then one of the editors of *The Smart Set*, who has since consistently reviled almost everything which I or my colleagues have ever done in the theatre. Speaking of *The Family Exit*, he wrote:

> . . . Langner is a writer with a lively mind and a knack for adult wit. One of these days, unless all tokens fail, he is going to write a genuinely fine American satirical comedy.

The play closed after four weeks. In passing, I may say that it is a pity that Nathan's mental capacity has been limited by the four walls of the theatre, on which subject he has written for many years with apparent erudition. Of all the critics who were writing during my theatrical adolescence, he is the only one who both supported and survived this vital period in which the Players came to life. This was also the period when the Provincetown Players, headed by George Cram Cook and Eugene O'Neill, came into being and cradled the early works of O'Neill and Glaspell. This latter theatre was always a more personal expression of the authors behind it than was our group, with the result that it tended to develop its authors rather than its audiences—a worthy and important objective, difficult to achieve, and deserving of the greatest praise. It was frankly experimental as to plays while the Washington Square Players were attempting to present productions which would be in healthy competition with the plays of Broadway. The Washington Square group fought the issue of the art theatre *versus* the commercial theatre; it sought to produce its plays at the Comedy Theatre in competition with commercial attractions; it sent a traveling company on tour, and it operated a small and unsuccessful school of acting. It finally developed most of the producing talent which was later to become the Theatre Guild.

Among the acting talents which the Washington Square Players introduced to the American Theatre may be mentioned Katharine Cornell, Roland Young, Rollo Peters, José Ruben, Frank Conroy, Marjorie Vonnegut, Remo Bufano (of marionette fame), Arthur Hohl and Glenn Hunter; among its scenic artists, Lee Simonson and Rollo Peters. Edward Goodman and Philip Moeller both deserve special mention. Goodman held the helm of the Players with great discretion and artistry, and in later years has put his theatre talents into teaching acting at the American Academy of Dramatic Arts. Philip Moeller, as a result of his training with the Players, became one of America's most brilliant directors, and in the direction of comedies he was unsurpassed in this country.

While my title in the Players was "Business Manager," I was a member of its Board of Directors, in which capacity I helped select the plays, cast them and supervise the productions. Here was born the system, later imported into the Theatre Guild, which enabled me and the others to learn every branch of the theatre without having sole responsibility for what is, in essence, a cooperative effort. In the mornings and afternoons I put in a full day at patents, and my evenings and week ends were spent with the Players, or in writing plays for them. My work was stimulating, and was progressing well in both fields; and I managed the difficult task of starting two different careers with a maximum of enthusiasm.

In the short three years from 1915 to 1917, the Washington Square Players presented sixty-two one-act plays, many of which were outstanding.[2] The list included *In the Zone* by O'Neill, *The Magical City* by Zoë Akins, *The Girl in the Coffin* by Theodore Dreiser, *Suppressed Desires* by George Cram Cook and Susan Glaspell, *Trifles* by Susan Glaspell, *Neighbors* by Zona Gale and many other fine plays. I recommend any group of young people who are energetic and ambitious to try repeating that program in thirty odd months, and then throwing in for good measure the production of six long plays, including Chekhov's *The Sea Gull*, Ibsen's *Ghosts*, Shaw's *Mrs. Warren's Profession*, Andreyev's *The Life of Man*, Maeterlinck's *Aglavaine and Selysette* and last and undoubtedly least, Langner's *The Family Exit!*

Walter Prichard Eaton, then a drama critic, summed up the achievements of the Washington Square Players as follows:

... It accustomed a public, small perhaps, to look with interest on experimental work, and to relish the unusual, work done for the sheer joy of the doing. Finally, it left among the workers themselves a sense of incompletion, of a vision striven for but not attained, a realization of mistakes, but a belief nonetheless that the vision was a sound one, that in a spirit of cooperation and united purpose some day it was not unattainable.[3]

With the entrance of the United States into World War I, I was unable to give any more time to the Players, and regretfully resigned. One by one our best actors joined the armed forces, but Edward

[2] See appendix for list of plays of the Washington Square Players.
[3] *The Theatre Guild, The First Ten Years*, by Walter Prichard Eaton, Brentano's, New York, 1929.

Goodman held the fort, aided only by his wife Lucy Huffaker, until he too joined the Army. So the Washington Square Players came to an untimely end, leaving behind it a handful of trained amateurs who were ultimately to lift the bedraggled face of the theatre, as well as a substantial debt to the stage-struck Lee Shubert, who had long been inured to "holding the bag" for impecunious impresarios who attempted to fill his chain of theatres. Thus, with a record of artistic achievement and financial disaster, ended my first experience in the American theatre.

CHAPTER XI

A Village Wooing and Other Matters

IN THE fall of 1915, at the beginning of the second season of the Washington Square Players, I was dining at the restaurant in the back yard of the Liberal Club when Ernest Holcombe, our blond-bearded president, entered with an attractive girl who talked animatedly with him and his wife, Grace Potter. Her slim form, shiny dark hair, and broad forehead above smiling intelligent eyes, attracted the attention of most of the men present, including myself. They were seated at a table adjacent my own, and after dinner was over, adjourned to the Club premises. The electric piano and the liberally minded dancers were soon pounding out rhythm. There I encountered Ernest and his pretty companion, whom I was determined to meet. Ernest did the honors in true Liberal Club style. "Estelle, meet Lawrence," he said, and added, "Lawrence, meet Estelle." We shook hands, and I immediately detached her from her escort. "Do you mind telling me your last name, and I'll tell you mine." We promptly exchanged last names and a good deal of personal information about one another. Her name was Estelle Roege, and she was a mixture of Irish, Scots, German and French, had been born in Fredericksburg, Texas, and lived all over the South. At the moment she was studying singing in New York, a prominent citizen of Atlanta named Forrest Adair, who had known her family, having interested himself in her career. She was a graduate of Tallahassee State College in Florida, and had been a schoolteacher, but changed that vocation, for which she was temperamentally unfitted, for a musical career.

I immediately fell head over heels in love with Estelle, as did most of the other unattached male members of the Liberal Club, but on my first encounter, I was leading the pack, and I increased my head start from then on. I took her out to dinner and the theatre the next evening, and indeed wooed and won her so precipitously that she was figuratively carried off her feet and exhibited all the symptoms of having been struck by a minor tornado. Within three weeks, on Thanksgiving Day, 1915, we were married in Greenwich, Connecticut, at the side of a beautiful lake on Maurice Wertheim's estate. The ceremony was performed by a bewildered Justice of the Peace with gold-filled teeth, who was so confused by the fact that we had entirely rewritten the wedding service to accord with our modern ideas, that he asked Estelle if she took me to be her lawful wedded wife, to which she said "Yes." He also unintentionally asked her if she was willing to obey me until death did us part, which she had carefully deleted from the wedding service, to which she was too embarrassed to answer "No," so again answered "Yes," a promise she had no intention of keeping. In this idyllic open-air ceremony we were made man and wife, the occasion being unexpectedly concluded by the appearance of a large black bat which flew over us, and which Estelle laughingly assured me meant good luck, as the bat was the Chinese symbol of happiness.

Our marriage, completed so rapidly, was not accomplished as simply as it sounds. It was, for one who at the time had grave doubts as to marriage as an institution, a complete about-face. As for Estelle, who hardly knew me, it was contrary to all her training to look so hurriedly before she leaped. I persuaded her to take the step, however, by a specious reasoning which I do not recommend to others. "Why not agree to marry for three years?" I suggested, "and then if it's all a mistake, we can get divorced." Estelle fell in with this proposal, which seemed a logical compromise at the time, but the consequences of which were ultimately disastrous. On the eve of her wedding, she was given a stag dinner at the Liberal Club by Art Young, the cartoonist, and eleven other admiring Villagers, all of whom had been removed from the running by my dynamic tactics. We honeymooned at Lakeville, Connecticut, and Washington, D.C., by the end of which time we had known each other all of six weeks and were beginning to ask questions about each other's families. "I think my family will like you," she said, "for you remind me of my father, who is a schoolmaster." "I think my family will like you," I replied, "for you remind me of the pretty Welsh governess I was in love with as a boy."

We moved to an apartment at 113½ West Twelfth Street in the back yard of which stood another house in which lived Max Eastman and his wife Ida Rauh, while next door was a small experimental school conducted by Miss Caroline Pratt, which later became the City and Country School and still flourishes. We redecorated the apartment, and installed a dining room of white enameled furniture which was easy to keep clean, but reminded our guests of nothing more elegant than the Childs' restaurants of the period. One of our guests, the late Max Pam, a Chicago lawyer and art collector who had the unique claim to fame of owning the original painting of "September Morn," was highly amused by our white enameled dining table, which, he said reminded him of the celluloid collars worn by radicals, which could be washed off and worn month after month.

After we had been married a year, Estelle announced that our family would soon be augmented, and in the manner of girls in the Village, proceeded to demonstrate that she could have a baby without showing the least signs of pregnancy, a struggle in which Nature ultimately defeated her. Estelle, large as a pretty Southern mansion, ultimately went to a private hospital on Lexington Avenue, and presented me with a daughter, whom she named Phyllis for my sister and Adair for her friend Forrest Adair, then Chief Shriner of the United States, who was almost as surprised as I was to find himself the child's godfather.

In the summer of 1918, we moved to Woodstock in the Catskills. It was my first experience of a so-called artists' colony in America. There were two artists' settlements on opposite sides of the quaint little village of Woodstock. One of them was the Maverick, run by a gray-bearded iconoclast named Hervey White, with a penchant for building summer shacks and printing articles on esthetics on a small hand press; while the settlement on the other side of the town named Byrdcliff was made up of the more affluent artists, and run by a notable named Whitehead. Hervey White lived a hermit-like existence during the winter, but in the summer his colony blossomed out with Sunday Concerts in a large open barn, and later on, a theatre added its programs to the summer activities. Each year, on the day of the August full moon, the Maverick Festival held sway. It was an American attempt at a Saturnalia, and highly successful at that. Here the affluent artists from Whitehead's group, attired in fancy costumes of the most imaginative nature, mingled with the more impecunious painters, writers and musicians who made their homes in Hervey White's domain. Wine, champagne and the less costly but more potent spirits flowed freely.

Here I met, for the first time, George Bellows dressed soberly as a Pierrot, and Robert Chandler, giant painter with a shock of curly white hair atop his enormous head and shoulders, attired as Bacchus, and riding astride a gaily caparisoned donkey, followed by a throng of revelers clad in Roman togas and led by Louise Hellstrom, a red-haired maenad dressed as a Bacchante. The procession of merrymakers climbed the path up the adjoining hillside, to an open-air amphitheatre where sketches, songs and ballets were performed by the artists, after which the revelers dispersed. Throughout the moonlit night the woodlands rang with shrill female laughter and the cries of inebriated males. Next day the entire village of Woodstock was in the grip of a communal hang-over.

During my second summer in Woodstock I purchased a bungalow from Neil Reber located midway between the Maverick and Woodstock village, and a short distance from an elegant and handsome mansion where Alfred de Liagre, then a small boy, was being raised to become an elegant and handsome theatrical manager. Our household included my small daughter Phyllis, our cook Christine, and a superior English governess named Miss Higginbottom. To this bungalow I added a modern bathroom, something unique in the neighborhood, and rather shocking to the sensibilities of the rugged Maverick pioneers who were in the habit of performing their ablutions in an outdoor shower or a bucket of water. When the bathroom was built, I was called upon by a delegation from the Maverick led by Hervey White dressed in a lavender shirt, white trousers and sandals, who wished to inspect it. As our water supply was dependent on filling the tank by the hand pump, and the tank was usually empty, the bathroom was somewhat of a joke. I led the delegation to the bathroom door, rather shamefacedly, and remarking, "Here is our standing joke," I opened the bathroom door. Standing in the tub was the starkly naked figure of our dignified English governess, Miss Higginbottom, who let out a scream which stampeded the entire delegation. "Quite a joke," remarked Hervey. "Do you play this on everyone?"

Providence decreed that I should be punished for bringing so decadent a note as a bathtub into an artists' summer colony. A few years later, I rented the bungalow to a violinist named Gustav Tinlot. During an electric storm, the iron vent pipe attracted the lightning to the bathroom, and set the place on fire. Tinlot, awakened in the night, rushed into the flames like a true artist and saved his beloved violin and music, while his wife, being less of an artist, rushed into the flames and saved their beloved baby. I visited the blackened ruins a few days later and experienced a queer sensation. This was the first home I had ever owned, and all that remained were the charred foun-

dations, a chaos of bedsprings and a blackened bathtub. It was a challenge. I instructed Neil Reber to rebuild the bungalow. "With or
without a bathroom?" he asked. "With!" I replied, stubbornly.

While, in the beginning, there had been keen rivalry between the
Washington Square Players and the Provincetown Players, I had always maintained a personal friendship with George Cram Cook and
his wife Susan Glaspell, whose closest friend was Lucy Huffaker, the
Players' press agent. One of our programs included *In the Zone,* a one-
act play by Eugene O'Neill, prominently connected with the Provincetown group, while I was represented in the Provincetown group by
two plays written by me and produced by them.

Many of my Village friends were connected with the Provincetown
Players. Among these was James Light who, beginning as an actor,
ultimately became co-director of the Players with George Cram Cook.
Jimmy and his wife Susan spent two summers at our house in Woodstock, living in a small guesthouse we had built on the side of our
mountain. Inspired by an argument one morning between Jimmy and
Susan over the breakfast table, I wrote a one-act play which I called
Matinata. During the course of the argument, Susan arose and tripped
over Jimmy's foot. "You kicked me," she said, accusingly. "Nothing of
the sort," replied Jimmy. "You fell over my foot." "Your foot had no
right to be in the way," was Susan's somewhat illogical reply as she
stalked into the kitchen. Jimmy not only liked the play, but secured its
acceptance by the Provincetown Players for production. He also cast
himself for the leading part, which, since he was playing himself, fitted
him like the proverbial glove. O'Neill had just finished *The Emperor
Jones,* and a curtain raiser was needed to precede it. Jimmy suggested
that *Matinata* be given this position on the bill, to which I gladly
agreed. The opening night arrived, and *Matinata* went off well, Jimmy
and Norma Millay playing the leading parts. Then *The Emperor Jones*
burst like a bombshell on the audience. Nothing like it had ever been
seen in the theatre before. Charles S. Gilpin was magnificent as the
Emperor, and the insistent beat of the tom-toms worked the audience
and the critics into a state of hysterical excitement. When at last the
curtain fell, all remembrance of my fragile curtain raiser was buried in
the avalanche of applause for O'Neill's masterpiece. The following day
I looked through the newspaper notices; in vain I tried to find mention
of my play. One kind critic was good enough to add as a footnote to
his column that "*The Emperor Jones* was preceded by a one-act play
by Lawrence Langner entitled *Matinata.*"

Norma Millay, who appeared in my play *Matinata* and many other

Provincetown plays, lived at 25 Charlton Street, Greenwich Village, with her two sisters, Edna St. Vincent Millay and Kathleen Millay. The three beautiful Millay girls were something of an institution in Greenwich Village, and swarms of young painters, writers and poets made pilgrimages to their apartment on the top floor, where the young ladies were chaperoned by their mother from Maine, a bright little birdlike lady who regarded her daughters with all the bewildered surprise of a hen whose progeny had turned out to be, not chicks, but nightingales.

My special favorite was Edna, whose play *Aria da Capo* had won high success at the Provincetown Theatre. Norma, who married the painter and actor Charles Ellis, had real talent as an actress, while Kathleen was both poet and novelist. Evenings at No. 25 Charlton Street were a perpetual soiree with Edna holding court in one room, Norma in another, and Kathleen in the third, while Mother Millay fluttered on guard over her fledglings, hopping from one room to another. But daytime found the apartment transformed into a veritable ladies' academy. Edna told me that when she was working, she locked herself in her room each day with several packets of cigarettes, and wrote her sonnets with the same inspired precision that a sculptor chips marble, spending hours to achieve the perfection of fourteen matchless lines; Norma would be learning her latest part for the Provincetown Players, while Kathleen would be working over her latest novel.

Djuna Barnes, a contemporary of Edna, also wrote plays for the Provincetown Players which combined a startling sense of dramatic values with an incoherence of expression that made everything she wrote both exciting and baffling at the same time. Djuna was one of the most attractive girls of the Village; she was tall, beautifully built, with irregular features, a tilted nose, differently colored eyes and a small head set on a swanlike neck, yet all composed perfectly, and she gave such an effect of beauty that she attracted many of the eligible young men of the Village. She disappointed all of them but one by marrying a large and erudite gentleman named Courtenay Lemon who, later on, became one of the Theatre Guild's most able play-readers. I am rather proud of the fact that while I was conscious of Djuna's charms, I also believed in her talent to the extent of backing her financially for a short period, in order to enable her to devote herself entirely to writing a play. The play disappointed, but Djuna came through ultimately as a writer, and later won critical acclaim with her novel *Nightwood,* as well as *A Night Among the Horses* and *Ryder.*

No picture of those days in Greenwich Village is complete without mention of Harry Kemp, the Kansas hobo poet and his beautiful wife Mary Pyne, who worked for the Provincetown Players and played with moving success in O'Neill's *Before Breakfast*. Mary had Titian red hair, gray-blue eyes and the kind of creamy skin and red lips found in paintings by Henna. She combined the charm of Mimi in *La Bohême* with the spiritual beauty of a Della Robbia Madonna, and not only was she loved by all who knew her in the Village but her talents as an actress had won the interest of several "uptown" managers. Harry had a hard time earning a living as a poet, but what with selling a poem here and there, and with Mary's earnings in the Provincetown Players, they managed to lead a bohemian existence in the Village of those days, where everyone was poor and living was cheap. We considered Harry and Mary among our best friends, and we were thrown into consternation when we learned that Mary, who had to climb several flights of stairs to her apartment each day, had collapsed with a hemorrhage. Harry was in a pitiable state, and at a loss to know what to do. I passed him on Sixth Avenue one day carrying some small parcels. "I just sold a poem," he said, "and I've bought Mary some caviar, paté de foie gras, pickles and some other things she likes from the delicatessen." Mary steadily grew worse, for all the care Harry gave her so lovingly, and she had to be transferred to a sanatorium at Saranac where it soon became apparent that her condition was incurable.

Harry spent his time at her side in Saranac, broken by visits to New York in an endeavor to sell poetry to provide little presents for Mary and help defray the mounting expenses. One tragic day while he was at my apartment, the telephone rang and the long-distance operator asked for Harry. In a few moments he returned from the telephone, which was in our dining room, his eyes streaming with tears and his lips trembling. "My little Mary is dead," he said, then collapsed in a chair. Thus ended the unsung saga of Mary Pyne, a lovely rare person and one of the most promising young actresses of the Provincetown Players.

With the entry of the United States into World War I, most artistic activities in the Village came to an end. I offered my services to the Army Ordnance Department in Washington, D.C., where someone was needed to take care of international patent contracts. With the knowledge I had gained in England while working on inventions of the so-called Munition ring, including Skoda, Schneider-Creusot and Vickers, I was engaged as consultant to Major Amasa Holcomb, then in charge of patent matters for the U.S. Ordnance Department, and I worked on preparing the contracts for the British Stokes trench mortar and the French hand grenade, which had been adopted as standard equipment for our Army. I spent part of each week in Washington, and the balance in New York where our office staff was depleted by the draft. Moreover, we were now inundated by new war inventions, which pressed heavily on the rest of my time.

On one occasion, working on a contract for the so-called French fuse, I ran across a situation which I have often used to illustrate the difference between a discovery and an invention. The fuse cap of the shell, a thimble-shaped affair, had been made in France by cutting it with a milling cutter, an expensive operation which held up production. Contracts had been let to a number of American companies to make these caps by die pressing on a mandrel so as to save time. Only two companies were successful in doing this, however, and we had to investigate why they succeeded while the others failed. It turned out that the trouble arose from the red-hot cap sticking to the mandrel after it was pressed, so that it could not be removed. The inventor employed by one of the successful companies was a large Hungarian who worked for weeks on the problem without success, until, in despair, he went out and got thoroughly inebriated. He woke up the next morning to find himself in a disorderly house, without any recollection of how he came to be there. Hastily leaving, he noticed on the dressing table a large box of talcum powder. "If I put talcum powder on the mandrel, the cap won't stick to it," he surmised. He was correct. Thanks to the lady of easy virtue, the problem was solved, and the production of shells proceeded in the necessary volume. Finding the talcum powder was the "discovery," and using it on the mandrel was the "invention"!

In my work at the Ordnance Department, I was struck with the lack of cooperation which then existed between the Army and Navy. Inventors of devices which were used by both Army and Navy were often accorded entirely different treatment, and it was not unusual to find an inventor complaining that the Army refused to recognize his patent while the Navy had done so and was paying him a substantial royalty, or *vice versa*. I suggested to Goldthwaite H. Dorr, then Assistant Secretary of War, that a joint Board of Patent Control be set up with representatives of both Army and Navy on it. To my surprise, my suggestion was adopted and promptly put into practice. This was one of the first joint Army and Navy Boards to come into existence, and it lasted for many years under the title of Army and Navy Munitions Patents Board. I remember with a thrill attending the first meeting of the Board, with Mr. Dorr at its head and Army and Navy officers seated at opposite sides of a long table engaged in affable discussion and directing their hostility entirely toward the enemy, instead of at one another.

The spring of 1918 was a time of desperation in Washington, as the Germans gathered their massive forces for the mighty Hindenburg drive. The nightmare of the war drove me deeper and deeper into despair as I realized how tenuous was the thin line of trenches which stood between Western civilization and its destruction. At the lowest ebb, when I had given up all other interests and was spending all of my time in the Ordnance Department, an article appeared in the *New York Telegram* sneering at the Washington Square Players and their ignominious end. "Make no mistake," I wrote in a letter which was printed in this paper. "The Washington Square Players are no more dead than any other organization that is marking time on account of the war. The dramatic impulse which created it and kindred organizations is a living, breathing, real thing, much more alive than those who sneer at us. The doctors and wiseacres of Broadway and the newspaper offices who are busy analyzing the causes of the 'death' of the Washington Square Players must not be surprised if the corpse expresses its appreciation by registering a vigorous kick."

By the fall of 1918, the picture in Europe changed. The Germans were pushed back, and by November they were a defeated rabble. On Armistice Day, November 11, 1918, as I joined the happy crowd milling along lower Fifth Avenue, I celebrated not only because it meant the end of the war, but also because it meant, as far as I was concerned, beginning again where I had left off with the Washington Square Players.

Four weeks later I called a meeting of the most prominent members of the Players to start a new theatre.

CHAPTER XII

A Theatre Is Born

IT WAS Thursday, December 18, 1918, a month before Prohibition came incredibly into being, that I strolled into the Brevoort Hotel, at the lower end of Fifth Avenue, New York. The basement of the old hotel was divided into small airless rooms crowded with tables, and stocky Latin waiters rushed to and fro bearing trays of alocholic beverages to the guests, who seemed bent on drinking as much as possible before this simple pleasure became a criminal offense. The scene was joyous and animated, as befitted the most expensive restaurant in Greenwich Village. Even the oncoming of Prohibition could not dampen the spirit of gaiety which permeated the place, and was due to the fact that less than a month before, peace had come as a conclusion to what we then thought was the bloodiest war of all time, and with it the conviction that never again would the world be bathed in blood, since it was now "Safe for Democracy." We were prepared to put up with such petty inconveniences as Prohibition with the full knowledge that American liberty included the right of every citizen to break any law of which he did not thoroughly approve.

I personally faced the future with assurance, for now the way was clear to start a new theatre. Moreover, for the first time in my life I had invested in a modest wine cellar. In this happy frame of mind, I encountered Philip Moeller sitting with Helen Westley at one of the tables, the former debonair and vivacious, with his long cigarette holder punctuating his conversation like the baton of an orchestra leader, while the latter, handsome, dark and mysterious, dressed in a flowing robe obviously influenced by the Isadora Duncan mode, was sipping an exotic beverage and explaining that since her life was lived

Helen Westley and José Ruben in the author's one-act
comedy *Another Way Out*, presented by the Washington
Square Players at the Comedy Theatre, 1916.

Above: George Cram Cook, co-founder of the Provincetown Players, and Katharine Cornell, who made her stage debut with the Washington Square Players.

Below: Susan Glaspell, co-founder of the Provincetown Players, and Edward Goodman, Director of the Washington Square Players.

The Board of Managers of The Theatre Guild, 1923. *Left to right:* Lawrence Langner, Philip Moeller, Theresa Helburn, Maurice Wertheim, Helen Westley, Lee Simonson.

The Theatre Guild's first successful play, *John Ferguson*, by St. John Ervine, with Helen Freeman, Augustin Duncan and Helen Westley, 1919.

Richard Bennett and Margalo Gillmore in the Theatre
Guild production of *He Who Gets Slapped* by Andreyev,
1922.

Richard Bennett, Sidney Howard, Pauline Lord and Glenn Anders at a rehearsal of the Theatre Guild's production of Sidney Howard's play, *They Knew What They Wanted*, 1924.

EARLY THEATRE GUILD PLAYWRIGHTS.

Above: St. John Ervine, Franz Werfel.   *Below:* A. A. Milne, Ferenc Molnar.

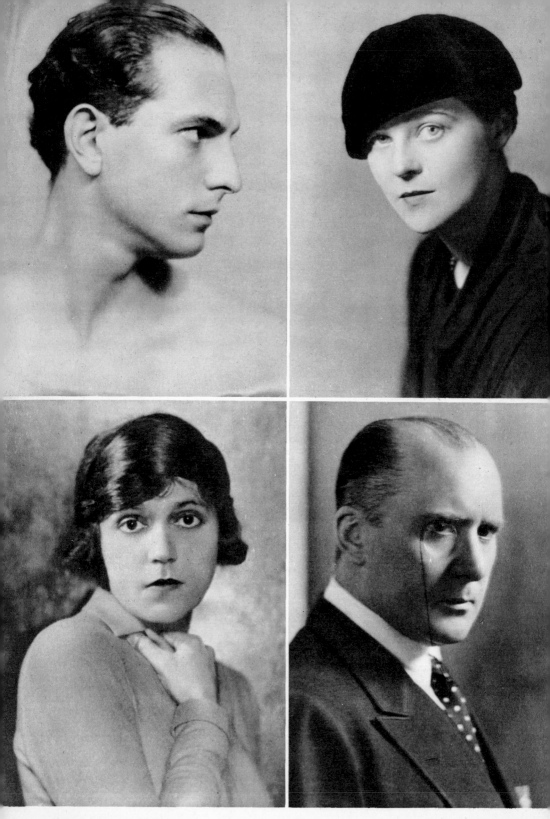

ACTORS AND ACTRESSES OF THE EARLY DAYS OF THE THEATRE GUILD.

Above: Joseph Schildkraut, Eva LeGallienne.   *Below:* Alice Brady, Arnold Daly.

on a higher plane than that of everyone else in the room, Prohibition would make little or no difference to the steady progress of her ascent upward and onward toward Nirvana. At their invitation, I sat with them, ordered some wine, and we conversed about the eternal verities, in which all three of us were soon deeply immersed, if not actually submerged.

The warmth of the room, in contrast with the crackling cold outside, the warmth of the wine, the warmth of the conversation, the warmth in Helen's handsome eyes—in fact, the general warmth of the occasion —contributed to a sensation of unreality, of having lived in an impossible world which had suddenly come to an end, so that now all nightmares were outlawed, and dreams could become real. In this atmosphere, artistic achievement became possible again, and the strivings of so many of us in the theatre, which had come to an untimely end with the advent of war, seemed suddenly capable of renewed life and vigor. Such thoughts stole through my mind, and they led me to make the announcement that I intended to start a theatre again, in which the dreams begun with the Washington Square Players would at last be realized.

It was fortunate that my companions were Philip and Helen, both of whom were possessed of the kind of impractical imagination which makes imaginative ventures practical. My thoughts were no sooner spoken than the new theatre became a living reality to both of them. "Why, of course," said Helen, "I want to act again!" "When do we start?" said Phil. "First," I replied, "we must have a meeting." "*That'll* be lovely. I adore meetings," said Helen. "I'll call one as soon as possible," was my answer. And thus, amid the clatter of glasses, the flow of wine, and the stimulation of conversation in convivial company, was started our new theatre—the Theatre Guild.

But birth is never as painless as conception. To start the new theatre into being involved a good deal of labor. I wrote to my friends of the Washington Square Players, some of them in Army camps, others overseas, and outlined my plans for the new theatre. "It must be a little theatre grown up," I wrote, "and should differ from the Washington Square Players in the following respects: It should be governed entirely by its Board of Managers, to which its director should be responsible. It should be a professional theatre, employ professional actors and produce only long plays 'which should be great plays.'" Nothing in this plan seems revolutionary today, but for those of us who had achieved their greatest success with one-act plays and had started in the amateur theatre, it represented a dangerous step into the unknown future. "And since you are so snooty about being 'professional,'" remarked one of my former colleagues, "who among you is really a professional?"

I called the first meeting at the home of Josephine A. Meyer, then quite ill. She was our spiritual godmother, however, and remained so until the time of her death. At this meeting, a few days before Christmas, 1918, were Helen Westley, Philip Moeller, Rollo Peters and myself, with Edna Kenton as witness at the accouchement, as she had been in the case of the earlier Washington Square Players.

The meeting was highly successful. We not only discussed the forming of an art theatre, we discussed very fully the kind of art theatre which we wanted to form. The conclusions set in writing after the meeting formed the Magna Charta of the Theatre Guild for many years until they became unworkable. For those who are interested, I quote the following which I noted down in a letter written directly after the meeting:

1.—That we would form a group to carry out the idea of an expert theatre; that is, a theatre which would be entirely different from the Little Theatre or Provincetown Players type of theatre, but would be made up only of artists of the theatre who are experts in their work.

2.—That we would either lease or secure the building of a theatre seating a considerable number of people, and certainly larger than the usual Little Theatre (between 500 and 600 seating capacity), in some place where the rents were sufficiently low not to make rentals a burden.

3.—To govern absolutely by a committee which will delegate its executive and administrative powers to members thereof.

After these policies had been formulated, a great many discussions took place at meetings which were held at the homes of Philip Moeller and myself. Remembering the famous medieval guild houses in Brussels, I suggested the name "Theatre Guild" to indicate the varied branches of stagecraft we intended to incorporate into our theatre. I was howled down at first, it being pointed out to me that the word "guild" in America had, up to that time, been mainly applied to charitable groups of sweet old ladies, such as Church Needlework Guilds and so forth. Finally, because nobody could find anything better, my suggestion was accepted. Since then, almost every organization in America has called itself a Guild, and we have had a Dramatists Guild, a Lawyers Guild, a Literary Guild, and a score of others all following our example, until the word has become as hackneyed as a weary old tune.

I have often been asked the queston, "Why did you start the Theatre Guild?" My motives were by no means simple. On the one hand, I did not want the pioneer work which had been done by the Washington Square Players to die merely because it had not been brought to a successful fruition. On the other hand, the conditions against which I and the rest of my friends had rebelled in the theatre were by no means conquered. The commercial theatre remained what it had been prior to the Washington Square Players, with the exception that Arthur Hopkins and one or two other "uptown" managers had been courageous enough to break ground for the production of plays of high artistic merit. The small "artistic" theatres, such as the Neighborhood Playhouse and Provincetown Players, were either no longer in existence or were operating in an erratic fashion, and to me it seemed essential that there should be a theatre in which plays of artistic merit and adult content could be given to compete with plays which were put on mainly for the amount of profit they could make for their producers.

I had faith in the desire of a large section of the American public for better things in the theatre, and I wished to test whether my faith was justified. To this extent there was involved in the formation of the Theatre Guild a crusading spirit which made what we were doing more exciting than the mere producing of plays as a matter of self-expression or profit. Along with the crusading spirit, there was, of course, a strong desire for self-expression on the part of most of us, including myself as a playwright.

It is an ironic commentary on my own career, and also an explanation of some of my frustration in the Guild, that it soon became apparent, after the organization had been running for a while, that neither I nor any of the other playwrights, including Philip Moeller and Theresa Helburn, would be permitted to have their plays produced by it. It soon became crystal clear, after putting the matter to a test, that if any of the Board of Managers wrote a play and wished to have it produced by the Guild, unless it was unanimously approved by the entire Board, it would cause extreme embarrassment and ultimately lead to the disintegration of the organization. As a consequence, Theresa Helburn, Philip Moeller and I found ourselves looking for other outlets for our plays, and we often placed such writing talents as we possessed to the furtherance of the plays of other American authors when needed.

As the work of the Guild proceeded, we found it more and more difficult to put into words a definition of what were our aims and ideals as far as plays were concerned. We finally hit on a phrase, "To produce plays of artistic merit not ordinarily produced by the commercial managers," and for a number of years this was a fair statement of our objectives. When, however, other managers began following our lead, it was even more difficult to differentiate our objectives, for what was the artistic theatre of those days has since become the most affluent section of the commercial theatre of today.

One of our most enthusiastic supporters at the beginning was Rollo Peters. Handsome, an accomplished actor and scenic artist, this son of Charles Rollo Peters, the California painter, was in his late twenties and brimming over with talent. Moreover, in the battle of "amateur" versus "professional" which was fought to a standstill at our original meetings, he was firmly on the side of the "professional," and the full weight of his influence was thrown onto the scales, and decided the question once and for all in these early days.

Another enthusiast was Lee Simonson, who, on his discharge from the Army, threw himself tirelessly into the work of organization. Lee, always a purist, had the most intensely logical mind I have ever encountered anywhere, but once it was made up, it was a Herculean task to get him to change it. Lee insisted, with excellent logic, that we should first raise forty thousand dollars, the sum which he deemed necessary to underwrite the theatre for a year, and having raised it, then to proceed. I, having an elastic mind, felt we would never be able to raise forty thousand dollars, and suggested that we start the theatre with what we had, and then raise the additional money later if we needed it. Arguments on this and other matters of policy went on for weeks.

I remember that Lee Simonson called upon me one afternoon to discuss ways and means of starting the new theatre. He spent the afternoon with me. I invited him to dinner. He spent all evening arguing with me, staying until two o'clock in the morning. It was then too late for him to go home, so I put him up for the night. He got up early the next morning, and continued arguing until lunch. I won my point, but almost lost my mind.

Lee's theory that we should find a benefactor like Mrs. Willard Straight, who had underwritten *The New Republic* magazine (which was Lee's Bible at the time) gained some support at our meetings. The idea was alluring to the impecunious young people of whom our group was largely composed. The plan was simple: First, you found a millionaire. Then you proceeded to throw salt on his tail by glowing accounts of the glamorous life of the theatre. And then you somehow separated him from forty thousand dollars, a mere trifle on which, since he would surely lose it, he could take a very satisfactory income-tax loss. I half-heartedly agreed that if such a person could be found, it would be wonderful, to which I added that hens might lay golden eggs but very seldom did. I secured the interest of an athletic young millionaire, who walked me up and down Fifth Avenue about ten times, during which I explained in detail all our plans, making them as glamorous as possible. But when we worked up to the point, he asked bluntly, "How much money have you got?" I replied vaguely, "Oh, between five hundred and fifteen hundred dollars," to which he replied with unanswerable logic, "You're doing it on a shoestring, Lawrence. I don't think I'd be interested." This was the moment when I should have brought the forty thousand dollars into the conversation, but I could no more ask for money than rob a bank. "I guess you're right," I replied, and returned home with sore feet and aching muscles, resolved that the Theatre Guild must never be dependent upon a subsidy from anyone.

Since nobody else found an obliging millionaire who could be seduced into helping us, my views regarding our finances ultimately prevailed, for the reason that there was no alternative. I suggested that we endeavor to find a few donors of five hundred dollars each, and as an inducement to others to follow suit, I put myself down for this amount, but paid in considerably more. We also agreed to raise money by selling tickets on subscription, as we had done before with the Washington Square Players. Thus was begun the Theatre Guild membership, a group of kindly disposed theatre lovers in most of the large cities of America, who have rejoiced with us in our successful accomplishments and have borne patiently with our failures over the past three decades. They made it possible for us to be independent of the whims of "patrons of the arts" (had we been able to find one with the right kind of whim), and to build our foundations solidly on the support of the intelligent theatre-going public.[1]

I do not mean to speak unkindly here of patrons of the arts. One of them, a most gallant gentleman, stepped in to help us at the very outset of our career. Looking around for a theatre, Rollo Peters and I decided that the old Garrick Theatre, which had been originally built for the famous comedians Harrigan and Hart, would be just the place

---

[1] The Theatre Guild was started with the incredibly small capital of $2,160, of which I contributed $1,610. All of this was repaid later. Our original subscriptions amounted to $474; our first week's receipts at the box office were $1,363, and our second week's receipts were $1,392. The opening night receipts were $403.35, and the following night we dropped to $281.45. Everyone worked for the same salary which, as I remember, was $25 per week!

for us, so we decided to plead our cause to the millionaire Otto H. Kahn, who had leased the theatre for Jacques Copeau just previously in a princely gesture intended to improve Franco-American cultural relations. Somewhat timidly we called on Otto Kahn, and on arrival were ushered into the enormous partners' room of Kuhn, Loeb & Company at Pine and William Streets. Here, seated at large shiny desks, were all the partners of this banking firm, and at the largest and most shiny of all sat Otto Kahn, a handsome, distinguished white-haired man with a curling mustache and velvety black eyes, who dressed and carried himself with European elegance, and looked for all the world like an ambassador. As we arrived at his desk, all the other partners looked up at us from their work, and I learned later that Mr. Kahn habitually enlivened their dull routine of making millions by interviewing at his office Metropolitan Opera divas, ballet dancers, painters and other glamorous souls who dispelled the gloom of Wall Street like rays of fitful sunlight.

Neither Rollo nor I possessed sufficient personal glamor to hold the attention of the other partners of Kuhn, Loeb & Company for more than a few moments, after which Mr. Kahn ushered us into a small office evidently reserved for matters too weighty for the rest of the partners to hear. After telling him our plans and our desire to rent the Garrick Theatre, he asked us what we could afford to pay. "As little as possible," we replied, making it unanimous. "Very well," he said, in meticulous English in which every word was pronounced distinctly, yet did not completely cloak his German accent, "when you make the rent, you will pay the rent. When you do not make it, you need not pay it!" "Just the kind of landlord we needed," I remarked to Rollo, as we passed out through the line of desks where the other partners were seated, no doubt wondering what new foolishness the head of the firm was up to.

Our meetings grew more and more frequent, and the numbers who foregathered grew larger and larger. Dudley Digges, Augustin Duncan, Edna St. Vincent Millay, Henry Herbert, Theresa Helburn, Justus Sheffield, Helen Freeman and many others began to appear and to join in the discussions. The meetings had the effect of separating the sheep who had creative ideas from the goats who hadn't, or who weren't interested, and ultimately we winnowed the mere talkers from the actual doers. Chief among the latter were Rollo Peters, Lee Simonson, Helen Westley and Philip Moeller. They became, along with myself and Justus Sheffield, a liberal lawyer with artistic impulses, the first working committee or Board of Managers of the Guild, while

Rollo, who threw himself wholeheartedly into the venture, was named its Director. Josephine Meyer was the playreader and Theresa Helburn was given the title of play representative. Had we realized the outstanding talents of Theresa Helburn at this time, she would undoubtedly have been made a member of the original Board of Managers. As it was, this took place later at a time of crisis. Plays were read and discussed and we ultimately settled on *The Bonds of Interest,* a Spanish *commedia dell' arte* costume play by the Nobel Prize winner, Jacinto Benavente, for our first production.

Our first play selected, we worked like beavers at the Garrick Theatre. Philip Moeller directed the rehearsals, while Rollo played the role of Leander and also designed and painted the sets out of old bits and pieces of scenery left on the Garrick stage by the Copeau players. Rollo also designed the costumes and supervised their fabrication out of all kinds of oddments and remnants, such as painted oilcloth, rubber, wallpaper and other materials which he seemed to conjure up out of thin air. I have a vivid picture of Rollo standing on a ladder on the stage, painting a palace wall while learning his lines, interrupted by questions from an aged sewing woman as to how a costume was to be made. Lee, who was presiding over the birth of his child at the inconvenient moment when we, too, were about to give birth, also came when he could, and splashed paint on the old canvas which was rapidly being transformed into Seventeenth-Century Spain. Dudley Digges, of the Abbey Players of Dublin, one of the world's greatest character actors (and earlier a fugitive from a Weber and Heilbronner store where he had been reduced to selling haberdashery for a living), was added to the company in the role of Polichinelle, while Edna St. Vincent Millay, elfin-like and delicate as a flower, abandoned her sonnets for the part of Columbine. We also engaged the professional Amelia Summerville to play the wife of Polichinelle, while Helen Freeman played the comely and graceful heroine Silvia. Helen Westley, dark and handsome in a velvet brocade (made no doubt from painted tissue paper), played the part of Dona Sirena.

At the final dress rehearsal, I stood in the wings and watched the stage from the side. The gaily painted scenery, the tinsel costumes, the actors moving in and out of the shafts of blue moonlight, brought back to me vivid remembrances of the toy theatre of my boyhood. I was nostalgically happy, living again in an enchanted world with far wider horizons than the everyday world in which I worked for my living. It is the fashion to speak of this kind of theatre today and my attitude toward it, as "escapist." It has never seemed to me that an enlargement of life was an escape from life. On the contrary, this kind of theatre opens vistas which are not to be found either in the realism of life or in the realism of the theatre which imitates life. In this theatre of painting, costume, music and poetry, the stage, as Shakespeare puts it, serves "to hold, as 't were the mirror up to Nature," rather than the camera. I had always been wedded to this kind of theatre, and wherever there has been a question or doubt about giving performances of the classics, I have usually thrown my weight on the side of the angels, although my voice has often been a voice crying in the wilderness.

On April 19, 1919, the magic curtain rose on the Theatre Guild's first play, *The Bonds of Interest*. I sat in the theatre surrounded by our band of one hundred and fifty courageous subscribers, and as the lights faded out on the curtain, there was a vibration of expectancy which made me feel that we would have a most responsive reception. The production was glamorous, the story was witty and enchanting, the acting was excellent. Only a small accident marred the smoothness of the performance. In the garden scene, Madam Polichinelle, played by Amelia Summerville, wore a magnificent hooped skirt of cloth of gold—at least it appeared to be cloth of gold. Rollo had actually made it out of oilcloth painted with gold paint. It looked very expensive from the front, but its actual cost was under thirty dollars. Miss Summerville was a lady of ample proportions, and she played her first scene sitting on a little wooden chair. It was a hot night, and—well, we all know what happens to oilcloth on a hot night. When the perspiring Amelia rose to make a dignified exit, the little chair stuck to her skirt and rose up with her. To our horror, as she crossed the stage, the chair clung tenaciously to the oilcloth until Dudley Digges, who followed her off stage, with fine presence of mind neatly plucked the chair from her posterior, leaving a large white patch in full view of the cheering audience.

When the curtain fell, the applause was clamorous and our hopes ran high. They were dashed to the ground the next morning by the drama critics who seemed in no mood to welcome our advent. Our money trickled away. "What shall we do," I asked Estelle, "buy a car, or give the money to the Theatre Guild?" "Give it to the Guild," was her unhesitating reply, and I met the losses of about five hundred dollars a week for three weeks. Then a surprising thing happened. Maurice Wertheim, a Wall Street banker who had worked in Professor Baker's '47 Workshop at Harvard and had just returned from Persia, visited the play. He came, he saw *The Bonds of Interest* and the theatre conquered. "This is exciting!" he said. "How is it doing?" "Badly," I replied. "It's losing five hundred a week." "I'm interested," he said, and after I'd explained the situation, he thought it over for a moment and remarked, "How'd you like it if I lose the next five hundred dollars, you the next, and so on?" and the fledgling theatre found a new collaborator.

We had promised to give two plays, and were having a hard time finding the second. Feeling rather depressed, I was walking along Fifth Avenue late one afternoon when I passed Brentano's bookstore and decided to look through the printed plays in the play department. As I looked over the shelves, I was attracted by the name St. John Ervine as the author of a play called *John Ferguson*. I remembered the time, more than ten years before, when I had met Ervine at the West London Parliament and he had voted for the Small Holdings Bill I had brought in.

I picked the book off the shelf, little thinking as I did that I held the future of the new Theatre Guild in my hand. I took it over to the saleslady and told her I would like to buy it. She said she was sorry, but it was too late, as the store had already closed. I pleaded with her, however, and by some stroke of luck, I melted her heart for she very kindly wrapped the book, which I took home and read.

It was just the play we were looking for! My fellow Board members were all as excited about the play as I was, and we decided to produce it at once. Before we could do this, however, we had to make our arrangements with the author. I therefore cabled over to St. John Ervine asking whether we might produce the play, signing the cablegram "Theatre Guild, Lawrence Langner." Ervine knew very little about theatrical managers on this side of the Atlantic and sent a telegram to Bernard Shaw asking him if he knew the Theatre Guild or Lawrence Langner. Shaw wired back a characteristic reply. "Don't know either. I advise you to get your money first." As a result, Ervine cabled me, asking for a thousand dollars advance royalty, and since we did not have any money in the treasury, we were at a loss as to what to do. In the meanwhile, I had written to Ervine, reminding him of my earlier association with him in the West London Parliament, and telling him of our aims and our comical financial situation. Ervine immediately cabled back that we might produce the play without making any advance payment, so we went right ahead.

On the opening night, we were literally down to our last penny. The play ended in an ovation to the cast, all of whom performed magnificently, especially Augustin Duncan in the title role and Dudley

Digges as James Caesar. *John Ferguson* wrung the emotions of the drama critics so hard that the next day their pens dripped ecstasy. The public rushed to the Garrick Theatre and stood in a line reaching out into the street. As I watched the people hungrily buying tickets, two or three friends who had offered to help in financing us, but had been unable to do so, came and offered me their congratulations along with their belated contributions. "Sorry," I said, "but it's too late, thank the Lord!"

After *John Ferguson* had been running a few months and accumulating a slender fortune for the Guild, the members of Actors Equity Association (the actors' union) and the theatrical managers started calling one another names. The name calling boiled over into a dispute which led to the memorable Actors' Strike. Since our sympathies were with the actors, we were the first to recognize Equity. They, in turn, decided not to call out our actors, with the result that for several months the only play in New York was *John Ferguson*. If you wanted to go to the theatre, you just *had* to see *John Ferguson*. We felt so prosperous that we decided we could afford to have a business manager, so we found ourselves a charming and handsome young man named Walter Wanger, who had no experience in the job but was brimming over with boyish enthusiasm. "Just the man for us," said Rollo, "*distingué*, if you know what I mean." He *was* just the man for us. He rushed *John Ferguson* out of the Garrick Theatre, planted us firmly at the Fulton on Forty-ninth Street, and after six months or so, learned enough about theatre production to become a successful theatrical manager himself, beginning his career with a play employing thirty young children among whom he looked like a slightly older brother. After this, his advance became meteoric, and I often encounter him in the more exclusive palaces of Hollywood, his boyish enthusiasm for the good old Garrick days only slightly dampened by the passing of years and quite unobliterated by the many million miles of photographic film which bear his successful imprint.

Before the opening of *John Ferguson*, Augustin Duncan replaced Justus Sheffield (whose interest in theatricals was sporadic) on the Guild Board, and Maurice Wertheim also joined the Board, and introduced the other members to such mysteries as double-entry bookkeeping, corporation reorganization, and other practical aspects of business gleaned from Wall Street. The group, although now successful beyond its dreams, had not yet sifted down into a coherent body. My feeling, based on my experience with the Washington Square Players, was that unless a genius could be found as Director, the theatre should be managed by a group. Augustin Duncan, a man of the highest artistic integrity, lovable and noble in character, and with far more professional theatre experience than any of the rest of us, felt otherwise, and soon the Board began to divide into two camps, with Augustin Duncan, Rollo Peters and Helen Freeman on one side, and the rest of us on the other.

The gap was widened by the fact that Duncan and Peters were our best actors, and quite properly, the best parts fell to them, Duncan playing the older leads and Rollo playing the juvenile leads. This, in turn, affected discussions on the choice of plays, and since the opposing camp was not as tough-skinned as ours, the situation split wide open. I tried in vain to pour oil on the troubled waters, but the oil merely caught on fire and added to the general conflagration. Soon, to my regret, they resigned from the organization, leaving us, the less sensitive souls, in possession. I regretted particularly the loss of Rollo Peters, to whose great talents and accomplishments the Guild, in its early days, owed so much.

We were now faced with the problem of running the Guild without a Director. Lee Simonson took over the office temporarily, and with the best of intentions, imported with him the organizational methods he had learned recently in the United States Army. "Verbal orders don't go," was his watchword, and soon each member of the staff was sending written memoranda to the others headed in military fashion, "From A—— B——, Press Agent, To C—— D——, Secretary." After a little while, the entire Guild was so wrapped up in red tape that it was almost impossible to unravel us. Lee, who had no appetite for the job, eagerly awaited a successor; so did the rest of us.

At this time, Theresa Helburn, who was a graduate of Bryn Mawr and Baker's '47 Workshop at Harvard, was serving as our play representative. She was also the dramatic critic of *The Nation,* a career of crime she has since expiated by long years honorably spent in reading the criticism of others. She was, at the time, aged about thirty, with soft brown hair and warm twinkling eyes, a high forehead and generous mouth. Her personality was friendly and charming, and despite her small rounded stature, exuded an air of importance and intellectual honesty. No one seemed particularly surprised when, after she attended a few meetings, it was suggested that she take over the executive functions of the Guild with the title of Executive Director. She was engaged for a few weeks but has stayed for over thirty years. Before long we found ourselves a smoothly running organization, for while Terry had had no previous business or theatre experience, she was quick to learn. She possessed the faculty of conscientiously carrying out the decisions of the Board, yet at the same time holding to her own opinions, and I often wonder how she survived so difficult an assignment. But if her appearance was soft and comfortable, her nerves were like whipcord and her will power like steel; it could bend, but did not break under the strain of carrying out the decisions of the hydra-headed creature which was to guide the Guild's destinies during one of its most successful periods.

But it is not to be supposed that a woman of Terry's ability would, for long, merely content herself with carrying out the wishes of the Board. As soon as she picked up the complex threads of theatre production, her voice was just as effective as anyone else's, if not quite as loud or strident. It was not long before most of us realized that her abilities were outstanding, and more and more of the executive work of the Guild was placed on her shoulders, while her talents in casting the plays, and her training under Professor George Pierce Baker made her invaluable. In addition to her artistic work, to her fell the task of carrying out the many impersonal decisions of the Guild, whether she believed in them or not. Many an actor fired from a play has blamed Terry for the fact to this day merely because it was her task to convey to him the unfavorable decision of the Board. That she was able to retain the measure of popularity she has under these circumstances, is nothing short of a miracle; nor did her colleagues (myself included) spare her by helping her out on occasion. "Let Terry do it" was our watchword.

Later on, after she was standing firmly on her own two feet, there was a certain amount of dissension in the group over the limits of her authority, and one day Simonson referred to her as having established a "Dictatorship of the Executariat." However, since our Board was made up of six Dictators who made it their business to see to it that no one dictated to them, while at the same time they each and every one did his best to dictate to every other Dictator, Terry dismissed the charge rather lightly, but ultimately resigned in disgust, after which the Guild suffered some of its worst setbacks.

With our third play, *The Faithful* by John Masefield, followed by *The Rise of Silas Lapham* by Lillian Sabine, there began a cycle which was to repeat itself with disastrous results every so often. Having money in the bank from *John Ferguson,* we splurged on these two costume plays and lost all our money. The first was an honorable failure; the second, which starred James K. Hackett, was not so honorable. Hackett fled to London, where he was engaged to play opposite

Mrs. Pat Campbell in a play of Shaw's. G.B.S. told me later that Hackett was introduced to the famous English actress who was noted for her rudeness. "James K. Hackett?" she repeated vaguely, looking him straight in the eye. "Why, I thought you were dead!"

Hackett, who was an old-fashioned romantic actor and a contemporary of James O'Neill and Richard Mansfield, had been engaged by the Guild despite its avowed hatred of the old "star" system. Under the "star" system, the play itself and the other actors all became satellites of the star, resulting in a general deterioration of the theatre, since the star, usually an "actor-manager," was often jealous of the other actors appearing with him, and took good care to see that no one outshone him in the public eye. The Guild was definitely hostile to this system, and from then on, for over twenty seasons, it "starred" its plays and "featured" its actors. This policy would have been continued right down to this day, had not a leading playwright insisted on "starring" our leading actors the Lunts, thus breaking down a Guild policy which had for years been based upon giving first importance to the play.

Almost down to our last penny again, we reached out in the direction of a great play. We engaged Emmanuel Reicher, formerly director of the Volksbühne Theater of Berlin [from which I borrowed the idea of a subscription system] to direct Tolstoy's *The Power of Darkness*. It was a powerful play on an important Christian theme and was splendidly acted, but the public responded not at all. We held a meeting of despair in the cellar-like smoking room of the Garrick Theatre.

"We are down to our last two hundred dollars," I remarked to the gloomy assembly.

Emmanuel Reicher, who was present at the meeting, pushed a printed play across the table. "Here is a play called *Jane Clegg* by St. John Ervine, the author of *John Ferguson*. I recommend that you do this as your next play," he said.

Jane Clegg had been under discussion for some time, but there had been differences of opinion which Reicher's admiration for the play resolved in its favor. *Jane Clegg* proved that lightning can strike twice with the same author, for it was just as successful and ran even longer than *John Ferguson*. The Guild was "saved" again by St. John Ervine, who there and then became our patron saint.

During our next season, following an unsuccessful bout with Pinski's *The Treasure*, we went with some trepidation to our first joust with Bernard Shaw, selecting *Heartbreak House* as our second offering. In order to secure the rights to *Heartbreak House*, I cabled Shaw for permission for the Guild to present the play; G.B.S., not having heard either of the Guild or of me, telegraphed curtly to St. John Ervine, "WHO ON EARTH IS LANGNER?" Ervine told Shaw that Langner and the Guild could be safely trusted with his play. Then G.B.S. wrote to Theresa Helburn that he wondered whether the Guild was "bold enough and clever enough to know that the alternative to pleasing an audience for two hours is to put the utmost strain upon their attention for three, and send them home exhausted but inspired." Just as we were about to open, Shaw cabled that we had to postpone the opening date until after November 2nd, the day of the Presidential election. In vain we pleaded. "Inexorable," he cabled, economizing as usual on his cable costs. Later on he told me that he had had a number of experiences which proved to him that before a Presidential election the theatre always did badly. No amount of argument would shake him from this belief, although it dated from the days of the old-fashioned elections when parades marched through the streets and campaign oratory was sufficiently entertaining to compete with theatre going. Warren G. Harding was duly elected to bring the country back to "normalcy," while *Heartbreak House* waited until November 10th, thus obeying Shaw's injunction to Theresa Helburn, "Better produce *Heartbreak House* with the first cast you could pick up out of the gutter on November 15, than to produce it on October 15, with Sarah Bernhardt, the two Guitrys, Edwin Booth, John Drew, Maude Adams, Mary Pickford and Charlie Chaplin." I shudder to think what would have happened to the play with this cast. As it was, our efforts were crowned with success, and the play was extraordinarily well received. The Guild was "saved" again.

As all those who lead a double life know full well, no sooner are you in trouble in one of your lives than you also find yourself in trouble in the other. And generally when you are busy in one life, you are even more busy in the other; so that you are like a man with two wives, each demanding your exclusive attention. I was able, by a species of personal legerdemain, to jump from my vocation of international patents to my avocation at the Guild by getting to the Garrick at 8:30 in the morning, working there until 10 A.M., then spending the day until five at the office, and returning to the Garrick for the evening. Not being the type of man who hankers in the evening for a comfortable armchair, slippers and a cozy fireside, I found the days all too short to encompass both my interests.

After the war, the patent practice called for increasing attention on my part. Inventors have a habit of keeping patent attorneys busy through all the ups and downs of life. When there is a depression, inventors try to think up new ways of making money; when times are good, they can afford to spend more money on their inventions. When there is a war, they make inventions to win the war; when the war is over they adapt many of the war inventions to purposes of peace. The accumulation of inventions which had been made or held over during the war, as well as the large number of new clients who entered into foreign trade for the first time, overwhelmed our office with work, and it became necessary for me to take a trip to England and the Continent to establish a London office for my firm, and also to make contacts with leading European authors, directors and actors who would be helpful to the Guild. So after our successful opening of Shaw's *Heartbreak House*, I set sail for England with the happy feeling that my office and the Theatre Guild were in good shape, and that I could devote some time and effort to strengthening the European connections of both. I also resolved to call on Mr. Shaw, to ascertain whether the Guild could represent him in the United States.

CHAPTER XIII

Shaw and Back to Methuselah

WHEN I was fifteen, and working in the office of Wallace Cranston Fairweather in London, he gave me a ticket to a lecture by Bernard Shaw at the Fabian Society, with the intriguing title "The Position of the Artist under Socialism." Shaw, aflame with his red beard and his subject, made a profound impression on me. The position of the musician, author or actor under Socialism, according to Shaw, would be that of a capitalist millionaire. "My income," said Shaw, "as a state dramatist would be enormous!" "And serve you right!" cried someone in the audience. Shaw was not entirely mistaken in his prophecy, for years later Stanislavsky told me that Chaliapin, a national hero in Soviet Russia, was paid handsomely for each appearance. One day he was set upon by robbers in a remote village. "I'm Chaliapin!" he announced imperiously to the footpads. They apologized profusely, gave him a handsome present and escorted him on his way to safety.

At the time we produced *Heartbreak House,* Bernard Shaw was anathema to the public because of his attitude toward World War I. Instead of being purged or shot, as would undoubtedly have been the case with this particular artist at such a time under Communism, he had retired to his home in the country to work in peace and quiet.

After Shaw gave us permission to produce *Heartbreak House,* I was informed by him that I was to communicate with his lawyer, Benjamin Stern, a charming and urbane gentleman who had represented Shaw's interests in this country for generations without showing any appreciable signs of accompanying wear and tear. Whether instructed to do so by Shaw, or as a personal favor to me, Stern in a fatherly

130

manner did his best to frighten me into a panic "I must warn you," he said, "that Shaw will not permit you to alter as much as one single word in his play. He once closed Faversham's production of *Getting Married* because the actor dared to cut it without his permission. And lest you think," he proceeded, fixing me with his penetrating eyes, "that you can tamper with the play without Shaw knowing about it, let me also warn you that he has the most uncanny way of knowing exactly what you are doing. Once Arnold Daly wanted to present one of Shaw's plays at the Maxine Elliott Theatre on Fortieth Street. Shaw cabled his refusal because the street was being repaired!"

I learned later from Shaw that a lady, one of his early admirers, had been in the habit of attending the performances of all his plays in New York with the book in her lap, and wrote Shaw instantly if anyone deviated from the printed word. She undoubtedly also kept him informed of the condition of the New York streets.

Armed with Shaw's ferocious contract, which no lawyer has ever dared to interpret, we proceeded to make the first production of *Heartbreak House*. The world premiere took place on November 10, 1920, and brought this playwright back to the living theatre after an absence of several years. But at the outset we were faced with a difficulty, for after engaging the beguiling blonde-haired Effie Shannon for the part of Hesione Hushabye, we noticed she was described by Shaw as having "magnificent black hair." In the text of the play, Ellie, another character, says to her, "Oh, you don't mean to say, Hesione, that your beautiful black hair is false." Effie was requested either to dye her hair black or wear a black wig, but her reaction to both proposals turned the approach into a retreat, if not a rout. The six Guild Directors put their heads together and hit upon the ingenious plan of having the line slurred in the reading.

I had corresponded with Shaw regarding *The Devil's Disciple*, and he had invited me to communicate with him when I arrived in London, although he expressed the belief that Richard Mansfield had "squeezed the last farthing out of the *D's D*" and that the play was essentially a "star melodrama and, as such, not so much the Theatre Guild's business as, say, Barrymore's."

Arriving in London in the winter of 1921, I called on St. John Ervine, who gave me some advice as to how to achieve my objective. "He's really a very kind man," said St. John. "When I lost my leg in the war, he sent me a postcard saying that every tree is better off for a little pruning. This was his way of telling me not to dwell too much on my troubles."

This did not sound very reassuring, and I left Ervine with the impression that a difficult task lay ahead of me. The morning arrived when I was instructed to call at 10 Adelphi Terrace, and I walked up the stairs to the entrance to Shaw's apartment. A low fan-shaped grill of sharp iron spikes separated the staircase landing from the lower floor of the building, and I speculated on how easily a precipitous retreat might result in one's being impaled on this formidable barricade. The door opened, and I was shown into the study, a comfortable Georgian room, crowded with photographs and busts of Shaw himself, and dominated by a cheerful fireplace on the white mantel of which was carved the words "They say—what say they—let them say!" I innocently supposed that this was Shaw's own personal formula for iconoclasm, but learned from him years later that this legend was on the mantelpiece before Shaw moved into the apartment. Paraphrasing the motto, I said to myself "Shaw says—what says he—let him say!" and I waited with a little more courage as a result.

After a few minutes, Shaw came in, lean, white-bearded and erect, looking rather like Father Christmas on a hunger strike, minus only the red cloak and the bell. His face was pink and red, his eyes alive and keen, and his manner very cheerful and sprightly. He greeted me warmly, put me at my ease, and after discussing the production of the play, asked to see the photographs I had brought with me. His sharp blue eyes scanned the very handsome set Lee Simonson had provided—"Quite good," he said, rather severely, in the manner of a schoolmaster appraising an examination paper, "only the room should look like a ship's cabin, and Simonson has made the tops of the doors rounded instead of flat. Doors on ships are never rounded." I murmured apologies, and said that it hadn't hurt the play—no one had noticed the tops of the doors anyway, they were so engrossed in his dialogue! His severity relaxed until he came across a picture of Effie Shannon. "Isn't she playing the part of Hesione?" he asked, sharply. My heart momentarily stopped beating. The vision of being permitted to produce more Shaw plays began to fade. I nodded, and the sharp blue eyes regarded me angrily. "But she has fair hair—you must have cut one of the lines!" "Well, not exactly," I replied. "We just mumbled it—what would you have done?" The fate of my mission hung in the balance. Shaw smiled. "That's all right," he said, and the crisis was passed.

I broached the subject of producing more of his plays. He evaded me—plunging into an account of his latest work, *Back to Methuselah,* which he had been writing during the war, and which he assured me was probably the longest and best play ever written. It was based on the theory that mankind could extend the span of human life from the Biblical threescore and ten to many thousands of years, by leading a Shavian existence on lines laid down by Shaw himself and which succeeded to the extent of carrying him into his nineties with no mental idiosyncrasies other than those which have been habitually associated with him. The play itself was in five separate parts, and since it began with Adam and Eve and stretched over millions of years, it seemed that no member of our Theatre Guild audience was likely to live long enough to be able to disprove any of Shaw's prophetic conclusions. My interest was excited, and I asked for a copy. "On your way back from the Continent, drop in to see me again, and I'll have the plays ready by that time."

After a while, Mrs. Shaw entered. She was a gentle gracious lady with plain, pleasant features, and of medium height and comfortable build. She was about the same age as Shaw, whom she seemed to regard in much the way a mother would a brilliant young son who needed careful guarding. Perhaps her maternal attitude came from the fact that she married him after nursing him through a rather dangerous illness. Shaw seemed a little quieter in her presence, as though on his good behavior, but I sensed a relationship between them which I was to learn afterward was based upon the deepest respect for each other's qualities. Upon the death of Mrs. Shaw many years later, the American newspapers printed a ridiculous story that she had left her personal fortune "to teach the Irish good manners" because of Shaw's lack of them. During the years I was to know them both, I was constantly amazed at Shaw's courtly old-fashioned manners. If Mrs. Shaw started to leave the room, Shaw would leap from his chair, dash like a sprinter to the door with his beard waving, so as to arrive ahead of her, and he would hold it open with a deep bow until she had passed into the hall. On the occasion when I first met her, Shaw introduced her in the grand manner, like an impresario displaying a prima donna, a role which did not fit Mrs. Shaw in the least. He ostentatiously seated her in a chair, and showed her the photographs of the production, which she admired appreciatively. However, when Shaw pointed out his objection to the doors with the rounded tops, she replied simply, "What difference does it make?", to which the great man made no reply. I was to learn from many years' friendship with Mrs. Shaw that "the Genius," as she lovingly called him, was guided by her excellent common sense, which often served as an antidote to his tendency to explode fireworks on all occasions. Moreover, she suggested the subjects of some of his best plays, including *The Doctor's Dilemma* and *Saint Joan*. Mrs. Shaw was most kind to me and invited me to lunch with them when I came back from the Continent.

Returning to London a month or so later, I called again on the Shaws. The iron spikes had lost their terror, and seemed even a little friendly as I rang the bell. After being told politely by Shaw that I was not to smoke in the dining room (a wholly unnecessary precaution, since I did not smoke at all then), we had lunch, during which G.B.S. gave me his views on the war and the peace which was in the making. "I have seen the end of the German Empire," he said, devouring a goodly helping of cabbage, "the end of the Russian Empire, and as for the British Empire—" he winked, and ate some more cabbage.

We talked about *Back to Methuselah*, and the best way to present it. Shaw's idea was to have all five plays produced consecutively, so that the audience would have to take the entire dose in one helping. On leaving, he said he would send me the printed proof sheets, and I asked for a contract. "Don't bother about a contract," he said, as I stood at the door taking my leave, "it isn't likely that any other lunatic will want to produce *Back to Methuselah!*"

And he was right, as usual.

Shaw had evolved the idea of certain individuals living for several hundred or even thousands of years from studying some of the experiments made in Austria by Dr. E. Steinach, and this was the main theme of the play. In due course, the proof sheets arrived at my hotel together with a letter dated March 9, 1921, reading:

At last I have got a complete set of proofs of the forthcoming volume. You will understand that I am breaking faith with my publishers in letting them out of my own hands for export and that I must place you under the most blood-drinkingly sacred obligation not to show them to a soul except in confidence to your colleagues and the T.G. of America. If any account of them or quotations from them reach the press in either country there would be the devil to pay for me. Further, as they are not finally corrected for press will you send them back to me when the book is published or else write me an assurance that you have destroyed them with your own hands. If you once let an imperfect text loose, you can never overtake it and I always have to destroy my unused proofs with the greatest care. Bon Voyage!

His postscript read:

> The final corrections will not involve any change that you need take into account. Also you may regard the dialogue as drastically cut, so the producer has nothing more to hope in that direction.

My heart fell as I read the postscript. I was to regard these plays, running into thousands upon thousands of words, "as drastically cut"! I studied the proof sheets on shipboard, and whether due to a bad storm which lasted for several days, or to the plays themselves, no Atlantic crossing ever seemed longer. Nevertheless, I was highly excited by the adventure of producing so imaginative a work, and I wrote him en route telling him so, and also calmly suggesting that he rewrite the second play of the series, which struck me as too local. My first task on arrival in New York was to ensure the secrecy which Shaw had imposed on me as a "blood-drinkingly sacred obligation," whatever that might mean.

One of the difficulties of the youthful Theatre Guild arose from the fact that six tongues can wag six times more frequently than one, and the problem of keeping theatrical news out of the New York newspapers was almost as difficult then as it is today, when some of our newspapers employ reporters with all the talents of private detectives to spy on our doings. On arriving in New York, I swore my colleagues to secrecy and then let them read *Back to Methuselah*. They did, and realizing the length and expense involved, as well as the fact that we were nearing the end of the theatrical season, the decision to produce the play was postponed over the summer. Meanwhile, Shaw wrote me that he wanted the play published in book form, which seemed illogical in view of his earlier admonition to make no mention of the plot before its public performance. I suggested he postpone publication until after the play had opened, and I added:

> If you would like to come over to the States at the time when we give the play, the Guild would be prepared to pay for your passage and expenses in New York. We would shield you from all publicity by every possible method. What suggests itself immediately is that you enter the country clean-shaven, so that nobody will recognize you. What could be simpler?

Shaw's reply explained that he was certain that the first part of the play could be tremendously effective on the stage and that to perform it along with the second part at the same performance would be impossible. We would have to resign ourselves to putting on *Back to Methuselah* on three evenings and two matinees. He added:

You must sell tickets in batches of five, all five tickets on one sheet with perforated card divisions. If people buy them that way they will not throw them away. They may be bothered and disappointed by the first two plays, as you expect; but their bewilderment will not take the form of throwing their tickets in the fire, especially if you charge enough for them. You can warn them that the prologue in the Garden of Eden will last only an hour (or perhaps 50 minutes; you can time it at rehearsal) and that no assumptions must be made as to the duration of each part of the play. The wording of your programmes and announcements must always rub in the fact that what the public is going to see is one play, with sections of various lengths.— Later on we can see about giving separate performances of the sections; but for the first ten performances (say) it must be impossible to take less than the whole dose.

The book will be published on the first of June or thereabouts. I note your calm suggestion that it should be held back until you are ready to produce. I told you you wanted the earth. If you want to produce simultaneously with the publication you must hurry up very smartly, indeed.

In the meantime, the question of the expense of this enormous undertaking was bothering us considerably. While published in book form as one play, *Back to Methuselah* is in reality five separate and complete plays, calling for quite different sets, actors and costumes. We had the Garrick Theatre, the seating capacity of which was so small that it was impossible to operate on a profitable basis there, no matter how well the play was attended. While we were debating the matter, I reported to G.B.S.:

The general consensus is that it is a stupendous piece of work, and the Guild stands awed. The greatest difficulty seems to be the second play. The majority of the Guild are in favor of putting it on next season during a lull, so that we can all work on it, but we are all worried about the second play. I have never heard from you about this, and hope I may do so shortly.

My next letter to Shaw explained what had been happening over the summer. Carpentier, the French boxing champion, had battled with Jack Dempsey, the American heavyweight champion, and had been "knocked out" notwithstanding Shaw's published opinion that Carpentier would win. I reported at considerable length on our production plans, on how we were proposing to present the huge play, and how we were arousing interest in it. I suggested that he could help us with the press by sending us copies of any articles in England condemning him as unscientific, together with his answers to his critics. We could place them in the newspapers. I added facetiously that he had lost a great deal of prestige over here as a result of his having picked Carpentier to win the fight. We were now inclined to doubt his scientific accuracy.

G.B.S. answered this letter while touring in Yorkshire, and my remarks on the prize fight seemed to interest him far more than *Back to Methuselah.* He wrote:

I must insist that I did not pick Carpentier to win the fight. I very expressly warned the punters that Carpentiers had been beaten by Dempseys very often, instancing Mace by King, as I might have instanced Corbett by Fitzsimmons and Johnson by Willard (if that was genuine). What I *did* say was that the betting was absurd, and that though I had never seen Dempsey and knew nothing about him at first hand, it was humanly impossible that he could be so superior to Carpentier as to justify odds of 4 to 1. I said that on Carpentier's achievements the betting was 50 to 1 on him; and after the fight I said it should have been 500 to 1 on him. Dempsey, according to the reports and the films, made no defence at all: Carpentier literally smashed his fists on him, but this time had not the luck to get on the elusive spot which he found in Beckett. Dempsey is one of those terrors whose simple plan it is to take whatever the other fellow can give him and hammer him to pieces afterwards. But that is a very chancy plan when the other fellow is such a tremendous hitter as Carpentier. Dempsey escaped falling to C's right by a millimetre; and that is not quite good enough to back 4 to 1. The next step would seem to be to put up a gorilla for the championship.

By the way, if Carpentier had been an Englishman he would quite possibly have gone ten rounds by keeping on the retreat when he found that hitting was no use. But Carpentier will fight; and this silly infighting which he picked up from the Americans enabled Dempsey to thump him on the back of his neck and serves him right, too. In the old days the champions were all middle weights, and the giants mere chopping blocks for them. However, all that is stale drivel now; that fight has disgusted everybody with the ring.

In the meantime, my colleagues and I at the Theatre Guild, who had been holding back a decision because of the artistic and financial problems involved, finally decided to present the series of plays on a "Festival" basis, which I jubilantly reported to G.B.S.:

July 28, 1921

The lunatic has prevailed. God and yourself willing, the curtain will ring up on *Back to Methuselah* in February or March of the coming year (unless some dire financial calamity happens to the Theatre Guild).

We shall, of course, perform the play without any cuts (unless you, yourself, want some), and will endeavor to give the very best possible production.

Back to Methuselah was put into rehearsal early in the year 1922. We decided that the first four plays should be given two at a time, which made a somewhat lengthy evening, and they opened a week apart. As this called for more work than our stage director Philip Moeller could possibly put in, we decided to share the production with the Neighborhood Playhouse, connected with the Henry Street Settlement, and the directors Alice Lewisohn and Agnes Morgan staged the first play *In the Beginning*. The costumes of Adam and Eve presented a problem, since they were in the pre-figleaf period of the story, and the difficulty was to find a compromise between stark-naked realism and what the New York Police Department would permit to appear on the stage of a so-called "legitimate" theatre.

Our scenic artist, Lee Simonson, decided to swathe Ernita Lascelles, who played Eve, in heavy pink tights with hair of cloth of gold, while Adam, played by George Gaul, was given a pair of bathing trunks of the same gold material. On the day of the dress rehearsal, the Garrick Theatre was filled with spinsters from the Neighborhood Playhouse, who brought with them an atmosphere of Social Welfare and Higher Morality not usually associated with the theatre. On the stage Margaret Wycherly was trying to hide herself behind a bush out of which her arm, garbed as a Serpent, protruded as she moved it in sinuous undulations—it being our intention that Margaret's head should be hidden by the bush, but the bush was not quite large enough. "I can still see your head," cried Theresa Helburn from the rear of the theatre. "Can you see it now?" asked Margaret, shrinking into an impossible position behind the bush. Suddenly George Gaul, resplendent in his cloth-of-gold loincloth, appeared from the wings as Adam. As he walked into the spotlight, nothing was visible on stage but his highly illuminated gold loincloth which sent a gasp through the assembled ladies. "If you think we *can't* see it, you're very much mistaken," shouted Theresa Helburn to Margaret Wycherly. George Gaul, thinking the remark was addressed to him, rushed off the stage in frightened embarrassment, while the Social Welfare and Higher Morality ladies rocked with unashamed laughter for ten minutes before order was restored.

Finally, on February 27, 1922, the first two plays of the cycle opened. They were enthusiastically received by the audience, but not by the press. The second bill included the play, *The Tragedy of the Elderly Gentleman*, which contained one of the most long-winded parts ever written, and the strain on the audience listening to the play was excessive. One day a Guild director asked William, our enthusiastic colored doorman, how the play was going. "Fine!" said William. "Less and less people walk out on it every night."

After the opening of the third play of the cycle, I left for Europe, and called on G.B.S. with the intention of securing his permission to cut *The Elderly Gentleman* so that the play would have a chance for a New York run. I was met very cordially by Shaw, and also by Mrs. Shaw, who stayed and chatted with us while we looked over the photographs of the production. "Look, Charlotte," he said to Mrs. Shaw, as he examined the picture of Albert Bruning as the Elderly Gentleman, "they've given the actor a make-up so that he looks like me! Why, the Elderly Gentleman was an old duffer. Why on earth did you suggest me?" "Because he talked on and on and on," I replied. "Besides, he said he could not live in a world without truth, by which we of course assumed you had written yourself into the character." This was a bad beginning for an interview in which I wished to persuade him to cut the play, but encouraged by Mrs. Shaw, I persevered. "The reason I object to cutting my plays, is this," said G.B.S. "I write a certain amount of deadly serious dialogue, and when I have given the audience as much as they can possibly take, I throw in some humor as a reward. Now when my plays are cut, the actor or other person who does the cutting always takes out the serious dialogue, and leaves the funny parts, so that the whole purpose of the play is defeated. Besides," he said, "you can never trust an actor to cut a play." "But I suggest you cut this yourself," I replied, "and I'll cable the changes to New York." "You shouldn't have given the two plays in one evening," was the retort. "But people can't come in the afternoon," I replied, "and it's so long, they really suffer."

Then G.B.S. began to suffer too. "This goes against all my principles," he said, looking at Mrs. Shaw. "G.B.S.," she said, "perhaps the Americans don't always know what the Elderly Gentleman is talking about. There's that long piece about John Knox and the Leviathan; hardly any English people know about that, either." I unashamedly and unscrupulously followed Mrs. Shaw's lead, and suggested that there was a great deal more in the play that wasn't understood by Americans—or by anybody else either. "Besides," I added, "at least half a dozen times the Elderly Gentleman starts to leave the stage. Each time the audience settles back delighted, but each time he turns around and comes back for another ten minutes of monologue."

"After all," said Mrs. Shaw, "you did intend him to be an old duffer, and it *is* hard to listen to an old duffer going on and on." G.B.S. squirmed and twisted, but finally gave in. "Very well," he said.

"We'll go over it line by line." "I have some cuts suggested," I said, quickly offering him the printed version on which I had marked my deletions. In a few minutes he grew so interested in cutting the play, that he took out at least half as much again as I had originally hoped for. An hour later I left, trying to stop from looking too pleased with myself, for I had been told in New York that I would be wasting my time, as no one had ever been able to persuade Shaw to cut one of his plays before. And I doubt very much whether I would have succeeded without the help of Mrs. Shaw.

The play was considerably improved by the cutting, but the run of the cycle was not greatly prolonged as a result, and it closed after nine weeks of playing. I returned to New York in August, and wrote G.B.S. as follows:

August 25, 1922

On arriving here I inquired into what loss had been incurred in respect of *Back to Methuselah,* and found that it had amounted to about $20,000. It was not announced, but the news leaked out as such news sometimes does leak out. Part of this loss was due to the fact that it ran two weeks longer than it should have run; it is not a total loss because most of the materials, etc. which we used can be used over again, and anyway, the Guild is not the least bit worried about it. In having ventured to tackle so big a job we have made a tremendous number of friends and shall have nearly double the number of subscribers for the coming season as we had for this season so it will all come back to us eventually.

Shaw, however, never quite forgave us for not making a financial success of *Back to Methuselah.* I did my best to take the blame on ourselves, feeling that he should not be discouraged (as if that were possible!) and later on in 1924 I wrote him:

I have been somewhat depressed by your letters, because I think you are angry with the Guild over *Back to Methuselah.* You do not realize that over here it was regarded as a great success, and not as a failure. When you take into consideration that it ran for nine weeks in a small theatre, playing every night, you must appreciate that this was a magnificent achievement. The fact that we lost money was not due to any arrangement of the parts, but because the Garrick Theatre was too small for us to make money out of the play. If we had had a theatre twice the size, there would have been a profit instead of a loss. I hope you will not feel badly any more about this. I am quite certain that if Goethe had seen *Faust* presented in parts one and two every evening for nine successive weeks, he would have stood on his head with amazement.

When Lee Shubert, some years later, financed the production of *Jitta's Atonement,* he wrote a letter to Shaw questioning the royalties. Shaw replied to Mr. Shubert that he underestimated the value of Mr. Shaw's name, which had been proved to be worth at least $10,000 to a play. He explained this by stating that the Guild had expected to lose $30,000 on *Back to Methuselah,* but had lost only $20,000, thus showing that Shaw's name alone was worth $10,000!

CHAPTER XIV

I Visit the Playwrights

URING the first few years of the Theatre Guild's career, there were no playwrights in America of the stature of Chekhov, Shaw, Galsworthy and Granville Barker, with the sole exception of Eugene O'Neill, who was connected with the Provincetown Players and later with a management consisting of himself, Robert Edmond Jones and Kenneth Macgowan. It was my feeling, as well as that of the rest of the Guild Board, that we should produce the important plays of European authors to set a standard for American writers, and we did, *force majeur*, until our own native dramatists, including Maxwell Anderson, S. N. Behrman, Robert Sherwood and Philip Barry entered the field and we began to produce their plays. In the meanwhile, since my international patent practice took me over to Europe each year, I set myself the task of cementing our relations with the important dramatists of England and the Continent.

One of the first authors I visited was my old friend St. John Ervine who, with his attractive wife Nora, lived in a comfortable, unpretentious apartment near Hampstead Heath. St. John had grown somewhat heavier than the young man I had known in the West London Parliament, and owing to the loss of his leg in the war he walked with the aid of a cane. We discussed *John Ferguson* and *Jane Clegg* and the success these plays had won in the United States—a success far greater than they had attained in England. I expressed the hope that he would be able to write again with the same dramatic force. "When I was writing *John Ferguson* and *Jane Clegg*," he said, "I used to walk all day long, sometimes as much as twenty miles at a time, and during these long walks I thought over my characters and worked myself into a state of emotion which I was able to put into my plays. Now that I am no longer able to walk I wonder whether I will ever be able to write as well again. . . ."

I believe that St. John was a martyr of World War I, for while he has since written a number of successful plays, they were in the field of comedy, such as *Mary, Mary, Quite Contrary* and *The First Mrs. Frazer,* and he never again struck the rich emotional vein which made *John Ferguson* and *Jane Clegg* his masterpieces.

Ervine was a great admirer of Bernard Shaw, but he had some doubts about the Irish seer's infallibility. "My God, Lawrence," he remarked once, "suppose the old boy's wrong. He'll have led almost half the civilized world in the wrong direction."

In order that I might meet Arnold Bennett, for whom I had expressed considerable admiration, Ervine invited him to dinner and I sat at table next to Mrs. Arnold Bennett who had been a successful actress and diseuse in Paris. She was a strikingly handsome Frenchwoman of statuesque proportions, with regular features, high forehead, shiny dark hair pulled tight back on her head and a deep strong voice of compelling intensity. Arnold Bennett himself was a small man of very undistinguished appearance, almost chinless, and looked for all the world like a small-town grocer. Ervine had seated him next to an attractive young girl because, as Mrs. Bennett explained to me afterward, "Arnold is writing a novel about young people and wishes to meet some young girls so that he can draw his characters from life." Mrs. Bennett paid more attention to Arnold and the young girl than to me and seemed a little put out by the proceedings. I learned later that there was a rift between them which was ultimately to blossom into a separation.

I found it extremely disconcerting to carry on a conversation with Bennett owing to a curious impediment in his speech. He could talk quite volubly until he arrived at a word which he had great difficulty in bringing out. His face would then become as red as a turkey cock's, and even though you knew exactly the word he wished to say and politely indicated that you knew just what he was driving at, he nevertheless persisted in the most painful manner until, with explosive effect, he finally brought the word into being like a bombshell, after which he talked quite fluently again until the next impediment was reached. Despite these difficulties he managed to ask me a great many questions about the New York theatre, mostly from a play-marketing standpoint. I told him that my own life had been considerably influenced by reading his newspaper play, *What the Public Wants,* in which one of his characters, a newspaper publisher, ascribed his success to surrounding himself with men who knew more about the business than he did, while he also built up his business organization so that it could get along perfectly well without him. Bennett, who was nothing if not a practical businessman, suggested that if the play had influenced me to such an extent, it might well have the same effect on others, and calmly asked me why we did not produce it. On my return to the States I was successful in interesting my colleagues in the play and we produced it in the spring of 1922, but apparently without influencing any of the handful of people who saw it.

Arnold Bennett invited me to dinner at his apartment where I was introduced to Mr. Gilbert Miller who was just beginning a managerial career and was regarded as the white hope of the English theatre. Gilbert, looking like an oversized cherub wearing coattails and a white tie, dominated the conversation which was peppered with the names of Lords, Earls and Kings with whom he and Arnold were apparently on familiar terms. After dinner Mrs. Bennett took me to the library where she showed me some of Bennett's manuscripts. She handed me, with particular pride, the first manuscript copy of *The Old Wives' Tale.* "Arnold learned calligraphy from studying the manuscripts written in the old monasteries by the friars of the Middle Ages and did not start to write this book until he had mastered the art. As you see," she continued, "each page is like an illuminated manuscript, for Arnold wanted each page to be a work of beauty, not only beautiful in expression but also beautiful in appearance." I looked over the manuscript with amazement. There were very few deletions or corrections and even these were made neatly and with the same exquisite penmanship.

Bennett was an indefatigable worker and as I grew to know him better I learned how strong was the will power behind his enormous literary output. "Had a good day today," he once remarked to me. "Turned out nearly ten thousand words!" I felt that his novels and plays had deteriorated greatly since he stopped writing about the Five Towns and had started writing fashionable novels about fashionable people. I pointed out to him, somewhat timidly, that his roots were in the healthy soil of the common people of England and that he was on sure ground when he wrote about them. I told him that our American audiences were less and less interested in English drawing-room comedies of the type in which a handsome aristocrat (usually portrayed by Sir Gerald Du Maurier) balanced a porcelain teacup on one knee while he made love in epigrammatic phrases to someone's porcelain wife seated on the other. Bennett noted my opinion in his diary, which, when published, revealed his interpretation of my remarks in the following language:

Lawrence Langner came to see me yesterday. He said positively that the American taste was against drawing-room plays and decidedly in favour of what he called "genre" plays, i.e., plays of character strongly developed, middle class or lower middle class. He urged me to write a Five Towns play, even if I did it specially for U.S.A.[1]

Nevertheless, Arnold did not heed my advice. He was seemingly too deeply involved in British society to return to the soil from which sprang his best work.

Another British author whose work I admired immensely was John Galsworthy and I decided I would try to bring him under the Theatre Guild banner. I was invited to come to his home for an interview. Buoyed up with high hopes I arrived at the appointed time at the Georgian manor house near Hampstead Heath in which he lived. I was ushered into a large, luxuriantly furnished living room by a silently moving butler and, after waiting a few moments, Mr. Galsworthy entered and invited me to be seated. He was a tall, grave, distinguished man who reminded me of a barrister in his formality and correctness of speech. I explained the aims and aspirations of the newly formed Theatre Guild and told him of our successes with the plays of Ervine and Bernard Shaw, doing my best to excite his interest. He listened to me politely but appeared to be equally interested in polishing his carefully manicured fingernails which he seemed to admire immensely. Finally, I asked him whether he was thinking of writing a play in the near future and if so whether the Theatre Guild might present it in New York. "No," he replied, quite definitely, "I don't think I will ever write a play again. I find that they are not nearly as lucrative as novels. Indeed," he added, "I don't know why anyone should write plays when they pay so badly." In vain I endeavored to rouse in him a response to my enthusiasm for the theatre —to say nothing of the Theatre Guild. "Actually," he said, "I've been looking over the proceeds of all the plays I have written and I find that I would have done far better financially had I spent the same time in writing novels. I shall never write a play again." Nothing I could say had any effect on him and I left wondering how anyone of his artistic stature and financial independence could possibly be so

[1] *The Journal of Arnold Bennett,* The Viking Press, Inc., Copyright 1932.

dominated by the question of box-office returns. Not long after my visit he wrote *Old English,* one of his most successful plays which, I may add ruefully, he turned over to another management. His story about never writing another play was probably a good way of getting rid of me, I thought in retrospect.

Having produced A. A. Milne's *Mr. Pim Passes By* and with other plays by him under consideration at the Theatre Guild, on one of my visits to London I telephoned him for a luncheon appointment. On the morning we set for this I received a call from Bernard Shaw asking me to lunch. "I'm sorry I can't come," I said, "I'm lunching with A. A. Milne." "Bring him along," said the genius at the other end of the line. "I'd like to meet him." "But suppose he doesn't want to come?" I asked. "Don't you worry about that," said G.B.S. "I'm sure he'd like to meet *me.*" Milne, of course, was delighted and we met at Mr. Shaw's apartment.

Milne was a slight, boyish-looking young man, genuinely bashful and an excellent listener. This suited Shaw to a tee and we sat there listening to G.B.S. discoursing on the subject of playwriting. "Now take *At Mrs. Beam's,*" said Shaw. "C. K. Munro, its author, has done a good job, but his observation is not good. He has a character remark that he dislikes going to church and sitting among a group of smelly people in dirty clothes. Now, as a matter of fact," said Shaw, "the people who go to church usually take a bath on Saturday night—their only bath in the week—and put on their 'Sunday best' clothes, so church is probably the only place where these people are ever clean. Good observation is essential to good playwriting." Milne was charming and self-effacing and when at last we were alone together he showed me a snapshot of his wife and child with a butterfly flying over them, of which he was inordinately proud, being an amateur photographer, and apparently far more interested in the detail of the butterfly than in his wife, his child, his plays, or me. My visit ultimately resulted in the Guild's producing two other plays by him, neither of which caught on. He then wrote *Winnie the Pooh* which made him famous in every English-speaking nursery for a generation and won him a larger portion of immortality than any of his whimsical comedies for grown-ups.

One of my trips through Europe took me to Vienna two years after the end of World War I. My friend James N. Rosenberg had given me a letter of introduction to a certain Frau Eugenie Schwarzwald, the head of one of the most important girls' schools in Vienna, who was noted for her literary and artistic salon as well as for her good works among the Viennese artists and writers who were suffering bitterly for lack of food and fuel. Frau Eugenie invited me to her home. She was a large, pleasant, gray-haired woman with an imposing manner, obviously used to managing others and anxious to help her Viennese author friends by finding some plays for me to take back to the Theatre Guild.

"I will invite some of the theatre people of Vienna to meet you next Sunday," she said; so next Sunday came around and Estelle and I attended at her home. There we met many of the leading Viennese actors and actresses, as well as some of the important authors, but my interest was most aroused by a thin, dark, distinguished-looking man with hair graying at the temples who at once reminded me of Eugene O'Neill. We were introduced by Frau Eugenie to the gathering and I learned that this distinguished guest was the novelist Jacob Wasserman. Since Frau Eugenie introduced us to everyone as Americans who were in Vienna hunting for plays, manuscripts began pouring in by the dozen at our hotel the next day. In the course of a long and animated conversation between Jacob Wasserman and Estelle he confided to her that he, too, had written some plays and would send them to our hotel. "What luck," I said on our way home, "three unknown plays by the author of *The World's Illusion.* Won't that be a major event when the Theatre Guild announces our treasure trove!" The next day the plays arrived from Wasserman; all three of them in a neatly-bound volume of one-act plays! My hopes were dashed to the ground. I still treasure the volume but I had to write the illustrious author that it was against the Guild's policy to produce one-act plays.

My visit, however, was far from unproductive. During the soiree which Frau Eugenie gave for us I was introduced to a charming young woman whose name I have forgotten but whose beauty and intelligence I shall always remember. She did me and the American theatre-going public a service for which I shall be eternally grateful. "Who do you think is the best playwright in Vienna today?" I asked her in what passed for light conversation among the Viennese intelligentsia. "What do you mean by 'playwright'?" she replied, her eyes flashing brilliantly and making it difficult for me to keep my mind on the conversation. "We have two kinds of playwrights here," she said. "*Dichter,* which means poet and *Schauspiel-schriftsteller,* which means merely the writer of a play. The *Dichter* is always the best." By this time I had decided that she had a charming smile and a delightful Viennese manner. "And who is your best *Dichter?*" I asked nonchalantly. "Franz Werfel," she replied. "He is represented here on the stage by two plays, *Böksgesang* and *Spiegelmensch.*" By this time I had decided she was one of the prettiest women in Vienna. "*Böksgesang*—what does that mean?" I asked. "You know what is a *bök?*" "Something you drink?" I ventured. "No, a little animal with long horns." "Oh, a goat!" "Yes, *Goat Song!* That is the name of the play. It means tragedy song. It is one of the most artistic plays of our theatre." I wrote the title in my memory and we talked of less important things—after which we drifted out of each other's lives never to meet again. Before leaving Vienna I ordered copies of all of Werfel's plays and brought them back to New York with me. My sister-in-law, Ruth Langner, translated *Goat Song*, and the Theatre Guild produced it at the Guild Theatre early in 1926.[2] The play was an outstanding artistic success, but as it was also grimly tragic and vaguely sociological, it upset the sensibilities of many of our wealthy subscribers who kept popping off our subscription list like firecrackers. "Please take my name off your membership list," wrote the then Mrs. Vincent Astor, resigning with a resounding protest.

Goat Song marked the beginning of a new career for Franz Werfel, for after we and others had imported more of his plays, he followed suit and came over here himself, accompanied by his handsome wife, a famous Viennese beauty who was formerly married to Gustav Mahler, the composer and conductor. The Werfels made several visits here and finally settled in Hollywood after the clouds of doom began to gather over Europe. My first meeting with Franz Werfel took place on his first visit to New York, after we had produced *Goat Song* and *Juarez and Maximilian.* He was a round, cheerful man with a round head and curly hair, short body and pudgy baby features which gave him the appearance of an intellectual Cupid, since he habitually wore glasses. When he smiled, his eyes half closed, and one felt the warm geniality of his personality. Years later, when I met him in Hollywood, I felt that in spite of the vicissitudes which he had undergone as a refugee from Vienna (many of which are so humorously described in *Jacobowsky and the Colonel*), he nevertheless retained a cheerful, optimistic demeanor. At the same time, Hollywood affected him little, for he lived in complete detachment in an Old-World atmosphere which he brought with him and maintained with the help of Mrs. Werfel.

On this same trip we met in Vienna the then President of Actors' Equity Association—John Emerson and his petite wife Anita Loos,

---

[2] Alfred Lunt, Lynn Fontanne, Edward G. Robinson, Henry Travers, Zita Johann, Helen Westley, George Gaul, Blanche Yurka, Philip Loeb and Herbert Yost were in the cast of *Goat Song.*

famous as the author of *Gentlemen Prefer Blondes*. They were staying at our hotel and together we made the delightful boat trip down the Danube to Budapest. Here we introduced them to our friends the Barnas who had become millionaires from their sale of the Longchamps Restaurants in New York which they had established after their success with the French Pastry Shop on the corner of Eleventh Street and Sixth Avenue. Mr. Barna, no longer a pastry cook, was now a Budapest banker and sported a handsome Daimler car which he placed at our disposal, along with Mrs. Barna who turned herself inside out to make us happy. As one of the producers of *Liliom*, I was wined and dined, taken to restaurants and pastry shops in the Park for afternoon tea, and shown a little vista of the gay life of the city.

As our production of *Liliom* was still running in New York, I decided to call on Ferenc Molnar, its author. I had heard a great deal about Molnar, rightly regarded as the leading Hungarian playwright, and since the writing of plays seemed to be a major industry, if not an art, in Budapest during the first quarter of this century, to be the acknowledged master of all his fellow craftsmen was no mean honor. Moreover, I was told that this Molnar was a wit, a gay dog, a *bon vivant*, a Casanova, and had all the other attributes which go to make up a fascinating Hungarian *literateur*. When Estelle and I drove over to his apartment at the hour Molnar appointed for meeting us—which was two o'clock in the afternoon—we were prepared for almost anything. We were ushered into a living room by a manservant who informed us in German that Mr. Molnar expressed his regrets for keeping us waiting but he was still in bed and would arise shortly and be with us.

As we expected the unexpected we were not at all surprised, so we made ourselves comfortable and examined our surroundings. The living room was large and comfortably furnished, and its outstanding feature was a long refectory table on which stood a collection of carved wooden statuettes of the Virgin Mary interspersed with handsome old pistols and revolvers. "What is the Freudian significance of these?" asked Estelle, examining the collection on the table with her critical American eye. "Perhaps he's going to write a play about an innocent virgin held up by an armed robber," I suggested. "Nonsense," said Estelle, with finality. "It has something to do with sex!"

With an anxious glance at the door she then proceeded to psychoanalyze Molnar, building up a startling picture of the symbolic significance of virgins and revolvers which was interrupted by the appearance of our host, a chubby rounded man in his late forties wearing a dark dressing gown of imposing design and gazing at us rather sleepily out of one half-closed eye while the other, which appeared to be propped open by a monocle, appraised us alertly. "Excuse me, please," he said in French, "for being late. You see, this is an early hour for me for I stay awake all night long and I sleep nearly all day." This seemed like a good beginning. "Not a very healthy life," I remarked, for want of something better to say. "No," said Molnar who by this time had seated himself in a comfortable armchair and looked as though he might go back to sleep again at the drop of a hat. "You see, I am about to die." This startled us both and we glanced uneasily at the revolvers. It startled even Molnar for he seemed to come rapidly to life. "I am about to begin to write a new play. In order to live in the lives of my characters I have first to stop living in my own life. I give up going to theatres and restaurants and seeing my friends, and this is, in effect, dying." "At which stage are you now?" I asked. "Well, I do not actually give up life for nearly two weeks," he replied with a charming smile, "and I should like to take you out one evening and show you something of the artistic life of Budapest, as well as what goes on in our theatres."

We said we were glad to learn that he would be living long enough to take us on this excursion into Budapest night life, for which he seemed so eminently fitted to guide us. "And what is your new play about?" I asked, scenting another prize for the Theatre Guild. "It is about a sort of girl *Liliom*," he replied. "I will have my Berlin agent, Zisser, send you the manuscript when it is finished." "Has he not a bad reputation?" I asked. "Yes, terrible," was the reply. "He is one of the most dishonest men in the business, but years and years ago he sold my first play for me and I am so grateful to him that I have allowed him to cheat me a little ever since." This seemed fair enough, but I should add that the agent did not send me the play and it was produced unsuccessfully in New York some years later with Pauline Lord under the title of *Launzi*. After a conversation in which Molnar plied me with questions about *Liliom* in New York, I, in return, secured his opinions about happenings on the Budapest stage. We brought our visit to a close and left with the feeling that our host would go right back to bed and wake up a few hours later thinking that we were probably no more than shadows in a passing dream.

When the appointed evening came around, and Molnar called for us at our hotel, we realized that we were no dream figures. The vivid personality who awaited us in the hotel lobby, attired in evening dress, opera hat and black cape, was fully awake and reminded me of one of the elegant guests at the party in *Fledermaus*. Molnar was definitely dressed to go places and Estelle and I felt provincial by comparison. "Shall we have dinner?" I ventured after we had sat for some time drinking apéritifs at the hotel café. "Dinner!" said Molnar in horror-struck tones. "Why, I've just finished breakfast. I have arranged a real Hungarian dinner for you at my favorite restaurant at midnight." Ah, one of those gay Hungarian supper parties, I thought to myself, such as I had often read about in so many Hungarian plays. No doubt the girls will be drinking champagne out of their slippers and dancing on the tables. "And now we shall go to the theatre," said Molnar, and we set off for a playhouse, the name of which sounded like "Big Sin House," but was later translated to me as meaning Comedy Theatre.

It was fun going out in Budapest with Molnar. The hotel porters smiled, the taxi drivers hailed him, theatre doormen bowed, maîtres d'hotel prostrated themselves, waiters scurried hither and yon, and pretty ladies flirted as we passed them by. It was easy to see that Molnar was not merely their best dramatist, he was also a living symbol of a delightful mode of living which had been nearly destroyed during World War I, and which has now been completely liquidated by those grim locusts, the Nazis and the Soviets, who swarmed over the laughter-loving city and stilled its witty voices. Out of this civilization which is gone there is little left to bear witness to the gaiety, tenderness and charm of those happier times, and what there is lives mostly in the pages of the plays of Molnar, Biro, Lengyel, Fodor, Vajda and a few others, whose best creations, I hope, will live on long after those who destroyed their civilization are lost in oblivion.

On that evening, many years before the holocaust, Molnar entered the theatre like a king entering his realm. The manager rushed to greet him and the ushers attended him solicitously. "We shall not sit down," he said, then turned to us. "This is a play about little people, an imitation of my play, *Liliom*. It's hardly worth seeing all through." We stood in the back for a few minutes listening to the Hungarian actors, all of whom looked like duplicate copies of Liliom, Julie and Marie. Then Molnar conducted us to another theatre. "This play is about royalty, a poor imitation of my play, *The Swan*. It's not worth staying longer than ten minutes." So we stood up again for a short while until we were whisked off to another theatre. "This play," said Molnar as we entered, "is an imitation of my play, *The Guardsman*," and the costuming of the officers and women on the stage brought that comedy vividly to mind. "No need to stay here," said Molnar. We

were whisked from theatre to theatre, all of which seemed to be playing either Molnar or imitations of Molnar. At one of these theatres
where we stayed during an intermission, we were introduced to a
beautiful, dark-haired woman dressed in a svelte evening gown who
was standing behind a curtain in a parterre box, apparently hiding
herself. "This is the authoress of the play, the Baroness Lily Hatvany,"
said Molnar as he introduced her. She was most gracious to us and,
peeping out from behind her curtain, invited us to dinner at her castle
in Pest, on the other side of the Danube. "Why does she hide herself?"
I asked Molnar. "Is the play as bad as all that?" "Not at all," said
Molnar, "the girl is talented but she is a Countess and it is bad form
for a Countess to write a play so she must hide herself from the public." I examined with new interest this girl who had broken the con-
ventions; obviously, no true Hungarian aristocrat should degrade
herself by writing for the theatre. This story threw a different light on
Hungarian society and I began to realize that all was not glamorous
that glittered. The Hungarian authors, actors and actresses, most of
whom, along with Lily Hatvany and Molnar, have now happily moved
to the United States, have possibly regretted the number of times the
beautiful actresses in their plays have succumbed (on stage) to the
charms of the handsome Counts and Barons, who in real life embraced
Fascism with even greater enthusiasm than they embraced the actresses in their dressing rooms.

After leaving the last of the theatres, Molnar brought us to his
favorite restaurant for his favorite dinner. The scene which met our
eyes was plebeian in the extreme. We walked over to a small enclosure passing between tables at which were seated heavily upholstered
Hungarians and their mattress-like wives eating goulash and drinking
beer. Waiters rushed us swiftly into the enclosure laden with food
calculated at the hour of midnight to dispel any possibility of sleep,
and we waded through a dinner which makes me, even at this late
date, hungry even to think of; the potato soup was divine, the veal
paprika was heavenly, the noodles and chicken Hongroise with
dumplings was sublime, and the rest of the six-course meal deserving
of every weighty panegyric which could be applied to solid food. Our
only regret was that we, too, did not live like Molnar between the
hours of seven at night until seven in the morning so that we might
have attacked all this heavy Hungarian food without the uncomfortable feeling that it would result in our immediate deaths from acute
gastric convulsions. These highly seasoned comestibles were washed
down in heavy drafts of heavier Tokay which made the fact that the

girls were not dancing on the tables both irrelevant and immaterial. Indeed, had the ladies present taken it into their heads to do so, there would have been such a crashing of furniture as would have startled the entire neighborhood.

Replete with good food and liquor we dragged our bodies behind the irrepressible Molnar who rose from his meal as lightly as a phoenix from its ashes and conducted us to the famous Artists Club of Budapest, of which he was the most prominent member. Here we were made welcome as the producers of *Liliom* in New York, the success of which had been blazoned all over Budapest, and had resulted in a happy revival of the play in that city. We were introduced to a gay throng of actors, actresses, writers and singers. It seemed to me that most of the actors were named Bela, the actresses Mitzi, the writers Ladislaus, and most of the singers a combination of all three; but by this time my memory was becoming hazy and I have only a confused recollection of meeting all these happy people, each one of whom in turn took me into a corner, told me that the theatre in Budapest was in a terrible condition and did I think I could arrange for them to come over to New York or Hollywood? Had I been producing a Hungarian spectacle I could have signed up a shipload of actors on the spot; as it was, I could do little to help, and as consolation offered the opinion that the theatre in New York was in an equally bad condition and always would be. No one took this part of my conversation very seriously, however, for since that time most of those same artists have come over here and are all doing very nicely, while our own theatre and motion pictures have been greatly enriched by their coming. At about four in the morning, half-dead with fatigue, Estelle and I crawled into a taxi leaving the monocled Ferenc Molnar and his fellow club members, for whom the day was yet young, playing cards and drinking brandy.

The Guild's connection with Molnar, which began with *Liliom,* was followed by *The Guardsman* and *The Glass Slipper.* Meanwhile, my cross-continental rival, Gilbert Miller, who was living in London and had a good head start on me, began to bring Molnar's plays to New York and added *The Swan, The Play's the Thing* and other greater and lesser works to the list, after which Ferenc Molnar himself, luckily for us all, came to the States and settled here.

Many years later found the same Ferenc Molnar, now white-haired but with the jaunty monocle still holding his left eye open, sitting in our office at the Theatre Guild while Theresa Helburn and I proposed to him that *Liliom* be made into the musical play *Carousel.* "I have refused many offers to make *Liliom* into a musical play," said Molnar, "including one from the great Puccini himself. Why should I now permit this to Richard Rodgers and Oscar Hammerstein?" "Will you please go to see *Oklahoma!*" we suggested, "and then come back and talk with us again?" Molnar promised to do this and in a few weeks we met him again. "After seeing *Oklahoma!*," he said, "if you can promise a musical treatment which does not violate the spirit of the play, you have my permission, if Rodgers and Hammerstein are willing." Thus began a new life for *Liliom* in the musical theatre as *Carousel*, the form in which it has won a fame that almost equals the renown of the masterpiece from which it is fashioned. And not a little of the pleasure I have enjoyed in watching it is a nostalgic recollection of the attractive Hungarian ruffian played for us by young Schildkraut and the spiritual Julie of Eva Le Gallienne which will always live in my memory.

During this same period I made many visits to the Paris theatres which were divided between the "Boulevard" playhouses devoted to the subject of adultery in all its Gallic varieties, and the art theatres of André Antoine, Jacques Copeau, Firmin Gemier, Dullin and Pitoëff, with all of whom I became acquainted. The rest of the French theatre was largely under the impression that there were no playwrights other than the French, and no subject of interest in the theatre other than jumping in and out of someone else's bed, accompanied, of course, by someone else's wife. Most of the Parisian art theatres made their beginnings in the same way as the Theatre Guild, by importing the best plays written by foreign authors. Later on, some of the French playwrights followed the standards of the new theatre, and such men as Lenormand, Giraudoux, Géraldy, Bernard, Amiel, Obey and others, began writing plays which were of international interest. I met Lenormand and his Dutch actress wife in Paris prior to our production of his play, *The Failures*. He was a lean, cadaverous, grave-faced man, given to airing his metaphysics in the theatre. As a young man, he had traveled around France with a small touring company in which his wife played the leading roles. He was sneered at and jeered at as a failure. He put his experiences and his feelings into this fine play, *The Failures*, the title of which was so uninviting as to keep most New Yorkers out of the theatre in which we were playing it. Under the direction of Stark Young, and with Winifred Lenihan in the lead, we presented the play at the Garrick Theatre, and made all our friends who were not on the top rung of success extremely unhappy by doing so. I overheard a young novelist of fair-to-middling fame say to his wife as he left the theatre one evening. "You can't say

I'm a failure!" "Who said you were?" she replied. "Why, the play, of course," said the young man angrily. The play, one of the finest we have ever presented, was not a success. It is hard to sell failure in these United States.

Our success with *Liliom* resulted in its being played all over Europe, and in Paris it was presented by the Pitoëffs. Pitoëff himself played the title role, while Madam Pitoëff, who made a point of bringing a little Pitoëff into the world with a regularity which was in strong contrast with the Parisiennes of the period, played the part of Julie. Playing in scenery which looked for all the world like something made from ribbons bought at the Bon Marché, Madame Pitoëff's appearance was such that when, later on in the play, Liliom made the remark, "I'm going to be a father," one thought to oneself, "I knew it when the play began!"

Firmin Gemier, who was the director of the Odéon Theatre, was a large, deep-voiced, warmhearted actor-manager who looked more like an industrialist than a man of the theatre. He was the first to introduce O'Neill to the French stage and we became fast friends. On the occasion of his producing *The Emperor Jones,* I helped him with some of the details of production, including a demonstration of the drum rhythms which form an accompaniment to the play.

Dullin, one of the finest actors in the French theatre, conducted his own playhouse in Montparnasse, and also introduced many plays from other countries. At his theatre I saw a splendid production of Pirandello's *Right You Are If You Think You Are.* This so impressed me that I brought back tidings of the play to New York, and later on we produced it successfully at the Garrick Theatre with a cast which included Edward G. Robinson, Laura Hope Crews, Helen Westley, Henry Travers, and in the role of the lunatic wife, Armina Marshall!

Antoine, who had been a pioneer in the French art theatre years before all the others, and had introduced Ibsen, Strindberg and Shaw to French audiences, was an old man at the time when I first met him at his theatre in Paris. I thought he seemed tired and disillusioned. The plays for which he had fought and bled in his youth had become accepted during his later years, and he shared the fate of all successful pioneers in the arts. The cause for which he had given his youth had become so accepted in his old age that the younger generation barely appreciated the battles that had been fought to break the ground of the past so as to pave the way for the future.

As the years roll by, it seems clear that the Theatre Guild's early policy of importing the best artistic plays and production ideas of Europe, which was often bitterly opposed at the time, sowed the seeds which later bore a harvest of American plays and productions that have since then compared favorably with those of the rest of the world.

CHAPTER XV

The Theatre Guild Grows

THE early and middle twenties found the young Theatre Guild producing an average of three or more outstanding plays each year; indeed, the average from 1920 to 1925 was higher than that of any other management.[1] In our first six years we had produced over twenty important plays, a record which was beaten only by the Guild itself when in one period of two-and-a-half seasons with our Acting Company, we produced fourteen noteworthy plays in succession. Our dreams of the theatre came true with amazing rapidity, and when I look back, I marvel at the creative vitality we expended on our activities. But the entire American theatre was possessed of enormous vitality during those days. They were the days when there were over eighty legitimate playhouses in New York City, and hundreds throughout the country, which formed a huge battleground over which dozens of touring companies roamed, while the Shuberts fought Klaw and Erlanger, and Erlanger seemingly fought everybody. The critical world was becoming more critical, the Alan Dales and Louis De Foes were eclipsed by Alexander Woollcott, Heywood Broun, John Anderson and Percy Hammond, who wrote of the theatre with excitement and artistry, and, with the notable exception of George Jean Nathan, hailed the Theatre Guild as the white hope of the American theatre. Young people from all over the country were pouring into Broadway, as they later poured into Hollywood, and

---

[1] *Heartbreak House, Mr. Pim Passes By, Liliom, Ambush, He Who Gets Slapped, Back to Methuselah, R.U.R., Peer Gynt, The Adding Machine, The Devil's Disciple, St. Joan, Fata Morgana, The Failures, The Guardsman, They Knew What They Wanted, Processional, The Garrick Gaieties, Arms and the Man.*

creative movements were everywhere in evidence—in writing, in stagecraft, and, later on, in acting.

Here, my own story becomes, to a considerable extent, the story of the Theatre Guild, and of the other members of the Guild's Board with whom I collaborated. I shall not attempt, however, to include here a history of the Guild, but will confine myself to those activities in which I was personally most interested. The Guild was, until the year 1939 when Theresa Helburn and I became the administrative directors, strictly a group expression, and each person contributed his best to the results as a whole. Each Board member was talented in a particular field, and our results were, so to speak, the sum of these talents.

At first, it was the function of the Board to select the plays, directors, actors and scenic artists, and to supervise all the details of production, acting and revision of the plays. Later on, the production supervision was left to the Production Committees or Supervisors, and finally it all devolved on Terry and myself. Many plays were turned over to the Guild because of the assistance we were able to render an author. Most adept at this were Terry, Phil and myself.

In order to perfect myself in the technique of playwriting, I took private lessons for a season with Hatcher Hughes, who conducted the playwriting course at Columbia University. 'Gene O'Neill once remarked to me, regarding Professor George Pierce Baker's famous Workshop '47 course at Harvard which he took, as did Terry Helburn and Maurice Wertheim: "You can be taught everything about playwriting except the most important ingredient, which is life itself." I was constantly receiving lessons in this ingredient, however, which I augmented with courses on sociology by Thorsten Veblen, and on psychology by Dr. Alfred Adler, at the New School for Social Research. Armed with the impressive new vocabulary and techniques gained in this way and from experience, I specialized, along with Terry, in working with our authors.

One of the most interesting of these was Thomas Wolfe whom I met in the year 1923, long before he was "discovered" as a novelist. I remember Wolfe as a tall, shy, gangling youngster whose play about a Nordic Southern politician with Negro blood sprawled in the same way as did his novels later on. In a letter to his mother, written about Christmas, 1923, after his interview with me, Wolfe wrote:

He (Langner) told me I was a fool if I gave this play up; he said that in a week's time I can make it into a play which will sell. It needs no rewriting, he said,—the stuff's all there—it needs . . . cutting down thirty minutes, and from ten scenes to eight, and "tightening" it up,—that is, making the main thread of story, the plot, more plain in every scene.

And Wolfe added, with reference to a suggestion made by someone that he give up writing and go into business, that I advised him:

There are thousands of bank clerks, and real estate men everywhere making $35 and $40 a week, . . . But there aren't three people in America who are doing the same class of writing I am. Therefore, it was a matter of pure business, artistic considerations aside, to stick to it. The best plays made the most money in the end.[2]

While my advice did not help Wolfe's playwriting career, it was nevertheless equally applicable to his novels which came later. He did not put his play into satisfactory shape. As I met him from time to time, and I read his novels, as big, sprawling and disorganized as their author, I doubted whether he would ever possess the discipline to observe the hard rules which the theatre imposes upon its writers. My last meeting with Wolfe was in the subway a few weeks before his death. He told me he was writing in Brooklyn—to get away from New York!

During this period of working on productions, I began to draw away from my patent practice and to devote myself more fully to the Guild, which was bitterly criticized at the time for not producing more American plays, but we stuck to our guns and insisted on maintaining the standard we set for ourselves. Later on came the American writers, consisting of Eugene O'Neill, Elmer Rice, Maxwell Anderson, Sidney Howard, Arthur Richman, S. N. Behrman and Robert Sherwood, but most of these attained their highest level of writing in the latter half of the twenties and the early thirties.

I was also acquainted with another group of writers who had little or no kinship with the Theatre Guild and made up the famous coterie of the Algonquin Round Table. These included George S. Kaufman, Marc Connelly, Charlie MacArthur, Franklin P. Adams, Robert Benchley and others who were graduated mainly from newspapers, and hence consorted largely with the drama critics, a practice which I disdained along with the general chitchat and high-stakes poker games in which many of the Round Table members indulged themselves. The restaurant in the Algonquin Hotel was a sight to see in those days: on guard at its entrance stood George, the handsome Greek headwaiter who used to ask my advice on patents. The large Round

---

[2] *Thomas Wolfe's Letters to His Mother,* Charles Scribner's Sons, Copyright 1946.

Table was at the back of the restaurant where sat the famous coterie; and around the fringes of the Round Table were set smaller tables, like planets arranged around the sun, and at those sat the lesser luminaries of the theatre, the actors and actresses, the managers, the directors, the literary crowd, the publishers, and myself on the occasions when I lunched there. Passing from table to table was our genial host, Frank Case, tall, handsome and appreciative of good theatre and good cooking. A casual visitor might encounter, on almost any day in the twenties, such notables as Alex Woollcott, Heywood Broun, Robert Benchley, George S. Kaufman, Franklin P. Adams, Harold Ross, the tall Robert Sherwood and his miniature first wife Mary, Marc Connelly, the bearded Ernest Boyd, the publisher Horace Liveright, his brother Otto, the shock-headed Conrad Bercovici, and Carl Van Vechten and his animated wife Fania Marinoff.

Whether it was because we were too serious-minded or too busy at the Guild, or just unimpressed, we never became a part of the so-called Algonquin crowd, which made a brilliant contribution, both critical and creative, to the Broadway theater of this period.

For the first years of the Theatre Guild's history, each play was produced by the Board acting as a whole. Let nobody imagine that this was a painless process. On the contrary, each point of view was fought over *ad nauseum*. Fond as we then were of one another, each of the six members of the Board of Managers was an extremely self-opinionated individual, and never particularly happy in giving in to any of the others. It was our custom during these years to have dinner together each Thursday evening at Henri's, a crowded French restaurant permeated with a strong odor of chocolate, then situated on West Forty-fifth Street, where a special table was conspicuously reserved for the six Board members. During dinner we would argue many points, and often the noise from our table was so excessive that diners in the vicinity would complain to the manager. After dining, we removed to the apartment of one or other of the Board members, and finished the meeting, which was usually over by midnight, leaving most of us exhausted and disappointed, for if we won one important battle, we were sure to have lost another. And these were really battles. Out of this extremely painful method of conducting our affairs came most of the early successful productions of the Theatre Guild.

In the production of our plays, it was our practice after the rehearsals had reached a certain point of completion, for the six of us to attend a "run-through" of the play at the theatre, and take notes of the progress. Then we would adjourn to the stage itself, when the poor actors had gone home, and inform the director where we felt his direction was at fault, or where the actors were not properly interpreting the play. This ordeal was extremely painful for the actors, and they deeply resented the method by which so many good results were obtained. They christened the Guild Board of Managers "The Death Watch," and many an actor refused to play for the Guild again after having experienced these excruciatingly painful rehearsals at which the six members of the Board, each armed with pencil and note paper, sat like silent executioners watching the actors play their parts while they were still in a state of unreadiness. Years later we abandoned this method of producing plays, but I must add in all fairness that our new method, while less objectionable to the actors, was not productive of any better results.

Our first successful play after Shaw's *Heartbreak House* was the charming English comedy, *Mr. Pim Passes By,* by A. A. Milne, for which we rescued the brilliant comedienne, Laura Hope Crews, from. retirement, and in which Phyllis Povah played the young fiancée. Phyllis, who had recently married, started to have a child of her own, and as the play had a long run, her condition became so obvious to the audience that the play began to be about the plight of an unmarried mother in a polite English household, and something quite foreign to the author's intention. Alarmed at the gossip overheard by the ushers, the six Guild directors attended a matinee performance and solemnly decided that Phyllis would have to leave the cast. She did, and just in time, for the baby was born a few days later.

He Who Gets Slapped by Leonid Andreyev was an especially interesting early Guild production, the play being laid in a circus and having a curious dreamlike quality. The part of the embittered clown, "He," who sought a new life in a circus, was played by the famous actor Richard Bennett, father of Constance Bennett and Joan Bennett of the movies, who gave a brilliantly romantic performance but seemingly hadn't the least idea of the character he was playing. During rehearsals, the translator, Gregory Zilboorg, a Russian of formidable intellect who has since become famous as a psychoanalyst, undertook to explain this complex Russian soul in detail to Bennett, who merely became more confused than ever. "Can I have lunch with you, Lawrence?" he asked one day during rehearsals, after having heard a long discourse from Zilboorg. We sat at a table in a small restaurant on Sixth Avenue. "Lawrence," said Dick, a troubled expression on his handsome face, "this high-brow fellow Zilboorg keeps talking to me for hours about the character's psychology, and I simply don't know where the hell I'm at, he confuses me so. Now, tell me simply: is this a Bassanio part, or a Mercutio part?" I decided it was a Mercutio part, and as no one else could make Dick see it otherwise, that is how he played it with enormous success. In a later revival by Tyrone Guthrie, in which the glamorous sets of Lee Simonson were replaced by a sordid background, and the production was made with a greater emphasis on "symbolism," the play failed to interest our audiences. I feel sure that it was Richard Bennett's failure to understand the character which, along with Simonson's *mise en scène* and the beautiful and talented Margalo Gillmore's moving portrait of little Consuelo, made our first production of the play so great a success.

Through his father, Rudolph Schildkraut, the great German actor, we were introduced to Joseph Schildkraut, a young man who had recently arrived in the United States, and who was known among his friends as "Pepi." It was young Schildkraut who suggested that we should produce Molnar's play, *Liliom,* in which he wished to act the title role. When the play was presented, it became one of our outstanding successes, with Eva Le Gallienne as Julie, and Joseph Schildkraut as Liliom. The performances of these two were unforgettable; Eva with her great spiritual quality and wistful tenderness, and Schildkraut whose flashing physical beauty, bravura, and fresh vitality made the part of Liliom both hard and sympathetic at the same time. Young Schildkraut not only possessed great acting talent, but was high-spirited and temperamental, and not one of the least difficulties in securing a long run for the play was to keep him on his good behavior, something which took the combined efforts and patience of us all.

Pepi was a realistic actor, and imbued with the spirit of Liliom, it was his practice to spank Helen Westley, who played Mrs. Muskat, with considerable vigor on her posterior throughout the play. Helen, no less a realistic actress, enjoyed the vigorous spankings which she received, and, indeed, seemed to respond best when struck hardest. Later on, Helen stepped out of the cast into another play, and was replaced by a new actress who bruised more easily and was less appreciative of Schildkraut's attentions. After making numerous complaints to him, she decided to take matters into her own hands. One evening, at the end of the scene in which Pepi administered his first spanking, he came running off the stage nursing his hand. "What do you think that woman did?" he complained to the stage manager. "She put tin inside her pants, and if she continues, I'm not going to play with her any more." "If Mr. Schildkraut intends to continue to strike me so violently," retorted the current Mrs. Muskat, "I'm going to continue to play with tin in my pants." Pepi desisted, and the play continued its run, but the character of Liliom became considerably milder from then on.

In the season of 1923–24 we engaged Arnold Daly, one of the most famous actors on the American stage, to appear in special performances of a German play entitled *The Race with the Shadow* by Wilhelm von Scholz. In addition to being a magnificent actor, Daly could justly claim the honor of having first introduced many of the plays of Bernard Shaw to America. Arnold, who had been extremely handsome in his youth, was a middle-aged man when I first met him. He was of medium stature, with dark hair and dark eyes which constantly danced under his bushy brows as he would recount one amusing story after another about his relationship with Shaw, with whom he ultimately quarreled violently in London. He once described to me how Shaw directed his own plays. "All that it is necessary for you to do, Arnold," said Shaw, "is to say my lines so slowly and clearly that the audience can understand every word." "What about my acting?" asked Arnold. "As long as they can hear my lines, you can act or not as you please." This, of course, was Arnold's version of the story. "After I write my plays," Shaw once told me, "I take a chessboard and move the pieces from position to position. Each piece represents an actor, and I write the stage directions into my plays after I have worked them out in detail on this chessboard. If the actor follows the stage directions exactly as they are written in the play, he cannot possibly go wrong." Shaw's stage directions are, indeed, masterly, but they do not leave the actor and director enough latitude. A creative artist with the temperament of Arnold Daly was constantly in hot water with Shaw for departing from his instructions. After the break between them, Shaw vowed that Daly should never again appear in a Shaw play. They were both Irish and explosive about one another, Shaw being the more tolerant of the two while Arnold took to drink, being at heart deeply unhappy over the rift.

Before we engaged Daly to appear in *The Race with the Shadow,* Arnold had been drinking heavily, but he seemed then to be on his good behavior. He was magnificent in the part, having the ability to hold the interest of the audience with an intensity which is found only in the greatest of actors. Alas, one Sunday afternoon, Arnold arrived at the theatre tragically inebriated; he could barely repeat his lines even though the stage manager, Philip Loeb, fed them to him one by one from the wings, until the pages of the prompt script fell out of his hands and scattered all over the stage. We were forced to ring down the curtain on the pretense that Arnold was ill. Despite this, we engaged him for other plays after he had had a long spell of good behavior, so greatly did we admire his acting talents.

Unfortunately, Daly won the ill-will of Alexander Woollcott, the dramatic critic, who fluctuated between being an angel to his friends and a hellion to those he disliked, with an emotional instability which made it impossible to know at any given moment whether he was going to kiss you on the cheek or stab you in the back. Daly appeared in two failures in succession, followed by a third. "Arnold Daly went down last night for the third and last time," wrote the irrepressible Woollcott, going far beyond the bounds of dramatic criticism and human decency. Arnold never recovered, and died horribly in a sordid rooming house, by accidentally setting fire to himself with a cigarette, apparently while in a state of intoxication. Thus, lonely and without friends, one of the greatest actors this country has ever known made his tragic final exit.

The day after his body was discovered, there were blazing headlines on the front pages of the newspapers, "Shaw says of Arnold Daly's death, that spontaneous combustion, while rare, sometimes occurs!" I could hardly believe my eyes when I read these cruel words. Surely Shaw was misquoted, I said to myself, and the next time I saw him I raised the question. "G.B.S., I don't believe you actually made that statement about Arnold Daly dying from spontaneous combustion, and I've told people so." "No, you are wrong, Lawrence," he replied. "I did say it, and for this reason. Arnold was no more sentimental about death than I am. He adored publicity, and his death was getting very little of it. Had I made a few pious remarks, they would have gone unnoticed, but I knew that if I made a sensational statement it would make front-page headlines, so I invented the story about spontaneous combustion sometimes occurring (which, by the way, is true), and it had exactly the desired effect. Arnold, had he been alive, would have been delighted to see his name in large headlines in every important newspaper in the English-speaking world." I looked at G.B.S. in amazement, but I had no reason to doubt his sincerity. I had seen so many instances of his kindness as to believe him incapable of intentional cruelty.

In the season of 1923–24 we produced another play of which I was inordinately fond: this was *Fata Morgana* by Ernest Vajda which gave the exotic Emily Stevens one of the finest parts of her career. Emily, a tall, handsome woman with a mass of blonde hair, was one of the greatest actresses of this period. A niece of Minnie Maddern

Fiske, she had the comedic flair of her famous aunt, but she also had a deep tragic undercurrent which made her playing of Hedda Gabler the greatest portrayal of this role in our era. In *Fata Morgana* she was exquisitely sensitive as the wife who fell in love with the young boy, and her playing contributed greatly to the play's success. Off stage Emily was moody; in one mood she was gay, witty and penetrating in her observations while in another she was sad and tragic to a degree. In one of these latter moods, she forgot to make her entrance on stage when Orlando Daly, her husband in the play, called "Tina, Tina!" at the climax of a big scene with Morgan Farley. Josephine Hull and some of the other actors went running to her dressing room, and when they opened the door they discovered Emily standing without a stitch of clothing on, casually lighting a cigarette. Orlando Daly and Morgan Farley kept on arguing ad lib onstage and calling "Tina! Tina!" intermittently in the wings. Emily was rushed into her clothes and onto the stage a full three minutes later—and all this happened without the audience being the least aware of the panic which the actors were experiencing on the stage in front of them.

Alfred Lunt and Lynn Fontanne, whose names have since been written in capital letters all over the history of the American theatre, came to us in the Guild season of 1924–25. And it was something of a feat for our Executive Director, Theresa Helburn, to bring these two players together in their first play, *The Guardsman* by Molnar, for the play had been produced before and was a failure, and the play's owner understandably did not want it to fail again. So he insisted on our using two "commercial" stars while we insisted on using Alfred and Lynn. Both of them had recently won acting honors, Alfred in *Clarence* and Lynn in *Dulcy,* but neither had yet achieved so-called "stardom." However, fortune was on our side, for whenever the play was offered to a woman star, she turned it down on the ground that the man's part was better than hers, while the men stars turned it down for the reason that the woman's part, in their opinion, was better than the man's. This dilemma left no alternative for the play's owner, but he astutely required that the Guild pay an extra percentage for bringing Lunt and Fontanne together. As Alfred wished Lynn to have the better part and Lynn wanted Alfred to have the better part, they were not disturbed by any of the questions which had kept other actors from appearing in the play.

On October 13, 1924, at the Garrick Theatre, the curtain rose on a crackling comedy performance of a kind which had never been seen before in our theatre. With colorful settings by the youthful Jo

Mielziner and the brilliant direction of Philip Moeller, this performance of Alfred and Lynn, aided by Dudley Digges as the Sardonic Critic, and Helen Westley as the vituperative "Mama," was a high watermark for the young Theatre Guild and established the beginnings of an Acting Company which, later on, climaxed this period of our career.

They Knew What They Wanted, the first of a series of magnificent plays which were to flow from the pen of Sidney Howard, a tall handsome Californian who had recently come East, was also produced this same season, and its locale in the Napa Valley was quite new to the American theatre. I was deputed to try to induce Pauline Lord to play the part of Amy, and I called on her one afternoon at her apartment just off Riverside Drive. Pauline, whose expressive features and eyes changed so greatly from moment to moment that one glimpsed only fleeting impressions of her elusive personality, seemed frightened to death at meeting me, and I felt quite overcome by her fear and became equally frightened. It seeped out during the timid conversation that passed between us that she would be willing to play the part. I fled as soon as I had this information and in due course she was engaged. Pauline had the same quality on the stage as in life. Her method of playing a love scene was always, as it were, to shrink, to be always on the point of moving back, as contrasted with the more usual type of actress whose tendency was to move toward the loved one. This hesitancy on her part, shared by a few others of the same school, led me to divide actresses into two groups, "the shrinkers" led by Pauline, and "the pushers" led by Judith Anderson, who developed this form of acting into high art in *Medea*. Pauline shrank so magnificently in *They Knew What They Wanted* that she received all the requisite sympathy from the audience, while Glenn Anders as her lover took the fullest responsibility for pressing his attentions on her; the handsome Richard Bennett relieved the monotony of his part by introducing far more swear words than the script called for. The play, which won the Pulitzer Prize and firmly established Sidney Howard on the road to success, ran for the entire season, so that, with *The Guardsman* and *Fata Morgana*, we had three plays running simultaneously in New York.

Not all of my experiences with the theatre in the exciting early nineteen twenties were at the Guild. The entire theatre was alive in those days, and I still recall with interest meetings with the fabulous impresario Morris Gest, with the leaders of the Moscow Art Theatre on the occasion of their American visit, and with Reinhardt. Moreover,

I was also involved at the time with my own efforts at playwriting and play production under other auspices than the Theatre Guild's.

In 1923 the brilliant Morris Gest brought the great Russian actor, Constantin Stanislavsky, and the Moscow Art Theatre to New York for a season of repertory. Morris, with his black velvet hat, flowing black necktie and opera cloak, looked like an impecunious painter from the *Quartier Latin* in mourning for some long-lost model, and no matter how happy the occasion there was always something tragic about his eyes—possibly the result of importing too many Russian temperaments into the United States. Morris Gest, like his contemporary, Sol Hurok, could not resist importing Russians, and in addition to bringing over the Moscow Art Theatre, he also imported the Chauve-Souris with Nikita Baliev, and the Musical Studio of the Moscow Art Theatre. The last time I saw him, he had imported a company of midgets for the World's Fair at Flushing Meadows. Rex Smith, then the redheaded editor of *Newsweek*, wanted to introduce me to a charming Spanish lady midget, and we visited her home in the Fair Grounds by the uncomfortable expedient of crawling in through the front door of her little house on our hands and knees. She told us that the midgets were of all nationalities, and hated each other just as heartily as larger folk. There were Fascist midgets from Italy and Germany, she said, who despised the Communist midgets from Russia, and of course they all treated the Jewish midgets abominably.

As I crawled out of her house, I ran right into Morris Gest, looking more funereal than ever. "Imagine, Lawrence," said he, in tones of deep despair, "after the Moscow Art Theatre, now I have midgets." "Why?" I asked. "Well," said Morris, "it was this way. In Paris a friend said to me, 'Morris, do you want to make a million dollars? Take these midgets to the World's Fair.' Now, Lawrence, you know a midget means bad luck in show business, and I wouldn't touch midgets for even two million dollars, so I said 'No,' and left Paris for Warsaw to put some flowers on my poor father's grave. I hired a carriage and drove to the cemetery, and as I stepped out on the sidewalk, who should be standing there but a midget! I realized at once it was a message from my poor father beyond the grave, telling me I should make maybe a million or so out of these midgets, so I wired Paris and booked the attraction—and that's why I'm here today, handling midgets."

Aided by Otto H. Kahn, Morris Gest did a great service to the American theatre by bringing to New York Stanislavsky and the Moscow Art Theatre, and later his co-director, Nemirovich Dantchenko,

and the Musical Studio of the Moscow Art Theatre. Since our earlier
efforts with the Washington Square Players had been largely inspired by
what we had heard of the Moscow Art Theatre, we visited all the performances. Here, to our surprise, we found that instead of Chekhov's
plays being produced as murky tragedies, every ounce of comedy was
extracted from them. Where all American productions of these plays
had been done in gloomy darkness, the Russians turned on the lights
and actually let the audience see what was happening. This was so
revolutionary in American art theatre circles that some of our foremost
scenic artists began to show suicidal tendencies. They could not question the famous Moscow Art Theatre, but what logical reason was
there, for example, for playing the cellar scene in *The Lower Depths*
of Gorki in full light? After hearing a long discussion on the subject,
I decided to ask Stanislavsky the reason. "So the audience can see the
expressions on the actors' faces," he replied. A new generation of scenic
artists has since sprung up which has not seen the Moscow Art Theatre.
I meet them all the time designing sets for the Guild, and as fast as
they turn down the lights I turn them up again. This becomes a sort
of duel between me and the director or scenic artist, as the case may
be, but having on several occasions seen plays ruined on their opening
nights by being played in gloomy darkness, I have become a fanatic
on the subject, and paraphrasing the Book of Genesis, my watchword
is "Let there be light!"

While Stanislavsky was in New York in 1923, he came to see all the
Theatre Guild plays, and as his hotel was almost opposite the Wyoming Apartment on Seventh Avenue where I then lived, he came to
supper after the theatre on several occasions. We carried on our
conversations in French, which we both spoke sufficiently slowly and
badly to make ourselves clearly understandable to one another. Stanislavsky was a tall, handsome, white-haired man with Old-World manners and a fine physique. He gave the impression of a nobleman of
the court of Louis XIV rather than the dean of modern actors. Added
to his great personal charm was a sincere and kindly interest in those
members of our family he met at our home. One afternoon he entertained my daughter Phyllis, then a small child who spoke French
better than either of us, by making a doll of his hands, using his
knuckles as the face and a handkerchief which made the dress and
bonnet. This kept them both amused and occupied for the better part
of an hour.

One of the subjects which he discussed often, as he sat in front of
the fire after his play was over, was the production of plays in the

United States as compared with that of his own troupe. "You have here, so far as I can see, only theatre 'spectacles,' " he said. "The difference between such a spectacle, and performances by the Moscow Art Theatre lies in this, that in a spectacle the actors are only partly motivated by their imagination and that of the director, while in our theatre the actors are so deeply imbued with their roles that they become the actual characters in their imagination, and it is impossible for them to be either partly or wrongly motivated." "How does this happen?" I asked. "It is because during our rehearsal period, which can take anywhere from six months to a year, the actors go over, in their imagination, the past lives of the characters they are playing and actually live their parts. Also, if the play is laid in a certain part of the town, they go there and become habituated to the way of life of the characters they are playing." "No wonder you take so long to rehearse," I remarked. "Our Actors' Equity Association, the actors' union, allows us only four weeks' time." "Then you are doomed forever to produce only spectacles in the American theatre," he replied.

I did not agree with him then, nor do I agree now. Our method of producing plays "out of town," with anywhere from three to six weeks of playing before the play is brought into New York, often results in a total period of from seven to ten weeks of rehearsal. I admit that one or two actors and actresses I *could* mention take almost all that time to learn their lines. Moreover, Russian theatre characters are much more complex than American, and probably more difficult to portray on the stage. Sergei Soudeykin, the Russian painter who designed the sets of *Porgy and Bess,* once told me that Dostoyevsky, in his novels, had created so many complex characters who spent their time suffering over their souls that for three generations most of the Russian intelligentsia were trying to complicate themselves into being Dostoyevsky characters. The reaction to this is for the present-day Soviet Russians to act like tough extroverts.

Stanislavsky at this time was my god in the theatre and I tried to learn all I could from him. "What is your method of teaching acting?" I asked. "There is no way of teaching acting if the actor has no underlying talent. One can only assist the talent which exists to become greater," he replied. "This can be done in many ways; for instance, by exercises of the imagination. I suggest to a young actor that he is outside a room, the door of which is closed. Now, he must open the door under a number of different conditions. For instance, he may imagine that his sweetheart, whom he has not seen for many months, is in the room. Or he may imagine that there is a tiger in the room." "Then why should he open the door?" I asked. "Perhaps, if he has enough imagination, he won't," was the smiling reply. "Such exercises are simple and are followed by more complex ones along the same line; but don't imagine one can become an actor by exercises. Above all there is the basic personality, and more is learned from actually living a rich and deep life so as to gain understanding than in any classroom. In loving, suffering, discussion, interest in the arts, and in the poetry of marriage, the soul of the artist is developed." "What do you mean by 'poetry of marriage'?" I asked. "Marriage—a true marriage—has a poetry of its own which gives a background of harmony to the artist for his creative work." I reflected on my own marriage, then running into difficulties. There was certainly no poetry there. . . .

"Whom do you consider your greatest actor, Kachalov or Moskvin?" I asked. "Moskvin," he answered, unhesitatingly. "God was good to Kachalov. He created him handsome, winning, and desirable to women. Moskvin had no such God-given gifts; he is small, ugly, and in appearance insignificant. Yet by the power of his own imagination and art, which are of the highest order, he has overcome all these defects and made himself the greatest actor in our troupe. God made Kachalov—Moskvin made himself."

Stanislavsky suggested to me one evening that if the Guild would select a group of talented young people he would take them back to Moscow for two years and train them in a number of plays. I took the matter up with our Board of Managers, but the idea was thought to be impractical, as well as too difficult for us to swing financially. In retrospect, I greatly regret this for it was an adventurous plan from which great things for our theatre might have resulted.

Stanislavsky was co-director, with Nemirovich Dantchenko, of the Moscow Art Theatre for many years, Stanislavsky having the veto on the acting, and Dantchenko on the plays. Dantchenko, the more scholarly man of the two, came to New York several years later with the Moscow Art Theatre Musical Studio, bringing many brilliant musical adaptations, such as *Carmencita and the Soldier,* which combined effective dramatic staging with operetta and opera. Dantchenko, a heavy-set bearded man with strong features, a high forehead and a deliberate manner of speech, also visited at our home, and we had some talks of his personal problems with the Art Theatre which were not so different from my own at the Theatre Guild. The "veto" system (now in operation with the United Nations) gave him considerable frustration, and he was able to create freely in the theatre only after he started the Musical Studio in which Stanislavsky was not particularly interested.

Dantchenko told me of his initial difficulties in getting anyone to appreciate the value of Chekhov's *Seagull* as a play, for it was originally a failure in Petrograd (now Leningrad), and it was only after strong persuasion on his part that Stanislavsky agreed to produce the play as the first offering of the Moscow Art Theatre. It was an immediate success and from then on the genius of its author was recognized by the entire world. "There is only one road for the playwrights of the future," said Dantchenko to me one day, "and that is the road of Chekhov." I did not agree. The theatre is as wide as life and there are as many roads as humanity is capable of creating. I would personally prefer to travel on the road of Shakespeare who will live long after the futilitarians of Chekhov are but dimly remembered.

While the Moscow Art Theatre was playing in New York another distinguished visitor, Max Reinhardt, arrived here on the magic cloak of Morris Gest to arrange for a production of *The Miracle*. Reinhardt was a middle-aged man of short stature whose head impressed me as having been carved out of granite for he changed his expression but seldom, and it was hard to guess what he was thinking. He was always accompanied by Dr. Rudolph Kommer, a little roly-poly figure of a man with a moonface out of which round eyes peered at you through round spectacles. He acted as a sort of theatrical midwife for Reinhardt, assisting in the accouchements of his master's ideas, and he was as volatile and talkative as Reinhardt was phlegmatic and taciturn. Kommer was almost as spectacular in his way as Reinhardt. He was the eternal promoter and promoted everything from theatrical productions to the marriages of his actress friends to English aristocrats or American millionaires.

Reinhardt at this time, and indeed until his death, suffered from what may be unkindly termed elephantiasis of the imagination. His simple and beautiful productions at the Deutsches Theater which had so influenced my attitude toward the theatre some years earlier were now buried in the past and his interest seemed to thrive only in the spectacular. I had seen some of his enormous productions in the Grosses Schauspielhaus in Berlin in which hundreds of extras came charging into the circus arena that served as the stage, and from his discussion of *The Miracle* I realized it was to be another huge spectacle. Kommer suggested that Reinhardt produce a play for the Theatre Guild and discussed the matter at some length, but we did

not succeed in getting together. I was not too enthusiastic, as I preferred a few good actors to five hundred to a thousand indifferent ones.

Since Reinhardt seemed sad and rather lonely, I suggested to
Estelle that we ask him and Dr. Kommer to our home for Thanksgiving dinner. They came and in due course were initiated into the
mysteries of roast turkey, cranberry sauce and pumpkin pie, the latter
two comestibles being quite unknown in Europe. We had a delightful
dinner, and Reinhardt and Kommer vied with one another in telling
us amusing stories of the European theatre and entertaining our
small child Phyllis. A few months later when I told Kommer that
Estelle and I had divorced he remarked, "I must tell Max at once. He
will be so surprised." "Why?" I asked. "Well, after your Thanksgiving dinner on our way back to our hotel he said to me, 'There is a
happy man, surrounded by his wife, his child, his turkey, his cranberry sauce and his pumpkin pie, while you and I sit alone in our
lonely New York hotel!' The tears came into his eyes, and he felt
sorry for himself for days!"

While all these happenings were taking place in the theatre, our
New York and Chicago patent practices were growing, and we also
opened a Washington office under the management of E. F. Wenderroth. It seemed desirable, therefore, to strengthen our London connections to handle the increasing volume of work we were sending
there. Harold Stevens, a young Chartered Patent Agent who had
worked with John Parry and myself in London, had been recently
released from World War I, and John suggested that it would be a good
idea to form a London firm with our English correspondents, A. E.
White and Harold Stevens. John and I went over to London and
discussed the situation with them and we formed the firm of White,
Langner, Stevens and Parry, which, upon the death of Mr. White,
became the firm of Stevens, Langner, Parry and Rollinson, now one of
the foremost firms of British Chartered Patent Agents.

I continued during this period to devote a great deal of my time to
playwriting. I made a practice of spending each summer on the
Continent, and for two or three months each year I settled in a small
town in France with Estelle and Phyllis, and here I spent my time
working on my own plays. In the village of Le Croisic in Brittany I
completed my play, *Moses*, which was published by Boni and Liveright.

Returning to New York, I promptly submitted it to the Guild. *Moses*,
in my opinion, was just as good as many of the plays of other
authors which we had produced, but in this opinion my colleagues

regrettably did not concur. After some heated discussions in which I was torn between the desire to withdraw the play from the Guild or withdraw myself from the Guild, I finally decided to withdraw the play. I offered it to the rest of the New York theatre, which examined it politely without becoming at all excited and then declined it with thanks. Soon after, the writing members of the Board began to realize that if the Guild did not produce their members' plays, the plays immediately received a black mark in the eyes of all the other managers. "Surely if the play is any good the Theatre Guild would produce it!" they would say. "Not so," I would reply, "we want to avoid fighting with one another." "But you do that already," was the skeptical reply. My answer was that the quickest way to break up the Guild would be to become involved in arguments over each other's plays.

The other members of the Guild finally gave up playwriting, but I stuck to my guns with dogged obstinacy and continued to write, notwithstanding the handicaps which I had imposed upon myself, until some years later, by building my own theatre with Armina Marshall in Westport, I could try out my own plays without a "by your leave" from anyone.

CHAPTER XVI

Shaw, Saint Joan *and Stresa*

O N MY visit to the Shaws in 1922, I had asked whether there was any new play in the offing. "The trouble is, we haven't been able to find a good subject," said Mrs. Shaw. I must have looked astonished, for she continued, "Yes, I sometimes find ideas for plays for the Genius. If we can find a good subject for a play, he usually writes it very quickly."

Some months later, Mrs. Shaw found a good subject. She told me about it later. "I had always admired the character of Saint Joan, so I bought as many books about her as I could find, and left them in prominent places all over the house. Whenever the Genius picked up a book on the table or at the side of his bed, it was always on the subject of Saint Joan. One day he came to me and said quite excitedly, 'Charlotte, I have a wonderful idea for a new play! It's to be about Saint Joan!' 'Really,' I replied, 'what a *good* idea!' " Mrs. Shaw's eyes twinkled as she told me the story.

I first became acquainted with the fact that *Saint Joan* was being written by a letter I received from St. John Ervine in the summer of 1923. I then wrote G.B.S.:

St. John Ervine has just written me that he has heard you have finished a new play on the subject of Joan of Arc. Provided that this is not the chronicle play in five hundred scenes, I think we shall want to do this, and I hope you will let us see it.

Meanwhile, *Back to Methuselah* was to be produced in England by the Birmingham Repertory Theatre, under the management of Sir Barry Jackson. I had written to St. John Ervine suggesting that we

174

visit Birmingham together, and he had agreed to accompany me. Shaw wrote:

Dear L.L.

Saint Joan is finished except for revising and inserting stage business. It's a star play for one woman and about twenty men. Sybil Thorndike is to play it in London.

Incidentally, I fell on the rocks in Ireland, and cracked a couple of my ribs, besides tearing one of them nearly out of my spine; and though I have kept going I realize that 67 is too old for such games. . . .

Shaw's ribs suggested a "press release," but I was careful to write for permission. This came with the following letter:

Provided you don't suggest to the insurance companies that I am too much disabled, my rib can bear a little publicity.

The scenes in *Joan* can all be reduced to extreme simplicity. A single pillar of the Gordon Craig type will make the cathedral. All the Loire needs is a horizon and a few of Simonson's lanterns. The trial scene is as easy as the cathedral. The others present no difficulty. There should be an interval at the end of the Loire scene and one (very short) after the trial scene, and even that makes an interval too many: the act divisions should be utterly disregarded.

Early in October St. John Ervine and his wife Nora accompanied me to Birmingham, where *Back to Methuselah* was produced consecutively for five performances, each afternoon and evening for three days. The effect of seeing all these plays one after the other was murderous, but G.B.S. was triumphant. "This," he said, "is the way you should have done it in New York!" I replied that the title should be changed to *Back and Back and Back to Methuselah*.

One wet afternoon we were all invited for tea at Sir Barry Jackson's home, and sat drying ourselves in front of the fire; for luckily for Shaw and Sir Barry, it rained so hard all the time the plays were being presented in Birmingham that the theatre was one of the few dry spots where the public could congregate, and the alternatives to seeing the plays were too damp and dreary to contemplate. Shaw, perky as ever in spite of his broken rib, was explaining how none of the respectable medical men in Ireland diagnosed his trouble correctly, and only when he got in touch with an unorthodox individual known as an American doctor, was the fact discovered that his ribs were injured. This, G.B.S. hastened to assure me, was not because the doctor was American, but because he was unorthodox.

"Tell us something about *Saint Joan*," said Ervine. Whereupon Shaw, his tall figure standing before the fireplace, head erect, white beard waving and blue eyes twinkling, launched into the story of Joan, and what he had done with it; his conversations with an Irish priest who had been most helpful, and the impact of his own keen mind upon the original source material. For at least two hours St. John, his wife Nora, myself and Mrs. Shaw, grouped around the fireplace, listened with rapt attention as G.B.S. told us not only the story of the play, but threw in practically all the contents of the Preface for good measure.

All of us were exhilarated by his lively stories, which happily seemed endless; and while he talked, Mrs. Shaw, seated on a low chair at one corner of the fireplace, appeared to be engrossed in her knitting, pausing only to smile now and again, like a kindly mother whose grown son was distinguishing himself before an appreciative audience. During one of the lulls in the conversation, which were infrequent, and came only when G.B.S. had reached the end of one anecdote and waited for the chorus of "How wonderful!" before going on to the next, Nora Ervine leaned over to Mrs. Shaw, looked at her knitting and asked with some concern, "Whatever are you making, Mrs. Shaw?" "Nothing," replied Mrs. Shaw in a whisper. "Nothing, really. But I've heard the Genius tell these same stories at least a hundred times, and if I didn't have something to do with my hands, I think I'd go stark raving mad!"

One might imagine from this little story, that there was not the greatest understanding and sympathy on Mrs. Shaw's part toward her husband. But that would be erroneous. She regarded him with amused admiration, and never lost her sense of humor about him. On one occasion when Alfred Lunt and Lynn Fontanne were lunching with the Shaws, I was seated next to Mrs. Shaw. G.B.S. presided at the other end of the table, and proceeded to entertain Alfred, Lynn and Philip Moeller with a stream of amusing anecdotes of the theatre. I asked Mrs. Shaw why G.B.S. always refused to visit America. "I'm afraid he's liable to get overexcited, meeting so many people, and getting so much publicity," said Mrs. Shaw. "But we could arrange to protect him," I replied. A particularly loud burst of laughter came from the other end of the table. "I'm sure you'd do *your* best to keep him quiet," she replied, "but you see, there's Mr. Shaw himself!"

Mrs. Shaw's influence was always directed to the more human, emotional side of G.B.S.'s work, and I felt that had it been even stronger, G.B.S. might have written many more plays of the stature of *Saint Joan*, for her warm human quality was a good antidote for his tendency to theorize on political, social and every other subject under the sun. "All Italian women are stupid," he once remarked in her presence at Stresa. "How can you say that," she replied. "You know only three or four Italian women, and you can hardly speak enough Italian to carry on an intelligent conversation with any of them." The Genius subsided. He disliked admitting that *Saint Joan* was his best play. It was not iconoclastic, and G.B.S. had built his reputation on iconoclasm. A year later he was to write me, "Everyone, to my disgust, assures me it is the best play I have ever written."

Some years later at Stresa, G.B.S. told me that he felt that *Saint Joan* was directly inspired by the Saint herself. "As I wrote," he said, "she guided my hand, and the words came tumbling out at such a speed that my pen rushed across the paper and I could barely write fast enough to put them down." Since G.B.S. wrote *Saint Joan* in Pitman's shorthand, according to his secretary Miss Patch, we must assume that the words came rushing out in torrents—and that the Maid of Orleans was as long-winded as he was. In an editorial written on G.B.S.'s death, one of the leading New York newspapers described him as an atheist. I thought of his remarks about Saint Joan as I read the editorial. No atheist could have written *Saint Joan,* nor could an atheist have believed it to be divinely inspired. G.B.S. did not believe in the orthodox religions, but he believed in religion, and I offer this story as evidence of his belief in the after-life, no matter how often, on occasion, he pretended to be bored by the prospect of spending eternity in heaven with his friends.

During the dripping interludes between plays at Birmingham, and later in London, G.B.S. discussed some ideas about casting *Saint Joan.* He had recently seen Alla Nazimova in the moving pictures (they were silent in those days) and thought she might be right for the part. Despite her accent I felt, however, that some quality of the character would be lost if it were not played by a young girl. Eva Le Gallienne had been playing the part of Julie in *Liliom* with a great deal of spiritual quality, and I suggested her as the best possibility for the part.

In due course at my hotel in London there arrived a printed paper-backed copy of *Saint Joan* marked in G.B.S.'s meticulous handwriting, "Private and Confidential, to Lawrence Langner." I took a measure of the play; it was terribly long. "Another long-winded one," I thought; but soon lost myself in admiration as I read it. I mailed the book to New York, and followed soon after. I rushed from the boat to the

Garrick Theatre where the play had been read immediately on receipt by the rest of the Guild Board. Where *Back to Methuselah* found us hesitant, *Saint Joan* galvanized us all into quick action.

After a debate as to who should play the Saint, which lasted with undiminished violence for many days, the Board finally selected Winifred Lenihan for the part—a selection which was excellent, for I have seen five productions of *Saint Joan* in three languages, and I have yet to see a performance to equal hers. This was due to the fact that she possessed in herself the attributes of courage, fervor and youth which the part called for. The keynote of the Guild's production was its essential simplicity. Simonson's scenery and costumes gave it a stark hard masculine quality which I have never seen in any other production, and the English presentation which Shaw raved about, and which I saw later, struck me as very prettified and feminine indeed.

We all felt that the play was far too long, and remembering our unhappy experience with *Methuselah* decided to write Shaw begging him to make some deletions, mentioning the fact that many persons in the audience lived in the suburbs, and would miss the last train home if they waited for the end of the play. Shaw's laconic cable in reply was as follows:

London, November 19, 1923

THE OLD OLD STORY BEGIN AT EIGHT OR RUN LATER TRAINS AWAIT FINAL REVISION OF PLAY—SHAW

As we were all set for rehearsals, Shaw's reference to a final revised version of the script dropped like a bombshell in our midst. Cables passed back and forth, resulting in the demand by Shaw that we stop rehearsals immediately and postpone the opening. We protested by cable that to postpone for a week would cost £400, and requesting G.B.S. to send the revised draft as soon as possible. Shaw's irate reply arrived a week or so after we received the corrected copy:

3rd December 1923

I enclose a letter just received from my printers. I presume you have had the corrected copy by this time.

The worse part of dealing with you T.G. people is that you are each and all half and half very superior beings and exasperating idiots. When I heard that you were actually rehearsing from a copy which you knew to be an unrevised first proof I tore my hair. I should not have trusted you with it. A man who would play *Methuselah* in three nights is capable of anything. But at least I did tell you very expressly that what you had was not the play in its final form. Only, you never attend to what I say; and if the stoppage of the re-

Heartbreak House production of Bernard Shaw's *Heartbreak House*, 1920; set designed by Lee Simonson.

Roeder, Fred Eric, Lucille Watson and Albert Parry.

The Theatre Guild production of Bernard Shaw's *Back to Methuselah*, 1922, with George Gaul, Eleanor Woodruff, Ernita Lascelles and Albert Bruning.

Winifred Lenihan in the Theatre Guild production of *Saint Joan*, 1923.

Above: Lynn Fontanne in the Theatre Guild production of Bernard Shaw's *Pygmalion,* 1926. *Below:* Romney Brent and Alla Nazimova in the Theatre Guild production of Bernard Shaw's *The Simpleton of the Unexpected Isle,* 1935.

Alfred Lunt as Dubedat in the Theatre Guild's production of Bernard Shaw's *The Doctor's Dilemma*, 1927.

Beatrice Lillie and Hope Williams in the Theatre Guild's production of Bernard Shaw's *Too True to Be Good*, 1932.

Above: G.B.S. at Stresa, 1929.
Below: G.B.S. and Armina Marshall at Stresa, 1929.

Both photos by the author.

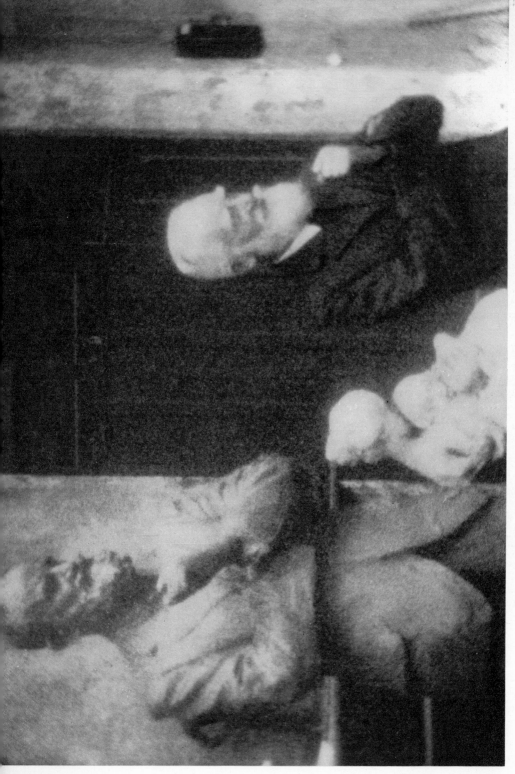

Bernard Shaw posing for statue by Prince Paul Troubetzkoy, Stresa, 1929.

Photo by the author

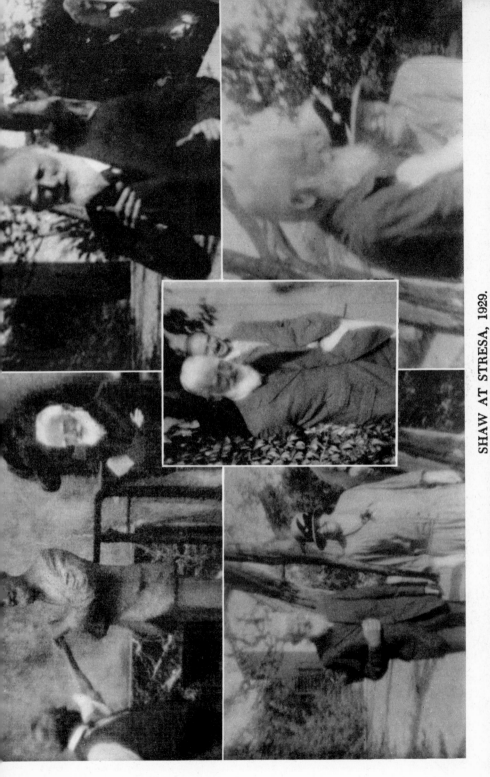

SHAW AT STRESA, 1929.

Prince Troubetzkoy working on statue of G.B.S.   G.B.S. expostulating.

G.B.S. walking with Mrs. Shaw.   The author and G.B.S.   G.B.S. embracing Mrs. Shaw.

SHAW AT STRESA, 1929.

He flirts with Armina Marshall.   He talks with the author.

He dries himself.   He expounds his views on women's clothes.

Camera study of G.B.S. by the author.

hearsals (not that I have any hope that you really stopped them) cost you £400, which is great nonsense, my only regret is that it did not cost you £4000, an all-too-slender penalty for such criminal recklessness.

I read the play to Sybil Thorndike from the second set of proofs; and the dialogue occupied exactly 3 hours 3 minutes. Since then I have made another and more drastic revision which has, I think, got the last bits of dead wood out of the play, and have certainly saved the odd three minutes. I think therefore it should be possible to begin at 8 and finish at 11:30. The English edition of *Heartbreak House,* uniform with the proofs just sent you, contains 110 pages, including only two specifications of scenery. Joan contains seven different scenes. Compare the number of pages and you will see that your estimate of four hours is far over the mark.

Simonson must not make the scenery fantastic. It may be very simple; but it must suggest perfectly natural scenery. Joan was an extremely real person; and the scenery should be keyed to her reality. Simonson must also be limited to three cigarettes a day.

As can be imagined, I was between two fires; Shaw on the one hand, and the rest of the Guild Board on the other. But lest any of my readers should be under the impression that Shaw had greatly reduced the length of the play, let me add that he had omitted very little from his first copy. *Saint Joan* was, and still is, a long long play.

On December 14th I wrote G.B.S.:

As to never attending to what you say, I can only say that I listened most attentively at Birmingham; in fact, you never gave me an opportunity to do anything but listen, nor anybody else either. Not that I wanted to do anything but listen, but if I forgot something of what you said, please put it down to torrents of rain in Birmingham, torrents of conversation in Birmingham, and fifteen waking hours out of forty-eight spent at the theatre . . . my mental processes must have been paralyzed.

After our first dress rehearsal we decided to make one more attempt to have G.B.S. cut the play, and cabled him as follows:

JOAN OPENS FRIDAY EVENING. CONSENSUS OF OPINION AT FIRST DRESS REHEARSAL FATAL DROP OF INTEREST DURING TENT SCENE AND BEGINNING TRIAL SCENE. WERE YOU HERE SURE YOU WOULD AGREE WITH US. WE WILL NOT DROP ONE LINE WITHOUT YOUR CONSENT BUT FOR GOOD OF PLAY AND TURNING POSSIBLE FINANCIAL LOSS INTO ASSURED ARTISTIC FINANCIAL SUCCESS STRONGLY URGE YOUR CABLING CONSENT OUR EXPENSE FOLLOWING OMISSIONS. . . . OUR DUTY TO GIVE YOU OUR FRANK OPINION. FINAL RESPONSIBILITY YOURS. PLAY MAGNIFICENT.

THE GUILD

My readers will note that we suggested Shaw's cabling at our expense, but even with this inducement, he maintained an obdurate silence. On Friday, December 28th, *Saint Joan* made its first appearance on any stage. It was enthusiastically received by its audience. But as usual the critics complained of its length. Also, on the opening night, many of the audience left before the final curtain, which came down at 11:35.

While many good things were said about the play, the complaints about its length from the press, coming after the disappointment of *Back to Methuselah,* the failure of which we felt was largely due to its overlength, caused us to cable to Shaw the next day for permission to cut the play. Alas, we had bitten granite. My own personal cable, equally unsuccessful, was as follows:

ONE CRITIC COMPARING YOU WITH SHAKESPEARE SAYS THAT JOAN CANNOT BE SUCCESSFULLY GIVEN UNTIL AFTER YOUR DEATH BECAUSE IT CAN THEN BE CUT. SPLENDID OPPORTUNITY TO PROVE AGAIN THAT YOU ARE GREATER THAN SHAKESPEARE BY CABLING THE GUILD TO USE ITS DISCRETION IN MAKING SOME OMISSIONS OF UNESSENTIALS. GUILD HAS DONE SPLENDID WORK. SURE YOU WOULD AGREE IF YOU WERE HERE

We even persuaded Winifred Lenihan to cable in her own name, asking him to shorten the play. To this G.B.S. replied:

THE GUILD IS SENDING ME TELEGRAMS IN YOUR NAME. PAY NO ATTENTION TO THEM.

SHAW

Ben Jonson wrote of Shakespeare that he was one of the most long-winded of men. I venture to say the same of Shaw, and that many of his plays will never be seen at their best until after the copyrights have expired. In latter years, I felt a relaxing of the relentless rule. On one occasion Shaw said to me, "If only you would not bother me with asking for permission—!"

This reminds me of a remark once made to me by Mrs. Shaw. "Of course, Mr. Shaw is a strict vegetarian, but I've noticed that when he is traveling, he doesn't inquire too closely into the origins of the soup!"

Despite the length of *Saint Joan,* the large theatre-going public came to see it. A few weeks later I was writing G.B.S. as follows:

It is extremely annoying to have to admit that you are right. People are coming in droves to see *Saint Joan,* and it is a great success. I have complete confidence in your business judgment. I still hold my own opinions about the length of the play.

Having heard nothing from G.B.S. for some time, I was convinced he was too annoyed with me to write. However his letter was finally forthcoming. It covered many points concerning the production, including some inevitable complaints of a very minor nature. It also contained one paragraph of more than passing personal significance to me:

I am not at all anxious about *Joan;* but I am somewhat concerned about you. You could hardly have been rattled by Heywood Broun and Alan a Dale *et hoc genus omne* if you had not been rattled already. As a matter of fact you were rattled at Birmingham before *Joan* came into operation at all. I sympathized, but did not like to say anything, as it was evidently some private grief that had disconcerted you. What about that pretty lady who called on me and said she was Mrs. Langner, and did not take the smallest interest in the theatre, nor, as far as I could make out, in me? Has she been giving you trouble; or have you been giving it to her? You need not answer this impertinent question: I put it only to show that my recent assumption that you were not *compos mentis* at the theatre was not founded on your panic over *Joan.*

G.B.S.'s intuition regarding the pretty lady (Estelle) who was not interested either in the theatre or in him, was correct. I replied to his questions:

Either you are a mind reader, or St. John Ervine has been talking, because the fact is, that the pretty lady who called on you and did not take the smallest interest in the theatre, nor in you, also took no interest in me, which was very disconcerting, as we had been married for eight years and have a little daughter.

G.B.S. also wrote me further on the subject of publicity for *Saint Joan.*

The great press feature of the production was the notice by Pirandello, which you never even mentioned. The *N.Y. Times* has sent it to me specially with an invitation to comment. Perhaps I will; in the meantime let Terry sit tight on that article that I sent her when you had cabled a ghastly failure. She had better send it back to me.

By the way, you must stop your people from giving away my private business letters to the press. It is impossible to correspond on such terms. Nothing requires greater tact and knowledge of what is allowable than giving to the press matter not meant for it; and the silly young folk who become press agents because they are congenital unemployables are the last in the world to be trusted with such delicate business. You must give a flat instruction that nothing that I write, past or present, is to be given to the press without my express permission.

Terry's latest is a request for a new play to open the new theatre next January. She should have saved up *Joan* for it. I have no more *Joans* in me. Are you going to put in a revolving stage? It would have come in very handy for *Joan*.

He also gave me his views on the photographs we sent him:

The pictures have arrived. I had a long letter from Simonson, the Reformed Smoker (or *has* he reformed?), about it. On the whole there is nothing to complain of, which is a pity, as I complain so well. However lots of things are wrong; so here goes.

In Act I the steward should be much older than Baudricourt; and both Baudricourt and Poulengy should be in half armor and be obviously soldiers and not merchants. This is important, as it strikes the note of France in war time. As it is, Poulengy's coat should not be belted. Baudricourt should be smart, a *beau sabreur*. The steward should not be a zany, but a respectable elderly man whom nobody nowadays would dream of assaulting. Otherwise B's handling of him becomes mere knockabout farce.

In the second act Joan's hair should be bobbed; and she should be dressed as a soldier, quite definitely masculine in contrast to her girlish appearance in the first act. And at the end of the act she should be in front of all the rest, in command of the stage in the good old fashioned way from the point of view of the audience, and not beautifully composed in the middle of the picture with all the other people turning their backs to the spectators. Why don't you carry out my directions and get my effects instead of working for pictorial effects. As to the Dauphin I believe his wig is wrong. His portrait shows that his hair was completely concealed by the fashion of the time, giving him a curiously starved and bald appearance that would be very effective on the stage.

The Bishop looks about right for the Inquisitor and the Inquisitor for the Bishop. My effect of a very mild and silvery Inquisitor and a rather stern Bishop has been missed as far as the makeup is concerned. The altar and candles in the middle of the cathedral scene are feebly stagy, and do not give the effect of a corner of a gigantic cathedral as my notion of one big pillar would. And it leads to that upstage effect, with a very feminine operatic-looking Joan in the centre, which I wanted to avoid. The drag towards the conventional is very evident; and is the last word in operatic artificiality (an angry woman tears a thing downward and throws it to the floor); but still, it is all very pretty in the American way, and might have been worse. I am going to see Charles Rickett's plans and sketches for the London production this afternoon; and it will be interesting to see what he makes of them.

Meanwhile, the demand for seats for *Saint Joan* had increased to such an extent that we had to move to another, larger theatre, of which fact I informed G.B.S.; and we requested him to write us some articles and letters that we could use to publicize the play at its new home. I also sent him a copy of a skit I had written on *Joan*.

My last letter from G.B.S. on the subject of *Saint Joan* was as follows:

What an unreasonable chap you are, wanting your letters answered! I never answer letters: if I did I should have no time for anything else.

The skit on *Joan* tempts me to write it up for London. The Play has repeated its American success here: it is going like mad; and everyone, to my disgust, assures me it is the best play I have ever written. Sybil Thorndike's acting and Charles Rickett's stage pictures and costumes have carried everything before them. I am convinced that our production knocks the American one into a cocked hat. Why don't you come over and see it?

I had a letter (among many others) about your production from Rebecca West, in which she makes the astonishing remark that I ought to amplify the Inquisition speech, and goes on to complain that though it is "quite beautifully delivered," people don't get the meaning of it. As it lasts seven or eight minutes and is one of the successes of the production here, I am surprised. Is there anything wrong with it?

The press notices here were just like the American ones: play too long: cut out the epilogue; magnificent play only needing the blue pencil to be a success etc. etc.

Cardinal Hayes's medal was a Godsend, as a press correspondent named Thomas had just written to the French papers to say that I had "bafouée" Joan. The medal brained him and left him for dead.

I received Terry's demand for articles and so forth with the composure of a man swimming the Niagara rapids and being asked casually for a light. Terry thinks I have nothing else to do but job about as her press agent, and throw in a play occasionally. She should thank God for having done so well.

Who keeps the daughter? Hadn't you better marry Terry until the other lady finds that all husbands are equally dull, and comes back? Meanwhile, why not run her through half a dozen plays like Strindberg?

I didn't marry Terry (Theresa Helburn) who was already married, and still is; but after Estelle and I were divorced, I did take the suggestion to run the lady through a couple of plays. One of these was called *These Modern Women* which ran for a brief three weeks in New York, and which most of my married women friends thought I had written about them. A particularly virulent attack on the play appeared in Heywood Broun's column, to the effect that he had never in all his dealings with modern women met one like the lady depicted in the play. A few days after, I met him and asked him how he had happened to review the play, since I had been told he had not seen it. "Well, Lawrence," he said, "you see, Ruth Hale thought you'd written it about her and me, so I let her review it for me. I hope you don't mind." I did!

The difficulty in introducing a personage like Bernard Shaw into one's autobiography is that he tends to take the bit in his teeth, and instead of writing your own story, it turns out that you are writing his. From the time the Theatre Guild produced *Heartbreak House* in 1920 until our production of *The Simpleton of the Unexpected Isles* in 1935, the world premieres of all of Shaw's plays (except *The Apple Cart*) were presented by the Theatre Guild, and a considerable amount of correspondence passed between myself and Shaw on the subject of these plays.

During my annual trips to Europe to visit my London office, I always called on the Shaws. It was my desire that the Guild should cement its relationship with him, and I tried in vain to have this set forth in writing. Notwithstanding the fact that the Theatre Guild has produced sixteen plays by Shaw, the only contract we had with him, other than the original *Heartbreak House* document, was the following written on a half sheet of notepaper:

June 14, 1922

My dear Langner,
    Yes: your letter of the 12th correctly summarized our understanding except that though I have stood out for a minimum payment of $2500 win lose or draw I have never asked for an advance, or been in a hurry for a contract. Of course I have no objection to either; but I wish to affirm that it is the Guild and not the Author that gets these attacks of nerves. . . .
    Meanwhile I am not to deal with the plays in New York without giving the Guild a look in unless I yield to an overwhelming impulse to treat them shabbily and lose my reputation for being the most reasonable man now living.

To this should be added the following legend on the back of a picture post card from Madeira in 1923:

Now the Actors Theatre, which has done pretty well with *Candida*, wants to reap the harvest you have sown; but I am telling them and all other applicants that you have an option on all my plays, and that they can have only your leavings, if any.

Shaw was always an excellent businessman. His business advice to Ervine, and undoubtedly to all other authors, was stated tersely "Build up your copyrights." I have retailed this advice to many an author flushed with success in Hollywood, when he had either sold his stories outright, or worked for a salary; had he done the same amount of work and held on to his copyrights, in time these would have worked for him, as they did for Shaw.

G.B.S. was the backbone of the Guild in its early days, and I coined the slogan "When in doubt, play Shaw," which served us well for close on twenty years. Maurice Wertheim, the Guild's financial genius, once prepared a detailed balance sheet showing how the high Shaw royalties made it impossible for the Guild to make any profit out of his plays. I showed Shaw the figures, but he barely glanced at them. "I remember seeing a balance sheet like this," said Shaw, "prepared by the Shuberts in connection with Forbes-Robertson's production of *Caesar and Cleopatra.* It came to me along with a letter saying they couldn't possibly keep the play running unless I reduced my royalties. I refused, and the play ran for several months longer!" I admitted we would continue to present his plays even though we lost on them, and the matter was dropped.

When I was in London in the summer of 1922, Shaw told me of the unhappy plight of his Austrian translator, Trebitsch, now ruined by the war, who had written a drama called *Jitta's Atonement.* "But how could you translate it when you don't know German?" I asked. "I have a smattering," he replied, "besides," he added, with a twinkle, "translating isn't just a matter of knowing the language. The original play was a tragedy—which was all right for Austria—but it would never go that way in England and America, so I turned it into a comedy!" Shaw offered this play to the Guild and while it was being considered, Bertha Kalich approached us for the American rights. We acquiesced and Shaw wrote me:

The Guild has cabled to me to give *Jitta* to Madame Kalich, probably blessing her for having extricated it from a difficult situation. But I am not at all happy about it. She seems the right woman for it; and she is very keen on it; but from what she has said to me I suspect that if the production is left in her hands she will suppress the comedy side of my version, and revert to the unrelieved gloom of the original; and I don't think this will succeed in America, because it means that the last two acts will merely wallow gloomily in the memories of the first.

I saw your press communication about the play; but I do not want it suggested that it is 95% Shaw and 5% Trebitsch. Novelty is always valuable; and novelty is the one quality that I have lost hopelessly with the affirmation of my reputation. The line to take is to boom Trebitsch in New York (steps are being taken to that end on this side), and to suggest that as what has been lacking in my plays is HEART, the combination of the emotional Trebitsch with the intellectual Shaw is ideal, and will make the most dramatic event of the season. . . .

Alas, *Jitta's Atonement,* which the Theatre Guild rejected, didn't succeed even as a comedy, but the play stands as evidence of the kindness and loyalty of Shaw to his friends when in trouble, financial and otherwise. The famous French actor Gemier once told me that Shaw had been so atrociously translated into French by his authorized translators, that his plays were seldom given in France, but that his loyalty to these translators was so great that it was impossible to have better versions made by other translators.

After I was married to Armina, I dropped a line to G.B.S. telling him we would be visiting my sister Gladys at Milan. He thereupon invited us to visit him and Mrs. Shaw at Stresa on Lake Maggiore.

About the middle of August we arrived at Stresa and put up at Shaw's hotel, the Regina Palace, an ornate buff-colored barracks-like structure overlooking the lake. G.B.S. had reserved our room for us, and greeted us on arrival.

"You must stay here for a few days," he said, and added, "but Americans are not very welcome here, on account of the Sacco-Vanzetti case."

It was the ironic fact that in Italy, where my brother-in-law in Milan a few days earlier had solemnly stopped me in a café from making a derogatory remark about Mussolini ("We call him Mr. Smith," he added), the populace was nevertheless in a state of tremendous tension over whether Sacco and Vanzetti would receive the death penalty. Perhaps this was because they were inured to injustice in their own country but could not bear to believe that the same thing could happen in democratic America.

After settling comfortably in our room for the night, we were awakened at what seemed to be an unearthly hour by a loud knocking at our door.

"Come along, wake up!" cried Shaw from outside. "It's seven o'clock, and if you want to come swimming with me, you'll have to hurry up! See you at breakfast!"

"Do you want to get up this early?" I remarked drowsily to Armina.

"Of course," she cried, leaping from her bed like a gazelle. "How often will you have an opportunity of swimming with G.B.S.?"

I was stumped. First of all, I don't swim very well—about fifty strokes, and I am winded. Secondly, it was blowing quite hard the night before, and I was sure the lake would be full of waves, which have an irritating habit of getting into my eyes, ears and mouth.

"Up you get," she cried, "you can't keep Shaw waiting for you!"

So I got up, protesting mildly, and down we went for breakfast. G.B.S. was waiting for us. It was his custom each morning to cross

the lake in a motorboat, then moor this boat off the estate of Albert
Coates, the conductor, swim for the shore and end up with a sun
bath on a grassy meadow which sloped down to the beach. We
boarded the motorboat dressed in our bathing suits, crossed over toward the other side of the lake, and at what seemed to me to be an
enormous distance from the shore, G.B.S. dived in off the side of the
boat. As his head and shoulders emerged from the lake and he shook
the water out of his white hair and beard, the sun caught his pink
cheeks and blue eyes, and he looked for all the world like Father
Neptune emerging from the waves.

"Come on in, it's fine!" he shouted.

Armina, like most California-bred girls, was somewhat of a mermaid,
and in she dived, showing off with a very effective scissors stroke. I
cautiously lowered myself down the side of the boat, looking nervously
at the shore which seemed to be miles away. I suppose the motorboat
will keep moving slowly behind us, I thought, throwing discretion to
the winds and timidly striking out in the direction of Father Neptune
and the Mermaid. I kept going for a while, as the waves waved wildly,
and the other swimmers swam rapidly ahead of me toward the shore.
I looked back to reassure myself that the motorboat was following me.
It was not. The Italian boatman had stopped his engine and was
settling down to a comfortable siesta. I was torn between the choice
of drowning or calling for help. I called for help. The motorboat
started up, G.B.S. and Armina swam back, and between the three of
them I was heaved out of the water and ignominiously ferried to the
shore. Some years later, when recounting this incident, G.B.S. remarked
that it was the greatest compliment ever paid him.

"Lawrence Langner," he said, with a twinkle in his eye, "followed
me to such an extent that when I jumped into Lake Maggiore, he
jumped in after me without being able to swim a stroke, evidently
thinking that my mere presence would save him from drowning."

Arrived at Villa Intragnola, the estate of Albert Coates, G.B.S. disappeared behind some convenient bushes and returned a few moments
later wearing what seemed to be an old pair of white underdrawers.
By this time a young lady had appeared on the scene. She was Sylvia
Ray, Mr. Coates' secretary, and she was in the habit of joining G.B.S.
for his morning sun baths. The three of us grouped ourselves appreciatively on the grass while Shaw expounded his views on one subject
and another.

Not unnaturally, since the aging philosopher was in a state of next
to nudity, the question of modesty came up for discussion, since the

Pope had recently forbidden all Italian women to enter churches in dresses without sleeves and skirts which did not cover the ankles.

"What on earth do priests know about morality!" Shaw asked impatiently. "The trouble with these men who try to adjudicate upon what is moral or immoral, is that they really know nothing about the subject. Any man who attempts to decide that one style of clothing is seductive while another style of clothing is not, must know something about the art of being seductive, and priests who rail about the theme of women's costumes are obviously the very last persons to be in a position to express an opinion on the subject. I remember in my young days when women dressed in accordance with the dictates of the clergy, they were literally swathed in clothing so that they resembled feather mattresses more than anything else, and I may add the women who wore these clothes looked considerably more seductive than the half-clad girls of today. There are really only two competent judges of what is seductive in women's clothing, and they are the women who make it their business to be seductive because they study it, and playwrights like myself, because it is our business to *know* what women must wear in order to be seductive."

He thought the clergy, and playwrights too, might turn their attention from women's clothes to an abuse of marriage which he noticed had been growing recently:

"That is, the selling of husbands by their wives to wealthy women who, in return for the husbands, paid handsome sums by way of damages for alienation of affection. This new trade in husbands is gaining considerable headway."

"Every afternoon," he informed me, "I go to Prince Paul Troubetzkoy's studio to sit for a statue of myself. It's very tiring but I have to do it."

"Why?" I asked.

"Well," he replied, "the Prince's wife died last spring, and he was very upset over her loss, so in order to get his mind off his troubles, I decided to commission him to make a statue of me, not that the statue isn't very good," he added. I was impressed by this example of G.B.S.'s personal kindness.

Later we met Prince Paul Troubetzkoy, a tall, distinguished Russian who seemed very sad and serious. He was an old friend of Shaw's, and had done a very fine head of him some twenty years earlier. The Prince dined with the Shaws and ourselves at the hotel. He was an ardent vegetarian, and joined Shaw in his choice of soup and greens.

Most vegetarians I have met have a habit of proselytizing and the Prince was no exception.

"If you are guest of my house," he said solemnly at dinner, in rounded Russian accents, "and you wish to eat lamb chops, I give you big knife and take you into garden and show you little lamb, and you can assassinate him!"

As I had no desire to assassinate a little lamb with a big knife, I was glad I was not a guest in his house. Still I felt I should defend my taste in lamb chops, so I ventured to remark that but for our habit of eating lambs, they would probably have no existence whatever, and I instanced the fact that up to the time of their deaths, domestic animals were fed, cared for and relieved of all anxiety by their owners, who even supplied them with mates in order that succeeding generations of lamb chops might be perpetuated.

"I violently object," said Shaw, "to being a procurer for domestic animals. But," he added, "unlike the Prince, I don't advocate vegetarianism for anyone but myself. You see, I'm really a sort of saint!"

"I tried vegetarianism, but had to give it up a long time ago," said Mrs. Shaw quietly to Armina. And then she whispered, "It's very bad for the teeth." I glanced sidewise in the direction of Mr. Shaw's teeth, but saw no evidence of any disastrous results. "Can anything about G.B.S. be false?" I asked myself, but I feared to carry the inquiry any further.

Prince Troubetzkoy invited us to his studio, not to partake of lamb chops, but to see the statue for which G.B.S. was posing, and one fine afternoon we accompanied him and Mrs. Shaw down the lake on a small steamboat to the little village where the Prince made his home. I brought my 16mm. movie camera along with me, and had a field day taking pictures of G.B.S. posing for his statue. Then I asked him and Mrs. Shaw to allow me to take a picture of them walking together, and they both kindly obliged. As they approached the camera, G.B.S. suddenly embraced Mrs. Shaw and kissed her. Mrs. Shaw, taken by surprise, remarked, "What on earth did you do that for?" "Don't you know that every movie ends up in a clinch!" was the reply. And thus I came into possession of the only picture extant of Mr. Shaw kissing his wife!

We took our departure soon after, but before leaving I asked G.B.S. whether I could not obtain a duplicate of the early Troubetzkoy bust to place in the lobby of the Guild Theatre.

"I have two already," was the reply, "but there's no sense in my giving you one, because in a year or so, if you go on producing my plays, you'll ultimately become bankrupt, the Guild Theatre will fall into the hands of the Shuberts, and my bust will be your only asset!" However, Mrs. Shaw said she thought something might be arranged.

A month or so later I heard from Mrs. Shaw in reply to a suggestion that we might consider purchasing the bust:

Now about the bust. You speak of purchasing—but, you know, at Stresa we had an idea of letting you have one of the two we had here! Of course, if there is any probability of the Theatre Guild *buying* it would not be right for us to come between Prince Troubetzkoy and a sale! If that was to come about you would have to write to him and ask him his price (Prince Paul Troubetzkoy, Villa Cabranca, Suna, Lago Maggiore, Italy). But the other idea is this: G.B.S. does not want to give the bust unconditionally to the Theatre Guild. He says (ironically) "you never know what will happen in the theatre—they may come to grips or . . . something may happen." I tell you what he suggests. He might lend the bust to *you,* and give you a free hand to do what you like with it; show it whom you like, or make what arrangements you think best: with the private arrangement between you and him that you put it up in the theatre as long as the theatre is in a satisfactory state. If it should ever happen that you wished to withdraw it from there—then you could arrange with us as to its future disposition: but you could have full power to withdraw it at any time, on your own private judgment.

The bust of Shaw arrived in due course and was placed in the lobby of the Guild Theatre. The bronze of the bust has since turned bright green, either out of deference to the Emerald Isle, or to show Shaw's passionate addiction to vegetables. The bust was originally made when Shaw's hair and beard were a flaming red, and great clouds of flame and smoke proceeded from his mouth as he expressed his explosive views to a startled Victorian world.

In November of 1928 I wrote G.B.S.:

Your statue looks very well indeed in the Guild Theatre lobby. Unfortunately, however, a vendor of cigarettes has placed his stand underneath it so that you look for all the world like the patron saint of nicotine. I think we shall have to hang a card around the neck of the statue bearing the words, "Mr. Shaw does not recommend these cigarettes."

Upon our leaving the Guild Theatre (the mortgage on which is now owned by the Shuberts as Shaw prophesied years before) we took the statue with us. It now ornaments the entrance hall of the Theatre Guild building, and is placed in front of the elevator; it wears an expression which suggests to the passer-by that it is healthier to walk upstairs than to ride. After G.B.S.'s death, I learned that he stated in his will that we might keep the statue, but since the Theatre Guild is not a "permanent" institution, upon our passing out of existence, the bust is to be given to the Metropolitan Museum in New York. Every time I pass it now, I say to myself, "Well, Shaw, we're still here!"

CHAPTER XVII

Art and the Prohibition Era

THE period of 1920–29, known as the Prohibition Era, had a marked effect on American arts and letters. It sent a pack of writers and painters from the right bank of the Hudson to the left bank of the Seine, from whence, after imbibing French literature and countless apéritifs and Scotch-and-sodas in Montmartre and elsewhere, they returned home and left their incisive marks on American literature and painting. The most distinguished of these was Ernest Hemingway and their ranks included F. Scott Fitzgerald, John Dos Passos, Glenway Westcott, Louis Bromfield, Harold Stearns and other children of the so-called "lost generation," a generation which I do not think was lost at all, but merely exiled in revolution against the revolting law of the land which attempted to decide what kind of liquid you might or might not pour into your own personal insides.

The possession of a bottle of good liquor in those days was an enormous achievement, and a good man often risked his life and eyesight when he accepted a drink from an unknown source. Poets have sung of the courage of the battlefields, but few have penned the courage displayed at New York cocktail parties in the twenties. I have seen strong men drink and turn white, and putting caution to one side, go on and drink and drink again, and later on suffer from hang-overs which have lasted literally for weeks. Yet grimly they drank, and the grimness of their drinking underlay the gaiety of these parties, so that while the pleasure seekers on the surface seemed intent only on having a good time, beneath the surface there was a solemn and couragous dedication to the cause of the Goddess of Liberty.

192

The slanderers of this era are forever harping on its superficiality, yet it will go down as one of the most fecund in the history of American art. It ushered in some of our best novelists, Sinclair Lewis, Sherwood Anderson, Ernest Hemingway, Joseph Hergesheimer, Carl Van Vechten, James Branch Cabell, Willa Cather, Ellen Glasgow, Louis Bromfield, Scott Fitzgerald; our best playwrights, Eugene O'Neill, Maxwell Anderson, Elmer Rice, Philip Barry, Robert Sherwood, S. N. Behrman; writers of comedy such as George Kaufmann, Marc Connelly, Charles MacArthur, Moss Hart; and the new prophets of modern music, Aaron Copland, Roy Harris; and in lighter vein, George Gershwin, Jerome Kern and Richard Rodgers.

One of the most fabulous characters of this period was the famous mural painter, Robert Chandler, known to his friends and the newspapermen as "Sheriff Bob," because in his youth he had been a sheriff of Dutchess County, New York. Bob was a man of Gargantuan stature and girth; at the time I knew him best, he had a crown of curly gray hair which surmounted his ruddy countenance, and his appearance suggested Pan, Bacchus, Falstaff and all the other symbols of lusty hedonism. His good friends Clemence Randolph and John Colton immortalized him in the character of Joe Horn in their play *Rain*, adapted from Somerset Maugham's short story. Joe Horn was the Rabelaisian trader who conducted his affairs from the bowels of an enormous armchair under the seat of which was stowed away a veritable vintner's supply of whisky and rum. Bob's home on East Nineteenth Street, off Gramercy Square, consisted of two houses connected together, as though a single house were too small to accommodate his gigantic proportions, and the two top floors made an enormous studio in which he painted his large murals, as well as his famous screens, found today in art galleries all over the country. On the floor below, the houses were divided into living and sleeping quarters which were alive with humanity in the raw, for Bob was always surrounded with friends who came from all walks of life. Here one met prize fighters, vaudevillians, painters, sculptors, members of the Social Register, writers, newspapermen, critics, actors, actresses and female impersonators, all mixed together like odd assortments in a salad—yet blended into a palatable whole by the dressing of Bob's inexhaustible hospitality.

Life with Bob and his entourage was a crazy pattern of humanity painted in staggering strokes on an enormous canvas reeking of bad alcohol. Bob had an unlimited supply of rotgut whisky which he obtained from a mysterious source, and as the whisky held out indefinitely, so did his friends. Fortunately, Bob was solicitous of those of us whose stomachs were more delicate than the ex-barflies who fluttered around his buffet, and out of consideration for us, he kept some bottles of excellent whisky under the enormous chair in which he was customarily seated, attired in a resplendent dressing gown and pajamas.

On my first visit to his apartment Bob took me upstairs to his huge studio around the walls of which were hung enormous murals, partly finished. Picking up a large paintbrush and a bucket of paint, he sketched in some details, holding the paintbrush with both hands as he worked. Everything Bob did was on a giant scale. Small things frustrated him, and after painting the huge ceiling of Grand Central Station, most things must have seemed small to him.

For all his great girth and monumental size, there was something very boyish, almost childlike, about Bob. He was simple and sincere, and hated the stuffiness of the New York society from which he had graduated. One day when I was alone with him, he told me the story of his marriage to the famous Italian opera singer, Lina Cavellieri, a woman whose beauty was legendary on the Continent of Europe. His marriage to her had been the occasion of his receiving the famous telegram "Who's loony now?" from one of his brothers, about whose own sanity there had been some considerable public doubt. The marriage turned out unhappily. "I really loved her," said Bob, "but I believe she had the evil eye, and it affected me!" But he denied vigorously that she had married him for his money. "All she got out of me was two hundred thousand dollars," said Bob, as though this was a mere nothing. The outcome of the marriage made him very unhappy. "I went to Bermuda," he told me, "to brood over my misadventure. One day as I sat on a bridge looking over the water, I saw a school of fish swimming below me. The flashing beauty of their form and coloration thrilled me, and I started painting again. I studied countless varieties of fish swimming in the clear tropical waters, and came back to New York and started to work on my screens."

With the passage of the years, Bob tired of his screens and murals, and tried portraits. The portraits were always interesting, but unfortunately did not look at all like the persons who were sitting for them. He loved the theatre and came to see many of our plays at the Theatre Guild. One of his favorites was Pirandello's *Right You Are If You Think You Are,* in which Armina played the part of the veiled wife. Bob painted her in her costume, and the portrait, I thought, was very successful, especially, since she wore a veil, it was impossible to tell whether or not it was a good likness. Later on, shaken with illness due to the inroads the life he led had made on his constitution, as well as disappointment over his failure to receive recognition as a portrait painter, he was taken to the hospital in Kingston, his life being despaired of. Armina and I were journeying to Woodstock when I learned of Bob's illness, so we visited the hospital. He seemed pitifully weak, but we tried to minimize his illness and in order to inspire some hope in him, I asked him if he would paint my portrait as soon as he was well, for which I felt I could afford to pay him the sum of $500. "No one has ever offered to pay me for a portrait before," said Bob cheerfully. "I'll get well and do it." And he kept his word. He rallied, returned to New York, painted my portrait, and then, a few weeks later, he died—a little happier, I hope, for having sold his first portrait.

Carl Van Vechten was another fabulous party giver of this period. He had just reached the pinnacle of his career as a novelist with the publication of *Nigger Heaven* in which for perhaps the first time, a white man who had the courage to learn to know Negroes as human beings, had also the courage to write about them as human beings, instead of lovable servants. He discovered the city of Harlem within the city of New York where it had been lost for generations, and introduced it lovingly to the people of America. Carl's influence led to an entire new literature on the subject of the Negro, to which white and Negro authors alike contributed, and made easier our task of producing such masterpieces as *Porgy* and *Porgy and Bess,* and the production of Negro plays by other producers. It is difficult for theatre goers of today to realize that, as Eugene O'Neill told me, during the presentation of his play, *All God's Chillun Got Wings,* the producers were constantly threatened by the police because miscegenation was dealt with in the play.

In the early twenties, very few white men met a Negro socially. The Negro was relegated to the place of shoeshiner, janitor, servant, ditchdigger or minstrel-show entertainer. To Carl's eternal honor, he was among the first to meet the Negro on terms of friendship, and he spread the gospel of his humanity among his friends. At his home I met on terms of complete equality some of the finest people I have known, both white and Negro. Outstanding among these was James Weldon Johnson who, with his wife Grace, became our friend. Johnson had the features and bearing of the most aristocratic of Americans, and would have been recognized as a leader of men anywhere in the world, except in certain parts of the South. Poet, writer, musician, and one-time American consul, James Weldon Johnson will always be remembered as a noble symbol of his race, and how it has enriched the cultural world from which it had been barred prior to this Prohibition Era on which so much contempt has been poured. Under the noteworthy leadership of James Weldon Johnson, the Negro race was surging toward its great contribution to American music, art and letters. His brother, Rosamond Johnson, was also one of our friends of this period, and a feature of our parties was the singing of Negro spirituals by Johnson and Taylor Gordon, which—believe it or not—was a novelty in those days, before the American Negro's contribution to folk music had been publicly recognized. Rosamond Johnson in his youth had been a member of the vaudeville team of Cole and Johnson, and he consulted me as to whether I thought he and Taylor Gordon singing spirituals would receive sufficient support to justify giving a concert of this kind of music. I advised him strongly to go ahead, and arranged for them to give a recital at the Garrick Theatre, the first of its kind, so far as I know.

Others I met at Carl's parties included Langston Hughes and Countee Cullen, both slight, sensitive and boyish, representing Negro poetry; Richmond Barthé, the sculptor; the attractive writer of Negro novels, Nella Larsen; the red-haired singer Nora Holt, half-Scotch, half-Negro, who was the toast of Paris and the Riviera, and Ethel Waters, who could sing a naughty song with the same inner purity that she gave to her spirituals; the urbane blond-haired Walter White, now Secretary of the National Association for the Advancement of Colored People, and a young actor and singer of prodigious proportions named Paul Robeson, whose Othello for the Theatre Guild, years later, was the most thrilling portrayal of this character I have ever witnessed.

Carl, at his parties, was always a striking figure; tall, pink-faced, with a mass of fluffy white hair like whipped cream atop a strawberry ice cream, and wearing a magnificent cerise and gold mandarin robe, he resembled the Dowager Empress of China gone slightly berserk, and he usually amused himself by going from guest to guest offering them refreshment while intermittently pinching Helen Westley who let out wild trumpetings of joy! Fania Marinoff, Carl's wife, who had enchanted New York audiences by her deft portrayal of Ariel in Winthrop Ames' magnificent production of The Tempest, was a petite, vivacious hostess who darted about amidst her guests like a tropical humming bird, and was even more gorgeously caparisoned.

As Armina and I had many of the same friends, the crowds at our own parties were not so different from those at Carl and Fania's, ex-

cept that we entertained more theatrical people, who were possibly
not quite as unrestrained as the others. One of the frequent visitors to
our parties and to Carl's and Fania's was the poetess Elinor Wylie,
tall, beautiful and ethereal, who invariably insisted at some time during the evening on hushing everyone up, and then reciting in ecstatic
tones Shelley's *"Ode to the West Wind,"* after which she would re-
sume her normal occupation of talking about herself. She often irritated me by her supreme egotism, and I remember on one occasion,
on being told at our home by Herbert Gorman, the novelist, that his
wife Jean typed his stories for him, Elinor turned to her husband
William Rose Benét, one of the most brilliant men of letters of our
time, and remarked, quite seriously, "Bill, I don't see why you don't
type *my* stories for *me!"* However, Elinor Wylie will be remembered
for her novels and poems long after people have forgotten that she
imagined she was the incarnation of Shelley, and if I was irritated because she was always talking to me about herself, you may be sure
that one reason for my irritation was probably because I wanted to
talk to her about *myself.*

In the early twenties, I moved from Greenwich Village to a formal
apartment house, The Wyoming, on Seventh Avenue near Carnegie
Hall. I did not care for living "uptown," however, and except for this
brief period of two years, I lived most of my life in the Village below
Fourteenth Street. At the Wyoming I met new friends, "uptown"
folks from all the professions, who were also friends of Carl and
Fania. Among them were Alfred and Blanche Knopf, the former one
of New York's most accomplished publishers, whose misfortune it was
to be constantly mistaken for me by irate actors who snubbed him,
only to realize later that his handsome Persian countenance was his
own, and not mine—while his wife, Blanche, who was a partner in his
business, retained a sylph-like beauty and an intelligence which grew
even keener as her form grew trimmer. Also at our parties, and at the
Van Vechtens', were the current literary crowd, often including Louis
Bromfield, looking like a literary Boy Scout, with his charming wide-
eyed wife, wide-eyed with admiration of her talented husband; Fanny
Hurst, statuesque, beautiful, whose classic brow seemed to conceal
some mysterious age-old wisdom; the bubbling Bill Bullitt, then respected as a novelist before he became an Ambassador; Rebecca West,
an odd mixture of beauty, unconventionality and respectability on her
frequent visits to the States; Horace Liveright and his literary henchman, T. R. Smith; Frank Adams (F.P.A.) quipping with the ele-
phantine Heywood Broun; brown-bearded Ernest Boyd and his French

wife Madeline; and red-bearded Joseph Wood Krutch and his French wife Marcelle; and occasionally the ebulliently youthful Scott Fitzgeralds. The theatre's contingent included Judith Anderson, looking intense and passionate; Constance Collier, both vague and incisive at the same time; Lenore Ulric, whose dark beauty was aggressively provoking; Marguerite D'Alvarez who specialized in aphorisms; and sometimes, though rarely, Kit Cornell, receiving the homage due her with a placid calm which contrasted with the nervous elegance of her husband Guthrie McClintic.

One of the most fascinating characters of the Prohibition Era was Horace Liveright, founder of the publishing firm of Boni and Liveright, who, during the turbulent twenties, was the most daring of the New York publishers, and speculated on the relatively unknown Theodore Dreiser and Eugene O'Neill and rode them through to success and popularity. Boni and Liveright owed its success to the intuitive hunches of Horace backed up by the sound literary judgment of his henchman T. R. Smith. They promoted the Modern Library and among their authors were Henrik Van Loon, Gertrude Atherton, Ernest Hemingway, Sherwood Anderson, Ludwig Lewisohn and Samuel Hopkins Adams, and they also nurtured the brilliant young publisher Bennett Cerf who later formed the successful firm of Random House. Liveright was a tall, handsome dark-eyed man with the persuasive powers of a Svengali and the forensic qualities and attractive appearance of a Sir Henry Irving. I was first introduced to him during the early days of the Washington Square Players by his brother Otto, who had obligingly played the part of the corpse in my one-act play *Licensed.* Horace had recently left the New York Stock Exchange, married the daughter of a prominent New York envelope manufacturer and entered with wholehearted enthusiasm into the manufacture of paper. He was romantic, enterprising and a devotee of the arts, and it was always my boast that I started him off in the role of publisher.

On the occasion of one of my frequent trips to Chicago I ran into him at the Blackstone Hotel and took him along with me to Maurice Browne's Little Theatre in the Fine Arts Building, where we witnessed the performance of a Greek play. Since the auditorium was so small in this miniature temple of the arts, even the rustling of programs detracted from the performance, so Maurice Browne hit upon the unique idea of having the programs printed on Japanese tissue paper so that they would not rustle and disturb the superesthetic actors. Horace was enthusiastic over the performance, and asked me to introduce him to Browne when the play was over. Maurice was flattered with Horace's highly complimentary remarks about the play and production, and his enthusiasm even included the programs. "And where," said Horace, "did you get this particular kind of tissue paper?" Browne informed him, and asked why he wanted to know. "I feel," said Horace, "that this would make an excellent brand of toilet paper."

Horace's next step in the direction of literature came a few months later when he called me on the phone and said, "Lawrence, I want you to take out a trade-mark on a new brand of toilet paper we are making. It's to be called 'The Pick-Quick Papers'!" A few weeks later, a sad-looking little Hungarian man appeared at my office carrying a large parcel. "I have been sent by Meester Horace Leeveright," he said with a strong Magyar accent. "He wants you should patent this new invention of mine, in which he is interested financially." He opened the parcel and revealed a monumental roll of toilet paper which was made of paper on one side and absorbent cotton on the other. "But," I remarked dubiously, "this will be extremely expensive." The little Hungarian shrugged his shoulders sadly. "Naturally," he said, "it is only for the rich." A week or so later Horace called me on the telephone in great excitement. "Lawrence," he said, "we want you to change that patent immediately." "Why?" I asked. "We find it better," he replied, "to use it for the tops of chocolate boxes!" You will find it being used for the tops of chocolate boxes to this very day.

A little later, Albert Boni with whom I had shared the Washington Square Book Shop, called at my office and asked my advice as to whether he should go into partnership with Horace Liveright in the book publishing business. "I strongly advise you against it, Albert," I said. "Horace is a wonderful promoter, and will bring a great deal of enthusiasm to the firm, but you will need a partner who can work fifteen hours a day, if necessary, reading manuscripts and making editorial decisions." A few days later Horace came to see me and asked my advice as to whether he should enter into a partnership in the publishing business with Albert Boni. "I strongly advise you against it, Horace," I said. "Albert is a wonderful promoter and will bring a great deal of enthusiasm to the firm, but you will need a partner who can work fifteen hours a day, if necessary, reading manuscripts and making editorial decisions." They immediately formed the firm of Boni and Liveright, and remained together as partners for barely six months, after which they quarreled violently. Albert left and started half-a-dozen other enterprises, while Horace went into partnership with T. R. Smith, a man of encyclopaedial knowledge and excellent editorial capacities, as well as editor of a collection of improper poems entitled

Poetica Erotica, which launched Horace in a field which seemed a logical extension of his experience as a paper manufacturer.

Horace had a flair for making literary personages, such as Eugene O'Neill and Theodore Dreiser, vividly exciting to the public. He had a habit of constantly asking my advice but never taking it, so when I tried to deter him from entering the theatrical world, he responded by producing such successful plays as *The Firebrand* and *Dracula.* With his untimely death, New York became a more sober but less exciting place to live in.

Early in 1924 the circles in which I moved were struck dumb by the work of a group of dancers just arrived from France. On the stage of the Neighborhood Playhouse, they danced indifferently well, but on a signal from their leader, a dark-complected mystic with piercing black eyes named Gurdjieff, they stopped dead like statues in whatever position they happened to be. My interest in the group was not in how well they danced, but how well they stopped. Gurdjieff's first appearance with his group of dancers was not at all what the New York audience expected to see. He was called a mystic, a "monument to human thinking and creativity" and this was a performance of students of movement combined with mental exercises and set in ancient ritual diagrams to the music of ancient monasteries. His famous "stop" exercise was what excited the audiences who watched ignorantly but avidly. When the "Stop" signal sounded from the wings each dancer stopped in the exact angle in which he found himself while his mind remained alert for the next facet of thought. Gurdjieff claimed this control was taught by his system of living (since referred to as "The Movement") of which Ouspensky was the custodian in England, while the late A. R. Orage, once the brilliant editor of *The New Age,* was entrusted with the task of making American converts. Courtney Lemon, our playreader, was friendly with Gurdjieff and suggested that if I happened to be in Fontainebleau, the headquarters of The Movement, I might enjoy meeting him.

In the spring of 1922, at a time when my marriage with Estelle was breaking up, I was working on a play at Montreux and decided to finish it at Fontainebleau. For relaxation I paid a visit to the attractive historical mansion in which dwelt Gurdjieff and his disciples, where, I was told later, Katherine Mansfield had died.

On my ringing the old-fashioned bellpull, a lady with a Russian accent half-opened the door in a high wall and after regarding me suspiciously, let me in when I uttered the magic name of Courtney

Lemon. "You can see M. Gurdjieff," she said, "but I must warn you he had an automobile accident last month, and has been in a trance for twenty-three days." "How is he now?" I asked, thinking how incongruous it was for the leader of a new religion to have an automobile accident, just like a common or garden variety of mortal.

Her reply set my mind at rest. "He is still in a trance," she said, "but his mind is so sharp, he can see people and work just the same. At the present moment he is building a Turkish bath in the garden." And she conducted me to where the prophet was seated, giving instructions in bad French to a group of obvious Greenwich Villagers of the long-haired men and short-haired women variety. Gurdjieff, appearing none the worse for his accident, looked handsome and intelligent in his simple workman's clothes. He courteously asked me to sit beside him, clapped his hands and ordered black coffee, and then I watched the builders. They were nailing planks to a wall. A girl stood on a chair, a youth held the plank in position, another youth held the nails, another girl held the hammer, and still another youth held the chair. The girl with the hammer handed it to the girl on the chair, who drove the nail in the plank. I noted all this carefully, for never in my life had I seen so many people engaged in one simple operation.

Gurdjieff explained that these amateur carpenters were would-be poets, actors and others who never used their hands, and that this work cured them of the neurotic ailments from which they suffered. He asked me questions about mutual friends in the United States, and then, greatly to my surprise, attempted to interest me in a project to carry out his teachings by opening a hotel or establishment in the South of France. He then showed me over his Temple, a strikingly designed building, the roof of which was suspended from high posts while the floor was covered with furs and rugs. I was invited to stay for dinner, a meal which was served to me sitting alone in solitary magnificence in a huge dining room, at a mahogany table which might easily have seated fifty people. After dinner, the prophet conducted me to the Temple to listen to some music which he had composed. It was almost dark when we entered the building and we mounted a large dais on one side of which was a couch, while all over the floor sat men and women who, after Gurdjieff motioned me to be seated, gazed up at him with adoring admiration. As Gurdjieff clapped his hands for cups of fragrant Turkish coffee, and the organ began playing mysterious strains in the Greek scale which might have been composed by Debussy had he decided to write gypsy music, the waves of adoration which were directed by the listening audience to Gurdjieff seeped over to me, sitting on the couch at his side. Looking over the heads of the men and women turned upwards in postures of worship, I started to feel that I too might become a prophet, if only by contiguity. I, too, began to pass into a trance, and to dream of Temples spread all over America, with myself as a sort of minor Mystic of the Movement, the import of which I did not clearly understand, but felt vaguely was to turn neurotics into normal people and normal people into neurotics. I was rudely awakened from my trance, however, by the voice of Mr. Gurdjieff bidding me goodnight and asking me to come again. The cool night air washed all the dreams out of my brain, and as I walked home to my hotel, I marvelled at the unplumbed depths of the human soul and its unceasing search for spiritual truth. Many of my friends, whose intelligence I respect, belong to the Movement, and I hear that its following continues to grow, but I fear that I am not the stuff of which Prophets are made, although for a moment I felt myself potentially one for all the wrong reasons.

One of the towns where we lived in France was Hendaye, on the Bay of Biscay, with a beach that seemed a hundred miles long, and a low stone wall over which one could see the gardens of Pierre Loti. Another was Antibes, where I have many recollections of a life that is no more; the Philip Barrys with their villa at Cannes; the Charles Bracketts and Gerald Murphys at Cap d'Antibes; the Hotel du Cap, where Dwight Wiman and his wife Steve gave elaborate parties; and the small bathing beach on which, in the mornings around eleven, one could see (if one wanted to) the elderly Elsie de Wolfe taking her exercises, after which she went swimming, wearing a large picture hat and a veil!

Here I met again my uncle Leopold Orsay of Paris and Buenos Aires, whose example had caused me to leave England and seek my fortune in the States. He now lived in retirement near Nice and told me that the greatest mistake he had made in his life was to realize his childhood dream, and lead a life of idleness on the Riviera. "Take my advice," he said. "Don't ever retire. I have nothing to do now but take a daily promenade, drink cognac and argue with my family." His words made a strong impression on me, and I decided to continue to work as long as I was able, and to enjoy such leisure as I could obtain, as an accompaniment to living, instead of as an anticlimax.

Another "character" I met during the period of boom prosperity was the famous astrologer Evangeline Adams, a pleasant-faced, plebeian-looking little old lady who dispensed forecasts of the future on a wholesale basis, and conducted a business which netted her an enormous income from the speculative Stock Exchange gamblers who thrived in that crazy era. Soon after meeting the illustrious Evangeline, who invited me out to her country place, I decided, for the fun of it, to consult her upon my own future. Estelle had just sailed to Europe, and it was no surprise when the lady astrologer, after making a number of mathematical calculations which could have made sense only to a lunatic, informed me that Estelle would meet a man on the steamship with whom she would fall in love. Estelle did exactly as was prophesied, and on my arrival in Europe it was decided between us amicably that we should divorce, and that in order to do so expeditiously, I should take an apartment in Paris, so as to be able to avail ourselves of the provisions of the French divorce laws. The divorce with its comic accompaniment of notaires, reconciliation proceedings, and other peculiarities of French justice, was finally granted. Estelle married her handsome Englishman, and like the princess in the fairy tale, has lived happily ever after. I returned to the United States determined never to marry again.

Fate decided otherwise. Some years previously, André Fontaine of Camp Airey fame, had sent an attractive young actress named Armina Marshall who was looking for a job, to see me at my office on William Street. She walked into my room just before lunch, and I retain a vivid impression of her smiling brown eyes set wide apart over high cheekbones, and of her open honest face, warm with friendliness, yet bashful to the point of extreme shyness, something which she soon overcame. Later on I was to learn that this honesty and friendliness was the key to her character, and that her modesty concealed her very considerable talents as an actress, writer, teacher and organizer. She handed me a letter from André Fontaine praising her work on a play she had produced at Roslyn, and she apologized for taking up my time. I told her to see Theresa Helburn and on the back of André's letter of introduction to me, I wrote a note to Terry. "This is Miss Marshall. Will you please do what you can for her?"

The Guild was casting Paul Claudel's *The Tidings Brought to Mary* at the time, and Armina had learned that the famous Russian director Kommisarjevsky was looking for six tall, dark-haired girls to play the parts of nuns. She took my note to Theresa Helburn who asked her to come the following week, when the final selection of the six nuns would be made. On the fateful day, Armina arrived with about twenty other tall brunettes who were ushered into the small casting office at the Garrick Theatre. Terry Helburn, rounded and fuzzy-haired, followed by a frighteningly tall secretary, entered the room and looked appraisingly at the anxious girls. "Will the young lady Mr. Moeller sent kindly step to one side? Thank you." The young lady separated herself from the others. "And now, the young lady sent by Mr. Simonson?" said Theresa. This particular young lady stepped over to the first girl selected, making a smaller group to one side. "And now, the young lady I sent. Ah, yes! Excellent! Please join the others. And now the young lady sent by Mr. Wertheim. Step over please. And the young lady sent by Miss Helen Westley—" Two handsome brunettes stepped forward. "Please, we're twins!" "Oh, how nice," said Miss Helburn, sweetly. "Now, you other girls, I'm sorry, but the parts are all filled. Come back another time and I hope we'll have something for you." As she started to leave, Armina, taking her courage in both hands, said, "But Miss Helburn, I'm the young lady Mr. Langner sent." "Oh, are you?" Terry replied. "Well step over, too; I guess we'll have eight nuns instead of six."

On the slender thread of this incident which led to Armina being engaged by the Guild, hung one of the most important chapters of my life. She played several parts with the Guild, and as these grew larger and larger, they brought her more prominently to my attention, until her engagement with the Guild included me as well. After we were married, she acted only intermittently, but her excitement and interest in all my theatre work has always equaled my own. She has collaborated with me in the writing of plays, and in productions at the Guild and at Westport. Later on Eugene O'Neill became devoted to her, and she served as Associate Producer of *The Iceman Cometh* and *Moon for the Misbegotten;* she also became the Producer of "Theatre Guild on the Air," our radio theatre program, which, under her guidance, has achieved a listening public of many millions.

Our engagement was partly responsible for the little musical revue, the first of its kind, known as *The Garrick Gaieties*. Armina was one of the younger actors appearing in Guild plays who organized themselves into a junior group under the encouragement of Terry Helburn, who always had a warm spot in her heart for the younger generation and did her best to help them. This group included such talented players as Romney Brent, Philip Loeb, Edith Meisner, Sterling Holloway, Betty Starbuck and June Cochran.

It was the practice of this group to rehearse experimental plays on the Garrick stage at night after the regular play was over and to show their plays when ready to the Guild Board. One of these was *Fata Morgana* which we afterward produced. During the summer of 1923 many of the members of the group, including Armina, came to visit me at a house I had rented from Max Eastman on Mount Airey at Croton-on-the-Hudson. Dudley Field Malone and his wife, Doris Stevens, lived on the opposite side of the road, and on Sunday evenings our visitors would entertain us with "stunt" parties, each doing little sketches or songs which displayed their particular talents for the particular edification of Dudley, Doris and myself. About the same time, Paul Moss, who later became Commissioner of Licenses for New York City, and his friend Ben Kaye, who practiced law and wrote plays, proposed to Theresa Helburn that they give some Sunday night performances of sketches and songs for charity, using the younger group of actors as the performers, and they introduced to Terry a young composer named Richard Rodgers and a young song writer named Lorenz Hart, who had been writing musical shows for Columbia University. Young Rodgers had been trying to make up his mind whether to accept a position in the women's underwear business, in which a brilliant future was said to await him, beginning at a secure salary of fifty dollars a week, or whether to take a chance on starving in an attic as a musical composer. Dick hesitated, then decided that once the revue was placed on a business basis, he would gamble on his music.

Thus, using the young actors and actresses who performed at my home, and the brilliant talents of Rodgers and Hart, with sketches by Ben Kaye and others, there was produced the first *Garrick Gaieties,* a youthful revue in which the young actors kidded their elders mirthfully, while such tuneful melodies as "Manhattan" and "Mountain Greenery" announced to the world that in Richard Rodgers and Lorenz Hart a new musical team of major importance had been discovered.

After Armina and I were married, my life was no longer my life, but rather "our" life, since we worked so closely together in the theatre. Armina was born in Oklahoma, and was the daughter of Chalmers Marshall, a picturesque Western pioneer who as a youth drove a stagecoach through Kansas, and later became a federal marshal in the Indian Territory. After running in the opening of the Cherokee Strip, he became sheriff of Pawnee County, Oklahoma. There, in the town of Pawnee, Armina lived as a child, next to the jail where her father kept his prisoners. Armina's father often went in pursuit of bank robbers, and his career included an affray with a famous bandit, Tom Jordan, in the town of Keystone, where the sheriff killed the outlaw in a shooting duel while he was in the act of robbing the local bank. This killing broke the sheriff's long record for bringing home his quarry alive, and so preyed on Chal Marshall that he left the State of Okla-homa and moved his family to the Pacific coast.

Armina's first step toward the theatre was to qualify as a teacher of English and Drama under the California state school system, and she attended the University of California, Los Angeles Branch, and later took summer courses in drama at Berkeley. Then she returned to the Imperial Valley and was appointed schoolmistress in a remote spot at the edge of a lonely desert, to which she rode weekly on a white horse for eighteen miles over the flat desert from her home to the solitary one-room schoolhouse. Here for two years she taught eleven nonde-script children of all ages, grades and races, who had, she found, but one attribute in common, an unholy desire to make things as difficult as possible for her. Out of this pioneering life came that forming of character which produced the determination which is one of Armina's most marked characteristics. When she finally saved enough for her tuition at the American Academy of Dramatic Arts in New York, she announced her intention of leaving California to her father and mother, who resolutely forbade her to do so. Young as she was, she overcame all opposition with the ruthlessness of a bulldozer demolish-ing a stone wall. Accompanied by a girl friend, Jeanne LaGue (who later married the actor, Philip Loeb), she entrained for New York with her father's final admonition ringing in her ears, "Whatever you do, beware of those wicked New York theatrical managers," and to that warning against the predatory behavior of New York theatre managers, I owe my wife. For who could resist a girl who remarked grimly, when, after an evening of dancing, I first kissed her good night in a taxicab, "Is that necessary, Mr. Langner?"

I decided as I went home that night that it was not necessary. I further reaffirmed my decision never to marry again—though nobody had suggested that I should. I sat down at a table with an exercise book and wrote out twenty reasons why I should not marry again, all of them compellingly convincing. And to nail the whole thing down, I consulted the famous Jungian psychiatrist, Dr. Beatrice Hinkle, who agreed with me that I was not the marrying type, and that as a writer I should put my art first and marriage second.

"What a wonderful thing psychiatry is," I thought, as I left my last consultation with the clear resolution to remain a bachelor for the rest of my natural life. Three months later, I married Armina. I was puz-zled to know why Dr. Hinkle was so pleased to learn the news. "I knew if I advised against it, you'd be for it." She laughed her merry laugh, which began in her eyes and spread over her entire body. And she is still laughing.

After Armina and I were married, we set sail for Europe, our destination being Italy where we planned to tour before going to London to visit my mother, and to pick up my daughter Phyllis with whom we planned to spend the summer at Annecy, in Haute Savoie. Just before sailing, my lawyer drew my attention to the fact that I had married Armina during the period when I was prohibited from doing so under my French divorce decree. "All you need to do is to remarry again after July 15th," was my lawyer's advice, "but keep it quiet so as to avoid any publicity." So off we sailed for Naples, blissfully figuring that we would casually drop into a magistrate's office and remarry. Our tour took us to Rome, where we visited the theatre which was the home of Luigi Pirandello, the greatest of all Italian playwrights, and we saw a production of *The Chief Thing* by Evreinoff which so intrigued us that a few years later the Guild produced it in New York, where it was a resounding failure!

As we entered the theatre, Pirandello, a short man with a high forehead and pointed features, a beard which was even more pointed, and a sweet smile, stood at the box office to welcome us. He told us that he was indebted to Mussolini who had set him up in this theatre where he produced both his own plays and the plays of foreign authors. I had been particularly pleased to learn that my one-act play on the subject of free love and marriage, *Another Way Out,* had been translated into Italian by Louis Howe, and had been successfully presented by Pirandello in this theatre; this, however, without affecting the Italian marriage customs to any appreciable extent. After the Evreinoff play was over, we discussed with him our contemplated production of *Right You Are If You Think You Are,* and we asked if we might produce some of his other plays, to which he was agreeable.

Some years later, Pirandello visited us at our country home near Westport, at the time when we were producing *If This Be Treason,* by our good friend the Reverend John Haynes Holmes, in which Armina played the part of the wife—this time the President's wife. The play dealt with war between the United States and Japan, which was easily averted on the stage by our President, played by McKay Morris, flying over to Japan, and having a nice cozy talk with the Son of Heaven, as a result of which the war was called off. Pirandello was incensed by the idea of this play. "The Japanese are insects and must be exterminated like insects," he remarked to me after the play was over. His words returned to my memory many times afterward, first when Japan joined the Axis and later, when, during the war, as Secretary of the National Inventors Council, I hunted ceaselessly for some kind of insect powder to be sprinkled over them.

While in Rome I decided to make inquiries as to our remarriage. I appeared at the License Bureau and was told that under the Italian law, I would have to produce Armina's parents' consent to the marriage. This was decidedly awkward since they were living over six thousand miles away in the Imperial Valley, California, fondly imagining that their daughter was legally married to me in the first place. There was no use attempting to remarry in Italy under these circumstances.

I found later on that in France, too, the question of domicile was paramount, and there was no casual method by which strangers could be married informally. We decided to visit Geneva, only a few miles away, and to investigate the situation in Switzerland. Driving up to the Mayor's official habitat, I left Armina and my daughter Phyllis outside in our car and went in to discuss the conditions under which foreigners could marry in that country. Here I found matters far worse. According to the stolid Swiss official, not only must I produce my French divorce papers; I must also have a long domicile and Armina's parents' consent into the bargain, as well as an agreement on her "dowry." I returned to the car despondent. The difficulty of getting married again was becoming a nightmare. We had now tried three different countries, to no avail. Having written so many plays attacking marriage, was marriage catching up with me and revenging itself? I decided our best bet was to return to London, stay there long enough for our domicile, and then get married. There my old friend George Taylor advised me to marry in a Registry office in the heart of London, rather than in a small village, if we wished to avoid publicity; so betaking ourselves to Covent Garden and driving through mountains of vegetables and fruit baskets, we arrived at the Registry Office on Henrietta Street at opening time. The charwomen were scrubbing the ancient floors and regarded us suspiciously; and in the presence of the sleepy-eyed Registrar and George Taylor as our witness, we were duly remarried. On our return to New York we were met at the docks by the reporters, and congratulated ourselves that our second marriage had not been detected by the papers. The next morning our pictures appeared in the *Daily News* over the caption "New York Theatrical Producer Marries Same Wife Twice!"

We settled down to housekeeping in a house I owned with Arthur Garfield Hays at 47 West Twelfth Street. This house we purchased together some years before, intending to divide it into two duplex apartments, one for each of our families, but as our first marriages both culminated in divorces, we somewhat cynically nicknamed the place "Divorce Villa." Here Armina and I lived quite happily in a strange community. On the top floor lived Herbert Gorman industriously writing novels; on the floor below, Robert Keith, a promising young actor of the time, industriously studying parts for plays; on the first and second floors, ourselves, while the basement apartment was occupied by Peter Arno, the *New Yorker* artist who made sleep impossible for us all by giving parties night after night for members of *The Garrick Gaieties,* and playing their songs on his piano, which was horribly out of tune, until, driven almost distracted, we complained; after which he adopted the simple expedient of inviting us to his parties, so that from then on we had to hold our peace.

To add to the excitement of living, one of my plays went into rehearsal at this time. I called it *A Fine Suburban Lot* but my manager shortened it to *Henry Behave,* a title to which I reluctantly assented, and have ever since looked back upon with a feeling of shame. It opened with Gladys Robertson, now a successful painter, in the feminine lead, while her husband, Edward G. Robinson, supported her in a minor role; also appearing on the professional stage for the first time was Pat O'Brien, later to become a noted Hollywood star. Unfortunately, the minor roles were better cast than the major, and the play catapulted itself to critical disaster on its opening night, August 23, 1926. On leaving the theatre my wife was taken to the hospital, not, she assured me, on account of the play, but because a baby was clearly on its way. The obstetrician, who was at the theatre for the opening, informed me the next day that I was the father of a nine-and-a-half-pound son, and that in his view, Armina's production was far better than my own.

During this period I was continuously writing plays, and three of them were produced in New York. My first was a musical comedy which was given the title *Tangerine* by its producer, Carl Carlton, a former band leader, the reason being that he had an earlier successful play called *Irene,* and he was superstitious enough to believe this title, which he pronounced "Tange-Irene," might bring him similar luck. The idea of the play arose out of a conversation I had with William H. Davis, the well-known patent lawyer who later became head of the War Labor Board. We agreed that if women had to support their husbands, the men would soon develop all the so-called "feminine" vices, while the women would be far more successful in the men's jobs and probably have a much better time of it. I recounted the idea to Phil Bartholomae, a writer of musical plays. He was very enthusiastic about it. We worked well as collaborators by the simple expedient of never meeting each other, but working according to a system which I recommend to all collaborators. I wrote the first draft of the play. I then sent it to him. He wrote the second draft and returned it to me, whereupon I wrote the third draft. In this way, by the time we arrived at the fourth draft, we had a fairly good musical comedy on the subject of feminism. The play was put into rehearsal while I was in Europe in 1922, with Vivienne Segal in the lead. By the time I returned to the States, the play had already opened out of town, had closed as a failure, and the scenery by Lee Simonson had been sent to the storehouse.

Carl Carlton, however, was not the man to go down under defeat. He decided still another collaborator was needed, and he called in Guy Bolton, another well-known writer of musical plays. Being an astute man, as well as a good band leader, Carlton decided on using strategy. He told me that Bolton could not possibly rewrite the play, and that I should write my own new version; and he told Bartholomae and Bolton the same story. As a result, I made one version, Bartholomae made another, and Bolton a third; Carlton then pieced all the best material from the three versions together, and opened the play in New York with Julia Sanderson, Frank Crummit and Jack Hassard, all very successful artists in the musical theatre.

Tangerine was a great success and ran for two years on Broadway at the Casino Theatre, and Julia Sanderson and Frank Crummit played together so well that they finally married, and were an ornament to the theatre and radio for a round decade when they left *Tangerine* after an additional year's run on the road. I was especially grateful to Frank Crummit, for he brought to the musical a song of his own entitled "Sweet Lady," which was played on the dance floors for years, and helped immeasurably in putting over the play.

CHAPTER XVIII

The Guild Theatre
and the Acting Company

DURING the third year of our occupancy of the Garrick Theatre, I and other Guild members became acutely aware of the necessity for a permanent home for the Theatre Guild. Alas, I was also acutely unaware, at the time, of the troubles which lie ahead for those who seek to enshrine an ideal into a building —and especially in our own case the ideal of an Acting Company which we had not yet been successful in embodying in our own work.

I had been raised on the theory that the only kind of art theatre worthy of the name was one in which the actors appeared in a repertoire of plays, as was the case with the Moscow Art Theatre, so that the actors did not become stale through playing the same part every night, and also had the opportunity of playing widely diversified roles.[1]

As the Guild Theatre was dedicated to repertory, in order that there might be plenty of room for a number of different productions, the stage of the theatre was made so large that there was hardly enough space left for the actors' dressing rooms, and certainly not enough room for the audience, for we made the ghastly mistake of providing a theatre with all the stage space necessary for a repertory of plays without enough seating capacity to provide the income needed to support the repertory. Blame this on our inexperience, but suffice it to say that we had plenty of room for the scenery, but not nearly enough for the actors and audience.

---

[1] Eva Le Gallienne made a number of gallant attempts to operate this kind of dramatic theatre in New York, but despite the artistic advantages from the acting point of view, the difficulties and expenses have been so great that no repertory company in New York has lasted over the years.

211

In March, 1922, when we celebrated our fourth birthday, we announced our plans for building the Guild Theatre. It received the hearty acclaim of our friends and supporters, and everybody proceeded to work with the greatest enthusiasm on raising the money to build. Along with Maurice Wertheim, I was strongly opposed to asking for private subsidy, and we raised over a half million dollars by the sale to the theatre-going public of Second Mortgage bonds at a high rate of interest, and every penny of interest due on these bonds was ultimately paid, notwithstanding the real estate slump caused by the depression which wiped out the Second Mortgage bonds on all the other New York theatres, and eventually cost the kindly bondholders a considerable part of their equities in the Guild Theatre Bonds. Thus the generosity of our friends, as well as the depression which took place later, resulted in our unwittingly handicapping our fortunes early in our career; and if we succeeded in maintaining the artistic standards we set for ourselves in starting in the theatre, it was in spite of the burden of the Guild Theatre rather than because of any help it rendered to us. There was a value in having a home, however, no matter how much of a misfit it turned out to be, and I firmly believe this home kept us together in the same way that a Southern family is kept together in an ancestral mansion from which it is too poor to move elsewhere. Nevertheless, I write down the Guild Theatre today as one of our greatest failures. At the time of its opening, however, the enthusiasm for its possibilities was tremendous, and since we were not possessed of a crystal ball into which we could gaze into the future, my colleagues and I enjoyed the genuine pleasure of seeing before our eyes a magnificent building planned for our own kind of theatre, and in which we hoped that all our dreams were to be realized. The American National Theatre and Academy (ANTA) has now taken it over, and are operating it on a tax-free basis with subsidies and concessions from all the unions, which will make their burden far less than ours; and I wish them better luck with the building than we had.

As the theatre began to reach completion and took shape in a pseudo-Italian style of architecture which was fashionable at the time, we decided to ask Bernard Shaw to open the theatre, and Maurice Wertheim invited him to stay at his estate, which I described as "one of the most beautiful places near New York." I approached him while I was in London, but he refused. I thought Mrs. Shaw might be more amenable so I wrote her as beguilingly as I could, but my blandishments were of no avail. I received a picture post card from Madeira showing a chromo of Reid's Palace Hotel, and the following in Shaw's neat handwriting on the back:

January 25, 1925

This also is one of the most beautiful places near New York: flowers, sunshine, bathing, and no theatres to open. I have written to Mr. Wertheim to acknowledge his very handsome invitation. I may be the means of shutting the new theatre some day; but as to opening it, I leave that to the President: it is his job, not mine. We expect to be here until the middle of February.

In due course President Coolidge opened the Guild Theatre by pushing an electric button in Washington, and, blessed in this way by the Apostle of Taciturnity, our new theatre opened with Shaw's brilliant comedy, *Caesar and Cleopatra,* in which Helen Hayes and Lionel Atwill played the title roles, while Philip Moeller directed the play.

The year before, in order to raise money to purchase two beautiful tapestries to decorate the walls of the theatre, we gave a subscription ball at the Hotel Commodore which we called "The Tapestry Ball." Our efforts were successful, and on the opening of the new theatre, the tapestries were hanging on the walls of the auditorium.

The opening night was a brilliant affair, and the first play, under other circumstances, would have merited high praise, for Helen Hayes was delightful as the child Cleopatra, Atwill was satisfyingly romantic as Caesar and Helen Westley incredibly magnificent in the role of Ftatateeta. But the critics, who had been our good friends up to this point, after noting the palatial appointments of our new home, began to fear that our new theatre would go to our heads; and Alexander Woollcott coined the phrase, apropos of the tapestries hanging in the auditorium, "The Gobelins will get you if you don't watch out!"

In discussing the play later with G.B.S. he remarked that the best Caesar was Forbes-Robertson, who had opened the Shubert Theatre with the same play. "Unfortunately," said G.B.S., "I gave Forbes-Robertson the business of eating dates during an important scene, not knowing that he had false teeth. On the opening night his teeth stuck together, so that he became speechless, and had to rush off stage to take them out, and replace them again."

After *Caesar and Cleopatra* we tried again with another Shaw play, this time *Arms and the Man* in which Alfred Lunt played Bluntschli and Lynn Fontanne played Raina. The play was a great success and was later moved to the Garrick. Apropos of this play, Alfred told me he always liked to find a place in a part where, at one brief moment, he could make the audience feel sorry for him. Alfred said the point came in Act I of *Arms and the Man* where he was almost dead from fatigue, on his first entrance; and he certainly made the most of it. His Bluntschli was probably the finest this generation will see; the same part was originally played by Mansfield, and I doubt if it was played better. I have my acting heroes, and Alfred heads the list.

Since by this time we were comfortably established in the Guild Theatre, one may wonder what had become of our ideas about repertory. The question which puzzled us all was how a system of repertory, in which the plays were changed nightly, could be made compatible with our subscription system, for which we then had over twenty thousand subscribers requiring six weeks of playing time for each play to take care of their seating. I suggested a plan which I termed "The Alternating Repertory System" which was a compromise between repertory as understood by the Moscow Art Theatre, for example, and our own system of long runs. This plan of modified repertory consisted in producing a play for a week, and then using the same actors in a second play for the second week, then back to the first play, and so on.

This Alternating Repertory System was adopted in the Guild season of 1926–27, and gave us the following advantages: The actors played a different part each week, so they did not become stale; it lengthened the run of a weak play, since the box office was open for two weeks in point of time to sell seats for each playing week of the play; good actors were willing to play in smaller parts one week, if they appeared in larger parts the following week; the labor costs were reduced as compared with the cost of ordinary repertory; the best actors were not tied down to a single play, but were used in two or more plays; and when the plays were sent on tour under this system, railroad fares were reduced as each company played two or three plays, and stayed longer in each town.

Our first problem was to establish our Acting Company. Starting with Helen Westley as the original nucleus, the Theatre Guild Acting Company included Alfred Lunt, Lynn Fontanne, Dudley Digges, Henry Travers and Ernest Cossart; to these were added later Claire Eames, Margalo Gillmore, George Gaul, Glenn Anders, Earle Larimore, Tom Powers, Edward G. Robinson, Claude Rains, Edgar Stehli, Erskine Sanford, Philip Loeb and others. All were fine artists and most of them have since risen to positions of the highest eminence in the theatre or motion pictures. Indeed, to engage such an acting company today would cost at their present salaries at least $35,000 per week, something no management could possibly afford!

While I was in London in 1925, I saw a delightful comedy named *At Mrs. Beam's* by C. K. Munro, in which the talented actress Jean Cadell played the amusing landlady. We brought her over from England, and Alfred and Lynn delighted our audiences with a series of fireworks ending in an informal tussle on the floor which began, so to speak, a career of affectionate duels which the Lunts, in one form or another, are still continuing on the stage.

Our Acting Company opened the season of 1926–27 with the play *Juarez and Maximilian* which had been sent to us by its author, Franz Werfel, following our production of his *Goat Song*.[2] During rehearsals, our play seemed headed for a long run, the final run-through of the play without scenery and costumes being so moving that all of us who witnessed the rehearsal were dissolved in tears. A curious thing happened, however, when the full dress rehearsal took place in the scenery and costumes. Whether this was due to the height of the scenery, which tended to dwarf the actors, or because the uniforms and costumes seemed to make a wall between the emotions of their wearers and the audience, I do not know, but the fact remains that the play was no longer the touching experience that it was during rehearsals, and while it received considerable artistic acclaim, it was written down as a distinguished failure.

Since *Juarez and Maximilian* could not serve as a basis for our Alternating Repertory System, we immediately put Shaw's *Pygmalion* into production with Lynn Fontanne in the part of Eliza Doolittle. She was superb in the role, looking the living image of Hogarth's impish "The Shrimp Girl" which hangs in the National Gallery in London. *Pygmalion* was immensely popular, and we were now ready to put our shiny new plan into operation. Having separated Alfred from Lynn, we put Alfred in rehearsal with Claire Eames in *Ned McCobb's Daughter,* an amusing play about bootleggers from the pen of Sidney Howard, and we opened this in the John Golden Theatre, which we rented in order to carry out our plan. We now had two plays running which employed all the members of our Acting Company—*Pygmalion* at the Guild Theatre and *Ned McCobb's Daughter* at the John Golden Theatre.

---

[2] In *Juarez and Maximilian* translated by Ruth Langner, Alfred Lunt played the sensitive Austrian Archduke Maximilian; Edward G. Robinson played Porfirio Diaz, and Claire Eames the Empress Charlotte; Margalo Gillmore was the Princess Salm, while Arnold Daly played the Marshal of France and Dudley Digges the Archbishop Labastida. Also included were a number of youngsters who were later on to make their mark in the theatre: Cheryl Crawford, Harold Clurman, Sanford Meisner and Morris Carnovsky.

Dizzy as it sounds, our next step was to produce two plays which could alternate with *Pygmalion* and with *Ned McCobb's Daughter*. We were able to do this by engaging Laura Hope Crews, and adding her to our Acting Company in another magnificent play by Sidney Howard, *The Silver Cord* which title has since become part of the American language. We were able to play both *The Silver Cord* and *Ned McCobb's Daughter* at the John Golden Theatre; and we sent over to Paris and secured the services of Jacques Copeau to direct his own version of *The Brothers Karamazov*. This play alternated with *Pygmalion* in the Guild Theatre, and employed the services of Alfred Lunt, Lynn Fontanne, Claire Eames and Edward G. Robinson.

By this time we had produced five out of the six plays which we had contracted for with our subscribers, and this left us with the necessity of finding one more play which could employ Laura Hope Crews, who was playing in *The Silver Cord* at the John Golden Theatre every other week, but was idle during the alternating week and complaining of having too little to do!

We solved the problem by producing a play which I had been urging for a considerable period, Pirandello's *Right You Are If You Think You Are*, and this opened at the Guild Theatre for special matinees, where it proved immediately successful, costing us the total sum of $1,500 because of our use of a "unit" set. Soon, however, the attendance at *The Brothers Karamazov* began to drop off, so we produced a new play by a new writer, S. N. Behrman, called *The Second Man* which employed Lunt and Fontanne every other week. Later on, we revived *Mr. Pim Passes By* which kept Laura Hope Crews busy between this play and the Pirandello play. We now had six plays running in three different theatres, and all these plays were popular.

The achievement of this Alternating Repertory required considerable juggling, as most of the actors had to play one week at one theatre, and the next week at another. Each Saturday night they packed up their make-up boxes, and off they traipsed from the one theatre to the other. It was, indeed, during this period, quite difficult for an actor to remember in exactly which play or theatre he was playing. But there were marvelous compensations, for each actor appeared in a diversity of roles, and each play seemed to take on added dimension under this system. Indeed, it can be described as an actor's dream, for during a period of twelve months, Alfred Lunt appeared in five good roles, while Lynn Fontanne played in four, and the other actors had a similar variety of roles. We closed our tenth season in a blaze of glory, and with a subscription list which had grown to twenty-three thousand members in New York.

Under this system of Alternating Repertory, the Guild achieved the greatest period of its entire career. The system, though it had certain aspects of a jigsaw puzzle, actually worked to produce the results we had aimed at. With the exception of *Juarez and Maximilian*, all fourteen plays [3] produced by the Acting Company were financially as well as artistically successful, and the Guild coffers began to fill. To the credit of all connected with the venture, however, no dividends were declared, and the money which accumulated was held as a reserve for future losses. This record of producing fourteen artistically successful plays one after another has, I believe, never been exceeded in the New York theatre, and probably has been encountered in reverse only by the Guild itself which, later on, managed to produce almost as many unpopular plays one after another.

There are many reasons for this "Golden Era" of the Theatre Guild, as some of my friends have called it. The Alternating Repertory System was largely responsible for its success, for when you have an Acting Company with such actors as Alfred Lunt, Lynn Fontanne, Dudley Digges and all the rest, you are like the owner of a magnificent orchestra, and whatever music the orchestra plays will be played much better than when you throw a group of artists together who barely know one another, and have had no experience of playing together as a team. When plays could command the services of such fine actors and actresses, half the battle was won; but the astonishing thing is that the plays themselves were for the most part excellent works of art which have remained eminently playable down to the present day. Later on, *Porgy* and O'Neill's *Strange Interlude* did not lend themselves to alternation, so they were permitted to play continuously at other theatres. The plan had considerable elasticity; so much so, indeed, that it permitted us to take our eye off the ball to such an extent that, in the end, we failed to realize the importance of what we were doing, and allowed opportunism to take the place of clear thinking and planning.

In order to make Alternating Repertory possible on a financial basis, I suggested building the sets on the stage by the use of standard flats

---

[3] From April, 1926, with *At Mrs. Beam's* to October, 1928, the Guild produced the following plays: *Juarez and Maximilian, Pygmalion, Ned McCobb's Daughter, The Silver Cord, The Brothers Karamazov, Right You Are If You Think You Are, The Second Man, Porgy, The Doctor's Dilemma, Marco Millions, Strange Interlude, Volpone* and a revival of *Mr. Pim Passes By.*

or units of neutral color, so that one set of these could be used like children's building blocks for different plays, by changing the position of units containing doors, windows, etc., and using different draperies. These units provided some highly effective sets, but the scene designers hated them. Simonson wittily christened them "Eunuch" sets, but there was desperation in the disdain of the scenic fraternity, for we proved conclusively by the popularity of most of these plays which used unit sets, that the audiences are mainly interested in the play and the acting, and will seldom stay away from the theatre on account of the scenery.

Now that the Alternating Repertory plan was highly successful, I lived in a seventh heaven of delight. However, the plan meant far more to me than to some of the others involved. For instance, play agents began to calculate how much more their clients could earn were the plays presented for the usual Broadway run. Scenic artists gibed at the use of the scenic units; and even some of the actors who were playing smaller parts the one week, as compared with the alternating parts the following week, were complaining of the system, forgetting Dantchenko's adage that "There are no small parts, only small actors." Our playreader, Courtenay Lemon, complained that we were becoming an actors' theatre and remarked, "Our only salvation is to remember first, last and all the time that the play's the thing; that up and down, backwards and forwards and sideways; the play is forever the thing, and that without a sound play, no amount of acting can save you from deserved damnation." I, on the other hand, defending our Acting Company, wrote angrily in the Guild's magazine asking what kind of music the Philharmonic Orchestra would play if every time it gave a concert, Toscanini had to engage an entirely new company of musicians. We were both right, but these two forces, the pro-Play and the pro-Acting Company, were in constant opposition because we lacked the unity of purpose to keep both forces working together.

Part of the achievement of the Acting Company was due to the plays of Sidney Howard, which will be given long after his untimely death. Howard wrote at least part of his autobiography in his master-piece, *The Silver Cord,* in which his first wife, Claire Eames, played a leading role. Claire, tall, distinguished and vibrant, with features and mannerisms which reminded one of Queen Elizabeth, descended on the New York theatre from Cleveland like a hurricane blowing from the Great Lakes, and swept us all off our feet with her brilliant acting, directing and sheer joy of living. We made her a transient member of the Guild Board, and her enthusiasms often carried us along when we began to feel tired and bedraggled. "He wasted a precious hour of my valuable time," she said to me once, speaking of a person who bored her; and indeed her hours were precious and her time valuable, for she died far too young for a theatre that needed her fresh vital artistry.

In the winter of 1927, we brought over from France the distinguished artist Jacques Copeau of the "Theatre de Vieux Colombier," to make the production of *The Brothers Karamazov* for our Acting Company. Copeau was a sad, serious, long, lean Latin who took himself and the art of the theatre—which he regarded as more or less synonymous —very seriously. The production of *The Brothers Karamazov* proceeded smoothly enough up to the dress rehearsal, when all the actors suddenly appeared in beards and it took us quite a time to recognize them as they stepped out on the stage. Alfred Lunt, looking divinely handsome as Dmitri Feodorovitch Karamazov, was told by Copeau that he must have the mark of a wound on his cheek. "But I have one," replied Alfred pointing to what appeared to be a large scratch on one side of his face. "I want a big large wound right across your cheek, at once!" replied Copeau, getting a little temperamental. "Very well," said Alfred gaily. "You shall have it!" Twenty minutes later he sallied forth from his dressing room with an enormous gaping wound painted in bright green right across his cheek, which gave the effect of a gangrenous protuberance. "We will have no wound at all," was the response of Copeau. Alfred left the stage and returned later with a fair-to-middling scar across his cheek. "I've made a compromise," he said, as he presented himself to the smiling Copeau, who learned a lesson on how to handle American actors.

In the year 1926, I was called on the phone by the ubiquitous Harold Freedman who informed me that our playreader, Courtenay Lemon, had returned a play which he thought I should read; he added, rather shrewdly, that had I read it, it would not have been returned. I read the play. It was *The Second Man* by S. N. Behrman; I liked it enormously, and enthusiastically recommended it to my colleagues. Theresa Helburn and Philip Moeller seconded my enthusiasm for the play, and soon we were in rehearsal with Alfred Lunt, Lynn Fontanne, Earle Larimore and Margalo Gillmore. The play was well received and S. N. Behrman was launched on his career.

Sam, when I first met him, was short, slight, and rounded in build, and the passing of the years have merely added a number of layers to his body and a more pronounced ovality to his head, perched on his neck and accentuating his sensitivity. Soft, round, curved, all the words which suggest a horror of exercise and a love of personal comfort (two qualities which I share with him) are applicable to Sam's physical make-up, but only words like hard, sharp, incisive can be used to describe the mind which looks out at you through keen dark eyes under a broad high forehead. Indeed, the clumsiness of his body is always in contrast with the nimbleness of his wit, while his sybaritic appearance is in marked contrast with his mental austerity. The second man who dwells in the rounded body of Sam Behrman is sharp and angular, and but for the saving grace of his penetrating humor, might have attacked the follies of our times with guns and pistols rather than with weapons of wit, satire and ridicule. Writer of the most incisive dialogue of our day, S. N. Behrman has chosen his characters from among those who speak his language, and has written over fifteen comedies, most of them brilliantly conceived; of these the Theatre Guild has produced eleven.

After the success of *The Second Man,* Alexander Woollcott scornfully depicted Behrman as a small boy standing outside a stately mansion and peeking in at the windows to learn how life was lived by the upper crust. Woollcott, who peeked into many windows himself, intended his remark to be derisive, but in fact it was complimentary. Had Sam been born in a stately mansion, he might have been blind to the vested injustice and intolerance against which, unlike Woollcott, he wielded his sharpened pen. *The Second Man* was not only popular when it was first produced by us, but is often revived, and it still remains one of the best American examples of high comedy.

One of my happiest experiences at this time was in working with Helen Westley, one of the most original and delightful members of our Board. She appeared in so many of our plays that it was jokingly said that she *was* our Acting Company. Every so often Helen, the only member of the Board who, so to speak, led the higher spiritual life under the combined influence of Yogi and Bernarr Macfadden, would be heard to express herself on this subject or that with never-failing clarity. Once, Jane Heap of *The Little Review* informed Helen that she had brought with her from Paris a phonograph record of James Joyce reading *Ulysses.* "Was he reading out loud?" asked the inimitable Miss Westley. One Christmas Eve, Helen, in pursuit of her cult of spiritual and bodily health, retired to bed at 9:30, leaving her guests disconsolate by her withdrawal. Some wag suggested that it might be appropriate to the spirit of the occasion to sing a Christmas song under her window. Carl Van Vechten, Philip

Moeller and the rest of us went out into the cold night and standing under Helen's window, proceeded to sing "O, Tannenbaum." After a few moments, her window opened and she inquired, "Who is Tannenbaum?" "We're singing you a Christmas carol," said Carl. "Well, Tannenbaum sounds Jewish to me!" said Helen, slamming the window and returning to bed.

Other interesting experiences happened between 1926 and 1928. Several of them are worth noting in some detail.

One day in the winter of 1926, a Chicago Public Utilities magnate named Samuel Insull dropped in at the office of the Theatre Guild and unintentionally influenced our entire future. Mr. Insull called on our business manager, Warren Munsell, and informed him that his wife was acting in a Chicago theatre venture in which he was interested, and he suggested that if the Theatre Guild Acting Company came to Chicago the following fall he would underwrite the undertaking, which was to be on a subscription basis; the first four plays were to be produced by the Guild, the last two by the local Chicago company.

While we had from time to time sent out sporadic touring companies this was the first time a subscription series had been proposed out of town, and Samuel Insull was willing to back his faith in us with his money. A few months later I met him in Chicago; he was a pleasant vigorous man of affairs, small in stature but large in vision, who, like the late Otto Kahn, thought it was his public responsibility to subsidize the arts, such as the opera and the theatre. Few of such benefactors exist today. Perhaps they have been taxed out of existence.

Insull told me that as a young man he lived in England representing the Edison Company, and that a tall lanky young Irishman named Bernard Shaw worked for him as an electrician; he knew very little about electricity and caused so much trouble that he was soon fired from his job. I checked this story later with G.B.S., who told me it was correct, even admitting that he knew very little about electricity. Mr. Insull introduced me to his attractive wife, who belonged to that familiar feminine order which will move mountains in order to act in the theatre. Indeed, she it was who primarily moved us out to Chicago.

In the fall of 1927, we began our Chicago engagement with the Lunts in *Arms and the Man* and *The Guardsman*. Our plays were a brilliant success, and our season started off auspiciously. As I walked along Michigan Boulevard with Philip Moeller after the opening of *The Guardsman* at the Studebaker Theatre, we looked out over the broad expanse of Lake Michigan and talked of the United States as our field for future activities, rather than the New York City which gave us our start. Our dreams of bringing Theatre Guild plays to the four corners of the U.S.A. seemed grandiose at the time, but many of them have since been realized.

The Chicago engagement was so popular that the shrewd Mr. Insull who underwrote us actually received a profit from our engagement. ". . . and the first time I ever made a profit in the theatre or opera in my life!" he told me smilingly. Insull's memory was sullied by his losses in the 1929 financial crash, but I shall never cease to be grateful for his enthusiasm which brought the Theatre Guild into a far larger field of activity than it might have had otherwise. Our first Chicago season was further made memorable by opening *The Doctor's Dilemma* there, with Alfred and Lynn and the rest of our Acting Company, which we later brought back to New York.

In our dream of covering the United States, we made a humble beginning by playing the following season, that of 1928–29, in Baltimore, Boston, Cleveland, Pittsburgh and Philadelphia, and we sent *Marco Millions, Volpone* and *Porgy* to Chicago to follow our first two plays with the Lunts. Then, in Boston, we opened with Alfred and Lynn in a new play, Sil-Vara's *Caprice* which, apart from a few headaches in rehearsal, was the most joyous event in the Guild's eleventh season.

In the spring of 1927, a representative of the Judson Concert Bureau suggested that we send out an Acting Company to bring artistic plays to a large number of cities which were already in the habit of receiving concerts. We engaged an excellent acting company led by Florence Eldridge, George Gaul and Frederick March. Their repertory included *Mr. Pim Passes By, Arms and the Man, The Silver Cord* and *The Guardsman,* and the scenery could be used in theatres, schoolhouses, auditoriums or what have you. This traveling company played in a hundred and thirty-two cities in 1927–28. We visited them on their return at Danbury, to congratulate the actors on their tour, and I have seldom met such a group of indignant, overworked people. What they particularly disliked was that, in the words of Freddy March, now one of our greatest character actors, "The hotel accommodations in most of the small towns were so bad that even when we did have an opportunity to sleep, the beds and the inhabitants thereof often made it impossible to do so," and while the fire has now died out of Freddy's eyes and flames no longer burst out of Florence's nostrils, the verbal chastisement which I have received from time to time at the hands of these two artists has taught me a lesson I will always remember. I mention this tour to warn others who may have the wild idea—which is suggested every so often by the Concert Agencies—that theatrical companies can play "one-night stands" all over these United States without adequate rest periods.

With the rapid growth of our subscribers we felt it was necessary to have some means of keeping more closely in touch with them, and I suggested that we publish for this purpose a magazine which would stimulate interest in the theatre. There was already in existence a magazine known as *Theatre Magazine* which was in its declining years, largely because the theatre was also in its declining years, at least quantitatively if not qualitatively. *Theatre Magazine* was owned by two charming Frenchmen, the brothers Meyer, and the old volumes of their magazine remain as touching as old valentines, or faded flowers pressed between the leaves of an old book. After serving several months as Associate Editor, during which I tried to slant the publication in the direction of the modern theatre, I felt that the Theatre Guild should either purchase the magazine, or I should bow out. The brothers Meyer, however, were not in a selling mood, so I regretfully retired from the field of theatrical journalism—or at least I thought so at the time.

As the number of subscribers kept on increasing, the need for our own magazine grew more apparent. With over 25,000 subscribers in New York alone, my colleagues in the Guild readily agreed that we should publish our own magazine. So we brought out a quarterly magazine of which I was the Editor, called *The Theatre Guild Quarterly*. As we had provided very little in the way of funds to pay others for articles, I found myself obliged to write not only the editorials but also many of the articles, for which I adopted various pseudonyms. After a while, we decided to change the magazine into a monthly called *The Theatre Guild Magazine* which in its first two years achieved a circulation of fifty thousand. But the amount of work involved in bringing out this magazine, on top of everything else, was beginning to overwhelm me, for while I continued to write articles and editorials, there was the insistence of a deadline in getting out the issue each month, which made what had been fun before, in the case of a quarterly, into a real task monthly.

It so happened that an old journalist friend of mine, Hiram Modderwell, who had written one of the best books on the theatre in the old Greenwich Village days, had just returned from Italy. I captured him and submitted his name (which he changed to Motherwell) as

Editor to our Board, and he was cheerfully accepted. The magazine continued to grow, not only in size but also in circulation. I confined my literary efforts, however, to one article a month and a page of editorials.

One of my ideas which bore fruit in the magazine was to have the plays reviewed by persons specializing in the field to which the play related; thus, we had a psychologist review a psychological play, a politician reviewed a political play; and so on until we were stumped when we sent Djuna Barnes to obtain a review by a gangster of our bootlegging play, *Ned McCobb's Daughter*. She just couldn't find one willing to become a dramatic critic!

The Theatre Guild Magazine had been running for some years when we were approached by John Hanrahan, who was connected with *The New Yorker;* he felt that what America needed was a good magazine of the theatre, and that *The Theatre Guild Magazine,* which suffered from the stigma of being a house organ, might afford a solid foundation for his purpose. I gladly recommended the cutting of the umbilical cord between the magazine and the Theatre Guild, and in its issue of May, 1932, the name of the monthly was changed to *Stage Magazine,* and Hanrahan took over the parental duties which had heretofore fallen on my shoulders. The magazine fell on evil days along with the rest of the American theatre during the depression, and with the issue of June, 1939, Mr. Hanrahan reluctantly abandoned the venture, and *Stage Magazine* came to an untimely end. Every so often a wide-eyed enthusiast comes into my office and remarks, "Why doesn't the Theatre Guild start a new magazine?" My reaction is to look embarrassed and to reply, "We did, and we'd rather not do it again."

About this period in the Guild's history, we also decided to start a School of the Theatre. The leading proponents of this idea were Theresa Helburn and myself, and we steam-rollered it over the mild opposition of some of the other Board members. It was conceded that if we could find a good teacher we might proceed with the school, which was to be a non-profit making institution; and we were to use the surplus from the wealthier pupils' tuition to pay for scholarships for the poorer pupils. We managed to enlist the services of the beautiful, talented but argumentative Winifred Lenihan, an excellent actress who was full of enthusiasm for the job. But alas, Winnie did not have the patience needed for a schoolmarm. She was much too temperamental to fit into the routine involved; she would fly into a passion at the drop of a hat and be as sweet as an angel the next minute.

The students were supposed to have some contact with the Guild Board members, but so far as I could observe, this contact resolved itself mainly in eating their lunches on the stairs of the office building, and blocking the passage of the Guild Directors up and down the stairs, to their constant irritation. Statistics taken many years later showed that the school, in its three seasons of operation, produced no startling results. Its most successful acting pupil was the popular actress Sylvia Sidney who was also the one and only pupil to be expelled from the school, thus proving that expulsion from an institution of learning is often the sign of talent, as in the case of Eugene O'Neill who was expelled from Princeton.

Sylvia was then a darling child of sixteen or so. One morning her mother brought her to my home. "Mr. Langner," she said, "a grave injustice has been done my child! She has been expelled from the Theatre Guild Summer School for coming home an hour late at night." "The car broke down," said Sylvia, wide-eyed and as innocent as a babe in arms. "I'll see Miss Lenihan," I replied, "and justice will be done." When I spoke to Winnie, somewhat in the manner of St. George facing the dragon, she looked me squarely in the eyes and said, "But you are always complaining about lack of discipline! I was simply carrying out *your* ideas—discipline!" I was, of course, defeated; Sylvia was not reinstated and probably owes her success in the theatre to this concatenation of circumstances.

We did produce some other talents, however, a gifted young ballet dancer named Lucia Chase, who was later to shepherd the Ballet Theatre, and the talented Cheryl Crawford who helped start the Group Theatre, and is now one of New York's most potent producers. The following year we graduated two other talented youngsters, Arlene Francis and Linda Watkins. Winifred Lenihan, tired of fighting a losing battle against the lack of interest on the part of the Guild, finally resigned, leaving the school and its future an unresolved problem on our collective hands.

The providence which guided our destiny now brought us into touch with a gifted individual who not only helped solve our school problem, but later on, many others as well. In the year 1926, we brought the Rochester American Opera Company, sponsored by George Eastman of Kodak fame, to play a short season in New York City, and I met its impresario, Vladimir Rosing, and a tall bespectacled young man, half-Russian, half-Armenian, named Rouben Mamoulian, who was associated with him, and conducted classes in the drama in Rochester. Mamoulian begged us to visit him and see some of his work.

Later on I saw some of his pupils performing in a play in Rochester, and was impressed with his ability as a dramatic teacher, and with his striking personality and enthusiasm for the theatre. As my patent practice brought me to Rochester at least twice a year, I usually spent the days with my clients and the evenings with Mamoulian, who walked my legs off pacing the streets of Rochester, telling me all he planned to do in the theatre if I would only bring him to New York.

Winnie Lenihan was succeeded by Hamilton MacFadden as head of the Theatre Guild School, and I bethought myself of the long-legged Mamoulian as dramatic teacher. He agreed, and soon after arrived in New York, set up shop, and began to pester the Guild directors in a most efficiently irritating manner, to come and see the plays given by his pupils and, of course, directed by himself. Finally he prevailed, and we went to a school production of *The Seven Keys to Baldpate* at the Garrick Theatre after carefully explaining that we could stay only a few minutes because of other appointments! The play was so well directed by Mamoulian and so well acted by his pupils, that the Guild directors stayed to the unbitter end.

Meanwhile, circumstances were adding up in Mamoulian's favor. At a dinner party given by Alma and Alonzo Klaw, I met Du Bose and Dorothy Heyward. Du Bose had recently written the novel *Porgy*, and together they had dramatized it. I secured the manuscript from them, and the Guild decided to produce it. When the question of staging the play came up, a number of well-known directors were approached, but all fought shy of an all-colored cast, for at that time there had been few Negro plays done on Broadway, and there were many tales (mostly untrue) of the irresponsibility of Negro actors. Terry and I suggested Rouben Mamoulian for the job, and the rest of the Guild, in despair, accepted him. Mamoulian went to Charleston, South Carolina, the scene of the play, where he absorbed the atmosphere of the place like a sponge. Returning to New York, he put on a production which made theatre history, and later on, when Warren Munsell suggested that *Porgy* be made into a musical play, the famous *Porgy and Bess* by George Gershwin, it was Mamoulian again who staged it and launched this American musical classic on its long career.

Meanwhile, the Theatre Guild School found itself without a head again, for once Mamoulian had directed *Porgy*, other important directorial assignments fell in his path. The youngsters continued to clutter up the stairways of the Guild Theatre office building, and the directors continued to stumble over them. After some further efforts were made, one bright director suggested at a Board meeting, "Why not dissolve

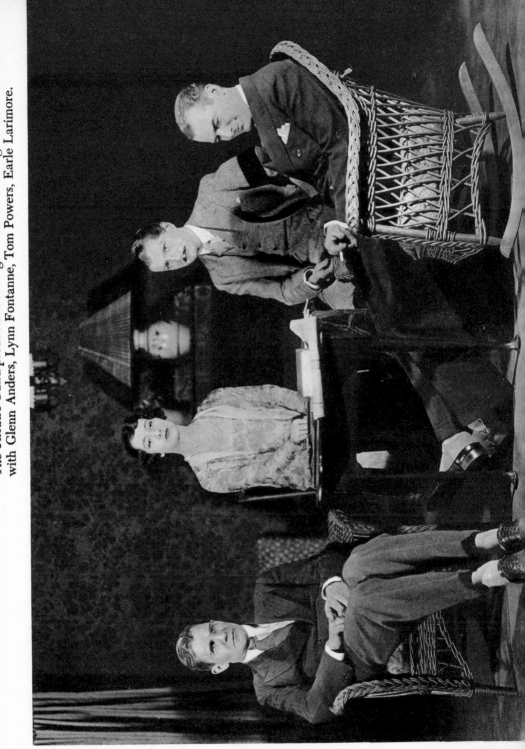

The Theatre Guild production of Eugene O'Neill's *Strange Interlude*, 1928, with Glenn Anders, Lynn Fontanne, Tom Powers, Earle Larimore.

Alla Nazimova and Alice Brady in the Theatre Guild production of Eugene O'Neill's *Mourning Becomes Electra*, 1931. Setting by Robert Edmond Jones.

EUGENE O'NEILL IN HIS TWENTIES.

Portrait by Nickolas Muray.

Eugene O'Neill at his home at Spithead, Bermuda, taken by the author on the day he received the original copy of *Strange Interlude* from O'Neill, 1927.

Above: Gene Lockhart and George M. Cohan in the Theatre Guild production of Eugene O'Neill's *Ah, Wilderness!,* 1941. *Below:* A re-hearsal of the Theatre Guild production of Eugene O'Neill's *The Iceman Cometh,* 1946. *From left to right:* Nicholas Joy, Carl Benton Reid, James Barton, Eugene O'Neill, Marcella Markham, Dudley Digges and Eddie Dowling.

LAWRENCE LANGNER AT THE AGE OF THIRTY-FIVE.

the school?" Over the negative vote of Theresa Helburn and myself, the resolution to wind up the affairs of the school was carried by the majority, and the Theatre Guild School came to a final and inglorious end, which both Terry and I greatly regretted. "Some day," we muttered to ourselves, "we'll start that school again."

The end of our 1927–28 season found the Guild at the peak of its career. We had the finest Acting Company to be assembled in New York since the days of the famous Augustin Daly Stock Company. Our system of Alternating Repertory was working out excellently, and we had seven "hits" running to capacity business in New York City. Our receipts were such that we were able to redeem many of the bonds on the Guild Theatre (we redeemed over $200,000 of bonds at this time). Plans for the conquest of the road had begun. We had attracted the best of the native and European playwrights under our banner. Walter Prichard Eaton had been commissioned to write a book covering our first ten years, and our School and Magazine were flourishing. All in all, at the end of our 1927–28 season we were riding high, wide and handsome, and well on our way to accomplishing what we had set out to do in the American theatre.

CHAPTER XIX

O'Neill and Strange Interlude

I FIRST met Eugene O'Neill at Provincetown in the summer of 1917. He lived on the edge of the ocean in an abandoned Coast Guard Station, which was formerly the home of the famous Mabel Dodge, and to reach his home it was necessary to trudge for about three miles across the sand dunes. Rumor had it that Robert Edmond Jones had decorated the house in the gay blue-and-white color scheme which it then wore, and the large room which formerly contained the coast guard lifeboat was now the living room.

On the beach just below the house was the wreck of a large schooner, and O'Neill, costumed in a bathing suit, took me onto the beach where, somewhat superfluously, I emptied the sand out of my shoes. The resounding surf, the background of the wrecked sailing ship, and the lithe, muscular body of O'Neill, his dark Irish eyes set deep in his sun-tanned face, made an appropriate O'Neill setting for my first meeting with our foremost playwright, with whose destiny my own was later linked for so many years. We talked over the production of *In the Zone* by the Washington Square Players, after which he invited me to join him in a swim. This I refused, being no swimmer in a high surf (or even in a low one), whereupon O'Neill plunged in and displayed his prowess with a swift overarm stroke of which he was very proud. Like Bernard Shaw, O'Neill's favorite sport is swimming; indeed it is the only form of athletics in which he has indulged during the time I have known him. My last view of him, as I bade him farewell at this first meeting, was his silhouette at the side of the house, the ocean behind him and the wind blowing his hair awry. It was also my last view of the old Coast Guard Station, for the restless Atlantic swallowed it up a few years later and not a trace now remains but the endless ocean and the lonely dunes.

Ever since I read O'Neill's first volume of one-act plays, I regarded him as our outstanding American dramatist. In the days of the Washington Square Players I helped bring about the rapprochement between that organization and O'Neill, which resulted in our producing his *In the Zone* which was later booked in vaudeville by Al Lewis and Max Gordon. O'Neill once expressed the opinion that the Provincetown players were artists while the Washington Square Players were an "uptown" commercial theatre and not worthy to be regarded as competition. We in turn regarded the Provincetown Players as "amateurs" in everything except their playwrights, O'Neill and Susan Glaspell.

I was determined to bring the Theatre Guild and Eugene O'Neill together, but all my early attempts ended in failure. 'Gene, on his side, wanted to work with the Guild.

One day in 1919 not long after *John Ferguson* had opened, as I was standing in the Garrick Theatre lobby, Agnes O'Neill, then 'Gene's wife, came in with a manuscript of his new play, *The Straw*. "'Gene wants you to have this," she said to me. As I left the lobby, one of the Guild directors asked if he could read the play over the week end. A few days later I asked for it. "I returned it to O'Neill," he said. "It's all about consumptives. I decided we'd never do it." I was furious. I tried to get the play back, but it had already been sent to another management.

My next attempt was with *Anna Christie*. I had concluded all arrangements with 'Gene for our production of the play, when I had to leave for Europe. On my return I found that some of our temperamental directors had been scrapping with O'Neill as a result of which he withdrew the play and gave it to Arthur Hopkins. On November 15, 1921, I wrote 'Gene as follows:

I have been having an orgy of your plays in the last week having seen both *Anna Christie* and *The Straw*. I was fully prepared to rave about *Anna Christie,* but certainly not to come out and lose almost a night's sleep after seeing *The Straw*. In spite of an uneven production, it thrilled me and held me to the end. I had not read the manuscript so did not know what was coming. The New York critics who called this play gloomy are only fit to criticize a meal and its effect on their mental attitude. Anything serious is gloomy. I am sending everybody I can to see *The Straw*. I wish to God the Theatre Guild had done it.

I know the Guild stands with a large black double cross against its name as far as your plays are concerned, but let me tell you that our troubles have been due to honest differences of opinion and nothing else. I want you to regard me as your representative in the Guild (although I admit so far I haven't put anything across), but we can give the plays a 90% production and we do command a definite audience.

I received a telegram from 'Gene on November 26, 1921, which read as follows:

ONLY JUST GOT YOUR LETTER OF THE FIFTEENTH. THANKS FOR YOUR SENTI-MENTS AND APPRECIATION. I AM SENDING YOU PLAY I SPOKE OF LAST SUMMER. THINK YOU WILL LIKE IT. ALL BEST REGARDS FROM US BOTH.

EUGENE O'NEILL

This was followed with a letter sending us a play called *The First Man* which was again turned down, thus scoring another black mark against the Guild.

Later on, hearing that 'Gene was writing a new play, I got in touch with him and learned that he was working on *The Fountain* and *Welded.* We were much interested in the actor Jacob Ben Ami at the time and were looking for a play for him. I visited 'Gene at his home in Ridgefield, Connecticut. It was called Brook Farm, and was a low-lying colonial farmhouse with Revolutionary associations. 'Gene met me and was very cordial. We talked about the Provincetown Play-ers and the necessity for better acting of their plays. Later on, he permitted the Guild to read *Welded* which did not meet with the Board's approval. Finally, we bought *The Fountain* but decided later not to produce it. Thus, all my efforts to bring the Guild and O'Neill together had failed. Five plays were offered by 'Gene and five refusals were made by the Guild.

"What do you think is the finest thing I could do to help the Ameri-can theatre?" Maurice Wertheim asked me with enthusiasm one day as we walked down Sixth Avenue toward the Garrick Theatre. "Sub-sidize Eugene O'Neill so that he can write plays for the next two years without any financial worries," I said. "All right," said Maurice, "go ahead and sound him out." I passed on the suggestion through a friend and this resulted in my receiving the following from 'Gene dated Janu-ary 10, 1921:

Indeed I'll be glad enough to talk it all over with you when I get to town again—the first part of February probably. I'll confess your proposition has me puzzled. Granted its generous interest, it yet seems to me inconsistent. I am in no dire straits for money, as you must know. Even if I were, my poverty-stricken years of the past are proof enough that there is no danger of my street-walking along Broadway. I simply ain't that kind of a girl.

But, after all, all that part of it is immaterial. I know what you were driving at and, as I have said, I appreciate the interest. However, the whole thing, to my mind, boils down to this: Either you have faith in my plays, or you haven't. If you have, you produce them. If not, not. And you have turned down three of mine already. In rejections of my work you have a clear lead over any other management. These facts, you must acknowledge, are a bit inexorable.

Your committee's judgment is not in question here. Perhaps they were right, perhaps wrong. A jury of our peers might well disagree forever on that point. And certainly they—the committee—were entitled to their verdict made in good faith. The thing is, how do you expect me to reconcile your adverse judgments with your alleged appreciation? It is all very well to talk of my future work, but if everyone had done that I would have no past nor present to build a future upon. The only help I need or would accept from anyone is a hearing—a fair hearing as in *Jones* or *Anna Christie*. And my obligation, both as a man and as a playwright, lies toward those who have helped me to that hearing and thereby proved their faith in me in the one way it can be proved.

So there you have my side of it; and it seems to me there is little else that can be said.

All this without any trace of hard feeling on my part, I know I don't have to tell you that. It is merely a question of unprejudiced disagreement, but I am afraid the evidence indicated that your committee and I are doomed forever to disagree.

Later on, O'Neill, Robert Edmond Jones and Kenneth MacGowan formed a producing firm which had considerable success and which produced O'Neill's *Welded, All God's Chillun Got Wings, Desire Under the Elms* and *The Fountain*. O'Neill went to live in Bermuda and came to New York from time to time.

In the spring of 1927 I suffered from a severe cold and was advised by my doctor to take a couple of weeks off to recuperate. By this time the producing firm with which O'Neill had associated himself had dissolved, and O'Neill spent most of his time in Bermuda. I had a hunch that a visit to Bermuda might not only restore me to health but also enable me to restore the personal relation which had formerly existed between O'Neill and myself, and which had very naturally become cloudy for the reasons I have explained above. My hunch turned out to be correct.

O'Neill welcomed me warmly and we had some talks about the possibility of the Guild producing *Marco Millions*. From that he went on to discuss the future of the American theatre, and what he hoped to contribute toward it. Walking up and down the sandy beach near his white-roofed coral house which had been built by a Seventeenth-Century privateer, and stood at the edge of the sea, 'Gene explained that he was experimenting with ways and means to break down "realism" in the theatre, and had just finished a play in which the characters not only talked to one another but also spoke their thoughts in a form of aside which he thought the audience would accept. The idea fascinated me and I asked him if I might read the play, which he informed me was called *Strange Interlude*. He also told me that it would take six hours to play it. In view of our experience with *Back to Methuselah,* this did not daunt me.

A few days later I was invited to O'Neill's home for a swim and dinner afterward, and I spent the evening with him discussing the theme of the play. He told me that he had already promised it to a well-known American actress who was his first choice, but that if I liked the play and she did not, I might have it for the Guild. Meanwhile, I could read it and let him know what I thought of it. He then handed me the first six acts of the manuscript, which I still possess. It was half again as thick as an ordinary play, for not only was it a double-length play, but so long that nearly forty pages were subsequently cut out of it. Clutching the precious manuscript to my bosom I returned in the horse cab which had been ordered for me (there were no automobiles in Bermuda at the time) and drove along the shore road in a gale which at times seemed so strong that I feared horse cab, *Strange Interlude* and myself would all be blown together into the sea.

I went to bed intending to read at least part of the play before I fell asleep; the storm outside grew more and more violent as the play grew more and more exciting. The tropical thunder and lightning, and the fierce howling of the gale which began to assume hurricane proportions, failed to interrupt me. All night long I read and read, and at four o'clock in the morning, my eyes strained and throbbing, I finished the sixth act. Before I went to sleep I examined my feelings about the play as far as I had read. I judged it one of the greatest plays of all time.

The storm died down during the night, and the next morning was bright and clear; as soon as I was awake I telephoned 'Gene and told him how enthusiastic I was about the play. He invited me over to his home again. This time he definitely promised me that if the actress to whom he had offered the play did not care to do it (and he thought there were certain reasons why she might not), the Theatre Guild could have it. Then he gave me a breath-taking exhibition of his over-arm stroke which I photographed with my cine-kodak. 'Gene at this time was about thirty-eight years old, and at the height of his mental and physical powers. He was built like an athlete, his deep black eyes set in a sunburnt Irish face, as handsome as one could hope to see anywhere, and the skin of his lean body was the color and texture of mahogany with underlying muscles of whipcord. At no time before or since have I seen him in such good health. I luckily recorded his appearance at the time with my movie camera.

After my return to New York, I wrote Gene telling him I had stirred up some interest in *Marco Millions* and asking him to send us a copy of *Strange Interlude*. On the arrival of the manuscript, I circulated it among my fellow directors. To my horror, they did not all share my enthusiasm. One of them even went so far as to say that if all the asides were taken out, the play would be greatly improved. I wanted to choke him, but restrained myself.

At about this time I had completed a comedy about Lady Godiva which I had submitted to the manager of the actress to whom O'Neill had sent *Strange Interlude*. A few weeks later he invited me to lunch and informed me, in charming phrases, why he didn't like it. I understood perfectly. He was not the first manager who had not liked it, so we discussed this topic and that, and the conversation turned to O'Neill. "I'm glad to say Miss ——— made an excellent decision today. She has decided *not* to do a new play which Eugene O'Neill has sent her—a very long affair that just goes on and on!" I nearly fell out of my chair—but recovered and did my best to look unconcerned. I am no poker player, and have often wondered since whether my host noticed the gleam which came into my eye, and the speed with which I finished my dessert and tossed down my coffee. I rushed back to the Guild Theatre and gave my fellow directors the good news. They were, I felt, with some exceptions, quite unreasonably unmoved.

At the next Board meeting I pressed the matter with enthusiasm, having also heard from O'Neill that the play was now released for us if we wanted it. Many and varied were the objections to the play at the Board meeting, and I became frantic. To quiet me down they offered to bring O'Neill to New York to discuss the play, and in the meantime bought his play *Marco Millions*. These tactics did not suit me at all. Aided by Theresa Helburn and Maurice Wertheim, I conducted a frenzied campaign to secure the production of *Strange Interlude*. On April 21st, I wrote the Board a stinging letter:

In *Strange Interlude* we have probably the bravest and most far-reaching dramatic experiment which has been seen in the theatre since the days of Ibsen. O'Neill's genius was never more clearly shown than in this play. . . . This play contains in it more deep knowledge of the dark corners of the human mind than anything that has ever been written before. It proclaims O'Neill the great dramatic genius of the age. As an important experiment, it knocks *Back to Methuselah* into a cocked hat. . . .

None of O'Neill's plays is as perfectly written as this play; if the Guild did it, none would be better produced. If we fail to do this great experiment, if we lack the courage and the vision, then we should forever hang our heads in shame, for we will have lost one of the greatest opportunities in our history. Indeed, the theatre being what it is today, it almost devolves upon the Guild to produce this play, as the only surviving art theatre in America, for the demise of the other art theatres, such as the Neighborhood Playhouse, places upon us the solemn responsibility of being the first to recognize the work of genius and to dare to experiment, even if it be accompanied by financial loss, if that experiment be in the direction of greatness. One thing we can never lose by such a course—our prestige and our self-respect.

My letter had its effect. The Guild Board decided that the play would be produced if 'Gene was willing to cut it sufficiently, but that *Marco Millions* should be presented first. I wrote 'Gene on the subject of cutting the play, to which he replied:

You should have enough confidence in my ability to trim this play down to be able to predict for yourselves what the final product will be. After all, you are not dealing with any novice in the theatre, and anyone who has ever worked with me—Bobby (Robert Edmond Jones), Kenneth (Kenneth Magowan), Arthur (Hopkins), etc.—will testify that I don't have to be urged but am always on the lookout for helpful cuts right up to the last week of rehearsals. And the legend that I don't attend rehearsals is all rot. I didn't in the old Provincetown Players days because I was never in New York and when I was I was never "on the wagon." But of late years it has been different. Except in cases where I saw that my play was being given no chance and it didn t matter whether I was there or not, I have been very much on the job. *Beyond the Horizon, Anna Christie, Hairy Ape, All God's Chillun, Glencairn* cycle, *Desire Under the Elms* and *G.G. Brown* are examples of when I was. And I should most decidedly be there from the first day to last if I were doing stuff with you people because I would be genuinely interested.

O'Neill, after condensing both *Marco Millions* and *Strange Interlude,* came to New York, and he stayed at our home on Eleventh Street. He was with us for about two weeks, and we went into all phases of the two plays. He saw very few friends while with us but he finally consented to our giving a small party for him. "The reason I avoid parties is because I'm extremely bashful," he told me. "In my younger days I used to drink in order to get up the nerve to meet people. Since I've quit drinking, it's become worse. When I once started, I was like a sailor on shore leave—a holdover from my seafaring days." He told me in Bermuda that he had entirely sworn off drinking, and gave as one reason the effect of alcohol on the brain as explained to him by a doctor friend. "It's just like turning the albumen in your brain into the white of a poached egg!" This vivid and horrible picture made me a hesitant drinker for the many years which have intervened.

During all the time I knew O'Neill, and this goes back to when we were both in our twenties, I never saw him drink any kind of liquor. However, he assured me that he was, in his youth, a notoriously stalwart drinker, and he, in my opinion, built this up into the proportions of a legend. He told the story that at one time he was seated in the Provincetown Playhouse watching one of his plays when a young woman in the seat in front of him remarked to her escort, "Do you know that Eugene O'Neill, the author of this play, is a terrible drunkard?" "No," replied the young man. "Yes, and not only does he drink to excess, but he takes drugs, too." This was too much for 'Gene. "Excuse me, Miss," he said to the young lady, "you are wrong there. I do *not* take drugs!"

During the many visits I had with 'Gene I learned to know him not merely as a writer but as a person. I always felt in his presence that I was in the presence of greatness and nobility of thought. The kindness of his smile, the gentleness of his spirit, the philosophical detachment of his mind, his Olympian view of human destiny, were not only inspiring but so endeared him to you that you wanted to lay down your life in his service. This ability to inspire hero-worship in me, which both he and G.B.S. had in common, was not always conducive to my doing my best work in their interests, for I was often too willing to give in to their foibles when my own better judgment told me to put up a tougher fight against them for their own good.

Our first choice for the part of Nina was Alice Brady, then one of our greatest emotional actresses, and Maurice Wertheim carried his own personal enthusiasm for the play to the point of visiting her with me at her apartment. We tried to talk to her about appearing in the play while her seven dogs were climbing all over us in an ecstasy of affection. "Would you mind putting these dogs outside?" asked Maurice in desperation, as he removed two dogs from his lap and a third from his foot. "Not at all," said Alice, "if they disturb you!" From then on we discussed the play more quietly and Alice darted from one reason to another for not playing the part of Nina. Years later, she told me she had made the mistake of her career in not playing it, and she made reparation by her unforgettable performance in *Mourning Becomes Electra*. Meanwhile, Alfred Lunt appeared with great success in *Marco Millions* at the Guild Theatre, which was warmly acclaimed by the critics and audiences.

It seems difficult to realize, now that *Strange Interlude* is regarded as an American classic, that we had great difficulty in securing an actress to play the role of Nina, but at that time the Freudian implications of the play were, generally speaking, unknown in the theatre, and Nina was generally regarded as an unsympathetic role. We were fortunate in finding in Lynn Fontanne an actress who was courageous enough to essay the role. Fearing that Lynn might not like the part, Theresa Helburn and I made a special trip to Baltimore where she was playing at the time, and on the train we went over each and every argument we might be called upon to use, to convince her that she should play the role. We were invited to supper with Alfred and Lynn after the performance and arrived at the Lunts' apartment at the Belvedere Hotel so charged with our arguments that we were almost ready to pop. We were somewhat chagrined to hear Lynn tell us that she had decided, without any question, to play the part, for we were so intent on convincing her that we were almost disappointed to learn that she had already convinced herself without our help.

With an excellent cast which included Earl Larimore, Glenn Anders and Tom Powers, the play went into rehearsal and opened at the John Golden Theatre on January 23, 1928. The rehearsals were marked by considerable argument, for time after time 'Gene insisted on cutting out comedy lines or "laughs" when, in his opinion, they interfered with the emotional build of a scene. Philip Moeller, who directed the play so brilliantly, adored the comedy and every time 'Gene solemnly cut out an amusing line, Phil would plead vociferously for its return. "I hope he doesn't realize that line is funny," Phil once remarked to me, "for if he does, out it'll go." Every now and again 'Gene would retire to the lounge with me, and give vent to his feeling about some of the acting in language he certainly did not learn in school at Stamford. He was never too pleased with his actors in rehearsal, and once told me that he adopted the technique of asides which showed what the characters were thinking in *Strange Interlude* because the majority of actors were incompetent to do so. This, however, can be taken with a grain of salt, like some of Shaw's remarks on the same subject. No author ever succeeds in getting a complete realization of the part he has created, and he blames the actor because the actor is unable to achieve the impossible. On the other hand, I have seen many creative actors add dimensions to a part of which the author never dreamed.

Matters were not made more harmonious during rehearsal by the fact that one of the members of the company loaned a copy of the play to Alexander Woollcott, then dramatic critic for the *New York World,* which enabled him to write an article for *Vanity Fair* holding the play up to ridicule, and making fun of the asides, O'Neill and the Theatre Guild for producing the play. Owing to a mishap in timing, which we learned later was not Woollcott's fault, the *Vanity Fair* article was published a few days before the play opened. Herbert Bayard Swope, Editor of the *World* at the time, was extremely upset that their dramatic critic should have condemned the play in another periodical before it had actually opened, and in the ensuing ructions, he forbade Woollcott to review the play and sent Dudley Nichols in his stead. Nichols adored the play and when he went to Hollywood and made a successful career as writer-producer and director, he devoted himself to the cause of bringing O'Neill's genius into motion pictures. Woollcott angrily resigned from the *World.* The *World,* not long after, went out of business, but the two facts were unrelated.

The night *Strange Interlude* was presented to a waiting world I ran out to a neighboring drugstore during each intermission and gave a blow-by-blow account to 'Gene who was waiting in his hotel to hear how the play was received. The next day the dramatic critics outdid themselves in praising this play which, although it ran for nearly five hours, did not seem a minute too long.

Instead of our patrons objecting to going out for dinner during the long intermission after Act 5, they seemed on the contrary to enjoy it. Going to the John Golden Theatre became a sort of adventure which not only enriched the Guild and the author, but also all the restaurants in the neighborhood. One of these prepared a sandwich in half-a-dozen layers and called it the "Strange Interlude Sandwich"! Later on, when the touring company played Quincy (Wollaston), Massachusetts, just outside Boston, a restaurant near the theatre was tottering on the brink of bankruptcy; the play brought the owner so many customers that with the cash he accumulated he started a chain of restaurants all over the country known by his name of Howard Johnson!

The asides in the play were the cause of much comment. "One reason *Strange Interlude* is such a success," a wag was heard to say, "is because many of the audience learn for the first time the surprising fact that people actually think." I was personally amazed at the success of the play, for while I knew it to be a great play, I did not dream it would command the popular success which it was to achieve. Indeed, it earned nearly three hundred thousand dollars for O'Neill, and a little more for the Guild, all of which we lost later.

I thought that *Strange Interlude* would achieve a revolution in the theatre, but in this I was mistaken. O'Neill himself was the only writer to follow this technique, and this only in his later play *Dynamo*. Nevertheless, it is being used today on the radio and in motion pictures in so-called "streams of consciousness," and it is also being used in television.

'Gene's happiness over the success of *Strange Interlude* and *Marco Millions* was marred by difficulties in his personal life which ultimately culminated in his divorce from his wife Agnes. Added to his troubles, there was hardly a day when the reporters were not trying to interview him to secure more gossip. Finally the situation interfered with his peace of mind to such an extent that he determined to set sail for Europe to put all this painful publicity behind him. He left the States early in 1928.

As *Strange Interlude* settled down for a steady run in New York, thus introducing an embarrassing hiatus in our alternating repertory plans, we decided to send out road companies of the play, and we found that the rest of the United States was just as excited about *Strange Interlude* as was New York. Pauline Lord and Judith Anderson in turn played the role of Nina on the road, while later on Mary Ellis and Basil Sidney took a company of the play to London where, however, it achieved only a moderate success.

The Boston Censors, who, being usually Irish-American, for some obscure Irish reason have always resented their great fellow Irish-American, served notice on us that we must not bring the play to their city. With Theresa Helburn, I went to Boston, and together we instituted a whirlwind campaign both by publicity and by forming Boston committees to fight the censorship of the play. What upset the censors particularly, we were told, was the reference to an abortion in Act 3 of Part I, and we were led to believe that this was due to the activity of the late Cardinal O'Connell, who was said to rule New England with the power of a medieval prelate. Notwithstanding every effort to trace the rumor to its source, we were never able to do so, and I firmly believe this was merely a ruse to cover the real situation, which actually was venality on the part of certain local political bosses, for we were given a message that the matter could be settled by paying the sum of $10,000 as a legal fee. Terry and I searched all around Boston's suburbs to find a city administration which was not subject to the same sinister influence and we found this in Quincy, a few miles outside the Boston city limits. As the result of running motor busses from Boston each day, which transported the audience to and from the theatre, the play was an enormous success and played for far longer than it would have in Boston without interference from the censors. The phrase "Banned in Boston" which was broadcast as a result of this experience, helped to attract audiences throughout the country.

Years later the fact that the attack on the play was not due to the Catholic Church was confirmed by the successful production of the play in Rome and Milan under the auspices of the Vatican through Catholic Theatre Action.

In September, 1928, I received a letter from 'Gene sending me a copy of his new play *Dynamo,* from which I quote:

> ... I've finished *Dynamo* and feel it's the real stuff. You will judge when you read it. . . .

> ... One thing I want to make plain about *Dynamo* (perhaps on the program) is that it's the first of a trilogy written on the general subject, more or less symbolically treated, of the death of the old God and the spiritual uneasiness and degeneration into which the sterile failure of Science and Materialism to give birth to a new God that can satisfy our primitive religious cravings, has thrown us. . . .

'Gene also wrote that he intended to take a trip around the world, hoping to find an isolated spot where he could settle down to writing. He decided to try Hong Kong first.

On October 4, 1928, I cabled 'Gene:

DYNAMO ACCEPTED WITH ENTHUSIASM. ALL WISH YOU BON VOYAGE.

I received a post card from 'Gene, mailed in Egypt in November reading as follows:

> This is written three days out from Marseille on a balmy Mediterranean. Your cable was delivered just as I sailed and did much by way of a cheery bon voyage. I feel safe about *Dynamo* now and am already starting preliminary work on the next one. This voyage is going to mean a lot to me. I'll write a letter as soon as I'm settled in Hong Kong or wherever it is to be. I hope *Interlude* is holding up. Write me about it, will you? All my best to all the Guild!

Hong Kong, however, did not turn out to be the haven he was looking for, and in December he sent me a post card from that city saying:

> Have decided not to stay here. Not very interesting and climate hot now
> and damp and enervating. No place to work. So, on to Shanghai, Kobe and
> Yokohama. Will probably settle in Japan.
> Love Armina and you. Hurry up *Dynamo!*

After 'Gene arrived in Shanghai, the newspapers were full of the
news that he was seriously ill, and I cabled our patent and trade-
mark law associate, Mr. A. Krisel, to get in touch with him and see
that he had the best medical care. Mr. Krisel sent me a newspaper
clipping, showing how unsuccessful 'Gene had been in hiding his identity. I quote from the *Shanghai Times* of December 20, 1928, as follows:

EUGENE O'NEILL FOUND NO REST STAYING HERE

Says There Are Too Many Snoops
And Gossips in Shanghai

IS LOOKING FOR PEACE

Famous Playwright Says He Will
Go to South Pole to Find It

Manila, Dec. 19. The well-known American playwright Eugene O'Neill,
author of *Emperor Jones, Anna Christie, Desire Under The Elms* and other
well-known plays, has arrived here on the German steamer *Coblentz*. He is
travelling under the name of the Rev. William O'Brien.
Mr. O'Neill was under the care of a well-known medical practitioner in
Shanghai when he suddenly disappeared a week ago leaving behind him a
letter in which he stated that "he came to China seeking peace and quiet" and
"hoping that here, at least, people would mind their own business and allow
me to mind mine, but I've found more snoops and gossips to the square inch
here than there are in any New England town of a thousand inhabitants. I am
going to Honolulu and then, perhaps, to Tahiti, if Honolulu adopts the same
attitude as Shanghai that I'm a politician whose life must be public. At any
rate I'll find peace and solitude to work in if I have to go to the South Pole."

My worries as to the state of 'Gene's health were fortunately set
at ease by a cable I received from him from Singapore on December
24, 1928:

YOUR CABLE FORWARDED HONG KONG. FEEL WELL NOW. MUCH IDIOTIC PUBLIC-
ITY SHANGHAI MANILA MY DISCOVERY DISAPPEARANCE KIDNAPPED BANDITS
DEATH ETC. MERRY CHRISTMAS TO ALL.

                                                                    GENE

We produced *Dynamo* at the Martin Beck Theatre with an excellent cast.[1] Philip Moeller directed the play, but it was diffused in effect and the meaning was difficult for the audience to understand. We greatly missed 'Gene at rehearsals for clarification and cutting, and had to do the best we could.

Dynamo, although it excited considerable interest, was not popular, and we were reluctantly forced to close the play after fifty performances. *Dynamo,* with its intuitive foreknowledge of what was to be discovered later as to the universal nature of energy, was produced in 1929, the same year that we presented *Wings Over Europe,* an extraordinary play that foretold the discovery and probable results of the atom bomb fifteen years before the bomb was actually exploded at Hiroshima. This play, of which Maurice Browne of Chicago Little Theatre memories was the co-author with Robert Nichols, was successful, while *Dynamo* was not, and this notwithstanding that in Claudette Colbert we used a very beautiful and talented actress in the lead. After we closed *Dynamo* she left immediately for Hollywood with such impetus from the play's failure that she has never since returned to the legitimate stage. We had asked 'Gene to come to New York to help us stage the play but he decided not to do so, a decision he regretted later, as is explained in the following letter received after we notified him that the play had closed:

I'm quite resigned to its being a failure—for many reasons. First, I'm sure now, from the reaction, that any play of mine that followed *Interlude* was almost bound to be—unless it enormously topped *Interlude* (a hard job but *Lazarus Laughed* could have, with its exultant spiritual message, if properly produced and acted).

Secondly, I blundered horribly in shooting off my mouth about a trilogy and the meaning of it. I didn't mean what is usually meant by trilogy, of course, and I didn't mean "message," "solution" or anything definite. But it gave them all a clue as to how they should misinterpret—and, as they were gunning for my next play, they seized on it eagerly. My own fault, though!

Thirdly, I never should have let the play out of my hands so soon after completing it—contrary to my usual practice. Besides being in a distraught state of mind at the time I went over the script, I had no perspective on it. When I read it over—after settling here—too late—I was appalled by its raggedness and, in the third part, vagueness and complicatedness. It was in no shape for production. You will see what I mean when you read the book.

Fourthly, I should have been there and all I'm doing now would have been done at rehearsals. Or, more to the point, I should have held over the play

---

[1] The cast included Claudette Colbert, Glenn Anders, Dudley Digges, Catherine Doucet, George Gaul, Helen Westley, Hugh Forrester and Edgar Kent.

until next season when I could be there. This is no beef against Phil, of course. I know he did a fine job with what was there—but he couldn't be expected to read my mind and rewrite from it!

After the failure of *Dynamo,* 'Gene never stayed away from the initial production of any of his plays.

CHAPTER XX

Trouble Ahead

MY FATHER taught me as a child the famous lines which Shakespeare wrote in *The Rape of Lucrece*, "We oft neglect the thing we have, and all for want of wit, make something nothing by augmenting it." By spreading out over the country we strengthened the Theatre Guild but we weakened the Theatre Guild Acting Company, now made up of over thirty performers. It was impossible to send our Acting Company on tour, and have them play in New York at the same time, so that while we gave our out-of-town subscribers our best actors during the season of 1928–29, this left us with too thin a fare to provide proper sustenance to our New York members. To avoid this dilemma we planned to satisfy our New York audience by increasing the size of our Acting Company so that we could produce four plays in Alternating Repertory, with part of the Company in New York while the other part was on tour.

Our first play, *Faust,* Part I, included Dudley Digges, George Gaul and Gale Sondergaard, but it was not successful and could not form part of our alternating plan; nor was the following play, Shaw's *Major Barbara* with Winifred Lenihan, Eliot Cabot, Dudley Digges and Percy Waram. Our next play, *Wings Over Europe,* was an immediate success, but the cast was made up entirely of men, and it was impossible to alternate it with another play. Then came Sil-Vara's delightful comedy *Caprice* with the Lunts, and Eugene O'Neill's *Dynamo,* but the latter ran only for a short period and the former was so popular that we hesitated to alternate it with anything else. In this way, the Acting Company, so important to the achievement of this phase of our work, began to crumble away, and our councils were divided. We had, without realizing it, overreached ourselves, and so, as I appreciated only in retrospect, we began to move backward instead of forward.

Edward G. Robinson, one of our most important character actors, left our Company for another management. Later on, he went to Hollywood. Eddie lived across the street from me in Greenwich Village, and one evening he came to my home and asked me if the Guild would increase his salary to $250 a week. I was unable to secure the increase from the Board, which amounted to a mere $25 a week. He regretfully left us, and a few years later was earning thirty to forty times his weekly stipend.

I saw only one way to prevent the disintegration of the Acting Company, and this was to bring them all together again in their original repertory of plays and send them to London, where we had a proposition from Charles Cochran for a season's engagement. The Board adopted this plan, but alas, it fell through because of a disagreement with our actors on the subject. Later on I made some desperate attempts to revive the Acting Company, but my efforts were unsuccessful, for soon after the beginning of the next season we were laid low by the panic of 1929.

Other factors were also beginning to operate unfavorably against the Alternating Repertory system. The new authors did not like it because it cut down the length of the runs of their plays, and it became increasingly difficult to get new plays for this system. For this, and for a number of other reasons, the alternating system was ultimately dropped. In my opinion, the Guild's light never shone as brightly thereafter.

Money in the bank is not the capital of an art theatre. Its real capital is the creative energy of its workers. With artistic capital, financial success follows. The success of the Acting Company, for which I fought and bled, resulted in our being able to accumulate a capital of $750,000 at the time, as well as to redeem over $200,000 worth of Guild Theatre bonds. With the depression, this capital began to dwindle, and what was worse, so did our creative energies, which were our real capital.

We started the twelfth season of 1929–30 with three failures in a row, including Romain Rolland's excellent play *The Game of Love and Death* beautifully acted by Alice Brady, and S. N. Behrman's *Meteor*. Sam Behrman's comedy must be written down as less than triumphant, despite the fact that its leading parts were played by

Alfred Lunt and Lynn Fontanne. *Meteor* was a brilliant study of a brilliant business man, but somewhere in the rehearsal period, it became transformed from a four-act play into a three-act play, and lost itself in the transformation. Sam Behrman's sense of dramatic structure has never been his strongest point, but his characters are always fascinating and his dialogue scintillating. Given a basic structural skeleton, his plays spring into vivid life. Ina Claire, who appeared in several of them, was particularly successful in helping his construction of the play, by the simple expedient of standing in the center of the rehearsal room, looking him squarely in the eyes and saying, "Sam, this play is about me, isn't it, so what do I do next?" In this manner she kept the backbone of the story intact, with herself in the center of it, as a result of which his comedy *End of Summer* (which we produced during the season of 1935–36) was transformed by Sam during rehearsals into a moving and well-constructed play.

Meteor, however, failed to respond to treatment, and at one of the conferences which took place after midnight at Boston's Ritz-Carlton (the hotel where more plays have been rewritten than in any other place in the world), it was decided that Lynn and Alfred needed stronger scenes of conflict and more moments of tenderness. Sam, who rose each morning at seven and produced a few pages of beautiful dialogue before breakfast, appeared at the theatre the next day with some sheets of paper. "Here, Lawrence," he said, "are six pages of conflict, and here are three pages of tenderness!" Notwithstanding our efforts, the play refused to come together, and nerves became very tense as the days wore on, and the dreaded New York opening came closer and closer. One afternoon, at a rehearsal which had the ominous stillness of an oncoming storm, Philip Moeller who was directing a scene which was obviously impossible to direct or act, suddenly began to sob and cried out, "I can't stand it any more! I can't stand it!" He then threw a fit of hysteria which had me running for water while others dragged him over to a couch. "Get him home as soon as possible," said Alfred Lunt, taking charge of the situation. "It's been too much for him, and I don't wonder at it." We helped the trembling Philip to his feet, and I started to walk back to the hotel with him. No sooner were we out on the street than Phil pulled himself together. "How do you feel now?" I asked. "Fine," he said, striding along and smiling happily. "If I hadn't thrown that fit of hysterics just when I did, some of the actors would have done it a minute later."

This same season we also produced *A Month In The Country* by

Turgenev, the first realistic play in the history of the modern theatre, in which Alla Nazimova and Katharine Hepburn first appeared with us. Our final play was *Hotel Universe,* a poetic fantasy by Philip Barry which was especially championed by me, and in which Ruth Gordon gave one of her finest performances, but it also finished in the red. The Guild was having its own financial crisis of 1929, to parallel that of Wall Street.

I was not, at first, personally affected by the Wall Street panic. What savings I had accumulated I had put into railroad bonds at the suggestion of a cousin of mine. During the "boom" era which ended in 1929, this cousin had conducted a banking business and made me a director. This gave me a curious feeling, for while I had no ambition to be a banker, here I was being consulted about the promotion of new companies about which I knew very little. We had some clients, however, who came over from Europe with inventions which needed financing, so I introduced them to my banking partners. One of these inventions was the Hofgaard electrical calculating machine brought over from Norway by Ove Collett of Oslo, and a company was floated for it.

When the stocks and shares came tumbling down, I walked through the New York financial district to sense its atmosphere. There was a kind of calm over Wall Street which was in striking contrast with the foreboding headlines in the newspapers. Yet it seemed as though, despite the calm, the foundations under the proud tall skyscrapers were trembling, and I felt that man's footing on the earth, for all his pride, was as insecure as it must have been in primitive days. I turned away from this scene, which seemed so unreal, to the theatre whose esthetic values alone seemed to stand firm in a tottering world. A few days later, my secretary was sobbing at her desk. All her savings had been put into the stock market and she had no money to put up for further margins. I agreed to underwrite her. My losses on this slight transaction alone were equal to a year of my earnings. To my secretary, it spelled the loss of all her savings.

Armina and I proceeded to purchase the farm at Cannondale, Connecticut, which we christened Langnerlane, and without any fears faced the depression which was beginning. I was still living in a fool's paradise. The farm contained over a thousand apple trees. I bought a book on apple raising, and found that apple trees had thousands of different diseases. The first year I had the orchard, a horde of field mice with a taste for apple bark destroyed over a hundred of the trees. Even a field mouse can upset all one's calculations I found; so can blights, moths, caterpillars, apple worms, borers and a host of other pests. The apple orchard cost hundreds of dollars each year until I happily abandoned the trees to the savagery of nature.

As though the theatre had not enough on its hands to weather a panic of first magnitude followed by a long and arid depression, Fate found a sharper stick to beat us with in the invention of the talking pictures. These, in spite of being pooh-poohed in the early experimental days of Al Jolson singing "Mammy," very quickly robbed us of our most experienced talent both in acting, directing and writing. The Gold Rush of the forty-niners was paralleled by the Gold Rush of the nineteen thirties; Hollywood became, overnight, a Mecca for the second-raters and a graveyard for some of the first-raters. Eugene O'Neill showed me a final telegram he sent to Warner Brothers after refusing a flood of offers to write movie scenarios. It read "No, no, no!"

Some years earlier, in the days of the silent pictures, I had been offered a position by Paramount Pictures to take the place vacated by Walter Wanger. "I might take it," I replied, "if I can bring along fifty of my friends with me." "Why do you want to do that?" I was asked. "In order to have my own gang to fight *your* gang to make the kind of pictures I'd like to make," was my reply. Needless to say, my proposal was turned down. Now that silent pictures had given way to talking pictures, I was again approached, this time by the same Walter Wanger, our former business manager. He took me over the picture studios at Astoria, and showed me how the new invention worked; and then he asked me if I would come to Hollywood and work in the new medium. I must admit I was tempted by the possibility of reaching the masses with productions of Theatre Guild caliber, and I was also fascinated by the technical and scientific aspects. Without actually saying "Get thee behind me, Walter," I nevertheless put the temptation aside, for I felt that I was dedicated to the theatre, and that this was no time to leave for the greener pastures on the other side of the fence.

But with dwindling business and lower salaries as the only sure prospects in sight, some of the members of our Acting Company left for the Coast. Dudley Digges, Ernest Cossart, Claude Rains and Henry Travers did so reluctantly. But as we had abandoned the system of Alternating Repertory which gave them opportunities for playing varied roles, we had no artistic compensation to offer them in return for their sacrifices in staying with us.

From now on, internal squabbles added to our troubles. A Chinese actor in *Roar China,* one of our productions, used to remark, "It looks black from where I sit," and during this period, this became our favorite slogan. In order to function with less friction, it was decided to place each play under the management of a Production Committee of two members (later called supervisors) who, however, were subject to the whims and fancies of the entire Board, exercised at so-called "Managers' Rehearsals." Good results were often obtained in this way, but it afforded no final solution to the problems of group production.

There was no lack of creative suggestions, however, for we were literally bursting with creators. We had acquired Rouben Mamoulian after his success with *Porgy* and *Marco Millions:* we also acquired another young director named Herbert Biberman who was broad, brawny and heavily bespectacled. Both Mamoulian and Biberman were later elevated to the Board of the Guild, so that with Philip Moeller, there were now three stage directors in our management.

Then began the "Regime of the Directors." Biberman had spent several months in Russia under the Dictatorship of the Proletariat, and came into the Guild replete with such words as "Dynamic," "Agitprop," and some other resounding new words, all of which were very impressive, especially as Biberman seldom talked any quieter than in a loud shout, and had a disconcerting way of emphasizing what he was saying by banging his clenched fist on anything handy. As he was physically big and muscular, and on occasion could bellow like a bull, our meetings became more and more like conferences of a baseball team, and the most fruitful topics of disturbance were when we decided which of the three staff directors was to direct a given play. This was a sporting event in which anything might happen, and often did. While an exciting argument went on as to who should direct the Russian play *Roar China,* Lee Simonson began pacing back and forth in my living room speaking his mind in such volumes of oratory that my little black Scottie, thinking that I needed protection, suddenly darted at him and bit him on the ankle.

In addition to Philip Moeller, who was liked by all of us, we each had our favorite directors, and we backed them much as one backs his favorite horse. My favorite was Mamoulian against Biberman, and I backed him, together with Terry and Maurice. The others backed Biberman, and it was neck and neck as to which horse would win. As often as not, they tied, with Phil Moeller quietly coming in ahead of them both. When Biberman was in the saddle, the Guild really became "dynamic." His method of directing was the same as Ellen Terry's, but the results were different. He showed the actors how he,

Biberman, would play the part, and then told them to imitate him. After seeing a run-through of a play which he was directing, I remarked, "These are not actors, they are bibermans," and indeed there was something not quite human about them; they were like robots or homunculi.

It was decided that Biberman, being as fresh from Russia as the latest shipment of caviar, should direct *Roar China* which I promptly renamed "Roar Biberman," whereupon Mamoulian, after making a dignified speech about minority rights, oppressed directors and his prior claim to direct anything of Russian origin, retired gracefully to Hollywood, much to my personal regret and consequent loss to the Guild.

Nor was our new policy of emphasizing the director rather than the play or the acting ensemble producing satisfactory artistic results. Most of the plays this season of 1930–31, except for *Elizabeth the Queen*, directed by Philip Moeller, were failures artistically, and financially were disastrous. Our season's loss was over $180,000. Something was radically wrong.

While away on a business trip I had time to mull deeply over this situation, which, if it continued, must bring our enterprise to ruin, and on April 2, 1931, from Akron, Ohio, I wired my secretary:

PLEASE WRITE IMMEDIATELY FOLLOWING LETTER ALL GUILD BOARD. I WISH TO GIVE NOTICE THAT I SHALL INTRODUCE THE FOLLOWING RESOLUTION AT THE NEXT BOARD MEETING. RESOLVED THAT THE GUILD ITS POLICIES AND METHODS OF OPERATION REQUIRE COMPLETE REORGANIZATION. I ASK THAT THIS BE MADE THE FIRST ORDER OF BUSINESS OF THE DAY AND THAT THE MEETING BE STRICTLY LIMITED TO BOARD MEMBERS.

At the meeting I behaved very badly, attacking everyone for the state of affairs with equal violence. I particularly attacked the conception of the dictator-director as exemplified by Biberman. Terry Helburn and Maurice Wertheim were on my side, but they put forth their arguments with considerably less hysteria. It had become manifest in the operation of the Guild with its group of three stage directors that there was no way of providing "management," since the others could be outvoted on any issue, yet were required to take the responsibility for failure if a project did not succeed. I suggested the restoration of the Acting Company as our most vital need, but this issue was compromised in a proposal on which all could agree. The most important part of this read as follows:

All titles of members of the Board of Managers to be abolished.

Production committee of two members of the Board selected for each play by a majority vote of the entire Board; said committee to be in charge of each play and have the right to call the full Board to rehearsals for advice.

Biberman's contract not to be renewed for next season.

No advance commitments to members of the Board for production of scenic work.

Definite agreement by all on basic principles of Guild policy.

Biberman left the organization for Hollywood and with him went the theory of the God-given director; expenses were cut down and the operation of the Guild was put on a businesslike basis. We came out of this crisis in a far healthier condition, and its good results were shown in the improvements in our productions and personal relations between the directors in the seasons which directly followed.

But the Guild's travails were not ended. We had as our play-reader a brilliant young man I had suggested for the job named Harold Clurman, who was bursting with creative ideas, while our talented Casting Direc.r Cheryl Crawford who was sponsored by Theresa Helburn was habitually in a similar state of creativeness. Encouraged mainly by Terry and myself, they dreamed up a Studio which produced, in the spring of 1930, with a great deal of vitality, a play called *Red Rust* which depicted quite vividly the uncomfortable lives lived by students in Soviet Russia. During this period Harold and Cheryl may be depicted as living (like myself) in a state of healthy fermentation, which was likely to erupt into a rebellion at any moment, and I respected their enthusiastic attitude toward the theatre, and their supreme disrespect for their elders. Now in order to stage a successful rebellion, it is necessary to have something to rebel against, and since our conduct of the Guild as a kind of dogfight was calculated to serve as an example to be avoided by the young, it was not surprising that the most immediate and vulnerable subject to stage a rebellion against was ourselves. Adding to their number a third exponent of their theatrical ideals, Lee Strasberg (who had acted for us in *Green Grow the Lilacs*), they laid down some artistic principles with which most of us were in sympathy, and their plea for the revival of an Acting Company was especially dear to my heart.

The best that the parents of a child can do when that child wants independence is to help it on its way; and this the Guild Board did, even though it was apparent later on that our offspring regarded us as old-fashioned fogies running around the theatre in circles. When they formulated their plans to start the Group Theatre, Terry Helburn was particularly active in helping them to get on their feet. In addition to providing half the funds for their first two plays, we turned over to them a play by Paul Green, *The House of Connelly*, with something of a pang, as well as another play, *1931*, by the Siftons, with a feeling of relief by at least one member of the Board. The umbilical cord thus cut, the Group Theatre began to function, and during much of the time when the Theatre Guild was in the doldrums, artistically speaking, the Group Theatre with its playwrights, Clifford Odets and Irwin Shaw, wrote a brilliant page in the annals of the theatre of the thirties, and its individual directors have continued to influence the theatre long after the Group Theatre ceased existing as an entity.

While the Guild now continued to function more fruitfully, yet the compromise settlement, on which I and all my fellow members of the Board were able to agree, left out what I regarded as an important basis for the future of the Guild, the formation of a new Acting Company. Although happy to see the end of the regime of the God-given directors, I was inwardly seething. I ultimately exploded.

In the spring of 1932 Armina and I decided to form our own Acting Company away from the Theatre Guild, to build a summer theatre for it near our home at Westport, Connecticut, and to prepare a repertory of plays to bring to New York the following season. In this way I would show the Guild members the value of an acting company and prove to them the error of their ways. We bought a barn with seven acres of land off the Boston Post Road; we remodeled it as a theatre with a full-size stage; we organized an acting company, and we started them in a repertory of six plays including Shakespeare and Ibsen; and Armina and I did this in the few months intervening between March and July. The fact that I was launched in an enterprise in which I did not have to be subservient to the wishes of five other collaborators no doubt was responsible for the release of so much energy on my part. I named the theatre "The Westport Country Playhouse," and the Acting Company "The New York Repertory Company."

From now on I no longer became frustrated and emotional when my ideas were turned down at the Guild. I simply took them to Westport and tried them out in our own theatre. My disposition was positively sunny, for now not only could I work on plays for the Guild each winter, but each summer I could produce anywhere from eight to ten plays which I liked, as I liked, and with whom I liked. I thoroughly enjoyed this strange freedom which tied me down to do more work than I had ever done before. There was a positive joy in selecting a play, casting, choosing the director, the scenic artist, the décor, molding it, shaping it until it came to life on the stage—a life of its own which might be long or short as the case might be, but was nevertheless a living thing created from some words on paper, a handful of actors and the other ingredients which were the recipe for the most enchanting dish a cook, to my mind, could enjoy making. Horse racing may be the sport of kings, I thought to myself, but play producing is the sport for me, and I did not envy the kings.

During the Guild's 1930–31 season, we produced Maxwell Anderson's *Elizabeth the Queen* in which Alfred Lunt and Lynn Fontanne gave such magnificent performances as Essex and Elizabeth; Philip Moeller staged the play and Lee Simonson contributed the splendid sets and costumes. I first met Max Anderson just after we had purchased this play. Max, who in his younger days had been a newspaper editor, was a big heavy-set man, clumsy in his movements, lovable as a person and very pleasant to work with.

When we opened *Elizabeth the Queen* in Philadelphia, the play showed certain rather obvious deficiencies, which we discussed with Max who said he would rewrite some scenes and add some others. "How did you make out?" I would ask Max each morning before lunch. "Sorry, Lawrence," he would answer. "I had no luck. I just didn't feel like writing." The weather was fine in Philadelphia, and waiting for Max was an enjoyable interlude, but as the fateful day for our New York opening drew closer, and no rewriting was forthcoming, we began to grow more and more anxious. Finally we postponed the New York opening and moved to Baltimore. A torrential rainstorm which assaulted Baltimore and drenched us as we came to and from Ford's Theatre added to our depression. On Tuesday morning after the Baltimore opening I met Max in the foyer of the Belvedere Hotel, and regarded him as an anxious farmer would a favorite cow that had gone dry. "How about today?" I asked, bitterly. "Here's what you wanted for Act One." He handed me some sheets, folded together. "Here's Alfred's new speech." Another sheet was handed to me; and so on until I was clutching in my hands the entire revision of the play. "When did all this happen?" I asked in amazement. "Well, Lawrence," replied Max with an enigmatic smile, "I really only write well when it rains." No drought-ridden farmer was more grateful for rain than I was.

On the opening night in New York I stood on the stage of the

Martin Beck Theatre by the side of the curtain man as, for a count
of seventeen curtain calls, he exhausted himself raising and dropping
the curtain, while Alfred, handsome and graceful in the black costume of Essex, and Lynn, wearing the lustrous copper-colored robe of
Elizabeth, which gave her the appearance of a metallic statue, bowed
to the applause which roared in successive waves from the excited
audience.

The next season, that of 1931–32, united the Guild forces in a
magnificent production of O'Neill's *Mourning Becomes Electra* with
Alla Nazimova and Alice Brady. Old wounds were healed, and working to bring out the best in O'Neill's high drama brought out the best
in us. The play lifted our season out of the quagmire into which we
had dragged it with a shaky opening production of Alfred Savoir's
He with Claude Rains.

Robert Sherwood's delightful comedy *Reunion in Vienna,* brought
Alfred, Lynn and Helen Westley together again in a *mise en scène*
reminiscent of their earlier efforts in *The Guardsman.* Helen, as the
counterpart of the famous Madame Sacher of Vienna, was trenchantly
acidulous, and a high moment in the performance came one evening
when Alfred Lunt, who was required to lift her skirts and spank her
across the seat of her red bloomers, discovered to his horror that she
had forgotten to put them on.

Reunion in Vienna was the first play by Robert Sherwood produced
by the Guild and as I was on the production committee of this play
with Terry, I had many opportunities to meet and work with him.
I found him to be one of the most idealistic of our playwrights, and
a man whose attitude and conception of the theatre is on the highest
plane. Indeed, I remarked once, facetiously, that anyone as tall as
Robert Sherwood would have difficulty in writing anywhere except
on a high plane, for he stands head and shoulders taller than the
ordinary man, and from this altitude the world must look different.
Sherwood, with his long head and solemn face which belies his sense
of humor, speaks with great deliberation, each word lingering on his
lips as though it has a separate identity and meaning. His desire to
make the world a better place to live in motivates his plays, and his
training as a dramatic critic has undoubtedly helped him to analyze
his material, and to write plays which have excellent dramatic structure calling for very little help from others. Indeed, with the exception of Eugene O'Neill, I know of no other playwright who produces
a manuscript which, on first reading, is so ready for production.

In the case of *Reunion in Vienna,* Bob ran full tilt into our Theatre

Guild Board system and did not like it at all. One of our members regarded himself as an authority on psychoanalysis, and began an acrimonious argument with Sherwood as to whether the analyst in the play was really orthodox or not. I tried to smooth out this situation, and succeeded for the time being, but it was not an easy matter. The play was directed by Worthington Miner, and Alfred, Lynn and Helen Westley were enchanting in their respective roles. The play opened out of town and a certain amount of revision was necessary— more than was usual later on in Sherwood's plays.

Once again my fellow Board members attended a performance. Once again Bob, Terry and I listened to long tirades on psychoanalysis, and on how little Bob understood the subject. The net result was to irritate our author with the organization, and as this kind of irritation added up from author to author, I believe it contributed considerably to the disaffection of such playwrights as Anderson, Behrman and Sherwood, from the Guild, until ultimately they formed their own producing organization.

Reunion in Vienna opened in New York November 16, 1931. Its gaiety and its contrast of the romantic appeal of old Vienna with the point of view of the psychoanalyst made this comedy one of the high points in the careers of Sherwood, Lunt and Fontanne. Some years later they took it to London where it ran for an entire season.

During our next season (1932–33), we produced S. N. Behrman's *Biography,* one of the best comedies ever written in this country, and Maxwell Anderson's *Both Your Houses,* which won the Pulitzer Prize. *Biography,* excellently directed by Philip Moeller, also brought us into association with the brilliant comedienne, Ina Claire, who seemed especially fashioned by providence with the rapid-fire tongue to speak Behrman's iridescent sentences as though they were mere commonplaces of language. Ina ranks with the best actresses of this period, her style reminding one of the expert comedy acting of the earlier Minnie Maddern Fiske and Marie Tempest. She was one of the prettiest women I have ever known, with blond hair, laughing Irish eyes, piquant features, a beautiful figure, and a sense of humor that worked without ceasing, both on the stage and off. But beyond this, she had a deep emotional quality which, alas, she seldom permitted herself to display. Had she done so and played such roles as Hedda Gabler with which Eva Le Gallienne and I often tempted her for Westport, she would have gone far beyond the role of comedienne which she chose for herself. With her disappearance from the stage in recent years, a style of acting has disappeared along with her, and unless some new genius of comedy appears on the horizon, the generations of today and tomorrow will never know the joy of witnessing the lightning timing, the flash of wit, the grace of movement, or the high excitement of acting which are Ina's.

Unfortunately, Ina could never learn her lines in a hurry, and it took several prompters located behind convenient pieces of scenery to ensure that she would eventually deliver a memorized performance. And the extraordinary thing was that as she flitted from one part of the stage to another, to pick up one line here and another there, nobody in the audience was faintly aware of what was going on, for she was completely unhurried and relaxed. "I learned this by watching Duse," she once informed me. "Whenever she forgot a line she simply went over to the prompter's box, picked it up and went right on."

Biography opened in Pittsburgh during a week of fog and rain, and rather than stay in our dismal hotel rooms, we gathered in the cheerful studio set designed by Jo Mielziner, pulled down the theatre curtain and had tea on stage each afternoon after rehearsal. One actor irritated Ina by his empty performance: "How can I play the scene," she expostulated, after he left the theatre, "with that man snorting at me like a prop stallion!"

Ina's personal kindness and instinctive knowledge of the theatre was shown some years later when, in another Behrman play, a young actress who appeared with her tried every device to attract attention from Ina to herself, including the trick of appearing on the opening night with her blond hair dressed in the same striking way as Ina's. "I understand her perfectly," said Ina without the slightest concern, when I discussed this with her. "But she doesn't understand that it took me twenty years of hard work to make the audience keep their eyes on me when I come on the stage, and nothing she can do can affect that." And she was right.

Another play of this season was *The Good Earth*, adapted by the veteran playwright Owen Davis and his son, Donald, from the novel by Pearl Buck. The leading character, a Chinese peasant woman, was played by Alla Nazimova, who at this time was in her early fifties and at the height of her powers. Alla was a woman of medium height with dark hair and penetrating eyes, a woman of great charm and beauty. One of her most surprising characteristics was that she never looked the same. At one time she dazzled you with her beauty and smartness, at another time she looked completely drab and ordinary, a third time she suggested the *maîtresse* of a French Baron. Brought over here from Russia many years earlier, Nazimova's voice had never lost its Russian flavor. It was warm, soft and velvety and was one of her most fascinating qualities on the stage.

Nazimova had a disconcerting way of playing a part differently from night to night. In *A Month in the Country* she sometimes played the character of Natalia as a charming and delightful woman; at other times, she would play her as a sulky and lovable creature, while another time she would make her positively mean and disagreeable; and what was more extraordinary, whichever characterization she happened to choose on the particular night she was playing it, this characterization was completely consistent from the beginning to the end of the play. On one occasion when she was playing in Shaw's *The Simpleton of the Unexpected Isles* I remarked that her performance of the night before was the best she had given. "What did I do last night, Lawrence?" she asked, "and tell me how it differed from the way I played it tonight?"

The highest point in Nazimova's career, in my opinion, was her portrayal of Christine in O'Neill's *Mourning Becomes Electra*. In this part, she combined feminine allure with a strength of passion which made entirely credible the love affair between herself and the sea captain, Adam Brant, a man considerably younger, while her ability to arouse the sympthy of the audience made one almost forgive her the murder of her husband, General Ezra Mannon, while hating her for doing it. Thus she became the victim of the Mannons rather than their oppressor.

Eugene O'Neill, Maxwell Anderson, S. N. Behrman and Robert Sherwood all gave us plays for our next season, that of 1933–34. On the same day that I received *Ah, Wilderness* from Eugene O'Neill by mail, I was handed *Mary of Scotland* by Maxwell Anderson in person.

We produced *Mary of Scotland* with Helen Hayes in the title role, Philip Merivale as Bothwell and Helen Menken as Elizabeth, with Theresa Helburn directing the play. As was usual with Max Anderson's plays, some slight rewriting was necessary. In Pittsburgh, when we opened *Mary of Scotland*, we were in difficulties with the end of the second act. Helen Hayes invited us all to supper in her sitting room one night at the William Penn Hotel. "I have an idea for that scene at the end of the second act," she said, after we had eaten. "That's why I asked you up here. I thought I'd feed you first in case you didn't like my idea." And then she explained that in the scene as written, she had too much to say and do as Mary, while Bothwell, played by Philip Merivale, had too little. "By this time," explained Helen, "they're all tired of me. I know I shouldn't say this as an actress, but take most of the scene away from me and give it to Philip." Helen's instinct was right, and Max accepted her suggestion, which, far from weakening her part, made her big scene in the third act more powerful than before.

Max, in his point of view, his individualism, and his love of Jeffersonian democracy, continues to represent the traditions of that finest of American institutions, the independent small-town editor. Had he not written for the theatre, he might have become another William Allen White. Max, like Shaw, usually gets good notices on his last play when the dramatic critics review his new play. After he joined the Playwrights' Company, I worked on none of his later plays except for *Candle in the Wind*. Whenever I hear that a new one is being produced, I feel an inner pang, like someone whose friend is giving a party to which he will not be invited. And I always watch the weather for rain.

While some of our plays were doing well in New York during this season, others were failures, and those that failed were dire failures. There was no halfway mark. We were still in the darkest days of the depression. Most of the subscription cities which I had worked so hard to build up, lecturing and visiting them year after year as I took trips around the country for my firm, began to slip away, and soon we had to abandon all of them except Chicago, Boston, Philadelphia, Pittsburgh and Washington. In Detroit and Cleveland, when the banks closed, we lost all our subscription money, and it was repaid only years later, in the late thirties, when the tide of the depression began to turn.

To add to our misfortunes, after the Lunts had finished their road tour of *Reunion in Vienna*, they left the Guild to go into management with Noel Coward, and opened in his new comedy *Design for Living*. This was heartbreaking at the time, but I never gave up the hope that one day they would return to the Guild. A couple of years later Helen Westley and I called on them in their dressing room at the theatre where they were playing in Coward's *Point Valaine* and we began to tempt them to return to our fold in a Shakespearean production; they had also been thinking of something of the sort, and we finally agreed on *The Taming of the Shrew*. In the early part of our eighteenth season, they returned to us in a gala production of this comedy, so gay, so boisterous and so colorful, that it remains one of my happiest memories; with them came Richard Whorf, to whom I introduced them, and Sidney Greenstreet, both magnificent actors.

Along with several other actors, they formed the nucleus of a new Acting Company under the Theatre Guild banner.

Meanwhile, the Theatre Guild suffered another severe loss. It was one of the ironies of fate that during the time when Helen Westley was young and beautiful, she had difficulty in obtaining parts, but in her fifties, her salty and lovable personality was so popular that she was given opportunities which enabled her to reach the height of her acting career. She was offered an excellent Hollywood contract, and although her heart was still with the Guild, she felt that since she was being used as an actress only sporadically, and did not enjoy working for other managers, she could not afford to turn down the opportunity. This was a great handicap to the Guild, for we all adored her, and her influence was always in the direction of greatness. Helen Westley's charm, vitality and integrity in the selection of plays, her insistence that the Guild should produce only the finest, and her ability to evaluate the second-rate and to distinguish it from that which was first-rate, were invaluable to the Board. After she passed away, George Jean Nathan (with whom I occasionally agree), when puncturing an "experimental" play which we had produced recently, mourned her loss from the Guild in the following terms:

. . . Whenever any such play shows up, it induces people who are bored stiff by it nevertheless flatteringly to remark that it took courage to produce it. What it takes, of course, is not courage but dumbness. Which recalls the late Helen Westley, who for many years was a member of this same Theatre Guild's board of directors. On the Guild's opening nights, the grand old girl, begauded as ever like the gypsy queen in an 1890 comic opera, always deposited herself in a seat on the aisle in one of the rear rows of the theatre. On the various occasions when her Guild associates saw fit to put on plays like this exhibit, it was her pleasure to hail me on my way out at the first intermission and loudly to assure me that if I didn't think the play was a polecat I was crazy. At the second intermission, she would lean over as I went up the aisle and beamingly yell, "See, I told you! It's getting even lousier." And at the evening's end she would grab me by the arm and gleefully shout, "My God, did you ever see anything like it?" I miss her.

During this same period Philip Moeller was offered the post of director for three motion pictures in Hollywood, and for protracted intervals of time he also was absent from the Guild. Theresa Helburn, who had given up her position as Executive Director of the Guild, was offered a tempting post with Columbia Pictures, and took a leave of absence of nine months.

The depression of the thirties, which created so much havoc within the Theatre Guild, was also responsible for troubles which threatened the entire American theatre. Notwithstanding the average citizen's lack of spending money, the handful of so-called "hit" shows were un-available to most of the theatre-going public because the theatre tickets were largely in the hands of ticket speculators. In the fall of 1930, I received a call on the telephone from Winthrop Ames, the famous Bostonian who occupied a unique position as an artistic pro-ducer in the theatre. On arriving at his office, Ames, tall and thin, with sharp features looking not unlike the redoubtable Sherlock Holmes, assigned me to an armchair, poured me a Scotch-and-soda, and told me that he had been asked to serve on a committee which would put a stop to theatre ticket speculation. He stated, however, that on account of ill-health he was unable to do so, and asked whether I would serve in his place. I assented, little knowing what I was letting myself in for. I flung myself into the fight with all the zeal I could muster, and it was decided, as part of the campaign, that we would control the sale of tickets ourselves in such a way as to avoid these getting into the hands of the "speculators."

Remembering that Keith Prowse in London used to send messenger boys in uniform to deliver theatre tickets, it occurred to me that the American telegraph companies might be willing to undertake the sale of theatre tickets. I therefore called on the Western Union Telegraph Company and met Mr. J. C. Willever, head of their Special Services Department, and he in turn introduced me to Newton Carlton, the President of the company, a large cherubic-looking elderly gentleman wearing a fancy vest and a carnation in his buttonhole. "Why, I remember in England," said Carlton flamboyantly, "the messenger boys used to deliver flowers and theatre tickets. Do you imagine that a great American corporation like the Western Union Company would stoop to send theatre tickets and flowers from a gentleman to his lady friend?" "I don't know what you mean about stooping," said Willever. "As a matter of fact, Western Union performs exactly that service right at the present moment." While Mr. Willever was very willing that every Western Union office throughout the country should become a theatre ticket office, he could not secure the cooperation of his Board of Directors.

I decided to visit the rival company, the Postal Telegraph Company, and here my efforts met with greater success. I made an arrangement between this company and the embattled theatrical managers, and almost overnight there was a battalion of over seventy-five clerks selling theatre tickets by wire at a central ticket office off Times Square.

The advent of Postal into theatre ticket selling broke the situation, and the ticket agencies were glad to come to terms. Later on they signed an agreement known as the "Ticket Code" between themselves, Actors' Equity Association, and the League of New York Theatres which regulated these practices.

While this fight was progressing, together with a number of other managers, I made an impassioned plea at one of the meetings for the formation of a permanent managers' organization, so that we might help one another for the benefit of the theatre. As a result of this meeting there was formed the League of New York Theatres, and I have served on its Board of Governors since its inception. The League is not as creative as I would like it to be, yet it has lasted longer than any other managers' association and has made considerable progress in securing good practices in the theatre. Together with Actors' Equity Association, it has enforced the Ticket Code, which has to some extent limited the amount of ticket speculation.

Years later, while *Oklahoma!* was running in New York, I discussed the subject of ticket speculation with the late Mayor Fiorello La Guardia. He asked me to give him a practical suggestion as to how to stop one of the evils which arises immediately when all the tickets are left at the theatre box office for sale to the public. Individuals who are known as "diggers" present themselves in the line at the box-office window, and buy tickets which they then turn over to the speculators. They then return again and buy more. I told the Mayor that if he would station a policeman in front of each box office, this policeman could spot the so-called "diggers," follow them to the offices of the ticket speculators, and then arrest them both under the law. "I could never do that," said the vivacious little Mayor. "Inside of three days the policeman would know the racket, and inside of a week the ward leaders would all be in the ticket speculation business."

Our Theatre Guild subscription system avoided ticket speculation on a limited scale by placing the best tickets directly in the hands of theatre goers. The depression hurt the subscription series very badly, and we were, moreover, fighting an opposition system initiated by the Messrs. Shubert, since the Theatre Guild did its booking through their rivals, Messrs. Klaw and Erlanger.

As the depression deepened, the road situation became desperate. The Shuberts and Klaw and Erlanger continued to wage their relentless war, and it was destructive for the theatre as a whole, for when a successful star or play was booked into a town by one organization, another star or play of equal importance was usually booked to play against him or it by the other, and what was left of "the road" by the depression was being killed by the war between the two circuits.

When Franklin D. Roosevelt came into office and closed all the banks, admonishing the public that the only thing to fear was fear itself, he signed the National Recovery Act (NRA) out of which came a number of benefits for the theatre. One of these was a closer coopera- tion between the unions and the managers, while another was the bringing together of individuals who, instead of working solely for themselves, began to work for the general good of the theatre.

In my work with the Klaw and Erlanger office, I had met Erlanger's partner, Marcus Heiman, who had invested a considerable amount of his fortune in theatres at a time when such investment was not the most happy experience in the world. Heiman, however, was doing his best to straighten out matters so that what was left of the American theatre could exist during these dark depression days when every week brought news of the tearing down of another theatre building. By a coincidence it happened that Earle Bailie, a partner of Seligman & Co., bankers for the Shuberts, was my next-door neighbor in the country. I brought him and Heiman together with the suggestion that it might be to the best interests of the dying American theatre for the two circuits to cooperate in providing a continuous theatrical season for each town with the plays spread out so that there would be a twenty-five to thirty-five week season throughout the large cities of the country.

Later, Lee Shubert and Heiman met and Mr. Shubert suggested the United Booking Office, which now serves to book plays throughout the country, irrespective of who owns the theatres, and in such a man- ner that the plays are distributed week by week to each city throughout the season, instead of being played destructively against one another. This new arrangement had the effect of saving many theatre buildings, including the fine Colonial Theatre in Boston, because so few of the theatres either in or out of New York City were earning even their taxes during this period that their owners were tearing them down and converting them into parking lots by the dozen. The younger generation in the theatre today does not realize what it owes in this respect to the efforts of Marcus Heiman and Lee Shubert, who in a single deal changed the co-called "road" from a liability and a head- ache for everyone in the theatre, into an asset which, while it may not please everybody, is nevertheless a great deal better than before the United Booking Office was formed.

In the reorganization of the road, the Theatre Guild Subscription and the Shubert Subscription were merged in the American Theatre Society, of which I became President. With the improvement in conditions in the late thirties, we began to reinstate the cities which had dropped out, and today the Theatre Guild-American Theatre Society subscription system reaches from coast to coast, and now includes twenty-one cities with a total of well over one hundred thousand subscribers.

In the beginning, the main burden of supplying plays for these cities fell on the Guild, but when the American Theatre Society was formed, other managers joined the movement, so that today the Theatre Guild usually supplies only three of the plays while other managers supply the balance. Many of the cities throughout the country would be starved for plays were it not for the fact that the subscription audience underwrites the sending of four or five good plays a year to their towns.

My experience in the operation of the National Recovery Act in connection with the theatre taught me the value of group cooperation, and I sincerely regretted the passing of this organization which encouraged all the members of a craft to get together and endeavor to iron out their difficulties and to improve conditions without government interference. It may be true that adversity makes strange bedfellows, but one of the results of having strange bedfellows is that one attempts to adjust one's position in the bed to make room for all. In the American theatre, with its artists and craftsmen all eager for the improvement of their own lot without reference to the lot of others, it is a pity that this lesson of cooperation learned from the depression has been forgotten. One of the efforts at cooperation which I suggested was an annual Theatre Convention. I proposed that all the people engaged in the theatre, including both employers and employees, sit down together each year and try to work out suggestions for the benefit of the theatre as a whole.

My proposal was adopted by all the elements of the theatre and there was formed a national organization called the American Theatre Council, and under the auspices of this body, we called the first Convention of the American Theatre which lasted for three days at the Hotel Astor, beginning May 24, 1937. Hundreds came from all over the country to discuss how to increase our audiences, to improve our productions and finances, to fight outside interferences such as censorship, and, in general, to deal with all the other problems of the American theatre, except those which would create internal dissension. The three-day meeting wound up with some constructive results, and the personal friendships which we had gained by working together in the Convention helped us over many difficult places in dealing with one another later on.

So well did the first Convention of the American Theatre work out, that a second Convention was called, and this met at the Hotel Astor a year later. Unfortunately, and without the slightest intention of hurting the Convention, Brock Pemberton let slip some criticism of the attitude of the newspapers toward the theatre. The press reacted unfavorably and when the time approached for the calling of the third meeting, we realized that it would be impossible to recapture the spirit which had animated our earlier meetings. A handful of enthusiasts are now hard at work to reestablish these annual gatherings of the late thirties. But perhaps we shall have to fall upon more evil days again before this is possible.

The dark days of the depression were also having a bad effect on the playwrights. Most of the plays which were being written by the younger authors, following the success of Odets' *Waiting for Lefty,* were of the type which were labeled "socially significant," and while of immediate propaganda value, had no lasting interest as works of art. Furthermore, the threat of Hitler's mounting ambitions was constantly before us, and we essayed time after time to produce plays which would publicize the blessings of democracy to an audience skating on the thin ice of financial distress. I was in entire sympathy with the rest of the Guild Board in producing such plays as *Valley Forge* by Maxwell Anderson, which went back to the beginnings of American democracy with a human portrait of George Washington and ended with the ringing words "This liberty will look easy by and by when nobody dies to get it."

At the end of the season in 1935 our future seemed to me very dark. Except for Margaret Kennedy's *Escape Me Never,* produced in association with the London manager Charles B. Cochran, with which we introduced Elisabeth Bergner to the Broadway public, we had suffered serious reverses from several of our productions—especially from a "socially conscious" musical revue *Parade,* which lost about $100,000 for us, and this without any artistic justification other than possibly the fact that it set the example for later musical revues with social content, such as *Pins and Needles* and *Call Me Mister.* Our bank balance began to look alarmingly small. Worse still, Philip Moeller, Theresa Helburn and Helen Westley were all in Hollywood, leaving me to hold the fort with no good plays to produce, and with the ebullient Lee Simonson as the only other active collaborator.

CHAPTER XXI

Inner Tensions and Contact with Youth

M Y PREMONITIONS of disaster for the Guild were contradicted by the following season. It seemed as though the Guild was heading indeed toward a renascence after the staggering blows it had suffered from the previous season.[1] Fortunately for the Guild, a group of excellent new plays arrived, and at the same time our directors who had left us for Hollywood happily returned to the fold, richer in experience, but chastened in spirit by their West Coast adventures.

Among the plays of this season, *Porgy and Bess* proved to be a landmark in the American musical theatre and *Idiot's Delight* was a memorable expression of that concern with the dangers of war in Europe which Sherwood and I shared with others who gave thought to Hitler's designs and policies. My own state of apprehension, intensified by my interest in international affairs in connection with the firm of Langner, Parry, Card and Langner, used to keep me awake at night wondering what was to be done. It was my business to keep *au courant* with what was happening in Europe. I took courage from the fact that in my years of international experience I had seen very few fine inventions come out of Germany, while this country was the source of the most important inventions. Inventively, I thought, we can beat Hitler if we are ever faced with a state of war. I began to plan how we

---

[1] Five of our six productions were successful; the series of 1935–36 included *The Taming of the Shrew,* in which the Lunts scored a triumph, and laid the basis for a new acting company, *Porgy and Bess,* S. N. Behrman's charming and provocative high comedy *End of Summer,* in which Ina Claire excelled, Robert Sherwood's *Idiot's Delight* and Dodie Smith's comedy *Call It a Day.*

could use our inventors in case we became involved in war, and I continued to advocate the production of plays which would serve to draw the attention of the country to the dangers ahead of us.

Porgy and Bess, based on our earlier play *Porgy,* has since become the classic American Negro Folk Opera. The idea of using George Gershwin, then a recognized composer of musical comedies, but whose *Rhapsody in Blue* had made a great impression on the musical world, was the brilliant suggestion of Warren P. Munsell, our business manager, who has never received the credit which, in my opinion, is due him for having promoted this important work.

I visited George Gershwin a number of times while he was writing the music, and he was very proud of a desk he had invented which enabled him to sit at the piano and write down his music while he was composing it. George's apartment was adorned with a large number of his paintings, of which he seemed to be prouder than of his musical achievements, and I felt he rather resented the fact that I lavished my praise on his music instead of on his painting.

The opening of *Porgy and Bess* in New York on October 10, 1935, at the Alvin Theatre was unforgettable. In colorful settings by Sergei Soudekine, which were just far enough away from realism to provide the requisite picturesqueness, with a magnificent orchestra conducted by Alexander Smallens, and under the superb direction of Rouben Mamoulian, whose handling of the crowd scenes remains a vivid recollection, one of the most excited audiences in the history of the New York theatre attended the opening, and their expectations were fully realized. With such magnificent songs as "Summertime," "I Got Plenty of Nothin'," "Bess, You Is My Woman Now," etc., history was being made not only in the musical theatre, but also in the world of the American folk song. Brilliant performances were turned in by Todd Duncan as Porgy, John W. Bubbles as Sportin' Life, and Anne Brown as Bess, which started a new group of careers in the theatre. When the opera came to an end, the curtain rang down to tumultuous applause, but as we left the theatre, we did not realize how great a classic this play was ultimately to become.

Bob Sherwood's play *Idiot's Delight* was directed by Alfred Lunt and at one of the run-through rehearsals, I expressed the feeling that the play seemed too light for its significant content. Lynn put her finger on the pulse of the situation, and suggested to Bob that he write an important scene for her and the manufacturer of munitions, with the result that a great deal of weight was added to the play which, up to that time, had drifted perilously between the delightful story of a group of chorus girls lost in Italy, and the more serious implications of the oncoming war.

The high light of our 1937–38 season was the scintillating comedy, *Amphitryon 38*, adapted for us by S. N. Behrman from the French of Jean Giraudoux. With Lunt and Fontanne in the leading roles, it opened in San Francisco before one of the most attractive audiences I have ever seen assembled in a theatre. Alfred, in a sky-blue toga designed by Valentina, with beard and curls to match, cavorted about the stage in the character of Jupiter while Lynn looked enchanting and acted enchantingly in the role of Alcmene. The fantasy of Giraudoux was embellished by the wit of Sam Behrman, and when I met the famous French author of the 38th version of this play on his visit to New York to see our production, he expressed himself as delighted with it. While we were working on the play in Frisco, we spent some time with the talented blond-haired weaver, Dorothy Liebes, who, with seven beautiful girls, turned out exquisite hand-woven fabrics which have since set the fashion for modern textile design all over the country. What with the weavers, the wines, the restaurants, the Golden Gate, and those special flavors of living which make San Francisco our most picturesque and romantic city, our production of *Amphitryon 38* was a highly enjoyable affair, and has always made me wish to open other plays in that city.

During this season, at a time when none of us were too happy about the state of the world, Sam Behrman brought us his new political comedy, *Wine of Choice*. I believe that we produced this play largely because I had once told Sam's play representative, Harold Freedman, that no matter what Sam wrote, he could rewrite it so brilliantly during rehearsal that it would ultimately emerge as a good play. There were three important roles in *Wine of Choice*, as well as the part of the young liberal who usually married the boss's daughter in Sam's plays. One of these roles was that of a Senator from New Mexico played for some reason or other by a well-known English actor, Leslie Banks, with a well-known British accent which was not remotely connected with New Mexico; there was a sarcastic newspaper correspondent played by the well-known newspaper correspondent, Alexander Woollcott; while the boss's daughter was played by Miriam Hopkins, one of the more versatile actresses of the stage and screen, with a gift for rapid-fire dialogue both on and off the stage. Miriam, whose acting I admired greatly, was not at all happy in her part and had no hesitation in saying so. Neither was Leslie Banks. Nor was Alexander Woollcott.

The play was being directed by Philip Moeller, who was also not at all happy, and all of us were marooned at the Ambassador Hotel in Chicago with the Christmas holidays facing us and with very bleak prospects for returning to New York in time to celebrate them with our families.

There was a good deal of revision under way, and each morning Sam would appear at the theatre with his few sheets of paper which contained the rewriting which had been agreed upon the night before. At the termination of each rehearsal, I was visited by Leslie Banks who remarked, "Really, Lawrence, I see from the way this is being rewritten that you don't need me in this play. You can replace me easily with a hundred-dollar-a-week actor." Miriam would invite me to discuss the rewritten pages over the supper table, and together with her husband Anatol Litvak would comment until the small hours of the morning on how unfavorably her part had been affected. Alec Woollcott, on the other hand, scorned to criticize where he thought he could create. His method of showing his dissatisfaction was to take his typewriter and rewrite all his scenes using his own dialogue—which, considering how light and limber was his usual conversation, was singularly heavy and repulsive.

Woollcott lived in one wing of the Ambassador Hotel called the Ambassador West, while Philip Moeller, S. N. Behrman and I lived in the other wing called the Ambassador East. These two wings were connected by a long tunnel through which I was constantly running from one wing to another, carrying sheets of paper on which Woollcott had typed his proposed rewriting of his scenes, and returning with Sam's more brilliant treatment of the same scenes and situations. One evening Sam walked into the theatre at the end of the play in a tragically unhappy mood. "What's the matter?" I asked. "Why don't you cheer up?" "Cheer up?" he said. "How can you expect me to under these conditions? Alex keeps rewriting his scenes, and remarked to me this evening that if he could not write better than I can, he would jump into Lake Michigan." This was a great help.

Matters went from worse to worse as the play left Chicago for a despairing week at Pittsburgh. Here in the gloomy grandeur of a sitting room of the William Penn Hotel, Miriam informed me that under no circumstances would she play the part in New York and she happily handed in her resignation. Then Philip Moeller decided to leave the play in Philadelphia, for which I could hardly blame him. But Behrman's loyal mentor, Harold Freedman, with the tenacity which has made him famous, stuck to the play, and asked the talented

Herman Shumlin to serve as director, which was like asking a serious-minded professor of philosophy to dance on egg-shells. Claudia Morgan replaced Miriam, and Herman made a brave effort, but *Wine of Choice* lasted in New York only a little longer than the few weeks covered by our subscription audience.

During the following season, tensions within the Guild Board of Managers mounted, and the schism which had been partially healed a few years before became increasingly apparent as our difficulties in operating the Guild became increasingly burdensome. These began to approach a climax in the spring of 1938, when four of our most prominent authors, Maxwell Anderson, S. N. Behrman, Robert Sherwood and Sidney Howard, for whom we had produced sixteen plays, most of which were successful, joined forces with Elmer Rice to form the Playwrights' Company. I remember calling at the office of Harold Freedman who represented Behrman, Sherwood, Howard and Anderson, suggesting somewhat bitterly that they take over the Guild subscription as well, since I saw little prospect of the Guild being able to run the theatre any longer without the support of these representative playwrights. Eugene O'Neill, who had been asked to join the group, refused to do so, but since he was hard at work on the cycle of six long plays which, according to him, would take years to complete, we could not count on his help. Moreover, notwithstanding our sporadic successful plays, our financial condition was growing desperate. Our capital had been diminishing despite the fact that we had produced, on an average, at least one popular play each year. Since, however, we still continued with a program of six plays, it took more than one successful play to meet the losses of the balance. Road conditions were indescribably bad, and only the so-called "smash hits" were able to earn profits on a nation-wide tour. The Guild Theatre itself was one of the severest drains on our resources. The theatre, with its limited audience capacity and oversized stage had become a white elephant. The leading actors and actresses insisted on a salary based on a percentage of the intake of the theatre, and since the Guild Theatre's intake was relatively small, the actors preferred to play in a theatre with a large capacity, such as the Shubert Theatre, where they could earn almost double their earnings at the Guild Theatre.

Furthermore, the authors of successful plays did not care to have their plays presented at the Guild Theatre, since their royalties, too, depended upon a percentage of the gross. Indeed, some authors gave us their plays only on condition that they were *not* produced at the

Guild Theatre. In only two years of our history had we made any profit at all in the Guild Theatre, and the payment of interest and taxes was a painful load. Our dream theatre became a nightmare theatre.

The first play of our twenty-first season, 1938–39, was a tender comedy about a marriage between adolescent youngsters, called *Dame Nature,* by André Birabeau, adapted from the French by Patricia Collinge, which had been an immediate success in my summer theatre at Westport and introduced a young actor, Montgomery Clift, to the New York stage. If any play seemed headed for a happy reception in New York, this was it. It was received with so much acclaim at Westport that Sam Harris, one of the most astute of managers, had offered me $50,000 for a half interest in the comedy. We opened it in the Booth Theatre on September 26, 1938. As the audience was seated in the theatre, the news was breaking that Hitler had invaded Czecho-Slovakia. During the intermissions, I and others in the audience rushed down Forty-fifth Street to Times Square, where we could see the horrible news of doom and destruction traveling in electric lights on the sign around the New York Times Building. Needless to say, our insubstantial comedy died in front of our eyes.

Soon after this occurred one of our wildest adventures. One of our Board members, in an objective mood, analyzed our situation and decided that what we needed was more contact with "youth." Most of the members of the Board had reached forty and over, and certainly were not growing any younger. Our Board member's suggestion passed from the general to the specific. "I think the best thing that could happen to the Guild right now," said he, "would be to make a contact with Orson Welles, the young director who has just done so brilliantly with the Mercury Theatre, and I believe that from this contact with youth, the Guild may become rejuvenated."

We called upon the youthful Orson Welles, who immediately suggested that the Guild should help finance his proposed production of an agglomeration of Shakespearean plays which would be entitled *The Five Kings* and would contain all the best scenes from *Henry IV, Henry V, Henry VI, Richard II* and *Richard III.* As the kind of contact with youth which we had in mind was not merely that of supplying our dwindling funds to youth, we suggested a collaboration, to which Orson Welles replied that he would be delighted. He thought that the collaboration should consist in our giving advice, so that his youth might have the benefit of the experience of our age, with the proviso, of course, that he was under no obligation to take our advice. With certain strong qualms on the subject, I let myself be beguiled into the belief that I would, in some mysterious manner, recover my zest for the theatre which at the moment had been dulled to some extent by a long series of failures.

My first intimation of danger came at the offices of the Mercury Theatre, where I was introduced to a young lady who showed me a large model consisting of a rotating stage carrying miscellaneous-looking structures made out of pieces of cigar boxes connected together into something that resembled a medieval city made of banana crates and painted dark brown. I remarked that it would be quite impossible to tour the play, as it would take at least two days to set up this cumbersome scenery in a theatre, in traveling from one town to another over a week end.

As touring was an essential part of Orson's plan, my advice to the young lady—said in tactful terms—was to design another set which was adapted for travel. She replied that Orson had worked out this revolving stage for the purpose of having the exciting duel between Hotspur and Prince Hal played while the stage rotated, and that as the actors dueled around the stage in one direction, the stage itself would rotate in the opposite direction, thus producing an effect of seeing double or complete seasickness on the part of the audience, to say nothing of the effect on the actors. In due course the scenic scheme was put into work despite my advice, and it was the scenic scheme which defeated *The Five Kings* in the end.

We were invited to attend the dress rehearsal in Boston. On arriving at the Colonial Theatre, I was presented with a bill for seven thousand eight hundred odd dollars for overtime and rehearsal expenses incurred during the week previously—my first contact with youth.

I passed hurriedly from the manager's office into the half-lit auditorium where I perceived quantities of electric cables extending from the stage in every direction like the strands of a gigantic spider's web. Many of the strands led to an improvised table in the center of the orchestra, at which, standing before a group of four microphones and surrounded by a corps of assistants, was the large form of Orson Welles who from time to time bellowed into a loud-speaker, "I want that cue! What is the matter with that cue? How many times do I have to set a cue? Don't you know that I gave the cue? Isn't there anyone among you who knows this cue?" Finally, in a burst of rage, he jumped away from the loud-speakers, rushed to the aisle, ran down it and leaped onto the stage shouting at the top of his voice, "Will the seven stage

managers and their assistants please come out here?" From out of
the wings, from under pieces of scenery, and from behind curtains,
there appeared fourteen or fifteen curious-looking individuals each
and all wearing short beards and resembling nothing so much as
brothers to the seven dwarfs. I learned later that all these stage managers had to appear in the play, and Orson had insisted that everyone
should grow their own beards so as to look thoroughly authentic in
their roles.

"I have seven stage managers," bellowed Orson, "and each one
of them has an assistant, and yet I cannot get a simple cue correctly
set in this play. I have been twenty-five minutes trying to get this cue
set. Now, what is the matter?" It transpired that each of the seven
stage managers thought that one of the other stage managers was
going to attend to the cue, while the seven odd assistant stage managers thought likewise. Orson leaped from the stage leaving behind
him the impression that all the seven stage managers had to attend to
the cue simultaneously, and at least another twenty minutes was spent
cleaning up the situation again. The dress rehearsal took all of Saturday, and continued late into the night. It continued all day Sunday and
Monday right up to the time of the opening performance, and finally,
after the opening performance was over, the dress rehearsal was
finished on Tuesday. The stagehand bills were enormous. Our contact
with youth was turning out to be an expensive experience.

The opening performance, which may be properly described as an
interruption to the dress rehearsals, took place before the elite of
Boston, who came to the theatre to pray, but remained to scoff. Orson
had assembled a motley crew of vaudeville actors, amateur actors,
himself, John Emery, Burgess Meredith wearing a beard almost as
large as himself, and a distinguished actor from England named Robert
Spaeth. Spaeth spoke with a cultured British accent and appeared to
be the most distinguished member of the company, for his speaking
voice was musical and poetic, and his carriage and deportment was
dignified and austere. Indeed, he seemed to be entirely out of place
in the oddly assorted company, and as the opening performance
showed, the production and Robert Spaeth never did get together.

Playing the part of Chorus, it was Spaeth's function to read to the
audience portions of history; playing the role, so to speak, of a
Shakespearean Master of Ceremonies. Spaeth, dressed in dignified
monkish costume resembling the pictures of Dante gazing upon his
Beatrice, appeared on the forestage for his first speech, which he had
not committed to memory, since it was to be read from a book. Un-

fortunately, wherever Spaeth stood with his book, there was no spot-light, and when he moved into a spotlight, the light capriciously disappeared, so that the poor man was left sputtering and chasing the spotlights from point to point on the forestage. His prologue ultimately over, he tried to get back onto the revolving stage, only to be struck by a passing piece of scenery which caused him to step back hastily; he then stepped onto the revolving stage again, which transported him to the wings in imminent peril of his life. The traveler curtains were then drawn open, disclosing a large group of stagehands running off the stage, after which the play proper began. Orson played the part of Falstaff with a certain lusty, gusty New-World quality which swept the winds of his birthplace in southern Illinois into the banana crates which simulated a London pothouse. Fearing Shakespeare had not made the character of Falstaff sufficiently coarse, Orson thoughtfully added a water closet to the tavern scene to which he, from time to time, betook himself with proper delicacy of spirit.

The first scene over, Robert Spaeth again came on the forestage and declaimed his lines, this time finding the spotlight, but unfortunately losing his place in the book, so that some agonizing moments passed before he was able to find the page and continue. At the end of his lines, he made for the center of the traveler curtains, but as the re-volving stage had already begun to rotate, and remembering that he had been struck by the scenery the previous time he ventured on it, Spaeth unfortunately thought he would walk along the forestage to the side, and then go off at the corner between the traveler curtain and the proscenium arch. Unluckily for him, there was no opening at this point, and by the time he tried to struggle through, the curtains were flung back and covered him in his corner. The next time the cur-tains were drawn together, Spaeth was revealed crouching in the corner. He immediately made an attempt to get off stage by breaking through the center of the curtains. Here, however, he was balked by the turntable rotating again, so that ultimately the poor man jumped off the forestage into the orchestra pit, and so escaped, to the applause of the delighted audience. And to make matters worse, on each occa-sion that Spaeth came out after this to read a new speech, the audience began to laugh, wondering what new calamity would befall him.

In order to reduce the play to playable length, Orson had to remove several of the kings, which he finally did with considerable ruthless-ness. The duel between Hotspur as played by John Emery and Prince Hal as played by Burgess Meredith, emerged as a piece of highly imaginative stagecraft. On my return from New York to Boston toward the end of the engagement, I was met by Burgess Meredith in his dressing room, and he told me in the most dejected manner, "I don't know how I'll ever be able to give a performance tonight. I have a temperature of 102°." A few minutes later I remarked to Orson, "I admire the wonderful spirit of Buzz Meredith. He has a temperature of 102°, and yet he is going to give a performance tonight." This seemed to irk Orson considerably. "Why, that's nothing," he replied, not to be outdone by Burgess, "I have a temperature of 104° and I'm going right on immediately."

The company left Boston and entrained for Washington, leaving behind an enormous bill which it was the Guild's privilege to pay, including one from the Ritz-Carlton Hotel which covered repairs to the chandeliers, venetian blinds and other items which our confreres, in the exuberance of their youth, had demolished. Orson eliminated some of the scenery along with some of the kings, but notwithstanding this, when we arrived at Washington, the curtain was delayed almost two hours after the audience was seated. After playing two weeks more in Philadelphia, our patience and money ran out, as did the audience, so *The Five Kings* came to an untimely but not ignominious end. In spite of all the drawbacks, this contact with youth provided a refreshing interlude, and if any of us were complacent before the episode, we were shaken out of it by the time *The Five Kings* was packed up and sent to the storehouse to await that day, yet to come, when Orson Welles will revive it.

Our next offering was *Jeremiah* by Stefan Zweig. Never was a play more aptly titled, for it was produced during the apprehensions and tensions which accompanied the beginnings of the great European disaster, and when it opened, its gloom and prophecies of miseries to be visited upon the sons of Man were portentous, both for the world and for the Guild. Again we received a discouraging press, but this time our financial resources had reached rock bottom. The play, which was as ill-omened as its leading character, was an expensive failure, and its closing found the Guild in debt to its directors for $60,000. Alas, the author of the play, Stefan Zweig, was equally ill-fated. He committed suicide with his wife in Brazil only a few months before the Allies turned the tide of battle against Hitler. Had he been able to hold out a little longer, he might have put together again, in a happier pattern, the broken pieces of his life.

Jeremiah marked a crisis in the relations of the Guild's Board of Managers. The old rule of having two members serve as Production Committees, and the Board as a whole participating in productions, had broken down with the constant bickerings between the Board, the Committee, the authors and the actors. Moreover, certain of the Board members were desperately unhappy working with other Board members. One of our members, believing that none of us had anything more to offer in the theatre, suggested that the Guild be dissolved at a large public dinner to which the Mayor of New York would be invited, and indeed moved a resolution to this effect. I fought vigorously against this voluntary demise, and was seconded by the rest of the Board. A stringent reorganization was indicated, however, and plans for a new regime were being drawn by the Board during the entire spring and summer of 1939.

CHAPTER XXII

O'Neill, Ah, Wilderness!
and Days Without End

URING the thirties the Theatre Guild produced three of
O'Neill's plays, *Mourning Becomes Electra, Ah, Wilderness!*
and *Days Without End.* I worked on all these plays, and
acted, when he was not in town, as liaison between him
and the Guild.

'Gene was happy again in his domestic life. He had met and fallen
in love with Carlotta Monterey, one of the most beautiful women I
have ever known. Carlotta was a tall, dark-haired girl with classical
features, flashing black eyes, and a habit of tilting her head as she
looked at you. She had acted in numerous plays, including 'Gene's
The Hairy Ape, but unlike many actresses, her interests were not
bounded by the three walls of the stage.

On my return to New York from England in the summer of 1929 I
received the following cable from 'Gene:

GRAND NEWS. CARLOTTA AND I MARRIED YESTERDAY. ALL OUR BEST.

They settled in a beautiful French chateau at Le Plessis, Saint Antoine-
du-Rocher, Indre-et-Loire about four hours journey from Paris. I cabled
them our felicitations and received the following letter in reply:

I haven't got a hell of a lot of work done in the past two months, as you can
imagine, what with moving, settling down, plagiarism suits, and getting married, but from now on I'll be hard at it. I'm attempting something big and new
—the most ambitious stuff I've ever tackled, but it sure looks good.

275

The French civil ceremony proved to be quite impressive—we liked it, felt it meant something—not like our buy-a-dog-license variety in U.S.

All our best to you both!

The "something big and new" referred to in this letter turned out to be *Mourning Becomes Electra* while the plagiarism suit was that brought by a writer named Gladys Adelina Lewys who had sent me a copy of her pseudo-classical novel entitled *The Temple of Pallas-Athenae* which she had had privately printed. Miss Lewys' charges against O'Neill were described in the *Herald Tribune* of May 8, 1929:

> In her complaint Miss Lewys says the book was published on May 18, 1924, and that in November of that year she delivered a copy of it to Lawrence Langner, director and manager of the Theatre Guild, Incorporated. In the same year, the complaint continues, she personally delivered a copy of it to the agents for Boni & Liveright "for the purpose of negotiating for the publication of a cheaper edition." (Her privately printed copy was a $20 edition.) In February, 1925, another copy was delivered to the Theatre Guild with a complete outline for its dramatization, she charges.
>
> . . . Miss Lewys says that she was subsequently notified that the Guild would not produce a play based on her novel.

She was also quoted as stating:

> "I wrote 100 love sonnets to one man recently and I turned out seventy-two of them in one month—all in the Elizabethan style.
>
> "Picture my shock and amazement when I went to see *Strange Interlude* for the first time three months ago. Eugene O'Neill had used my material but used it all wrong. He took a beautiful ideal and brought it so low that I was shocked and scandalized. He has pandered to the licentious. He made a travesty of my work and turned pure English into the argot of the day."

When I looked in my library, I found the book was there and the pages were still uncut! I reported the trial to 'Gene and drew the obvious conclusions concerning the plaintiff's state of mind.

Judge Woolsey gave the decision in the case, which was entirely favorable to O'Neill. The decision has become a classic, for in it, for the first time, the Judge awarded heavy costs to the author who was unjustly accused of plagiarism. This put an end to the constant bringing of plagiarism suits against successful authors, an evil which existed so commonly before this suit, that almost every time we produced a successful play, we were immediately sued for plagiarism.

Shortly after the trial, I had a long letter from 'Gene containing cryptic references to a play that later turned out to be *Mourning Becomes Electra*.

As for work, I am at it in my tourelle every day from nine or quarter to, until lunch time at one-thirty and I am getting a lot done and hope to have the first draft of the whole opus finished by the middle of February, if my present gait keeps up. I worked on the preliminary doping out all last summer and then got off to a couple of bum starts that ate up time. Also there were interruptions like having to go to Paris for three weeks, every day of which I was in the dentist's chair. But now I am off on the right foot and well into it. It involves a lot of hard labor—more than there was in *Interlude*—but I think it will be worth it. No, I am not going to tell you what it's all about. Suffice it that it's the most ambitious thing I have undertaken. This doesn't mean that there is any elaborate new experiments in technique involved, or that I am trying to evolve a new language like Joyce. There isn't that about it. And I'm not coyly withholding the secret for any other reason except that, remembering my blundering about *Dynamo*, I simply have a reaction against saying a word about this in advance. I would rather wait until it is all done as well as I can do it and then let it do the talking for itself. Also I want to let it become exactly what it wants to be and not be forcing it into my preconceptions. It might very well turn out to be nothing like what I would describe it as at this stage of creation.

The letter also contained interesting references to the reception of *Strange Interlude* in Europe. The Berlin critics had been severe toward the play and its author. 'Gene, however, took comfort in the fact that the public reaction was entirely in his favor. His comments deserve to be recorded:

Did you see what the Berlin critics did to *Interlude?* My, oh my! But their bad intentions evidently misfired for the play has been running now nearly two months and the management assures me that it is one of the few hits this season in Berlin. I also get the same dope from outside sources that are reliable.

Elizabeth Bergner made a terrific success as Nina and the rest of the cast is fine, I believe. She got all the credit for whatever the boys found good in the play. I wonder what they'd say if they knew that every gal who has played Nina, in the U.S., Sweden, Denmark, and Budapest, has also made a great hit. Three successes for *Interlude* out of three starts so far in Europe—Sweden, Budapest and Berlin—isn't so bad, what? I omit Denmark because I have no dope on that except that it caused the leader of the Conservative party in their parliament to make a public speech of his alarm and disgust, which sounds all to the good! You had better try London with it next summer while the going is good. It will probably drive the Limie critics into a fury but I think it might go—in fact, probably would go. What is your opinion?

To get back to the Berlin critical uproar. I was accused of imitating every German dramatist they could drag up, including Schiller, and then they threw in Ibsen, Strindberg (the Scandinavians made no such accusation), and Shakespeare for good luck. One critic got real peeved because I had so obviously imitated Shakespeare—which is the finest compliment I have ever got. But his tone, as I got it via translation, seemed to indicate that he sniffed at

the Bard as old hat. Another got mad because Charlie says in Act One that
"Europe is dead, etc." He attributed that to my upstart Yankee effrontery
mocking at the motherland of culture. In fact, what got under my skin was the
obvious chauvinistic anti-Yank color to the critiques. It was the same in Paris
with *The Hairy Ape*. They all began on the line of "this American playwright
who the naive Americans think can write, etc." and then let me have the anti-
American "works." Some that praised me got around it by saying I was Irish
. . . The various Authors Leagues rant and sniff at the "Yankee invasion" as if
they were a carpenter's union in Australia . . . I only hope my dear land ap-
preciates the beatings I am taking in the first line trenches! (Pardon! I forgot
Boston!)

His next letter, dated February 19, 1930, again referred to *Mourning
Becomes Electra*. He was pleased with the progress he was making
on it. He was not certain when it would be in shape to be shown to
the Guild, as he intended "to write the whole thing from cover to
cover three times in longhand in order to get all there is out of it."
He added that he was going to follow this procedure henceforth with
all his plays. When Theresa Helburn and her husband, John B.
Opdycke, visited him at his chateau at Le Plessis, she obtained from
him an outline of the play, which she passed on to me on her return.
But 'Gene warned me by letter that he had bitten off "a hell of a
mouthful" and that he hadn't yet masticated it. He was certain only
that it had dramatic power. He was also beginning to feel homesick
and intended to return to America after spending the spring at
Plessis.

The manuscript of the new play, *Mourning Becomes Electra*, which
was actually three plays in one, arrived in New York just about the
time we received the decision that 'Gene had won the *Strange Interlude*
plagiarism suit. After reading it, I wrote him:

. . . I could not put it down, once I started reading, and had to go on and
read the three plays, one after the other. The effect was to knock me silly for
the rest of the day.

The play was enthusiastically accepted by the Board and 'Gene
agreed to come over and assist us in the production. We felt that Alice
Brady was the finest actress available for the part of Lavinia, but we
were afraid of losing her because of her peculiar reaction to *Strange
Interlude*. Theresa Helburn and I therefore set out for Atlantic City
where Alice was playing at the time, and did our best to woo her into
accepting the role. We were helped in this by her father, William A.
Brady, the famous theatrical manager, a great admirer of O'Neill, and
a friend of his father, James O'Neill. "Papa" Brady, as we called him,

proved a helpful ally, and in the Ritz Hotel in Atlantic City, we signed Alice to her contract, the details of which we negotiated over the telephone with her father. She did not sign, however, until the last moment, on Sunday morning, just as our train was about to leave. Consequently, Terry and I arrived at the station just as the train began to pull out, and we caught it only by making a running leap. Sitting in our Pullman panting from our exertion, we surveyed with satisfaction our contract with Alice. *Mourning Becomes Electra* was on its way!

Mourning Becomes Electra is thought by many discerning critics to be O'Neill's greatest play. The effect on me, when I saw it at its best, was as though I had been kicked by a mule at least a dozen times in my solar plexus, for as the play progresses, one passes from ever-increasing climax to climax with a crescendo effect which leaves you staggering at the end of the play. The fact that the play ran for five hours was all in its favor, for to see it was such an experience for playgoers that for days after, they could talk of nothing else, and consequently sent all their friends to the theatre to see it, too. *Mourning Becomes Electra* was not only one of our greatest artistic successes; it was also a financial success, and carried us through one of our most difficult seasons.

Seven weeks were given to rehearsals, and at the end of this both Philip Moeller who directed the play and O'Neill who stood by for all rehearsals, were in a state of exhaustion. On the opening night the audience sat enthralled by the magnificent play, acting, and settings. During the first intermission I saw Papa Brady, then in his seventies, bounding up the aisle like a schoolboy, his eyes bright with joy. I congratulated him on Alice's performance. "She should have done *Strange Interlude,* but she didn't ask my advice on that," he remarked. Alla Nazimova gave an unforgettable performance in the role of Christine while Earle Larimore's Orin was so flawless that you felt Orin in person was appearing on the stage. With their acting, the magnificent direction by Philip Moeller, the inspired support of the cast, and the stark Grecian columns and Victorian interiors of Robert Edmond Jones, *Mourning Becomes Electra* was a high watermark in the American theatre.

The day after the opening the New York drama critics saluted its advent with an accolade of praise which has never been surpassed or even equaled. If any of my readers are so ill-advised as to wish to become drama critics, they will gain a liberal education in how to write readable reviews under conditions of great mental excitement, by consulting, in the libraries, the New York daily papers for October 27, 1931. The following excerpt from Brooks Atkinson's review in the *New York Times* will illustrate:

> . . . Using a Greek legend as his model, Eugene O'Neill has reared up a universal tragedy of tremendous stature—deep, dark, solid, uncompromising and grim. It is heroically thought out and magnificently wrought in style and structure, and it is played by Alice Brady and Mme. Nazimova with consummate artistry and passion. Mr. O'Neill has written overwhelming dramas in the past. In *Strange Interlude* he wrote one almost as long as this trilogy. But he has never before fulfilled himself so completely; he has never commanded his theme in all its variety and adumbrations with such superb strength, coolness and coherence. To this department, which ordinarily reserves its praise for the dead, *Mourning Becomes Electra* is Mr. O'Neill's masterpiece.

Joseph Wood Krutch, writing in *The Nation*, declared:

> It may turn out to be the only permanent contribution yet made by the twentieth century to dramatic literature. . . .

Sixteen years later found me walking over the R.K.O. lot in Culver City, California, where Dudley Nichols was making the film version of *Mourning Becomes Electra*. As I watched the cameras clicking and the hordes of Hollywood workmen flitting around with their machines, lights, sound equipment, cameras and enormous sets, I seemed to feel the ghosts of Nazimova and Alice Brady, who have since passed away, looking over the scene with bewilderment and even terror. Yet they must have been thrilled as I was to see the tall figure of Dudley Nichols, his eyes lit by his passion for his work and his adoration of O'Neill, commanding the scores of technicians and actors who carried out his every wish. Yet the inability of some of his actors to achieve the emotional values of O'Neill's play prevented this picture from becoming, as Nichols hoped, a permanent monument for O'Neill in the field of motion pictures.

When 'Gene returned to this country in 1931 with Carlotta, they took an apartment at 1095 Park Avenue, New York, and his joy at having his own home again was quite characteristic, as was also his dodging the attendance at any theatrical opening, including his own. But despite his excitement over his New York apartment, he and Carlotta did not live there long. 'Gene could not write in New York. He had to live somewhere where he could find solitude and the ocean. Hunting for an all-the-year-round climate, Sea Island, Georgia, was recommended to them by Ilka Chase, a mutual friend. Together they hied there in the spring of 1932 and began building a house on the beach which they called "Casa Genotta."

In the spring of 1933, 'Gene and Carlotta invited us to spend a week with them along with Fania Marinoff, who was one of Carlotta's good friends. In due course we arrived at Casa Genotta, a beautiful home in Spanish style which the O'Neills had built a few yards from the broad sandy beach. The house was arranged around a courtyard, and Carlotta had the architect design one wing so that the end which looked out over the ocean was in the form of the stern of a medieval sailing vessel, and in this end was located 'Gene's study in which he wrote his plays.

Carlotta, one of those rare women who was born beautiful and will remain so all her life, had spent a considerable part of her early life in England and the Continent, and was at home anywhere. All her talents and efforts at the time went into making an attractive home and surroundings in which 'Gene could have privacy for his work, and to this she dedicated herself with almost fanatic fervor. Her home at Sea Island was decorated with unerring taste, and her mixture of Danish and Dutch blood made her a meticulous chatelaine. Armina, who prides herself on her housekeeping, always returned from the O'Neills' with a feeling of inferiority. "I'll never be able to run a household as smoothly and successfully as Carlotta," she would say in despair.

In Casa Genotta the household revolved around 'Gene's writing. In the morning he worked in his study until noon. Then, attired in his dressing gown, he came down to the beach where Carlotta, Armina, Fania and I were sunning. After a while we went swimming in the sandy colored water which is, to me, one of the most unattractive features of Sea Island. 'Gene was the best swimmer and swam far out to sea, followed by Armina; the rest of us hugged the beach.

The island was at its best at the time of year we were there, but it was humid and hot in summer and by no means the paradise the O'Neills expected it would be. Indeed, so damp was the atmosphere that special bronze had to be used for all the window hardware, for ordinary metal would rust away. Another unpleasant feature of the island came to light when I asked Carlotta why all the bushes in the charming patio were clipped up from the ground for a foot or so. "That's so we can see if there are any snakes under them." Then she explained that the island abounded in rattlesnakes, and 'Gene added smilingly that these were relatively harmless compared to the pretty little pink coral snakes which also disported themselves in this paradise. Fania, who hated snakes even more than I did, trod very gin-gerly around the countryside after this, and I was never quite at ease either. But our visit was happy and restful, and we talked over plans for the future.

'Gene, it appeared, was writing a new play, *Days Without End*, which would show that love could last beyond life. In writing it, it seemed as though he had gone back to his early religious feelings and was affirming his belief in the afterlife. I have always believed that this play was inspired by Carlotta and that in it 'Gene sought to express his hope for a love which transcended mortal life and could last forever. This romantic desire for the permanence of love on the part of both of them could be explained by their earlier unhappy ex-periences, as well as by the romantic streak which made 'Gene sail before the mast and roam around the world. The regularity of home life at Casa Genotta made for ideal working conditions, and just as Le Plessis had produced a background for the enormous task of *Mourning Becomes Electra* so, here on Sea Island looking out over the ocean, 'Gene brooded over other plays to be written in the future.

A few weeks after our return I received 'Gene's letter of May 15th from which I quote. The play, first called *An End of Days*, became later *Days Without End:*

For heaven's sake, don't count on this opus for next fall—or even next sea-son. When I read it, I may feel so sick of it I won't want to touch it again for six months or so—or I may be too enthused about the one I'm outlining now to work on the other again for a while. Or— But there are so many "ors." The best thing for you all to do is go ahead with your plans without considering it even as a possibility—but with the assurance (I *can* speak surely here)—that if there is no play from me next season there will *surely* be *two* (perhaps three) for the following season. If you go ahead on this basis, then if I get *An End of Days* right in time for next season and you *can* cast it and make room for it—well, all the better! But I would not be playing fair with the Guild or myself if I did not make the extreme uncertainty about the next session abso-lutely clear. Sabe?

'Gene's next letter was unexpectedly more optimistic. The play was finished and he thought it "a damned interesting piece of work." He also made reference to "another play." This was *Ah, Wilderness!* While he was struggling with *Days Without End* and under the usual strain which his writing imposed on him, he awoke one morning supremely happy, having dreamed an entire play which reminded him of his own childhood. He literally rushed to his study, poured out the play on paper and finished it in less than four weeks. "It was," he told me, "like a holiday from the other play."

'Gene and Carlotta arrived in New York in due course and we received the manuscript of *Ah, Wilderness!* which we all read and liked. There were some differences of opinion about *Days Without End,* however, and 'Gene sensed the controversial nature of the play and was greatly worried as to which of these plays should be produced first. On August 7, 1933, he wrote me from Faust, New York, putting his anxieties into words:

Days Without End is nothing if not controversial, especially in its Catholic aspect. It is sure, fail or succeed, to arouse much bitter argument. It will be well hated by the prejudiced who won't see the psychological study end of it but only the general aspect. And, technically too, there will be much argument pro and con. Now I feel strongly that such a post-production atmosphere, if *Days Without End* were done first, would be fatal for *Ah, Wilderness!*

Give all this careful thought, all of you, and I know you'll agree.

A day later he was still confused and wrote me again:

There is a lot to be said on both sides, and I've been saying it all to myself until I'm quite gaga and confused and my opinion is worthless. All I know is that any play of mine that immediately follows *Electra* is in a bad spot—no matter how good it is; and I'm so close to both these two plays that I really don't know just how good or bad either of them is. This is particularly true in the case of *Ah, Wilderness!* which is so out of my previous line. Has it got something finer to it than its obvious surface value—a depth of mood and atmosphere, so to speak, that would distinguish it from another play of the same genre, the usual type? I felt it had when I wrote it. (Nathan, for example, says most emphatically yes.) But now, frankly, I'll be damned if I can trust myself to judge. I simply don't know. It's up to you Guilders to decide. Has it charm and humor and tender reminiscence enough to disarm the people who will feel that dramatically it is a terrible let-down after *Electra?*

On August 14th I wrote him that, for a variety of reasons, we preferred to produce the comedy first. During the rehearsals of *Ah, Wilderness!* 'Gene attended the theatre regularly and made considerable cuts. Indeed he was usually extremely co-operative in regard to cutting, and once he was in a cutting mood, he cut faster than the director asked in rehearsals. He was not at all happy, however, when the play took to the road, and he had to spend a week in Pittsburgh. I had the greatest difficulty in getting him to come to the theatre at all after the dress rehearsal, and even then he would come in only for certain scenes. I asked him why he had this phobia against attending performances of his own plays, and he told me that it did not relate to his own plays, but to being present in a crowded theatre, which made it very difficult for him to sit still and watch the play. On other occasions, I have been with him in crowded arenas such as Madison Square Garden where he would spend hours watching the six-day bicycle race, and more recently at prize fights in Madison Square Garden, where he did not appear to have the slightest discomfort in mixing with crowds of thousands in a large arena.

Ah, Wilderness! opened at the Guild Theatre October 2, 1933, and was received with delight on the part of the critics and audiences. All 'Gene's fears about the reception proved to be unfounded, for the play's quality of nostalgic sentiment made it overnight a piece of Americana as indigenous to our soil as a folk song. And with the passage of time, this play has proved the most endearing, if not the most enduring, of his works. The story of the boy who was 'Gene, his adolescent adventures and the tender understanding of his father and mother make a picture of the decencies of American family life which no play has surpassed in the theatre. It continued to run for a whole season with George M. Cohan at his best, until his bad habit of elaborating the comedy made the play seem unnecessarily long. Later it was played on the Coast by Will Rogers, and by Walter Huston in the motion picture. 'Gene felt that we used the wrong emphasis in employing these outstanding actors for the father, for he regarded the boy as the leading character.

After the successful opening of *Ah, Wilderness!* we went to work on *Days Without End.* 'Gene seemed to be especially timorous about this play, mostly I believe, because it represented a very deep change in some of his views of life and also because it might be possibly interpreted as a return to his early Catholic faith. His struggle over this was shown not only in the difficulty he had in writing the play, but the first version had a Protestant minister, which he later changed to a Catholic priest. This was the right thing to do, for surely this play sprang out of a deeply rooted sectarian revolt. 'Gene's letter to me on October 29, 1933, shows some of his doubts in the situation:

I'm especially anxious to have your sympathetic backing on this particular play, not only because it's a tough one to get over and is bound to arouse a lot of antagonism, but because I want to lean over backwards in being fair to it and getting it the best breaks. For, after all, this play, like *Ah Wilderness!* but in a much deeper sense, is the paying of an old debt on my part—a gesture toward more comprehensive, unembittered understanding and inner freedom —the breaking away from an old formula that I had enslaved myself with, and the appreciation that there is their own truth in other formulas, too, and that any life-giving formula is as fit a subject for drama as any other.

Days Without End opened in New York on January 8, 1934, at the Henry Miller Theatre and was as badly received by the critics as *Ah, Wilderness!* had been well received a few months earlier. I fear that these gentlemen were afraid that O'Neill was going back to his early faith, and attacked him from that point of view as much as for the play itself. This, of course, was not correct, and had they been able to take a more objective view of the play, it would have fared much better, as indeed it did in such countries as Sweden, Italy and Germany. 'Gene was bitterly disappointed with the reception of the play, and returned soon after to Sea Island. Before going he confided to me that he had plans for executing a major work in the theatre which would take years of his time to write, and I left him with the feeling that although he was discouraged, he would nevertheless soon forget what had happened to *Days Without End* in the excitement and interest in this new major work. When the book of *Days Without End* was finally published 'Gene sent me an autographed special edition of uncorrected proofs on the title page of which, in his neatest of neat handwriting, appeared the following inscription:

Dear Lawrence:
    Again, thanks for your fine cooperation in helping this opus to a fine production! Whatever its fate in the Amusement Racket which New York vaingloriously calls The Theatre, it will have been heard by a few of them it was written for, thanks to the Guild, and will live for them. So what the hell!
                                    'Gene
January 27, 1934

In the spring of 1935, Russel Crouse, our press agent at the time, since distinguished for his brilliant co-dramatization of *Life With Father* and other plays, went down to visit 'Gene, and brought back the news of the new cycle of plays on which 'Gene was working. In March Armina and I spent some days at Nassau, and on our way back we paid a second visit to the O'Neills. I found 'Gene deeply engrossed in his new cycle (I called it his six-day bicycle race) for which he was stripped for action like a pugilist. His habits were most regular, and everything ran like clockwork in Carlotta's comfortable and tastefully decorated home.

The first morning I was there, after doing his morning's work, 'Gene came out and sat on the beach where I was taking a sun bath and as we both looked out over the ocean, the waves breaking at our feet a few yards away, he told me about his plan for his new plays. They would take literally years to write. We were not to expect to receive the first of them until the last was completed because he would be making changes in them until the very last one was done. Each play would be complete in itself, yet each of the plays would be part of a whole, which he called *A Touch of the Poet*. The plays would deal with several generations of a family, an admixture of old Puritan New England stock and Irish-American blood, and it was the Irish in the admixture which gave the cycle its title, for the touch of Irish blood gave the touch of the poet. Characters were to be in their youth in one play while they would be parents or grandparents in later plays in which the main stories were based on the lives of their children and children's children. Galsworthy's *The Forsyte Saga* seemed like child's play in comparison, as 'Gene traced the effect of the grandparents on the children and their grandchildren, reminding me of the Biblical prophesies as to the sins of the parents being visited upon their children unto the third and fourth generations. I marveled at the scope of the work he was attempting, and wondered whether, in the hot damp climate of Sea Island, he would have the strength to last out the ordeal he had set for himself. Later on, Carlotta and Armina joined us. We went in swimming and 'Gene swam out far into the sea, his head and powerful arms pushing through the green-brown water like a lonely amphibian, belonging neither to the sea nor to the land. But I was troubled about the climate of Sea Island and its effect on 'Gene. No matter how hard Carlotta tried, she fought a losing battle against the dampness coming from the warm sea air laden with salt moisture, and the continuous heat of summer. 'Gene continued with his work and reported the progress he was making in a letter to me of August 12, 1936.

I hope you yourself don't believe the Cycle is "an American life" in any usual sense of the word, or you're going to be disappointed. I mean, I'm not giving a damn whether the dramatic event of each play has any significance in the growth of the country or not, as long as it is significant in the spiritual and psychological history of the American family in the plays. The Cycle is primarily just that, the history of a family. What larger significance I can give my people as extraordinary examples and symbols in the drama of American possessiveness and materialism is something else again. But I don't want anyone to get the idea that this Cycle is much concerned with what is usually understood by American history, for it isn't. As for economic history—which so many seem to mistake for the *only* history just now—I am not much interested in economic determinism, but only in the self-determinism of which the economic is one phase, and by no means the most revealing—at least, not to me.

He added:

Try a Cycle sometime, I advise you—that is, I would advise you to, if I hated you! A lady bearing quintuplets is having a debonair, carefree time of it by comparison.

A hell of a hot oppressive summer here. Carlotta and I are neck and neck toward the Olympic and World's sweating record! We just continually drop and drip.

The dropping and dripping ultimately became too much for 'Gene, and with considerable reluctance, they left Sea Island in the hopes of finding a better climate in the Pacific Northwest. It was during this period that 'Gene won the Nobel Prize for literature, which of course pleased all of us greatly. Later, at my request, he showed me, with almost childlike pleasure, the black box which he opened to display the large gold medallion symbolizing the greatest honor awarded to an American playwright. There was not the slightest suggestion either of undue pride or modesty on his part. He took it in his stride.

Carlotta, writing from Seattle, Washington, told me that they had a really lovely house on a high bluff on the sound with a charming garden in terraces down to the water. "The view across the sound with the Olympics in the background (when it is clear!), is beautiful," she wrote, and "'Gene loves to watch the boats go by and hear the sea gulls and the foghorns." Later, in November, Carlotta wrote me that if Seattle had a sunny climate it would be as famous as the Riviera. "Geographically it is amazingly beautiful but in the winter there is much fog and rain." Carlotta continued, "We must find a place to live if we ever sell our present home. And northern California seems best in many ways. But, we'll just look everywhere and be very sure." I pitied 'Gene and Carlotta. They seemed doomed to spend so much of their lives hankering for a home where they could be on the sea, with plenty of sunshine both in summer and in winter, have complete privacy and yet be somewhere near a city. All through 'Gene's life he had been searching for this spot, but seemed never to find it.

Finally they moved on south into California, where Carlotta designed and built the modest but extremely handsome home known as Tao House, facing Mount Diabolo in Contra Costa county, about an hour out from San Francisco. Here, for the first time in years, 'Gene was able to enjoy bearable weather the year round. And here he settled down to write on his cycle.

CHAPTER XXIII

Shaw and His American Visit

HAVING worked on so many of the plays of O'Neill and Shaw, the two outstanding theatre geniuses of our time, I was interested in learning their opinions of one another and in comparing their attitudes toward their work. I once asked O'Neill to what extent Shaw had influenced his own writing. 'Gene said he had been more influenced by Shaw as a man and as a writer than as a playwright. When he went to prep school in Stamford, Connecticut, he was wildly excited about Shaw's *Quintessence of Ibsenism*. It was his favorite reading during his last year at school, and he kept underlining the points with which he agreed with Shaw in red ink to such an extent that the book was almost entirely underlined. Whenever 'Gene indulged in an argument, he would slay his opponents by quoting from Shaw, and, indeed, he gained a reputation for being Mephistophelian among the other boys by his apt quotations.

'Gene remarked that he had never been unwilling to admit that he had been influenced not only by Shaw but even to a greater extent by Strindberg. Notwithstanding the fact that Shaw's *Quintessence of Ibsenism* had greatly predisposed him in favor of Ibsen, he drew a sharp line of distinction between his own plays and those of Ibsen, stating that he had sometimes been referred to as a "naturalistic" or "realistic" writer whereas he had never actually written along these lines except on rare occasions. Notwithstanding O'Neill's interest in Ibsen, he is no disciple of the gloomy Norwegian dramatist. On one occasion he stated to me, "Ibsen has set back the theatre for many years by his very success in developing a so-called 'naturalistic' method which in reality is not naturalistic at all. Ibsen's realism in the theatre is just as much manufactured as the theatre of Sardou which preceded it." Throughout his writing career, O'Neill has constantly attempted to break down the realism or naturalism of Ibsen and to add to the dimensions of the theatre by the use of masks as in *The Great God Brown,* asides as in *Strange Interlude* and *Dynamo,* and sheer fantasy as in the case of *Days Without End.*

Shaw greatly admired O'Neill's work as a dramatist, but with his old-maidish temperance attitude, could never quite get over being shocked at 'Gene's early drinking. When I told him at Stresa that 'Gene had not touched a drop of liquor for years, and had "sworn off" it for life Shaw replied, "He'll probably never write a good play again." I explained that 'Gene had already written many good plays since he had stopped drinking, which seemed to make very little impression on G.B.S., for a few years later he asked me the same question again.

"How is O'Neill feeling?" asked Shaw when I was in England in 1947. I stated that he was well, but that he took a pessimistic view about the state of the world, and was of the opinion that our present civilization was on its way downhill, and headed for ultimate disaster. "Tell him not to worry about that," said Shaw cheerily. "If mankind turns out, as I suspect, to be a failure, it will destroy itself and be replaced by some other creature." Their outlooks appeared to be the same, but O'Neill, the writer of tragedy, was tragic about it, while Shaw, the writer of comedy, was cheerful, and this difference in attitudes existed notwithstanding the difference in their ages, Shaw being the older man by over thirty years.

In the summer of 1929, when the Lunts were playing *Caprice* with so much success at the St. James Theatre in London, Armina and I were visiting there with Philip Moeller, and we all received an invitation to lunch with Mr. and Mrs. Shaw. The occasion was hilarious; Philip Moeller, Alfred Lunt and Lynn Fontanne were seated at one end of the table, at the head of which sat G.B.S., while Sir Barry Jackson, Armina and I were seated around Mrs. Shaw. G.B.S. regaled the listeners at his end of the table with one story after another, to the accompaniment of shouts of laughter.

Among the topics of conversation during lunch was the production of Mr. Shaw's latest play, *The Apple Cart,* in which there were a number of British Cabinet Ministers. He asked me why we were producing it in New York so late in the season, to which I replied that we had a large number of actors who were playing Cabinet Ministers in *Wings Over Europe* on tour, and since it was hard to secure men whose intellectual appearance suggested Cabinet Ministers, we intended to wait for the tour to come to an end before producing *The Apple Cart*. "But that is all nonsense," said G.B.S. "Where did you get the idea that Cabinet Ministers look intelligent?"

We took G.B.S. to see *Caprice,* and he was delighted with it, and with the performance of the Lunts. As we stood on the pavement with Carl Van Vechten after the play was over, waiting for a taxi, G.B.S. expounded his views on the play and performances to the edification of a throng of admiring onlookers who gathered around us. As he continued to speak, the crowd continued to grow, and G.B.S. watched it out of the corners of his eyes. When the number approached that which usually attends upon Royalty or movie stars, G.B.S. said, "Look here, I've got to move on"—and move on he did, after smiling and bowing to the appreciative onlookers.

In March, 1930, *The Apple Cart* opened in New York City, and the critical notices were mixed. The part of King Magnus was played by Tom Powers and his mistress by Violet Kemble Cooper. Years later Shaw complained that we should have waited for Sir Cedric Hardwicke, whose performance made the play a great success in London.

The next new play we received from G.B.S. was *Too True to Be Good.* On receipt of this manuscript I remembered what Shaw had once said on the subject of plots. "In my opinion," he stated, "it's quite unnecessary for a playwright to bother himself about a plot. I believe it would be quite possible for a writer to start two people off with a conversation and bring in other people and keep the conversation going and fill the entire evening." "Yes," I replied, "provided the conversation is good enough. But of course you're the only one able enough to write such a conversation." "Naturally," he replied, "I don't recommend this for anybody except myself." When I read *Too True to Be Good* I thought, "At last! Here is the play which Shaw has been thinking about." Unfortunately, notwithstanding the fact that we cast it with the very best available actors, and achieved somewhat of a sensation by having Beatrice Lillie play the Nurse, while the part of The Patient was played by Hope Williams, the play had a mediocre reception and must be counted a failure.

In the spring of 1933, Shaw passed through New York City on his way back to England from a world cruise on the S.S. *Empress of Britain.* On his arrival in California he annoyed some of his liberal friends on this side of the water by putting himself under the sponsorship of William Randolph Hearst, the newspaper publisher, and having himself extensively photographed with him for the Hearst papers. When I mentioned this to Shaw on his arrival in New York, G.B.S. tossed it off and showed me some of the photographs. "You'll notice," he said, "that my white beard catches all the light and no one even notices that Hearst is in the picture!"

On the day of Shaw's arrival in New York none of the Guild Board members was at the Guild Theatre, and in the early morning G.B.S. dropped by and had a talk with our Business Manager, Warren Munsell, inspected the theatre and the bust of himself in the lobby, and returned to the ship. Had we been informed of the possibility of this visit we would have had the red carpet out, but perhaps this is just what he wished to avoid.

Shaw's visit to New York was sponsored by a women's organization, The Academy of Political Science, that was quite unknown to us and we were equally unknown to it, so that the Guild Board was not invited to the gathering given in Shaw's honor at the Metropolitan Opera House, nor were we able to purchase seats. I was able, however, to hear the speech over the radio, and although G.B.S. was not in his best form, I doubt whether many who heard his clear, crisp, hard-hitting Irish-English diction over the air waves will ever forget the quality of his voice. Though he was but four years short of eighty, it was as clear, as young and unquavering as that of a man half his age.

The following morning Armina and I visited Shaw on the beautiful *Empress of Britain* and breakfasted with him. His other guests were Robert Lorraine, veteran of a dozen Shaw comedies and one of his oldest friends in the theatre, Princess Kropotkin, and Agnes de Mille's mother, Mrs. William De Mille, who was the daughter of Henry George, the Single Taxer, whom G.B.S. had greatly admired. Despite his speech of the previous day delivered before an audience of many thousands at the Metropolitan Opera House, and his tiring trip up the harbor and through the streets of New York, the veteran playwright was up early and in top form. Breakfast was scheduled for eight o'clock, and with the usual promptness which prevails in the Langner family, we arrived breathless at eight-fifteen, stumbling over casks, packing cases and like obstacles which were dotted all over the pier as though the Fates were quite determined that we should be even later than usual.

When we arrived in the ship's dining salon, G.B.S. was already there. Mrs. Shaw begged to be excused as she had had but one meal in New York and it gave her ptomaine poisoning. We sat at the table and G.B.S. talked—the rest of us listened.

"I witnessed a performance of a play in a Chinese theatre," he remarked. "While the show on the stage was interesting, the show put on by the audience was even more enjoyable. Throughout the performance the various members in the audience would raise their hands, and a skillful attendant stationed at the back of the theatre would throw a hot, wet towel to them, with which they washed their faces and the backs of their necks and, thus refreshed, settled down to enjoy the performance again." G.B.S. suggested that a somewhat similar idea might well be introduced in the European and American theatres, as undoubtedly nothing would be more calculated to wake up an audience during a play than the application of hot towels as a stimulant. I reminded G.B.S. that during *Back to Methuselah* we were in the habit of serving black coffee to the audience during the intermissions, which was probably just as stimulating and undoubtedly more sanitary.

As we proceeded with breakfast, straggling figures began to appear among the tables. When we had risen, several newspaper reporters stepped forward. "Mr. Shaw," said one, "I am the man who got into your cabin yesterday. Do you mind my having my photograph taken with you?" "Not at all," replied G.B.S. "I am ready for anything."

Then G.B.S. rose and went on deck to meet the reporters, who seemed like old-fashioned gentlemen compared with the gang of hoodlums who now began to take movies and photographs of him. Evidently under instructions to "get Shaw's goat," they did everything possible to irritate and disconcert him, in one instance a lout letting off a flashlight almost in his face, amid loud guffaws, and taking advantage of Shaw's shocked surprise to snap an absurd picture of him which was later published in a New York journal. Not one of these hoodlums showed the slightest respect for the man who was perhaps the most brilliant thinker and dramatist of our day. Although a number of intelligent questions were asked by the reporters of the New York daily press, those put to G.B.S. by some would have been a discredit to the lowest grade of an elementary school. Here is a sample: "Would you like to go to the Zoo?"

Someone brought up the old joke about Shaw and Shakespeare. "What did you mean when you said that you were better than Shakespeare?" he was asked. G.B.S. replied: "He and I were drawn to write a play on the same subject—Caesar and Cleopatra. When I wrote my play I put the words 'Better than Shakespeare?' with a note of interrogation. This started the entire controversy which raged for many years. Of course I did not mean that I am a better dramatist than Shakespeare. I merely raised the question. Nobody could possibly beat Shakespeare in his own line. For example, I think that no one but Shakespeare could have written as great a play as *King Lear*. However, Shakespeare's ideas are of no use to young persons nowadays. They must read Shaw in order to get a liberal education. If they read Shakespeare for social ideas, they will get nothing which will help them today. Each nation must produce its own literature for its own time."

Then someone asked, "Do you think there should be a sort of overdictator for the whole world?" Shaw replied, "I haven't contemplated that."

"And if there were such a dictator of the world, do you think you would be competent to fill the job?" asked the same great mind. To which G.B.S. replied, rising, "Gentlemen, the time is up." We left the boat sadly wishing that G.B.S. might have taken away with him a better impression of our national manners.

Our next Shaw play, *The Simpleton of the Unexpected Isles,* was produced in the spring of 1935. Like *Too True to Be Good,* it was a conversation piece, only the conversations were longer and longer. Notwithstanding an excellent cast which included Alla Nazimova, Romney Brent, Lawrence Grossmith, McKay Morris, Rex O'Malley and Viola Roache, the play was again received with indifference on the part of the critics, and registered a further financial loss for the Guild. In spite of this, I believe that it contains some of Shaw's most inspired writing, and at some future time a public will be found for this magnificent allegory.

In August of 1938 I received from G.B.S. a privately printed copy of his latest play, *Geneva*. By this time the possibility of a war with Germany was on everyone's mind, and the Theatre Guild had been, wherever possible, producing plays which would arouse the nation to the dangers to democracy everywhere, should Hitler's dream of world domination by the German "superman" come to be generally accepted. On reading the copy of *Geneva* I was furious with the way Shaw had dismissed Hitler's heartless treatment of the Jews—a treatment which was later to culminate in the killing of over four millions of them in the concentration camps of Buchenwald and Oswiecim. I delivered a frontal assault on G.B.S. by letter on August 26, 1938, which, believe it or not, caused him actually to revise the third act of the play, and to change the character of the Jew. "To please you, Lawrence," he replied, "I have written up the part a bit." Shaw also wrote me, "You may now put the copy I sent you in the fire as useless, or, better still, sell it as a curiosity!" [1]

We did not produce *Geneva* even in its revised form, for it seemed to us to be merely another conversation piece, and we felt that we could not risk the financial sacrifices involved. Later on Terry and I went to Canada to see *Geneva* as produced by Maurice Colbourne, but it did not interest us sufficiently to bring it to New York. However, Colbourne and Gilbert Miller took the chance, and the play opened in New York on January 30, 1940, and met with the failure which we had anticipated.

Later on, Shaw sent us his play, *The Millionairess*, which the Guild also decided not to produce. As I liked the play, I put it on at the Westport Country Playhouse, in the summer of 1938, with Jessie Royce Landis in the title role of Epithania Fitzfassenden. The play was delightful and was extremely well received by the audiences. I should add that in addition to producing *The Millionairess* at Westport, we also produced there *Fanny's First Play, Captain Brassbound's Conversion* and *You Never Can Tell.*

In 1938, Armina and I wrote a play called *Suzanna and the Elders* which was partly suggested by the Oneida Community. We dedicated it to Mr. and Mrs. Shaw, and were deeply touched by a sentence written by G.B.S. at the end of a post card acknowledging our dedication:

We are dreadfully old, and forget everything; but we have not forgotten you.

Mrs. Shaw's health began to fail in the latter part of the thirties. The last time we saw her was on our visit to England for the London production of *The Pursuit of Happiness.* We tried to take G.B.S. with us to see a matinee, but he pleaded that he had read the play, which he found rather shocking, and that he now avoided the theatre as the plague. We learned through the newspapers of Mrs. Shaw's death in 1943. Armina and I wrote G.B.S. letters of sympathy, which he did not answer. Instead he sent us a beautiful photograph of Mrs. Shaw, as though words were meaningless on such an occasion.

Some years later, the story of Mrs. Shaw's funeral service was recounted to Armina and myself by someone who heard it from one of the two persons who attended. Accompanied by Lady Astor and

---

[1] See Appendix II, p. 454, for copies of this correspondence.

his faithful secretary, Miss Patch, they drove to the service. Shaw was silent and preoccupied. Then some of Mrs. Shaw's favorite music was played on the organ. After the resounding tones of Handel's *Largo* rang out, Shaw began to sing as though inspired, his eyes shone and his voice sounded young and clear, his spirit soared as though he was singing to his beloved Charlotte, as though he felt that her presence was near him and she did not wish him to grieve for her. After this, purged of his grief, Shaw became himself again, and on making some passing quip on his way home, Lady Astor is said to have remarked, "You really *are* a wicked old man!" When this story was told me, I remembered again Shaw's telling me that Saint Joan herself had guided his hand as he wrote his play about her. Behind the philosopher and the poet stood the mystic. Perhaps he felt that Charlotte Shaw was not really dead—but had merely passed over into another dimension of space in which they would again meet.

CHAPTER XXIV

The Westport Country Playhouse

WHILE the Theatre Guild was undergoing periods of varying fortunes during the depression of the thirties, Armina and I were carrying on parallel activities during the summers at the Westport Country Playhouse. We built the Playhouse in the year 1931, in order to establish a Repertory Company of our own, and to carry out our own ideas as regards plays and production.

The Westport Country Playhouse is situated in a hundred-year-old orchard just off the Boston Post Road. A more attractive spot for a country theatre could hardly be imagined. This red barn nestling amid old, gnarled apple trees was a haven of peace and tranquility compared with Broadway, and some of the happiest days of my life have been spent driving to and from our farm to the Playhouse and rehearsing in the open air under the old trees.

There we were free to try out our creative ideas without interference, and without facing financial disaster if they failed. New plays and the classics could be essayed without reference to the tastes of Broadway. Actors could attempt new roles without facing the terrors of the New York opening nights, and new directors and scenic artists could be given a first chance to show their talents. And furthermore, the younger generation could have an opportunity to gain experience in the theatre. The dramatic critics of the local papers welcomed us as a relief from the tedium of movie going and transmitted their pleasurable experiences to our audiences, who enjoyed us as a gay addition to the life of the community. Even the stagehands, the traditional enemies of the managers in the large cities decided, after a few preliminary skirmishes, to make their peace with us, and became our personal friends and collaborators in our happy undertaking. And the spirit which animated the beginnings of the Country Playhouse continues right down to today, as each new season brings fresh talents into the theatre and offers new opportunities in untried fields to the older actors and stage directors.

Some of this spirit of pleasurable accomplishment undoubtedly springs from the atmosphere of the Playhouse itself. Remembering the toy theatre of my youth, and especially the "tuppence-colored" theatre with its gay proscenium of bright red and gold, its bright red curtain and red-and-gold-curtained side boxes, I asked Cleon Throckmorton, noted scenic designer of the Provincetown Players, to carry out this idea in a barn theatre. Throckmorton, who had designed the famous Cape Playhouse at Dennis, Massachusetts, responded with enthusiasm and made the stage the same size as that of the Times Square Theatre in New York so that plays could be moved from Westport to New York and elsewhere. This gave our Playhouse a distinction over most summer theatres, and made it possible to use it as an incubator for plays for the theatres in other cities.

The first experiment in Westport was to be Repertory with an Acting Company which was to compensate me for the loss I felt with the disbanding of the Theatre Guild Acting Company. Armina and I threw ourselves with enthusiasm into forming this company, which we christened the New York Repertory Company.

I asked Rollo Peters, who had done such invaluable work in the early days of the Theatre Guild, to become a member of the Company and to put his varied talents as scenic artist, actor and stage director at our disposal. He did so, and also helped find the large red barn and unearthed the script of Boucicault's old Victorian melodrama, *The Streets of New York,* which was to form our first offering. Other actors who joined the Acting Company were Romney Brent, Dorothy Gish, Winifred Lenihan, Moffat Johnston, Fania Marinoff, Armina Marshall, Jessie Busley and Tony Bundsman. As I wished to open the Repertory Company in a great hurry, for sixteen hours a day the carpenters and electricians were busy at work transforming the red barn (which had formerly been used as a tannery for leather hatbands) into our theatre.

Our opening play, *The Streets of New York,* which had been played all over the world, and which appropriately dealt with the depression of 1837 and was hence topical in the depression of 1931, was produced with incidental music selected by Sigmund Spaeth, and colorful Victorian painted scenery and drops by Rollo Peters, who also played the leading role opposite Dorothy Gish. On Monday night, June 30, 1931, the theatre was opened by old Daniel Frohman, then in his eighties and Dean of American producers, who made a charming speech with a crackling thunderstorm as an obligato accompaniment. But the storm subsided, and soon the audience fell under the spell of the delightful acting and singing, and the colorful costumes and scenery. Both our play and our Playhouse were instantaneous successes, and the play itself was performed twenty-one times in our repertory. It was followed by *The Comic Artist* by Susan Glaspell and Norman Matson. Then came *As You Like It*, with Rollo playing the part of Orlando and Armina as Rosalind, followed by Ibsen's *Pillars of Society* and Will Cotton's *The Bride the Sun Shines On*. At the end of the season we had a repertory of these five plays running in Westport and ready to bring to New York, and I conceived the daring plan of opening them one right after another in the same week, just to show New York what an Acting Company could actually do.

One of the plays I enjoyed most during this first season at Westport was *As You Like It*, directed by myself and Charles Jehlinger, the beloved Dean of the American Academy of Dramatic Arts, and in it I tested many of my theories regarding Shakespeare. We used an Elizabethan set and a deep apron stage which enabled us to bring the actors out among the audience, so that they were out of focus with the scenery. To our surprise, this produced almost the same effect as the "close-up" in the movies. I was impressed by what I discovered about the fluidity of the Shakespearean stage, which enables the play to be played continuously without any interruption or dropping of curtains, one group of characters going off stage as another group comes on, thus giving the same continuity as a motion picture; and I have used a modification of this form in many Shakespearean productions with which I have since been associated. The Acting Company played with great zest and simplicity, with Rollo Peters as Orlando, Armina Marshall as Rosalind, Dorothy Gish as Celia, Romney Brent as Touchstone, Fania Marinoff as Phoebe, Moffat Johnston as Jacques and Winnie Lenihan as Audrey. The Westport production so intrigued me with the play that I ultimately persuaded Katharine Hepburn to play the part of Rosalind, and in it she recently achieved her most successful role, breaking records for attendance in theatres all over the country.

Our Company was especially enlivened by the presence of Dorothy

Gish, one of the most entertaining actresses of our time, who, with her sister Lillian, had just finished her career in silent pictures as the aftermath of a stage career begun as a child actress. Dorothy had a habit of coming to the Playhouse wearing an old sweater and a torn skirt, with her hair in curlers, and looking for all the world like a cleaning woman. One evening we were invited to a dance at the Southport Yacht Club and Dorothy joined our party wearing a sumptuous white satin evening gown with her curls in ringlets, and she outshone in beauty all the other girls there. "How wonderful you look!" I remarked. "Compared to the way you usually go about, the transformation is miraculous!" "I'm glad you like me," she replied dryly, "but I have a funny feeling from so many years in the theatre and pictures, that whenever I dress myself up like this, I ought to be paid for it."

From time to time one or more of the inmates from a sanitarium next door paid us visits and watched our rehearsals, behaving very correctly. We had, however, one frightening experience. During a performance of *The Comic Artist* we noticed a number of strange-looking men and women stealthily entering the theatre after the curtain had risen. The men were bearded and the women were miscellaneous. We thought at once there had been a break from the sanitarium, and wondered what to do. At intermission I went up to one of the more harmless-looking men, and asked him who these strange people were. "Don't you know?" he answered. "We are summering near here and you told Cheryl Crawford we could all come to see *The Comic Artist*. We are the Group Theatre!"

Some years later, as Harry Wagstaff Gribble, the author of *March Hares*, was entering the Playhouse, a jolly-looking inmate of the sanitarium called over the wall and asked, "Are you Lawrence Langner?" to which Harry answered, "No." "I know that," was the happy response from the inmate, "because I am."

Toward the end of our first season, with all five plays readied for Repertory, I began to prepare our plans for our New York debut. Alas, the moment we began to consider the future of our Repertory Company in New York, the fears and bugaboos which always attend New York openings began to pervade our Acting Company. There was a feeling on the part of some of the actors that, having struck a great success with *The Streets of New York*, it would be foolish to jeopardize this success by continuing with a repertory of plays in New York. We were at the bottom of the great depression and what was for me an artistic experiment, was for most of the Acting Company a question of their next day's bread and butter. I did my best to allay their fears and my efforts were loyally seconded by Romney Brent and most of the actors, who were in sympathy with my objectives. Meetings of the actors took place to which I was not invited, as a result of which the company finally agreed to follow my lead and to bring the plays into New York as a Repertory Company. However, in order to meet the physical difficulties of my plan to open the plays one after another in a single week, I decided to open *The Streets of New York* first, and to follow it with the other plays two weeks apart.

We presented *The Streets of New York* in the fall of 1931 at the Forty-Eighth Street Theatre as the first production of The New York Repertory Company. The next day we were overjoyed to find that the New York critics had given us a rousing welcome, and our business at the box office was excellent.

Toward the end of this first season at Westport, William M. Chadbourne, a noted New York lawyer, spent the week end with us, and told me he was writing an article on the subject of "The Recent Decline of the Bond Market." As I had been entirely absorbed in producing the five plays at Westport, I did not realize that there had been any such decline, and I decided on the following Monday to look into my financial situation. I was horrified to find that the money which I had hoped to use to cover any losses of the Repertory Company in New York no longer existed. In view of this, our second play, Ibsen's *The Pillars of Society,* was an unfortunate choice, for it required a style of acting which was neither "naturalistic" in the Ibsen sense nor "artificial" in the sense of Boucicault. We fell between two stools so far as the New York critics were concerned, for they damned our acting as well as our play.

Many other troubles beset us in New York. We had to employ for *The Pillars of Society,* a play in one set, the same number of stagehands as we employed for the large production of *The Streets of New York.* I appealed to the head of the Stagehands' Union. He listened to a passionate oration by myself and by Winifred Lenihan, whose own father was a labor leader, but this left him unmoved. The last straw was reached when the ticket sellers in the hotel ticket offices began telling prospective customers for *The Streets of New York* that this play had closed, and had been replaced by *The Pillars of Society.* I realized then the difficulties of educating the six hundred or more persons who sell theatre tickets in New York City in the intricacies of Repertory. Meetings were held with the Acting Company and it was decided among us all that it would be better to proceed with *The Streets of New York,* drop *The Pillars of Society* and then introduce another play into the repertory. Looking back with the perspective of the passing years, my own Acting Company demonstrated the improvidence of attempting repertory in New York City under present-day conditions, and particularly under the conditions imposed by the Stagehands' Union.

The next summer at Westport, that of the year 1932, I formed another Acting Company headed by Osgood Perkins and June Walker, both excellent actors. Our ingenue was a young girl, Jane Wyatt, who came to see me wearing a very pretty hat with violets, which seemed to be the same color as her eyes, and despite the protestations of my director, after testing her acting talents, I insisted on engaging her. She responded with a very creditable job of making a career for herself, both then and later on in motion pictures. Unfortunately for my Repertory plans, at the end of the season we had developed only two plays worthy of a New York opening; these were *Chrysalis* and *The School for Husbands.*

My ill luck with these two Repertory Companies affected my attitude toward this form of theatre, which I had so strongly advocated at the Guild. Examining the facts in the light of experience, I decided that in reality my main interest in the theatre was not so much in an acting company as it was in good plays. From the beginning I had approached the theatre from the point of view of a playwright, and when a conflict arose as to which came first, the play or the acting company, my inherent tendency was to put the play first and the acting company second. Further soul searching on my part, and an examination of the great acting companies of other countries made me realize that these (other than Shakespearean companies) had generally derived their permanence from the presence in them of a great actor or director who served as its leader, and by his presence inspired the actors to the point where they were perfectly willing to make sacrifices for the sake of their art. Thus, after two unsuccessful attempts at Westport, I abandoned my plan of a Repertory Company, and found myself with a loss of over $100,000 in cash and a substantial gain in experience. The Westport Country Playhouse, however, remained intact out of the debris of our dream, and Armina and I decided to use the theatre thereafter for the production of plays—my own plays and other plays—in which we were particularly interested.

During our second season at Westport, looking through my own manuscripts gathering dust in a desk drawer, I selected a light comedy I had written in France entitled *For Husbands Only,* another of my diatribes on the subject of marriage, and both Osgood Perkins and June Walker were extremely funny in it. The play amused *me* immensely, but failed to have the same happy effect on other people, so it departed this life on the stage of the Country Playhouse.

The adaptation of Molière's *The School for Husbands* which I wrote with Arthur Guiterman in rhyme came from the same desk drawer. As a boy, I was familiar with the French Bergerette songs which were beautifully sung by my cousin Lillian, and I used these songs throughout the play. To my surprise, I found that both Osgood Perkins and June Walker of our Acting Company possessed excellent singing voices. The play was very popular in Westport, and so impressed my colleagues in the Theatre Guild, that they decided to break their rule and produce a play at least partly written by one of their own members; I think they salved their consciences by regarding Molière as the real author rather than Langner and Guiterman. Arthur and I decided that Molière did not know how to complete the play, however, so we added another half-hour of playing time to it, and introduced many new scenes which must have caused its originator to roll over in his grave.

Thumbing through some of the old ballets written by Molière, I found one called *Le Rêve de Sganarelle* from *Le Mariage Forcé,* and we placed this ballet in the middle of the play. I secured the services of Doris Humphrey and Charles Weidman who invented some very charming dances in the manner of the period, and danced in it with their troupe. *The School for Husbands* was presented by the Theatre Guild at the Empire Theatre, and notwithstanding the fact that it received good notices, was able to stay there only for a few months, after which it went on tour over the Theatre Guild subscription system.

During the next summer of 1933, we produced at Westport the comedy, *The Pursuit of Happiness,* which I had written in collaboration with Armina. It was brought to New York under the management of Rowland Stebbins. We also produced a version which I wrote of Strauss' *Die Fledermaus* with lyrics by Bob Simon, and I found in Dwight Wiman a producer who brought it to New York under the title of *Champagne Sec.* As a result, during the fall of 1933, I was represented as a collaborator in these three plays on Broadway. This was indeed compensation for having given up my dream of an acting company.

The story of *The Pursuit of Happiness* is an indication of the extent of the part played by luck in the theatre. A friend of ours, the same Alice Raphael who was so largely responsible for my coming to the United States, spoke to Armina about the extraordinary forecasts made by an astrologer in Toronto, and suggested that she have her horoscope made. Armina, more or less to amuse herself, wrote to the astrologer with the necessary check, and in due course received her horoscope. This solemnly stated that she would find she had a talent for writing for the theatre. Without more ado, Armina asked me if she might collaborate on my play, *The Pursuit of Happiness,* which had been reposing for a couple of years in my desk. She did so, and made what had been a play on the serious subject of equality under the Declaration of Independence into a gay comedy which had its high point in a "bundling" scene which she conceived in terms of comedy where I had been quite serious on the subject.

Our cast at Westport was headed by the charming young actress Peggy Conklin and a young actor named Tonio Selwart who played the role of the Hessian with the Continental grace which the part called for. On the evening of the dress rehearsal, our staff came to see the play, and as they filed out of the theatre after the final curtain with glum faces and polite congratulations, I felt that the situation was desperate. Not so Armina. She turned to me with a grim look on her face. "Let's ask the director to take tomorrow off, and let me work with the actors. Those kids haven't the faintest idea how to bundle!" And the following morning all three of them, Armina, Tonio and Peggy, were seated in the four-poster bed, restaging the now famous bundling scene. Armina and I worked all day with the actors. The pace was changed, the timing of many of the lines altered, and in general, a thorough overhauling was accomplished. On the opening night, the laughter was continuous, and the play was enthusiastically received by the audience. The second night's performance was seen by Rowland Stebbins, the producer of *Green Pastures,* and he immediately bought the play and production. It was finally brought to New York, after opening in Philadelphia under the direction of Miriam Doyle, with only one change in the original Westport cast.[1]

The vestigial remains of my original serious play still appear in the *Pursuit of Happiness,* but the public took to the "bundling," hook, line and sinker, and the play became known as "The Bundling Play." It enjoyed immediate popularity in New York, where it ran for the entire season. After this, it was taken to London along with Rowland Stebbins, its producer, and ourselves. It received excellent notices there, but did not achieve the popularity it had in this country. Later on a

---

[1] In the original New York cast of *The Pursuit of Happiness* were Peggy Conklin, Tonio Selwart, Dennie Moore, Seth Arnold, Charles Waldron, Hunter Gardener, Eleanor Hicks, Oscar Polk, Raymond Walburn, R. G. Kirchner and David Harte.

motion picture was made, in which Francis Lederer and Joan Bennett appeared. Since its original production, the play has been given hundreds of times in stock and summer theatres, where it still remains a popular favorite, and it was also made into a musical play. Today the serious implications of *The Pursuit of Happiness,* in its handling of the problems of equality and freedom, are more topical than when it was originally written.

Lady Godiva, my next play, was based on the hitherto unrealized importance of wearing clothes, not for keeping warm, but to enable Man to claim a kinship with God. The title role was played by Violet Heming, an eminently beautiful and talented comedienne who has since married an eminently respectable United States senator. Violet seemed to be more concerned that when she rode the horse, she would be completely covered from head to toes with her hair, than she was with the more intellectual aspects of my play. We borrowed from a neighbor, Philip Dunning, an old wooden horse which formerly stood outside a saddlery store, and on this we planned to seat our hirsute but shrinking Godiva. The climax of the play was a discussion between Lady Godiva and her horse. Unfortunately, Violet's own flowing golden locks were insufficient to envelop her beyond all possibility of criticism, so at the last moment we hurriedly sent to Bridgeport for large quantities of yellow upholstery stuffing which we pinned all over her clothes. When she finally appeared on horseback on the opening night, there was a sigh of disappointment from the audience, for to all intents and purposes Godiva's head and shoulders were appearing from the top of a blonde-colored hair mattress.

My next collaboration with Armina was a comedy which we called *On to Fortune.* It was produced in Westport in the season of 1934, and was thought to be good enough to bring to Broadway by Crosby Gaige, a former partner of the Selwyns, an excellent connoisseur of cooking, and of the fine art of type setting. As Gaige was a man of impeccable taste, it seemed to us that *On to Fortune* could not be in better hands. The play opened in New York on February 4, 1935, with Ilka Chase, Myron McCormick, Glenn Anders and Roy Atwell in the leading roles and while it made its satiric point and was likened by one of the less-informed drama critics to the works of Molière, it departed from the boards after a short life, unmourned and unremembered. However, our friend Ilka Chase, one of the theatre's most versatile actresses, rose from the ashes of the play like a rocket and later on, showered the world of literature, radio, television and the lecture platform with the explosion of her talents.

As I had always been interested in Restoration comedies, which paved the way for the work of Sheridan, Wilde, Shaw, Noel Coward and a host of others, I decided to try producing some of them. I first selected Wycherley's *The Country Wife*—one of the most brilliant comedies written in the English language, as well as one of the most risqué. Aided and abetted by Ruth Gordon, who played the title role, I adapted and directed the play myself. In the high light of the play— the famous letter-writing scene—Ruth gave one of the most delightful comedy performances I have ever witnessed. The play was well received by the sophisticated Westport audience, and Helen Hayes was so delighted with Ruth's performance that she wanted to back the play for New York. Ruth introduced me to the talented Jed Harris, whose exotic genius blossomed in the theatre like the deadly nightshade. After a few interviews with Harris, we agreed to work together, and he amused himself at odd moments by alternately insulting me and insulting Lee Shubert, whom he had fascinated into providing the necessary financial backing.

On the day Ruth Gordon's contract was signed, Jed telephoned me to drop in to his office. Announcing that all plans were ready, he thereupon tore the contracts into shreds with a happy gleam in his eyes, and informed me that he had decided he would proceed no further. I was not too upset over his decision and so informed the disappointed Ruth, who promptly sailed to London and made a great success in the play with the Old Vic company. Gilbert Miller ordered a new acting version for London, but it was seemingly impossible to make this without using some of the rearrangement I had made for Westport. Backed by Helen Hayes, Gilbert Miller brought Ruth and the Old Vic version to New York with Roger Livesy and Irene Browne in the supporting cast, but before doing so, he arranged to pay me a royalty for the use of part of my Westport arrangement. Wycherley's ghost must have been furious at my receiving a royalty on his play!

Ruth Gordon, who gave so brilliant a performance in *The Country Wife,* is one of the most expert comediennes of our time. In her first play, *Mrs. Partridge Presents,* she was almost eccentric in appearance, yet when her career called for it, she waved a magic wand over herself and became beautiful and *chic!* In between acting many important roles, Ruth wrote some successful comedies, and she now makes a habit, which I hope will continue, of playing at our Playhouse in Westport at least once each season.

Joseph Wood Krutch, one of the best drama critics this country has ever produced, has for many years shared my affectionate interest in the playwrights of the Restoration. One evening I was discussing with him the production of another Restoration play at Westport, and mentioned my preference for Congreve. "Which of his plays do you like best?" I asked Joe. He replied, "I think *Love for Love* has the best plot, but *The Way of the World* has the best characters." I reread both plays, and decided that if I could transpose the main characters of *The Way of the World* into the plot of *Love for Love*, I would have an excellent play with the best features of both. I immediately perpetrated this act of sacrilege, and the following season I produced my own version, a combination of both plays. Beautifully acted by Eva Le Gallienne and Dennis King, the play met with immediate audience response.

One evening Ina Claire came out to Westport to see the play, and afterward went back with me to Eva's dressing room. Eva was delighted to see Ina, whom she greatly admired, and she remarked, "Ina, I think you ought to be playing this part instead of me. Don't you think so, Lawrence?" I was taken aback for a moment, then replied, "I think Ina would be very good in it." I returned home and remarked to Armina what an objective artist Eva Le Gallienne was. "Here she is appearing in an excellent part," I said, "yet she has the extraordinary honesty to say that Ina would be better in it than she was." I marveled at Eva's idealism and her willingness to go through sacrifice after sacrifice for her art. At the end of the engagement Armina went into Eva's dressing room to say good-by, and to thank her for her lovely performance. "Lawrence doesn't like me in this part," remarked Eva. "He said that Ina Claire would be better in it than I am!" "Thank God she's human," was my comment.

One of our friends, Anna May Wong, the California-born Chinese actress, confided the fact to me that she longed to appear in a new play, and that she wished someone would write one for her. I immediately obliged by collaborating with John Gerard on a new version of Gozzi's *Princess Turandot,* and the play opened at the Summer Theatre in Mount Kisco, after which it was brought to Westport during the season of 1937. Anna May Wong played the Princess, while McKay Morris, resplendent in Oriental costume, acted the role of her imperial father. On the opening night at Westport, the audience was enlivened by the presence of some of America's leading actresses— Ethel Barrymore, Ina Claire, Eva Le Gallienne and Alla Nazimova. A

Above: The Westport Country Playhouse. *Below:* Some of the original New York Repertory Company at the Westport Country Playhouse. *L. to R.:* Rollo Peters, Armina Marshall, Knowles Entrekin, Dorothy Gish, Romney Brent.

Above: Peggy Conklin and Tonio Selwart in the bundling scene of *The Pursuit of Happiness* by Armina Marshall and the author, Westport, 1933. *Below:* The author, Armina Marshall and John C. Wilson, Directors, Westport Playhouse.

Ruth Gordon in the famous letter-writing scene from *The Country Wife*, produced at Westport, 1935, and later by the Old Vic in London and Gilbert Miller in New York.

Above: Violet Heming in the author's comedy, *Lady Godiva*, Westport, 1933. *Below on the left:* Jose Ferrer in *The Silver Whistle*, Westport, 1948. *Below on the right:* Thornton Wilder, Betty Field and Armina Marshall in *The Skin of Our Teeth*, Westport, 1949.

Langnerlane
Farm, Cannon-
dale, Weston,
Connecticut.

Oval swim-
ming pool with
island designed
by the author.

Leo Godowsky and the author, 1930. Olivia DeHavilland and Marcus Goodrich on their wedding day at Langnerlane, 1946. Philip Langner, the author's son, at the Westport Country Playhouse, 1950. Luigi Pirandello and the author, Weston, Connecticut, 1935. (*inset*) Tallulah and her lion cub, Weston, Connecticut.

congenital idiot who was connected with the enterprise went backstage to Anna May Wong's dressing room just before the curtain rose
and told her with enthusiasm that all these important ladies of the
theatre were present. This was enough to put a far more experienced
actress in a state of panic, and its effect on Anna May was immediate.
Instead of giving the restrained performance which had won her
plaudits in Mount Kisco, in her understandable nervousness, she
overplayed with results which were disastrous both for her and the
play. When it closed, I had little enthusiasm for reviving it again. Other
plays on which I collaborated with Armina, and which were presented
in Westport were adaptations of *The Keyhole* by Andre Kadar, and
Doctor Knock by Jules Romains.

Some years earlier I had been attracted by a reference in Shaw's
Man and Superman to the interesting experiment of John Humphrey
Noyes at the Oneida Community. I selected as a subject for collaboration with Armina, a play based upon American communism as it had
been practised in many old communities such as Oneida, New Harmony, Brook Farm and Amana. In the course of writing the play,
which we called *Suzanna and the Elders,* we decided to visit Oneida,
New York, the home of the former community. We were cordially
received by John Pierrepont Noyes, the president of the concern which
continues the business originally established by the old community.
He allowed us to inspect the beautiful old buildings and theatre, which
is a gem of American Victorian architecture, and should, in my opinion,
be turned into a National Museum. Mr. and Mrs. Noyes came to
Westport when we produced the play and enjoyed our performance
there, with Uta Hagen and Onslow Stevens heading the cast and
Terry Helburn playing an important part. Later on the play was produced on Broadway by Jack Kirkland, with his wife Haila Stoddard in
the part played by Uta Hagen, and by the curious metamorphosis
which sometimes occurs when a play which has been popular in a
country theatre is made ready for Broadway, the emphasis of the play
changed. It became much more concerned with the physical life of the
Community than with its spiritual values. As a result, the play opened
in Princeton with these distorted values, and in the course of playing,
its humor became broader and broader.

When *Suzanna* finally opened in New York, Armina and I were
chided by Brooks Atkinson of the *Times* for having written a "vulgar"
play. Its message as to the failure of Communism was ignored by the
critics (we were twelve years ahead of the times), and we both unconsciously decided that it would be a long time before we went

through all the agonies of writing a play again. Our decision was helped by the fact that it had become increasingly difficult for us to collaborate, largely (according to this collaborator) because, as Armina learned more and more about playwriting, our arguments grew longer and longer. The next summer our son Philip, home for vacation from Hotchkiss School, inquired plaintively, "I hope you two are not going to be writing a new play, so I can have some fun on my holidays."

Up to this time, I had written fourteen full-length plays, of which six had been produced; I had collaborated on ten more, all of which were produced, and I also made two arrangements of other plays which were presented. Seven of my one-act plays have also been produced.[2]

The Westport Playhouse was enlivened by the presence on two occasions of Laurette Taylor, one of America's greatest actresses, who, had she devoted herself to important plays such as *The Glass Menagerie* in which she last appeared, could have easily surpassed all the other actresses of her generation. Laurette, with blonde hair, round face and enormous eyes, was of light build, but her voice had a musical quality and her sense of humor, which danced in her expressions and added perfect timing to her speeches, was something at once indescribable and unforgettable. Making her reputation in a light comedy, *Peg O' My Heart,* by her husband, Hartley Manners, she acted infrequently and then usually in plays which were unworthy of her talents. She tried out a play at Westport and so enthralled were Armina and I with her acting, that we watched her every performance during the week. She would come on stage doing three things at once: carrying a remembrance of whence she came; recognizing the other characters on stage, and bringing in her main motivation in the play; and she could project all these feelings to the audience as she entered. Each night her performance varied slightly but was always spontaneous and creative. "How do you do it?" I asked her in her dressing room. "Good acting, Lawrence," she replied, "starts from the behind up!" In this answer, bluntly put, lies the true reason why the intellectual processes have very little to do with acting.

Jane Cowl, one of our most popular actresses, was also fond of appearing at the Country Playhouse, and the second season I directed her in Ashley Duke's *The Man With a Load of Mischief.* Jane knew far more about direction than I did, and I found myself within a few hours agreeably carrying out her wishes under the hypnosis of her charm. One day I remarked, "The best way to get along with you,

[2] See Appendix IV, p. 463, for list.

Jane, is to let you do exactly as you please!" "Exactly!" purred Jane, in her rich velvety tones. She brought her own electrician with her in all her plays, and he in turn carried a large mirror which he held at the footlights so that she could see herself at the lighting rehearsals, and in this way, right up to her last appearance, she was always lighted to look young and beautiful to her audience.

During the first years at Westport, I always managed to lose a considerable sum each season, but I charged this off to personal enjoyment, and assumed that I would have lost considerably more had I been really interested in farming. I produced many of the plays largely to please myself, and usually booked in plays to please that part of the audience whose taste differed from mine. I made several attempts to overcome the difficulty of operating without loss. One season George Abbott and Philip Dunning, distinguished producers of Broadway hits, shared the responsibility of the theatre with Armina and myself. They put on a play one week while I put on a play the next week. During the rehearsal of one of my plays, I saw George Abbott sitting in the auditorium with a pained expression on his face. "Don't you feel well?" I asked. "I was just wondering how on earth you can select such plays," he answered. "I know just how you feel," I replied. "Every other week I wonder the same thing about you."

During the seasons of 1937–38, we conducted the theatre in partnership with Day Tuttle and Richard Skinner, a most amiable and talented team of summer impresarios, and the plays were given both at Westport and Mount Kisco. John Haggott and John Cornell, my son-in-law, ran the Westport Theatre for the 1939–40 seasons, doing excellent work. When I was spending a large amount of time in Washington during the year 1941, Armina, who was never far from the foreground, stepped fully into the picture. "Let *me* run the Playhouse with Jack Wilson," said Armina, "and you'll find yourself with an income instead of a deficit each year." So together they began to operate the Playhouse for the season of 1941.

John C. Wilson, who has since become an accomplished stage director, had been associated for a number of years in London and in this country with Noel Coward and the Lunts. He had bought a home in Southport, and together with his attractive wife, Natasha, had been a frequent visitor at our first nights. Indeed, Jack Wilson, tall and handsome, whose premature gray hair contradicted his boyish appearance, not only brought an air of distinction to our theatre, but his friends gave our Playhouse a *cachet* enjoyed by no other summer theatre of its kind. Thanks to Jack, it was not unusual to meet at the Playhouse Noel Coward, Tallulah Bankhead, Terence Rattigan, Anita Loos, Pamela Brown, Bea Lillie, Valentina and Mainboucher; while our own theatre neighbors, who include Richard Rodgers, Eva Le Gallienne, Mary Martin, Edna Ferber, Joshua Logan, Nedda Harrigan, Elia Kazan, Bobby Lewis, Cheryl Crawford, Rose Franken, Bill Maloney, Marian Anderson, Gladys Swarthout and many others, have made Westport an interesting gathering place on both sides of the footlights. Jack's first *coup* was to inveigle Tallulah Bankhead into playing *Her Cardboard Lover* as the opening play of the season, and so rapidly did he progress in the art of stage direction, that at the end of his first Westport season, he directed Noel Coward's comedy *Blithe Spirit* with such excellent results that it was an outstanding New York success.

Tallulah Bankhead arrived at the first rehearsal of *Her Cardboard Lover* with a lion cub she had found with a circus in the wilds of Nevada, and he was a constant attendant throughout the rehearsals. On the opening night at the Playhouse, after romping around the stage in a particularly alluring negligee, Tallulah took her first curtain call alone. The next curtain call she appeared with the baby lion in her arms, her tawny hair picking up the color from his, or *vice versa*, but in any event making a pleasing picture of actress and lion meet audience. Naturally, the curtain calls multiplied, for with each call Tallulah displayed her lion in a more imaginative manner. Tallulah carried the lion on stage with her as she toured from one summer theatre to another, until by the end of the season the lion had grown almost as large as a St. Bernard and weighed over thirty pounds, and under these conditions he was led, not carried, to the footlights.

After the season was over, Tallulah invited Theresa Helburn and myself to call at her hotel to discuss a play we had sent her. We found the lion reclining on a small balcony with a French window between us. "I love having him here," said Tallulah. "We understand one another, but the hotel people are so silly, they object to his going up and down in the passenger elevator." I felt a strong wave of sympathy for the hotel people. A few moments later Tallulah left us to bring a manuscript out of her bedroom. The lion, who had been watching us through the window, no sooner saw her disappear than, pushing the window doors aside, he bounded into the room, came over to me and began pawing playfully at my legs. I looked apprehensively at Terry who was seated in an armchair with her glasses on. The lion perked up his ears, also looked over at Terry, and apparently fascinated by her horn-rimmed spectacles, bounded across the room and up on her lap with the evident intention of batting off her glasses and raising hell generally. By this time, Tallulah returned to the room and took in the situation at a glance. With quick presence of mind, she seized her lion by the tail, dragged him off Terry's lap and hauled him bodily into her bedroom where she locked him in.

"Don't pay any attention to him, Terry!" said Tallulah, straightening out the furniture. "He loves to do that to people. He's just having fun." Two weeks later the hotel management prevailed and the lion was presented to the Zoo.

The same season was enlivened by the appearance at the Westport Playhouse of the successful young picture actor, Tyrone Power and his wife Annabella in Molnar's *Liliom*. On the Friday before the Monday opening night, Ty received a telephone call to return to Hollywood immediately to make some retakes of a recent picture. Ty protested, but the Hollywood people were obdurate. "Let me call them up," I asked Ty. I did so, and asked why they demanded his immediate return when they had given Ty permission to sign an Equity contract to play with us. "That was only a gentleman's agreement," was the bewildering reply.

Our lawyer, Kenneth Bradley of Bridgeport, told me that under an old Connecticut law, one could stop a man leaving the State if, by so doing, he broke a contract. I called in a Bridgeport sheriff, and introduced him to Ty at the theatre. "Ty," said Jack Wilson, "you cannot leave the State of Connecticut without breaking your contract, and the sheriff is here to stop you!" "You mean I am *forced* by law to stay in Connecticut until I open in the play?" asked Ty, with a happy grin. Ty explained his dilemma to Hollywood on the long-distance phone. After some legal skirmishes, the matter was settled the way we originally offered to settle it, and Tyrone Power opened in triumph as Liliom with Annabella as Julie.

Westport was often the scene of unexpectedly colorful incidents. In the twenties I was acquainted with Marcus Aurelius Goodrich, a *New York Times* book reviewer who was later to achieve fame as the author of the excellent novel *Delilah*. He was now engaged to Olivia de Haviland, the noted picture star, whose father had been a patent attorney practising in Japan, and had represented our office there many years previously. Olivia had come East to play the lead at Westport in Barrie's *What Every Woman Knows*, and on the Saturday evening before the Monday opening night, she and Mark asked me to arrange for their wedding the following day! I surmised that this was too fast, even for Connecticut, but on the Monday morning, Olivia and Mark were married at our home, the wedding taking place in the flower-decked pavilion on the small island in our swimming pool. "Lawrence," said Olivia, "since you knew my father, you must give me away," and walking together to the strains of Mendelssohn's *Wedding March* played on a harp by a lady harpist from the *Oklahoma* orchestra hurriedly imported from New York (and brought to our farm on a truck), Olivia and I crossed the bridge to the island and she and Mark were married. Olivia, married that morning, opened in triumph with a splendid performance at the Westport Playhouse the very same evening—a real trouper, I thought, as I watched her taking a dozen curtain calls at the end of the play.

Not all our experiences at the Westport Playhouse were as happy for all concerned as those recounted here. In the summer of 1949 the Playhouse witnessed a performance of the fine young actress, Mary MacArthur, with her mother, Helen Hayes, in a gay comedy entitled *Good Housekeeping*. Mary, a sensitive attractive girl, gave a splendid portrayal of a university president's daughter, and revealed a genuine talent which promised on maturing to carry her far along in the theatre. Alas, this was not to be, for she was taken tragically ill the evening after the closing of the play. Mary's passing was mourned as that of the Theatre's child, for she was beloved by all who knew her. Her memory will be kept everlastingly alive by the Mary MacArthur Polio Fund, of which a Chapter has been organized by the young people of Westport in her honor.

Jack Wilson introduced us to a talented young stage director, Martin Manulis, who acted as Managing Director of the Westport Theatre, and brought with him, from previous experiences, the apprentice system used in many summer theatres. Since then, a group of theatre-loving youngsters are selected each year from the most successful young graduates of the dramatic departments of colleges and schools of acting, and these boys and girls receive a thorough training in every branch of the theatre. The apprentices particularly enjoy being in contact with the professional people, and are encouraged to take notes of what they learn. One young would-be actress informed me that she had lost her notebook and was terrified that someone might find it. "Why are you so worried?" I asked. "Well," she replied, "I was helping on Sunday when Tallulah Bankhead's costumes arrived for *Private Lives*. She said she hated them, threw them on the floor and stamped on them, and I wrote down in my notebook *everything* she said. I'd be so embarrassed if anybody found it."

Today the Westport Country Playhouse is more truly a center of theatre than any other producing center I know. At Westport the scenery is designed, built and painted on the premises, instead of being let out to a contractor, and often the costumes are made there too. With the apprentices busily at work, the actors streaming in and out of rehearsal, the scenery being laid out on the grass to dry the paint in the sun, and the props being built in the shop, we work together in the same way as Shakespeare must have worked when he served his apprenticeship in London. And if he served as an ostler, as rumor has it, it must have been the apprentices' duty to "park" the horses and carriages, the counterpart of parking the cars today. One of the pleasantest sights I know is the audience streaming out of the theatre at intermission, the men and women dressed in summer clothes, and the spirit of gaiety which they bring to the Playhouse enhanced by the social gathering which forms part of the evening's enjoyment. What a contrast with the sober demeanor and almost belligerent attitude of New York audiences!

The triumvirate consisting of Armina, John C. Wilson and myself, have continued to operate the Playhouse since the war, with Martin Manulis as its managing director and our son Philip as its general manager.[3] Almost every important stage actor and actress of our time has played at Westport. The Playhouse was the first to bring prominently to the attention of the managers and the public such young talents as Jane Wyatt, Patricia Neal, Gene Kelly, Stewart Chaney, Montgomery Clift, Zachary Scott, Danny Mann and many others. We have also striven to make the Playhouse more interesting than the usual summer theatre by reviving the classics and worth-while plays of the past. And as long as I am in the minority, I believe it will continue to be solvent.

At the opening of the Summer Season of 1951, we celebrated the twentieth anniversary of the founding of the Playhouse, and prepared for a gala opening night. Before the audience arrived, I sat in the theatre in the semi-darkness, and as I looked out over the auditorium onto the empty stage, I called to mind some of the high moments of the past: Ethel Barrymore, with her patrician carriage, grace of movement, rich voice tones and deft comedy timing in *The School For*

---

[3] See Appendix III, p. 459, for list of the important plays and players who have appeared at the Country Playhouse, Westport.

Scandal; Otis Skinner, romantic to the end, playing the last perform-ance of his career in *The Nobel Prize;* Eugenie Leontovich in *Tovarich* and *Romance,* in both of which she played with great delicacy, warmth and personal charm; Jimmy Savo, whose comic pantomime and rolling black eyes and curls made our production of Molière's *Would-be Gentleman* an hilarious experience; Eva Le Gallienne in the contrasting roles of *Love for Love* and *Camille;* Alla Nazimova giving her heart-breaking performance of Mrs. Alving in *Ghosts;* Laurette Taylor, whimsical and pathetic in *Outward Bound;* Ruth Gordon in a number of brilliant comedic performances, of which that of *The Country Wife* was outstanding; Jane Cowl in several roles, of which I remembered best *Captain Brassbound's Conversion;* Thornton Wilder, no mean actor, in his two best plays, *Our Town* and *The Skin of Our Teeth,* the latter including brilliant performances by Betty Field and Armina Marshall; the beloved Mr. and Mrs. Charles Coburn in *The Yellow Jacket,* which they carried to every corner of America; and Helen Hayes giving one of her best comedy performances in *Good House-keeping.* I might have dreamed on indefinitely but for the rumble of distant thunder. I left the theatre and looked heavenward. A storm was obviously on its way. The curtain rang up at 8:45 and precisely five minutes before, we experienced a downpour of torrential rain similar to the one which baptized us on our original opening night twenty years earlier. Our audience, drenched to the skin, settled down to try to enjoy the beginning of our second twenty years, while the actors on the stage, Kim Hunter, Nina Foch, Karl Malden and Scott McKay, shouted the lines of Phil Barry's play *The Animal Kingdom,* at the tops of their lungs in an abortive attempt to make themselves heard over the din of the elements.

The twentieth season of the Playhouse marked a change in its gen-eral management, which was turned over to my son Philip, after he had taken the islanders of Nassau in the Bahamas by surprise by moving part of the Westport staff across the Caribbean and giving the first season of plays in the history of the West Indies.

During the last few seasons, we have increasingly used the West-port theatre for experimental purposes, and as a laboratory, so to speak, for new plays by young authors for the Theatre Guild and John C. Wilson. This policy is being continued with growing success, and during the past season the majority of plays given at Westport have been new plays, mostly by new authors. We hope in this way to introduce new writers to follow in the footsteps of those giants of the twenties and thirties who are no longer contributing to our theatre.

This has made Westport a *rendezvous* for the younger people of the theatre, and fortunately for us, our audience contains an unusually large number of adventurous souls who would rather follow us into the realm of artistic speculation than imbibe the usual summer-theatre fare. And if they don't enjoy the play, they can always enjoy the scenery provided by Nature, the best scenic artist of them all.

CHAPTER XXV

The New Regime

M Y WORK in the Theatre Guild may be roughly divided into three periods of ten years each. The first ten years witnessed the rising curve of the Theatre Guild, culminating in the production of a large number of successful plays by the Theatre Guild Acting Company. This was followed by the next period of ten years ending in the spring of 1939, which may be regarded as the ten wavering years of the Theatre Guild, although during this period, many of the finest American plays were produced by us. The next ten years marks the operation of the Theatre Guild with Theresa Helburn and myself acting as the Administrative Directors, and Armina Marshall serving as Assistant Director and later on as Associate Director.

The fact that the Guild was able to survive for this third period was due to a number of circumstances, and first among these must be mentioned the advent of Katharine Hepburn. This spectacular young woman flashed like a comet across the theatre when she made her first appearance in a play entitled *These Days* by Katherine Clugston which was produced by Arthur Hopkins. I remember vividly her opening-night performance, and realized at the time that an electrical personality had arrived. Later on she was engaged to play the maid and to understudy the ingenue in our production of *A Month in the Country*. I saw little of her during this time, when occasionally she would swoop cyclonically through the office with her mop of red hair awry in all directions. After a relatively brief interval she married and went to live in Philadelphia. I remember on one occasion when she flitted through our office, asking her whether she would appear again in a play with us, to which she replied that since she had married she had given up the theatre. The next time I met Kate was at a luncheon appointment I had made with Miriam Howell, one of the most attractive Actors' Representatives in the United States, who had called me up saying that she was bringing Katharine Hepburn along with her, as Kate was leaving that afternoon for Hollywood where she had just signed a contract. We lunched together, Katharine was very quiet and subdued, and entirely unlike the girl I came to know later. I wished her good-by and good luck, and hoped that she would come back to the theatre some day, and that was that.

Hepburn made a spectacular success in Hollywood, her first assignment being the young girl in Clemence Dane's *A Bill of Divorcement* with John Barrymore. This was followed by many others, but the theatre was in Kate's blood, and in the year 1936 she returned to New York, and we agreed on the production of Helen Jerome's dramatization of *Jane Eyre*. Kate made a very appealing figure in the person of Jane, and pleased us by her attitude toward the theatre. When the play was having its final dress rehearsal in New Haven, she remarked to me with considerable force that she was irritated to find that her name was appearing in larger letters on the billboards than any other member of the company. "I want it understood," she said, "that I object to having any more billing than the other actors." "That's very generous of you," I replied. "Generous!" she said scornfully, "I just don't want to stick my neck out!"

I joined *Jane Eyre* at Cleveland and took train with the company to Pittsburgh. When a company is not tired of traveling, the trooping from one city to another on Sunday is usually enjoyable. There is a sense of bustle and fun at the railroad station, the company either has a Pullman or a car reserved for it, and it is everybody's opportunity to visit, play games or catch up with reading. It brings back something of the life of the old strolling players in England, when the actors and actresses moved from town to town and could perform only by license of the Lord Chamberlain.

When we arrived in Pittsburgh, Kate, her attractive friend Laura Harding and I went for a long walk in Schenley Park, which was covered with snow, and although we were in the center of a residential section of the town, we might have been in the wilds of Canada, so deserted were the snowbound streets and paths. As we trudged for miles through the park, Kate talked about her plans for returning to the theatre, and I was captivated by her sincerity, gaiety and high spirits. She showed us how to make a mask of her face in the snow, by burying her face in it, from which she emerged with her clear skin pink and tingling. I respectfully declined to accept her invitation to do the same.

After the Pittsburgh opening performance, Kate gave a party to which I was invited along with some of the company in her sitting room, and she decided to put on a Fashion Show of the summer clothes she was going to wear in Florida after the tour was ended, and which had just arrived at the hotel. Outside the weather was vile. It had started to snow again, and Pittsburgh never looked more dismal. We felt greatly cheered as Kate appeared in dress after dress of summery material, and when the Fashion Show was over, we all had a happy supper together. Kate was never destined to wear these clothes again, for she sent the trunk containing them to await her arrival in Florida, and it was stolen in transit.

It was eventually decided that we would not bring *Jane Eyre* into New York, but that Kate would at some future time appear in another play for the Guild. A couple of years went by, and in the spring of 1939, Theresa Helburn received a call from Philip Barry, who informed her that he had been having some discussions with Kate, after she had appeared in the screen version of his play, *Holiday*. They had met and talked over the possibility of his writing a play for her, and this play was partly completed under the title of *The Philadelphia Story*. Barry had felt that our system of producing plays with six Guild directors was extremely confusing to the author and insisted that if the play was to be given by the Guild, he would like to have Theresa Helburn and myself alone concerned with its production.

The Guild was still in debt to the tune of about $60,000 at the time, while *Jeremiah* with its cry of doom was still on the boards, and there was nothing on the horizon that looked nearly as promising as *The Philadelphia Story*. We agreed to Phil Barry's conditions, and he deposited two acts of the play with us. At this time Kate had been having difficulties in Hollywood owing to the fact that she had been cast in a number of indifferent pictures. Some individual with a gift for phrasing had described her as "poison at the box office," and she had just received an offer for her services in a new picture in Hollywood at a salary which was so small as to be almost insulting.

We read the two acts of Phil's play eagerly and noted that it was a high comedy of unusual quality, so without further ado, Terry and I began work on the casting while Phil addressed himself to the task of writing the third act. This arrived later but it was not entirely up to expectations. The play, nevertheless, went into rehearsal while Phil continued to work on it. We opened in New Haven, and then went to Philadelphia, where the play was received with great acclaim. The third act, however, was still not right, and Phil went to his home in Florida to rewrite it. He came back just as we were about to play Washington, D. C., and this time the third act met all requirements.

We then had an extremely difficult decision to make. The play was doing unusually well on the road. If we brought it into New York, however, and it received bad notices, this would destroy any possibility for a road tour later. There were many counsels to keep the play out, tour it all over the United States, and then bring it into New York. When Terry and I arrived in Washington, the discussion was raging. The Guild was on its last legs, Hepburn was on her last legs, and Phil Barry had not written a successful play for years. Should we take a chance on the situation and bring the play into New York, or should we duck it and establish it all over the country and then come to New York later? The fate of all of us hung in the balance. Both Terry and I sweated through this decision, which was one of the hardest we have ever had to make, but we both agreed. Kate's first views on the matter, which she changed later, were expressed picturesquely by her. "If I have a barrow and I'm selling my fruit very well on the side streets, why should I go to the market place where all the other barrows are, and where I may not do nearly as well?"

On the opening night at the Shubert Theatre I passed through many moments of anguish, realizing that the future of the Guild was at stake. The reception was cold and hostile at first, but gradually the play's charm, and the excellent acting of Kate, Joseph Cotten, Van Heflin and Shirley Booth broke down the reserve of the audience, and by the end of the second act I felt that everyone was with us. At the end of Act 3, there was that kind of enthusiastic applause which you know is not coming from politeness, and the following morning we were overjoyed to find that our press notices were excellent. The Theatre Guild had another big hit on its hands and the three derelicts were miraculously on their feet again.

Nearly three years after its opening *The Philadelphia Story* finally closed after its third engagement in the city for which it was named. Kate gave a party for the cast and stage crew at the Berkley Hotel to which I was also invited. It was one of those happy-sad affairs where everyone was glad about leaving the play after so many performances, and unhappy about saying farewell to one another and to Kate. The party dwindled but I stayed to the end, along with Red, our property man, Emily Perkins, Kate's secretary, and Kate. "What shall I do next?" said Kate, addressing herself partly to Red and partly to me. Red, who was sitting on the floor with Kate, did not seem to know the answer. With the wisdom which comes so readily at three in the morning, I suggested that she do something dangerous. "What do you mean by dangerous?" she asked me belligerently. "A play in which you'll aim high but risk falling flat on your face if you don't come through with a great performance," I replied. "Shakespeare or Ibsen, for instance." Red agreed with me, and we left Kate completely convinced. Later on she decided to play *As You Like It*, an enterprise which looked surprisingly dangerous at the time she undertook it, and in which she added new laurels to her career as an actress.

The Philadelphia Story marked an epoch in the affairs of the Guild, not only because of its success which paid off the Guild's debts, but also because it was the first play to be produced by the Guild without using the services of the Board of Managers. Terry and I worked together as producers of the play without friction and with complete sympathy and understanding of each other's point of view, and we in turn were similarly *en rapport* with the author. Thus was born the new system of Guild management which has lasted down to today, with Terry and myself usually working as supervisors of the play. At the inception of this new plan any group of two members of the Guild Board were permitted to produce plays in this way, provided the play itself was not vetoed by the Board as being below Guild standards. No other Board members availed themselves of this opportunity, however, and from this time on the selection and production of plays became solely the responsibility of Terry and myself.

In the spring of 1939 the Group Theatre produced William Saroyan's short play *My Heart's in the Highlands*, and in order that it might be seen by as large an audience as possible, we took this play under our wing and presented it to our New York subscribers. The run of the play was considerably prolonged, for which we received the thanks of the dramatic critics. During the summer I was visited at Langnerlane Farm by Eddie Dowling, who informed me that he had received a copy of a new play from Saroyan with excellent parts for himself and Julie Haydon. The play was called *The Time of Your Life* and we read it with great relish. Terry and I decided to join forces with Dowling and to produce the play, which we regarded as one of the finest of the period. Saroyan was in California, and it was decided to place the production in charge of Bobby Lewis who had done such an excellent job with *My Heart's in the Highlands*.

When the play opened in New Haven, it was in a state of incredible chaos. By this time William Saroyan arrived on the scene, and appeared to be a man of varying amiability, at one time having the charm of a romantic Eastern potentate and at other times displaying all the sensitivity of a U.S. Mail truck driver. As he switched rapidly from an Eastern Potentate to a Western truck driver, it was difficult for me to keep up with his moods, but I will say this for him, that he knew what he wanted, and many a situation which had been missed was immediately remedied by Saroyan. He attended the opening at New Haven, accompanied by the ever-present George Jean Nathan, who regarded himself as "the discoverer" of Saroyan, and hovered around him like an oracular fairy godmother. Nobody at the New Haven opening seemed to know what the play was about, including the actors, and a bewildered audience left the theatre and learned from the papers the next day that the dramatic critics were equally bewildered. At a late conference in the Taft Hotel after the opening night, Bobby Lewis handed in his resignation. In retrospect, it is a pity that Saroyan was not present from the first rehearsal, for the director is greatly handicapped when the author is not present. With Lewis out, a council of war was held and it was decided that Dowling, Saroyan and myself would endeavor to put the play into shape, giving Saroyan billing with Dowling as the director.

I was soon to learn that Saroyan had never directed a play in his life, had not the slightest idea of how to talk to the actors in such a way that they understood him, and that his method of dealing with them varied from acting their parts himself in the most amateurish manner and requesting them to imitate him, or else bellowing at them. He knew what he wanted, but he did not know how to get it. We opened in Boston two or three days later, throwing out the entire scenery, and building a new realistic set. Furthermore, we decided that eight of the actors selected with Mr. Lewis' blessings were inadequate, and we replaced them with new actors from New York. The goings and comings between New York and Boston for the next two weeks have since become legendary. Actors were shuttling back and forth, being tried out in New York, sent up to Boston and thereupon accepted or rejected as the case might be.

Meanwhile, Armenian friends of Saroyan began to arrive from the Pacific coast. One of them, an attractive boy by the name of Ross Bagdeserian, was introduced to me by Saroyan as his cousin, and the former added that he was writing him into the play because he knew how to sing an Irish song, "When Irish Eyes Are Smiling." Another Armenian friend was delegated to play the mouth organ, which he did exceedingly well, and he was also used to sweep the stage at the beginning of the play. "We can't ask my friend to be sweeping the saloon when the curtain rises," said Bill to me one day. "Why not?" I asked. "He's one of the most distinguished Armenian painters in this country! He can't do anything so menial as to be a bar attendant." We finally compromised by having his friend sweep the stage with his back to the audience so that he should not be recognized. Meanwhile, to make matters worse, Nathan wrote and published an article blaming the entire debacle at New Haven on the Theatre Guild, and prophesying that it would be a dire failure when it opened in New York in view of what had been done.

Matters seemed to be in a state of crisis so I decided to stay every minute the play was in Boston, and I determined to extract every ounce out of it no matter what happened. Some of the ideas Saroyan had regarding the staging of the play were good, others were dreadful. Dowling, Terry and I got together on the essentials, and the recasting of the play was done between myself in Boston and Terry in New York. One of our ideas was to use William Bendix who played the Policeman, in which he gave an unforgettable performance; indeed, a performance so magnificent that later on, when he played the part in Los Angeles, he was given a contract for motion pictures, and has since become a picture and radio star. Another unknown young man who was suggested by Armina and myself was Gene Kelly who had done some "hoofing" in a little revue at Westport. He was put in the cast despite the protests of Saroyan, and was so successful in the role of Harry that Richard Rodgers and George Abbott, seeing him, starred him in *My Pal Joey* from whence Hollywood snatched him, and he, too, began a career in pictures. Terry suggested a gifted young actress, Celeste Holm, for the part of Mary Ell, which she played with telling effect, and her blonde beauty, tenderness and sense of humor made this the starting point for her successful career in the theatre and talking pictures.

For the first week in Boston, the play seemed to be getting steadily worse. None of the critics had a good word to say for it with the exception of Elliot Norton of the *Boston Herald* who used to drop into the theatre from time to time and give me words of advice and encouragement. At rehearsals, I would sit on the stage with Dowling, while Saroyan sat to one side, generally eating pears, apples or other fruit, which he peeled with a murderous-looking pocket knife. Every now and again he would shout at an actor or show an actor what to do, while I endeavored to keep the peace as we worked out the various changes of movement, renditions and so on. There was a good deal of reconstruction to be done on the act formation of the play, on which I worked, as well as on the "curtains."

One fatal evening, when everyone in the company was completely discouraged, the electrician decided to change the amber gelatins, and put in new ones. He did not, however, burn them out first, which is customary with ambers, and as a result, when the curtain went up on this particular evening, the actors' faces were all positively yellow, as though they were suffering from jaundice. Moreover, since they were busy remembering everything they had been told, and were also under the general restraint which actors feel when they have no confidence in what is happening, the performance was depressing to a degree. At the end of the evening Saroyan came up to me in the lobby of the theatre and, bellowing like a bull, shouted, "What the hell is the matter with the actors?" "Do you really want to know," I replied, equally sore. "Yes," he said. "What is it?" "*You* are what is the matter with the actors. If you'll keep out of the theatre the next three days, we will be able to bring this play into good condition. Otherwise, we won't." Saroyan ran around to Dowling's dressing room and asked whether I had any right to keep him out of the theatre, to which Eddie replied tactfully that he thought it could be arranged for him to sit in the orchestra, instead of on the stage.

We were in serious difficulties over the last act, however, and each time we discussed the matter with Saroyan he would state, "The climax of this play is the pinball machine. If you don't have a good pinball machine the play has no climax!" We scoured everywhere to find the right pinball machine but there were none available. I finally decided to try to invent one. I had a machine built by a model-maker who was often employed by our firm in New York in connection with patents, and it was arranged in such a way that at the right moment red, white and blue lights flashed, the noise of clashing machinery was heard, and an American flag was waved, when the pinball fanatic finally succeeded in winning. I painted the machine myself on stage, despite the Union rules to the contrary, and for this I received grudging thanks from the distinguished author. Saroyan had great difficulty in ending the play, and by a piece of luck, Philip Barry, who had come up to Boston to see Terry and me, was able to suggest a brilliant solution by the simple expedient of having Eddie Dowling, who had been sitting in his chair for practically the entire evening, get out of his chair, walk across the stage and wave good-by to everybody!

Over the week end we brought the play to New York. Saroyan was very critical of the Booth Theatre, and asked if it might not be possible to push the walls out on either side, in order to accommodate more people, and to improve the sight lines on the sides. As we were opening on the next Wednesday, I informed him that it would not be possible to carry out his wishes in time.

The day before the opening he appeared with a little Armenian girl from his home town, Fresno, and asked if she might be permitted to appear in the play. "What do you want her to do?" I asked him. "Well," he said, "when the old Italian woman comes in I would like this young girl to be with her, and I've written a couple of lines for her." "Why must this little girl appear in the play?" I asked. He thought for a moment, and replied, "I have every kind of person in this play, an old man and an old woman, a middle-aged man and a middle-aged woman, a young man and a young woman, and I have a little boy, but I have no little girl." I thought this was a fairly logical reason, but since we were opening the next night I told him this was impossible. The following morning, he came rushing into the theatre and said that Nathan had decided that the scene which took place in Julie Haydon's bedroom should actually be played in the saloon itself. As this would have involved restaging the entire scene the day the play was opening in New York, I politely suggested that Nathan should mind his own business, and we intended to produce the play the way we had rehearsed it in Boston, and as written in his manuscript.

The Time of Your Life, which is undoubtedly Saroyan's best work in the theatre, received both the Pulitzer Prize and the Critics' Circle Award, and until *Streetcar Named Desire,* was the only play which had won both of these honors.

Saroyan never forgave me for the fact that I kept him at arm's length from the actors during the latter part of the Boston engagement. When the play was published, he omitted all reference to the Theatre Guild as the producers of the play. He furthermore placed the scene which, in his original manuscript, was located in Kitty Duvan's bedroom, in the saloon itself, which is of course absurd.

Love's Old Sweet Song, also by Saroyan, was also given this season, and was jointly directed by Saroyan and Eddie Dowling, with Armina Marshall as Associate Producer. This play, one of Saroyan's most charming efforts, was written in loose form. Any eccentric actor who appeared at our office might stimulate him to write in scenes for that actor, very much as one might build a vaudeville show by putting in a "number" for any comedian who applied for a job. The danger into which we were drifting became very apparent when, one fine day, a lady parachute jumper appeared at the Guild office and was shown in to Saroyan. "Could you jump from the roof of the stage with your parachute and land on the stage at the end of the second act?" asked Saroyan. "Because if you can, I will make you one of the characters in the play." Since the lady couldn't without breaking her neck, we were mercifully spared this addition to the play. However, Saroyan discovered an old friend on the street, a Greek comedian, who had appeared as a comic in some films, and by providing him with a lawn mower and an American flag, Saroyan introduced him into the play with extremely happy effects!

We finally opened in Philadelphia with sad results, for while the first half of the play was excellent, it reached a climax in the middle of the second act after a long speech by Walter Huston as a medicine vendor, and from there on this act ran steadily downhill. The feeling of the audience at the end of the second act was one of extreme disappointment, for they had just seen the weakest part of the play where they should have seen the strongest. After Saroyan made a number of attempts to remedy the situation, it finally occurred to me that if the play, which was in three-act form, could be played as a two-act play, our intermission could take place in the middle of the play, and at the point about halfway through where the second act reached its climax. It is never possible to tell whether an operation of this kind will turn out successfully, and the only way to ascertain is by trying. Saroyan therefore agreed to slice the play in half, and it became a two-act play instead of a three-act play. Since it was extremely loose in form, this operation, instead of hurting it, turned the trick and converted what had been a failure into a success. That part of the play which was weakest, instead of being at the end of the second act, now became the beginning of the second half of the play, and from this point on the play steadily improved until the final curtain.

When we opened in Baltimore, we received excellent notices, not an easy matter, for Baltimore is a town where the critics are not noted for their indulgence. I felt happy as we brought the play to New York, feeling that the out-of-town tryout, with its consequent financial losses, had nevertheless justified itself since we had apparently solved all our problems. Alas, however, I had reckoned without our Saroyan. Two days before the play was due to open in New York he arrived at the theatre with his play agent, Pat Duggan, and the two of them sat down in the smoking room of the Booth Theatre and expounded their point of view to the rest of us. Saroyan, it appeared, had demonstrated his ability to write a two-act play with *The Time of Your Life*. It was now considered desirable that he should demonstrate his ability to write a play in three acts—yet here we were putting it into two acts! Terry and I pointed out that we had already demonstrated that the play was extremely weak in three-act form, but was excellent in two-act form. We were met on all these scores with stubborn obstinacy by Saroyan.

As we teetered in the face of uncertainty, Saroyan made an impassioned speech: after all, it was his play and if it was a failure, he would have to take the responsibility for it. His reputation was at stake, and he felt that he must insist on his right as an author that the play should be presented in three-act form. Finally, to make his point very clear, he added, "And I'll be very glad to buy out everyone here who has money invested in the play, so that I will own the entire play myself." Pat Duggan, who, thank the Lord, preserved his Irish sense of humor, winked at me and suggested that we have a chat in the hallway. "I just want to explain one thing to you," said Pat. "Please don't take up his offer. He hasn't the money to buy you out, and even if he had, I wouldn't let him."

The matter was discussed back and forth, and it was agreed that since Saroyan's reputation was more important than anything else, we should accede to his request rather than "destroy a great work of art." The result was that *Love's Old Sweet Song* opened the following night with a weak second act, and the critics, except for one or two, lashed it severely. The next day Saroyan called me on the telephone and remarked, "You had better put the curtain back the way it was in Baltimore!" Alas, we had missed the train. Thus was "lost" one of the most delightful plays Saroyan has ever written, and if someone wishes to revive it some day, I strongly recommend that he present it in the two-act form with which we should have opened the play in New York.

It is one of my regrets that Saroyan has written so little for the theatre since the war. In retrospect, he was always an exciting and colorful personality, right in many big ways and wrong in many small ones. He has never been mediocre, dull or conventional, and I would gladly put up with his temperamental antics for the sake of another good play.

Not all our experiences with talented playwrights were as turbulent as our collaboration with this unbridled genius. During the same exciting period, we had the gratification of working again with Robert Sherwood, who had previously given us such noteworthy plays as

Reunion in Vienna and *Idiot's Delight.* This time, moreover, a Sherwood production was something more than putting on another play with the Lunts. The play was not merely another theatrical triumph; it launched us all in a minor crusade, as became the period of high tension when Europe was engulfed in World War II.

After the Lunts returned from a tour with their acting company, which included Richard Whorf, Sidney Greenstreet, Bretaigne Windust and Thomas Gomez in *Idiot's Delight* and *The Taming of the Shrew,* it was decided to bring the latter play back to New York, and it opened toward the end of the season at the Alvin Theatre. As the result of the Lunts' continuous playing of this Shakespearean comedy, it had been greatly improved, and many who had seen it originally, flocked to the Alvin again to find their performances even funnier, and the play more charming than in its original presentation. About this time Helen Hayes asked me to help her with the Finnish Relief Fund which was being raised by the American theatre, under her chairmanship, in order to aid the Finns who were being attacked by the Russians, and I served as assistant chairman. Alfred and Lynn were greatly interested in this movement, for in addition to their natural sympathy, Alfred's mother had been born in Finland. I asked them if they would give a benefit performance and join with us in donating one evening's profits to the Fund. They responded by saying that they wished to give not merely one evening's, but an entire week of profits, and this resulted in our jointly turning over to the Fund a substantial amount.

Before the Lunts played their return engagement in New York, I had been in touch with Bob Sherwood of the Playwrights' Company, asking him if he would make some revisions of his play *Acropolis* which I had always admired, but which I thought needed some changes in order that it might build structurally to make a better play. Bob listened with approval to my suggestions regarding a possible rewriting of the play for the Lunts, and said he would get to work on it and try to finish it so that it would be available for Alfred and Lynn the following season. I felt very happy that I had arranged this with Bob, for I regarded the theme of this play as extremely important for our era. For the benefit of those who have not read *Acropolis,* I should add that it presents the collapse of Athenian democracy; and this was a timely subject while Nazism was continuing to extinguish freedom in Europe. The play also shows, through the immortal story of Pericles and Aspasia, that art endures while time obliterates most of the other efforts of man. Bob informed me that he expected to have the play ready about May, and we made arrangements to close *The Taming of the Shrew* in order that the Lunts might have a rest before beginning *Acropolis.*

On the eve of the closing, Bob appeared at the Alvin Theatre and handed Alfred and Lynn the new manuscript, and they left the next day for their farm at Genesee Depot, Wisconsin. A few days later, on reading the *New York Times*, I was amazed to see a notice to the effect that Sherwood had written a new play for the Lunts called *There Shall Be No Night*, and that he was at Genesee consulting with them regarding casting. I called Alfred on the telephone and read the notice to him. He informed me that Bob Sherwood had recently arrived, and they had just finished reading the new play about which they were greatly excited. He put Bob on the telephone, and he explained that on his return to New York he would work out an arrangement between the Playwrights' Company and the Theatre Guild by which there would be a joint presentation of the play.

Bob arrived a few days later and explained that he had conceived the idea of writing this play about Finland in the throes of war with Russia, as a result of listening to a radio broadcast around Christmas time. He had decided to tell no one about it, neither the Lunts nor any of the members of the Playwrights' Company, but to work in great haste and secrecy, feeling that if he discussed it with anyone it would impede his creative flow. *There Shall Be No Night* turned out to be one of Sherwood's most effective plays, and in it Alfred and Lynn gave their finest acting performances. They employed in the company Richard Whorf who had belonged to the Acting Company, as well as Maurice Colbourne, Edward Raquello, Phyllis Fraser and Thomas Gomez.

This play was not merely a theatre success. It was a stirring indictment against the encroachment by a large totalitarian country upon a small democracy, and was as applicable to the encroachments of Hitler as to those of Soviet Russia. The Lunts played this play around the country as though they were conducting a crusade—as indeed they were. Wherever it was played, it stirred the audiences to an affirmative belief in democracy, and a determination to maintain what they had against totalitarian tyranny. Later on, during the actual warfare, the play was taken by the Lunts to London, but by this time the Finns had thrown in their lot with Hitler. By a deft rewriting of the play, which set the locale in Greece instead of in Finland, with German aggressors instead of Russians, it became just as topical and *apropos* as an indictment of the Fascist brand of tyranny as it was against the Communist brand. The Lunts, as part of their contribution to morale, courageously played *There Shall Be No Night* in London for a period of nearly a year while the war was on, and while bombs were falling all around the theatre, and they also played in camps all over England putting heart into the thousands of soldiers on leave or preparing to depart for the front.

Another play which we produced at this time, and which formed part of the theatre's crusade against Fascism, was *The Fifth Column* by Ernest Hemingway, written in Madrid under the fire of Franco's siege guns. After some considerable difficulties in straightening out the manuscript, due to the fact that Hemingway had retired to Cuba, and had left the additional dialogue to be written by his adapter, Benjamin Glazer, the play came to New York and received excellent notices. Like the Lunts, Franchot Tone was also a crusader, but unfortunately he was intermittently in and out of the cast due to laryngitis, so that the run of the play came to an untimely end. In producing this play, we were aided and abetted by Billy Rose, the successful producer, columnist, song writer and restaurant and theatre owner. Rose, who was a personal friend of Tone, made a substantial investment in the play, and impressed me greatly with his likable character, his intelligence and good sportsmanship.

The Guild's second season (1940–41) under the sole management of Terry Helburn and myself did not match our first season. For one thing, the European war was on, and we were operating under increasing difficulties. Also, I had begun to spend the greater part of my time in Washington organizing the National Inventors Council, while Terry and Armina were also engaged in war activities with the American Theatre Wing as well as carrying the greatest part of the load in New York.

Our first production of the season, *Twelfth Night,* was actually suggested by Helen Hayes. This came about in the following way. One of Shakespeare's plays which I have always loved is *The Winter's Tale,* and I was determined that at some time in my life we would produce it. I felt that Helen would make an excellent Hermione, and in the second half of the play, could portray her daughter Perdita. The play had been presented years before in this manner by Mary Anderson and also by Viola Allen, and both times it had been a great success and had played all over the United States. In order to attract Helen, Stewart Chaney, the scenic artist, entered into a conspiracy with me to prepare some colored sketches of the sets and costumes showing just how she and the production would look, and Helen, Terry and

I had lunch together at the Plaza. She admired the pictures, but said she felt she would much rather play *Twelfth Night* than *The Winter's Tale*, for she felt that while in *Victoria Regina* it was relatively easy for her to grow older and older as the play progressed, it would be considerably more difficult to grow younger and younger in *The Winter's Tale.*

We therefore prepared a production of *Twelfth Night*, which Helen liked, and in due course our play was launched, Gilbert Miller being taken in as a silent partner because of his former relationship with Helen as her manager in *Victoria Regina.* The play was excellently directed by Margaret Webster, and in my opinion was as charming and likable a performance of this comedy as I have ever seen. Helen, I felt, was extraordinarily good in every phase of her acting, and as I would sit in the theatre at a matinee watching the glow of enchantment on the faces of the children who were brought there by their parents, I felt something of the same glow which I myself had experienced when I first saw Ellen Terry so many years before in *The Merchant of Venice.* Helen, one of the most natural, lovable and effortless actresses I have ever known, a tireless trouper, and a woman who never complains about anything unless her reasons for complaint are monumental, is nevertheless extremely sensitive about her performances. Many times I have gone into her dressing room after a play is over, enthusiastic over her performance, only to be met by the remark as I entered the door, "Oh, dear, were you out front? I was terrible tonight." "I don't know what you are talking about," I would reply. "I thought you gave one of your finest performances." "Either you are crazy or I am," she would reply, "I just felt I was terrible the entire evening." When one is a natural actress, with a technique as superb as Helen's, it is almost impossible, even for a trained member of the audience, to notice differences which she feels in her performance, and of which she herself is keenly aware.

The first time I met Helen, she came to my apartment with her mother, Mrs. Brown, to discuss playing in *Caesar and Cleopatra,* and I remember her telling me how, after giving her support to Equity in its famous strike, she felt lost in the rupture of her relationship with her former manager, George Tyler. Although she was just out of her teens, I felt in talking with her a loyalty and strength of character which has since made her outstanding as a woman and as a leader in the theatre.

I have since worked with Helen in several plays, and have come to know and to admire her. She has always accepted the challenge of life with gallantry and high purpose. As I was her assistant chairman for Finnish Relief, while Armina was her acting chairman at the Washington Stage Door Canteen, we both were able to observe how generously she gave of herself to the causes she was called upon to serve. She has been able to play the part of great women, such as Queen Victoria and Mary of Scotland, because of the greatness within herself. One of the high moments of the theatre of our time is the last act of *Mary of Scotland* when Helen, despite her petite stature, towers above Elizabeth, as played by Helen Menken, and in tones which resound like the ringing of a bell, denounces her: "Still, still, I win. I have been a woman, I have loved as a woman loves, lost as a woman loses. . . . My pride is stronger than yours, and my heart beats blood such as yours has never known. And in this dungeon, I win here—alone."

In the American theatre, I believe that Helen Hayes has won too, not only because of the quality of her art, but because of the quality of her life.

Maurice Evans played the part of Malvolio brilliantly in *Twelfth Night,* and spoke with a slightly cockney accent, which did a great deal to make the play understandable. By accentuating the class difference in this way between Malvolio and Viola, the play was given an added dimension, just as a dimension was added to *Othello* by having the part played by "a blackamoor" which is the expression Shakespeare used for the character and which may be applied, without offense, to Paul Robeson who gave so miraculous a performance as the jealous Moor.

Twelfth Night ran for 129 performances in New York City and played for seventeen weeks on tour. I personally enjoyed it greatly, and it left me with an unsatisfied yearning for a Shakespearean company which was appeased several seasons later in a very expensive manner.

This same season was also notable for the fact that we produced Tennessee Williams' first long play, *The Battle of Angels.* John Gassner, the critic and teacher who had succeeded Harold Clurman in our Play Department in 1931, first introduced me to Tennessee, who was studying at the New School Playwriting Seminar, which was under Terry's and Gassner's supervision, and I read the play with considerable enthusiasm, but hoping that some rewriting would straighten out its defects. Terry Helburn agreed with me in believing that while the play needed revision, we should nevertheless produce it as Tennessee seemed to us to be the most promising young playwright we had come across in a number of years. The play was submitted to us in the spring of 1940 and I invited Tennessee to stay at our farm where he could work quietly on bringing about such improvements as were possible before the play went into rehearsal.

Tennessee, a modest young man with a poet's sensitivity, a gift of imagination and a feeling for trenchant dramatic dialogue which reminded me of O'Neill, was a charming guest and rapidly completed his work, using a little summer house to write in. We finally went into production and selected to play the part of the leading character, a woman storekeeper in a small Southern town, the talented stage and screen actress Miriam Hopkins. It looked as though this part suited her perfectly. Margaret Webster was engaged to direct the play. As her knowledge of the South of England was far superior to her knowledge of the South of the United States, we sent her on a visit to Tennessee, and she returned brimming over with local color. The theme of the play was not unlike that of *Streetcar Named Desire*, and it contrasted the decadence of the old Southern families against the violent emotions of the sexually virile Cajuns.

Unfortunately, Miriam was not at all modest about suggesting revisions, and on one occasion, in talking over the play at my home, became so excited that she took careful aim at my head with the manuscript, which happily missed me by a couple of inches. But Miriam, who wanted only what was best for the play, was always an excitable girl; I understood her perfectly, and was ready to duck when occasion called for it.

Margaret Webster had returned from the South accompanied with a large number of recordings of bird cries, the humming of cotton mills, noises of sawmills, the street cries of Southern hucksters, wheelbarrows rattling around, and so forth. Also, as the entire scenery was supposed to go up in smoke at the end of the play, our technical director, John Haggott, had accumulated an enormous quantity of storage batteries and other electrical equipment which made it difficult for the actors to walk around the back of the stage without tripping over the wires.

On the fateful opening night in Boston, Miriam, attired in a small-town woman's plain dress, made by Bergdorf-Goodman, came on stage and the play began. As it progressed, it transpired that she used the back room of the shop to conduct her amours, while her husband lay paralyzed upstairs and kept knocking on the floor with a cane. Each time Miriam said to Wesley Addy, who was playing her crude lover from the swamps of Louisiana, "Meet me in the back room—" the staid

Bostonian audience shrieked with laughter, which was horribly disconcerting to the actors and the author, as the play was intended to be received seriously. In time we eliminated the causes of this undesirable laughter. But our opening night was a calamity. The play was very frank, and we were notified by the Boston censor to delete certain parts of it. There were a number of hysterical meetings with all concerned, and Terry and I felt that a continuation of the production with the people involved would merely produce further hysteria without solving our problems.

Tennessee felt with us that some rewriting was needed, and this could best be achieved by him under conditions somewhat less exciting than those prevailing at the Ritz-Carlton Hotel at this particular moment. We also felt that the play needed some recasting as well as rewriting, so we reluctantly withdrew it, but I sent the scenery to Westport where it was stored at my Playhouse pending Tennessee's revisions. When these revisions finally came in, they obviously did not solve the problem, and were discarded by him in the printed version of the play.

Not only did *Battle of Angels* provoke the Boston censor, but many of our subscribers attacked us to such an extent that we leaped to Tennessee Williams' defense in a letter to our Boston members in which we admitted that the play had some technical defects, but denied that it violated good taste. In this letter Terry and I ventured a prophecy, a dangerous pastime. Speaking of Tennessee we said:

We chose to produce *The Battle of Angels* because we felt the young author has genuine poetic gifts and an interesting insight into a particular American scene. The treatment of the religious obsession of one of the characters, which sprang from frustration did not justify, in our opinion, the censor's action. It was, we felt, a sincere and honest attempt to present a true psychological picture.

. . . *The Battle of Angels* turned out badly but who knows whether the next one by the same author may not prove a success?

With *The Battle of Angels*, the Guild introduced one of the two most talented new writers of the nineteen-forties. Unfortunately, it was left for others to reap the harvest we had begun to sow. After our Boston fiasco, we lost the opportunity to produce such successful plays as *The Glass Menagerie* and *A Streetcar Named Desire*. This, I might add, was not our only unhappy experience with young talent. One of Terry's proteges, discovered through her Bureau of New Plays as early as 1937 and encouraged by Terry and John Gassner, was Arthur

Miller. But his first fully realized plays, *All My Sons* and *Death of a Salesman,* went to other managements. We offered him a production on the first of these, but he chose another producer, and the second of these was not submitted to the Guild.

There being no particularly good new plays on the horizon, we decided to fill out our next season of 1941–42 with revivals of older plays, and engaged as our director Eva Le Gallienne, whose ability and integrity we both admired.

Our first revival was O'Neill's *Ah, Wilderness,* in which the screen actor Harry Carey played the George M. Cohan part with distinction. The production received an excellent press, too. Yet for some reason which I have never been able to understand, the public showed complete indifference. We clenched our teeth, swallowed our losses, and went ahead with the next production, which was Sheridan's *The Rivals* with America's greatest comedian, Bobby Clark as Bob Acres, Walter Hampden as Sir Joseph Absolute, and Mary Boland as Mrs. Malaprop.

The combination of the idealistic Eva Le Gallienne and the comedian Bobby Clark had us all bewildered. During rehearsals, Bobby, with the most solemn face in the world, spent most of his time walking around studying positions, measuring the distance between one place and another, and in general, acting more like a carpetmaker about to put down a carpet than an actor about to deliver a comedy performance. I asked Eva if he was possibly out of his element in playing in a classic comedy, but Eva said, "No, I know he is thinking all the time, and he probably is going to do something quite surprising when we get to the dress rehearsals." Just as soon as the furniture and costumes arrived on the scene, we suddenly realized what Bobby was up to. He appeared on his first entrance with a long riding whip, and he had been measuring the distances to see how closely he could come to moving the whip around without actually tickling a bystander in the face. Everything had been worked out with great exactness, and he then began to deliver his real performance, aided by the hand props and furniture. I doubt if Bob Acres has ever been played as hilariously as it was by Bobby.

While *The Rivals* was well received, it was not a financial success, and by mid-season our two productions left us with a deficit of over $50,000. We therefore decided it was time to call a halt on revivals. Just after we had made our decision, we received a call from Cheryl Crawford who asked if she might revive *Porgy and Bess* at her summer theatre, with the option to produce it afterward in New York and elsewhere. We promptly agreed to this, with the result that she put on a most successful production, and netted a very large profit which would certainly have paid for our losses on all the other revivals many times over. This story illustrates that in this exasperatingly capricious theatre of ours, one should not give up too easily. We had a number of failures in a row before we produced *Oklahoma!* If there should be any rule regarding the backing of a series of plays, it is to stop when one is winning and not when one is losing.

When we were busily arranging for Helen Hayes to go on tour in *Twelfth Night* following its Chicago engagement, the Playwrights' Company was busily tempting her with a new Maxwell Anderson play called *Candle in the Wind.* As Helen felt that this play had an important message for the war, we got together with the Playwrights' Company, and Helen was cast in the leading part, while Alfred Lunt directed the play. Unfortunately, *Candle in the Wind* struck a dry period—and during dry weather, rewriting a play on the road was always difficult for Max Anderson. The play was brought to New York and ran its course briefly, its flickering flame unable to withstand for long the cool winds of Broadway.

After the New York drama critics had rapidly polished off Patterson Greene's charming play *Papa Is All,* laid in a farmhouse in the Pennsylvania Dutch country, we brought in another farmhouse play called *Hope for a Harvest* by Sophie Treadwell, the talented flashing-eyed California writer who was the author of *Machinal* and one of the closest friends of Terry and myself. Sophie's play was laid in a farming community near Stockton, California, in the San Joaquin Valley, where she had been raised by her parents, who were pioneers in the settlement of California. Fredric March and Florence Eldridge played the leading parts, and the play dealt with the consequences of putting too much effort into machinery, and too little in building human character to handle the machinery. Wherever this play was presented outside New York—in Boston, in Philadelphia, in Baltimore, in Washington, D.C., and elsewhere, it received magnificent critical notices and acclaim. But the New York critics came to the play, heard something discussed about agriculture, and promptly decided that it could not be of the slightest interest to New York audiences. When I read the notices the next day, I felt my ire rising—something I try to avoid, but my temperature was sufficiently high that I placed a large advertisement in the New York papers printing enthusiastic notices from over thirty out-of-town drama critics who had liked the play. The results were instantaneous. Even those New Yorkers who had bought tickets seemed to want their money back!

During this season, Philip Barry, overcome with the desire to write something which would aid the war effort, decided that the Irish were not doing enough to help the United States and its allies, and thought he could goad them into action with a play which was entitled *Without Love*. Katharine Hepburn, who by this time was nectar or ambrosia at the box office, agreed to play the leading role. Hepburn's popularity was now such that her public bought their tickets in advance, so that by the time we arrived at a town, all the seats were sold. After our opening in Princeton, it was apparent that some rewriting was needed. We were doing very well on tour, however, and decided to finish the season after playing a number of the large cities, so that the play would open in New York the following winter. We traveled through the country like a circus, all the comings and goings of Kate being accompanied by the wildest demonstrations on the part of tumultuous admirers.

One day Kate remarked to a group of us who were commenting on the phenomenal success of the tour, that she was no longer an actress, she was now an attraction! Bob Sinclair, the taciturn stage director who was afraid that this feeling might get to Katharine's head, replied, "Kate, you may be an attraction, but you'll never be as big a one as Gargantua!" Gargantua was the huge gorilla which the Ringling Brothers-Barnum and Bailey Circus transported from city to city in a large steel cage, and who never failed to bring out the crowds in numbers which certainly exceeded Kate's box office draw. From then on Kate, somewhat crushed, referred to herself as Gargantua.

The change in the functioning of the Guild Board which took place after *The Philadelphia Story*, resulted a year or so later in the reorganization of the Guild structure with the consequent resignation of Philip Moeller, Lee Simonson and Helen Westley who by this time was residing most of each year in Hollywood. Neither she, Moeller nor Simonson were active in producing plays, although they were free to do so with the business assistance of our manager, Warren Munsell; and the producing work fell entirely on the shoulders of Theresa Helburn and myself. We were, however, a minority on the Board, and subject at any time to the whims of the majority. Since for the first time in years the Guild was functioning smoothly and without unhappiness on the part of everybody concerned, Terry and I not unnaturally desired to continue in this manner, and after long drawn-out negotiations, this was effected by a reorganization, under which Terry and I were made co-Administrative Directors with full artistic

control. Maurice Wertheim also continued as a member of the Board
of Directors until his resignation in 1946. Moeller, Simonson and Helen
Westley, who had contributed so notably to the Guild, were given
pensions and preferred stock in the company from which they derived
considerable financial benefits. Thus ended, with many regrets and
much relief, the system of group management which had been so successful in the early days of the Guild, but had become increasingly
destructive as we left our growing pains behind us.

Our next season, our twenty-fifth, began with *Without Love*. Notwithstanding a divided press, it played to full houses for an engagement of sixteen weeks, and would have played all season but for Kate
Hepburn's Hollywood commitments. The Irish government did not
take Phil Barry's play seriously, however, and did not go to war against
Hitler as he suggested.

The ethereal-appearing Lillian Gish, of whom I am a devoted admirer, acted for us this season in *Mr. Sycamore*. Ketti Frings, a strikingly handsome girl from California, dramatized this fantasy about a
man who turned into a tree, and since the war was raging pretty
violently at the time, it seemed like rather a nice idea; but let us face
it, the escapism which it suggested was a little too remote. Our audiences could hardly identify themselves with the tree into which one
of the leading characters, played by Stuart Erwin, metamorphised
himself, while the girl played by Lillian sat under it and mourned
her loss.

Lillian Gish, whose delicate beauty is known all over the world,
is one of the most interesting women in the theatre, as well as one of
its most versatile actresses. The two sisters, Lillian and Dorothy, who
are close friends of Armina and myself, together with their mother,
fragile and beautiful as a piece of old Dresden, made an endearing
little family which included three dogs, two Siamese cats and a
masculine-looking parrot named John, who gave raucous imitations of
Jed Harris and George Jean Nathan, and surprised everybody, at the
age of thirty, by laying an egg.

Another play produced by us in the season of 1942–43 with Lunt
and Fontanne was *The Pirate* by S. N. Behrman, based on an original
play by Ludwig Fulda. Some years earlier, Alfred Lunt, who had
played in the Fulda play, had suggested the possibility of our prevailing upon Behrman to make a version. We had made our arrangements with Behrman before he joined the Playwrights' Company, but
his first version of the play had not been accepted by us. Later on,

Theresa Helburn visited the Lunts at their home in Genesee Depot, and suggested to Alfred and Lynn that *The Pirate* be resuscitated and Behrman set to work on it again. This was done, but we were later met with a claim by the Playwrights' Company that under their contract with Behrman they were entitled to the play. After a good deal of acrimonious discussion back and forth, the matter was finally settled by our making a joint production, with the Playwrights' in charge.

The play was put in rehearsal by the Playwrights' Company, all of whose playwrights visited the play while it was out-of-town, and made their suggestions for such rewriting as they thought it needed. Terry and I were not invited to participate, but after the lapse of several weeks, I received a telephone call from a member of the Playwrights' Company suggesting that the play be closed out of town, as it would be a hopeless failure if brought to New York. Since half the capital invested in the play was ours, he felt we should be consulted before this final action was taken. I answered that before we could come to a decision, I would go to Washington to see the play, and Terry and I would then decide whether or not it should be dropped. I left for Washington and visited Alfred and Lynn at the National Theatre. I found them in a state of deep depression, after more than ten weeks of work. I watched the play with great interest and found it very entertaining. After the play was over, I went to Alfred's dressing room and told him that I was not at all despondent about the play, and that I thought Behrman could readily set it right if certain things were done. Sam was sent for in haste, a scene at the beginning of the second act was moved to the end of the second act, and with some additional rewriting, it played extremely well. The play moved on to Boston and Philadelphia and thence to New York, where it received some good notices and ran for the rest of the season. After the play opened in New York, the picture rights were sold by Harold Freedman for the sum of $275,000! I cherish the telegram which I received from the author on the New York opening night. It read, "Thanks for bringing my play to New York."

By mid-winter of 1942, we were deeply engaged in the war, and the city of Stalingrad was under siege, and its heroic resistance, which was the turning point of the war, had us all in a state of apprehension. We read a play written by Konstantin Simonov called *The Russian People*, which had been presented by over two hundred Russian theatrical companies behind the lines, to bolster the morale of their

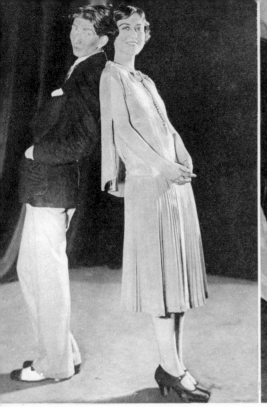

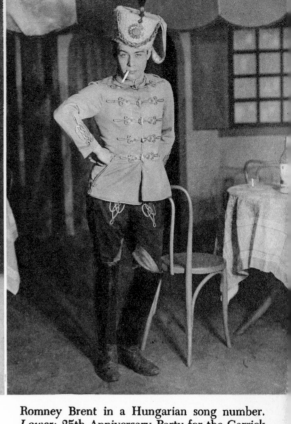

The Garrick Gaieties which brought Rodgers and Hart together, produced by the Theatre Guild, 1925. *Top left:* Sterling Holloway and ne Cochran singing "Manhattan." *Top right:* Romney Brent in a Hungarian song number. *Lower:* 25th Anniversary Party for the Garrick Gaieties, 1950. *Left to right:* Theresa Helburn, Richard Rodgers, Lawrence Langner.

Ina Claire in S. N. Behrman's *Biography*, produced by the Theatre Guild, 1932.

Michael Bartlett, Osgood Perkins and June Walker in an adaptation of *The School For Husbands* by Arthur Guiterman and the author, produced by the Theatre Guild, 1933.

Helen Hayes and Philip Merivale in Maxwell Anderson's
Mary of Scotland, produced by the Theatre Guild, 1933.

Above: Alexander Woollcott in S. N. Behrman's *Wine of Choice* produced by the Theatre Guild, 1938. *Below:* William Saroyan, Eddie Dowling and Gene Kelly in Saroyan's *The Time of Your Life*, produced by the Theatre Guild and Dowling, 1939.

Katharine Hepburn in Philip Barry's *The Philadelphia Story*, produced by the Theatre Guild, 1939.

soldiers. The play was a journalistic melodrama, a good documentary picture of the kind of courageous fighting which was being done by the Russians with their backs against the wall, and we felt that it might be of great value in making everyone alive to the need for stiffening the war effort. We therefore decided to put on the play, and engaged Clifford Odets to make an acting version.

Odets, now a prosperous Hollywood writer, who resembled in appearance a well-groomed capitalist playboy, turned out a good acting version of the play, and in due course it was put into rehearsal under the direction of Harold Clurman. One of the Russian characters was played by the fine character actor Luther Adler, while his sister, the beautiful Stella, who was married to our director Harold, was in constant attendance. The play that had done so much to keep up the morale of the Russian armies, did not seem to be having the same effect upon the Theatre Guild, for we had considerable misgivings as to whether it was being treated as a psychological character study or a rip-roaring melodrama.

As there was a great deal of rehearsing to be done in Washington and little time to do it, we asked Harold's wife, Stella, to assist us. Shortly after, in New York I received a long-distance call from our watchful stage manager, Elaine Anderson. "I wish you'd come down at once, Lawrence," she said, "Harold Clurman is rehearsing some of the actors on the stage for psychology, while Stella is rehearsing the others in the cellar underneath the stage, and telling them to play it for melodrama." I returned to Washington and tried to straighten out the situation, but no matter how much Harold tried to bring out the psychology, the melodrama came out on top, for melodrama, like murder, will out, and Stella in the cellar wasn't so wrong after all.

Just before the play left Washington, we received an invitation from the Soviet Ambassador Maxim Litvinoff and his wife to attend a reception in honor of the occasion at the Soviet Embassy. The invitation included Miss Helburn, myself and the entire company. At the time, the newspapers had been full of the extraordinary receptions which had been given by Stalin to Winston Churchill and other European dignitaries, and it was rumored that French champagne flowed freely in the Soviet Embassy to wash down enormous helpings of caviar which was flown by military plane direct from Russia. Our actors, living under wartime conditions, were looking forward to a sumptuous repast at the Embassy, but were regaled only with hors d'oeuvre of a fishy character which seemed to have been purchased from a neighboring delicatessen. Litvinoff and his wife were extremely cordial to us all, though Litvinoff's remarks about the "artistic" theatre did not strike me as very impressive. "Why do you not put on plays with a lot of pretty girls, like Max Gordon does?" he asked me, his keen eyes smiling out from under his enormous forehead. "I don't like these highbrow plays which the Theatre Guild does." And the attractive Madam Ivy Litvinoff told me, in good middle-class English, that she had written a motion-picture scenario, and wondered if she could sell it to Hollywood. All in all, they seemed as bourgeois a couple as one could meet anywhere, with very little in common with "the proletariat."

Several years later the author of *The Russian People*, Konstantin Simonov, accompanied by Ilya Ehrenberg and two or three Generals, visited the United States, and because of our production of his play, we were asked to act as hosts to him at our musical play *Oklahoma!* We did so, and after the final curtain I conducted the party backstage. Simonov, a tall, handsome young man in his late thirties, with jet-black curly hair and a dark mustache, made a rather striking figure, though he was obviously considerably less sophisticated than Ilya Ehrenberg, who impressed me as a seedy overeducated neurotic who had sold his soul for a mess of Soviet roubles. Our company, made up of eager young actors, singers and dancers, gathered around the group of visitors and listened to Simonov, who addressed them in Russian. The speech, as translated by an interpreter, was hollow and formal, completely lacking in humanity or humor, in which he referred to the theatre as "an unexportable product of civilization," and added a lot of high falutin' language which signified nothing. Of course, what the young people would have liked him to say was, "I enjoyed your play, and I'm happy to meet you all." Evidently this was too informal for a great Russian author. I remarked to a friend standing at my side, "Why on earth couldn't he just thank the actors and the authors graciously?" "There's a pretty good reason," said my friend. "If he said he liked *Oklahoma!*, two or three of those Russian fellows in uniform standing by would make a note of it, and when he returned to Moscow he'd probably be shot for praising a play which upholds property rights in Western ranches on a non-collective basis."

Later Simonov made some remark to a columnist derogatory to *Oklahoma!*, and when we met him at a luncheon party in Hollywood after a few weeks, Armina asked him whether he had really enjoyed our American musical. He replied with a polite evasion, contrary to the usual rudeness in Soviet diplomacy. Armina said, "In the United States we like to put all our cards on the table, and say what we really think. How did you like *Oklahoma!?*" "Well," he replied, "true art must not contain mixed elements of comedy and tragedy. *Oklahoma!* is a musical play, and there is no artistic justification for the killing of anyone in such a play." Thus he echoed exactly the same conventional criticism which one of our most commercial managers had expressed when we first produced the play.

All through the months of November and December, 1942, on my frequent visits to New York, I found Theresa Helburn wrestling with the problem involved in the production of this same *Oklahoma!*, based on the Theatre Guild's earlier play by Lynn Riggs called *Green Grow the Lilacs*.

CHAPTER XXVI

Double Life

BEFORE recounting the story of *Oklahoma!* I must interrupt this part of my narration to tell some of the happenings on the other side of my life. During the early days of the Theatre Guild, I traveled over the country two or three times each year, interviewing clients during the day, and lecturing at local Drama Leagues, Junior Leagues, Women's Clubs and so forth at night on the subject of the theatre, and I also lectured at many Patent Law Associations and universities on international patent and trade-mark law. During my European trips I divided my time in the same way—visits to the Patent Offices by day, and the theatres at night. I was thus able to lead a double life on two continents without appreciable wear and tear, or too much clash between one activity and the other.

On one of my frequent visits to Dayton, Ohio, during World War I, I was introduced by Mr. Kettering to Thomas Midgley, Jr., who had been a schoolmate of Eugene O'Neill in Stamford, Connecticut, and who was working on the task of finding some way by which gasoline could be compressed to a high degree in an engine cylinder without blowing the top off it. He found after long research that by adding a small amount of certain compounds, notably tetraethyl lead, this trick could actually be accomplished, thereby making possible the modern automobile and the huge airplanes of today, and developing billions of horse power from gasoline which would otherwise have been wasted. Tom was a lovable devil-may-care romantic, the last person in the world one would imagine as a painstaking research chemist; indeed, he always claimed he was a physicist who had become a chemist by accident, notwithstanding that he won the most coveted

342

awards in chemistry and was for a number of years President of the American Chemical Society. Tall, curly-haired with a high forehead, blue eyes and a happy smile, Tom would go into a recitation at the drop of a hat, and in his spare time wrote poetry of the James Whitcomb Riley school. He and I became good friends, a friendship which was to lead to our engaging in many interesting activities together and ultimately to our forming the National Inventors Council which examined the inventions for our Army and Navy during World War II.

At the time I first met him, Tom was working at his test tubes in an old converted residence in the center of Dayton. "What do you think of the word 'Ethyl' as the name of the new substance?" he asked me. "Terrible," I replied. "It will sound to everybody like a girl's name!" "Correct," he replied, "that's why I like it." "But you'll have great difficulty protecting it," I ventured. "Not at all," was his answer, "any decent man will protect a girl's name."

In the invention of Freon, the non-toxic, non-combustible refrigerant gas which revolutionized air conditioning in homes and trains, Midgley told me that he had tested out five batches of the gas on five groups of rats to determine whether it was poisonous. The first group of rats lived happily after being exposed fully to the gas, but the succeeding four groups of rats departed this life. "Imagine our good luck, Lawrence!" said Tom in telling me this story. "We found later on that the first batch of gas was pure but the other four batches contained a deadly impurity which killed the rats. Had we started our experiment in the reverse order and killed four groups of rats, I think we would have given up before the fifth." On this stroke of luck hung the fate of the huge home-refrigeration, deep-freeze and air-conditioning industry, which could not have operated with a poisonous and explosive refrigerant.

Another inventor with whom I became acquainted on my numerous trips to Dayton, Ohio, was Orville Wright, co-inventor with his brother Wilbur of the airplane. We often met for dinner at the home of the debonair patent lawyer Greer Mareschal, and Orville, a slight, white-haired man with a quiet unassuming manner, would tell us stories, in a high thin voice, of the early days of the airplane and the difficulties he had to overcome. When war was threatened by Hitler, I asked him whether he or his brother had realized, at the time when they invented the airplane, how many hundreds of thousands of people would be killed in war as a result. He replied that he and his brother had often talked it over, and had come to the conclusion that "the airplane would make war impossible, because you could not carry it on without killing women and children." From the point of view of 1903, when the airplane was successfully tested, this was correct. Our ideas of civilized warfare have slipped pretty far backward since then.

I worked on the foreign patents of many of the revolutionary inventions of this period. Once Armina and I were in Detroit, and breakfasted with "Boss" Kettering at the Book-Cadillac Hotel. We had just come off the train from Chicago, and complained of the heavy soot from the locomotive. "It won't be long now before I'll run a Diesel train from San Francisco to New York without a stop," said Kettering, "and it'll be as clean as riding in an automobile." And to everyone's amazement, this happened within the year. Some of the revolutionary patents on which I worked, along with many that were not so revolutionary, were those for the stainless-steel Diesel trains and the pressed-steel automobile bodies and wheels of the Budd Company; the tremendous strip mills of United Engineering Company by which the sheet steel for these bodies was rolled; the first continuous rayon spinning machines and processes of Industrial Rayon Company; and the basic Birdseye inventions which revolutionized the entire frozen-food industry. It is hard to believe, in these days of deep-freeze packaged food, that when I took away from Boston a sample of some lamb chops from the first Birdseye deep-freezing machine, and gave them to our cook Annie, she refused to cook them on the ground that they were as hard as rocks, obviously not fresh, and would give us all ptomaine poisoning!

Because of my knowledge of munitions inventions, and my work in the Ordnance Department during World War I, I was often called upon to help the government in matters relating to international patent law.

At the end of World War I, Walter Lippmann, then acting as an assistant to Woodrow Wilson, formed a committee consisting of Judge Learned Hand and Judge Charles M. Hough to prepare clauses to be inserted in the Treaty of Versailles relating to Patents, Trade-Marks and Copyrights. I was asked by them to join with William Wallace White, another international patent attorney, in advising them, and in preparing a compilation of all the war laws of the belligerent countries, which was published later by our government. Some of our recommendations were embodied in the Treaty of Versailles, and in the Nolan Act which enabled the inventors and authors who had been prevented from taking out patents or copyrights because of the war, to file their applications for protection later on, and thus secure their rights which would otherwise have been lost.

After the war, the United States Patent Office was in shocking condition because large numbers of examiners were leaving the service due to the low salaries. A committee under the chairmanship of William Houston Kenyon, a leading New York patent lawyer, was organized to endeavor to secure the passage of a bill through Congress to increase these salaries. I was put in charge of propaganda for this bill, and in due course our delegation of patent lawyers arrived in Washington where we met Mr. Mondell, a typical politician who was floor leader of the Republican Party, and was determined to delay taking any action on our bill. I in turn determined that he was our main adversary, and that we should center our propaganda against him.

Taking a leaf out of the books of the woman's suffrage campaign, just before the Bill came up on the floor of the House, I sent telegrams to the patent lawyers in each State, asking them to get ten of their leading clients to wire to their representatives in the House instructing them to go to see Mr. Mondell and also to vote in favor of the Bill. On the day when the Bill came up for consideration, such a barrage hit Congress as it had not experienced for years. Mondell rose from his seat waving a sheaf of telegrams, and accused us of conducting propaganda for our cause. Representative Walsh of Massachusetts asked, "Since when were the industries of the United States not permitted to express themselves to Congress when the Patent System was being jeopardized?" After two days of debate, the Bill was carried by a large majority.

After this, the patent lawyers of New York formed the New York Patent Law Association, and elected William Houston Kenyon as its first President. The Association began its career with a dinner at the Waldorf tendered to the federal judges of the New York, Connecticut, New Jersey and Pennsylvania circuit courts, for which I prepared the Menu in the form of a Patent Specification describing the courses as devices for appeasing hunger. After attending a few of these Annual Dinners, I realized they could be enlivened by some kind of entertainment which would relieve the tedium, especially as many patent lawyers, judges and inventors never seem to be able to say anything in half an hour if they can take a full hour to say it. I therefore decided to write and produce a play for the next Annual Dinner, and I wrote for this a one-act comedy under the title of *Patent Applied For.*

This playlet was based upon an experience I had with a woman who invented a corset and wished me to patent it. This inventor, a tall blonde, attractive Australian lady, came into my office carrying a paper package and wearing a long full coat. After introducing herself, she opened the package, and showed me a corset which seemed to have several corners, and a cord attached to each corner. "Mr. Langner," she said, "I've invented a new corset, the purpose of which is to liberate women from the tyranny of fashion. Each season a woman has had to buy a new corset according to what everybody else is wearing. But with my corset, she is freed from the dictates of fashion, and for this reason I call it the 'Liberator.'" I examined the bundle of strings and stays rather gingerly, and asked how the contraption worked. "I'll show you," she said, and thereupon she began to remove her coat and blouse and revealed that she was wearing a lace chemise or slip underneath. "It's quite all right," she said, noting my embarrassment. "I've been in the corset business so long, I don't mind demonstrating it for you." She then put on the corset, and proceeded to show how it worked. "Suppose," she said, "I want to have a flat front. I just pull on these two strings and there you are!" There was no denying that her "front" was flattened out considerably.

Then she undertook to show me a more complicated use of the corset: "Take this year, Mr. Langner," she said. "Waists are high, fronts are in, hips are out and backs are flat. First of all we'll get the waist high by tying this string, then we pull the front in by these short strings, and we let the hips out by unlacing here at the sides and pull the back in on these cords which tie on the back." The illustration was very effective, and this little incident served to make a hilarious comedy which was well acted by the patent lawyers, among whom I found several excellent actors, who, had they been less rational, might easily have earned a living in the theatre.

So popular was this play, that it was presented later on by the Patent Law Association of Chicago with one of its leading patent lawyers, Frank Parker Davis, in the principal role. The success of this ultimately produced a number of other plays written by other lawyers on the subject of patents and trade-marks, as well as by myself.[1] These patent plays became so popular that I was called upon to write one each year, and I soon found the task far too arduous. However, from time to time, when I had a good subject to satirize, I wrote other

---

[1] On one occasion the Patent Law Association of Chicago sent its actors to New York in an excellent play by Lynn Williams and Harvey Boettcher which was given at the Annual Dinner of the New York Association, thus introducing the odd feature of a touring company of patent lawyers.

plays, usually in collaboration with one of the leaders of the Bar engaged in the particular type of practice.[2]

As a member of the New York Patent Law Association, and later one of its Board of Governors, I served on a number of legislative committees of our Association, the Merchants Association and other out-of-town Patent Law Associations; and since I was a specialist in international patent practise, I was responsible for introducing some of the valuable features of foreign patent laws into the United States patent system, as well as keeping out some of the objectionable ones, such as Compulsory Workings, which were often suggested by others. Nor was my legislative work limited to the United States. On one occasion I was asked to prepare a suitable trade-mark law for the Republic of Venezuela; on another occasion I collaborated with my partner Dr. Steven Ladas in drawing up a suitable patent law for China, now doubtless discarded by the Communists.

My international patent work sometimes led me into political complications. In the winter of 1933, Armina and I decided to take a trip to Cuba, since my firm wished me to look into certain Cuban patent and trade-mark situations which were causing difficulties. We stayed at the Nacional Hotel, and on my signing the register, the hotel clerk remarked, "You are the living image of our Prime Minister, Orestes Ferrara, and I would advise you to be careful, as there are the beginnings of a revolution here against President Machado, and many people have sworn to assassinate the Prime Minister on sight!" This was cheerful news. "What do you advise me to do?" I asked the clerk. "Well," he replied, "if you see any suspicious-looking people, get as close to them as possible so they will see that you are an American, because the further away you are, the more you appear to resemble Ferrara."

I decided to treat the matter as a joke, but as I began to meet the various Cuban lawyers who represented our office, and visited the Casino and Race Tracks with friends, I noticed that I was always the center of interest for the crowds, and a good deal of discussion was going on as to whether I was or was not the original Prime Minister or just a carbon copy. Fortunately, no one attempted to assassinate me at the time, and I learned a year later that Ferrara barely escaped with his life by boarding a waiting airplane and lighting out for Miami.

I was very much outraged by the tales of bloodshed and cruelty

---

[2] Patent plays on which I collaborated were *No More Inventions* with W. Houston Kenyon, *The Saturday Night Soap Company* with Edward H. Rodgers, *National Kink Safety Pin Co., etc.* with Frank Parker Davis.

imposed by the Machado regime on the students of Havana University and all those who opposed the government, for I heard many inside stories from my friends which had not appeared in the censored Cuban press. I was the more shocked because the Machado regime was receiving considerable financial aid from the United States government. Three days before we left Cuba, Machado refused to permit the *New York Times* and the *New York Herald* (now the *Herald-Tribune*) to appear on the newsstands. By a coincidence, I had been studying the history of the early days of the Mormons at the time, and I remembered what had happened when the Prophet Joseph Smith broke up the office of the Nauvoo newspaper which criticized him. Instantly, the newspapers throughout the United States rose to the attack like a swarm of hornets, and I envisioned something of the same sort happening to Machado with the suppression of the *New York Times* and the *New York Herald* in Havana.

On my return to New York, I immediately telephoned Arthur Sulzberger, owner of the *Times,* and Walter Lippmann, then of the *Herald,* and told them of what I had learned in Havana, and asked if this story could not be told in all its horrible details to the American public. The *Herald* responded immediately by flying a reporter to Cuba for a story, while the *Times* published a series of crusading front-page articles by Russell Porter on the Machado regime which caused such a stir that our government withdrew its financial support; indeed, these *Times* articles and editorials contributed to no slight extent to the ultimate overthrow of the Machado regime.

While in Havana I argued a trade-mark case before the Cuban Patent Office. Unfortunately for us, our trade-mark was infringed by one of Machado's generals, whose son-in-law, a charming fellow, was the Chief of the Patent Office. He told me confidentially that he longed to give a decision in our favor, but since he owed his job to his father-in-law, he was "caught between the Sword and the Wall!" His words proved to be prophetic, for a few months later he was shot down and killed along with a number of Cuban officers who were trying to escape from the Nacional Hotel in which they were barricaded by Battista's army. With the advent of the new regime, we finally won our case.

When an investigation into the industries of the United States and the workings of the Patent System took place under the name of the T.N.E.C. investigation, I was asked to testify to the operation of the British patent laws as regards Compulsory Licensing of inventions, and I gave testimony before this commission for a couple of days. A misinterpretation of my testimony by some of the representatives of the Department of Justice who were then present, led to extremely serious consequences when, under the guidance of Assistant Attorney General Thurman Arnold, the Department of Justice launched a frontal attack on the Patent System a year or so later.

My theatrical and patent activities ultimately came together with curious results. In the winter of 1937, I was invited to attend a public dinner at which the American theatre was discussed, given under the chairmanship of Alvin Johnson, head of the New School for Social Research. I was seated at the Speakers' Table, and at my side was a distinguished-looking physician by the name of Dr. William Sirovitch, who, in addition to representing in Congress the borough in which my home was located, was also the Chairman of the House Committee on Patents, Trade-Marks and Copyrights. Dr. Sirovitch had brought himself into the public eye a year or so earlier by introducing a bill which put a little salt on the tails of the dramatic critics, by requiring that before a newspaper was permitted to escape scot-free of liability for damages in connection with dramatic criticism, it should publish a brief paragraph setting forth the critic's qualifications for his job! The doctor contended that for most of the then-current reviewers, the paragraph would be very brief indeed!

When Sirovitch learned that I was one of the directors of the Theatre Guild, he informed me over the dessert that he had written a play about Spinoza, and would like to send it to me. The learned Doctor had a habit of punctuating his conversation by poking me in the ribs from time to time as he made his points, and by the time the dinner was over, my right side was almost black and blue. Learning that I was also a patent attorney, he invited me to come to Washington, as he intended to conduct an investigation of the Patent System, and he asked me later if I would accept the chairmanship of an Advisory Committee which would assist him in this work. By this time I had read *Spinoza* and while it showed the Doctor's erudition and admiration for the great philosopher, it also showed that he was no master of the art of playwriting.

The Doctor, who had been a professor of philosophy at the College of the City of New York, and was one of the best speakers in the House, informed me that even though I did not care for his play, he nevertheless wished me to head the Advisory Committee which he felt should include not only well-known inventors and industrialists but also representatives of the American Federation of Labor and the

Congress of Industrial Organizations. I refused the chairmanship, but agreed to become its Executive Secretary. Our first chairman was Richard Eyre (who had originally introduced me to Agnes De Mille) and we included on the Council Major Edwin H. Armstrong, famous radio inventor, Judge Learned Hand, William H. Davis, then head of the National Mediation Board, Edward S. Rogers, the leading authority on trade-marks, John P. Frey, representing the American Federation of Labor (AFL), Walter A. Schmidt, chemical engineer, and a number of important patent lawyers from coast to coast. Later on, the chairmanship was taken over by the noted industrial chemist John Van Nostrand Dorr of the Dorr Co., and we added the composer Richard Rodgers as a representative of the Dramatists' Guild. Thus, in this Advisory Committee, there was combined all of my activities, both patents, trade-marks and the theatre.

The Advisory Committee functioned excellently for a number of years, during which the Patent System of the country was subjected to the most vicious attacks it has ever received, at the hands of Thurman Arnold, head of the Anti-Trust division of the Department of Justice. Arnold was an idealistic man with political ambitions who had written a stimulating book entitled *The Folklore of Capitalism* and in it had expressed some rather extraordinary views of the Patent System. He knew little about the subject, but this did not prevent him from having many theories and doing everything in his power to discredit the Patent System in the press. I was particularly upset over Arnold's proceedings, because he sought to introduce into the American Patent System the same Compulsory Licensing clauses which had done so much to vitiate the patent systems of Europe, and this was due to sheer inexperience on his part. The theory behind this proposal was that, once an invention had been made and patented, anyone should be able to manufacture and sell it as long as he paid the inventor a royalty.

The ineptness of this proposal can be easily shown if the same idea is applied to books and plays. Supposing that once a successful novel or play is published or produced, any other publisher or theatre manager could copy it by paying a royalty to the author. Since probably only one book or play out of ten is successful, while the other nine are published or produced at a loss, it can readily be seen that the most successful publishing house or theatre manager would be the one who waited for other concerns to bring out successful novels and plays, and then copied them. This would put a premium on piracy, and destroy the man of enterprise.

There is no doubt that many abuses existed in industry which contravened the Sherman Anti-Trust Act rather than the patent laws, but Thurman Arnold preferred to spend much of his time vilifying the Patent System and blaming it for the existence of conspiracies in restraint of trade. Indeed, later on, when a number of these cases reached the Supreme Court, after Arnold tried his cases ably in court instead of in the newspapers, the Judges showed by their decisions that the Sherman Anti-Trust law was inherently capable of meeting the situation, and due to the pronouncements of the Supreme Court many of the objectionable practices were removed.

During the war my differences of opinion with Thurman Arnold were to assume considerably greater importance. Arnold now attacked many of the leading American corporations for having agreements with German corporations for the exchange of inventions. This had been normal procedure for many years of peace, but Arnold now accused these corporations of helping Hitler. I pointed out, however, that due to these agreements, we received from the Germans such chemical inventions as synthetic rubber, atabrine (the quinine substitute), synthetic toluol for TNT, 100-octane aviation gasoline, plexiglass and many others, without which we would have had great difficulty in prosecuting the war. In a series of blasts at each other, in the pages of the *Atlantic Monthly* in 1942, I succeeded in showing that the Yankees had outtraded the Germans in the exchange of inventions and had received far more than they had given. Eventually Thurman Arnold let up on his private war as the public war effort engulfed him, and the virulent attacks on our patent system ceased with his resignation.

In the spring of the year 1936, Thomas Midgley, Jr., the inventor of Ethyl gasoline and collaborator on Freon refrigerant, phoned to tell me that Dr. Kettering, by this time Chief of the General Motors Research Laboratories, had been asked to take the chairmanship of the Sesquicentennial celebration for the United States Patent Office, and that he wished me to help him with the festivities. Tom felt that with my theatrical knowledge, we could stage some sort of a play or pageant which would demonstrate the role which invention had played in the development of the industries of the country.

With an eye to obtaining the publicity which they desired, I suggested the idea of staging a small pageant at the Sesquicentennial Dinner to be held at the Mayflower Hotel, Washington, and I further suggested that the most likely way to secure publicity was to engage a group of beautiful girls wearing specially designed costumes which would symbolize the various industries which owed their inception and progress to the Patent Office. A more blatantly banal idea could hardly be imagined, but the alternative, which consisted in publicizing pictures of the famous but unphotogenic scientists who had contributed to the inventions of the country seemed to lack mass publicity value, while my idea had the merit of appealing to the editors of the rotogravure sections of every newspaper in the country and to their millions of readers.

Consequently, sixteen famous beauties were engaged from a model agency in New York, and I asked Irene Sharaff, one of the most artistic theatrical costume designers, to design for the girls a group of costumes which would symbolize the various industries founded on invention, and at the same time would be striking and artistically beautiful. Irene Sharaff did a brilliant job and the results were most effective. On the day of the celebration, the sixteen beautiful models arrived in Washington, were duly costumed, and paraded about in the ballroom of the Hotel Mayflower after the dinner, to the accompaniment of volleys of flashlights from the photographers. These pictures were ultimately spread all over the newspapers of the United States.

We had but one casualty, Miss India Rubber, a tall buxom girl who was dressed entirely in rubber, from a kind of halo in the shape of a rubber tire on the top of her head, to a rubber girdle around her middle, and rubber shoes on her shapely feet. Unfortunately, at the last moment she was presented by an enthusiastic rubber company with some rubber stockings, the effect of which was to constrict the poor girl's circulation to such an extent that it became necessary for her to discard a considerable amount of her costume before the evening was over. Miss Calculating Machine, an attractive wide-eyed blonde bedecked with ribbons from adding machines, was the hit of the evening, while Miss Chemical Industry, wearing a hat in the shape of a retort, and a dress of spun glass, ran a close second; Miss Electricity, brightly illuminated from pocket batteries, came in third. The idea was, as I said, banal, but it worked beautifully.

The celebration brought together an excellent working committee consisting of Dr. Kettering, Thomas Midgley, Jr., Conway P. Coe, Commissioner of Patents, and myself. The fact that we worked together in connection with the Sesquicentennial of the Patent Office was of considerable value when, some years later, the so-called "phony war" came to an end with the dramatic march of the Germans into Belgium and France in the spring of 1940, and the four of us came together again to mobilize the inventors of America for the war effort under the egis of the National Inventors Council.

CHAPTER XXVII

The National Inventors Council

ROM the moment Hitler was elected Reich Chancellor in 1932, I became apprehensive for the future of the world. My mind early began to work on the problem of what this country could do to defend itself in case Hitler should actually lead the Germans on the warpath.

In the year 1938, I lunched with Dr. Arnold Seligsohn, the leading German patent lawyer, a handsome middle-aged man of great nobility, who told me of his efforts to help his Jewish people to leave the country, and who later paid with his life for so doing. When Hitler marched into Austria, my ideas began to take form. We could, I felt, beat the Germans by means of inventions, for in my thirty-odd years of handling inventions throughout the world, I had learned to regard the Germans as definitely inferior as an inventive race to the peoples of the United States, Great Britain and France. This was contrary to the popular belief at the time, when it was fashionable to regard the Germans as almost equal to ourselves in scientific achievement. However, there is a great difference between scientific achievement which is the result of research, and that which is the result of invention. This is an important point to remember. Research is a careful investigation by trial and error to achieve a desired result. Invention is the application of ingenuity by the exercise of the imagination to achieve a desired result. A research chemist makes an invention by patiently mixing substances in test tubes, and subjecting them to laborious tests. The Germans were adept at this painstaking work. But my friend Charles F. Kettering made one of his most important inventions while he was shaving himself. Indeed, he became so excited over his idea that he forgot to shave more than half his face.

The Germans, I knew, were long on research but short on invention. Americans, I knew, were good at both. In my years of experience in international patent practice, only a handful of first-rate German inventions had passed through my hands in contrast with the dozens of first-rate inventions originated in this country as the combined result of research and invention. Ever since World War I, I had been preaching the importance of industrial research, and in the twenties I wrote a pamphlet on the subject for the American Manufacturers Export Association in which I strongly urged that the words "Research Department" should appear on a door in the establishment of every progressive American manufacturer. I was not alone in preaching this idea, which caught on rapidly through the thirties, and by the time we entered the war we had an array of American research workers and inventors larger than those of all the rest of the world combined. My idea was to mobilize these research workers and inventors for our national defense.

My work in Washington on the Advisory Council to the House Patents Committee took me there frequently, and toward the latter part of the year 1939, a Bill was introduced dealing with the subject of secrecy of inventions likely to be useful to Hitler. I attended these hearings, and while there I met a young Lieutenant Commander from the Navy who was in their patent division. In the course of our discussion, he ridiculed the idea that inventions of any value to the Navy could come from civilian inventors, and he informed me that, although his office received about fifty inventions a day from the public, they were hardly worth examining. I instanced the fact that some of the most important inventions from a war standpoint were made by civilian inventors, and not by Army or Navy men. Among these I mentioned the torpedo, the armored battleship, the bombing airplane, the machine gun, the tank and others. The argument ended in a friendly way, and that was that. This discussion, however, set me thinking very seriously. "If this spirit permeates the Army and Navy," I thought to myself, "we will make a very poor showing, should war come."

Early in May, when Hitler struck at France and Belgium, I realized along with millions of other Americans that if Hitler conquered the Western powers, the United States would be in great danger. I decided to put my plan to mobilize American inventors for our National Defense into operation immediately. I telephoned Tom Midgley at

Columbus, Ohio, where he lived, and told him of my plan, and I asked him if he would come to Washington with me and meet Conway Coe, the Commissioner of Patents. I also wrote a proposal to establish an "Inventors Council for National Defense" to President Franklin D. Roosevelt on May 14, 1940, and on the next day to Conway Coe, both on note paper of the National Advisory Council of the House Committee on Patents.

The Commissioner of Patents responded to my call with enthusiasm, and by return mail invited us to meet him, suggesting that Dr. Vannevar Bush, President of Carnegie Institution and Chairman of the National Advisory Committee for Aeronautics, be requested to confer with us.

In view of Conway Coe's interest, Tom Midgley and I went to Washington the same week and discussed the situation with him at the Patent Office, after I had first consulted with a friend, Senator James Byrnes, then head of the Senate Appropriations Committee (and the uncle of the actress Frances Fuller), and received his blessings on the project. At the meeting at the Patent Office, we thought up the name "National Inventors Council" and Conway stated that he would take up the matter with Harry Hopkins, Secretary of Commerce, to ascertain if the Department of Commerce would cooperate in the formation of such a Council.

I discovered later that when the matter was brought to the attention of Harry Hopkins, he talked it over with the President and received his approval and in part these plans stimulated the formation of the National Research Council under Dr. Vannevar Bush.

According to Robert Sherwood in his brilliant footnote to history entitled *Roosevelt and Hopkins*,[1] Dr. Vannevar Bush had a somewhat similar plan for the development of new weapons and methods of warfare and this was also brought by him to the attention of Harry Hopkins. According to Sherwood, when Dr. Bush submitted his idea to Hopkins, the latter was already interested in the subject and "had received a suggestion along somewhat similar lines offered by Lawrence Langner, a public-spirited New Yorker, who divided this time between the practice of patent law and directing the Theatre Guild." Vannevar Bush's program emphasized "research" which included invention, while my proposal was more related to "invention" than research. My proposal, however, was the first to call attention to the

---

[1] Robert E. Sherwood, *Roosevelt and Hopkins, An Intimate History,* Harper & Brothers, New York, 1948, pp. 153-6.

situation in high places, and to emphasize the mobilization of scientists and inventors in the National Defense. A month later President Roosevelt wrote a letter to Dr. Vannevar Bush, dated June 14, 1940, forming the National Defense Research Council, the organization which produced the atomic bomb. In one paragraph of this letter the President specifically turned over to this new Council the research program on fissionable uranium then being conducted by the Bureau of Standards of the Commerce Department, and in the next paragraph he appointed the Commissioner of Patents as "contact" between the two Councils.

Dr. Bush, a man of thin and almost emaciated appearance, with a keen hard face of Puritan aspect, struck me as a character who might well have stepped out of the pages of *The Scarlet Letter*. Later, I developed an unbounded admiration for Dr. Bush, not merely because of the tremendous job of scientific organization which he performed, but also because of his ability to keep a large group of men from divulging to the Germans the greatest secret that has even been kept in the history of man, that of the manufacture on a collossal scale of the atomic bomb. Dr. Bush's insistence that each man working for this Council should swear an Oath of Secrecy witnessed by his wife, was the occasion of some mirth in the Services, one General remarking to me that "the girl friend should witness it too!" However, it was Dr. Bush who had the last laugh.

I visited Dr. Bush with Conway Coe to discuss possible overlapping of the two organizations. He showed me the letter of June 14, 1940, which he had just received from President Roosevelt, and I noted in it the instruction to continue research in the field of fissionable uranium, indicating that from the very beginning Roosevelt was fully conscious of the importance of this research. This information, which I kept locked up in my own bosom, was a source of constant apprehension to me during the war, for I knew that the Germans were working on this fissionable material, and as time after time Hitler would vaguely describe some great German discovery which was going to win the war, I would wonder whether he had not hit upon the release of atomic energy by the atomic bomb.

During the course of this interview with Dr. Bush, he agreed with me entirely as to the difference between "invention" and "research," and stated that he felt that our body should function separately from the proposed National Defense Research Council. Actually, I felt his reasons for this were not motivated entirely by a respect for inventors as a class, but rather, because, as he expressed it, "We're already being inundated with all kinds of inventions, and I want to keep the public away from what we are doing here as much as possible."

The actual job of putting through the Council on an official basis was done extremely well by Conway Coe who, with the help of Harry Hopkins, secured the assent of both the Army and the Navy to the forming of the new office. Under date of July 11, 1940, Dr. Charles F. Kettering was invited by Harry Hopkins to form the Council. Dr. Kettering at once accepted this invitation, and I was appointed Secretary of the Council. I arrived in Washington in July, 1940, and was deputed to call on the various branches of the military and naval establishments, and to explain the project to the officers who handled inventions. When I arrived at the Ordnance Department to talk the matter over with a general who was in charge of the Army Tank program, he took me outside his room and pointed to a long line of men waiting at the door to the main office with parcels, envelopes and papers under their arms. He informed me that this line of people were inventors waiting to see him, and that they took up more than half his day, leaving him less than half to devote to redesigning the new American tanks. I thought to myself, as I watched this queue, that it reminded me somewhat of a line at box office of a fairly successful play, except that most of the individuals hardly looked as though they were there to enjoy themselves. The General was delighted that the Council was to be formed.

The Army, hampered by lack of staff, were most anxious to cooperate on all levels with the new Council, and within a few days, upon hearing that we had secured three rooms in the Department of Commerce and set up shop there, the Ordnance Department sent down three truck loads of assorted inventions in the form of papers, models and chemical compounds, which were all dumped on the floor in the middle of one of the rooms and tuned over to us with their blessings. I counted about two thousand eight hundred inventions submitted to us under these conditions, and as we had no staff but myself and Tom Midgley, Conway Coe provided us with a young Patent Office Examiner from the Classification Division named Norman Ball, a very efficient clerk named Tom Reynolds and a couple of stenographers. No sooner was our Council's name painted on our doors than we began to receive additional quantities of inventions, and they poured in long before we had an adequate staff to handle them.

In the meanwhile, we were selecting the various Council members who would assist in handling the work of the Council, which was to serve as the receiving end for inventions for the Armed Forces. These inventions were to be sifted by a civilian staff, the good ones to be passed on by the Council members, and those selected by them were forwarded to the Army and the Navy. The Navy was represented on the Council by Rear Admiral Harold G. Bowen, Chief of the Navy's Office of Research and Inventions, the Army by Brigadier General Maubergne, Chief Signal Officer of the Army, and the Department of Commerce by Conway P. Coe.

Other members of the Council included Dr. William Coolidge, then Director of Research for the General Electric Company, the inventor of the drawn tungsten filament used in all electric lamps, and the Coolidge ex-ray tube, Watson Davis, head of Science Service, Dr. Frederick M. Feiker, Dean of the School of Engineering at George Washington University, Dr. Webster N. Jones, Dean of the College of Engineering at Carnegie Institute of Technology, Pittsburgh, Dr. Fin Sparre, Director of New Developments for the Du Pont Corporation, Dr. Orville Wright, co-inventor of the airplane; Dr. George Lewis, Director of the National Advisory Council for Aeronautics, Frederick Zeder, Chairman of the Board of the Chrysler Corporation, George Codrington, head of the Winton Diesel Division of the General Motors Corporation, and George Bakeland of the Bakelite Corporation. I regret that space does not permit me to describe in detail this remarkable group of men, each a leader in his own field, yet banded together in a common cause. It would take an entire book to describe their exploits, and it would make good reading.

Kettering, Codrington and Admiral Bowen had worked together for a number of years developing Diesel engines for submarines, and these engines were the prototypes of the Diesel engines with which Dr. Kettering has revolutionized the railroads of the United States. Hal Bowen, a blunt out-spoken engineer of Welsh descent, had fought a single-handed battle in the Navy to secure the use of high-pressure high-temperature steam, and largely as a result of his work our Navy had a cruising range 25 per cent greater than that of any other Navy in the world. He was also responsible for the first development of radar by our Navy, and for many other important innovations. At the time when the Council was formed he was the Chief of the Naval Research Laboratory at Washington, and prior to his retirement, he was head of the Patents and Inventions Section of the Navy, after serving as special assistant for the greater part of the war to Mr. Forrestal, then Secretary of the Navy. Hal Bowen, who loved the theatre and folk songs, became one of my close personal friends, and his advice was invaluable to me when I began to get into difficulties.[2]

Tom Midgley performed a brilliant job as our Vice Chairman, and in examining inventions relating to fuels. We sustained a great loss when he fell a victim to polio which ultimately caused his death. Tom, who used to drink the Ethyl gasoline he invented just to show his contempt for the cowardice of humanity, had a habit of testing out all kinds of chemicals on his own system. "That man is full of floating benzine rings," a fellow scientist once remarked. "I wonder how he manages to stay alive!" Tom regarded his illness as another opportunity for experimenting, and took an objective, intellectual interest in testing out every possible cure on himself. He invented a special bed with a harness overhead to enable him to pull himself up into sitting position and died tragically by becoming entangled in the wires in his sleep.

Dr. Kettering was fond of saying, "The National Inventors Council must serve as an open door to the Army and Navy for the inventors of the country who wish to assist the war effort by means of inventions." This policy helped not only in stimulating invention, but also in improving the standard of quality of those submitted; and it also established good relations between the inventors and the Council.

I remember, on one occasion, a serious-looking gentleman from Chicago had taken the trouble to come down by train and to inform me that he had an invention which could destroy the enemy very readily, but the device was so secret that he could not disclose it to me. I said that I was sorry, but I did not see how we could handle it under these circumstances. He returned a day or so later and explained the invention to our clerk, Mr. Reynolds. I asked Mr. Reynolds how he managed to get this information from the inventor, and he informed me that the man had asked him if he was a Catholic, and when Reynolds told him he was, he then divulged the invention. This consisted of a balloon which was to be sent up during a thunderstorm, and carried a long copper wire attached to it. This wire was to reach from the balloon to the earth, and by suitable manipulation was supposed to spray lightning on the enemy forces!

---

[2] Other members of the Council during the war included General Tschappat, and (later) Dr. Roger Adams, President of the American Chemical Society, Dr. Oliver Buckley, Chief of Research, Bell Research Laboratories, Rear Admiral Julius A. Fuhrer, Brigadier General Walter Wood, Brigadier General Earle McFarland and the Honorable Casper Ooms.

One of our difficulties was to separate the so-called "screwball" from the sane inventor who seemed to have screwball associations. For example, a young radio mechanic named Hedden came to see us from Miami, Florida. He told us that his business was that of a treasure hunter. He had been working on a device for locating buried gold and had succeeded in making one. Had this idea, with its screwball implications, been presented directly to the Army or Navy, I doubt whether he would have been given the attention he received at the National Inventors Council. His claims were investigated, as a result of which it was found that he had developed a non-magnetic method of detecting buried metals. He was taken in hand, introduced to the Army Engineers' Board at Fort Belvoir and from his invention was developed the famous American land-mine detector, consisting of a device which looked like a pancake at the end of a long stick, and was so delicate that it could detect a mine buried three feet underground. When General Rommel retreated from El Alamein and sowed the African desert behind him with hundreds of thousands of mines, the British pressed on with this mine-detector and were able to dig them up almost as fast as Rommel buried them. This same detector was used with great success in all the landings on the Pacific and in Europe, and resulted in saving thousands of lives on the allied side, as well as shortening the war by a number of months. In my opinion this one invention alone justified all the efforts which were put into the Council.

I shall not endeavor here to recount all the activities of the Council itself. Its achievements have been made a part of the official records of the war. The part I played in it as Secretary was partly executive and partly stimulative. On the executive side I did not shine, and as soon as possible I asked to have myself replaced by men with government experience. Conway Coe, on behalf of the Department of Commerce, offered me the position of Director of the Staff, but I felt that I could accomplish far more as Executive Secretary to the Council, with freedom of action so far as the Department was concerned. Moreover, the Guild was continuing to produce plays of importance to the war effort and I did not wish to cut myself off from this work.

John C. Green, who has done an outstanding job as Chief Engineer for the Council, referred to me as "the gadfly," and remembering the part of Mosca (The Gadfly) in *Volpone*, it was an apt description of my function, which was to sting or stimulate others into action on inventions. When our Council was very favorably impressed by an invention, I made it my business to push it with the officers of the

Army or Navy, and I was personally not averse to doing a little competitive "selling." I also spent a considerable amount of my time pouring oil on troubled Army, Navy or Congressional waters.

When an inventor named Howard Barlow claimed that his new explosive was being cold-shouldered by the Army and Navy, he arranged a demonstration with a quantity of live goats tethered in the neighborhood of the explosion. After the explosion took place, the goats were examined and found to be smiling and undisturbed. Barlow, however, unlike the goats, was extremely disturbed; and under his pressure, a Senate enquiry took place on the entire method of handling war inventions. I was summoned before a subcommittee of the Senate Committee on Military Affairs under the chairmanship of Senator Thomas of Nebraska and when I took the stand he regarded me angrily and accused the Council of being "mere lackeys to the Army and Navy," an accusation I strongly resented. "Where do you get the money for the Council?" he asked, and in effect I told him I didn't know. He glared at me angrily as much as to say, *What a Secretary!* and to my relief, he let me go. Later on, some of our important scientists were called as witnesses, and we were given a clean bill of health.

On the stimulative side, I had ideas of my own. Ever since the first meeting of the Council I had been studying the subject of long-distance bombing as a means of bringing the war to a close with the least loss of life. I had remembered reading in the newspapers some years earlier of an aviator flying over the city of Chicago for several days, his fuel tank being replenished in the air from time to time by means of a refueling plane flying over it, dropping a rubber hose onto it, and the two planes then flying together at the same speed until the tank in the lower plane had been filled from the tank in the plane flying above it.

I secured copies of all the patents on "refueling in the air," and later I wrote to my friend Harris G. Luther, then patent attorney of the United Aircraft Corporation of Hartford, asking for some further information on the subject. He replied, informing me that this method of refueling was quite practical and he sent me some articles showing that it had been used successfully by Sir Alan Cobham in England in trans-Atlantic flight. I prepared my suggestions for the use of these British devices for long-distance bombing in October and November, 1941, and these were submitted to the National Advisory Committee for Aeronautics which, on December 8, 1941, pronounced the idea to be practical.

On December 7th of the same year, while spending Sunday afternoon at home in New York City, I received a telephone call from Eugene Mullaly of my office telling me that the Japanese had raided Pearl Harbor. I listened to the radio and suffered in common with millions of other Americans the shame and humiliation of this attack, a feeling which changed to anger and a desire to hit back.

I thought at once of the long-distance bombers with refueling tanker planes on which I had been working, and I immediately drew up a plan for bombing the factories of Japan as soon as possible by means of long-distance bombers. On December 13, 1941, six days after Pearl Harbor, I placed this plan in the hands of the Planning Branch G-3 of the General Staff. I enlarged on my plan with an additional seven-page memorandum dated December 23, 1941. My idea was a continuous series of bombing raids on Japan by means of long-range bombers starting from Alaska or Hawaii refueled in the air by tanker planes which accompanied the bombers for part of the distance and returned to their bases after the bombers had been refueled.

I used all my powers as a playwright to dramatize the idea, and my memorandum of December 23, 1941, started out stating:

The effect of the destruction of American manufacturing plants by a series of German bombing attacks across the Atlantic Ocean can readily be imagined. It would seriously impede America's war effort. A series of such attacks against Japanese industrial centers by American high-altitude long-range bomber planes within the next few months will have a still greater disruptive effect on the Japanese war effort. The present plan is daring, surprising and perfectly feasible. It calls for . . . , the special training of about a hundred men and the greatest secrecy.

The National Inventors Council itself received no proposal of this character before mine, and I was given immediate consideration by the Army represented by Colonel Charles E. Hurdis, Chief, The Planning Branch G-3 of the General Staff, Colonel G. F. F. Schulgen, of the same branch, Colonel Wm. G. Brown and Lieutenant Birely of the Army Air Corps. (This was before there was a separate Air Force.) Early in January, I attended an interview in Colonel Brown's office and there I met the resourceful and courageous Colonel James Doolittle who, later on, led the famous air raid over Japan. I explained my idea to him and he told me he knew all about the Cobham English equipment. On January 10, 1942, I wrote Colonel G. F. Schulgen of the Planning Branch G-3 of the General Staff who was studying my plan, as follows:

I discussed this situation briefly with Colonel Doolittle, who informs me that he actually was present at a tanking operation conducted by Sir Alan Cobham for a trans-Atlantic trip, and that the same was entirely successful and very easily accomplished.

Colonel Doolittle agreed with me that a great deal of time would be saved by bringing the English people familiar with this development over to this country. He felt this would result in a great saving of time since the English people know all the things not to do, and it would not be necessary to make the same mistakes all over again.

I felt my idea was extremely important and kept following it up with the various officers, and I also got in touch with Sir Alan Cobham in England through my London partners, as a result of which, later on, the Army Air Corps secured his equipment and tried out his ideas in this country.

A few weeks later on, I read the news of the successful Doolittle raid over Japan. There was no information at first as to how this had been accomplished, and I naturally thought that refueling planes had been used. It turned out, however, that the raid was actually made by bombers launched from an aircraft carrier. The blows struck on Tokyo undoubtedly played a large part in discouraging Japan from attacking Russia at a time when the Germans were pressing on Moscow. Had they done so, the history of the world might have been written differently.

In the year 1949, American military aviators using the combination of B-29 long-range bombers and "refueling in the air" were able to fly entirely around the earth without once touching the ground. Their flight, in my opinion, demonstrated that my suggestion for "refueling in the air" in a series of raids on Japan in 1942 was entirely practical.

That I was fully aware of the possibilities of refueling planes is shown in my second letter dated January 20, 1942, to Colonel G. F. Schulgen:

The question which in my mind is ultimately involved is whether the U.S. Army is going to fight offensively or defensively. If you have decided to fight offensively here is the way to carry the war right to Japan, and to do it at an early date with practically no modification of existing equipment. If you wait to design bombers with a flying range able to reach to Japan and back, you will wait three years and the cost will be measured in billions of dollars.

On the other hand, if this opportunity is seized swiftly, aggressively, and with a determination to take the initiative, it may well turn the tide in the Pacific.

The Army's crack flyer, Colonel James Doolittle, has actually been present at a refuelling of the trans-Atlantic service in England, and tells us the idea is completely practical. Over a month has gone by since this proposal was first submitted and I hasten to urge its immediate consideration by the highest authorities in the Army without delay.

We waited three years to build the B-29 in quantities, and the cost was measured not only in billions of dollars, but also in thousands of American lives.

I have sometimes wondered what would have been the ultimate result, had my idea been carried out in its entirety early in the war against Japan. It might not have been necessary to drive the Japanese out of the Pacific island by island, for by destroying the arsenals on the mainland of Japan by repeated heavy bombing attacks from Hawaii or Dutch Harbor, the Japanese on the Pacific Islands would have ultimately been starved out, and forced to surrender. And it might not have been necessary to explode the atom bomb at Hiroshima and Nagasaki. . . . Indeed, Japan might have surrendered before we actually produced the atom bomb. All this might have been, and then it might not have been. Men who were better equipped technically than I was, made the decisions and bravely carried them out, and Man's fate did the rest.

In connection with the bombing of cities, I made a suggestion which was used by the Army Air Force. It was to drop pamphlets from the air on a number of cities warning the inhabitants that the industrial areas were to be bombed shortly, and urging them to send the women and children out of the town. The warning was humane as to the women and children, but the purpose of the suggestion was also to intensify the fears and destroy the morale of the men working in armament plants who remained in the cities. This idea was employed both in Germany and Japan with what may be grimly termed "success."

Another of my suggestions was to use bombing planes to drop large bombs into harbors, thus producing tidal waves to capsize enemy shipping. I explained the idea to Colonel "Benny" Myers, now serving a term of imprisonment, but not for rejecting my idea, which he discarded on the absurd ground that it was easier to hit the ships one by one with small bombs than to carry bombs big enough to cause an upheaval of the entire harbor. Both he and the naval experts who rejected my idea were proved wrong by the British, who later on dropped six-ton bombs, termed "block busters," into French harbors and destroyed German shipping and submarines. Another of my ideas, endorsed by the Council, and of immediate value today, was to build municipal underground through-traffic tunnels with connecting chambers in all large cities to serve to relieve traffic and provide underground parking room in peacetime, and to serve as atom bombproof shelters in wartime.

Soon after Pearl Harbor I decided that an article in the *Reader's Digest* with its eight million or more readers, asking the American public for inventions to help win the war, might be productive of some excellent ideas. Accordingly, I communicated with the editorial staff, which selected Stuart Chase, the economist, to write an article on the subject. After its publication in the *Reader's Digest,* ideas came in by the thousand. For several months the average number of suggestions received were over six thousand a week, while for one record week we received over ten thousand. With our small staff, it was impossible to keep up with the incoming mail, and we asked for a larger staff, but it was not forthcoming. For months we labored to classify and evaluate the deluge of ideas which had snowed us under. One evening when our tired staff had gone home, Armina came over from the Washington Stage Door Canteen which she was managing, and noticed the disarray of papers around the offices. "What are those packing cases of unopened mail?" she asked. "Suggestions we just haven't been able to get around to." "Why don't you get more staff?" she asked. I replied that we'd been trying to for months, but just hadn't been able to for reasons of red tape. I was constantly frustrated by having old rules and regulations of the Commerce Department flashed in my face when I asked for extra stenographers, extra engineers and extra assistants, and I was always in a state of apprehension that possibly in one of the packing cases full of unopened letters which were awaiting attention, there might be an invention which would save thousands of lives.

I finally became so exasperated that I decided that the only way to secure prompt results was by taking the National Inventors Council away from the Department of Commerce, and placing it under the Office of War Emergency. However, since this office was headed by Henry Wallace, whose starry-eyed theorizing did not recommend itself to the hardheaded scientists who made up the Inventors Council, I received very little support for this proposal. It did serve, however, to cause the Council to exert pressure on the Commerce Department; my insistence on extra staff finally won out, and we ultimately caught up with the backlog. It is not usual to economize in wartime government offices, but the total cost to the country of the National Inventors Council was an average of $90,000 per year throughout the duration of the war! I offer this as an example of misplaced economy.

While I was having these personal troubles with the Council, I realized that matters had been getting on my nerves from sheer frustration, and I felt that I should take a few weeks off from my Council activities and devote my time to *Oklahoma!* On arriving in New York, I went immediately from the train to the rehearsal at the Guild Theatre, and threw myself heart and soul into the work, and did not return to Washington until six weeks later. Broad smiles greeted me at the next Council meeting, when everyone present had read of the success of *Oklahoma!*

At the end of the war with Germany, on May 22, 1945, I drew up a Report of the activities of the Council, showing that over 210,000 inventions and suggestions had been evaluated by the Council, and 11,040 files were passed on as "worth while" to the war agencies. Of these, over 100 were actually in use at the close of hostilities, and tests were being made on hundreds of others.[3] I ended my report with the following warning:

I feel that this work of evaluation should continue and that we should not discontinue the work when the war with Japan is over, for some of the best inventions may come from those who have the experience of the present war behind them. Nor should we forget that it was our defenseless position which encouraged the aggressors. Such aggression will be encouraged again if we again fail to remember that our own strength is our greatest guarantee for peace.

Alas, my warning went unheeded. However, after the war ended, the Secretaries of War and Navy requested that the Council continue in operation on a skeleton basis, so as to be ready for action in case the unhappy necessity should again arise.

At the end of World War II, the Council and all its members received commendations and citations from the President, Secretaries of War and of the Navy and others familiar with our work. But I value most a letter from General George Marshall stating: "The activities of the Council in evaluating the tremendous number of inventions submitted by patriotic Americans have been of immeasurable value both in relieving the War Department of the burden of this test and in providing able technical assistance. With the appreciation of the War Department, I want to express my personal thanks for the outstanding efforts of the Council in stimulating the inventive potential of the nation and for the large contribution its members have made to the war effort."

---

[3] See Appendix V, p. 466, for copy of Report.

Dr. Vannevar Bush also wrote the Council stating: "Your job has been a difficult and important one and you may well have a justifiable pride in your contribution to the over-all war effort."

Two international projects, unrelated to the work of the Council, were initiated by me after the war was over. One of these had to do with the Italian elections of 1948. At a dinner party given by my friends Judd and Mildred Creen, Dr. Alvin Barach informed me, about sixteen weeks before these elections were held, of a conversation he had had with a high official of the State Department regarding the imminent danger of Communism spreading over Western Europe should the Italian Communists win the election. I decided that if the Italians in America could present their own viewpoint, gained from living in a democracy, to their families in Italy, the tide from the East might be checked. I took the matter up immediately with the proper authorities. Soon after, articles were written and Committees were formed, and thousands of Italians living in this country wrote their families in Italy, speaking in favor of the democratic way of life. The resulting flood of letters from Italians in this country to their families was noted by many newspaper correspondents, who reported that the effect was spectacular and decisive. Unfortunately, this effort has not been followed up as it should have been, due to our hit-or-miss foreign policy. Another project, on which I am still working, and which has met with universal approval, is the possible purchase of all the real estate of the old City of Jerusalem, and its preservation and restoration as a shrine (similar to Williamsburg, Virginia), for the benefit of all the religions involved; viz., the Christian, the Jewish and the Mohammedan. The old city would thus serve as a spiritual center for over a billion people and might well be a greater factor for universal peace than either the League of Nations or the United Nations.

The Council met two or three times a year from 1945 to 1950, but since the beginning of hostilities in Korea it has become active again, and inventions are received at an accelerated pace. I continue to place my confidence in American invention, fostered under our Patent System, and firmly believe that so long as we continue to encourage our inventors and research programs, we shall maintain our inventive lead over the Communistic nations which now threaten to overrun the world.[1]

---

[1] Congress has recently given permanent status to the operation of the National Inventors Council.

CHAPTER XXVIII

Oklahoma!

WHILE the war was proceeding and we were all absorbed, in one way or another, in the war effort, I still had a theatre to keep going with Terry Helburn. And at the Theatre Guild there were crises, prospects of utter disaster and fortunately counter-measures that brought us out of extreme difficulties into the light of victory. The miracle that ensured the latter is no secret: it can be summed up in the magic word *Oklahoma!*, which will long remain a legend in the annals of the American theatre.

In our twenty-fifth season, that of 1942–43, our fluctuating fortunes were again at a low ebb. In December and January we had about thirty thousand dollars in the bank; our plays of the season before had lost a great deal of money, and because of the way the war was going, it was difficult to raise capital. This was the time which Theresa Helburn chose to launch her project to produce the new musical play called *Oklahoma!*, and it looked as though the gods were against us from the start.

Green Grow the Lilacs, the original play from which *Oklahoma!* was fashioned, was originally produced by the Guild in the season of 1930–31 and, as written by Lynn Riggs, it called for a colorful chorus which sang cowboy songs to cover the changes from scene to scene. Terry and I had long admired the musical genius of Dick Rodgers, and often tried to persuade him to write a musical play for the Guild. About four years earlier we had called on him at his home and suggester that *Lysistrata* by Aristophanes would make an excellent musical, and might be suited to the talents of the redoubtable Ethel Merman. Dick turned down the idea on completely practical grounds, but

I remember remarking at the time, "Dick, I think you ought to write something for posterity," to which he replied, "I'd like to, Lawrence, but I have a family to support."

When Dick Rodgers came to live near Westport, Terry Helburn suggested to him that *Green Grow the Lilacs* would make an excellent story for a musical play. At the time, Lorenz Hart, who had been Rodgers' collaborator in *The Garrick Gaieties* and a great number of other musicals, was in poor health, and this made it difficult for them to continue collaborating. Terry talked over a number of lyric and book writers with Rodgers, and he suggested as his first choice working with Oscar Hammerstein, whom Dick admired greatly. Terry agreed enthusiastically to his being engaged by the Guild, thus forming the association between these two which has since made history in the musical theatre and resulted in such inspiring works as *Oklahoma!, Carousel, South Pacific* and, I hope, many others. To Terry goes the full credit for having conceived the idea of producing *Oklahoma!* and for bringing together these two artists to create the work. In doing this she provided them with an American folk story which stimulated their creative energies in a direction away from the normal musical comedy field, in which both of them had been active for so many years. They, on the other hand, were quick to realize that in this American material, written by a genuine poet of the soil, Lynn Riggs, was a story and characters worthy of the very best they could create. Dick and Oscar, both of them poets, took this story and made it their own, and with such songs as "Oh, What a Beautiful Mornin'," "The Surrey with the Fringe on Top" and "Oklahoma!," a magnificent contribution to the folk music of America was made in their first collaboration.

I remember my first interview with Oscar Hammerstein after he had written the script. He is a big, slow-moving man with a broad kindly face—slow moving but quick thinking. Unlike so many men I have met in the musical field, his interests are wide, his reading extensive and his knowledge of philosophy, economics and world affairs, greater than almost any other man I have met in the theatre. Richard Rodgers is quick and volatile, a practical man of the theatre, and an excellent business man. Nevertheless, both men have this in common, that they are essentially artists in their approach to their work, have a simple, direct humanity, and take a warm personal interest in the lives of the dozens of men and women who work in the plays with which we have been associated. I think it is this generous endowment of friendliness for others which has been at the base of Oscar's poetic quality in his verses, and of Dick's popular appeal in his music.

The book of *Oklahoma!* was completed in the late summer of 1942, and all through the fall and winter thereafter, we held auditions in the Guild Theatre for singers and actors. It was soon decided that Alfred Drake, who had appeared in the Guild's production of *Yesterday's Magic* the year before, and had an excellent singing voice, would make a good Curly, and Joan Roberts who had appeared in a small part in one of Oscar's musicals was selected as Laurey. While we were auditioning actors and actresses for these roles, we were also engaged in financing the musical. As our own treasury was so depleted, it was obvious that we could not produce *Oklahoma!* without outside capital. It was also obvious, when we got in touch with our usual backers, that during this dolorous period in the history of the world it was going to be no easy matter to raise the money. We needed $90,000 to $100,000, and as I was often away in Washington, Terry bore the greater part of the task of raising this money. Indeed, our morale at the Guild was fairly low, for in addition to our failure with *Mr. Sycamore* (which ended in an arbitration with the author, which we lost), we also lost the services of our highly efficient business manager, Warren Munsell, who was invited by the Air Force to return to the Army, so that we were operating the Guild without a Business Department.

Marcus Heiman and Lee Shubert agreed to put up part of the money, but they themselves felt it would be necessary to secure considerable outside backing. We decided the best way to do this would be to have Dick, Oscar, Alfred Drake and Joan Roberts attend a number of tea parties or cocktail parties to which prospective backers would be invited, and then to play and sing the songs to them so that they would not be buying a pig in a poke. We took a studio in Steinway Hall on several occasions, and one of our first visitors, Joseph Swan, came with his young daughter, and they were so delighted with the music that he decided to invest 10 per cent of the capital needed.

We also tried to interest another friend, Mrs. Vivian Spencer, who had backed some of our other plays, but her own finances would not allow her to invest in this musical at the time. She generously gave us a large party, inviting guests who were in the habit of backing plays, and Dick, Oscar, Alfred and Joan—like a little band of itinerant musicians—played and sang the songs while Oscar explained the story of the play. Speeches were made about the fortunes which would result from a small investment in the new musical. Alas, neither the songs nor the speeches were persuasive, for among all those present,

Above: First anniversary party for *Oklahoma!*, March 31, 1944. Mayor LaGuardia presents an award to Richard Rodgers and Oscar Hammerstein on the stage of the St. James Theatre. *Left to right:* The author, Betty Garde, Mayor Fiorella LaGuardia, Joan Roberts, Richard Rodgers, Alfred Drake, Theresa Helburn, Os-car Hammerstein. *Below:* Fourth anniversary party for *Oklahoma!* Wearing regalia presented to them by the Kiowa Indians of Oklahoma, *left to right,* Theresa Helburn, Oscar Hammerstein, Agnes DeMille, Armina Marshall, Richard Rodgers, the author.

The finale of the original Theatre Guild production of *Oklahoma!* The principals, reading from left to right, are Katherine Sergava, Lee Dixon, Celeste Holm, Alfred Drake, Joan Roberts, Joseph Buloff, Betty Garde and Ralph Riggs.

The original can-can girls of *Oklahoma!* led by Joan McCracken.

The Theatre Guild production of *Carousel*, 1945. The principals, *reading from left to right*, are John Raitt, Christine Johnson, Jan Clayton, Jean Darling.

only two persons were found to invest in the play and this only to the tune of $2,000.

The money needed came in very slowly indeed, and I became very pessimistic, but Terry kept her chin up and continued to seek investors.

More cocktail parties were given, one in the home of Jules Glaenzer, a friend of Richard Rodgers', and little by little in checks of $1,000 to $5,000, we gradually raised the necessary amount. S. N. Behrman, whom Terry persuaded to invest in the play, told me later that he did it only as a gesture of good will, feeling his money would be lost, but that he owed the Guild something for being the first to present his plays!

Finally came the question as to who should direct the play and design the scenery and costumes. Rouben Mamoulian, the hero of *Porgy* and *Porgy and Bess,* came to town from Hollywood, and he was engaged as the director on our suggestion. Miles White, the costume designer, and Lemuel Ayers, the scenic artist, had been discovered by Alfred Lunt and Lynn Fontanne, and were used in our joint production with the Playwrights' Company of *The Pirate,* which was very beautiful and colorful to look at; it seemed a very natural move to engage them for *Oklahoma!* When the question of a dance director arose, there was some difference of opinion as to the style of production and the kind of dance director needed. It so happened that Agnes De Mille, remembering that I had wanted to use her for the choreography in my production of *The School for Husbands,* wrote me asking if we could use her in the new musical project. I passed her letter on to Richard Rodgers, and later on I learned that Agnes was in rehearsal with her ballet *Rodeo* for the Ballet Russe de Monte Carlo. She invited us to see this, and Terry Helburn took Dick and Oscar to the opening performance. They were enraptured with Agnes' work, and indeed I have always felt that her creation of *Rodeo* greatly influenced the style of the ballets of *Oklahoma!*

Richard Rodgers contributed an experienced musical comedy stage manager, Jerome Whyte, who had been a "hoofer" in his young days and had successfully worked as Stage Manager for George Abbott and on some of the Rodgers and Hart musical plays; we contributed John Haggott, our Technical Director, and Elaine Anderson, our Assistant Stage Manager. Early in January, we went into rehearsal at the Guild Theatre, every inch of space of which was thereafter crowded with activity. I remember particularly the ballet rehearsing in the lobby, with an impish-looking sprite named Joan McCracken who played "The Girl Who Falls Down," leaping through space in a tight-fitting, black jersey practice costume, while every evening on the stage, as the shadows began to fall and the tired company went home, one became aware of the presence of a weird-looking individual named Eric Victor, who, long, lean and bearded, practiced leaping goat-like from the stage at unexpected moments, and scaring the lights and liver out of anyone he happened to take unawares.

Oklahoma! was a new form of musical, for it included both the elements of the musical theatre and of the dramatic theatre, as well as the ballet. The marriage between the musical elements and the dramatic elements in the staging of this unique combination, was due to the genius of Rouben Mamoulian who held to the same kind of integrated production he had established for *Porgy and Bess,* and welded the varying elements together.

This was not an easy matter, and resulted in a number of controversies. For instance, it was the custom at the time for all musical plays to have so-called "specialty" dance numbers, and the original manuscript called for one or more dancers to appear in what were called "spots" in the play to interrupt the action with a dance. For this reason the lively leaper Eric Victor was engaged without there being any particular "spot" for him. As the style of the play evolved, it became apparent that no place could be found for such "spots" either in the play action or the choreography, with the result that the necessity for using the talents of Victor, who had a "run-of-the-play" contract (which meant that he could not be discharged for several months) weighed heavily on our shoulders. On the opening night in New Haven, he fell off the trellis work and fractured a wrist. This would have been enough to deter any other dancer. Not so the leaping Victor! He went to the New Haven Hospital, had a plastic cast made for his wrist, and turned up the following week in Boston. It was suggested that he might hide in a barrel in Act 1 attired in cowboy costume, and after the musical number "It's A Scandal," he could jump out and perform his anti-gravitational antics. Victor, wearing large green gauntlets to hide the plastic cast on his wrist, was introduced into the play, but with disastrous results. His appearance was so unexpectedly frightening, that it took ten minutes before the audience would laugh again, and moreover it so hurt the production stylistically, that we paid off his contract. I happily record that he has since made a great success in other musical plays and revues which were more suited to his talents.

While *Oklahoma!* was in rehearsal at the Guild Theatre, Oscar and

Dick were writing new songs without any apparent effort during the rehearsals, whenever they were needed. Terry and John Gassner, our playreader, suggested that some kind of rousing song of the earth would be helpful in the second act, and one day Dick and Oscar appeared at the theatre, sat at the piano where we surrounded them on benches and chairs, while they played for us the rousing melody of the song "Oklahoma!" Further excitement was provided when we went to the Brooks Costume Company and saw the costumes for the play. Both Rouben and I, along with the rest of the men, thought that the women were far too covered up, as their costumes stretched from the tops of their necks to the tips of their toes. So while the designer, Miles White, was not looking, we persuaded the cutter to reveal a little more of the girls' necks and bosoms, especially in the costumes of Ado Annie which were worn by the beautiful and talented Celeste Holm.

At the final dress parade on the stage of the Shubert Theatre in New Haven, we were somewhat appalled by the shirts which the cowboys were wearing; they included a number of fancy colors and designs, which would have been greeted by true cowboys with shouts of derision, and it was necessary to tone these down considerably before we could possibly open the play. "Can't you get rid of those 'bitch-pink' shirts," asked Lem Ayers. "They're killing my scenery." "They're killing our cowboys, too!" was the response.

After the dress rehearsal, there were a number of small adjustments, and the play opened with the title *Away We Go* on the evening of March 11, 1943, to an audience made up of New Haven play-goers, Yale students, a considerable number of New York managers, and finally the investors who came out of curiosity to learn the fate of their investment. The first half of the play flowed like a dream; indeed, except for a certain amount of cutting, it opened in New Haven very much as it is being played today.

The second act did not play so well, but when the final curtain fell, the play received warm applause from the audience. As I went back-stage after the cheering had subsided and the house had cleared, the curtain was raised and I stood at the footlights with Elaine Anderson, our attractive Assistant Stage Manager, whose eager face was glowing with delight. "Imagine, Lawrence," she said, in her rich Texas accent, "Ah've bin in nothing but failures with the Theatre Guild, and this is mah first reel success!" Being superstitious, I rebuked her. "Don't say it's a success until after our opening night in New York." "But ah just know it's a hit, Lawrence," she said. "Ah absolutely know it!" And she was right.

As the crowd of managers, backers, friends of the actors, the composer and author chatted on the stage after the play was over, a well-known musical comedy producer who seldom talks in tones quieter than a resounding shout, informed everybody present that Oscar would have to rewrite the second act completely. Another important musical comedy producer called me on the telephone the next day and spent twenty minutes arguing with me that the perverted farm hand Jud should not be killed in the second act, because, in his experience of twenty-five years of producing musical comedies, there had never been a killing in one of them! I stated gently but firmly that this was essential to the play, and we would have to let it go at that. So pessimistic were the reports that came out of New Haven regarding the second act, that we decided to sell some additional interest in the play in order to be prepared for staying out of New York longer, if that were necessary, or to take care of losses in New York.

After the play opened in New Haven, Theresa Helburn whose courage and ideas had been so largely responsible in bringing *Oklahoma!* through its period in swaddling clothes, was taken ill with a severe throat infection due to overwork, and during a considerable part of the Boston engagement we had to conduct our conferences at her bedside. Notwithstanding this handicap, she continued to keep her fingers on the pulse of what was going on throughout the many ramifications of production. I applied myself particularly to organizing the changes in the second act, taking charge of the rehearsal timetable, which made me unpopular with everybody, and attending the conferences with the authors and director which were held nightly after the performances.

By a rearrangement of the material in the second act, and with very little rewriting, within ten days of the opening of the play in Boston, it was in excellent shape, and in practically the exact condition in which it opened in New York. During the Boston engagement there was an outbreak of German measles in the company, but fortunately for us, this took a mild form; it did look, however, for a moment that we might lose Agnes De Mille for quite some time. One morning while she was rehearsing her dancers, I met her in the lobby of the Colonial Theatre and remarked, "I've managed to get you an extra half-hour today, and I expect a kiss for that!" "Very well," she said, pecking me reluctantly on the forehead. Three hours later she came to me and said, "The doctor says I have German measles and I guess you're going to get it, too. This'll teach you not to collect bribes from choreographers." She was laid up for two or three days, but I escaped.

I was impressed during the rehearsals with the extraordinary resourcefulness of both Rodgers and Hammerstein. One of the chorus girls remarked to Rodgers, "Why isn't there more chance for us singers to use our singing voices? We have a wonderful chorus, and not very much to do." At that time, the number "Oklahoma!" was being sung mainly by Curly and Laurey, and we were all calling for more excitement at this part of the play. Dick immediately conceived the idea of using the entire chorus for the number with explosive effect. Oscar had a similar ability to think on his feet. When he was asked for an additional verse for the song "All or Nothin'" I remarked, "You have such a wonderful second verse, I don't see how you can ever improve on it." "I shall have to, Lawrence," was his reply. "It's my job to write a topper." "What does that mean," I asked, thinking vaguely that it had something to do with silk hats which had been called "toppers" in my youth. "Just a verse that will be better than the one that goes before," he replied. And sure enough, a few hours later he came out of his room with a third verse, definitely a "topper" to the other two.

Mamoulian was equally brilliant in integrating all the talents involved in the production, and merging them into the final form of *Oklahoma!* This was illustrated not only in the way the songs were directed by him, rather than, as customarily, by the dance director, but also in the way the play was lighted. In the beginning, the scenery was lit in accordance with current so-called "musical comedy lighting," but as the play progressed in Boston, it was supplemented with the kind of lighting which is used in the dramatic theatre. Every day more and more lighting equipment would arrive at the Colonial Theatre, in order to produce the effects of dramatic lighting called for by Mamoulian. When we moved to New York, to my horror, on the dress rehearsal night, we found that the front of the stage of the St. James Theatre was inadequately lit, and that the moment we turned on the very strong front lights which hung from the balcony, we had shadows all over the ballet drop which completely destroyed the effect of the end of the first act. We held a council of war and the following morning at eight o'clock John Haggott and I were working at the theatre with the electricians who constructed booms which were placed in the boxes, and were left there for the entire five-year run of *Oklahoma!*

When we were in Boston, a musical play called *Dancing in the Streets*, produced by Vinton Freedley with the adorable Mary Martin in the lead, and with scenery and costumes by Robert Edmond Jones, was playing against us, and there was quite a question as to whether we should not try to race in to New York ahead of this play. Rudolf Kommer, Max Reinhart's shadow, the roly-poly gentleman whose name has appeared now and again in these pages, came to Boston and saw both *Oklahoma!* and *Dancing in the Streets,* and he was as loud in his praises of the latter as he was pessimistic about the fate of *Oklahoma!* I myself had been worried as to what would happen in New York, because *Oklahoma!* was so different from any of the musicals which were running at the time. Many of the New York musical producers were either graduates of burlesque, or produced slick musical shows, done with great professionalism, which by this time had hardened into a formula. Except for *Show Boat,* there was absent from them any of the poetry or mood of Americana which characterized *Oklahoma!*

One objection which had confronted us when we asked for capital to back *Oklahoma!* from the professional Broadway investors, was that the play was "too clean." It did not have the suggestive jokes, the spicy situations, the strip-teasers and the other indecencies which too often went with a successful musical of those days. Some of these objections must have been in my mind when, on the last matinee, the immaculate Vinton Freedley, producer of *Dancing in the Streets,* came to see *Oklahoma!* at the Colonial Theatre. "What do you think are its chances?" he asked me as he came in. "Well," I replied, "I don't know. A great many people think it's 'too clean' for Broadway." After the play was over, Vinton walked up the aisle and remarked, "I think this play will be a tremendous success! And," he added, "I don't think it's so clean either." There is, of course, a certain amount of lusty humor in *Oklahoma!* but it is never lascivious.

When the fateful day arrived for the opening of *Oklahoma!* in New York, we refused to allow anyone to be seated during the singing of the opening number, "Oh, What a Beautiful Morning," and it was apparent to me from the beginning of the play that it had started off on the right foot.[1] I wondered how a New York audience would respond to the fact that for nearly forty-five minutes, not a single chorus girl appeared on the stage. But as one beautiful song followed another, the audience took the play to its heart, and there was the most tremendous outburst of applause at the end of the ballet, as the curtain fell upon the first act. During the intermission, I noted there was that

---

[1] The principal members of the original cast of *Oklahoma!* included Alfred Drake, Joan Roberts, Celeste Holm, Betty Garde, Joseph Buloff, Lee Dixon, Howard da Silva, Ralph Riggs, Marc Platt, Katharine Sergava, Joan McCracken, Bambi Linn, Owen Martin and Vladimir Kostenko.

electric thrill which passes through an audience when it feels that it is attending something of exciting import in the theatre.

During the second act, after the gaiety of the "Cowman and the Farmer" songs and dances, there was no doubt about the outcome. At the end of the play, the applause was overwhelming. A lump came into my throat, for not for many years had any play of ours received such an ovation from its opening-night audience. The next day the newspaper critics wrote column upon column of praise for Rodgers, Hammerstein, Mamoulian and De Mille; there was not a single bad newspaper notice. And then the legend of *Oklahoma!* began to grow.

At first we knew that we had produced a successful musical play, but not one of us—Rodgers, Hammerstein, Mamoulian, De Mille, Terry or myself—had any idea of the popularity which the play was to achieve, and the bright page it was to write in the history of the American musical theatre. It was only as the enthusiasm grew month by month with the impact of the play upon the American public, along with the well-advertised difficulty of securing tickets which became a standing joke in the newspapers, that we began to realize that we had produced a theatre classic. On one occasion, Armina lost her little Tibetan terrier Chang, and in desperation, she gave out a story to the newspapers describing her dog, offering as a reward to anyone who found him, two seats to *Oklahoma!* Chang was returned to us the following day!

The queue at the St. James Theatre box office grew longer and longer, the appeals from the ticket agencies grew stronger and stronger, and Fiorello LaGuardia, Mayor of New York City, telephoned for reservations whenever any distinguished visitors came to New York. The visiting European generals were entertained by the stationary American generals from the Pentagon; Mrs. Roosevelt from the White House, Mr. Morgenthau from the Treasury Department, and Mr. Hull from the State Department entertained foreign diplomats and potentates by bringing them to the play. The Duke of Windsor and his attractive wife saw *Oklahoma!* half-a-dozen times, and on one occasion I conducted him backstage where he bashfully made a charming speech to the equally charming company. "There's your favorite," said the Duchess pointing to Joan McCracken, the little dancer who originally fell down, and with whom the Duke shook hands and made some stammering compliments like an admiring schoolboy.

It soon became apparent that *Oklahoma!* would stay at the St. James Theater for a number of years, and that it would be advisable to produce a touring company to go to Chicago. I disliked the idea of calling this a "road" company, so I christened our new company the National Company of *Oklahoma!*, and the name "National" has been appended to the company ever since.

The National Company,[2] which was brilliantly reproduced by Jerry Whyte, opened in New Haven and went to Washington, where Governor Robert S. Kerr, the six-foot-three Governor of Oklahoma, appeared on the stage at the National Theatre and made a speech in which he tendered the thanks of the people of Oklahoma for the service done the State. The actors and actresses were then entertained by the Washington branch of the Oklahoma Society in the ballroom of the Willard Hotel. The entertainment was lavish, the guests were charming and the food was excellent, but somebody had neglected to tell the actors and actresses that because Oklahoma was a "dry" state, tea, coffee and soft drinks were the only beverages which were served. This dampened the spirits of some of the members of the company, who were quite tired from their exertions. Consequently many of us not unnaturally slipped out of the ballroom to the bar downstairs.

This came to the attention of our friend Mrs. Perle Mesta, now Minister to Luxemburg, whose father was the owner of the Skirven Hotel in Oklahoma City. She immediately wired the Chamber of Commerce of Oklahoma City and they ordered another party for the National Company at the Sulgrove, which was a hilariously gay affair, and the Chamber of Commerce also tendered a party to the New York Company at the Stork Club on the occasion of its first birthday, sending a delegation from Oklahoma City to the party. From then on we were taken under the wing of the Oklahoma Legislature. All the actors, actresses and others concerned were made honorary citizens of the State of Oklahoma, a privilege which we were assured by a would-be humorist, would allow us to obtain divorces in that state without becoming residents.

When Governor Kerr of Oklahoma made the keynote speech for the Democratic Party at the famous Chicago convention which nominated Roosevelt and Truman in the year 1944, the orchestra played "Oklahoma!" as a prelude to the Governor's keynote speech, and "Oh What a Beautiful Mornin'" was employed to underline the Democratic optimism that Roosevelt would win the election, which he did. An enthusiastic member of the Oklahoma State Legislature moved to have

---

[2] The principal members of the cast of the National Company of *Oklahoma!* included Harry Stockwell, Betty Jane Watson, Pamela Britten, David Burns, Walter Donahue, Dania Krupska, Alfred Cibelli, Mary Marlo, Gemze de Lappe and Lou Polan.

the song "Oklahoma!" made the national anthem of the State, but he was thwarted by a woman member of the Legislature who pointed out that since the song stated "Every night my honey-lamb and I sit alone and talk," it might give the children wrong ideas.

We were constantly receiving invitations to visit Oklahoma City. November 25, 1946, was set for our opening, and Governor Kerr and the Chamber of Commerce of Oklahoma City prepared a Western welcome which was to be writ large in the saga of *Oklahoma!* We left from New York while Rouben Mamoulian and his wife Azadia came from Los Angeles. As we arrived at the station the rain was pouring, but the loud-speakers were booming "Oh, What a Beautiful Mornin'." An old stage coach with six horses was awaiting us. The streets were gaily decorated with flags flying and foliage entwined around the lampposts. The governor and citizens had prepared a parade which included several thousand horsemen, cowboys from all over the state, Indians, floats and livestock. The weather had been showery, and soon the streets were deluged with sleet and ice, which made them so slippery that it was deemed unsafe for the hundreds of horses and riders to parade over the icebound pavements. The town was full of the disappointed thousands who had poured in for the parade, but this did not disturb the indoor festivities, which continued for an entire week. The play opened in the Municipal Auditorium, and the attendance at *Oklahoma!* in this one week broke all records for attendance at any theatrical attraction, anywhere, up to that time.

One evening in Oklahoma City, at an unusual ceremony, Terry, Armina and I were adopted into the Kiowa Indian tribe. We were given costumes, feathered headdress, beads and regalia, as well as the titles "Little Woman Who Sees Far" for Terry, "Princess of the Plains" for Oklahoma-born Armina, and "Master of Entertainment" for myself. Dick, Oscar and Rouben were later adopted into the same tribe, the Indians having given the management priority under the impression that they were more important than the writer, composer and director. Later, my association with the Kiowa tribe almost caused a catastrophe. Traveling to Chicago, I met a huge drunken Indian on the train who insisted on conversing with me in tones seldom quieter than a shout. To calm him down, I told him I was a member of the Kiowa Indian tribe. This made him furious, and he rose, his huge bulk towering over me. "You Kiowa Indian!" he grunted. "You wrestle with me!" "I'm sorry," I replied, "it's my bedtime now!", and I beat a hasty retreat from the smoking car. After this experience I no longer tell Indians that I am one of their brothers by adoption.

The time came for us to open *Oklahoma!* in England. While I was in London during the winter of 1947, I had seen a production of Noel Coward's musical called *Pacific 1868* at Drury Lane, with Mary Martin in the lead. I decided that when we sent *Oklahoma!* to England, we would surprise the English musical theatre by sending over the principals and a chorus with the men all virile and over six feet tall, and with chorus girls who could not only sing and dance well but who were also attractive to the eye.[3]

To represent us in bringing *Oklahoma!* to London, I luckily made an arrangement with Hugh Beaumont, known to his legion of friends as "Binkie," the sprightly boyish-looking leader of the English managers, on whom success sits as lightly as a plume on a hat.

Then began a race to open in London before our thunder was stolen by another robust American musical, *Annie Get Your Gun.* We selected some of the best actors from both our National and New York Companies, and a new chorus and *corps de ballet,* and Jerry Whyte, who was now our Musical Production Manager rushed the London Company into rehearsal.

Then came the problem of getting passage on the over-crowded ships. Twelve of the Company sailed on a freighter, the S.S. *Malancha.* A large number flew over, while Jerry and his wife, Jeannette, and Armina and I took passage on the *Queen Elizabeth,* along with seventeen large cases full of costumes. Our voyage was uneventful until a few hours before arriving at Southampton, when the *Queen Elizabeth* struck a sandbank and was grounded. As the tide went out, there was the danger of the huge boat overturning, and I spent an anxious night as I watched the efforts of about twenty-five tugboats which attempted to pull us off the sandbank. This was a thrilling experience, as each little tugboat, chugging its hardest in a desperate effort to pull the great mass of the *Queen Elizabeth* off the bottom, eventually gave up, emitting short snorts of disgust as they turned back. Finally, we were all taken off on tenders and transported the rest of the way to Southampton, Beatrice Lillie leading the crowded procession off the ship wearing a hat with a long peacock feather which was continually getting in my eyes as she conversed with me and Terence Rattigan with staccato movements of her head.

The costumes for the play had to be left on board and we disembarked on Tuesday, and as we were to open in Manchester on

---

[3] The principal members of the original English Company were Harold Keel, Betty Jane Watson, Henry F. Clark, Walter Donahue, Dorothea MacFarland, Mary Marlo, Erik Kristen, Gemze de Lappe and Marek Windheim.

Friday night, we were quite disturbed, especially as we learned that fourteen automobiles were piled up on the top of the hold, and would have to be removed before the sailors could get to our costumes. The very efficient Tennent office who represented us in London arranged to have a special tender pick up the costumes later, and transport them by a convoy of trucks to Manchester, where the British Customs Officials obligingly examined them in the theatre as they were unpacked.

After a most auspicious two weeks' engagement in Manchester, we prepared for our opening in London. When the production was taken into the Theatre Royal, Drury Lane, we found ourselves in real trouble. Unaccustomed to the methods of the British theatre, our Chief Carpenter Abe Kurnit fretted and fumed. He had arrived during the worst cold spell England had had for years, to supervise the making of the scenery under incredible difficulties. All his preliminary work, such as explaining the blueprints to the British carpenters, was done by candlelight, with the workmen working in their overcoats, and with semifrozen hands and feet. He lost thirty pounds in weight as a result of the experience. At Drury Lane the stagehands walked in and out as they pleased, stopping every so often for a cup of tea or a glass of beer. The flymen got tired and went home; and it looked as though we could not possibly open by Wednesday, April 30, 1947, the date set for our opening night performance.

Owing to differences between their methods and ours, the Electrical Department was utterly confused. They transferred the production from the portable switchboard we had used in Manchester to the Drury Lane equipment which was then over forty years old and full of antiquated devices. It took half an hour to set a cue, and then they set it wrong. We finally ran our dress and lighting rehearsal on the day of the performance. The ballet dancers, although they had rehearsed on an inclined stage in Manchester, found the slope much greater at Drury Lane, and had to practice dancing up and down hill, which made them very nervous. Because of all these mishaps, we were all extremely anxious as to what kind of an opening performance we would give under these handicaps. We gave final instructions to the electricians, "If in doubt, turn on the lights!"

The opening night of *Oklahoma!* at Drury Lane is one which I shall never forget. At about half past six, the beautiful red-white-and-gold auditorium of Drury Lane Theatre began to fill with hundreds of men and women in evening dress, decked out for a gala occasion, one of the most festive since the end of the war. The women were wearing their prettiest clothes which, since they were still in the depths of austerity, made the occasion seem like the good old days to the war-weary people who attended. Armina and I were given the box known as the Duke of Bedford's, while sitting across from us in the Royal box was Prince Littler, the modest owner of most of the English theatres, and a group of his friends. Prince gave me a key to a private staircase by which I could descend to the stage in a hurry in case of need, and I was told that this staircase had been used in bygone times by defunct Dukes of Bedford to visit the actors and actresses (especially the actresses) on the stage during intermissions.

The audience was in at ten to seven, and sat quietly listening to the overture. Then, at seven, the curtain rose and disclosed Mary Marlo as Aunt Ella churning in front of her farmhouse, with the golden Oklahoma scenery behind her. Then Harold Keel as Curly the cowboy, in all the glory of his six-feet-two inches of height came on, and his voice filled the great theatre and his breezy Western charm captivated the audience. At the end of the song, Keel received prolonged applause. I never saw an actor do a better job of winning his audience immediately. Jerry Whyte and I, who had been standing at the side of the orchestra stalls, stole out into the passage, shook hands, and he remarked, "We're in." From then on it was a riot. At the end of the De Mille ballet there was a tremendous burst of applause, and this applause continued right down to the drop of the curtain of Act 1.

In the lobby, during the intermission, the audience was wildly excited, the men and women milling around, absorbing drinks and exchanging enthusiastic comments. The so-called British reserve was conspicuous by its absence. At the beginning of Act 2, "The Farmer and the Cowman" brought the house down again, and the applause at the end of the dance number was so great that the actors had to stop and wait. Finally, Mary Marlo, who played Aunt Ella, with rare presence of mind shot her pistol in the air, which stopped the applause, and the actors were then able to continue. From then on the applause kept building and building until we reached the song ensemble number "Oklahoma!" which was received with such tumultuous shouts and hand clappings that the Company had to repeat it over and over. The laughter of the audience during the last act was almost continuous, far more than we were used to in the States. Then the final curtain came down to a tremendous volley of applause. Prince Littler had suggested to me and our London partner, Hugh Beaumont, that instead of making speeches at the end (which was the usual London custom), we reprise some of the numbers. First the Company sang "People Will Say We're in Love." Howard Reinheimer, Dick and Oscar's lawyer, was sitting next to me in our box, and I remarked, "Howard, let us remember this particular moment in our lives. Its like will never happen again."

We were looking out over the large auditorium with its four galleries and masses of boxes. The two thousand people in the audience were shouting "Bravo, bravo!" and applauding like madmen, and each time the curtain rose, there was a rising roar from the audience. After taking a dozen more curtain calls, the Company went into formation and sang "Oklahoma!" again and again and again. By this time, the audience went really wild, standing up, cheering, applauding, laughing and weeping.

After twenty minutes of this, it was decided to call a halt, and when the curtain came down again and, quickly, before there was another chance for more curtain calls, the orchestra played "God Save the King" and ended the most exciting opening I have ever attended.

The saga of *Oklahoma!* still continues. It has already played in Australia, South Africa, Sweden and Norway and will doubtless be given wherever there is a musical theatre to house it. Our National Company, in which the Guild takes great pride, has been touring the United States for the past eight years, and unless present signs are deceptive, may continue to do so for many years to come.

CHAPTER XXIX

Tallulah, Carousel, *and the Lunts*

FROM 1943 on, after our success with *Oklahoma!,* Terry and I returned to the dramatic theatre much in the same way that the homing pigeon returns to its cote, making excursions, however, into the field of the musical theatre from time to time, where the grass sometimes seemed greener.

Our first play after *Oklahoma!* was Shakespeare's *Othello,* which Margaret Webster fashioned into a masterpiece of production, casting as the jealous Moor the Negro actor, Paul Robeson; Jose Ferrer was cast as Iago and Uta Hagen as Desdemona. By using Paul Robeson, who played the Moor with great sincerity and dignity, the play became extremely modern, and indeed he seemed to portray vividly the role of the Negro in the welter of our present racial problems. The flamboyant Jose Ferrer was also excellent in an unhackneyed interpretation of Iago.

Our last play of the season, the almost unpronounceable *Jacobowsky and the Colonel,* was written by S. N. Behrman, based on Franz Werfel's original play, in which the famous French actress Annabella appeared with the Viennese actor Oscar Karlweis and our own Louis Calhern, who played the part of the Polish Colonel.

This play passed through some strange metamorphoses before it was successfully presented on the stage of the Martin Beck Theatre. It came into being as a result of a story told by Werfel to S. N. Behrman and others at a Hollywood dinner party about a Jewish refugee who was running away from Paris to avoid being crushed under the heels of the Nazi invaders. The little refugee Jacobowsky meets the romantic Polish Colonel, and together this ill-assorted couple journey through France, Jacobowsky with his practical Jewish mind and the Colonel with his medieval Polish mind furnishing a comedic contrast against the somber background of the Nazi conquest. Werfel felt that to secure the best treatment of this idea, he should find a manager and an adapter; unfortunately for Werfel he chose the dynamic genius of Jed Harris, and the impact was so dynamic that Werfel was thrown off balance until Harris retired from the scene.

With *Jacobowsky and the Colonel* I first worked with the now famous director Elia Kazan who was engaged by us to direct the play. Kazan, known to his friends as "Gadget," had a slight boyish figure, a Mediterranean cast of features and an irresistible smile. He is a first generation Greek-American, and a graduate of the Yale School of Drama and the Group Theatre, both of which he had weathered successfully. His boyish appearance is deceptive, however, for he possesses great maturity. It was a constant pleasure to work with him, so enthusiastic were his responses, and so vivid his imagination, and there was always a sense of gaiety in everything he did. All these are adjuncts to a remarkable directorial talent which has carried him to the highest position in the theatre and motion pictures while still in his thirties.

With the team consisting of Kazan, Sam Behrman, Theresa Helburn and myself, we set to work producing *Jacobowsky and the Colonel* under extraordinary difficulties, Werfel being in California and too ill to come to New York, while he insisted on approval of the version, which he later transferred to me, so that I had to act as umpire, so to speak, between his ideas and Behrman's. Werfel's earlier difficulties with the play had affected his heart, and I was in constant fear that any controversy between himself and Behrman might produce another attack. Werfel wanted a "heavy" treatment of the subject, while Sam achieved the same results in comedic terms. I decided in favor of Sam's treatment, to which Werfel ultimately became reconciled, although he reserved the right to publish his own original version and actually did so later. The play opened at the Martin Beck Theatre, and ran an entire season there, and also on the road, to the acclaim both of critics and audiences. During the run of the play, our public had great difficulty pronouncing the Polish name "Jacobowsky" in the title. One day a Pole standing outside the theatre looking at the display sign reading "Jacobowsky and the Colonel" was heard to remark to his friend, "How on earth do you pronounce this word 'Colonel'?"

In the year 1944 we moved out of the Guild Theatre into the building which the Guild now occupies at 23 West Fifty-third Street. This building, which Lillian Gish christened "The Embassy," was occupied at the time we took it by a White Russian Social Club, and had had many ups and downs before it fell into our hands. At one time it was a private gambling club known as the Metropolitan Club, and there were rumors that the room which served as my office was the main gambling room. I sometimes reflect that while the Theatre Guild is the more respectable institution, the room is still being used for gambling. It was said that one time the building had been used as a disorderly house, and I was informed by an actor that after we occupied it, an old gentleman was walking along Fifty-third Street when he noticed a number of attractive young women entering the building. "Ah! They're still in business," he thought, as his mind went back to some years earlier. He entered the sumptuous marble lobby, and noted that the "house" was replete with modern improvements including a telephone switchboard operated by a girl. "I should like to see the Madam," he stated. "I'm sorry," said the telephone girl, "Miss Helburn in away in Europe!"

Despite its magnificence, our new home, said to have been occupied at one time by Whitelaw Reid, formerly ambassador to England, made a relatively inexpensive suite of offices for the Guild and its various activities. My own room, formerly the library, was so large and luxurious as to remind one of Mussolini's private office, and kept me in a constant state of apology to those who entered it. I decided to use it as the Guild library, and I placed my desk in one corner with a sign reading "Librarian." A large ballroom on the second floor was used as a rehearsal room, and the first play to be rehearsed there was *Embezzled Heaven,* based on Franz Werfel's novel, with Ethel Barrymore in the role of a Hungarian cook. As the cook worked for a Countess, and Ethel looked more like the Countess than the cook, this can hardly be said to have been a triumph of casting.

Another play of this season was *Sing Out, Sweet Land* by Walter Kerr, the first musical play to use the folk music of America. A few months before this production took place, on one of the very rare occasions on which I visited a night club, I had heard a relatively unknown singer named Burl Ives singing at "Café Society Uptown." Our production was memorable because it introduced Burl Ives to the American public as the greatest singer of American folk songs, but this was by no means easy. After two or three days of rehearsal, Burl simply refused to attend, and we sent a stage manager over to Long

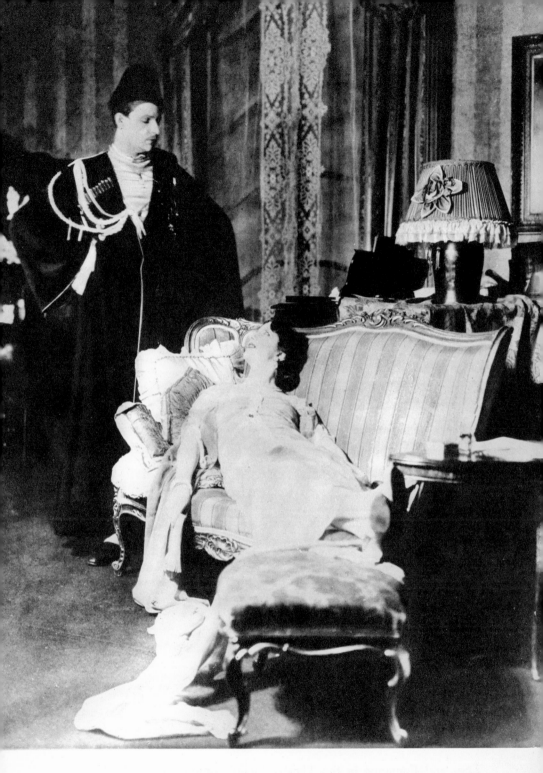

Lunt and Fontanne in their first joint appearance in the
Theatre Guild's production of Molnar's *The Guardsman*,
1924.

Lunt and Fontanne in the Theatre Guild's production
of Maxwell Anderson's *Elizabeth, the Queen*, 1930.

Above: Alfred Lunt, Lynn Fontanne and Henry Travers in the Theatre Guild's production of Robert Sherwood's *Reunion in Vienna*, 1931. *Below:* Lunt and Fontanne in S. N. Behrman's *The Pirate*, 1942.

Above: Alfred Lunt and chorus in the Theatre Guild's production of Robert Sherwood's *Idiot's Delight*, 1936. *Below:* Lunt and Fontanne in *Idiot's Delight*.

Lunt and Fontanne in S. N. Behrman's adaptation of
Giradoux' *Amphitryon 38*, produced by the Theatre Guild,
1937. Alfred Lunt as Jupiter and Lynn Fontanne as Alkmena.

Lunt and Fontanne in the Theatre Guild's
production of S. N. Behrman's *I Know My
Love*, 1949.

Island Sound to the barge on which he lived. The stage manager stood on the shore, waved to Burl and shouted, "Please come to rehearsal!" Burl rowed over eventually, and was persuaded to attend, but he definitely liked the barge better.

This season we also produced *Foolish Notion* by Philip Barry, which was notable for the fact that Tallulah Bankhead, for the first time in her career, acted for the Theatre Guild. In her early days in the theatre, and before she had achieved fame in this country, I had been attracted by her talent and, at her request, had given her a letter of recommendation to Basil Dean, the London producer, who was casting our play, *They Knew What They Wanted*. Tallulah called on him on her arrival in London and completely captivated him with her charm, and without bothering to give him my letter, secured the Pauline Lord part which was the beginning of her successful English career. I was particularly pleased to have her with us after so many years, and since her lion was no longer with her, I anticipated no particular difficulties. When the play opened in New Haven, it was apparent that a certain amount of rewriting of the third act had to be done and Phil Barry agreed that this would be finished by the time the play arrived in Baltimore. After the Baltimore opening, the entire company sat around on the stage with Tallulah in the center, while the stage manager passed around the rewritten third act. Tallulah read a few pages, and then threw the script violently on the floor and flounced out of the theatre. We were confronted with a first-class crisis. Tallulah retired to her hotel rooms with her entourage, while we retired to our rooms with ours. We all decided to see her that evening and have it out with her. This was a mistake. We should have known better.

When we arrived in Tallulah's rooms with John C. Wilson, she was in what may be delicately described as a high dudgeon, while her friend Dola (Mrs. Cavendish) was doing her best to soothe her. "You ought to have a great playwright like Noel Coward write you a great play!" said Dola with consummate tact as Phil Barry entered the room. "Darlings," said Tallulah, regarding me with a fishy eye, "The trouble with all you Theatre Guild people is—you are *too* normal!" She then went on to describe how all great writers from Shakespeare down to today were, to say the least, peculiar, and we left a few minutes later with the general feeling that matters had gone from bad to worse, for Phil could match Tallulah with his own brand of temperament, and indeed from every standpoint as an author he was completely justified.

In retrospect, I realize that both of our artists were justified from their own point of view, Tallulah because of her disappointment with the scene she had been promised, and Phil because of the display of fireworks which illuminated her displeasure.

The next morning we tried to calm Phil, but the more we tried, the worse matters became, for Phil grew progressively redder and redder in the face until finally his nose began to bleed, and I thought he was on the point of apoplexy, Armina rushed off to the doctor with him, and he was ordered to Johns Hopkins Hospital, as he had apparently broken a small blood vessel. Tallulah calmed down somewhat when she realized that no further changes in the third act were likely to be forthcoming with the author in the hospital. *Foolish Notion* continued its tour to Washington for two weeks while Phil recuperated. Meanwhile, Tallulah began to run a temperature. This did not seem to bother her. "The curious thing about me, darling," said Tallulah to me, quite seriously, "is that I give my best performances when I am slightly ill, because then my diaphragm is not quite so powerful." Tallulah, despite stories to the contrary, is extremely conscientious about her public. "I'm not worried about myself in this play, darling, but what I *am* worried about is what happens to the play when I'm not on the stage." This was a perfectly good comment, for Tallulah is a wonderful showwoman, and as long as she is on the stage she gives her public what it wants.

Tallulah telephoned me in New York one evening just before the end of the Washington run and said, "Darling! The doctor tells me that if I have a temperature of 102°, I won't be able to go on to-morrow, and I'm just *under* that now." I hastened to Washington the next day, and after the performance that evening Tallulah retired to her room, while Armina and I visited John C. Wilson, our director, in his room, which was on the same floor in the Willard Hotel. We shuttled back and forth down the long corridors for conferences from one suite to the other for an hour or so, after which Tallulah retired to her bedroom and returning a few minutes later, remarked, "Well, darlings, my temperature is 102° so I can't go on tomorrow." I went to bed feeling glum about the entire proceedings, for Phil was arriving the next day from the hospital with some new pages he had written while resting in contemplative convalescence. The following morning Dola telephoned Armina, who was acting as Associate Producer, and said, "Tallulah woke up this morning feeling much better, but she hasn't eaten for days. We've been trying to get a chicken at the hotel here, but there are none on account of the rationing." Armina scurried around Washington trying to locate a cold roast chicken, and ultimately found one. Tallulah ate it for her breakfast and thereupon behaved like an angel, accepted her new lines without any adverse comment, and played out the Washington engagement in the most beatific manner.

It so happened that the play called for a child actress, and under the Washington civic regulations, children under fourteen may not appear in plays there. Consequently, a midget is generally used to play such parts and a diminutive young lady was engaged for the child and appeared with Tallulah, which had the effect of upsetting her greatly. "I'm determined to play with the real child before I leave Washington," said Tallulah, "and I mean it!" We were all concerned at the chance of her breaking the law. "Why do *you* worry," she said, "By the time the police come after you, we will all have left town." Our tactful manager, Peter Davis, who was well versed in the art of getting along with Tallulah, said, "Tallulah, you know the Bankheads are famous in Washington for making the laws, not for breaking them. Don't you want to continue the family tradition?" He touched a tender spot. "You're quite right, darling," she said. "Dad certainly wouldn't want me to break a law." And she gave up.

A few years later Phil Barry called at my office, having just completed his last play, *Second Threshold.* He was in a benign mood and I thought I had never seen him so calm and happy. The next day I learned of his death. Working with Phil on a play was always an exciting experience. He was both a poet and a writer of deft comedy, and he used the English language as a composer uses point and counterpoint, achieving many of his effects from the timing and quality of word sounds as well as from their meaning. Phil, for the most part, especially in the day time, had the disposition of an angel, but at night conferences he could be difficult. His emotional involvement in his plays was great, but he was always helped by the presence of his wife, Ellen Barry, who with her tact, good taste and warmth was a calming influence on everyone during the hectic times when a Barry play was being born on the stage. Terry and I spent Christmas with Phil and Ellen in Paris in the year 1946, and Phil's sweetness and gentleness and Ellen's kindness and wisdom made memorable a Christmas Eve spent away from home in the otherwise cheerless atmosphere of a strange hotel. With his passing, the field of the American comedy of manners has become almost uninhabited.

Foolish Notion was indifferently received in New York, but did very well on tour. We were now riding high after having opened *Oklahoma!* followed by *Othello* and *Jacobowsky and the Colonel.* And better still, we prepared another Rodgers and Hammerstein musical which in some respects represented an advance over *Oklahoma!*

Soon after *Oklahoma!* opened in New York we began to talk with Richard Rodgers and Oscar Hammerstein about the possibility of working on another musical together. Dick Rodgers was very frank in regard to his attitude. "We will work for anyone who brings us a good idea," he replied. Terry and I worked hard to find another good idea for them. She and I agreed that *Liliom* would make an excellent libretto for a musical. However, there were a number of complications. First of all, neither Rodgers nor Hammerstein seemed to find the subject entirely to their taste, while Ferenc Molnar, the author of *Liliom*, was not at all enthusiastic about having his classic of the theatre transformed into a musical play. We decided that the best way to solve the problem was to arrange for Molnar to see *Oklahoma!* and then to make his decision. At an interview with Theresa Helburn and myself after he had seen the musical, he confessed that if Rodgers and Hammerstein could treat the subject of *Liliom* as tastefully and charmingly as they had treated *Oklahoma!*, he would give his consent.

Our only obstacle now was Rodgers and Hammerstein, and they were a tough obstacle, for it took almost nine months of discussion before they finally agreed that a story as foreign to the American scene as *Liliom* could be made into an American musical folk play. It was only when Richard Rodgers thought of using a New England background, that matters began to progress. We were helped in this by the fact that while Armina and I were in Los Angeles a few months earlier, Armina's niece, a young lady considerably taller than Armina who responded to the name of "Little Armina," told her of a very fine singer named John Raitt who sang at their high-school concerts, and had recently won a prize for singing in radio. Armina met this young man in Hollywood at a time when there was no piano available for her to hear him sing, but she had one of her "hunches," and came into the adjoining room where I was engaged in a conference, saying, "I wish you would meet a young man, John Raitt, who reminds me of Spencer Tracy in appearance, and is said to have a very good voice." I met John Raitt and was also impressed by his appearance, but had absolutely no idea as to how well he could sing.

Some months later, when we were looking for a replacement for the part of Curly in *Oklahoma!*, Armina insisted that we bring John Raitt from California and have him sing at an audition for Dick, Oscar and ourselves. The morning of the audition, Armina was very nervous. "Good Lord," she said, "supposing he can't sing!"

At the audition, John Raitt, a veritable young giant, came on the stage before the group consisting of Dick Rodgers, Oscar Hammerstein, Theresa Helburn, myself and Armina, who was sitting on the edge of her seat wondering what the outcome would be. Raitt stepped forward on the stage and said, "Do you mind if I warm up by singing the Barber's song from *The Barber of Seville* so that I can loosen up my voice?" He was told to go ahead, and stepped onto the apron of the stage and sang the Barber's song with such zest, execution, beauty of voice and clarity of diction, that we were all carried away by the excitement of the occasion. As he began to sing the second verse, Dick Rodgers, who was sitting behind me, leaned over and whispered in my ear, "There is our Liliom!" From then on the making of a musical play based on *Liliom* was assured.

In due course *Liliom* was transformed into *Carousel* by Rodgers and Hammerstein and with the integrated production by Rouben Mamoulian and ballets by Agnes De Mille, became, in my opinion, the finest American musical play of our time.

An unusual result of the uncanny collaboration of Rodgers and Hammerstein, was to make the musical play considerably deeper than the original play of Molnar, for they carried into it, through the ballet which was worked out with Agnes De Mille, and in the final scene of the play, a story of father-child relationship which is not to be found in the play from which *Carousel* was fashioned. Molnar was delighted with the work done by Rodgers and Hammerstein and attended one of the later rehearsals, sitting in the rear of the theatre. Nobody recognized him, and someone asked, "Who is that white-haired gentleman who is weeping so copiously?" It turned out to be Molnar. Indeed, everyone at the rehearsal was weeping so copiously that as I left to board a train with Terry Helburn, I remarked, "I'm afraid they have made the play far too sad. I doubt whether anyone will pay $6 for tickets to have their hearts completely broken."

The play opened in New Haven and the results were not unlike those connected with the opening of *Oklahoma!* The first act seemed to require the least amount of work while the second act was chaotic. Rodgers and Hammerstein had the idea of using a Mr. and Mrs. God in the proceedings, who turned out to be very gloomy indeed, for one could hardly be jocular on the subject. A number of changes were made in the play, including the elimination of a maternity scene in the ballet, in which Julie gave birth to her child—a scene which Agnes De Mille, not a girl to waste her ideas, promptly put into another ballet. With some excellent suggestions from Molnar and Mamoulian on the book, we arrived in Boston with a second act which was on its way toward the perfection which it later achieved.

Along with Dick Rodgers, I felt that a reprise of the love song "If I Loved You" was necessary toward the end of the play, but I met with considerable resistance to this idea. "Once you do this," said the authorities, "the members of the audience will reach for their hats and will never wait for the end of the play." However, I became quite obstinate on the subject, and to please me, or to silence me by proving their point, the reprise was put in. That evening I stayed in the theatre to watch the effect and I realized as I saw the audience reach for their hats and begin to rise and leave the theatre, that Dick and I were wrong, while the others were unquestionably right. I went backstage afterward to admit my error, when Dick Rodgers came up to me with a happy gleam in his eyes. "What sheet-music song do you suppose has sold the most copies of all those that are being offered in the lobby?" "I have no idea," I replied. " 'If I Loved You'! The sales went way up tonight, and it now looks as though it will be the hit song of the show," said Dick. "But you will have to take that reprise out," I said. "It just doesn't work. The people want to go home." "Take it out?" said Dick. "Not at all. We'll find some way to use it so the people won't want to go home." It took a week's work before this was achieved.

Finally, *Carousel* came to New York and was installed in the Majestic Theatre.[1] Things went quite badly on the dress rehearsal night, and I left the theatre thoroughly discouraged. I went home and the next morning I remarked despondently to Armina, "What an absurd occupation this is. Months have been spent on writing this musical, more months in producing it, $180,000 has been invested in it, yet on the basis of one evening's performance, all this may go down in defeat. This is the very last play I will *ever* do." Armina had heard this kind of talk before, and she knew that in time it would wear off, but nobody could have felt gloomier than I did on the opening of *Carousel* in New York City. Richard Rodgers, whose back had been hurt during the Boston tryout, had to be wheeled into the theatre on a stretcher, and I thought I never saw him look so much the very picture of a composer and artist as when he lay helpless with his hair ruffled on a pillow and listened to the wonderful score of *Carousel,* which I consider to be his masterpiece to date.

---

[1] The original cast of *Carousel* included Jan Clayton, John Raitt, Bambi Linn, Jean Darling, Jean Casto, Christine Johnson, Eric Mattson, Peter Birch, Murvyn Vie, Annabelle Lyon, Russell Collins, Robert Pagent, and Jay Velie.

This musical play again made history, and although it did not have the universally popular appeal of *Oklahoma!* it nevertheless ran a close second and played two successful years in New York at the Majestic Theatre, a considerably larger theatre than the St. James where *Oklahoma!* played for five years. It also toured for two seasons and played later in the Royal Theatre, Drury Lane, London.

After *Carousel*, indeed, it seemed as if the luck of the Theatre Guild was henceforth to be bound up with the fabulous fortunes of Rodgers and Hammerstein. As if destiny wanted to warn us against too much dependence on anyone, however, our last musical venture with Dick and Oscar was less fortunate, as we were to discover in the fall of 1947.

Allegro, the third Rodgers and Hammerstein opus, made by no means as happy a chapter as the earlier two plays. There was an extremely cumbersome scenic investiture, which made it difficult to operate the stage, and moreover Oscar Hammerstein had to devote a great deal of his time to helping the direction of the play. The same teamwork which had resulted in the success of *Oklahoma!* and *Carousel* was missing, and the results were unwieldy and unconvincing. This was unfortunate, because the play broke many traditions, and was moving in the direction of an advanced American musical theatre. Oscar's thesis was really an excellent one, and would have been appreciated by the very critics who misunderstood it, had not his message been obscured by the production.

Lessons in the mutability of fortune and in the impossibility of absolutely relying on any playwright or director or policy in the unpredictable theatre multiplied, indeed, for us at this time. Thus, we had a failure with a Behrman play, *Dunnigan's Daughter*, in spite of Sam Behrman's talent for high comedy and in spite of our having placed the direction in the hands of Elia Kazan, whose contribution to *A Streetcar Named Desire* and *Death of a Salesman* would have made it seem that a Kazan production was a passport to success. We also dropped about $100,000 in a venture, chiefly of my inspiration, to establish a Shakespeare Acting Company. We started with productions of *A Winter's Tale* with Florence Reed, Jessie Royce Landis and Henry Daniell, and *The Merry Wives of Windsor*, with Charles Coburn playing Falstaff. Alas, our Acting Company was not strong enough to overcome the public apathy to what were two of Shakespeare's weaker plays, and despite all our efforts, the Company ended in disaster.

Fortunately, however, the Lunts proved more beneficent to us than the Stratford bard, and it was their production of a new British comedy that saved our season of 1945–46 from being entirely disheartening.

But it was quite customary for the Lunts to rush into the breach when other trusty forces in the theatre failed us. This time they returned from the war zone bringing with them Terence Rattigan's comedy *O Mistress Mine,* which they played in London under the title of *Love in Idleness.* The play provided Alfred and Lynn with splendid acting parts, and in my opinion, was a far better play than the critics here admitted it to be. American audiences were by now deeply wedded to the Lunts, and the New York engagement and the subsequent tour was a triumphal procession, ending with the closing in San Francisco on account of Alfred's illness.

By this time Alfred Lunt and Lynn Fontanne had written a vivid page in the history of the American theatre. Before they joined the Guild in *The Guardsman* in 1924, I had seen Alfred on the stage only once before, in Booth Tarkington's *Clarence,* where his high spirits and gaiety made him the center of interest, and I had seen Lynn in the title role of *Dulcy,* her first major part in this country. The couple brought such zest and vitality to their acting, and there was such interplay of point and counterpoint in their scenes together, that soon one began to think of them almost as one personality—named Lynn-and-Alfred—a personality capable of miraculously endowing every couple they portrayed with the qualities of beauty, charm, wit, gaiety and enormous interest in one another. "How can any other actors expect to play together as well as Alfred and Lynn?" complained an actress bitterly. "They rehearse in bed!" "Would you like to meet Alfred and Lynn backstage and congratulate them on their acting?" I asked George Bernard Shaw after he had seen and liked them in *Caprice.* "It's not acting," said Shaw. "It's performing!"

Alfred and Lynn have made only one motion picture, *The Guardsman,* so that posterity may at least take a look at them as they were when they played in this masterpiece of light comedy. But no picture can convey the sheer delight which the audiences of our time have enjoyed in watching their virtuoso acting, which can range, as occasions demand, from delicate sentiment to deep emotion and tragedy, from moods of gaiety and light laughter to the savage laughter of satire or irony. When the Lunts played a comedy scene together, you felt you were watching the iridescent darting of lights and color all over the stage—the gods of the theatre were good to the public when they brought them together, and they were good to the Theatre Guild when all three of us joined hands for the future.

Alfred and Lynn, both of them tall, slender and invariably well-turned out, always appear calm and cool at the rehearsals of their plays. They work without sparing themselves, paying the minutest attention to the minutest details. If they are tired or worried over whether a scene is going properly or needs rewriting, it is Alfred who usually shows signs of nerves. No matter what Lynn may be feeling, she always keeps herself well in hand, and where Alfred might be emotional or temperamental, she can be counted on to calm him down and to express her own point of view with clarity, and if necessary, with asperity. Alfred and Lynn always show an unselfish attitude toward one another. If a play has an excellent part for Alfred, but not for Lynn, Alfred can be counted on to tell us that it is Lynn's turn to have the better part; and Lynn will be equally concerned for Alfred. This made it quite difficult to find plays for them, until Robert Sherwood learned the formula of making the parts substantially equal. "What is the secret of your success in the theatre?" someone once asked Sherwood. "I write plays for the Lunts," he replied.

Once the play has opened, Alfred and Lynn treat it in a manner which is rare in the theatre. No mother could take care of her babies more conscientiously than the Lunts take care of their plays. Each performance is for them of equal importance. "It's cheating the public to take their money and then let down," I have often heard Lynn remark. And they demand from their company the same attitude toward their work that they themselves bring to it. Fooling on stage, breaking up other actors, and other devices for relieving the tedium of consecutive performances, are taboo with the Lunts, who work ceaselessly to deepen their parts and to find better ways of playing them. When *The Taming of the Shrew* returned to New York after over a year's tour, it was played infinitely better by the entire company than at the end of the New York run. After playing *O Mistress Mine* for three years, during the last Saturday matinee Alfred said to young Dick Van Patten, playing the juvenile, "I have a new idea for this scene. I think it will improve it. We have one more chance to try it before we close the play!" This attitude is so rare in the theatre that it calls for special mention, for usually after playing for a long time, most actors lose all interest and become automatic or indifferent.

When Alfred and Lynn celebrated their twenty-first year with the Theatre Guild, we presented them with a silver plaque on which all the plays in which they had appeared were mentioned by name, a trophy which symbolized a friendship and working relationship extending for a period longer than any which has existed, so far as I know, in the American theatre. The names of twenty-four plays appeared on the plaque.[2] When we celebrated their twenty-fifth anniversary with the Guild, on October 14, 1949, an additional play, S. N. Behrman's *I Know My Love*, their twenty-fifth, appeared on the list.

As I write these lines, the Lunts are just completing a long tour of this play, during which they have encountered blizzards, railroad strikes, and other mishaps, while for the greater part of the tour Lynn played her part with a broken wrist, her left arm in a sling, an example of stoicism that is rarely encountered nowadays. Yet both Alfred and Lynn felt that in touring this play, they were repaying an obligation to their audiences who have enthusiastically supported them all over the country, which is in the great tradition of the great actors of America—a tradition which they have been the foremost to uphold in our time.

---

[2] See Appendix VII, p. 472, for complete list of plays in which the Lunts have appeared for the Theatre Guild.

CHAPTER XXX

O'Neill and The Iceman Cometh

DURING the latter part of the thirties, I had little news from Eugene O'Neill, who was busily engaged in writing the monumental cycle of nine plays he had projected for himself. In our conversations and his press releases, he had stated that he did not want any of these plays to be produced until all were completed, partly because he did not wish to take the time off from writing to spend on production, and partly because he wished to finish them as a complete work of art before any individual play was presented. In the early part of 1940 I wrote him suggesting that we make a start with the cycle the following season, to which 'Gene replied under date of March 10.

You can't begin producing the cycle until the first plays are ready, even if I wanted any of it done before it's all completed, which I don't. So I tell you again, forget it. Go on as if you had never heard of it. I've made myself put it aside for the past seven months. Had gone terribly stale, as I told you when we talked over the phone, and did not start the fifth play beyond getting it all ready to start. Since then I have been working on other things. But forget that, too, until further notice, because it does not mean I will have anything for you to consider in making your plans for next year.

Later on, a mention in the newspapers about a new O'Neill play called *The Iceman Cometh* aroused our curiosity; the situation was explained fully by 'Gene in his letter of July 17, 1940:

One reason I haven't sent you or Terry a script is that there are only two in existence. I have one and I sent the other to Bennett Cerf to lock in the Random House safe for safekeeping—but not for publication. Don't blame Bennett for not telling you or Terry. I made him promise to keep it dark from everyone, bar none. Frankly, I did not want you to see it yet—in New York. I was afraid you would want to produce it right away and I don't want the strain of any production now. There are other good reasons against it, too. On the other hand, if you or Terry happened out this way, as you thought you might, then I could give you the script to read with the proviso that production was out for the present, and do all my explaining why at the same time. But the idea of trying to do all this in letters simply had me stopped. Hence the secrecy. To tell the truth, like anyone else with any imagination, I have been absolutely sunk by this damned world debacle. The Cycle is on the shelf, and God knows if I can ever take it up again because I cannot foresee any future in this country or anywhere else to which it could spiritually belong.

Well, to hell with that. I'm writing this to explain my past few months secrecy re the completion of *The Iceman Cometh,* and to say if you and Armina, Terry and Oliver, want to read this opus you can get the script from Bennett. I'm writing to release him from his pledge of secrecy as far as you and Terry are concerned. But give it back to Cerf to lock up in the safe afterwards, and *please don't* let anyone else see it. Remember only two scripts exist and it's no time to let too many people, even in the Guild, really know about it yet. And forget about any production.

I'm working again on something—not the Cycle—after a lapse of several months spent with an ear glued to the radio for war news. You can't keep a hop head off his dope for long!

The crushing of France hit Carlotta and me hard for sentimental reasons in addition to the larger aspects of the disaster. When Tours was lost we felt almost as badly as if Danville, California, had fallen.

Terry and I both read the new play, and felt it to be one of 'Gene's major works. 'Gene replied to my comments in a letter dated August 11, 1940:

Many thanks for your letter regarding *The Iceman Cometh.* I'm damned pleased you liked it so well. Personally, I love it! And I'm sure my affection is not wholly inspired by nostalgia for the dear dead days "on the bottom of the sea," either! I have a confident hunch that this play, as drama, is one of the best things I've ever done. In some ways, perhaps *the* best. What I mean is, there are moments in it that suddenly strip the secret soul of a man stark naked, not in cruelty or moral superiority, but with an understanding compassion which sees him as a victim of the ironies of life and of himself. Those moments are for me the depth of tragedy, with nothing more that can possibly be said.

'Gene could not get the war out of his mind. Early in 1941 he wrote me:

Yes, you're right, the world chaos is always on one's mind no matter what one does, and the nearer spring comes with its invasion of England threat, the

Knitting Women would have told of their varicose veins, flatulence, flat feet and what not. Danton would have muscled in with a long harangue on the horrible hangover he had yesterday morning. Robespierre would have addressed the mob for two hours on the new pills he was taking to get rid of his pimples. The Revolution would have been forgotten. Louis would have become the Well Beloved again—a Royal Pal. The Bourbon dynasty would have been saved. In fact, I think the quickest way to stop Hitler is for some Allied agent, disguised as a good listener, to ask him, "Well, Adolph, how are the old hysterics lately?" Hitler will promptly ask for an armistice in which to start the tale properly, and then sue for peace at any price in order to gain leisure to relate all his symptoms.

Fantastic, you say? Not a bit of it. Nerves are the most absorbing ailment of all. There is practically no limit to their symptoms. As I know. Why, listen, Lawrence, only last night I woke up suddenly in a cold sweat. Everything was shaking. I thought, my God, an earthquake! But it wasn't. It was me. And then—

But I better stop or I'll be writing you a brand new farce. You know me. Always, as I've said, writing about character plus life!

Armina and I called on 'Gene again at Tao House during the summer of 1942, and found that his health had been considerably impaired by his long siege of work and the mental suffering he was undergoing. We had some discussions regarding the production of *The Iceman Cometh*. It was 'Gene's idea at the time that Eddie Dowling (who, while he was playing in San Francisco in Saroyan's *The Time of Your Life*, had visited 'Gene at Tao House) would be the right man to play the part of Harry Hope. 'Gene had run into difficulties in completing the cycle, and stopped to write another play, *The Moon for the Misbegotten*, as well as the play entitled *A Long Day's Journey Into Night* which was not to be published until twenty-five years after his death.

Armina and I left Tao House feeling quite depressed about 'Gene's health, and we found that Carlotta, too, was ill, due to arthritis and the strain of running the isolated household at Tao House without adequate help. 'Gene's health was a constant source of worry to her, and the additional burden of taking care of all his correspondence and typing his manuscripts, as well as her other household duties, bore heavily on her. Under these circumstances, they decided to sell Tao House and to take a much needed rest. Carlotta had no trouble in finding a purchaser for the house, for it was, like every house she built, extremely beautiful and desirable and livable. They moved into San Francisco, where they took a suite of rooms in the Huntington Hotel on Nob Hill.

In the early summer of 1944, Armina and I again visited the O'Neills when they were living at the Huntington Hotel. We found 'Gene and

Carlotta considerably healthier and happier and 'Gene was hard at work making final revisions on the new plays. We discussed what plays were in shape for production and were being typed in final draft in San Francisco. While Armina talked with Carlotta, 'Gene recited the titles of the plays which he had written. First of all came *The Iceman Cometh* which he was willing to allow us to produce a little while after the war was over. He felt the timing for the play's opening was very important, and that if it were to be produced immediately after the war was over, the pessimism of the play would run counter to public optimism, and would result in a bad reception by the audience. He thought a year or so after the peace, there would be considerable disillusionment, and that the public would then be more inclined to listen to what he had to say in this play.

Just as Armina and I were about to leave 'Gene's apartment, he handed me, with one of his shy smiles, two manuscripts, one of which was his new play *A Moon for the Misbegotten* while the other was a long one-act play entitled *Hughie*. "I would like you to read these while you are here in San Francisco," he said, "and tell me what you think of them."

On returning to our hotel that evening, we read both of the new O'Neill plays. I was particularly delighted with *A Moon for the Misbegotten* which I regard as one of the greatest plays O'Neill has ever written, and one of the few truly great tragedies written in our times. The play has, in its final act, and at the end of the second act, the spiritual uplift which is the characteristic quality of all great tragedy, and along with it is such a profound knowledge of the good and evil in humanity as to raise it head and shoulders above *Anna Christie*, which it resembles to some extent in its father-daughter and lover relationship. Indeed, the maturity which 'Gene had reached as a dramatist can well be measured by contrasting these two magnificent plays; the first, *Anna Christie* with its partly happy ending (and I am not averse to happy endings), and *A Moon for the Misbegotten* with its ruthless tragic finality.

After a second reading of the play I began to realize some of the troubles which awaited us in casting it, for the leading woman was to be a veritable giantess—indeed, exactly the kind of woman who, when she comes to see you and asks you to advise her whether she should attempt a career in the theatre—you look embarrassed and reply, "Well, I'm afraid you're rather a big girl—how are we to find a man tall enough to play opposite you?" Yet, here in this play O'Neill wrote the tragedy of an oversized woman, making it an oversized job for any producer to find the right actress for the part. In addition to the physical requirements of the actress, she must be tremendously experienced in the theatre and must have exactly the kind of emotional acting experience that it would be difficult for a girl of her stature to obtain. I made a mental note of all the very big girls I knew —emphasizing the Irish quality which was needed—and the following day I went around to see 'Gene again. I told him I had read both of the plays and gave him my opinion of them. The one-act play entitled *Hughie*, which was in the form of a long monologue by the rooming clerk of a cheap hotel, struck me as a magnificent task for any character actor. 'Gene told me that he had another one-act play which, together with this play, might make a full evening in the theatre, but he did not give me this other play as it needed some further revision. There were to be five other one-act plays in monologue form, and the series was to be called *By Way of Obit*.

After I had described my feelings about *A Moon for the Misbegotten* to 'Gene, he said, "Well, if you like it so much, Lawrence, you can have it." Naturally, I was overjoyed, and told him we would produce it any time he wanted, and that as I was going to Hollywood I would immediately get in touch with Barry Fitzgerald, as we thought he would be ideal for the father. After some discussion, it was decided that it would be better to produce this play before *The Iceman Cometh*, and we decided to go ahead immediately with the casting, and to endeavor to interest Dudley Digges in directing the play. During our interview that day 'Gene remarked, "As you like *A Moon for the Misbegotten* so much, you can read my other play *A Touch of the Poet*, and we'll talk about the casting of that play as well." He then gave me the manuscript of this new play, which had just been finally typed, and after I read it I realized that it, too, was one of 'Gene's greatest plays. *A Touch of the Poet* also carried with it some extremely difficult casting problems and we discussed these in considerable detail before we left San Francisco. It was decided, however, that *A Touch of the Poet* should be the last of the three plays to be produced, and that the long one-act play should await the completion of the other one-act play before production.

I left San Francisco highly elated with the prospect of producing these plays after the war was over, our only worry being the state of 'Gene's health. While he enjoyed living in San Francisco, he missed the swimming and the sun which had been an everyday occurrence at Tao House. As we left, it was decided that we would produce one of the plays soon after the war was over, probably *A Moon for the*

Misbegotten, and that the O'Neills would come to New York for the opening, it being 'Gene's idea that the play should open there, while I, on the other hand, wanted the opening to take place in San Francisco, so that he would not be forced to move to New York.

We arrived in Hollywood bearing the priceless O'Neill manuscripts, and set out in search of an overlarge Irish damsel with the acting abilities of a Duse, who could fulfill the following requirements of the author:

JOSIE is twenty-eight. She is so oversize for a woman that she is almost a freak—five feet eleven in her stockings and weighs around one hundred and eighty. Her sloping shoulders are broad, her chest deep with large firm breasts, her waist wide but slender by contrast with her great hips and thighs. She has long smooth arms, immensely strong although no muscles show. The same is true of her legs.

She is more powerful than any but an exceptionally strong man, able to do the manual labor of two ordinary men. But there is no mannish quality about her. She is all woman.

Our hunt began with the agents and, assisted by Dudley Digges and Dudley Nichols, we began to interview a varied assortment of Irish giantesses. Alas for all our efforts, we were unable to find one; our search was not successful in Hollywood, and later on, when we extended it to New York City, to London and to Dublin, all our attempts were without results. The few very large Irish girls we were able to find had, for a very obvious reason, very little acting experience. Indeed, from the very beginning, we experienced a sense of frustration in the casting of the play. Since we had planned to open the season of 1946–47 with *A Moon for the Misbegotten,* we were in a quandary as to what to do, for in addition to the difficulty of casting the woman, Barry Fitzgerald had a very lucrative radio contract which made it impossible for him to leave Hollywood, while James Dunn, whom we had discussed as a possibility for the leading male role in the play, was also involved in film commitments.

Finally, in the fall of 1945, 'Gene and Carlotta felt it was imperative for them to come East. When 'Gene arrived in New York, we were shocked by the change in his appearance. Since the time we had left him in San Francisco, he seemed to have lost a great deal of weight. It was decided that we would cast *The Iceman Cometh* and that this play should be the first of the O'Neill plays presented by the Guild at the opening of the following season. The winter was spent in casting the play, and Armina acted as Associate Producer and worked

unceasingly with 'Gene, Eddie Dowling, Theresa Helburn and myself
in securing the very finest cast we could possibly obtain for the play.
After a few weeks in New York, 'Gene's health improved, and especially after he began to work on *The Iceman Cometh.* He enjoyed his
visits to the Guild offices each afternoon, and he began to put his
manuscript into final shape. We all felt the fact that he was at work
again in the theatre was doing wonders in bringing him back to
health. One afternoon in May, 1946, we assembled in the large rehearsal room of the Theatre Guild building and read *The Iceman
Cometh* aloud. This was valuable not only for purposes of cutting,
but it also gave us an opportunity to hear how the actors fitted the
parts, and the parts the actors, how their voices sounded in the roles,
and how their personalities seemed to fit in with the words which
they uttered.

We were all impressed with the very sensitive reading given by
James Barton in the part of Harry Hope, the owner of the saloon.
At the same time we all felt that the task of directing the play would
be enormously difficult, and that Dowling would have about as much
as he could handle in that department without attempting to play the
part of Hickey as well. This was a disappointment for Dowling, but
he deferred to our collective judgment. Later on, 'Gene felt that James
Barton would be excellent for Hickey and thought that we should engage someone else to play the part of Harry Hope. During the summer
Armina and I went to Hollywood in an endeavor to cast the other
parts properly, and succeeded in interesting Dudley Digges in playing
Harry Hope.

During the month of September, 1946, *The Iceman Cometh* went
into rehearsal, and 'Gene attended each morning and worked hand in
glove with Dowling in the direction of the play. Every move of every
actor had been clearly thought out in 'Gene's mind, and he was of
enormous help in the staging of the play. He did a great deal of
cutting prior to going into rehearsal, but not, in my opinion, as much
as was needed, and there were some exchanges between 'Gene and
myself on the subject of reducing the length of the play. On one
occasion I told 'Gene that at my request my assistant, Paul Crabtree,
who played the part of Dan Parritt, had counted the number of times
a certain point was repeated, and this, in actual fact, was eighteen
times. 'Gene looked at me and replied in a particularly quiet voice, "I
intended it to be repeated eighteen times!"

'Gene was not willing to have the play open in an out-of-town city,
as was our usual custom, but insisted on following his own practice of

having the play open "cold" in New York. This called for considerably more time for rehearsal, but this was arranged for, and on October 9, 1946, the play opened at the Martin Beck Theatre, making a tremendous impression upon its audience. Owing to the length of the play, we began at 5:30 in the afternoon for the opening, took an hour and a half for dinner, and the play concluded at 11:30 P.M. Later on we started the play at 7:30 P.M. and ran straight through the evening, but while this pleased 'Gene, it did not please me, for in my opinion it put too severe a strain on the audiences.

During the opening night dinner intermission, unfortunately for us all, James Barton, the actor playing the part of Hickey, was forced to entertain a crowd of friends, including Babe Ruth, the famous baseball player, and his family, in his dressing room, instead of resting, so that by the time he came to make the famous speech which lasted nearly twenty minutes in the fifth act, he had little or no voice left with which to deliver it. As a result, the last act, which should have been the strongest of all, fell apart in the center. Notwithstanding this fact, the audience was deeply moved and there was a great ovation at the end of the play, while the critics, for the most part, gave the play the greatest acclaim.

At the opening performance, I telephoned 'Gene during the dinner intermission, telling him I felt the play was going well, and he suggested we all come up and see him after the play was over. When we arrived at the apartment, Carlotta had prepared a light supper, and I proceeded to recount the details of the opening night. I could not help remarking to 'Gene that, in my opinion *The Iceman Cometh* like *Saint Joan,* would never be properly presented until after the expiration of the copyright, when it might be possible to cut it. 'Gene smiled at me in his usual disarming way and said it would have to wait for just that. Later on I asked 'Gene if he would mark my copy of the play with the places where he would agree to cut and where he would not. It was astonishing to see how boldly he wrote the word "No" in blue pencil against most of my proposed cuts and how tremulously he wrote his infrequent "Yes." Then he wrote on the front page of the manuscript: "To Lawrence Langner, The hell with your cuts! Eugene O'Neill."

I recount these details to show that 'Gene has never at any time truckled to the box office. If, in his opinion, the play could not be cut without mutilating it, it mattered very little to him that its length affected the attendance at the theatre, for he wrote his plays for those who could take them and not for what he called the "entertainment racket." As it was, *The Iceman Cometh* had a considerable run, and one which I think would have been much longer had not James Barton developed a case of laryngitis, so that it became increasingly difficult to hear him during the latter part of the play. As he had a so-called "run-of-the-play" contract, which required him to continue in the play either in New York or on the road, we finally arranged to have him leave after the New York run, when the part was excellently played by E. G. Marshall. As we had to continue to pay Barton's salary under our contract with him, this placed a heavy financial burden on the undertaking. However, while this experience was unfortunate, it was nevertheless not such as to affect the magnificent quality of the play and the high place it occupies in the catalog of O'Neill's work. Dudley Digges gave the outstanding performance in this, the last play of his acting career.

The following fall, having searched incessantly for an Irish giantess to play the part in *A Moon for the Misbegotten,* we ultimately collected a cast together including Mary Welsh, a tall, handsome strapping girl of Irish extraction, and an excellent actress. She did not weigh nearly enough, however, and she had to fatten up for the proceedings, finally raising her weight to about 170 pounds so as to fill the bill in this regard. James Dunn was cast in the part of Tyrone and James M. Kerrigan in the part of Phil Hogan. The play was placed in rehearsal in February, 1947, and was directed by Arthur Shields, brother of Barry Fitzgerald. 'Gene at this time seemed to be dominated by a belief that in order to bring this play to successful fruition, it was necessary that everyone connected with it should be Irish.

During the first rehearsal, the actors sat around a table and began to read the play. Dunn read a few speeches and remarked, "I wish I had been taught to read in school." When we reached the third act, with its tragic situation, Dunn began to cry. "I'm sorry," he said. "This is just too much for me." "Take a rest," said Arthur Shields, the director, in his rich Irish voice. "No," replied Dunn. "I'll go right ahead." He continued to read, but was so overcome by tears that he could not continue. We all decided to take a rest. After a while Mary Welsh began to cry and had to stop reading, by which time everybody sitting around the table had tears in their eyes. Said Dunn, "We're *all* crying now. I guess it will be the management's time to cry later." How right he was.

After the play had been read aloud, 'Gene expressed considerable misgivings. Since all our contracts were signed and the scenery was already built, we suggested that the play be tried out in some of the Midwestern cities. This plan was agreed to with some reluctance by 'Gene.

On February 20, 1947, *A Moon for the Misbegotten* opened in Columbus, Ohio, and the town was in a state of great excitement. The play was received with mixed feelings on the part of the audience, being slightly overlong, a fault which 'Gene remedied later on. At the end of the second act I noticed that a group of people rose from their seats and left the theatre. I wondered whether they had been upset by some of the language in the play, and I asked the doorman whether they left on this account. "No," he replied. "They just said they were Irish." As was so often the case with 'Gene's plays, whenever he depicted Irishmen on the stage who were not models of sobriety, there was always a great outcry against him on the part of the Irish that he had libeled their race.

The play toured several cities and when it reached Detroit, I received a telephone call from Armina, who was acting as Associate Producer, telling me that the police had threatened to close the play unless some of the alleged profanity was removed. Terry Helburn was present at the Detroit opening and between the two of them, they withstood the threats of arrest. Armina's own account of the Detroit incident is as follows:

The morning after we opened, I wakened and ordered coffee, and the waiter brought in the morning paper at the same time. When I opened it, across the front page was the startling headline, "O'NEILL PLAY CLOSED FOR OBSCENITY." Later, Terry and I went to the Cass Theatre office to meet the Police Officer who acted as Censor. One of the objections he made was that the word "mother" was used in the same sentence with the word "prostitute." He mentioned other words which, he said, should not be used on the stage. He continued, "Now mind you, the actor can go ahead and say the sentence right up to the obscene word, and then he can make a gesture. But he cannot use the word." I said, "You've allowed the *Maid of the Ozarks* to play here in Detroit, and yet you will not allow a play written by Eugene O'Neill, the greatest playwright in America, who won the Nobel Prize?" He said, "Lady, I don't care what kind of prize he's won, he can't put on a dirty show in *my* town." I answered, "This is not a dirty show. This is a great play—which *Maid of the Ozarks* is not." "Lady," he replied, "when the *Maid of the Ozarks* came here, it was a very different play. I helped rewrite *that* play, and we finally let it stay here." To this I replied, "Well, I'm afraid you'd have your problems cut out for you to rewrite a play by Mr. O'Neill." This upset him considerably, for he burst out with "Listen, lady, I don't have to sit here and take that from a woman." Then Jimmy Dunn came in, and pacified him. He agreed to talk it over with Jimmy, but he said he wouldn't have women around, so Jimmy went with him and they actually deleted about eight words. By this time the reporters were there. The Police Officer realized he had made a laughing stock of himself, and to show that everything was all right, and that we were all happy about the affair, he wanted his picture taken with Terry and me, to which I said, "Over my dead body," and we didn't!

A Moon for the Misbegotten closed in St. Louis and it was decided to reopen it later with a new cast. However, because of his illness, 'Gene asked us to defer this until he was feeling better, and he also asked us to postpone the production of *A Touch of the Poet* for the same reason. This we agreed to, nothwithstanding the fact that two of the best directors in the country were eager to direct the plays. Other difficulties beset 'Gene, which culminated in his breaking his arm and spending some weeks at Doctors' Hospital. After his discharge, 'Gene and Carlotta gave up housekeeping in New York and went to live in Boston.

In the summer of 1948 I went to Boston to talk to 'Gene about reopening *A Moon for the Misbegotten.* He was staying at the Ritz-Carlton in a suite which overlooked the Common, and he told me how much he enjoyed living in Boston, where he had spent a year when he was studying in Professor Baker's class. He seemed relieved at being away from New York and was in excellent spirits but still wished to postpone the reopening of the play.

The state of 'Gene's health, due to the incurable Parkinson's disease, unfortunately grew worse, and apparently made him unwilling to risk the production of these unproduced plays, which are the only truly great plays which have passed through my hands in the past five years. I often visited him at his home in Marblehead, perched on bleak rocks and overlooking the ocean, and I would ask him not to postpone further our production of these plays, if not for his own sake, for the sake of the American theatre, which stood so badly in need of his greatness. However, about a year ago I again raised the subject. We were sitting together in his study and I asked if we might produce *The Touch of the Poet* with a certain director of whom he had approved. "I don't believe I could live through a production of a new play right now," he replied, and to my protestations that we would do everything possible to make things easy for him, he answered, "No, that's my last word on the subject."

CHAPTER XXXI

Shaw, the Latter Days

D URING World War II, our relations with Shaw were affected by a number of circumstances: first, the revival of his older plays, which required "star" actors who took a large percentage of the profits, while Shaw's own royalties amounted to 15 per cent of the gross with no picture rights included, and made the production of his plays an expensive luxury. But this was not the main reason why we no longer worked on the earlier adage "When in doubt, play Shaw." During the war Shaw constantly complained about the British income tax, and did not want his plays produced in the United States for this reason. Furthermore, he had begun to dabble in motion pictures, and with the assistance of the picture producer Gabriel Pascal, had made a fortune from *Pygmalion,* which remains one of the masterpieces of the motion-picture art.

From time to time Gabriel Pascal visited us in the United States and discussed various projects for simultaneous play and motion-picture productions, and we found ourselves being drawn into what appeared to be a series of fascinating ventures. Pascal—nicknamed Gabby—is a smallish man with a roly-poly body and a vivid imagination. In some other incarnation he must undoubtedly have been a religious leader, so intense is the fanaticism he puts into film making. With the eyes of an eagle, the rotundity of a Buddhasatva, the contemplative brow of a prophet and the relentless jaw of a Napolean, Pascal combines all the astounding qualities of the oriental, the occidental, and the accidental. He often visited us in New York, discussing one or other of the gigantic projects which made his mental life a series of grandiose acrobatics. G.B.S. loved to hear Gabby talk—

410

in fact his conversation is one of his most charming qualities. Within a few moments, he puts you at your ease and makes you accept him as one of the outstanding geniuses of all time, something which you continue to accept under the hypnosis of his charm, and recalling his superb filming of Shaw's *Pygmalion.*

Gabby's naive belief in his love affair with destiny is one of his most endearing qualities. Another quality is his power to project, from his vivid imagination, word pictures of what he would like to transform into motion pictures. Thus, in describing the story *The Snow Goose* by Paul Gallico, which he intended to make into a motion picture, Gabby informed me that he had made a trip to northern Canada and there had been introduced to a very beautiful snow goose. "Lawrence," he said, "I want to tell you this snow goose had the most beautiful face I have ever seen. In a close-up she will look even more beautiful than Garbo!"

Early in 1940 I wrote to G.B.S. and told him that Theresa Helburn and I were now the Guild's producers, and that matters were progressing favorably. We also suggested reviving *Saint Joan* with Katharine Hepburn. We received G.B.S.'s reply of April 3rd as follows:

I rejoice to hear that the Guild is up on its feet again. I had given it up as finished. It has, as you know, dropped me as an author. I did not blame it, as my plays did not seem to be bringing it any luck. The Press attack on *Geneva* and its flop has not improved matters. However, the sensational success of the *Pygmalion* film has suddenly brought me into vogue as a screen expert (I was supposed to know nothing about the cinema); and this bears on the Hepburn question.

St. Joan has been pretty thoroughly exploited lately by your new niece, Kit (Katherine Cornell). That irresistible lady called on me when she was last in London, and put me in her pocket in five seconds, not to mention that she had made a pot of money for me while the Guild was turning down my plays one after another and throwing me into the arms of the late lamented Federal Theatre. Is it not a bit soon to start a fresh tour of *St. Joan* on the heels of such a charmer?

Meanwhile my play *The Millionairess*, with Edith Evans in the title part, is next on the list at the Globe Theatre in London. In the original version I made the woman a boxer; but, on the stage, that was unconvincing and unladylike. So I have made her a Judo expert. Judo is what we vulgarly call jiujitsu, which is magnificently spectacular. The part requires just such a personality as Miss Hepburn. Has she ever read the play?

I discussed with Kate Hepburn the idea of appearing in *The Millionairess*, but she did not then see herself in the part, although she evinced some interest later on. G.B.S. refers in the above letter to

Katharine Cornell as my "new niece" because my daughter Phyllis had recently married her cousin, John Cornell, whom she had met at my summer theatre.

I wrote G.B.S. on August 30, 1940, at the time when the air raids over London were beginning to grow heavy, and I told him of the formation of the National Inventors Council. To this he replied:

Your National Inventors Council is all to the good. Our own people have been hard at work and expect to have something that will surprise Jerry after Christmas.

I gather that the Guild, after a narrow escape from extinction, has now regained some of its old success and prestige. The New York public can now subscribe to it without fear of suffering from my plays. The Federal Theatre experiment (I regret its untimely murder) seems to have proved that I am not a highbrow author and that my true sphere is where no seat costs more than fifty cents.

I am staying in the country at present, contemplating London from a distance of 30 miles. But as the German pilots cannot navigate as ours do, and, trusting to their instruments, are convinced that they are bombing the Houses of Parliament when they are in fact making me jump by shaking my dwelling with unpleasantly close explosions, the villages in the home counties are wishing they were in New England. However, as far as the bombing getting them an inch forward in the war, the Germans might as well be shooting the moon. Most of the houses they have destroyed we should have destroyed ourselves long ago as unfit for human habitation.

I wrote G.B.S. again on October 24, 1941, suggesting a revival of his plays and received a post card from him dated 28th of November, 1941, which can hardly be regarded as an answer. Here G.B.S. set forth his problems in regard to income taxes. I believe that all through this period he was under the impression that his American taxes would be added to his British taxes, and put him in the poorhouse:

William Brady also wants to revive *You Never Can Tell* with a magnificent cast; but I am sufficiently ruined already by Katherine Cornell's revival of *The Doctor's Dilemma* and the *Pygmalion* film, with royalties taxed 27% in the States and 95% here. I shall have to let Gabriel film *Arms and the Man* to keep him alive; but that is all for the duration: I may die at any moment now; and what is to become of all the people provided for in my will if my property is swallowed up by this infernal war? Don't mention another production to me unless you can guarantee a flop worse than *The Apple Cart* or the *Unexpected Isles*. However, I rejoice in the recovery of the Guild from its phase of apparent slow extinction. It sounds more like its old self now.

I heard no more from G.B.S. until he sent a post card on February 3, 1942, in reply to a letter of mine asking permission to revive one of his plays:

The war taxation forces me to ration revivals of my plays very drastically. But to throw away a good revival is as bad for the Guild as for me, or nearly so; as I presume the profits are taxed pretty heavily. Anyhow I am out of business until I can *reduce* my income to a point at which it becomes possible to live on it.   G.B.S.

In my reply I stated:

. . . Thanks for the information about the taxes. The reason why the Theatre Guild wants to put on your plays is not to make profits—we cannot do that, nor have we been very successful as profit makers—it is because of the lack of plays and the great need of the public for comedies. You force us back to Shakespeare and Molière. It is so long since the Guild made profits that we are not worrying about the taxes on them.

Nobody can tell me that you are out of business—especially yourself!

It is interesting to note that my letter was written while we were in rehearsal with *Oklahoma!*, and my reference to profits shows very clearly my state of mind at the time.

I had very little further correspondence with G.B.S. until 1945. Sir Cedric Hardwicke and Basil Rathbone both indicated to me in Hollywood they desired to act in *In the Days of Good King Charles*, and we in turn wished to revive *Saint Joan* with Katharine Hepburn. In replying to us, G.B.S. stated in a postscript: "In great haste. I am overwhelmed with business on the verge of my ninetieth year." We cabled G.B.S. on July 25, 1945, as follows:

AT NINETY IT IS IRONIC YOU SHOULD BECOME A BUSINESSMAN AS YOU HAVE NEVER BEEN ONE BEFORE. HOPE YOU WILL HAVE A BRILLIANT FUTURE IN THIS NEW CAREER. LOVE, TERRY, LAWRENCE, ARMINA.

On October 15, 1945, after a long hiatus in producing G.B.S.'s plays, Terry and I sent him a cablegram reading as follows:

RUMORS OF REVIVALS OF YOUR PLAYS BEING CIRCULATED AROUND BROADWAY. WE ASSUME WE ARE STILL ACTING AS YOUR AGENTS. ALSO IF YOU ARE RELEASING NOW FOR NEW YORK WOULD LIKE TO CONTINUE OUR CONTROL OF PLAYS WE HAVE PRODUCED ESPECIALLY PYGMALION ARMS AND THE MAN DEVIL'S DISCIPLE ANDROCLES AND THE LION SINCE WE MADE THE LAST SUCCESSFUL PRODUCTIONS OF THESE. WOULD FEEL VERY BADLY IF THEY WERE RELEASED TO OTHER MANAGEMENTS WITHOUT OUR HAVING FIRST CHANCE AT PRODUCTION OURSELVES.

To this we received a cabled reply dated October 22nd:

GO ON AS BEFORE SUBJECT TO MY RIGHT TO AUTHORIZE DIRECTLY WHEN ADVISA-
BLE. BERNARD SHAW.

Later on, other New York managers were in touch with G.B.S., and he gave them the right to perform individual plays. One of these was Maurice Evans, who discussed with me the possibility of making a joint production of *Man and Superman,* but afterward changed his mind and produced it independently. We received a post card from G.B.S. on the subject dated 7th of July, 1946, reading as follows:

Maurice Evans has a personal non-exclusive license to play *Man and Superman* in repertory on his tour. It is an express condition that the license will be withdrawn if he claims any further privilege or interferes with any new production. He has been reminded of this.

Obviously, however, it would be very good business for the Guild to cast him for the lead in its production.

My plays are now classics open to all managements like Shakespeare's, except for the royalties. First come, first served!

During the month of January, 1947, when Theresa Helburn and I were in London for the production of *Jane,* a play by S. N. Behrman based on a story by Maugham which we were unable to cast in America, we decided to call on G.B.S. and discuss our general arrangements with him. I called on Miss Patch who made the appointment with G.B.S. and gave us printed instructions on how to reach Ayot St. Lawrence.

The following day Terry and I hired a limousine and drove out to visit G.B.S. As we settled down in our car and drove through the winding roads which took us out of the London suburbs until we reached the Great North Road, we studied the printed directions which Shaw himself had written, showing us how to reach his country home. Only a playwright could have written such directions, and only a stage manager could have followed them.

Driving through the snow we read, "The lane twists about and rises and dips and rises again. At the top of the second rise, at a signpost marked 'to Welwyn,' bear left into the village of Ayot St. Lawrence. Drive through it past the ruined church; and at the end, where the road divides, Bernard Shaw's gate is facing you in the angle." Our chauffeur was no stage manager, and it is not surprising that we got lost several times in the snow. We finally arrived at the ruins of the church and descended from our car at Bernard Shaw's gate, fully expecting to meet the ruins not only of a church but also of a playwright.

As we drove towards the Elizabethan village of Ayot St. Lawrence, my memory strayed back to the first time I had seen G.B.S. when I was a boy of fifteen, lecturing at the Fabian Society on "The Position of the Artist Under Socialism." Here I was in England in 1947, and if England was not exactly under Socialism, at least Socialism was under way, and here was G.B.S. enjoying the income of a capitalistic millionaire. It would be interesting to see what had happened to him.

We walked through the snow to the porch of Shaw's red brick house, and the door was opened by a bored-looking housekeeper who had doubtless let in many boring callers during the past twenty years. She showed us into a comfortable little sitting room with four large chairs drawn up in front of a glowing coal fire. Around the room there was a good deal of bric-a-brac, a model of a small break-front desk, and a Chinese scroll on the wall. Theresa and I sat in front of the fire, and thawed out until G.B.S. appeared and greeted us. He was no longer the tall, handsome white-bearded figure I had once known, but resembled a Chinese philosopher or sage carved out of yellowing ivory, for his hair was streaked with yellow and his beard was shorter and irregular, as though he had bitten it off somewhat around the edges. I thought of Jaques' speech on The Seven Ages of Man in Shakespeare's *As You Like It*. At sixty-five Shaw had resembled "the justice . . . with eyes severe and beard of formal cut, full of wise saws and modern instances." As a vegetarian, however, he was lacking "the fat round belly with good capon lined." A lining of good vegetables, no matter how filling, can never produce the effect of a lining of good capon.

Shaw at the age of ninety was still in the sixth age of Man, wearing grey plus-fours in which he looked indeed "the lean and slipper'd pantaloon," and he walked, acted and thought like a man in his early seventies.

"How are you feeling?" I asked. "My legs are letting me down," he said, "but otherwise I am perfectly well." He motioned us to be seated, and sat in the large armchair at the side of the comforting fire. Then he put us at ease by discussing the English winter weather. Terry mentioned that she was going to Edinburgh with S. N. Behrman's play and that she dreaded the cold. "You should go a lot further north to the Orkneys," said G.B.S. allowing his imagination to run riot. "You will find a sub-tropical climate there due to the Gulf Stream which will astonish you," and he described a kind of island paradise where the winter warmth is so great that large fuchsia trees grow and bloom outdoors. "Why don't they make the Orkneys into a winter resort?" Terry asked me on the way home. "G.B.S. was probably romancing," I replied. "He still loves to discover something different from everybody else."

"What are you doing these days?" asked Terry. "I am being quite busy," said G.B.S. "First of all I am writing a new play for the Malvern Festival. There will be some plot and a good deal of conversation. I don't get so many new ideas now. After I had finished writing the play, I found that several of the things I had written had already appeared in some of my other plays. You know," he said, as though he was quite surprised at the fact, "it's rather hard to get new ideas at ninety. I rewrote the play and took out everything I had said before and now it's in fine shape." I asked if we might do it in New York after the Malvern production. "Certainly," he replied, "if you want to! It's called *The Unfinished Comedy*." (Later the play was retitled *Buoyant Billions*.)

I asked G.B.S. what he thought of the condition of the theatre in England under the Socialism which he had advocated.[1] "Dear me," he said. "We haven't Socialism in this country—merely Trades Unionism. Most of the Trades Unionists don't know what Socialism is. On the other hand it's a good deal better than what you have in the States. The average American has the mentality of the village blacksmith. He knows what is going on in his own community, but hardly anything about the rest of the world. In my opinion Henry Wallace is the only man in the United States who really understands world affairs." He hoped Wallace would run for President on the Democratic ticket, even if he couldn't be elected. He thought it would be good to have world issues debated on Wallace's level during the next Presidential campaign. I suggested that if the British were ever able to vote for an American President, Wallace might have a chance, but I doubted it otherwise.

Talking of world issues, Shaw didn't think it mattered very much whether every nation shared the secret of the atomic bomb. "One thing ought to be self-evident to everybody," he said. "None of the peoples

---

[1] I was never impressed by G.B.S.'s economic theories, which struck me as infantile. He advocated equal incomes for all, a conception about as impractical as the idea of dividing up all property, and distributing it equally among everybody. He called himself a Socialist when he advocated equal incomes in *The Intelligent Woman's Guide to Socialism and Capitalism*, but during his eighties he began to call himself a Communist. Actually, had he lived in Communist Russia, he would have been liquidated in the very first purge.

throughout the world want to destroy themselves. Indeed," he said, "from one point of view it's too bad the Japanese didn't appeal to the conscience of the world after the atom bombs were used at Hiroshima and Nagasaki. I think the conscience of the world would have stopped the United States from using any more of these bombs, just as the conscience of the world stopped the use of poison gas." I told G.B.S. I knew poison gas had been stopped not because of the conscience of the world, but because everybody had plenty of it. However, he stood his ground, as usual.

At about this time the housekeeper, no longer bored, entered with a tea tray and an appetizing assortment of cakes. Terry presided over the pouring, and offered G.B.S. a cup of tea. "No tea for Mr. Shaw," said the housekeeper sharply. "Mr. Shaw drinks this." And she handed him a glass of greenish-looking fluid which smelled like stewed acorn juice and which may have been the elixir of life for all I know.

Glass in hand, Shaw smiled benignly at us, and sipped his vegetable juice from time to time. "How is the theatre in America?" he asked. We told him our problems, and how the mounting costs were making it increasingly difficult to take chances in the theatre by way of experimental or non-commercial productions. "I see," he said with a smile. "You are caught between the cruel landlord and the *relentless* playwright." As we had hoped to persuade G.B.S. that his royalties, the highest in the world, ought to be reduced somewhat, I winced at the way he pronounced the word "relentless." "The theatre is not merely up against the landlord and the relentless author, but rising salaries as well," said Terry. "I agree with you," said G.B.S., and for a moment I thought, "Aha! Being a capitalist millionaire has taught him something." "The actors are overpaid," he said, "and it's entirely unnecessary. They would all be willing to work for less." And he instanced how Miss Gertrude Kingston told him that she had to ask a West End Manager £40 a week, in order that she might get a good dressing room, for they had a way of putting the inexpensive actors on the upper floors. However, she was willing to work for a third of that amount with Vendrenne and Barker because she was on a yearly contract and could count on work all the year round. "Until you get the theatre on that basis, you'll have to overpay," he added. "As to myself, I am now a classic. Of course I have to have my royalties, but if the royalty is only nine pence, why, I touch my hat and say 'Thank you.'" "How can anyone put on one of your plays and pay only ninepence royalty?" I asked. "Oh, some village amateur dramatic group," he replied. "They do the classics."

We expounded the theory that since it costs at least fifteen thousand dollars a week to operate one of Shaw's plays, his royalty of 15 per cent was too high. "I'll make you a proposition," said G.B.S. "I'll give you my plays royalty free up to fifteen thousand dollars." Our faces lit up happily, but only momentarily. "Any receipts over that, I'll take half—and of course," he added, "you'll have to play in a very large theatre." A rough calculation showed that G.B.S. would gain considerably more on this basis than before, so we said, "No, thank you. We'd rather pay the 15 per cent." As a capitalist millionaire G.B.S. hadn't changed so very much, I thought.

We discussed Gabriel Pascal who was making the Shaw plays into motion pictures. "How did you like *Caesar and Cleopatra?*" he asked. Then he added, the old twinkle coming into his eyes, "The picture shows you what a really good play I wrote."

I told Shaw I had again had a long conversation with Pascal on the subject of our doing his plays on the stage, after which they could be transferred to the screen. "I don't see how you could have a long conversation with him," said G.B.S. "I rather imagine that Pascal talked while you listened. That's what always happens with me. He's arranging to produce my pictures in Ireland now. As soon as the news was announced, I was inundated with requests from beautiful Irish girls to play the part of Saint Joan. They seem to think the only qualification they need is to be Irish." He dwelt on Ingrid Bergman's success in *Joan of Lorraine* in New York, and we reminisced on some of the other Saint Joans. He mentioned a continental actress and said of her, "I never liked her in the part. She made the audience weep, but for all the wrong reasons. She played Saint Joan like a servant girl who has to go to jail for three months for stealing milk for her illegitimate child. Now that is a tragic situation, I admit, but it is definitely *not* Saint Joan!" And speaking of this lady's success, Shaw quoted another playwright as saying, "Her great acclaim in the part of the Saint was due to the fact that her every gesture and intonation was directly contrary to the spirit and intention of the author!"

We talked happily of many more things until it was time to leave. "We'll be back here soon with *Oklahoma!*," said Terry cheerfully, as we put on our coats in the hall, "and you'll have to come to see it." "No," said G.B.S. rather sadly, "I'm afraid I won't. I've lost all interest in the theatre, and I'm not much interested in anything else either."

He insisted on coming out of the front door to see us off. The snow was all around us as he stood outside the door, the light falling on his bare head and hair, and giving him a translucent quality, almost

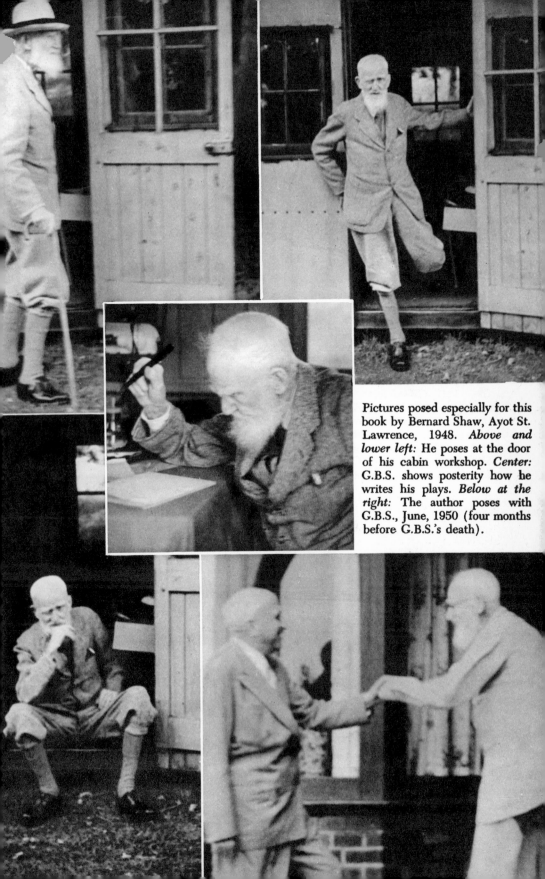

Pictures posed especially for this book by Bernard Shaw, Ayot St. Lawrence, 1948. *Above and lower left:* He poses at the door of his cabin workshop. *Center:* G.B.S. shows posterity how he writes his plays. *Below at the right:* The author poses with G.B.S., June, 1950 (four months before G.B.S.'s death).

Above: Charles F. Kettering at the wheel demonstrating the first Delco self-starter, Dayton, Ohio, 1912. *On the left* is William Chryst, Chief Engineer of Delco. *Below:* The first meeting of the National Inventors Council, Washington, D.C., September, 1940. *Seated from left to right:* Fred Zeder, Chrysler Corporation, Conway P. Coe, Commissioner of Patents, Dr. Charles F. Kettering, General Motors Research Corporation, Dr. Thomas Midgley, Jr., Ethyl Corporation, Dr. William Coolidge, General Electric Company. *Standing,* Dr. Fin Sparre, E. I. Du Pont De Nemours and Company, Dr. Webster Jones, Carnegie Institute of Technology, Dr. Fred Feiker, George Washington University, the author, and Watson Davis, Science Service.

Above: The N. I. C. visits the Willow Run Plant after completion. *Center,* Edsel Ford and the author. (*inset*) Council meeting at Washington, D.C., 1944. *Left to right:* George Codrington, the author, Dr. Roger Adams, Dr. William Coolidge, Dr. Charles F. Kettering, Rear Admiral Beuret, Major General Tchappat. *Below:* Meeting of the Council at Wright Field, 1943, *Front row, left to right:* N. I. C. meeting, Cleveland, August 24, 1943. *From*

left to right: Lawrence Langner, John C. Green, Dr. Fred Feiker, Dr. Fin Sparre, Dr. William Coolidge, Colonel B. Furuholmen, Rear Admiral Beuret, Dr. George Lewis, General William Tschappat, George Codrington, Colonel L. B. Lent, Orville Wright, Watson Davis, Dr. Charles F. Kettering, George Baekland, Fred Zeder, South Trimble, Admiral Hal G. Bowen, and Conway P. Coe, Commissioner of Patents.

THERESA HELBURN
Co-Administrative Director of the Theatre Guild.

ARMINA MARSHALL (Mrs. Lawrence Langner)

Associate Director of the Theatre Guild and Executive Producer,
Theatre Guild of the Air.

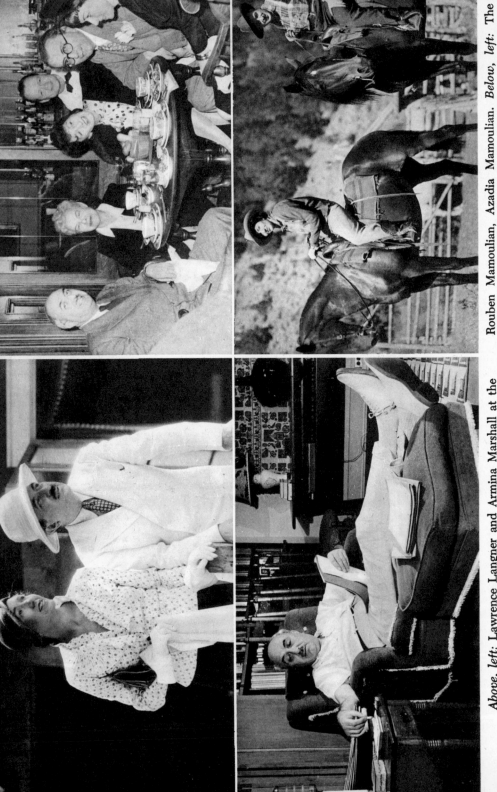

Rouben Mamoulian, Azadia Mamoulian. *Below, left:* The author at rest working on his farm in Weston, Connecticut. *Below, right:* The author at work resting on a ranch in Wyoming. *At left,* Armina Marshall.

Above, left: Lawrence Langner and Armina Marshall at the Westport Country Playhouse, 1935. *Above, right:* Boston, Massachusetts, rehearsal interlude from *Carousel,* 1945. *Left to right:* the author. Theresa Helburn, Armina Marshall.

saintly, like a halo. "I'm afraid you'll take cold." I called. "Nonsense," he said and he stood there, a friendly smile on his face. "Thanks for coming," and he waved good-by, smiling his charming old smile.

On our way back Theresa said that she thought he must lead a lonely life so far out in the country. I said I didn't think so—that I felt the key to his character was to be found in the Preface to *Man and Superman,* in which he wrote, "There are no passions like the passions of the mind." I thought that G.B.S. had indulged this passion all his life, and that as he grew older he had more chance to indulge it, and that with it he would never be lonely. He showed no symptoms of tiring, although our visit lasted nearly two hours.

A year later, in May of 1947, when Armina and I were in London for the opening of *Oklahoma!* at the Drury Lane Theatre, we had a pleasant visit with Pascal at his country place near Denham, where he lived in a beautiful old English farmhouse furnished in Italian antiques, an incongruity of style which was made possible only by Pascal's unique personality, which seemed to blend the two cultures together into a tasteful Anglo-Italian mélange. Present at dinner were several important members of the Irish government, who were nego-tiating with Gabby for making Shaw's motion pictures in Ireland. I gathered that a large Irish castle was being turned over to Pascal to be transformed into a Hibernian Hollywood. We told Gabby that we were going to visit G.B.S. on the following Thursday, and he volun-teered to come along with us. This was my first opportunity of seeing G.B.S. and Gabby together, and it was probably as amusing for me to witness G.B.S. laying down the law to Gabby, as it was for Gabby to hear G.B.S. reprimand me on the subject of the Theatre Guild and its shortcomings. We did not have much time alone with G.B.S., but we discussed the possibility of presenting *The Devil's Disciple* and *Heartbreak House,* which he gave us permission to produce; and he also asked us to continue looking after the amateur and stock rights of his plays, which at his request, we had handled for him in the United States for twenty-five years. "From a business standpoint you must now consider me as dead," he remarked with great vitality.

G.B.S. then took us for a walk through his grounds and showed us the little cabin where he wrote his plays. Although he complained about his legs giving way under him, he opened the French windows, and without any overcoat, despite the coldness of the weather, walked us down a little hill, on one side of which stood a statue of St. Joan which he had recently purchased from a lady sculptor living in the village. The walk to his cabin took several minutes, and when we arrived there, we looked through the window into the interior. The small, low shed in which he had written so many of his plays was entirely plain and without character, furnished with a couch-bed, a table and papers untidily scattered around. G.B.S. assured me that although over ninety-one, he continued to work in this cabin each day, writing articles or working on contracts for motion pictures and other rights, which he worked out in his meticulous Pitman's shorthand and sent to London for his secretary Miss Patch to type. He very seldom visited London, however, where Miss Patch conducted her office in his apartment in Whitehall Court.

After G.B.S. had given me a severe lecture on how to run the Theatre Guild, and Gabby a similarly severe lecture on how to make motion pictures in Ireland or elsewhere, he suddenly turned to me as though in distress, and said, "Lawrence, I have no photograph of you. I want to take your picture and I want to take Armina's, too." He then produced a small camera which seemed to require a great deal of adjustment, and took us out on the terrace outside the house. Here he posed us together, but I stopped him and said, "G.B.S., I want a picture of Armina and myself with *you*." "Who will take the picture?" he said. "Why not Gabby?" I replied. "He's a motion-picture maker." "Why, he doesn't know the slightest thing about photography," said G.B.S. with a twinkle in his eye, "I don't dare trust him." He handed the camera to Gabby with a show of protest, seated himself beside Armina and myself, and proceeded to instruct Gabby in the use of the camera. Later on I received a post card from Mr. Lowenstein, who was helping G.B.S. to classify his documents at Ayot St. Lawrence, and in it he wrote that the pictures which Gabby took turned out badly, so of course G.B.S. was right as usual.

In July of 1947 I wrote G.B.S. suggesting that we produce *You Never Can Tell*, *The Devil's Disciple* and *Arms and the Man*. G.B.S. replied on a post card:

Judith in the *D's D* is weakly sentimental: Katharine Hepburn is too strong for her.

Dick is not a raffish profligate: he is a tragic figure in black, like Hamlet, or Buckingham in *Henry VIII*.

I must let Alfred Fischer go where he chooses, as he did very well for me in Germany; but you should be able to give him as good terms as any other management, or better; and I should prefer yours.

Hardwicke would of course be perfect as the waiter. It would be wise to wait for him. G.B.S.

We informed G.B.S. that if and when we produced *You Never Can Tell,* we would take in Mr. Fischer as an associate producer, and an arrangement was made with Mr. Fischer. We finally decided not to wait for Hardwicke, but to produce the play with Leo G. Carroll in the part of the waiter. We made contracts to bring several players over from England and proceeded to put the play into rehearsal under the direction of Peter Ashmore who came over from London. After most of the actors' contracts were signed, a theatre engaged and the entire project was under way, we received a cablegram from G.B.S. on November 14, 1947, reading as follows:

TAXATION OBLIGES ME TO DEFER FURTHER REVIVALS. DISCIPLE IS OFF. ROBERT ALSO. G.B.S.

The Robert here referred to was Robert Montgomery, who wished to visit Bernard Shaw and talk with him about the possibility of making a motion picture of *The Devil's Disciple.* We naturally assumed that in stating that further revivals were to be deferred, G.B.S. did not include *You Never Can Tell* which was already under way, and which he had promised to us, and we therefore proceeded with this production, apparently to G.B.S.'s satisfaction. However, on January 10, 1948, when we were just about to go into rehearsal, we received a new cablegram from G.B.S. reading as follows:

PRODUCE NOTHING OF MINE UNTIL PRESIDENTIAL ELECTION IS OVER. SHAW.

Hindsight compels me to admit that it was too bad we did not cancel all the contracts, and follow G.B.S.'s instructions. It would have saved us a great deal of money and trouble. However, since we had already entered into the production contracts on *You Never Can Tell* with G.B.S.'s blessing, we cabled him that his request had come too late for us to stop the production. Moreover, Peter Ashmore, who had directed the play in London, was already at work.

Unfortunately, while *You Never Can Tell* was liked in Boston and Philadelphia by our audiences and the out-of-town critics, the drama critics of New York took it to pieces, notwithstanding the fact that it was, in my opinion, given an excellent production and was very much liked by our public; in fact, to test this out, we took a vote of the fifteen thousand odd subscribing New York members of the Theatre Guild, and well over two-thirds were delighted with the play. However, running expenses were very high, the summer was coming on, and we felt it expedient to close after a few weeks' run.

When this book began to reach completion, I asked G.B.S. if I might have permission to publish my stories about him and I sent him some of the chapters I had written for him to read over. In replying, he stated:

I can neither permit nor prevent the publication of books about myself. You must act on your own responsibility without asking my leave or anyone else's. Why should I grudge you that freedom?

But I implore you not to describe me as "a lovable human being." It will bring a million begging letters on me by the next post. Rather present me as detestable, avaricious, merciless, contemptuous, and everything else odious enough to discourage people from writing to me. Otherwise you may hasten my already imminent death.

G.B.S. was also good enough to say that he would pose for some pictures for this book, and his friend Mr. Lowenstein took these on some film I sent him. I particularly like the one in which Shaw posed, pen in hand, with furrowed brow, to show what the Genius looked like when he was working. His sense of humor stayed with him to the end.

During the summer of 1950, Armina and I were in London for the opening of Rodgers and Hammerstein's *Carousel,* and we asked G.B.S. if we might visit him. The answer came back on the usual post card, telling us to come, but that he had been ill with lumbago. This was destined to be our last visit.

We arrived at Ayot St. Lawrence in the late afternoon, and soon after, G.B.S. came into the room, looking frail and bent over, and walking with the aid of a stick. "Don't talk such nonsense," he replied to my remark that I thought he looked well. "I am decaying and disintegrating. I am not the man who wrote those plays." We sat and talked to him for a while, and he seemed gentler and more contemplative than ever before. In the course of our conversation he remarked, "Lawrence, I have told you several times now, you must regard me as being officially dead. I have made all arrangements so that my business affairs will proceed just as though I *were* dead." "But, G.B.S.," I replied, "whenever we want to do a play of yours, we still ask your permission, even though the Guild and the Westport Country Playhouse have produced over twenty of your plays." He answered in tones which sounded rather virile for one officially dead. "What, *only* twenty?" "Yes," I replied, "that's more than any other management has ever produced." By this time G.B.S. was coming to life rapidly. "I've written fifty," he said with a smile. "Why don't you do the other thirty?"

We then asked G.B.S.'s permission to produce *The Millionairess* with Katharine Hepburn, in accordance with his suggestion made some years earlier. "Is she a good athlete?" asked Shaw. "Indeed she is," said Armina. "She plays tennis every day, and takes long walks." And I added, hoping to clinch the matter, "She's as strong as a horse!" "Then you'll have to watch out," said Shaw, "for she'll have to play a scene where she applies jujitsu to her leading man, and she'll *kill* him if she isn't careful!" He then threw his head back and laughed heartily. This was the last time I heard him laugh.

He explained that he would never permit his plays to be done on television or in cut versions on radio, and when Armina remarked that cut versions of Shakespeare had been done successfully on radio, his eyes twinkled as he remarked, "My dear girl, it's bad enough to do that to Shakespeare, but it's sacrilege to cut Shaw!" I told him that I had brought a movie camera along to take a picture in place of the one which Pascal had muffed. "Come outside," he said. "If it's a movie camera, it calls for a director. Now you, Armina, will take a picture of the door to stimulate the interest of the audience. Then, after a moment of suspense, the door will open and I will come out. Then I will sit in my chair, Lawrence will come around the corner and I will rise and greet him cordially." G.B.S. acted the picture as planned, but when it came time for him to rise from his chair and greet me, the ninety-four-year-old actor was somewhat less than sprightly. I shall always cherish this picture, and the one that follows it. "I think I'd better not see you off," he remarked, and I remembered his old custom of walking down the driveway and standing in the road, waving at our car as it went by. But he changed his mind later on, and hobbled down the driveway to wave us good-by. My last picture of him standing by the roadside endeavoring to draw his bent-over body into the erect position in which he had always held himself, while he smiled and waved to us, brought the tears to my eyes. There will never be another of his ilk in our time.

During the past thirty years, the Theatre Guild has presented more of Shaw's plays than any other management, while the Westport Country Playhouse has presented seven. On balance, our relationship earned for G.B.S. somewhere in the neighborhood of $350,000 and has cost the Theatre Guild about the same amount. But had it cost the Guild ten times that amount, it would have been more than worth it to us. Our presentation of his plays to American audiences gained us a following which benefited all the other writers whose plays we produced during this period. But more than that, we counted his plays amongst the most precious contributions to the modern theatre, and in presenting them, we fulfilled one of our best reasons for existing.

I feel singularly ungrieved at G.B.S.'s passing, because I know he wanted to die. I know he felt that he had outlived his own brain and body, when he remarked to me, "Lawrence, I am not the man who wrote those plays," and he did not want to outlive that man. That man was a leader of our generation all over the world—in the theatre and out of it—and that man knew his days were over. The theatre has been very fortunate in the fact that some of the great geniuses of the world have written for it. One of these was Shakespeare, another was Shaw. The fact that Shaw was a great reformer, philosopher, thinker and humorist—the fact that he used the theatre as his medium of expression, has made the theatre a greater place for his being in it, and it will be a lesser place for his passing.

After we learned of Shaw's death, I suggested that the Theatre Guild sponsor a Memorial Service dedicated to his memory. This took place on November 19, 1950 at the old Guild Theatre. The speakers made the occasion one of high celebration that the theatre had been blessed with so distinguished a genius, intermingled with grief at his passing. But the best part of the service was Shaw's own words, for at the conclusion Peggy Wood, Burgess Meredith and Walter Abel played the last scene from *Candida;* John Gielgud read the "Statement of Faith" of Dubedat from *The Doctor's Dilemma,* while finally Katharine Cornell, with a sweep of emotion which carried the audience along with her, read the great speech of Saint Joan and ended the Memorial with the ringing words, so applicable to Shaw himself, "O God that madest this beautiful earth, when will it be ready to receive Thy saints? How long, O Lord, how long?"

CHAPTER XXXII

Widening Horizons

TERRY and I spent some time in England in the winter of 1946-7, where we were greeted on our arrival by snowstorms, gales, austerity and coal strikes. Our purpose was to re-establish our English connections, and also to produce a new play, *Jane*, in partnership with Tennent's. Our leading lady was Yvonne Arnaud, a charming and versatile comedienne who combined the talents of a first-rate concert pianist with the artful vivacity of a French vivandière, and our leading man was one of England's best actors, the suave and bearded Ronald Squire.

The author of *Jane* was my favorite playwright San Behrman, who had preceded us to London and was living in the Carlton Hotel in the magnificent apartment of his friend Sir Alexander Korda. Soon after my arrival, I called on Sam, and found him embedded in a luxurious armchair in a luxurious living room with a tray of exotic *hors d'œuvres* on a taboret to one side of him, and several bottles of whisky, *apéritifs* and so forth on the other. A waiter stood at attention in the back, while Sam beamed at me, and from time to time expressed his thoughts on the subject of England and the English. "I'm writing an article about the wonderful way the English are standing up under Austerity," our author informed me, helping himself to a serving of caviar; and indeed Sam wrote a very excellent article on the subject which appeared later in *The New Yorker*. However, he was soon to come in contact with some real austerity, for his play *Jane* opened in Blackpool in a blinding snowstorm which lasted for days, and we rehearsed in a cold theatre and returned to a cold hotel for our cheerless meals.

We spent New Year's Eve in a sad little hotel sitting room where the *Jane* company celebrated the oncoming year with some canned food and liquor which we brought over from America. One of the most interesting members of the *Jane* company was Ronald Squire, who delighted us all as we sat around the blazing fire with stories of his experiences in the theatre. His presence on New Year's Eve in the little sitting room in Blackpool made the evening memorable for me, for as we sat listening spellbound to his stories of Shaw, Barrie, Galsworthy and a host of others, the magic curtain of the theatre was raised again, and the little room became a realm of enchantment as we were transported from play to play and personage to personage in the exciting history of the English stage during the first half of the century.

Sam was having his troubles when *Jane* opened, for there was so little coal in the hotel that he did his rewriting in bed, and his hands were so numb that he could barely use the typewriter. Nevertheless, despite these hardships, which were slight compared to what the British people were suffering, the play was greatly improved by Sam, for when it came to London it received excellent notices and ran for the greater part of a year at the Aldwych Theatre.

While in London, I walked through that section of Chancery Lane in which I had worked as a boy, and found that the portions of Southampton buildings in which the offices of Cruickshank and Fairweather and Haseltine Lake & Co. had been situated, were now reduced to a gaping pit of rubble. As I regarded the senseless damage, I could not help but feel some inner satisfaction in the thought that no other youngsters would be required to spend their days in the cheerless, sunless offices in which I had passed so many unhappy hours as a boy. I also made a sentimental journey to Tavistock Square, where I had lived, and found that in place of the old house which had been our home, there was now only an ugly wound in the ground. On the other side of the Square, there was no trace of the house where formerly had dwelt the enchanting Pamela for whom I left England to seek my fortune in America. I decided to inquire where Pamela was living, disregarding an inner warning not to try to retrace my steps into the past. I called on her brother-in-law who remarked to me in surprise, "Don't you know what happened to Pamela? She has lost her mind, and is now in a sanitarium." I expressed my deep regret, to which he replied, "There's no need to be upset about her. She is far happier than any of us, for she doesn't know what is happening in the world." I could not share his simple optimism and felt depressed at the news, until I was able to turn my mind away from the past, and to begin making plans for the future.

One of these plans was to extend our relations with Hugh Beaumont to include the exchange of plays between England and the United States, so that we could find an outlet for our own plays in England, and in turn secure some of the best English plays for our subscription audiences in this country. Our first English importation under this arrangement was John Gielgud's English company in *The Importance of Being Earnest* by Oscar Wilde, in which venture we were associated with John C. Wilson. I crossed from London to New York with John Gielgud on the *Queen Elizabeth*. I found him a stimulating fellow traveler, perhaps the most erudite actor I have ever met. He seemed rather nervous as to whether his reception in New York would equal his first successful visit in *Hamlet*. As it turned out, both he and his company were given an enthusiastic reception in the Wilde comedy, so his misgivings were groundless. The actors shared a table together on board, and except for the times when the Atlantic behaved a little too roughly, we had a happy passage. His company included the charming actor Bobby Flemyng, Margaret Rutherford, Jean Cadell, Jane Baxter and Pamela Brown, a young lady who is already one of the leading actresses of the English theatre.

Pamela Brown, with reddish hair and enormous eyes, presented a weird but compelling appearance, being neither beautiful nor the opposite, but partaking of both qualities according to the particular mood she was in. As a conversationalist, she expressed more in monosyllables than any person I have ever met. She explained this as being due to the fact that when she was with me "she couldn't get a word in edgewise." Playing with John Gielgud in New York in *The Importance of Being Earnest,* she took the New York critics and audiences by storm, and when John, against our better judgment, insisted on reviving *Love for Love,* Pamela won the greatest critical praise in the part of Angelica. She was, I decided, a living testimonial to the British theatre which, by the existence of adequate stock and repertory companies, had enabled her to play over seventy-five parts in different plays during a period of time when an American actress would have considered herself lucky to have played a mere half dozen.

Encouraged by the reception given to Gielgud's company in the Oscar Wilde play, we organized a company which I christened Atlantis, consisting of the Theatre Guild, Tennents' and John C. Wilson, in order to bring fine English plays to the States. Terence Rattigan's *The Winslow Boy* was the first play to cross the ocean under this arrangement. Thanks to our subscription system, Atlantis was able to present this fine play all over the country—in over twenty-eight cities—something which could not have happened but for our membership support. Rattigan, a tall boyish-looking young man, with patrician features and a Seventeenth-Century grace of carriage, possesses in common with John van Druten a precision in the handling of language, a deftness in comedy, and a distinction in taste which is sadly lacking in the younger American writers of our period. But we should be thankful for the natural robustness of our own writers. There is room in our theatre for the lineage descendants of O'Neill, as well as for those of Galsworthy and Wilde. Atlantis' latest importation *The Lady's not for Burning* with John Gielgud and Pamela Brown, introduced the first long play by the important British poet Christopher Fry, who is, I believe, a spiritual descendant of Shakespeare, and may turn the English speaking theatre back to the poetic drama which is its highest expression.

I also began to think of the future of the Guild in terms of its contribution to the theatre's offspring—motion pictures, radio and television. It seemed illogical to be concerned with the artistic standards of the living theatre, and yet to be completely indifferent to what was done with plays presented to millions upon millions of Americans after they left the footlights. There were many instances where fine plays which we had produced in the theatre, were mangled or vulgarized in motion pictures and radio, and we felt that the American public was ready for something better than it was getting in both these fields—television at that time being still in its infancy. We therefore decided to interest ourselves to a limited extent in the production of our "subsidiary rights"—the name given to motion picture rights, radio rights, television rights, etc.—which had far greater audiences than existed in the Mother Church of the Stage.

At the time when we were working on *Jacobowsky and the Colonel*, we became acquainted with a young, able and intelligent lawyer named H. William Fitelson, who worked so well for our partners that we felt it would be valuable for us to have his help in connection with our proposed entry into these other fields—especially as he had specialized for a number of years in motion picture matters. With this end in view, we engaged him, and later on he became our general Counsel, following the resignation of Charles A. Riegleman who had served us ably in this capacity for many years. Prior to the war, we had discussed with radio experts, without success, the idea of producing a radio program based entirely on theatre plays. "The name of the

Theatre Guild is the kiss of death in radio," we were told by an important executive of the National Broadcasting Company. Some years later he lived to eat his words.

In 1945, Armina was made Associate Director of the Theatre Guild, and gave special attention to radio. Thanks to her efforts and those of Bill Fitelson, a contract was entered into with the United States Steel Corporation in the year 1945 to provide a radio program under the name "Theatre Guild on the Air," based on theatre plays, and which would attempt to spread an interest in the theatre into millions of homes throughout the country, and especially in places where the living theatre was not available to the listeners. Benjamin Fairless, the President, and Irving Olds, the Chairman of the Board, and his Chief of Public Relations, J. Carlisle MacDonald vigorously supported the plan, and they in turn informed us that their purpose was to make known the facts about their company to the American public, and that it was not intended to use the program merely as an adjunct to their advertising department.

We all attended a meeting of the officials of the Steel Corporation in their Board Room at 71 Broadway, and discussed the kind of plays we intended to present over the air. The Board Room was an impressive salon with handsome oak-paneled walls and massive oak chairs arranged around a massive oak table in the center of the room. Looking down on us, seemingly with warm approval, as we sat discussing the program, were gold-framed oil paintings of J. P. Morgan, Sr., Andrew Carnegie, Henry Frick and Judge Elbert Gary.

We began our first program in September, 1945, with Maurice Browne's and Robert Nichols' play about the atomic bomb, *Wings Over Europe,* and probably nothing could have been more timely and explosive over the air. For the first year, I acted as the Commentator and introduced the play each Sunday night. I found this a considerable strain, and much to my relief, reports came in from west of the Mississippi that this Langner who spoke over the air was obviously a dude, and one of the most objectionable features of the program. I did quite well, however, in the East where the traces of my English accent were not a complete liability. At the end of the season, I relieved the embarrassment of our sponsor by volunteering to resign.

"The Theatre Guild on the Air" became rapidly more and more popular with the listening audiences. We brought to the preparation of these plays our knowledge of the theatre, while we engaged Homer Fickett as director and George Kondolf as editor. As a result of combining the theatre and radio crafts, we were able to develop a form of radio theatre entertainment which conformed in performance to the standards of craftsmanship we had set for ourselves in the living theatre, and this resulted in bringing a higher type of play and performance into the homes of American families throughout the country. By the end of the season of 1950–51, we shall have produced over two hundred plays on the air, including the works of Shakespeare, O'Neill, Ibsen and other major dramatists, and our listening audience has at times reached the estimated figure of fifteen millions.[1]

We were unable to produce Shaw's plays on radio during his lifetime because of one of his characteristic quirks, that his plays may not be "cut." Before we launched our radio program, I wrote to G.B.S. in London and asked for permission to broadcast his plays over the air. His reply was terse and to the point:

My plays are mostly too long for radio; and the art of producing plays invisibly is a special one in which the choice of contrasting voices (the vocalists may be as ugly as Satan) is all important. I doubt whether you will find it possible to run the two distinct businesses together, and shall not commit myself to it until my doubts are resolved one way or the other.

I wrote G.B.S. in reply, telling him that Lunt and Fontanne were going to play in ten of our radio plays, and again asking for the rights. This was his cabled reply:

AGREED FOR YOUR PICK OF ALL MY PLAYS UNCUT AND UNCOOKED BUT THE LONGEST ARE TOO LONG FOR RADIO.

Of course, the joker in this was that unless we were willing to produce his plays in two installments, we would be unable to present them "uncut and uncooked" with the exception of his one-act plays. We found, as a result of producing a radio version of O'Neill's *Strange Interlude* in two installments, one week apart, that there was a distinct dropping off in interest from the first week to the second.

As might naturally be expected, from time to time I have been interested in the making of motion pictures by the Guild. As more and more actors left New York for the West Coast, the casting of plays called for annual visits to Hollywood to keep old contacts and to make new ones. On my many visits with Armina, we were entertained by the actors and actresses who had formerly been with us in the Guild.

---

[1] While Terry and I supervise the Radio program, the credit for its success belongs largely to Armina Marshall, its producer, Homer Fickett, its director, Mark Smith, its editor, and H. William Fitelson, its managing director.

Chief among these was Edward G. Robinson and his wife, Gladys, who had lived opposite us on Eleventh Street and were now living in a handsome home in which Eddie kept his pictures, of which he was very proud. Later he was even prouder of the excellent pictures painted by Gladys. One evening, as we were taking a drive after dinner, with Armina in the front seat with Eddie, while Gladys was sitting behind with me, Eddie drew up on a hillside, and as we admired the view Gladys sprayed some perfume over herself. Eddie turned around to me and drew in his breath. "Isn't Hollywood a wonderful place?" he remarked dreamily. "In what other city in the world could you smell the scent of beautiful flowers wafted from the gardens into our car?" "Sorry," said Gladys. "That was me."

I had long had a desire to meet Ernest Lubitsch, the famous European director who had made so many witty and engaging pictures, and our mutual friend Mady Christians was kind enough to arrange this. We were invited in to watch him make a picture with Marlene Dietrich and Herbert Marshall, and we stood in open-mouthed amazement at the lavishness of the settings, for every piece of furniture was an authentic antique, and the carpeting would have excited the envy of a pasha. Marlene Dietrich was wearing the handsomest of dinner dresses, and Herbert Marshall was standing at her side while she played the piano. The picture was taken and retaken about fifteen times, at the end of which Lubitsch, a short, chubby little man with laughing eyes, who smoked enormously large cigars, called a halt and invited us to have tea. I felt that the atmosphere was somewhat charged as we sat and discussed the legitimate theatre, Marlene remarking to me, as she smoothed the creases out of her magnificent silk dress, that she wished she could play a part in which she could appear wearing just a little black shawl and working-women's clothes. Lubitsch told us stories of the productions he had made in the German theatre, and tea was served leisurely to all of us as we sat there gaily chatting. I felt uncomfortable, however, not merely because I felt some strain in the atmosphere, but also because I had been informed just before we came on the set, that this picture was costing about $10,000 an hour to make, and I felt quite guilty at wasting at least $7,500 of Paramount's money in drinking a cup of tea and chatting with our host.

Weeks afterward, Mady Christians told me that Lubitsch and Marlene had had a violent quarrel about the picture, and neither had spoken to the other for several days, until our visit made it desirable to show a united front, and they acted as though they were the dearest of friends while entertaining us. The argument was over a hat which Marlene was wearing, as a result of which the picture had to be reshot for days, so that the cost of the hat added up to about $95,000! After learning this, I felt less guilty about that $7,500 tea party!

In discussing our making pictures with a number of would-be partners, I found at all times that the emphasis was on our making a single picture, which was entirely outside my conception of what a motion-picture program for the Theatre Guild should be. I realized from my knowledge of the theatre that unless there was a possibility of producing a program of artistic pictures one after the other, some of which would succeed while others would fail, our stay in this field would be of brief duration, and we therefore turned down some rather flattering opportunities to produce single pictures.

Later on, I received a visit in the winter of 1946 from an energetic young Englishman named John Wolff of the J. Arthur Rank organization, who was in New York City promoting the motion picture *Henry V*, directed by Laurence Olivier. Mr. Wolff informed me that *Henry V* had been shown to the leading executives in Hollywood and also to the exhibitors' representatives, and that they were unanimous in turning it down. "What we would like you to do, Mr. Langner, is to have the Theatre Guild get behind Olivier's picture, and recommend it to the Theatre Guild subscribers all over the country," said Wolff. "I would like to invite you and your colleagues to a private showing of the picture, and then you can make up your minds based on what you see." I explained that we were interested in anything which would increase the popularity of Shakespeare with theatre-going audiences, because we were at that very time developing our own Shakespearean company.

I invited Romney Brent, who was the director of our Shakespearean company, and his wife, Gina Malo, to meet Armina and myself at the screening of the picture. I was dubious as to whether we would want to stay throughout the entire showing, which we were told lasted nearly three hours. As a precaution, I mentioned that we had another engagement and would probably have to leave after the first hour. As the film unrolled, we were quite carried away with its beauty, imagination and poetry. It seemed to me to be quite the greatest motion picture I had ever seen, and proved what could happen in this medium if it could ever pass into the hands of artists.

I was quick to notice that the motion picture had been directed by a theatre actor and that practically every man and woman in it was a theatre actor and actress who also had motion-picture experience.

Needless to say, we stayed to the very end, and would have liked to see the picture all over again. After an hour, a young man interrupted me. "What about your appointment?" "Let it wait," I replied. "It isn't of the slightest importance."

Terry saw the picture later and seconded our enthusiasm, and we made an arrangement to promote it with our theatre audiences all over the country. We invited a number of theatre and literary celebrities to witness private screenings of the picture, and they were just as enthusiastic about it as we were. When *Henry V* was finally presented in the various theatres around the country, it made a tremendous success, and, indeed, until the production of Olivier's *Hamlet,* has played to larger audiences than any other British-made picture.

Eugene O'Neill was one of the greatest admirers of Olivier's *Henry V* and came with me to see it three times. Before he had seen this picture, he had made up his mind that he would nevermore permit any of his plays to be made into motion pictures, but *Henry V* converted him. He received an offer from his old friend, Dudley Nichols, to film *Mourning Becomes Electra,* and under the influence of his admiration for *Henry V* he assented. We were consulted in the making of this picture, and Armina, Theresa Helburn and I visited the studios in Hollywood while Dudley was making the latter part of it. It took a great deal of courage to make a picture from so tragic a subject, and while most parts were successful, other portions did not fare so well, largely, in my opinion, due to some errors in casting. *Mourning Becomes Electra* illustrates my point that in order to improve the quality of pictures, there must be room for failure as well as success.

The following year I visited England's famous motion-picture magnate, J. Arthur Rank, a big cumbersome man with a large nose and a shy smile, and he expressed his thanks for the successful promotion we had made of Olivier's *Henry V.* I told him I felt the picture had been of great value to the American motion-picture industry, because it had demonstrated that there was a large American public for artistic pictures. "Larry Olivier is coming in to see me this morning," he remarked. "He wants to discuss with me the possibility of making a picture of *Hamlet.* What do you think are its chances for success in the States?" I replied that they were excellent, and I added that I hoped he would give the Guild the opportunity of sponsoring *Hamlet* in the same way that we had sponsored *Henry V.* The next time I was in London, I was invited by Olivier to visit him at the studio at Denham where *Hamlet* was being screened. He led me through the maze of stone buildings, staircases, bastions and ramparts of Elsinore, and explained how he planned to make the picture. "I'm not making this in color," he explained, "because I think the contrast of black, white and the gray of the stone are more dramatic, and are more suited to tragedy than the color which inevitably tends to prettify everything it portrays." Olivier's hair was dyed light blonde, and as I saw him commanding groups of camera men, technicians, stagehands and actors while waiting for him, I thought he looked far more like the dictatorial Julius Caesar than the irresolute Hamlet of tradition. Indeed, I thought, if ever *Julius Caesar* is made into a motion picture, Olivier must do it. When *Hamlet* was finished, it was also sponsored in this country by the Theatre Guild, and more than fulfilled the prophecy I made to Arthur Rank.

These two great pictures are in my opinion, landmarks which may ultimately change the attitude of American motion-picture makers toward the production of motion pictures as works of art, for there is at least as large an audience for this type of production as there is for most of the claptrap which pours off the Hollywood assembly line. The "industry" responded to the idea by dropping their support of the "Oscar" awards when the grateful actors and actresses of Hollywood conferred it on Sir Laurence Olivier for his magnificent achievement.

We had failed, in the early days of talking pictures, to stamp the Guild imprint of quality on a type of motion picture, and so I decided that as soon as possible I would try to coax the infant television craft toward the Theatre Guild type of play and production. Before the war I had seen some theatre television productions made by National Broadcasting Company and Columbia Broadcasting Company but these ceased with the war, and at the time I returned from England in 1947, there were no plays being given on television other than a stock company (Kraft's) operated by an advertising agency.

When I was in London for the opening of *Oklahoma!* early in 1947, I visited the television studios of the British Broadcasting Company at the suggestion of John C. Green, Chief Engineer of the National Inventors Council, who had previously visited the London studios and thought they were far ahead of similar establishments in the United States. I found that Denis Johnston, author of *The Moon in the Yellow River*, which we had presented in New York, was in charge of the Program Department. I saw some television plays in London, and realized that while still technically imperfect, the medium would ultimately be capable of bringing the finest works of the theatre into the homes of the people. Terry and Armina shared my interest in the subject and together we decided to go forward.

I explained my ideas to Niles Trammell, John Royal and Warren Wade of the National Broadcasting Company, and they entered into an agreement with the Theatre Guild to produce a television play each month for seven months, each concern to pay its own expenses, it being our intention that each play should represent the best we could supply as theatrical producers, with the assistance of the television experts and directors provided by the National Broadcasting Company. We formed a small department headed by Warren Caro and we brought over from England Denis Johnston to direct our first play. We also decided, as a matter of sentiment, that we would begin our series with our first theatre success, St. John Ervine's *John Ferguson*, with Thomas Mitchell and Joyce Redman. We had to cut the running time of the play down to one hour, and the condensation unfortunately brought the emotional situations too close together and consequently turned this fine Irish drama into a melodrama. The general consensus was that our first experiment was far from successful. I had no quarrel with this appraisal, for we had to do our experiments in public. I knew, however, that if we proceeded with the program, we would learn from one play to the next just what the medium called for, and improvement would be shown. This turned out to be correct.[2] We were successful in securing permission from G.B.S. to present *The Great Catherine* exactly as written, and we engaged Gertrude Lawrence for the title role. It was directed by Fred Coe and produced by me, and the acting of Gertie Lawrence, Michael MacLiammoir, David Wayne and Joan McCracken was excellent. It was the first television play of Bernard Shaw to be performed, and it opened the first large studio of the National Broadcasting Company. A kinescope copy of the televised play reposes in the Museum of Modern Art.

Our seventh and last production, Thornton Wilder's *Our Town*, with Raymond Massey acting as narrator, was the most interesting television play produced in the series. John Gassner, writing in *The Forum* magazine, had the following to say on the subject of this production:

Unless I greatly miss my guess, the Theatre Guild's telecast of *Our Town* over NBC on Sunday, June 6th, will go down in history as the day when televised drama was really born. It was the first time that a play of quality

---

[2] Our next play was *Angel Street* by Patrick Hamilton, with Betty Field, which was staged by Edward Sobol. Other plays which followed included *Morning's at Seven* by Paul Osborn, produced by Armina and staged by Fred Coe, *Stage Door* by Edna Ferber and George Kaufman, produced by Terry and staged by Eddie Sobol, who also staged *The Late George Apley* dramatized by George Kaufman.

was televised in the new medium with style and distinction. Congratulations are in order to the producer Lawrence Langner, to the Guild's television executive Warren Caro, to Frederick Coe who directed, and to the good cast headed by Raymond Massey in the celebrated Frank Craven role. More importantly, however, it is possible at last to appraise a televised production without condescension and to draw conclusions as to its worth as a dramatic form. This is because the Guild's *Our Town*, while suffering from the as yet unsolved technical problems, accomplished what every art does; it turned the limitations of the medium into an advantage, just as the good sculptor takes advantage of the intractability of his materials instead of being defeated by the conditions of his art.

These seven plays were the first to be presented after the war and made television history. They set a pattern for other long plays which were produced for CBS by Worthington Miner, long associated with the Guild, who was one of the earliest pioneers and has made the greatest artistic contribution to television, along with Frederick Coe of NBC. Our program was followed by the Philco Theatre of the Air, which was produced by Actors' Equity Association for the benefit of its Actors' Fund.

Having started a trend in television toward the best works of the theatre, we had no great urge to continue on a commercial basis under which we were allowed only a single week to produce each play. We felt that each television play should be an event, with enough time for rehearsals to produce works of art, and this condition will, we hope, be present in any additional plays we may present in the new medium.

I often ask myself, after television, what? Having devoted myself for years to the living theatre, I found myself harassed by the very inventions I had helped to patent. One of my earliest clients was the American Biograph Company, with its stars, Mary Pickford and John Bunny, whose motion pictures gave the theatre some of its first competition. Then came another client, the Marconi Company, now the Radio Corporation of America, with the radio, which began to make working in the theatre more complex. Then came another client, Warner Brothers, who introduced the talking picture which made real inroads into the theatre. Then came a number of clients with television to make work in the theatre even more complex. I pray that with the perfection of television, the cycle of invention may come to an end. There are many who say that these inventions have helped the living theatre. They have greatly increased the reproduction and transmission of theatrical entertainment, but despite the advantage the living theatre has received, these inventions have, up to now, taken far more from the theatre than they have returned to it.

In the face of all these innovations, it requires a strong effort to keep from being confused by the different paths along which the theatre now seems to be traveling. As I look back over the past, and into the future, I affirm that those values which have made for the great theatre of the past will continue in the future, and that science has little to add to art in this respect.

Paraphrasing the Statement of Faith of Shaw's character Dubedat in *The Doctor's Dilemma,* I believe in Euripides, Aristophanes, Shakespeare, Congreve, Moliere, Sheridan, Ibsen, Strindberg, Chekhov, Shaw, Synge and O'Neill, and in the desire of audiences for beauty everlasting, and the message of art which has made the works of these authors eternal.

But believing is not enough. Conditions are such that the works of most of these authors, with the possible exception of Shaw, are seldom performed sufficiently today to satisfy the hunger of the ever-growing audiences of this country.[3]

In literature we are accustomed to buying in a book store the masterpieces of all periods. In the theatre, the very expression "revival" is generally regarded as a term of derogation. Yet it is largely by contact with the greatness of our past that we can enkindle the flame of art in our own generation and pass it on to the future. In England, stimulated by the excellent work of the "Old Vic" Company and the recently revivified Shakespeare Festival Company of Stratford-on-Avon, there has begun a renascence of the poetic theatre, which, although limited so far as this country has seen, to the efforts of T. S. Eliot and Christopher Fry, stems more from the theatre of Shakespeare than from Ibsen and the realists, and may have far-reaching consequences for the British and American theatres of tomorrow.

During the summer of 1950, Armina and I witnessed some performances at the Shakespeare Memorial Theatre at Stratford-on-Avon, and I came away with the feeling that it was extremely important for the American theatre to enlarge the appreciation of Shakespeare in the way this has been done in England. The Shakespeare Memorial

---

[3] The Theatre Guild's policy of presenting a classical revival from time to time has been limited mainly by the great costs involved, but in spite of this, we have given our audiences *As You Like It* and *The Relapse* within the past two seasons. Of these, *The Relapse* resulted in a loss of over $77,000, while the production cost of *As You Like It*, which exceeded $112,000 was recouped only because Katharine Hepburn, with characteristic gallantry, trouped it all over the country, breaking records everywhere, until a small profit was made.

Theatre, under the brilliant direction of Anthony Quayle, is now open for five months each season, and its Acting Company also tours the Colonies from time to time. Many Americans visit the birthplace of the Bard and attend the plays, but these are only a handful compared to the many thousands of theatre-hungry people in this country who rarely have a chance to view a fine Shakespearean production.

I have always felt that Shakespeare belonged as much to America as to England. It was the ancestors of the Anglo-Saxon settlers of America for whom his plays were written, as well as for those whose descendants remained in England. The English language which the venturesome founding fathers brought to America bears the imprint of his genius, and if it has been modified here by the passage of time, it has been almost equally modified in England too. (I hear a loud snort echoing across the Atlantic as I write these lines.) The theatre of America as well as the theatre of Great Britain has been built from its beginnings on the foundations of Shakespeare. One has only to recall that the reputations of most of our greatest American actors during the past hundred years were made in the playing of Shakespeare, and I believe this will continue far into the future.

To help in the rebirth of a Shakespearean theatre in this country, I have begun a project for an American Shakespearean Festival Theatre utilizing a building patterned after the Old Globe Theatre in London, but containing every convenience of modern adaptability.[4] Terry and Armina have seconded the proposal with enthusiasm. With such a theatre located in the country, many thousands of Americans who cannot afford a trip to England will be able to witness the finest Shakespearean productions during the summer vacation season, and afterwards the Festival Acting Company will also be able to tour the country during the winter. Such a theatre should belong to the nation, and in an era when our writers are confused by television, motion pictures, radio and the rest, it should serve as a beacon from the past to the future, illuminating the eternal verities of truth, beauty and poetic imagination.

---

[4] See Appendix VI, p. 468, for fuller information regarding this project.

CHAPTER XXXIII

Summation

I HAVE felt impelled to write this book because of my deep interest in the theatre to which I have devoted the greater part of my life. In writing it, however, I found that I was writing not merely a personal chronicle, but also the chronicle of a generation which started out with high hopes for American culture, of which the theatre formed an important part. This generation believed in the high mission of art not as a reform movement, but as an expression of civilized ideals, deep realization and a love of beauty, and it worked to preserve and advance these values within the framework of Western democratic society.

My generation started out with a belief in reason, good will and the high aspirations of the people, and working together through four decades, it produced a fellowship that brought forth good results in literature, the theatre and all the other arts. It passed through periods of high achievement often followed by disillusion, but it never was willing to succumb to despair and negativism.

It would be pleasant to be able to look back on a long life of work in the theatre, and to feel that one had accomplished all one had set out to do. Alas, that pleasure is denied me. Along with my earlier colleagues of the Washington Square Players and a band of pioneers, which among others included Arthur Hopkins, Winthrop Ames, George Cram Cook, Eugene O'Neill, and their colleagues of The Provincetown Players, the Lewisohn sisters of The Neighborhood Playhouse, and Robert Edmond Jones, Kenneth Macgowan and many others, we paved the way for a new professional theatre which was hospitable to works of art, and in this respect my colleagues of the Theatre Guild, along with Theresa Helburn and myself, were in the van of the revolution which changed the face of the American Theatre in the twenties and thirties. This change made possible the production and appreciation today all over the country, of plays that are works of art which might not otherwise have taken place. Again, the musical theatre was greatly improved by the influence of the Guild's productions of the *Garrick Gaieties,* the youthful mother of all the little revues, *Porgy and Bess,* a progenitor of America folk opera, and *Oklahoma!* which introduced to the world a new form of musical and ballet theatre, followed by *Carousel.*[1]

During the past thirty years, thanks to the talents of our playwrights, actors, scenic artists, critics and producers, the American theatre has risen to its highest stature, and one as high as any other theatre in the world. Since this renaissance of the American theatre, there have come to the forefront a group of playwrights second to none, led by Eugene O'Neill, and which includes Robert E. Sherwood, Maxwell Anderson, S. N. Behrman, Philip Barry, Elmer Rice, Paul Green, Thornton Wilder, Clifford Odets, Sydney Kingsley, Tennessee Williams, Arthur Miller, William Saroyan, Lillian Hellman, George Kelly, the English-born John van Druten, and many others, and such geniuses of the musical theatre as Richard Rodgers, Oscar Hammerstein, George Gershwin, Cole Porter, Irving Berlin and Jerome Kern. Another group of writers of delightful satiric comedies also developed under the leadership of George Kaufman, Marc Connelly, Ben Hecht, Charles MacArthur, Howard Lindsay and Russel Crouse.

In the march of History, all accomplishments in the theatre are ephemeral, except for the great plays which have been written and produced that will be a heritage for the generations to come, and the few rare instances where a great theatre company survives its initial impulse. The theatre can slip rapidly back into relying on the old type of commercial plays, and indeed, it always seems to be on the point of doing so. It is my hope that this chronicle may throw some light on at least a few of the important events of this era, and encourage others to continue to work with enthusiasm for a better theatre.

The resurgence which took place in the American theatre after about the year 1915 was part of a greater movement which began in Europe with the advent of Ibsen and his contemporaries, and grew into one of the great periods of the theatre, a period which can bear comparison with the great theatre of the Greeks and the Elizabethans, and the lesser theatre of the Restoration. Such periods of the theatre's

---

[1] See Appendix VIII, p. 473, for Theatre Guild plays and N. Y. opening dates.

blossoming are rare. Along with my colleagues at the Theatre Guild, I worked on the original productions of some of the greatest plays of this era—plays such as Shaw's *Saint Joan,* and O'Neill's *Mourning Becomes Electra,* and *Strange Interlude,* as well as many of the fine plays of Robert Sherwood, Maxwell Anderson, S. N. Behrman and other important American authors. I have not attempted to appraise these plays in terms of art—but rather to describe them and their authors in relation to their actual production in the living theatre. To some extent, this has been their story, as well as my own. It is also the story in part of the important actors of this period, such as Alfred Lunt and Lynn Fontanne, and many others with whom I have been associated. It is also, in part, the story of my colleagues in the Washington Square Players and the Theatre Guild, but particularly of Theresa Helburn, who has contributed so notably to most of the productions of the Guild, and of my wife, Armina Marshall, who has worked side by side with me in most of my undertakings.

With the passing of the years, as Terry has grown older, she has grown more resolute in accomplishment, more attractive in appearance and more mellow in temperament. Years ago she showed her contempt for middle-age by dyeing her hair a becoming shade of blue, to the admiration of the fashionable world, and the bewilderment of the rest of humanity. She became seemingly more energetic, more youthful; she played tennis better, swam better and worked better, until her very energy became a problem for us all. "What can we do to stop her producing more plays, seeing more actors, making more plans and trips?" we would say in councils of desperation. But we can do nothing to stop her. She arrives at the Theatre Guild building in the morning, takes the two flights of stairs at high speed, enters her feminine-looking office and proceeds to work on three things at a time. She dictates a sentence to her secretary, speaks another into the telephone, and with a third welcomes a bewildered playwright who sits glumly with his manuscript clutched to his bosom, awaiting the moment when she will pounce upon his cherished masterpiece. She will carry on interviews with three different persons in the same room or in three different rooms with equal ease, and as she flits from one to another, she will hum a happy little song. Nobody knows what song she hums; the melody is unrecognizable. But I rather suspect that what she sings to herself is:

> I am happy, really happy,
> Make it snappy—really snappy

In my office, in my bed,
I must quickly go ahead
With the projects in my head
I will be a long time dead!

Terry herself thinks the words she sings are, "I'm so tired, I'm so tired."
But one day, as she sang, blithely unaware of the fact, I stopped her
and asked what she was humming. Terry replied, to her own surprise,
"In the Shade of the Old Apple Tree." "Just a desire to desert Broadway for the quiet of country life," I suggested grimly. In the summer
of 1950, in attempting to lift the manhole cover at her swimming pool,
(something which only a superwoman would have attempted), she
sprained her back, which temporarily slowed down her physical pace
to that of a normal human being, but her mental drive is just as
energetic as ever.

As to Armina, she too continues to overflow with energy. She produces one play a week on the radio program, serves as associate producer on at least one dramatic play each year, and in her spare time
is a director of the Westport Country Playhouse, an excellent amateur
gardener and farmer, and accomplishes miracles in healing the wounds
which I cause unwittingly by my absent-mindedness. She is in so
many ways the exact opposite of myself that most of my so-called
good qualities or deeds (if any) are merely attitudes or actions into
which I, one of the laziest of men, have been shamed by her. Her
early life on her father's farm in the Cherokee Strip, and the many
hours of her youth spent in the saddle, have given her a love of
exercise and the great outdoors which I share, as it were, vicariously.
Thus, as I lie abed each morning and watch her exercise vigorously
for ten minutes on arising, my own muscles respond sympathetically—
such is the bond between us—and by the time she has finished I am
positively tired. But let no one imagine that she permits this condition to prevail without protest. Periodically she decides that exercise
would exhilarate me instead of tiring me, and it has almost cost me
my life to demonstrate that she is wrong. Thus, she has induced me
to exercise with a medicine ball, only to wrench a muscle in my arm;
to play "soft ball" baseball at Westport against a team captained by
Frederic March which ended in a strained ligament that put me out
of commission for a season; to spend a month on a dude ranch riding
a wide-backed horse named Katherine which resulted in my undergoing the agonies of parturition until a cowboy named Monty Montana adjusted my stirrups and saved me from splitting in two; and

finally to build an oval swimming pool with an island in the middle, so that, since I was too lazy to turn around and swim back and forth, I would be able to continue swimming around and around the island, a dream which never came true as I was always tired out about halfway around. Finally, in despair, she gave up, leaving me to lead my normal sedentary life, as a result of which I have been relatively healthy and hearty over the years.

As to myself, running in harness with two such teammates, what can I do but try to gallop along in order not to be left behind? Fortunately, on rare occasions, one or the other of them tires herself out, and then my old habit of endurance comes to the rescue, and I take over—for the moment. This has been useful in an organization where we seldom produce less than four or five plays each season, together with our radio program. And now other activities face me with an inevitable challenge. Among these are the operations of the National Inventors Council arising out of the threat of another World War under which we are now living. The danger is admittedly great, yet, in my opinion, not sufficiently great to justify closing down or greatly limiting our cultural activities. On the contrary, I envision an America which is strong both in the military sense and in the cultural sense.

Troubled as to how I might keep both of these objectives clearly in mind and at the same time preserve my sense of humor in a confusing world, I devised a philosophy for myself which I call "Leapism." A Leapist is one who leaps into the future with his imagination, and views each event of today both from its beginning in the present, and its ending in the future. In this way, the Leapist looks at what is happening in the world with some perspective, looking backward at it as well as forward. Take your newspaper today and read it as though you were reading it fifty years hence, and note how trivial are most of the happenings it records; and as to that new great war which everyone had expected, there is always the possibility, as Bernard Shaw once stated, that no great nation wants to commit suicide—so why should two of them want to do so?

Freed by this philosophy from listening too despondently to counsels of disaster, I affirm my belief in Twentieth-Century America. There is no place on earth where there is greater freedom for artistic or scientific accomplishment or more kindness and good will to strangers, and I am deeply grateful to the people of the United States who gave me the opportunity of living here and serving as a free citizen of this country.

Yet, despite all this freedom of accomplishment, we have barely scratched the surface of what should be done to foster the arts and to satisfy the artistic and spiritual needs of the American people, needs which have been accentuated by the leisure given by our highly developed scientific labor-saving economy. We cannot satisfy these needs merely by means of motion pictures, radio or television entertainment of the type now being purveyed to the public. (I except, of course, those artistic productions which are very much in the minority.) In my opinion, one of the vital needs of our times is for more creation in the field of the arts, whether it be in painting, literature, music, acting or entertaining others. To this, of course, should be added the actual participation in sports, which is diminishing while the public appreciation of exhibitions of expert sportsmanship and games is increasing. This has resulted in the ridiculous situation that we have millions of the public ready to turn out to see a prize fight, and scarcely a single prize fighter worth seeing. And if we fail to provide for richer creative opportunities than we are doing at the present, the same will be true of painters, musicians, playwrights, actors and entertainers. Indeed it is significant that most of our best comedians, and film and television actors, were trained in an entirely different medium, the variety shows, music halls or legitimate theatres, where the audiences were far smaller, but the opportunities for creative talent to develop were far greater than in the mass entertainment of today.

Many of my friends will protest in horror "What are you advocating? A host of amateurs—amateur painters, writers, singers, musicians, and, horror of horrors, amateur actors and amateur theatricals?" I am advocating just that. I believe that from a nation of amateurs can spring a theatre of professionals, and that if we insist on solely supporting professionalism, we will end up with nothing to support. In arriving at this conclusion I am naturally influenced by the fact that we who started the Theatre Guild, which has been accused of everything except a lack of professionalism, began as amateurs. It was the amateur efforts of the Washington Square Players, based on earlier amateur theatricals, which launched our theatre movement with all its consequences to the American Theatre. Moreover, Stanislavsky and the actors who formed the famous Moscow Art Theatre also began as amateurs, as did Lady Gregory's Irish Players of the Abbey Theatre, Dublin, and so were many of the world's best actors in their early beginnings.

The term "amateur" means one who works for love of the work, and it well described the spirit of our theatrical undertaking, and of the early efforts of many others who have developed into important professional art theatres. Out of a thousand amateur performers, many professional performers may develop, while out of a thousand radio or television viewers, nothing may develop at all. It is, in my opinion, one of the most heartening signs of the times that amateur theatre groups are developing all over the country into small professional acting companies, which in turn have produced such important local groups as the Cleveland Playhouse, the Pittsburgh Playhouse, the Dallas Theatre-in-the-Round, the Seattle University Theatres and a host of others. Looked down upon by the wiseacres of Broadway, this is the soil which is continually replenishing the American theatre, and which merits the major attention of the American National Theatre and Academy (ANTA).

There is, in my opinion, an untapped source of creative energy in the American people which could well be put into action and from which great spiritual satisfaction would result. This creative energy would be liberated once our people realized that within themselves are many facets, and that among these, in far more instances than are now realized, is the ability to create artistically. Unfortunately, we all tend to accept undue limitations about ourselves. At an early age we train our children with a limited objective. We give them a general education, and then implant the idea that men and women must specialize in one subject to earn a living, and that this is usually all it is possible to encompass in a lifetime. I do not believe this to be generally true, and my own life has been a denial of it. The capacity for all kinds of expression is, I firmly believe, latent in most of us if we do not shut our minds to it. Many a farmer's wife is a potential Grandma Moses, and if we doubt this, we have only to recall the beautifully artistic quilted bedspreads and originally designed rag rugs which were made in American farmhouses when the farmers' wives and daughters led a far more rugged, hard-working existence than they do today.

I believe that since our people's creative imagination is unbounded in the field of science, invention and art, we should be able to look forward to a far richer era of civilization than has yet been attained. Unfortunately, there are some factors militating against this in the field of entertainment. Among these are the pressure groups which exercise a censorship of motion pictures, radio and television. It is an ironic paradox that the pressure groups which most resent government interference with business, science, invention and religion, are often the very ones who are in the forefront in interfering with the free expression of creative artists. Thus it is too often only the second-rate artist who is willing to remain in fields such as motion pictures, television and radio, in which these pressure groups are constantly insisting that artists create solely along lines agreeable to them. A revolt against this condition, however, is already under way, and this revolt is spearheaded by the legitimate theatre, which has retained its freshness and originality by refusing to be censored except in the mildest way.

In making an optimistic forecast of the possibilities of our civilization, which affords freedom in science, invention and art, I do so at a time when we find ourselves forced to challenge the world dream of Communism with our own world dream of freedom of thought and imagination. We need not fear for the ultimate outcome, for inherent in the doctrines of Communism is the fettering of the imagination. The artist must create not what his imagination urges him to create, but what the State requires him to create. The scientist must relate his hypotheses to the Party Line. The inventor must invent along the lines of State interest; the novelist, the poet, the dramatist, the painter, the composer, all must wear the livery of the Party Line. What contribution to the future of civilization can be expected under these conditions?

In the field of drama, with which I am especially familiar, I know of no dramatist of any importance who has arisen in the past thirty years in Russia, despite the millions of rubles spent by the Soviet government in subsidizing the theatre. And in the field of modern industrial invention, with which I am also familiar, the Russian talent lags far behind that of the Western nations. Most of what the Soviet Union has in the way of industry and invention is copied from the West, and the pathetic efforts of the Communist Party to claim for Russia the invention of the steam engine, the electric light and the radio have deceived nobody but themselves. If we continue to maintain our inventive lead by constant vigilance and the application of more and more stimulus to our native talent for invention, we have nothing to fear inventively from the Russians.

Our own dangers, on the technological side, lie in overconfidence and a tendency on the part of our government and courts today to discourage inventors; to overcome this the National Inventors Council has just launched a vigorous campaign to secure the best treatment of inventors by the Government. While overconfidence is bad, too little confidence is even worse. I deplore the way we tend to frighten ourselves with our own atomic inventions. In my opinion, we should build a superior striking force and face the future calmly, secure in the knowledge that no one will dare to use such weapons on us first without reaping a tenfold more frightful harvest as a consequence.

Since World War II American research and invention have taken a tremendous leap forward, and the nation's resources in this field are now much greater than they were in 1940. This increase in inventive activity has been reflected in the expansion of the firm of Langner, Parry, Card and Langner, which now includes six younger partners in New York and Chicago, in addition to John Parry, Herbert Langner and myself. The additional partners are George von Gehr, Steven Ladas, Leonard Robbins, Del Valle Goldsmith, Sidney Deschamps and Verne Peterson, who have contributed notably to the firm's success.

What of the future of the American theatre under present conditions? It is often said today that our playwrights are confused and do not know what to write about. I disagree. I much prefer the work of the young American writers of today as compared with the young writers of the thirties and early forties, who too often mistook the stage for a political platform. Admitting all the incompetencies of our theatre, it still offers opportunities to the young writer, and these opportunities are growing rather than declining. In this connection, we appear to be coming to the end of a great era of playwriting. The writers who have followed O'Neill in this country, Shaw in England, Ibsen in Norway, Strindberg in Sweden, Pirandello in Italy, Rostand in France, Werfel and Schnitzler in Austria, Molnar in Hungary and Chekhov and Gorki in Russia, have been lesser men up to now. But the present world theatre continues to produce new writers of stature, except in the totalitarian countries. The light went out in Hitler's Germany and Austria, in Mussolini's Italy and in Stalin's Russia, and it has stayed out in all the countries behind the Iron Curtain whose art theatres more than ever before depend for their popularity on the classics and works of authors written before the Revolution.

It therefore devolves on all of us interested in a free theatre to give young playwrights a hearing and to produce their plays without reference to financial gain or loss. The Theatre Guild has been carrying on this experimental work at my theatre at Westport during the summer for several years past, and has been actively aided and abetted by our intelligent audiences. This project has already borne substantial fruit, and we have introduced some new writers of considerable merit. Among these is Robert McEnroe, author of *The Silver Whistle*, produced at Westport during the season of 1948 with the irrepressibly gay and versatile actor, José Ferrer, in the leading role, and William Inge, who wrote *Come Back, Little Sheba,* one of the best plays of last season's vintage which gave to Shirley Booth and Sidney Blackmer the best roles of their acting careers.

I regard as next in importance in the unfinished business of the theatre, new audiences to support the best plays. Here the Theatre Guild-American Theatre Society is constantly at work in the larger cities, finding a superior audience for a superior type of play. Our policy of not giving the public "what it wants," but what we consider the best, has generally met with success, as evidenced by the support of our members; and where we have failed, it has usually been our own fault for not holding sufficiently to our own standards or not finding sufficient plays of our own or other managements. It has not always been possible to hold to these standards. During our first ten years, we had all the literature of the world to choose from, and in this period we produced sixty-six plays of which fifty were by foreign authors, and only sixteen by American writers. Not unnaturally, we were bitterly accused of favoring foreign playwrights, but we stuck to our principle, which was to produce important artistic plays regardless of their national origin.

During our second period of ten years, our policy bore fruit, for the new American authors wrote up to our standards, so that approximately half the plays we produced were by American authors and the other half were by Europeans. During our third period of ten years, we produced over thirty-five American plays, and only twenty by European writers. Thus, in three decades, we passed from a preponderance of European plays to a preponderance of American plays. Having produced many of the masterpieces of the world theatre, our standards have necessarily fluctuated as the supply of good plays fluctuated. Our subscription audiences located in over twenty cities and now numbering over one hundred thousand members, remains a valuable asset in the American theatrical picture, and we have continuously given the producers of other plays of artistic worth, the benefit of our following. (Incidentally, the subscription system, ever since its inception, has been operated as a nonprofit venture.)

Further, in the unfinished business of the theatre, is the need for improvement in the art of acting. Our country has produced, in every recent generation, some of the world's finest actors. But the increasing mechanization of mass entertainment does not tend to produce great artists. The dramatic schools and the summer theatres are doing their best, but not enough, for too often no sooner does a talented young artist place his footsteps on the first few rungs of the ladder than he is sold across the continent to the sterile lots of Hollywood.

There is room for considerable improvement in the teaching of acting and especially in the schools and studios employing the so-called Stanislavsky method. These have contributed much to the training of young people in imaginative realistic acting, but in my opinion their methods have little in common with the training which produced the great acting of Stanislavsky and his original colleagues of the Moscow Art Theatre. Indeed, the Stanislavsky who wrote in his autobiography that "the operetta and vaudeville make the best school for actors" would have made short shrift with some of the American exponents of his methods.[1] Stanislavsky believed in training in voice, diction, gesture, movement and "a tremendous amount of outward technique" which, along with basic inner emotional acting, is also the proper way to train actors in the great tradition of the English speaking theatre. One shudders to imagine what actors trained in the American-Stanislavsky method would do to the plays of Shakespeare, for while their basic acting imaginations would no doubt be working properly, their lack of training in voice, carriage, diction and the music of poetry would handicap them hopelessly. The Actors Studio, which has done much praiseworthy work in the training of young actors, is alive to the dangers of this situation and hopes to remedy them. But perhaps there is a good reason why we lack such training at present. If the actors had it, where would they use it? Given a Shakespeare Festival Theatre, I believe the production of the classics would be greatly stimulated, and our acting schools and studios would soon have a good reason for enlarging their curriculum to include the proper training for such plays.

Finally, the effect of mounting costs on experimental or artistic productions must be met and conquered. This has already been partly accomplished in the summer theatres. The importance of this subject goes far beyond economics, for the theatre cannot progress without experiment or freedom for artistic achievement, and unless it can progress, it will ultimately pass into another period of sterility.

A self-appraisal of over thirty years' work in the Theatre Guild leaves me with the feeling that there will never be a time when the

---

[1] See *My Life in Art*, by Constantin Stanislavsky, Little, Brown and Company, Boston, 1924, page 122.

work is done. Fortunately, though we grow old, the theatre continues to be eternally young. What we have accomplished will soon pass into the limbo of forgotten things, and succeeding new generations have already taken over in places where we left off. Our generation has worked hard throughout long and busy lives, to influence the American theatre from time to time in the direction of the eternally great in art. To the extent to which we have succeeded, we shall have laid a foundation on which the theatre of the future can build.

For there is a new future for the theatre which belongs to the new generations. New ideas are constantly coming into the theatre and challenging the generations which evolve them. One of these is the theatre-in-the-round, or arena type of theatre, which eliminates the proscenium arch and the use of representational scenery. Who will accept the challenge of this revolutionary idea, descended from the ageless Greek theatre (in which some of the world's greatest masterpieces were originated), yet adapted to modern conditions in a form which may bring the costs of production down to a level where the living theatre may compete economically with all the reproducing inventions? For the first time in my life, the opportunity exists to build a large theatre of this type for repertory—a challenge which if accepted with the requisite vision, could produce a new acting company which could support itself without subsidy, since it has little or no expense in changing nightly from one play to another—the rock on which all American Repertory companies have foundered in the past. And then there is the idea of using television on large screens in large theatres. A superb play could be given by a great acting company on a stage in one city, and it may be witnessed in thousands of other theatres simultaneously in all the towns and villages of the country. What a challenge to the new generations to develop this new form of the theatre and to insist that it be not cheapened or abased. And finally, there are the new authors who will write the new plays for these new theatres. They must be inspired with the timeless spirit of the great writers for the theatre, so that their work can take its place along with the best the ages have produced. What great new vistas of the imagination lie ahead for the new workers in the theatre! What countless new opportunities for the creative workers with the will to create! I envy them!

THE END

APPENDIX I

The Washington Square Players

(See Chapter X, Pages 92 and 103)

The Washington Square Players was founded in the year 1914. Most prominent among the founders were Edward Goodman, Philip Moeller, Helen Westley, Josephine A. Meyer, Lucy Huffaker, Ida Rauh, Dudley Tucker, Albert Boni and Lawrence Langner.

Additional members who were active in the beginnings of the Washington Square Players were drawn from all the arts and crafts, and included Charles Boni, publisher, Walter Frankl, painter, Robert Miner, cartoonist, Floyd Dell, novelist, Edwina Behrer, musician, Remo Bufano, marionettist, Holland Hudson, writer, Karl Karsten, statistician, Ralph Roeder, writer, Florence Enright, actress, Bobby Edwards, Greenwich Village song writer, Sam A. Eliot, Jr., college professor, Edward J. Ballentine, painter, George Cram Cook, writer, Susan Glaspell, novelist, Robert Locker, illustrator, William Pennington, scenic artist, Mary Morris, actress, Daisy Thompson, housewife, and Edward Flanner, an enthusiastic businessman.

The actors in the opening performance of the Washington Square Players at the Bandbox Theatre included Ida Rauh, Josephine A. Meyer, and George C. Somnes. Other important actors who joined with the Players later on were Roland Young, Harold Meltzer, Lydia Lopokova, Arthur Hohl, Frank Conroy, Robert Strange, José Ruben, Elizabeth Patterson, Katharine Cornell and Glenn Hunter. There were many other excellent actors, too numerous to specify, but Margaret Mower, Gwladys Wynne, Noel Haddon, Kate Morgan, Michio Ito, and Mary Shaw in *Mrs. Warren's Profession* deserve special mention.

The following are the Playbills of the Washington Square Players:

First Bill, First Season (February, 1915)
   Licensed by Basil Lawrence (Lawrence Langner); *Eugenically Speaking* by Edward Goodman; *Interior* by Maurice Maeterlinck; *Another Interior* by an unknown author.
Second Bill, First Season (March, 1915)
   Love of One's Neighbor by Leonid Andreyev; *Moondown* by John Reed; *Two Blind Beggars and One Less Blind* by Philip Moeller; *The Shepherd in the Distance* by Holland Hudson; *My Lady's Honor* by Murdock Pemberton.
Third Bill, First Season (May, 1915)

In April by Rose Pastor Stokes; *Forbidden Fruit* by Octave Feuillet; *Saviors* by Edward Goodman; *The Miracle of St. Anthony* by Maurice Maeterlinck.

Fourth Bill, First Season (May, 1915)

The Bear by Chekhov; *Eugenically Speaking* by Edward Goodman; *Interior* by Maurice Maeterlinck; *The Shepherd in the Distance* by Holland Hudson.

First Bill, Second Season (October, 1915)

Fire and Water by Hervey White; *Night of Snow* by Roberto Bracco; *Helena's Husband* by Philip Moeller; *The Antick* by Percy Mackaye; *Interior* by Maurice Maeterlinck.

Second Bill, Second Season (November, 1915)

Whims by Alfred de Musset; *Literature* by Arthur Schnitzler; *Overtones* by Alice Gerstenberg; *The Honorable Lover* by Robert Bracco.

Third Bill, Second Season (January, 1916)

The Tenor by Frank Wedekind; *The Roadhouse in Arden* by Philip Moeller; *The Clod* by Lewis Beach; *The Red Cloak* by Lawrence Langner and Josephine A. Meyer.

Fourth Bill, Second Season (March, 1916)

Children by Guy Bolton and Tom Carlton; *Age of Reason* by Cecil Dorrian; *The Magical City* by Zöe Akins; *Pierre Patelin* by an unknown author.

Special Performance, May 7, 1916

Aglavaine and Selysette by Maurice Maeterlinck.

Fifth Bill, Second Season (May, 1916)

The Sea Gull by Chekov.

After this presentation, the Washington Square Players moved to the Comedy Theatre.

Summer Bill at the Comedy Theatre, June 5, 1916

The Honorable Lover by Robert Bracco; *Pierre Patelin* by an unknown author; *The Clod* by Lewis Beach; *Helena's Husband* by Philip Moeller.

Summer Bill, Third Season (August, 1916)

The Miracle of St. Anthony by Maurice Maeterlinck; *The Bear* by Chekov; *Literature* by Arthur Schnitzler; *Eugenically Speaking* by Edward Goodman.

First Bill, Third Season (October, 1916)

A Merry Death by Nicholas Evreinov; *The Sugar House* by Alice Brown; *Lover's Luck* by George de Porto Riche; *Sisters of Susanna* by Philip Moeller.

Second Bill, Third Season (November, 1916)

Bushido by Takeda Izumo; *Trifles* by Susan Glaspell; *Another Way Out* by Lawrence Langner; *Altruism* by Karl Ettlinger.

Special Performance, January 14 and 21, 1917

The Life of Man by Leonid Andreyev.

Third Bill, Third Season (February, 1917)

The Last Straw by Bosworth Crocker; *A Private Account* by Courteline; *The Hero of Santa Maria* by Kenneth Sawyer Goodman and Ben Hecht; *The Death of Tintagiles* by Maurice Maeterlinck.

Special Bill, March 12, 1917

Trifles by Susan Glaspell; *Lover's Luck* by George de Porto Riche; *The*

Death of Tintagiles by Maurice Maeterlinck; *The Hero of Santa Maria* by Kenneth Sawyer Goodman and Ben Hecht.

Fourth Bill, Third Season (March, 1917)

  Plots and Playwrights by Edward Massey; *The Poor Fool* by Hermann Bahr; *Sganarelle* by Molière.

Fifth Bill, Third Season (May, 1917)

  Ghosts by Ibsen.

Summer Bill (May, 1917)

  Pariah by August Strindberg; *Another Way Out* by Lawrence Langner; *Plots and Playwrights* by Edward Massey.

Special Bill, Fourth Season (September, 1917)

  The Family Exit by Lawrence Langner.

First Bill, Fourth Season (October, 1917)

  In the Zone by Eugene O'Neill; *The Avenue* by Fenimore Merrill; *Blind Alleys* by Grace Latimer Wright; *His Husband's Widow* by Jacinto Benavente.

Second Bill, Fourth Season (December, 1917)

  The Girl in the Coffin by Theodore Dreiser; *Neighbors* by Zona Gale; *The Critic's Comedy* by Samuel Kaplan; *Yum Chapab* (My Lord, The Dwarf) by J. Garcia Pimentel and Beatrice de Holthoir.

Third Bill, Fourth Season (January, 1918)

  The Sand Bar Queen by George Cronyn; *Suppressed Desires* by Susan Glaspell and George Cram Cook; *The Beautiful Legend of Pokey* by Philip Moeller.

Fourth Bill, Fourth Season (February, 1918)

  Youth by Miles Malleson.

Fifth Bill, Fourth Season (March, 1918)

  Mrs. Warren's Profession by Bernard Shaw.

Sixth Bill, Fourth Season (April, 1918)

  The Home of the Free by Elmer Rice; *Lonesome-Like* by Harold Brighouse; *Salome* by Oscar Wilde.

  In May, 1918, *Salome* was replaced on this bill by *The Rope*, by Eugene O'Neill, and *Close the Book* by Susan Glaspell.

APPENDIX II

"Geneva" Correspondence with Bernard Shaw
(See Chapter XXIII, Page 294)

For the benefit of those who may be interested in how I persuaded Bernard Shaw to rewrite parts of *Geneva*, I append our correspondence:

August 26, 1938

Dear G.B.S.:

Thank you very much indeed for sending me privately printed copy of *Geneva*. I read the play immediately, and while I enjoyed it very much in the main, I was so deeply hurt by certain parts of it that I feel I should write you immediately about same.

I refer especially to the part The Jew plays in this play, and which seems to me to contradict the attitude you have taken for over seventy years of your life. I do not believe that you will want future generations of Jew-baiters to quote you as part authority for a program of torturing, starving and driving to suicide of Jews all over the world. Yet, on Page 65, you give Battler (obviously Hitler) a speech in which he justifies everything that has been done recently in Germany and Austria, on the ground that in every country "the foreigner is the trespasser." As the thought is presented so convincingly by him, it seems that you do not take into account that Jews have lived in Germany for over 1700 years; that they have contributed largely to the cultural and scientific life of Germany; that during the last war alone over 30,000 Jews died in the German armies, and that but for a Jewish scientist, Haber, who invented the method of abstracting nitrogen from the air (which scientist later committed suicide) the Germans would have been defeated in 1916 instead of 1919. You give The Jew merely *the weak answer:* "For my race, there are no frontiers," as though the German Jew of today had anything to do with the historic reasons, beginning with the Roman armies and ending with Torquemada and others, as a result of which some of the Jews found themselves in Germany.

Furthermore, you justify Hitler as though he had merely opened his doors and allowed the Jews to depart, taking with them enough to start them off in other countries. However, . . . every schoolboy knows that, as a result of Hitler's actions, the German Jew who wishes to leave Germany finds every possible obstacle to departing with any means of subsistence or livelihood in another country, while those who remain there are subjected to increasing torture. You justify this torture on Page 66 by stating that Hitler is not responsible for what is done by his underlings. ("I cannot be everywhere, and my agents are not angels.") But, in a dictatorship, who is responsible? On Page 82, you have Battler state on this point: "I do not condescend to defend myself. I have already remarked that the Jews are obnoxious species,

454

which we refuse to tolerate just as we refuse to tolerate venomous snakes."
Instead of giving The Jew an historic answer backed up by facts, you merely
have him *present the weaker side* of his case; to wit: "We Jews have been
driven by persecution *into trade and finance* until we have become more
skillful at them than our lazy persecutors. This has made us their bankers
and employers, and to that extent their masters. The remedy is very simple.
They have only to cultivate their brains as energetically as they cultivate
their muscles. Then they will no longer be our slaves. . . ." etc., etc. The
idea implied by this weak answer, that all that the Jews have contributed
to German civilization can be expressed as "trade and finance," is an absurd
libel to a people which have enriched German culture in every field which
is higher than trade and finance.

Is not The Jew entitled to answer to the German accusation that the Jews
are obnoxious species, that nevertheless Germany and the rest of the world
have numbered among the brightest lights of German culture such men as
Albert Einstein, Hertz, Mendel and Frank, in science; Mendelssohn, Rubin-
stein, Gustav Mahler and Bruno Walter, in music; Wassermann, Ehrlich,
Freud and Adler, in medicine and psychiatry; Heinrich Heine, Feuchtwanger
and Zweig, in literature, and Franz Werfel, Schnitzler and Reinhardt in the
theatre? Yet you give The Jew only the pitiful answer of a reference to his
accomplishments in German "trade and finance." And can anybody properly
call the German iron-masters and bankers "lazy persecutors"? The Germans
as a race are probably the most industrious on earth. . . .

. . . how would you like it if all Irish books, and especially *your* books,
were burned by the English because the Irish were writers of radical literature of the kind calculated to damage the fighting instincts of the British
race? Incidentally, if you happened to be living in Germany instead of Great
Britain, you would find yourself in a concentration camp, and the penalty
for having written *Geneva* would undoubtedly have been a bullet through
your head, for dictators have very little sense of humor.

The final insult to the Jewish race which is contained in your play is
when The Jew, hearing of the end of the world, decides to try to buy up the
securities at a depleted value. Surely, no one would be so stupid, especially
The Jew, to whom, at least, you are willing . . . to ascribe superior intellect
in trade and finance! The Jew in your play is permitted to say nothing regarding the more spiritual aspects of his racial heritage; nor to act on that
heritage; nor show his contribution of such thinkers as Moses, Christ,
Spinoza, etc., all (like yourself) opposed to established tyrannies of power
and thought. He is the creation of Streicher, not of Shaw.

In the unpublished version of *Geneva* which you have sent me, you have
crossed out some of the passages on Pages 82, 83 and 84, which contain some
of the above. I do not know whether it is your intention that these passages
should appear in the printed version, but I know that it is your habit to revise
your plays before they are actually printed. In *St. Joan,* you actually deleted
nearly thirty pages. As one who has venerated you for practically all his life,
and has especially admired your fairness and, above all, your humanity and
kindness, I do most sincerely ask you to reconsider the position you have
given the character of The Jew in this play. Shakespeare, by the character of

Shylock, and Dickens, by the character of Fagin, have added greatly to the
cross of hatred which future generations of Jews must bear. You, who have
always been so understanding through your entire life, will surely not want
to add another figure to a collection which breeds intolerance and racial
hatred.

I am fully aware that whenever a comic Irishman is put upon the stage,
all the Irishmen rise in their wrath and write letters to the newspapers. When
anyone puts a comic Jew on the stage, the same thing happens. You and I
both come of races that are inordinately sensitive to this sort of thing, but do
not overlook the reason: Both races have had hundreds of years of living as
minorities in which they have constantly had to fight an assumption of superiority by the majority. This is a sufficient explanation for this hypersensitivity.
But my criticism of your character of The Jew does not spring from the fact
that you have made him a comic figure. You have not done this. You have
made him a pitifully inferior mouthpiece to express his case, thus playing
into the hands of the breeders of racial hatred by ranging yourself unconsciously on their side.

In a broader sense, judged by the standards of the latter speeches of your
own play, *The Simpleton,* I think you have missed even a more important
point in the present play. I refer to the fact that, while the Judge, at the end
of the play, excoriates both dictatorships and democrats in equal terms,
nevertheless, the impression is left strongly that you range yourself on the
side of the dictators. This is done especially in the character of Bombardine
and his magnificent speech on Page 72, which ends with the words: "Out
of the liberal democratic chaos comes form, purpose, order and rapid execution." But if you will send your mind back over the political history of mankind, you will realize that, out of dictatorships too comes ultimately the same
kind of chaos. It is merely postponed. Democracies breed liberalism and chaos,
and dictatorships breed tyranny and oppression, ultimately leading to chaos.
People will not tolerate tyranny and oppression more than a generation or so.
Then they come back to democracy, and later on to liberalism and chaos all
over again. Strong leaders like Mussolini and Hitler arise, and for a brief
moment in the history of the world, their regimes seem admirable from the
standpoint of efficiency and "getting things done." But does it last? You gave
the historic answer in *The Simpleton.* Looking out over the future, you saw
that man could never submit indefinitely to tyranny; that he would never be
willing to be a well-fed, well-housed political slave. The cry for liberty will
always ring out in the world, as long as the world exists. This is the ultimate
truth, the truth by which man has progressed upward and onward towards
his ultimate destiny. The present dictatorships are mere ephemeral halting
places on the way.

I wonder whether you have ever stopped to contemplate the part you
have contributed to this democratic chaos, with which you are now so im-
patient. St. John Ervine once remarked to me that you have more profoundly
influenced your generation than any other man. . . . The effect of your influence has been exactly the opposite of that of the dictators. You have
preached tolerance, justice, love of the common man, freedom, economic
fairness, elevation of women; and, in England and America, at any rate,
your disciples are numbered by the millions. Yet you seem to justify Fascism

with its intolerance, racial hatred, economic slavery, degradation of women, fanning of the war spirit, etc., mainly on the ground that its dictators are "Supermen" and the Supermen "get things done." Believe me, G.B.S., before you successfully attacked Victorian morality and economics, the plutocratic rulers of England were strong and "got things done." Why not have yourself brought before the bar at the World Court on the ground that you have preached liberalism, tolerance, justice and the other qualities which have permeated all your writings and made the liberal nations so largely what they are today? And make your accusers the very dictators whom you now seem to admire, and then justify yourself for what your teachings have accomplished. I believe that, if you do this, you would add a spice to the play, which to my mind it lacks at the moment. Now that you are restored to health again, I hope you will consider what I have said with your characteristic good humor. I especially hope you will forgive the length of this letter and will understand its spirit, which I am sure only echoes the thoughts of millions of others who love you as I do, and have had their lives and thoughts influenced so strongly by you.

Affectionately,
Lawrence Langner

On the 20th of September G.B.S. replied to this letter:

Dear Lawrence Langner,

Can you wonder at Hitler (and now Mussolini) driving out the Jews? Here am I who have written a play in which I make ruthless fun of British Cabinet Ministers, of German and Italian Dictators, and Cockney young women, of the Buchmanite Oxford movement, of Church of England bishops, and of the League of Nations. Everyone laughs. Not a voice is raised in their defence.

But I have dared to introduce a Jew without holding him up to the admiring worship of the audience as the inheritor of all the virtues and none of the vices of Abraham and Moses, David and Isaiah. And instantly you, Lawrence, raise a wail of lamentation and complaint and accuse me of being a modern Torquemada.

You ask me how I would feel if the British Government burnt my books because I am an Irishman, and then put Irish characters on the stage and made fun of them. Lawrence: the Irish *have* banned my books; and in *John Bull's Other Island* I myself have been far less kind to the Irish characters than I have been to the Jew in *Geneva*, who is introduced solely to convict the Nazis of persecution. But you will not allow him to do exactly what an able Jew of his type would do when Gentiles were swallowing a terrifying Press canard: that is, go into the money market as a bear speculator and make his fortune.

You really are the most thoughtless of Sheenies. However, to please you, I have written up the part a bit. Musso let me down completely by going anti-Semite on me; and I have had to revise the third act to such an extent that you may now put the copy I sent you in the fire as useless, or, better still, sell it as a curiosity. Only 40 copies of it ever existed; and most of them were worn to tatters at rehearsal in Malvern. So go in as a bull speculator.

Meanwhile wait until I send you a revised copy. You may show it to the Guild; but they had better leave it to the Federal Theatre and the 50 cent public, who are a much steadier source of income to me. . . .

Have you ever considered what would have happened to the United States if the Ku-Klux Klan had found as competent a leader as Hitler? There is a play for you in that.

Yours as always,
G. Bernard Shaw

I replied to this on October 7th:

Dear G.B.S.:

Thank you for your letter of the 20th September. If I am really one of the most thoughtless of "Sheenies," then you are one of the most inconsistent of "Micks."

Since you are rewriting the part of Mussolini, I hope that you will make it quite clear that his anti-Semitism does not spring from any nobler source than the fact that he believes it is a good way to stir up the Arabs against the British. This shows the tremendous value to the world of having supermen dictators, who at the stroke of a pen, can sacrifice the future of thousands of individuals on the altar of racial superiority. It is to laugh.

Practically all the great nations of the world have been racial mixtures. The mixture of the Nordic blood with the Latin blood produced the English and French races, the German blood, without Latin intermixture, producing the Junker.

The Irish as a race were greatly improved by the fact that many of the ships of the Spanish Armada foundered on the coast of Ireland, thus producing that group of the Irish people known as the "black Irish," a mixture of Celt and Spaniard, from which most of the men of genius of Ireland have been produced. A number of the Spaniards were Maranos—or converted Jews, which resulted in a certain admixture of Jewish and Irish people. Undoubtedly, you are one of the striking examples of this mixture, since you possess all the virtues of Moses, Spinoza, Heine and all the other Jewish prophets. Then, take your money-making ability. Nine-tenths of the radical playwrights starve to death; you make a fortune at it. Then look at your Socialism. Don't you know that, according to Hitler, all Socialists are Jewish? Yes, G.B.S., the truth will out. You too are a Sheenie; and as to that red beard of yours, did you not know that the medieval Jew always had a red beard? A friend of mine recently visited what remains of the Pharisees. He found that they had red beards and blue eyes. You are undoubtedly a Pharisee throw-back. . . .

Sincerely yours,
Lawrence Langner

APPENDIX III

The Westport Country Playhouse

(See Chapter XXIV, Page 313)

The Westport Country Playhouse is owned by the Langners, and is located just off the Boston Post Road in Westport, Connecticut. In the summer of 1951 it celebrated its twentieth anniversary. The Westport Country Playhouse was the first summer theatre to be constructed especially for the purpose of preparing plays for New York, and more than twenty-five plays have been transferred from Westport to the New York stage. Except for a break of four years (1942 up to and including 1945), the Playhouse has been open for at least ten weeks each season, and over 170 plays have been produced since 1931.

In the years 1937–38, Day Tuttle and Richard Skinner were associated with the Langners, and during 1939 and 1940 John Haggott and John Cornell were the managers. The present regime of Armina Marshall, John C. Wilson and Lawrence Langner began in the season of 1941, and continued after the war with Martin Manulis as managing director. The following is a list of some of the more important Modern Revivals, Classical Revivals and New Plays performed at the Westport Country Playhouse in the period between its first season in 1931 and its nineteenth season in 1950.

MODERN REVIVALS

Accent on Youth, by Samuel Raphaelson, with Paul Lukas and Katharine Bard (July, 1949)

Anna Christie, by Eugene O'Neill, with June Havoc, George Mathews, E. G. Marshall (July, 1948)

Arms and the Man, by G. Bernard Shaw, with Jose Ferrer, Kent Smith, Claudia Morgan (July, 1936)

Biography, by S. N. Behrman, with Ina Claire (July, 1940)

Captain Brassbound's Conversion, by G. Bernard Shaw, with Jane Cowl and Arthur Margetson (July, 1940)

Cradle Song, by Martinez Sierra, with Peggy Wood (August, 1933)

Curtain Going Up!, by Ivor Novello, with Constance Collier, Violet Heming, Glora Stuart (July, 1941)

Design for Living, by Noel Coward, with Jean-Pierre Aumont, Marta Linden, David Wayne, Francesca Braggiotti (July, 1946)

Fanny's First Play, by G. Bernard Shaw, with Claudia Morgan and McKay Morris (July, 1936)

Green Grow the Lilacs, by Lynn Riggs, with Betty Field, Mildred Natwick, Winston O'Keefe; dances staged by Gene Kelly (July, 1940)

Her Cardboard Lover, by Jacques Duval, adapted by Valerie Wingate and P. G. Wodehouse, with Tallulah Bankhead (June, 1941)

Liliom, by Ferenc Molnar, with Tyrone Power and Annabella (August, 1941)

Ode to Liberty, by Sidney Howard, with Ina Claire (July, 1935)

Our Town, by Thornton Wilder, with Thornton Wilder and Katharine Bard (August, 1946)

Outward Bound, by Sutton Vane, with Laurette Taylor, Bramwell Fletcher, Kent Smith (August, 1939)

Private Lives, by Noel Coward, with Tallulah Bankhead and Donald Cook (July, 1947)

Russet Mantle, by Lynn Riggs, with Dorothy Gish (August, 1936)

The Constant Wife, by W. Somerset Maugham, with Ethel Barrymore (July, 1938)

The Devil's Disciple, by G. Bernard Shaw, with Maurice Evans (July, 1950)

The Emperor Jones, by Eugene O'Neill, with Paul Robeson (August, 1940)

The Girl of the Golden West, by David Belasco, with June Havoc, Robert Stack, Murvyn Vye (June, 1947)

The Man with a Load of Mischief, by Ashley Dukes, with Jane Cowl (September, 1932)

The Petrified Forest, by Robert E. Sherwood, with Frances Farmer, Phillips Holmes (August, 1937)

The Philadelphia Story, by Philip Barry, with Sarah Churchill and Jeffrey Lynn (August, 1949)

The Second Man, by S. N. Behrman, with Franchot Tone, Margaret Lindsay, Cloris Leachman (June, 1950)

The Skin of Our Teeth, by Thornton Wilder, with Thornton Wilder, Betty Field, Armina Marshall, Fania Marinoff (July, 1949)

The Time of Your Life, by William Saroyan, with Eddie Dowling and Meg Mundy (June, 1949)

The Winslow Boy, by Terence Rattigan, with Basil Rathbone, Meg Mundy, Colin Keith-Johnston, David Cole (July, 1950)

They Knew What They Wanted, by Sidney Howard, with June Havoc, Kenny Delmar (July, 1946)

Tovarich, by Robert E. Sherwood, with Eugenie Leontovich (August, 1938)

What Every Woman Knows, by James M. Barrie, with Olivia de Havilland (August, 1946)

You Never Can Tell, by G. Bernard Shaw, with John Litel, Florence Britton, (August, 1935)

CLASSICAL REVIVALS

A Month in the Country, by Ivan Turgenev, adapted by Garson Kanin, with Ruth Gordon (August, 1949)

As You Like It, by William Shakespeare, with Rollo Peters, Dorothy Gish, Romney Brent, Winifred Lenihan, Armina Marshall, Moffat Johnston, Fania Marinoff (August, 1933)

Camille, by Alexandre Dumas, with Eva LeGallienne (August, 1936)

Ghosts, by Henrik Ibsen, with Alla Nazimova (August, 1939)

Le Bourgeois Gentilhomme, by Molière, with Jimmy Savo (August, 1936)

Love for Love, by William Congreve, with Eva LeGallienne, Dennis King (June, 1936)

Lysistrata '48, adaptation by Gilbert Seldes, with June Havoc, Joan Mc-Cracken, Bibi Osterwald, Maria Gambarelli, Homer Fickett (June, 1948)

The Beaux' Strategem, by George Farquhar, with Brian Aherne, Carmen Mathews, Maureen Stapleton (July, 1948)

The Country Wife, by Wycherley, with Ruth Gordon, McKay Morris (July, 1935)

The Pillars of Society, by Henrik Ibsen, with Rollo Peters, Armina Marshall (September, 1933)

The School for Husbands, by Molière, with Osgood Perkins, June Walker (August, 1932)

The School for Scandal, by Richard Brinsley Sheridan, with Ethel Barrymore (July, 1940)

The Streets of New York, by Dion Boucicault, with Dorothy Gish, Rollo Peters, Romney Brent, Fania Marinoff, Moffat Johnston (June, 1931)

The Yellow Jacket, by George Hazelton and Benrimo, with Mr. and Mrs. Charles Coburn, Louise Groody, Rex O'Malley (July, 1933)

NEW PLAYS

Angel in the Pawn Shop, by A. B. Shiffrin, with Eddie Dowling, Joan Mc-Cracken (June, 1950)

Chrysalis, by Rose Albert Porter, with Jane Wyatt, Elizabeth Risdon, Osgood Perkins, June Walker (July, 1931)

Come Back Little Sheba, by William Inge, with Shirley Booth, Sidney Blackmer (September, 1949)

Dame Nature, by Andre Birabeau, with Jessie Royce Landis, Montgomery Clift, Glenn Anders, Hugh Marlowe (June, 1938)

Dr. Knock, by Jules Romains, adapted by Lawrence Langner and Armina Marshall, with Richard Whorf, Claudia Morgan (July, 1936)

Dream Child, by J. C. Nugent, with J. C. Nugent, Ruth Nugent, Alan Bunce (June, 1934)

Finale, by S. K. Lauren, with Laurette Taylor (September, 1932)

For Husbands Only, by Lawrence Langner, with Osgood Perkins, June Walker (August, 1932)

Good Housekeeping, by William McCleery, with Helen Hayes, Kent Smith, Mary MacArthur (September, 1949)

Julie, by Frederic Arnold Kummer, with Lenore Ulric (August, 1934)

Lady Godiva, by Lawrence Langner, with Violet Heming (August, 1933)

Lady Jane, by H. M. Harwood, with Frances Starr (September, 1934)

Miss Mabel, by R. C. Sherriff, with Lillian Gish (August, 1950)

My Fiddle Has Three Strings, by Arnold Schulman, with J. Edward Bromberg, Maureen Stapleton, Steven Hill, Betsy Blair, Fritzi Scheff (August, 1950)

Princess Turandot, adapted by Lawrence Langner and John Gerard, with Anna May Wong, McKay Morris (August, 1937)

Suzanna and the Elders, by Lawrence Langner and Armina Marshall, with Onslow Stevens, Uta Hagen (August, 1938)

The Bride of Torozko, by Otto Indig, adapted by Ruth Langner, with Jean Arthur, Van Heflin, Sam Jaffe (August, 1936)

The Bride the Sun Shines On, by Will Cotton, with Dorothy Gish, Rollo Peters (August, 1933)

The Devil Take a Whittler, by Weldon Stone, with Carol Stone, Paul Crabtree, John Conte, Patricia Neal, Tom Scott (July, 1946)

The Difficulty of Getting Married, by Louis Vernuil, with Grace George (July, 1936)

The Millionairess, by G. Bernard Shaw, with Jessie Royce Landis and Onslow Stevens (August, 1938)

The Nobel Prize, by Hjalmar Bergman, with Otis Skinner, Armina Marshall (July, 1933)

The Pursuit of Happiness, by Lawrence Langner and Armina Marshall, with Tonio Selwart, Peggy Conklin (July, 1933)

The Silver Whistle, by Robert E. McEnroe, with Jose Ferrer, Billy Lynn, Doro Mirande, John Conte, Kathleen Comegys (August, 1948)

Traveller's Joy, by Arthur Macrae, with Gertrude Lawrence and Dennis King (August, 1950)

MUSICALS OR OPERETTAS

Champagne Sec, adapted from *Die Fledermaus* by Lawrence Langner and Robert Simon, with Peggy Wood, Kitty Carlisle, Helen Ford. Staged by Monty Woolley (September, 1933)

How's Your Code? by Gene Lockhart, with Gene and Kathleen Lockhart and Mitzi (August, 1933)

La Belle Helene, by Offenbach, in an all-Negro swing version by Stewart Chaney, with Anne Brown, Avon Long (July, 1941)

Texas, Li'l Darlin', by John Whedon and Sam Moore, music by Robert Emmett Dolan, lyrics by Johnny Mercer, with Kenny Delmar, Elaine Stritch, Danny Scholl, Harry Bannister (August, 1949)

The Chimes of Corneville, by Planquette, in a rhymed version by Arthur Guiterman with Helen Ford, Lucy Monroe, George Meader (June, 1934)

APPENDIX IV

Plays by the Author

(See Chapter XXIV, Page 308)

The following is a list of the plays written by the Author, or by him in collaboration with others, and produced on the stage.

ONE ACT PLAYS

Title	Produced by	Date
Licensed	Washington Square Players, Bandbox Theatre, New York	1915
Another Way Out	Washington Square Players, Comedy Theatre, New York	1916
Pie	Provincetown Players, Playwrights Theatre, New York	1920
Matinata	Provincetown Players, Playwrights Theatre, New York	1920
The Sire de Maletroit's Door (adapted from the story by Robert Louis Stevenson)	Montclair Little Theatre	1921
The Pyramid	Harry Irvine, Clare Tree Major's Theatre, New York	1922
Accidents Will Happen	Heckscher Foundation Theatre, New York	1924

FULL LENGTH PLAYS

Title	Produced by	Date
The Family Exit	Washington Square Players, Comedy Theatre, New York	1917
Holding Helen	Copley Theatre, Boston	1926
Henry Behave	Gustav Blum, New Amsterdam Roof Theatre, New York	1926
These Modern Women	Kenneth Macgowan, Eltinge Theatre, New York	1928
For Husbands Only	Westport Country Playhouse	1932
Lady Godiva	Westport Country Playhouse	1933

Plays written in collaboration with Armina Marshall:

Title	Produced by	Date
The Compromisers (adapted from Andre Kadar's The Keyhole)	Westport Country Playhouse	1934
The Pursuit of Happiness	Lawrence Rivers, Klaw Theatre, New York	1934
On to Fortune	Crosby Gaige, Fulton Theatre, New York	1935
Dr. Knock (adapted from the play by Jules Romains)	Westport Country Playhouse	1936
Suzanna and the Elders	Jack Kirkland, Morosco Theatre, New York	1940

Adaptations and collaborations:

The Red Cloak by Lawrence Langner and Josephine A. Meyer	Washington Square Players, Bandbox Theatre	1916
Tangerine, by Guy Bolton, Lawrence Langner and Philip Bartholmae	Carle Carlton, Casino Theatre, New York	1922
The School for Husbands (adapted by Lawrence Langner and Arthur Guiterman from Molière's School for Husbands)	Theatre Guild, Empire Theatre, New York	1933
Champagne Sec, adapted by Lawrence Langner and Robert Simon from Die Fledermaus	Dwight Deere Wiman, Morosco Theatre, New York	1933
The Country Wife, by William Wycherley, adapted by Lawrence Langner	Westport Country Playhouse	1935
Love for Love (combined with The Way of the World), adaptation from William Congreve's play by Lawrence Langner	Westport Country Playhouse	1935
Princess Turandot by Lawrence Langner and John Gerard	Westport Country Playhouse	1937
The Life of the Party, adapted by Lawrence Langner from Gogol's The Inspector General	Westport Country Playhouse	1950

Plays published but not produced:

Title	Published by	Date
The Broken Image (one act)	Frank Shay	1918
Moses	Boni and Liveright	1924

APPENDIX V

National Inventors Council

(See Chapter XXVI, Page 366)

The following is an excerpt from Lawrence Langner's Report, as Secretary to the Council, dated May 22, 1945, after the close of hostilities with Germany.

The Council was initiated almost immediately after the fall of France. By the time Pearl Harbor was attacked, we had already examined over 65,000 ideas, among which were found some of the most important of those which have since been adopted by the Army and Navy.

The following statistics, worked on by the Council and Staff, covered the period of 4½ years from October, 1940, through April, 1945:

Approximately 210,000 inventions or suggestions evaluated by the Council.
11,040 files submitted as including worth-while suggestions to the war agencies, divided as follows:

Army	6,876
Navy	1,772
Others	2,392

Total proposals, interviews, and inquiries dealt with by the Council and Staff exceeded 347,968.

The worth-while suggestions were placed in a Library of ideas. This now contains nearly 12,000 files.

Of the 11,000 odd files sent to the war agencies, 670 were selected for detailed investigation with development and tests. Accepted by the war agencies for production and use, between 90 and 100. It is highly probable that, when the conditions of secrecy are relaxed, it will be found that considerably more than this number are in actual use by the Army or Navy at the present time.

The cost of operating the office of the Council has averaged about $90,000 a year, the highest amount being in the year 1943 when $112,446 was expended. The Council members have contributed their services gratis.

Between 25 and 30 models have been built or tested by the Bureau of Standards under the auspices of the Council.

Over 200 problems of the Army and Navy have been circulated among inventors and engineers. It is estimated that from 20 to 30 per cent of these have been solved.

Hardly any instances have been found where the members of the Staff or Council turned down an invention which was later adopted by the Army or Navy. Nor have there been any general complaints about the failure of the Army or Navy to give proper consideration to new inventions since the advent of the Council. Viewed from this standpoint, the Council has done a serviceable public relations job for the Army and Navy.

Soon after Pearl Harbor, when it was apparent that there would be a dangerous rubber shortage, NIC, through Dr. Kettering and Mr. Fred Zeder, called a meeting in Detroit of the Society of Automotive Engineers and a committee of the Rubber Industry. As a result, a report was formulated which later formed the basis of the Baruch report and the present synthetic rubber program.

The Council has operated impartially without reference to the size or financial position of the inventor or corporation owning the invention; 90 per cent of the inventions which have been put into use by the Army and Navy were made by individual inventors in the employ of small companies.

Of the inventions adopted by the Army and Navy, over 40 per cent have peacetime industrial value as well as wartime value. Of the inventions in connection with which models were made by the Bureau of Standards, over 40 per cent had peacetime value.

Another invention sponsored by the Council, the Hedden land-mine locator, proved to be of great value to us and to our allies in the pursuit of Rommel across the desert in the North African campaign, in the landings in Sicily, and in general throughout all other landings and offensive campaigns in which the well-worked-out German defenses by means of land mines were completely defeated. The writer believes that this invention alone has saved thousands of lives and shortened the length of the war.

The work of the Council has been greatly facilitated by the Department of Commerce and the Commissioner of Patents, Mr. Conway P. Coe, who provided the Council with an excellent staff. Those difficulties which naturally arose in connection with the formation of a new organization were met and overcome in the process of time with relatively little friction.

Mention should be made of the valuable services rendered the Council by Mr. Conder C. Henry, Assistant Commissioner of Patents, Colonel Leon B. Lent, former Chief Engineer, Mr. John C. Green, the present Chief Engineer, and the very excellent engineering and clerical staff.

The Council members, many of whom did not know one another before the formation of the Council, have learned to regard each other with affection and respect and I believe I voice all their sentiments in expressing the hope that the Council will continue to meet for many years to come.

The war with Japan is not over and the work of evaluation must continue. While a lesser number of inventions is coming in, the standard is appreciably higher. Many of the inventions are coming from service men, and are based on first-hand observation of conditions at the various fronts.

I feel that this work of evaluation should continue and that we should not discontinue the work when the war with Japan is over, for some of the best inventions may come from those who have the experience of the present war behind them. Nor should we forget that it was our defenseless position which encouraged the aggressors. Such aggression will be encouraged again if we again fail to remember that our own strength is our greatest guarantee for peace.

APPENDIX VI

American Shakespeare Festival Theatre

(See Chapter XXXII, Page 438)

The following statement explains the project for a Shakespeare Festival in the United States, upon which the author is now working. There will be described in turn the theatre building itself, the Acting Company, the Academy and School of Acting, and other activities contemplated in connection with the proposal.

Unlike the Shakespeare Memorial Theatre at Stratford-on-Avon, which is a modern theatrical building of approved design, it is contemplated that the American Shakespeare Festival Theatre shall be patterned after the Globe Theatre at Southwark in which most of Shakespeare's greatest plays were originally presented to the public of his day.

The American Shakespeare Festival Theatre will accommodate approximately 1,350 people in the orchestra and balcony, and will also have a gallery accommodating approximately 250, making a total of approximately 1,600 seats. But the theatre auditorium will be elastic as to capacity, and by simple means will be closed in to accommodate audiences which are considerably smaller. It is contemplated that there shall be a specified number of free seats for school children during matinee performances.

While the American Shakespeare Festival Theatre will be equipped for the production of the plays on an Elizabethan stage in the settings of the period, yet the theatre building itself will be adaptable to any type of Shakespearean production, with or without the use of the proscenium. The stage housing will be large enough to contain a number of wagon stages so that the plays may be changed from night to night with a minimum amount of stage labor. The theatre will be provided with the latest lighting and technical equipment. A special feature of the theatre auditorium will be its adaptability so that it can serve for deep-apron stage productions, proscenium type productions, Greek type productions, and so-called "theatre-in-the-round," thus giving the stage directors the widest latitude in deciding how the plays shall be produced. The Globe Theatre was three stories high and had no roof over what we now call the orchestra section. Because of climatic conditions as well as the noise made by passing airplanes, this is not now practical, so the theatre will be provided with a roof. It will also be provided with air conditioning for cooling in the summer and heating in the winter.

The third floor of the theatre building will contain a number of school rooms which will house the Shakespeare Academy and School of Acting, rehearsal rooms, etc. Adjacent to the theatre will be a restaurant known as the Mermaid Tavern and a building which will house the scenery, scenery workshop, costumes, etc., so that all the scenery and costumes may be constructed at the theatre as was done in Elizabethan days.

I deem it fortunate that an American scholar, Dr. John Cranford Adams, President of Hofstra College, Hempstead, Long Island, has devoted many years of his life to the study of the original Globe Theatre and has consented to act as adviser in the building of the theatre, along with his collaborator, Mr. Irwin Smith.

Edward Howard, architect, of Westport, Connecticut, whose excellent remodeling of the Westport Country Playhouse has been greatly admired, has been engaged to prepare the plans of the American Shakespeare Festival Theatre, and he will be assisted by a committee of theatrical technicians, and scenic artists. Since the theatre building will be heated, it can be used for various cultural purposes during the Fall season and possibly into the Winter.

THE AMERICAN SHAKESPEARE FESTIVAL ACTING COMPANY

The American Festival will be patterned along the lines of the Stratford-on-Avon Festival which has proven so successful in England recently under the direction of Anthony Quayle. While the British Festival now runs as long as five months, it is not expected that at first the American Shakespeare Festival could be given for longer than ten weeks. It is therefore planned to begin the Festival about the latter part of June and to prepare the plays for the repertory one at a time so that by the latter part of July, all four plays will be presented each week. This repertory of plays will then be given during the month of August and the first week of September, making a total of five weeks. This will enable distant visitors who come East for the Festival to see all four plays in one week. (There is, of course, no connection between the Stratford Festival and the contemplated American Festival.)

The Acting Company will be made up of the best available actresses and actors who are schooled in Shakespearean acting. Many of the most prominent members of the acting profession have indicated their desire to participate in the Festival. The younger members of the Company will be selected for their acting ability and interest in classical acting.

Since the plays of Shakespeare were written for "star" theatrical performers, it is to be expected that there will be two or three "stars" at the Festival, as is the case with the Stratford-on-Avon Festival.

After the termination of the Festival, the Company will travel on an extended tour throughout the country supported by the Theatre Guild—American Theatre Society subscription. It is not expected to tour the entire repertory, but only the more popular plays. The company will play in the larger cities and return to the East in time to prepare for the following season.

It is also contemplated that a Junior Festival Company, similar to the "Young Vic" company in England, may be organized to carry a repertory of Shakespeare's plays to the smaller towns, colleges and communities using busses for transportation from town to town.

THE SHAKESPEARE ACADEMY AND SCHOOL OF ACTING

The Shakespeare Academy and School of Acting will be located in the theatre building or buildings. Particular emphasis will be placed upon the training of actors in the style of acting which is essential to the best performance of the works of Shakespeare and the classics. It is planned to engage the best available teachers in the United States and England to develop an American tradition of classical acting which will be a worthy counterpart to the British tradition. The school will be in essence a post-graduate course, and the students will be limited to graduates of other schools of acting and actors who already have stage training and experience. The summer seminar will include the following subjects :

a: Discussion and acting of Shakespeare's plays and characters.
b: Speech and diction.
c: Posture, fencing, dancing, etc.
d: Meaning of obsolete words and their restoration to the living language.

There will be one or more student productions during the season. The students who are full-fledged actors will also have an opportunity to appear in the plays themselves as extras or in bits. There will also be a technical apprentice group connected with the theatre which will be given opportunities for experience in the technical side of production.

A special course on direction, scenery, costumes, and history of Elizabethan theatre will be conducted by notable experts engaged to provide lectures each week as part of the curriculum for the students, and for the public particularly interested in the subjects.

APPENDIX VII

Plays in Which Alfred Lunt and Lynn Fontanne Have Appeared

(See Chapter XXIX, Page 396)

In the past century, no other stage couple has equaled the records made by Mr. Lunt and Miss Fontanne, outdistancing such celebrated stage partners as Sir Henry Irving and Ellen Terry and E. H. Sothern and Julia Marlowe. Starting with *The Guardsman,* they have been seen together in *Arms and the Man, Goat Song, At Mrs. Beam's, The Brothers Karamazov, The Second Man, The Doctor's Dilemma, Caprice, Meteor, Elizabeth the Queen, Reunion in Vienna, The Taming of the Shrew, Idiot's Delight, Amphitryon 38, The Sea Gull, There Shall Be No Night, The Pirate, O Mistress Mine* and *I Know My Love.* During the quarter of a century they have co-starred, they have averaged a tour every three years and an appearance in England about every four years.

Other plays in which they have appeared for the Theatre Guild are as follows: Alfred Lunt in *Juarez and Maximilian, Ned McCobb's Daughter, Marco Millions,* and *Volpone;* Lynn Fontanne in *Pygmalion* and *Strange Interlude.*

Mr. Lunt and Miss Fontanne also appeared together in *Design For Living* and *Point Valaine,* not produced by the Theatre Guild.

APPENDIX VIII

List of Theatre Guild Plays

(See Chapter XXXIII, Page 440)

The following plays have been presented in New York City by the Theatre Guild either alone or in association with others. From March 28, 1939, on, most of the productions of the Theatre Guild were supervised by Lawrence Langner and Theresa Helburn who, prior to this time, served either on the production committees or as members of the Board of Managers concerned in the production of these plays. This list of 173 plays probably constitutes the greatest number of art-theatre plays produced by a single management in this country in so-called "first class" theatres, which excludes stock companies, etc.

(A few plays produced by the Theatre Guild, but which were not brought to New York, are not listed here.)

Name of Play	Author	New York Opening Date
FIRST SEASON		
The Bonds of Interest	Jacinto Benavente	April 19, 1919
John Ferguson	St. John Ervine	May 12, 1919
SECOND SEASON		
The Faithful	John Masefield	October 13, 1919
The Rise of Silas Lapham	Lillian Sabine	November 25, 1919
Power of Darkness	Tolstoy	January 19, 1920
Jane Clegg	St. John Ervine	February 23, 1920
The Dance of Death	August Strindberg	May 9, 1920
THIRD SEASON		
The Treasure	David Pinski	October 4, 1920
Heartbreak House	Bernard Shaw	November 10, 1920
John Hawthorne	David Liebovitz	January 23, 1921
Mr. Pim Passes By	A. A. Milne	February 28, 1921
Liliom	Ferenc Molnar	April 20, 1921
The Cloister	Emile Verhaeren	June 5, 1921

Appendix VIII

Name of Play	Author	New York Opening Date
	FOURTH SEASON	
Ambush	Arthur Richman	October 10, 1921
The Wife with a Smile	Denys Amiel and Andre Obey	November 28, 1921
Bourbouroche	Georges Courteline	November 28, 1921
He Who Gets Slapped	Leonid Andreyev	January 9, 1922
Back to Methuselah	Bernard Shaw	February 27, 1922
What the Public Wants	Arnold Bennett	May 1, 1922
From Morn to Midnight	Georg Kaiser	May 21, 1922
	FIFTH SEASON	
R. U. R.	Karl Capek	October 9, 1922
The Lucky One	A. A. Milne	November 20, 1922
The Tidings Brought to Mary	Paul Claudel	December 25, 1922
Peer Gynt	Henrik Ibsen	February 5, 1923
The Adding Machine	Elmer L. Rice	March 18, 1923
The Devil's Disciple	Bernard Shaw	April 23, 1923
	SIXTH SEASON	
Windows	John Galsworthy	October 8, 1923
The Failures	H. R. Lenormand	November 19, 1923
The Race with the Shadow	Wilhelm von Scholz	December 14, 1923
Saint Joan	Bernard Shaw	December 28, 1923
Fata Morgana	Ernest Vajda	March 3, 1924
Man and the Masses	Ernst Toller	April 14, 1924
	SEVENTH SEASON	
The Guardsman	Ferenc Molnar	October 13, 1924
They Knew What They Wanted	Sidney Howard	November 24, 1924
Processional	John Howard Lawson	January 12, 1925
Ariadne	A. A. Milne	February 23, 1925
Caesar and Cleopatra	Bernard Shaw	April 13, 1925
The Garrick Gaieties	Richard Rodgers and Lorenz Hart	June 8, 1925
Arms and the Man	Bernard Shaw	September 14, 1925
	EIGHTH SEASON	
The Glass Slipper	Ferenc Molnar	October 19, 1925
The Man of Destiny	Bernard Shaw	November 23, 1925
Androcles and the Lion	Bernard Shaw	November 23, 1925
Merchants of Glory	Marcel Pagnol and Paul Nivoix	December 14, 1925

Name of Play	Author	New York Opening Date
	EIGHTH SEASON	
Goat Song	Franz Werfel	January 25, 1926
The Chief Thing	Nicholas Evreinov	March 22, 1926
At Mrs. Beam's	C. K. Munro	April 26, 1926
The Garrick Gaieties (2nd Edition)	Richard Rodgers and Lorenz Hart	May 10, 1926
	NINTH SEASON	
Juarez and Maximilian	Franz Werfel	October 11, 1926
Pygmalion	Bernard Shaw	November 15, 1926
Ned McCobb's Daughter	Sidney Howard	November 22, 1926
The Silver Cord	Sidney Howard	December 20, 1926
The Brothers Karamazov	Jacques Copeau, based on Dostoevsky's novel	January 3, 1927
Right You Are If You Think You Are	Luigi Pirandello	March 2, 1927
The Second Man	S. N. Behrman	April 11, 1927
	TENTH SEASON	
Porgy	Du Bose and Dorothy Heyward	October 11, 1927
The Doctor's Dilemma	Bernard Shaw	November 21, 1927
Marco Millions	Eugene O'Neill	January 9, 1928
Strange Interlude	Eugene O'Neill	January 23, 1928
Volpone	Stefan Zweig's version of Ben Jonson's play	April 9, 1928
	ELEVENTH SEASON	
Faust	Goethe (Graham and Tristan Rawson version)	October 8, 1928
Major Barbara	Bernard Shaw	November 20, 1928
Wings over Europe	Robert Nichols and Maurice Browne	December 10, 1928
Caprice	Sil-Vara	December 31, 1928
Dynamo	Eugene O'Neill	February 11, 1929
Man's Estate	Beatrice Blackmar and Bruce Gould	April 1, 1929
The Camel Through the Needle's Eye	Francis Langer	April 15, 1929
	TWELFTH SEASON	
Karl and Anna	Leonhard Frank (translated from the German by Ruth Langner)	October 7, 1929

Name of Play	Author	New York Opening Date
	TWELFTH SEASON	
The Game of Love and Death	Romain Rolland	November 25, 1929
Red Rust	V. Kirchon and A. Ouspensky	December 17, 1929
Meteor	S. N. Behrman	December 23, 1929
The Apple Cart	Bernard Shaw	February 24, 1930
A Month in the Country	Ivan Turgenev	March 17, 1930
Hotel Universe	Philip Barry	April 14, 1930
The Garrick Gaieties (3rd Edition)	(Various Authors and Composers)	June 4, 1930
	THIRTEENTH SEASON	
Roar China!	S. M. Tretyakov	October 27, 1930
Elizabeth the Queen	Maxwell Anderson	November 3, 1930
Midnight	Claire and Paul Sifton	December 29, 1930
Green Grow the Lilacs	Lynn Riggs	January 26, 1931
Miracle at Verdun	Hans Chlumberg	March 16, 1931
Getting Married	Bernard Shaw	March 30, 1931
	FOURTEENTH SEASON	
He	Alfred Savoir	September 21, 1931
Mourning Becomes Electra	Eugene O'Neill	October 26, 1931
Reunion in Vienna	Robert E. Sherwood	November 16, 1931
The Moon in the Yellow River	Denis Johnston	February 29, 1932
Too True to Be Good	Bernard Shaw	April 4, 1932
	FIFTEENTH SEASON	
The Good Earth	Dramatized by Owen and Donald Davis from Pearl Buck's novel	October 22, 1932
Biography	S. N. Behrman	December 3, 1932
American Dream	George O'Neil	February 20, 1933
Both Your Houses	Maxwell Anderson	March 6, 1933
The Mask and the Face	Luigi Chiarelli, translated by Somerset Maugham	May 1, 1933
	SIXTEENTH SEASON	
Ah, Wilderness!	Eugene O'Neill	October 2, 1933
The School for Husbands	Molière, adapted in rhyme by Arthur Guiterman and Lawrence Langner	October 16, 1933
Mary of Scotland	Maxwell Anderson	November 27, 1933
Days Without End	Eugene O'Neill	January 8, 1934

Name of Play	Author	New York Opening Date
	SIXTEENTH SEASON	
They Shall Not Die	John Wexley	February 21, 1934
Jig Saw	Dawn Powell	April 30, 1934
	SEVENTEENTH SEASON	
A Sleeping Clergyman	James Bridie	October 8, 1934
Valley Forge	Maxwell Anderson	December 10, 1934
Rain from Heaven	S. N. Behrman	December 24, 1934
Escape Me Never	Margaret Kennedy	January 21, 1935
The Simpleton of the Unexpected Isles	Bernard Shaw	February 18, 1935
Parade	George Sklar, Paul Peters and Jerome Moross	May 20, 1935
	EIGHTEENTH SEASON	
If This Be Treason	Rev. John Haynes Holmes and Reginald Lawrence	September 23, 1935
The Taming of the Shrew	William Shakespeare	September 30, 1935
Porgy and Bess	George Gershwin, Ira Gershwin, Du Bose and Dorothy Heyward	October 10, 1935
Call It a Day	Dodie Smith	January 28, 1936
End of Summer	S. N. Behrman	February 17, 1936
Idiot's Delight	Robert Sherwood	April 7, 1936
	NINETEENTH SEASON	
And Stars Remain	Julius J. and Philip G. Epstein	October 12, 1936
Prelude to Exile	William McNally	November 30, 1936
But for the Grace of God	Leopold Atlas	January 12, 1937
The Masque of Kings	Maxwell Anderson	February 8, 1937
Storm over Patsy	Bruno Frank	March 8, 1937
	TWENTIETH SEASON	
To Quito and Back	Ben Hecht	October 4, 1937
Madame Bovary	Gaston Baty, from the novel of Gustave Flaubert	November 16, 1937
Amphitryon 38	S. N. Behrman, from the French of Jean Giraudoux	November 1, 1937
The Ghost of Yankee Doodle	Sidney Howard	November 22, 1937
Wine of Choice	S. N. Behrman	February 21, 1938

Name of Play	*Author*	*New York Opening Date*
	TWENTIETH SEASON	
The Sea Gull	Anton Chekov, adapted by Stark Young from the Russian	March 28, 1938
Washington Jitters	John Boruff and Walter Hart	May 2, 1938
	TWENTY-FIRST SEASON	
Dame Nature	André Birabeau	September 26, 1938
Jeremiah	Stefan Zweig	February 3, 1939
The Philadelphia Story	Philip Barry	March 28, 1939
	TWENTY-SECOND SEASON	
The Time of Your Life (with Eddie Dowling)	William Saroyan	October 25, 1939
The Fifth Column	Ernest Hemingway (acting version by Benjamin Glazer)	March 6, 1940
There Shall Be No Night (with the Playwrights Company)	Robert Sherwood	April 29, 1940
Love's Old Sweet Song	William Saroyan	May 2, 1940
	TWENTY-THIRD SEASON	
Twelfth Night	William Shakespeare	November 19, 1940
Liberty Jones	Philip Barry	February 5, 1941
The Battle of Angels ⎫	Tennessee Williams	
Somewhere in France ⎬ (on tour)	Carl Zuckmayer and Fritz Kortner	
	TWENTY-FOURTH SEASON	
Ah, Wilderness! (revival)	Eugene O'Neill	October 2, 1941
Candle in the Wind (with the Playwrights' Company)	Maxwell Anderson	October 22, 1941
Papa Is All	Patterson Greene	January 6, 1942
Hope for a Harvest	Sophie Treadwell	November 26, 1941
The Rivals	Richard B. Sheridan	January 14, 1942
Yesterday's Magic	Emlyn Williams	April 14, 1942
	TWENTY-FIFTH SEASON	
Without Love	Philip Barry	November 10, 1942
Mr. Sycamore	Ketti Frings	November 13, 1942

Name of Play	Author	New York Opening Date
	TWENTY-FIFTH SEASON	
The Pirate (with the Playwrights Company)	S. N. Behrman	November 27, 1942
The Russian People	Konstantin Simonov (American acting version by Clifford Odets)	December 29, 1942
Oklahoma!	Richard Rodgers, Oscar Hammerstein II	March 31, 1943
	TWENTY-SIXTH SEASON	
Othello	William Shakespeare	October 19, 1943
The Innocent Voyage	Paul Osborn (Based on a novel by Richard Hughes)	November 15, 1943
Jacobowsky and the Colonel	Franz Werfel	March 14, 1944
	TWENTY-SEVENTH SEASON	
Embezzled Heaven	L. Bush-Fekete and Mary Helen Fay (Based on novel of Franz Werfel)	October 31, 1944
Sing Out, Sweet Land!	Walter Kerr	December 27, 1944
Foolish Notion	Philip Barry	March 31, 1945
Carousel	Richard Rodgers and Oscar Hammerstein II (Based on Molnar's Liliom)	April 19, 1945
	TWENTY-EIGHTH SEASON	
Dunnigan's Daughter	S. N. Behrman	December 26, 1945
The Winter's Tale	William Shakespeare	January 15, 1946
O Mistress Mine (with John C. Wilson)	Terence Rattigan	January 23, 1946
He Who Gets Slapped	Leonid Andreyev (Adaptation by Judith Guthrie)	March 20, 1946
The Merry Wives of Windsor	William Shakespeare	On tour
	TWENTY-NINTH SEASON	
The Iceman Cometh	Eugene O'Neill	October 9, 1946
The Fatal Weakness	George Kelly	November 19, 1946
The Importance of Being Earnest (with John C. Wilson)	Oscar Wilde	March 3, 1947

Name of Play	*Author*	*New York Opening Date*
	TWENTY-NINTH SEASON	
Love for Love (with John C. Wilson)	William Congreve	May 26, 1947
	THIRTIETH SEASON	
Allegro	Richard Rodgers and Oscar Hammerstein II	October 10, 1947
This Time Tomorrow	Jan de Hartog	November 3, 1947
You Never Can Tell	Bernard Shaw	March 16, 1948
The Winslow Boy (with Atlantis)	Terence Rattigan	October 29, 1947
	THIRTY-FIRST SEASON	
Set My People Free	Dorothy Heyward	November 3, 1948
The Silver Whistle	Robert McEnroe	November 24, 1948
Make Way for Lucia	John van Druten	December 22, 1948
My Name Is Aquilon	Jean Pierre Aumont; adapted by Philip Barry	February 9, 1949
	THIRTY-SECOND SEASON	
I Know My Love (with John C. Wilson)	S. N. Behrman; adapted from the French of Marcel Achard	November 2, 1949
As You Like It	William Shakespeare	January 26, 1950
Arms and the Girl	Book by Herbert and Dorothy Fields and Rouben Mamoulian; music by Morton Gould; lyrics by Dorothy Fields	February 2, 1950
Come Back, Little Sheba	William Inge	February 15, 1950
	THIRTY-THIRD SEASON	
The Curious Savage (with Lewis & Young)	John Patrick	October 24, 1950
The Lady's Not for Burning (with Atlantis)	Christopher Fry	November 8, 1950
The Relapse	Sir John Vanbrugh	November 22, 1950

Index

Abbey Players, 121
Abbott, George, 309, 322, 371
Abel, Walter, 424
Academy of Political Science, 291
Acropolis (Sherwood), 327-328
Actors Equity Association, 124, 148, 169, 260, 330
Actors Studio, 449
Adair, Forrest, 105, 107
Adams, Evangeline, 202-203
Adams, Franklin P., 159, 160, 197
Adams, Roger, 359n
Addy, Wesley, 332-333
Adler, Dr. Alfred, 158
Adler, Luther, 339
Adler, Stella, 339
Advisory Council to the House Patents Committee, 349-350, 354, 355
Aglavaine and Selysette (Maeterlinck), 103
Ah, Wilderness (O'Neill), 256, 282-284, 334
Akins, Zoë, 93, 103
Albertson, Florence, 47, 48
Albertson, Hazel, 47-49
Albertson, Ralph, 48-49
Albertson farm, 47-49, 92
Aldington, Richard, 81
Aldis, Arthur and Mary, 80
Aldwych Theatre, 426
Alexander, George, 30
Algonquin Round Table, 159-160
All God's Chillun Got Wings (O'Neill), 195
All My Sons (Miller), 334
Allegro (Rodgers and Hammerstein), 393
Allen, Viola, 329
Alternating Repertory Company, 214-227, 243-244, 400

Alvin Theatre, 265, 327
American Academy of Dramatic Arts, 102, 206, 298
American Biograph Company, 74, 436
American Chemical Society, 343
American Manufacturers Export Association, 354
American National Theatre and Academy, 212, 445
American Shakespearean Festival Theatre, 438, 449
American Theatre Council, 262
American Theatre Society, 262
American Theatre Wing, 329
Ames, Winthrop, 83, 196, 259, 439
Ami, Jacob Ben, 230
Amphitryon 38, 266
Anders, Glenn, 166, 214, 236, 241n, 304
Anderson, Elaine, 339, 371, 373
Anderson, John, 157
Anderson, Judith, 22, 166, 198, 238
Anderson, Margaret, 81, 84-86
Anderson, Marian, 310
Anderson, Mary, 329
Anderson, Maxwell, 142, 159, 193, 249, 252, 254, 256-257, 263, 268, 335, 440, 441
Anderson, Sherwood, 81, 82, 85, 193
Andreyev, Leonid, 97, 100, 103, 161
Angel Street (Hamilton) 435n
Animal Kingdom, The (Barry), 314
Anna Christie (O'Neill), 229, 402
Annabella, 311, 384
Annie Get Your Gun, 380
Another Interior, 96
Another Way Out (Langner), 85, 101, 207
ANTA, 212
Antick, The (Mackaye), 98-99
Antioch University, 52

Antoine, André, 154, 155
Apple Cart, The (Shaw), 184, 289-290
L'Apres Midi d'un Faune, 90
Arens, Egmont, 77
Aria da Capo (Millay), 110
Aristophanes, 368
Arms and the Man (Shaw), 213-214, 221, 222, 420
Armstrong, Edwin H., 350
Army and Navy Munitions Patents Board, 112-113
Arnaud, Yvonne, 425
Arno, Peter, 209
Arnold, Thurman, 349, 350-351
As You Like It (Shakespeare), 22, 298, 320, 415, 437n
Ashmore, Peter, 421
Astor, Lady, 294-295
Astor, Mrs. Vincent, 148
At Mrs. Beam's (Munro), 146, 214
Atlantic Monthly (periodical), 351
Atlantis, 427, 428
Atkinson, Brooks, 280, 307
Atwell, Roy, 304
Atwill, Lionel, 213
Away We Go (Rodger and Hammerstein), 373
Ayers, Lemuel, 371, 373

Back to Methuselah (Shaw), 132-141, 174-175, 178, 292
Bagdeserian, Ross, 321
Bailie, Earle, 261
Bakeland, George, 358
Baker, Belle, 74
Baker, George Pierce, 126, 158
Baker's '47 Workshop at Harvard, 122, 125, 158
Bakst, Leon, 90
Ball, Norman, 357
Ballantine, Stella, 72
Ballantine, Teddy, 72
Ballet Russe de Monte Carlo, 90, 371
Bandbox Theatre, 92, 95, 100
Bankhead, Tallulah, 310, 387-389
Banks, Leslie, 266-267
Barach, Alvin, 367
Barker, Granville, 76, 90, 94, 142
Barlow, Howard, 361
Barna, Mr. and Mrs., 149
Barnes, Djuna, 110, 224
Barrie, Sir James M., 311
Barry, Ellen, 389
Barry, Philip, 142, 193, 202, 246, 314, 318-319, 323, 336, 337, 387-389, 440
Barrymore, Ethel, 306, 313-314, 386

Barthé, Richmond, 196
Bartholomae, Phil, 210
Barton, James, 405, 406
Battle of Angels, The (Williams), 331-333
Baxter, Jane, 427
Beaumont, Hugh, 380, 382, 427
Before Breakfast (O'Neill), 111
Behrman, S. N., 142, 159, 193, 216, 219-220, 244-245, 254, 256, 266-267, 268, 337-338, 371, 384, 385, 393, 396, 414, 425, 440, 441
Belais, Rosie, 42
Beletti, Valerie, 66
Bel Geddes, Norman, 84
Bell, Josephine, 77
Bellows, George, 107
Ben Greet Academy of Acting, 18, 19-20
Ben Greet Shakespearean Company, 19
Benavente, Jacinto, 121
Benchley, Robert, 159, 160
Bendix, William, 322
Benét, William Rose, 197
Benjamin, Dr. George, 57, 87
Benjamin, Park, 43
Bennett, Arnold, 143-145
Bennett, Joan, 304
Bennett, Richard, 161-162, 166
Bercovici, Conrad, 160
Bergner, Elizabeth, 263, 277
Bergman, Ingrid, 418
Berkman, Alexander, 70
Berlin, Irving, 440
Biberman, Herbert, 248-250
Bill of Divorcement, A (Dane), 317
Binger, Carl, 47
Binger, Robert, 75
Binger, Walter, 44, 47, 75
Biography (Behrman), 254, 255
Birabeau, André, 269
Birch, Peter, 392n
Birely, Lieutenant, 362
Birmingham Repertory Theatre, 174-177
Blackmer, Sidney, 448
Blithe Spirit (Coward), 310
Bodenheim, Maxwell, 86
Boettcher, Harvey, 346n
Bohleber, William, 51
Boland, Mary, 334
Bolton, Guy, 210
Bonds of Interest, The (Benavente), 121-122
Boni, Albert, 49, 67, 69, 75, 76-77, 91-92, 93, 199
Boni, Charles, 49, 75, 76

Boni and Liveright, 75, 172, 198
Booth, Shirley, 319, 448
Booth Theatre, 269, 324
Boston Herald, 322
Both Your Houses (Anderson), 254
Boucicault, Dion Lardner, 297
Bowen, Harold G., 9, 53, 358
Box and Cox, 8
Boyce, Neith, 69
Boyd, Ernest, 160, 197
Brackett, Charles, 202
Bradley, Kenneth, 311
Brady, Alice, 235, 244, 253, 278-279, 280
Brady, William A., 278-279
Brent, Romney, 204, 293, 297, 298, 300, 432
Brevoort Hotel, New York, 67, 114
Bride the Sun Shines On, The (Cotton), 298
Bristol Channel, 1, 5, 7
British Chartered Institute of Patent Agents, 38, 40
British Museum, 26
British Patent Office, 24, 28, 36, 65
Britten, Pamela, 378n
Bromfield, Louis, 192, 193, 197
Brooks, Van Wyck, 46
Brothers Karamazoo, The (Dostoevsky), 216, 219
Broun, Heywood, 98-99, 157, 160, 183, 197
Brown, Anne, 265
Brown, Pamela, 310, 427, 428
Brown, William G., 362
Browne, Irene, 305
Browne, Maurice, 82-83, 92, 198, 241, 429
Bruning, Albert, 139
Bubbles, John W., 265
Buck, Pearl, 255
Buckley, Oliver, 359n
Budd Company, 344
Bufano, Remo, 102
Bullitt, William, 70, 197
Buloff, Joseph, 376n
Bundsman, Tony, 297
Bunny, John, 74, 436
Burne-Jones, Sir Francis Cowley, 33
Bouyant Billions (Shaw), 416
Burns, David, 378n
Bush, Vannevar, 355-356, 367
Bushido (Izumo), 101
Busley, Jessie, 297
By Way of Obit (O'Neill), 403
Byrnes, James F., 355

Cabell, James Branch, 193
Cabot, Eliot, 243
Cadell, Jean, 214, 427
Caesar and Cleopatra (Shaw), 185, 213, 330
Caine, Hall, 19
Calhern, Louis, 384
California, University of, 49, 206
Call It a Day (Smith), 264n
Call Me Mister, 263
Calvert, Louis, 22
Camden Town Theatre, 21, 22
Camille, 314
Campbell, Mrs. Pat, 127
Candida (Shaw), 184, 424
Candle in the Wind (Anderson), 257, 335
Cape Playhouse, Dennis, Massachusetts, 297
Caprice (Sil-Vara), 222, 243, 289, 290, 394
Captain Brassbound's Conversion (Shaw), 294, 314
Card, William, 29, 74, 89
Carey, Harry, 334
Carlton, Carl, 209
Carlton, Newton, 259
Carlyle, Thomas, 9
Carmencita and the Soldier, 170
Carnovsky, Morris, 215n
Carousel (Rodgers and Hammerstein), 153-154, 369, 391-393, 422, 440
Carpentier, Georges, 136-137
Carroll, Leo G., 421
Caruso, Enrico, 35, 43
Case, Frank, 160
Casto, Jean, 392n
Cather, Willa, 193
Cavellieri, Lina, 194
Cavendish, Mrs. Dola, 387
Cecil, Lord Robert, 32
Cerf, Bennett, 72, 198
Chadbourne, William M., 300
Chaliapin, Feodor, 130
Champagne Sec (Langner), 302
Chandler, Robert, 107, 193-195
Chaney, Stewart, 313, 329
Chaplin, Charles, 74
Chartered Patent Agency, 23, 28, 36, 172
Chase, Ilka, 280, 304
Chase, Lucia, 225
Chase, Stuart, 365
Chekhov, Anton, 45, 100, 103, 142, 168, 171, 447
Chesterton, G. K., 26
Chicago Little Theatre, 82

Chief Thing, The (Eoreinoff), 207
Christians, Mady, 431
Chrysalis (Porter), 301
Cibelli, Alfred, 378n
Claire, Ina, 245, 254-255, 264n, 306
Clarence (Tarkington), 394
Clark, Bobby, 334
Clark, Henry F., 380n
Claudel, Paul, 203
Clayton, Jan, 392n
Cleveland Playhouse, 445
Clift, Montgomery, 269, 313
Clugston, Katherine, 316
Clurman, Harold, 215n, 250, 331, 339
Coates, Albert, 187
Cobham, Sir Alan, 361, 363
Coburn, Mr. & Mrs. Charles, 314, 393
Cochran, Charles, 244, 263
Cochran, June, 204
Codrington, George, 53, 358
Coe, Conway P., 352, 355, 356-357, 358, 360
Coe, Fred, 435, 435n, 436
Cohan, George M., 284
Colbert, Claudette, 241
Colbourne, Maurice, 294, 328
Cole, Frank, 89
Collett, Ove, 246
Collier, Constance, 198
Collinge, Patricia, 269
Collins, Russell, 392n
Colonial Theatre, Boston, 261, 270
Colton, John, 193
Columbia Pictures, 258
Columbia University, 158, 205
Come Back, Little Sheba (Inge), 448
Comedy Theatre, 100, 102
Comic Artist, The (Glaspell and Matson, 298, 299
Commins, Saxe, 72
Coney Island, 44
Congreve, William, 306
Conklin, Peggy, 303
Connelly, Mare, 159, 160, 193, 440
Conroy, Frank, 98, 102
Convention of the American Theatre, 262-263
Cook, George Cram, 71-72, 92, 99, 102, 103, 109, 439
Coolidge, Calvin, 213
Coolidge, William, 358
Cooper, James Fenimore, 10, 40
Cooper, Violet Kemble, 290
Copeau, Jacques, 120, 154, 216, 219
Copeland, Aaron, 193
Cornell, John, 309, 412

Cornell, Katherine, 21, 101, 102, 198, 412, 424
The Corsican Brothers, 8
Cossart, Ernest, 214, 247
Cotten, Joseph, 319
Cotton, Will, 298
Courtney, William, 19, 20, 21
Covent Garden, 18, 34
Covent Garden Opera House, 34-35
Coward, Noel, 257, 305, 309, 310, 380
Cowl, Jane, 308-309, 314
Crabtree, Paul, 405
Crawford, Cheryl, 215n, 225, 250, 299, 310, 334
Creen, Judd and Mildred, 367
Crews, Laura Hope, 155, 161, 216
Critics' Circle Award, 324
Cronin, George, 47
Crouse, Russel, 285, 440
Cruikshank and Fairweather, 23-24
Crummit, Frank, 210
Cullen, Countee, 196
Currey, Margaret, 80-82

Daily News (newspaper), 208
Daily Telegraph (newspaper), 16
Dale, Alan, 157
Dallas Theatre-in-the-Round, 445
D'Alvarez, Marguerite, 198
Daly, Arnold, 163-164, 215n
Daly, Augustin, 227
Daly, Orlando, 165
Dame Nature (Birabeau), 269
Dancing in the Streets, 375-376
Dane, Clemence, 317
Daniell, Henry, 393
Dantechenko, Nemirovich, 167, 170-171, 218
Dante, Alighieri, 33
Darling, Jean, 392n
da Silva, Howard, 376n
Davidson, Jo, 71
Davies, Mary Carolyn, 69
Davis, Donald, 255
Davis, Frank Parker, 80, 346, 347n
Davis, Owen, 255
Davis, Peter, 389
Davis, Watson, 358
Davis, William H., 209, 350
Days Without End (O'Neill), 275, 282, 283, 284-285, 289
Dean, Basil, 387
Death of a Salesman (Miller), 334, 393
Deeds, Edward A., 52, 53-54, 77-79
DeFoe Louis, 157
de Haviland, Olivia, 311-312
de Lappe, Gembe, 378n, 380n

Delco electric self-starter, 51-55, 56, 57, 58, 65, 77-79, 86-89
Delco-Light equipment, 52, 77
de Liagre, Alfred, 108
Delilah (Goodrich), 311
Dell, Floyd, 70, 80, 90-91
De Mille, Agnes, 5, 291, 371, 374, 377, 391
De Mille, Mrs. William, 291
Dempsey, Jack, 136
Demuth, Charles, 71
Deschamps, Sidney, 447
Design for Living (Coward), 257
Desire Under the Elms (O'Neill), 231
Destinn, Emmy, 35
Deutsches, Theater, 57, 59, 63, 171
Devil's Disciple, The (Shaw), 131, 419, 420, 421
de Wolfe, Elsie, 202
Diaghilev, Sergei, 90
Dial, 71
Dickens, Charles, 81
Dies, Martin, 70
Diesel engines, 53, 344
Dietrich, Marlene, 431, 432
Digges, Dudley, 120, 121, 122, 124, 166, 214, 215n, 217, 241n, 243, 247, 403, 404, 405, 407
Dimitrov, Georgi, 49
Dixon, Lee, 376n
Doctor Knock, 307
Doctor's Dilemma, The (Shaw), 134, 222, 424, 437
Don Quixote, 9
Donahue, Walter, 378, 380n
Doolittle, James, 362-363
Dorr, Goldthwaite H., 112-113
Dorr, John Van Nostrand, 350
Dos Passos, John, 192
Dostoyevsky, Fyodor, 169, 216, 219
Doucet, Catherine, 241
Dowling, Eddie, 320-324, 401, 405
Doyle, Miriam, 303
Dracula (a play), 200
Drake, Alfred, 370, 376n
Dreiser, Theodore, 70, 91, 103, 198, 200
Drury Lane Theatre, 419
Druten, John van, 428, 440
Duggan, Pat, 325-326
Duke, Ashley, 308
Dullin (French playwright), 154, 155
Duncan, Augustin, 120, 123, 124-125
Duncan, Isadora, 54-55
Duncan, Todd, 265
Dunn, James, 404, 407
Dunnigan's Daughter (Behrman), 393
Dunning, Philip, 304, 309

Dunsany, Lord, 76
Dynamo (O'Neill), 238, 239-240, 241-242, 243, 289

Eames, Claire, 214, 215, 216, 218
Eastbourne, England, 7
Eastman, George, 225
Eastman, Max, 69, 91-92, 106, 205
Eaton, Walter Prichard, 103, 227
Edward VII, 35-36
Edwards, Bobby, 69
Ehrenberg, Ilya, 340
Eldridge, Florence, 222-223, 335
Eliot, Samuel, 49, 76, 92
Eliot, T. S., 81, 437
Elizabeth the Queen (Anderson), 249, 252
Ellis, Charles, 110
Ellis, Havelock, 33
Ellis, Mary, 238
"Embassy, The," 386
Embezzled Heaven, 386
Emerson, John, 148
Emery, John, 271, 272
Emperor Jones, The (O'Neill), 109, 155
Empire Theatre, 302
End of Summer (Behrman), 245, 264n
Enright, Florence, 92, 95, 99
Enter the Hero (Helburn), 97
Ervine, St. John Greer, 32-33, 123, 127, 131-132, 142-143, 174-176, 184, 435
Erwin, Stuart, 337
Escape Me Never (Kennedy), 263
Eternal City, The (Caine), 19
Ethyl gasoline, 52, 342-343
Eugenically Speaking (Goodman), 92, 95-96
Evans, Maurice, 22, 331, 414
Eureinov, Nicholas, 207
Ewing, Thomas, 89
Eyre, Richard, 350

Fabian Nursery, 31
Fabian Society, 26, 130
Failures, The (Lenormand), 154-155
Fairless, Benjamin, 429
Fairweather, Wallace Cranston, 23-27, 28, 130
Faithful, The (Masefield), 126
Family Exit, The (Langner), 101-102, 103
Fanny's First Play (Shaw), 294
Farley, Morgan, 165
Fata Morgana (Vajda), 164-165, 166, 204
Faust (Goethe), 39, 57-58, 243

Feiker, Frederick M., 358
Ferber, Edna, 94, 310, 435n
Ferrer, Jose, 384, 448
Festival Acting Company, 438
Fickett, Homer, 429, 430n
Field, Betty, 314, 435n
Fifth Column, The (Hemmingway), 329
Finnish Relief Fund, 327, 331
Firebrand, The (a play), 200
First Man, The (O'Neill), 230
First Mrs. Frazer, The (Ervine), 143
Fischer, Alfred, 421
Fiske, Minnie Maddern, 164-165
Fitch, Clyde, 45
Fitelson, H. William, 428, 429, 430n
Fitzgerald, Barry, 403, 407
Fitzgerald, F. Scott, 192, 193, 198
Five Kings, The, 269-273
Fledermaus, Die (Strauss), 60, 302
Flemyng, Bobby, 427
Foch, Nina, 314
Folies Bergère, 38
Folklore of Capitalism, The (Arnold), 350
Fontaine, André, 203
Fontanne, Lynn, 21, 148n, 165-166, 176, 213, 214, 215, 216, 217, 219, 221, 222, 236, 245, 252-253, 254, 257, 265, 266, 289, 327-329, 337-338, 371, 393-396, 430, 441
Foolish Notion (Barry), 387, 388, 389
For Husbands Only (Langner), 302
Forbes-Robertson, Sir Johnston, 213
Forrestal, James V., 358
Forrester, Hugh, 241n
Forsythe Saga, The (Galsworthy), 286
Forty-Eighth Street Theatre, 300
Forum, The (magazine), 435
Fountain, The (O'Neill), 230
Francis, Arlene, 225
Frank, Waldo, 44
Franken, Rose, 310
Fraser, Phyllis, 328
Freedley, Vinton, 375, 376
Freedman, Harold, 99, 219, 266-268, 338
Freeman, Helen, 120, 121, 125
Freon, 343
Freud, Sigmund, 92
Frey, John P., 350
Frings, Ketti, 337
Frohman, Daniel, 298
Fly, Christopher, 428, 437
Fuhrer, Julius H., 359n
Fulda, Ludwig, 337
Fulfillment (Raphael), 39

Fulton Theatre, 124

Gaige, Crosby, 304, 464
Gale, Zona, 103
Gallico, Paul, 411
Galsworthy, John, 142, 145-146, 286, 428
Game of Love and Death, The (Rolland), 244
Garde, Betty, 376n
Garrick Gaieties, The, 204-205, 209, 369, 440
Garrick Theatre, 119-120, 124, 136, 138, 154, 155, 165, 178, 196, 211
Gassner, John, 331, 333, 373, 435
Gaul, George, 138, 148n, 214, 222, 241n, 243
Geddes, Norman Bel, 84
Gehr, George von, 447
Gemier, Firmin, 154, 155, 186
General Motors Diesel Locomotive, 52
General Motors Research Laboratory, 53, 351
Geneva (Shaw), 293-294
Geneviève de Brabant, 35
Gentlemen Prefer Blondes (Loos), 149
George, David Lloyd, 10-11, 88
George, Henry, 291
Gerard, John, 306
German General Electric Company, 53
German Patent Office, 65
Gershwin, George, 193, 226, 265, 440
Gest, Morris, 166-167, 171
Getting Married (Shaw), 131
Ghosts (Ibsen), 103, 314
Gielgud, John, 424, 427, 428
Gilbert and Sullivan, 3, 5, 23
Gillmore, Daisy, 71
Gillmore, Inez Haynes, 70-71
Gillmore, Margalo, 162, 214, 215n, 219
Gilpin, Charles S., 109
Giraudoux, Jean, 266
Girl in the Coffin, The (Dreiser), 103
Gish, Dorothy, 297-299, 337
Gish, Lillian, 299, 337, 386
Glaenzer, Jules, 371
Glascow, Ellen, 193
Glaspell, Susan, 67, 70, 71, 92, 99, 102, 103, 109, 229, 298
Glass Menagerie, The, 308, 333
Glass Slipper, The (Molnar), 153
Glazer, Benjamin, 329
Goat Song (Werfel), 148, 215
Gods of the Mountain (Dunsany)
Goethe, Johann Wolfgang von, 39
Goldman, Emma, 84-85
Goldsmith, Del Valle, 447

Goldwyn, Samuel, 66
Gomez, Thomas, 327, 328
Good Earth, The, 255
Good Housekeeping, 312, 314
Goodman, Edward, 44, 45, 92-93, 94, 95, 97, 100, 101, 102, 103-104
Goodrich, Marcus Aurelius, 311-312
Gordon, Max, 229, 340
Gordon, Ruth, 246, 305, 314
Gordon, Taylor, 196
Gorki, Maxim, 447
Gorman, Herbert, 197, 209
Great Catherine, The (Shaw), 435
Great God Brown, The (O'Neill), 289
Green, John C., 360, 434
Green, Paul, 251, 440
Green Grow the Lilacs (Riggs), 341, 368, 369
Greene, Patterson, 335
Greenstreet, Sidney, 257-258, 327
Greenwich Village, 45, 65-79, 81, 85
Greet, Ben, 18-20
Grey, Viscount, 88
Gribble, Harry Wagstaff, 299
Grossmith, Lawrence, 293
Group Theatre, 225, 250-251, 299
Guardsman, The (Molnar), 153, 165, 166, 221, 222, 394
Guild Theatre, 190, 211-226, 268-269, 284, 291, 370, 371, 386
Guiterman, Arthur, 302
Gurdjieff, 200-202
Guthrie, Tyrone, 162

Hackett, James K., 126-127
Hagen, Uta, 307, 384
Haggott, John, 309, 332, 371, 375
Hairy Ape, The (O'Neill), 275
Hale, Ruth, 99, 183
Hamilton, Patrick, 435*n*
Hamlet (Shakespeare), 57-58, 427, 433, 434
Hammerstein, Oscar, 154, 369-375, 377, 379, 383, 390, 391, 393, 422, 440
Hammond, Percy, 157
Hampden, Walter, 334
Hand, Judge Learned, 344, 350
Hanrahan, John, 224
Hapgood, Hutchins, 69
Harat Export Company, 57
Harding, Laura, 317
Harding, Warren G., 128
Hardwicke, Sir Cedric, 290, 413, 421
Harrigan, Nedda, 310
Harris, Jed, 305, 385
Harris, Roy, 193
Harris, Sam, 269

Hart, Lorenz, 205, 369
Hart, Moss, 193
Hartley, Marsden, 71
Harvard College, 47, 48, 122, 125, 158
Haseltine Lake and Co., 28
Hassard, Jack, 210
Hatvany, Baroness Lily, 152
Havel, Hippolyte, 70
Haverhill, Mass., 47-49
Haviland, Olivia de, 311-312
Haydon, Julie, 324
Hayes, Helen, 21-22, 213, 256-257, 305, 312, 314, 327, 329-331, 335
Hays, Arthur Garfield, 49, 208-209
Hayward, John B., 51-52, 54, 80
Haywood, Bill, 72
He (Savoir), 253
He Who Gets Slapped (Andreyev), 161
Head, Cloyd, 82
Heap, Jane, 220
Hearst, William Randolph, 291
Heartbreak House (Shaw), 127-131, 184, 419
Hecht, Ben, 81, 85-86, 440
Hedden (inventor), 360
Heflin, Van, 319
Heiman, Marcus, 261, 370
Helburn, Theresa, 44, 45, 97, 101, 117, 120, 121, 125-126, 128, 138, 153, 158, 165, 183, 203-205, 219, 224, 226, 227, 233, 236, 238-239, 248-249, 250, 253, 256, 258, 263, 278, 294, 307, 310, 316, 318, 320, 329, 330, 331-332, 333, 336, 338, 339, 341, 368, 369-374, 379, 384-385, 390-391, 405, 408, 411, 414, 417, 419, 425, 430*n*, 433, 435*n*, 438, 440, 441, 442
Helena's Husband (Moeller), 98
Hellman, Lillian, 440
Hellstrom, Louise, 108
Heming, Violet, 304
Hemingway, Ernest, 192, 193, 329
Henri, Robert, 46
Henry V (Shakespeare), 432, 433
Henry Behave (Langner), 209
Henry Miller Theatre, 285
Henry Street Settlement, 138
Henty, G. A., 10
Hepburn, Katherine, 22, 246, 298, 316-319, 336, 337, 411, 413, 423, 437*n*
Her Cardboard Lover, 310
Herald-Tribune, 276
Herbert, Henry, 120
Hergesheimer, Joseph, 193
Herts, J. Russell, 44
Heyward, Du Bose and Dorothy, 226

Hinkle, Dr. Beatrice, 206
History of Tammany Hall (Meyers), 71
History of the French Revolution (Carlyle), 9
Hobohemia (Sinclair Lewis), 70
Hofgaard electrical calculating machine, 246
Hogg, Quentin, 13
Hogg, Quentin, Jr., 13
Hohl, Arthur, 102
Holcomb, Major Amasa, 111-112
Holcombe, Ernest, 68-69, 105
Holiday (Barry), 318
Holloway, Sterling, 204
Holm, Celeste, 322, 373, 376n
Holmes, John Haynes, 207
Holt, Nora, 196
Homestead Steel Mills, 50
Hope, Anthony, 16
Hope for a Harvest (Treadwell), 335
Hopkins, Arthur, 117, 229, 316, 439
Hopkins, Harry, 355, 357
Hopkins, Miriam, 266-268, 332
Hotel Universe (Barry), 246
Hough, Judge Charles M., 344
House of Connelly, The, 251
Howard, J. Bannister, 16, 18, 19, 20, 23, 24
Howard, Sidney, 159, 166, 215, 216, 218, 268
Howe, Louis, 207
Howell, Miriam, 317
Hudson, Holland, 98
Huffaker, Lucy, 70, 92, 98, 104, 109
Hughes, Hatcher, 158
Hughes, Langston, 196
Hughie (O'Neill), 402, 403
Hull, Cordell, 377
Hull, Josephine, 165
Humphrey, Doris, 5, 302
Hunt, John, 53, 54, 57, 58, 65-66
Hunter, Glenn, 99, 102
Hunter, Kim, 314
Hurdis, Charles E., 362
Hurok, Sol, 167
Hurst, Fanny, 197
Huston, Walter, 284, 325

I Know My Love (Behrman), 396
Ibsen, Henrik, 45, 103, 288-289, 298, 300, 430, 437, 447
Iceman Cometh, The (O'Neill), 70, 204, 397-407
Idiot's Delight (Sherwood), 264, 265-266, 327
"If I Loved You" (song), 392
If This Be Treason (Holmes), 207

Importance of Being Earnest, The, (Wilde), 427
In the Beginning (Shaw), 138
In the Days of Good King Charles (Shaw), 413
In the Zone (O'Neill), 103, 109, 228-229
Industrial Rayon Company, 344
Inge, William, 448
Ingersoll, Robert, 38
Insull, Samuel, 221-222
Intelligent Woman's Guide to Socialism and Capitalism, The, (Shaw), 416n
Interior (Maeterlinck), 96
International Business Machines Company, 54
Ives, Burl, 386-387

Jackson, Sir Barry, 174-176, 289
Jacobowsky and the Colonel (Werfel), 148, 384-385, 389, 428
Jane (Behrman), 414, 425, 426
Jane Clegg (Ervine), 127, 142-143
Jane Eyre, 317
Jehlinger, Charles, 298
Jeremiah (Zweig), 273, 318
Jerome, Helen, 317
Jerusalem, 367
Jitta's Atonement (Shaw and Trebitsch), 141, 185-186
Joan of Lorraine, 418
Johann, Zita, 148n
John Ferguson (St. John Ervine), 33, 123-124, 126, 142-143, 435
John Golden Theatre, 215, 216, 236
Johnson, Alvin, 349
Johnson, Christine, 392n
Johnson, Howard, 237
Johnson, James Weldon, 195-196
Johnson, Rosamond, 196
Johnston, Denis, 434, 435
Johnston, Moffat, 297, 298
Jones, Gwenyth, 4
Jones, Robert Edmond, 48, 76, 92, 142, 228, 231, 279, 375, 439
Jones, Webster N., 358
Jonson, Ben, 180
Journey's End, 83
Joyce, James, 81, 86
Juarez and Maximilian (Werfel), 148, 215, 217
Judson Concert Bureau, 222
Julius Caesar (Shakespeare), 434
Jungle, The (Sinclair), 69

Kadar, Andre, 307
Kahn, Otto H., 90, 120, 167, 221

Karlweis, Oscar, 384
Karsten, Karl, 95
Kaufman, George S., 98, 159, 160, 193, 435n, 440
Kaye, Ben, 205
Kazan, Elia, 310, 385, 393
Keel, Harold, 380n, 382
Keith, Robert, 209
Kelly, Gene, 313, 322
Kelly, George, 440
Kemp, Harry, 69, 111
Kennedy, Margaret, 263
Kenny, David, 89
Kent, Edgar, 241n
Kenton, Edna, 116
Kenyon, William Houston, 345, 347n
Kern, Jerome, 193, 440
Kerr, Gov. Robert S., 378, 379
Kerr, Walter, 386
Kerr, Page, Cooper and Hayward (patent-law firm), 51
Kerrigan, James M., 407
Kettering, Charles F., 52-54, 56, 57, 77-79, 342, 344, 351, 352, 353-354, 357, 359
Keyhole, The, 307
Keynes, John Maynard, 99
Kielty, Bernardine, 71
King, Dennis, 306
King, Fred, 46
Kingsley, Sydney, 440
Kingston, Gertrude, 417
Kirkland, Jack, 307
Klaw, Alma and Alonzo, 226
Klaw and Erlanger, 45, 157, 260-261
Knopf, Alfred and Blanche, 197
Kommer, Dr. Rudolph, 171-172, 376
Kondolf, George, 429
Korda, Sir Alexander, 425
Kostenko, Vladimir, 376n
Kreymborg, Alfred, 69
Kristen, Erik, 380n
Kropotkin, Princess, 291
Krupska, Dania, 378n
Krutch, Joseph Wood, 198, 280, 306
Kurnit, Abe, 381
Kuttner, Alfred, 44

La Coste, Renée, 77
Ladas, Steven, 447
Lady Godiva (Langner), 304
Lady's not for Burning, The, (Fry) 428
Lafayette Hotel, 67
La Grande Duchesse, 35
La Guardia, Fiorello, 260, 377
LaGue, Jeanne, 206
Lake, Simon, 25

Landis, Jessie Royce, 294, 393
Lang, Anton, 63
Langner, Arminia (Marshall) *see* Marshall, Arminia
Langner, Estelle (Roege) *see* Roege, Estelle
Langner, Herbert, 14, 47, 66, 74, 88, 447
Langner, Philip, 313, 314
Langner, Phyllis Adair, 107, 108, 168, 172, 207, 412
Langner, Ruth, 148, 215n
Langner, Parry, Card and Langner, 264
Larimore, Earle, 214, 219, 236, 279
Larsen, Nella, 196
Lascelles, Ernita, 138
Last Days of Pompeii, The, 9
Late George Apley, The, 435n
Lauder, Harry, 27
Launzi (Molnar), 150
Lawrence, Gertrude, 435
League of Composers, 39
League of New York Theatres, 259
Lederer, Francis, 304
Le Gallienne, Eva, 154, 162, 177, 211n, 254, 306, 310, 314, 334
Lemon, Courtenay, 110, 200-201, 218, 219
Lenihan, Winifred, 154, 178, 180, 224-225, 243, 297, 298, 300
Lenormand, H. R., 154-155
Leontovich, Eugenie, 314
Lewis, Al, 229
Lewis, Bobby, 310, 320-321
Lewis, George, 358
Lewis, Sinclair, 70, 193
Lewisohn, Alice, 138
Lewisohn sisters, 439
Lewys, Gladys Adelina, 276
Liagre, Alfred de, 108
Liberal Club, 67-73, 75, 90-92, 93, 105
Licensed (Langner), 79, 81, 85, 93, 95, 97, 198
Liebes, Dorothy, 266
Life of Man, The (Andreyev), 100, 103
Life with Father (Day), 285
Light, James and Susan, 109
Liliom (Molnar), 149, 150, 151, 153, 155, 162, 177, 311, 390, 391
Lillie, Beatrice, 290, 310, 380
Lindsay, Howard, 440
Lindsay, Vachel, 69
Linn, Bambi, 376n, 392n
Lippmann, Walter, 44, 76, 344, 348
Literary Digest, 46
Littell, Philip, 76

Little, Richard, 50
Little Bo Peep (Christmas pantomime), 5
Little Review, The (periodical), 81, 82, 84, 85, 86, 220
Little Theatre "movement," 82-83
Littler, Prince, 382
Litvak, Anatol, 267
Litvinoff, Maxim, 339-340
Liveright, Horace, 86, 160, 197, 198-200
Liveright, Otto, 97, 98, 160, 198
Livesy, Roger, 305
Living Corpse, The (Tolstoy), 59
Locker, Robert, 71
Loeb, Jacques, 72
Loeb, Philip, 148n, 163, 204, 206, 214
Logan, Joshua, 310
Lohengrin, 34
London Polytechnic school, 13-14, 28
Long Day's Journey Into Night, A, (O'Neill), 401
Loos, Anita, 148-149, 310
Lopokova, Lydia, 98-99
Lord, Pauline, 150, 166, 238
Lorraine, Robert, 291
Love for Love (Congreve), 306, 314, 427
Love in Idleness (Rattigan), 394
Love of One's Neighbor (Andreyev), 97
Love's Old Sweet Song (Saroyan), 324-326
Lowell, Amy, 82
Lowenstein, Mr., 420, 422
Lower Depths, The (Gorki), 168
Lubbock, Sir John, 9
Lubitsch, Ernest, 431
Lunt, Alfred, 21, 127, 148n, 165-166, 176, 213-217, 219, 221, 222, 236, 243, 245, 252-254, 257, 264n, 265, 266, 289, 290, 309, 327-329, 335, 337-338, 371, 393-396, 430, 441
Luther, Harris G., 361
Lyon, Annabelle, 392n
Lysistrata, 368

MacArthur, Charles, 85, 159, 193, 440
MacArthur, Mary, 312
McClintic, Guthrie, 101, 198
McCormick, Myron, 304
McCracken, Joan, 371-372, 376n, 377, 435
MacDonald, J. Carlisle, 429
McEnroe, Robert, 447
MacFadden, Hamilton, 226
MacFarland, Dorothea, 380n

McFarland, Earle, 359n
Macgowan, Kenneth, 49, 142, 231, 439
Machinal (Treadwell), 335
McKay, Morris, 207, 293, 306
McKay, Scott, 314
Mackaye, Percy, 98
MacLiammoir, Michael, 435
MacMillan, Charles, 23
MacMillan, Francis, 23
McNab, Forrest, 79
Maeterlinck, Maurice, 96, 103
Magical City, The (Akins), 103
Magowan, Kenneth, 439
Mahler, Gustav, 148
Mainboucher, 310
Majestic Theatre, 392, 393
Major Barbara (Shaw), 243
Malden, Karl, 314
Malo, Gina, 432
Malone, Dudley Field, 205
Maloney, Bill, 310
Mamoulian, Azadia, 379
Mamoulian, Rouben, 225-226, 248, 249, 265, 371, 372, 373, 375, 377, 379, 391
Man and Superman (Shaw), 307, 414, 419
Man With a Load of Mischief, The (Duke), 308
Mann, Danny, 313
Manners, Hartley, 308
Mansfield, Richard, 127, 131, 214
Manulis, Martin, 312-313
March, Frederick, 222-223, 335, 442
March Hares (Gribble), 299
Marco Millions (O'Neill), 222, 231-232, 233-234, 236, 238, 248, 400
Marconi Company, 436
Mareschal, Greer, 343
Margate Grammar School, 14
Marinoff, Fania, 160, 196, 281-282, 297, 298
Markham, Kirah, 91
Marks, Sir George Croyden, 73-74
Marlo, Mary, 378n, 380n, 382
Marshall, Armina, 155, 173, 186-187, 194-197, 203-209, 246, 251, 281, 285, 289, 291, 294, 296-315, 316, 322, 324, 329, 337, 340, 344, 365, 377, 379, 380, 382, 388, 390, 392, 399, 401, 402, 404, 405, 408, 419, 422, 429, 430n, 432, 433, 435, 437, 438, 441, 442
Marshall, Chalmers, 205-206
Marshall, E. G., 407
Marshall, George C., 366
Marshall, Herbert, 431

Martin, Mary, 310, 375, 380
Martin, Owen, 376n
Martin Beck Theatre, 241, 253, 384, 385, 406
Mary MacArthur Polio Fund, 312
Mary, Mary, Quite Contrary (Ervine), 143
Mary of Scotland (Anderson), 256-257, 331
Marylebone Town Hall, 31
Masefield, John, 126
Masses, The (periodical), 69, 91
Massey, Edward, 101
Massey, Raymond, 435
Masters, Edgar Lee, 82
Mathison, Edith Wynn, 19
Matinata (Langner), 109
Matson, Norman, 298
Matthews, Miss, 18, 19, 22-23, 24
Mattson, Eric, 392n
Maubergne, Brigadier General, 358
Maugham, Somerset, 193
Maverick Festival, 107
Maxim, Sir Hiram, 30
Medea, 166
Meisner, Edith, 204
Meisner, Sanford, 215n
Meldola, Raphael, 37
Meltzer, Charles, 98
Meltzer, Harold, 98
Mendes, Henry, 43
Mendes, Pereria, 38
Mendes, Raymond, 43
Mendes, Stella, 43
Menken, Helen, 256, 331
Merchant of Venice, The (Shakespeare), 20, 21, 330
Mercury Theatre, 269, 270
Meredith, Burgess, 271, 272-273, 424
Merivale, Philip, 256-257
Merman, Ethel, 368
Merry Wives of Windsor, The (Shakespeare), 393
Mesta, Mrs. Perle, 378
Meteor (Behrman), 244-245
Metropolitan Club, 386
Metropolitan Museum of New York, 191
Meyer, Josephine A., 44-45, 92, 99, 116, 121
Meyers, Augustus B., 71
Midgley, Thomas, Jr., 52, 342-343, 351, 352, 354-355, 357, 359
Midsummer Night's Dream (Shakespeare), 76
Mielziner, Jo, 166, 255

Millay, Edna St. Vincent, 69, 97, 110, 120, 121
Millay, Kathleen, 110
Millay, Norma, 109-110
Miller, Arthur, 334, 440
Miller, Gilbert, 144, 153, 294, 305, 330
Millionairess, The (Shaw), 294, 411, 423
Milne, A. A., 146, 161, 216, 222
Miner, Worthington, 254, 436
Miracle, The, 171
Mr. Pim Passes By (Milne), 146, 161, 216, 222
Mr. Sycamore (Frings), 337, 370
Mrs. Partridge Presents, 305
Mrs. Warren's Profession (Shaw), 103
Mitchell, Thomas, 435
"Modern Library" books, 75, 198
Moeller, Philip, 44, 45, 92, 93, 94-98, 102-103, 114-117, 120-121, 138, 158, 166, 176, 213, 219, 220-221, 236, 241, 245, 248, 249, 252, 254, 258, 263, 267, 279, 289, 336-337
Moissi, Alexander, 58, 59
Molière (*pseud.*), 5, 301, 302
Molnar, Ferenc, 149-154, 162, 165-166, 221, 222, 390, 391, 394, 447
Mondell, Mr., 345
Monroe, Harriet, 82, 86
Montana, Monty, 442
Monterey, Carlotta, 275, 280-281, 285, 286, 287, 399, 401, 402, 404, 406, 409
Montgomery, Robert, 421
Month in the Country, A (Turgenev), 245-246, 256, 316
Moods International (periodical), 44
Moon for the Misbegotten (O'Neill), 204, 401-404, 407-409
Moon in the Yellow River, The (Johnston), 434
Moondown (John Reed), 97
Moore, Owen, 74
Morgan, Agnes, 138
Morgan, Claudia, 268
Morgan, Etienne, 11
Morgenthau, Henry, Jr., 377
Morning's at Seven (Osborn), 435n
Morris, McKaye, 207, 306
Moscow Art Theatre, 6, 57, 166-171, 211, 214, 444
  Musical Studio, 167, 170-171
Moses (Langner), 172-173
Moss, Paul, 205
Motherwell, Hiram, 49, 223-224
Mount Kisco (summer theatre), 309

Mourning Becomes Electra (O'Neill), 236, 253, 256, 276-280, 282, 433, 441

Mudie's Lending Library, 13

Mullaly, Eugene, 362

Munro, C. K., 146, 215

Munsell, Warren P., 221, 226, 265, 291, 336, 370

Muray, Nickolas, 69

Murphy, Gerald, 202

My Heart's in the Highlands (Saroyan), 320

My Lady's Honor (Pemberton), 97

My Life in Art (Stanislavsky), 449

My Pal Joey, 322

My Theatrical and Musical Recollections (Soldene), 35n

Myers, Colonel "Benny," 364

Nathan, George Jean, 95-96, 102, 157, 258, 321, 322, 324

Nation, The (periodical), 125, 280

National Advisory Committee for Aeronautics, 361

National Advisory Council to the House Committee on Patents, 349-350, 354, 355

National Cash Register Company, 51, 53, 54

National Company of Oklahoma!, 378-379

National Defense Research Council, 356-357

National Galleries, 26

National Inventors Council, 53, 208, 329, 343, 353-367, 412, 443, 446

National Kink Safety Pin Co., etc., 347n

National Recovery Act, 261, 262

National Research Council, 355

National Theatre, 338

Nazimova, Alla, 177, 246, 253, 255-256, 279, 280, 293, 306, 314

Neal, Patricia, 313

Ned McCobb's Daughter (Howard), 215-216, 224

Neighborhood Playhouse, 117, 138, 200, 439

Neighbors (Zona Gale), 103

Neilsen, K., 71

New Age, The (periodical), 200

New Republic, The (periodical), 76, 77, 118

New School for Social Research, 158, 349

New York American (newspaper), 95

New York Evening Post, 97

New York Herald, 96, 348

New York Patent Law Association, 345-346

New York Repertory Company, 251, 297-301

New York Telegram, 113

New York Times, 96, 280, 307, 311, 328, 348

New York Tribune, 96, 98

New York World, 237

New Yorker, The (periodical), 224, 425

Nichols, Dudley, 237, 280, 404, 433

Nichols, Robert, 83, 241, 429

Nigger Heaven (Van Vechten), 195

Night Among the Horses, A (Barnes), 110

Nightwood (Barnes), 110

Nijinsky, Waslav, 90

1931 (Sifton), 251

No More Inventions, 347n

Nobel Prize, 287

Nobel Prize, The, 314

Nolan Act, 344-345

Norton, Elliot, 322

Noyes, John Humphrey, 307

Noyes, John Pierrepont, 307

O Mistress Mine (Rattigan), 394, 395

Oberammergau, 63

Obey, Andre, 21

O'Brien, Pat, 209

O'Connell, Cardinal, 238

Odéon Theatre, 155

Odets, Clifford, 251, 263, 339, 440

Oklahoma!, 5, 154, 260, 335, 340-341, 342, 366, 368-383, 384, 389, 390, 391, 393, 413, 419, 434, 440

Old English (Galsworthy), 146

Old Globe Theatre, 438

Old Wives' Tale, The (Bennett), 144

Olds, Irving, 429

Olivier, Laurence, 432, 433, 434

O'Malley, Rex, 293

Onto Fortune (Marshall and Langner), 304

Oneida Community, 307

O'Neill, Agnes, 229, 238

O'Neill, Carlotta (Monterey), 275, 280-281, 285, 286, 287, 399, 401, 402, 404, 406, 409

O'Neill, Eugene, 67, 70, 71, 72, 99, 102, 103, 109, 111, 142, 155, 158, 159, 193, 195, 198, 200, 204, 225, 247, 253, 256, 268, 275-287, 288-289, 342, 397-409, 428, 430, 439, 440, 447

O'Neill, Eugene—*Continued*
  Ah, Wilderness, 256, 282-284, 334
  Anna Christie, 229, 402
  Before Breakfast, 111
  By Way of Obit, 403
  Days Without End, 275, 282, 283,
    284-285, 289
  Desire Under the Elms, 231
  Dynamo, 238, 239-240, 241-242, 243,
    289
  Emperor Jones, The, 109, 155
  First Man, The, 230
  Fountain, The, 230
  Great God Brown, The, 289
  Hughie, 402, 403
  Hairy Ape, The, 275
  Iceman Cometh, The, 70, 204, 397-
    407
  In the Zone, 103, 109, 228-229
  Long Day's Journey Into Night, A,
    401
  Marco Millions, 222, 231-232, 233-
    234, 236, 238, 248, 400
  Moon for the Misbegotten, 204, 401-
    404, 407-409
  Mourning Becomes Electra, 236, 253,
    256, 276-280, 282, 441
  Strange Interlude, 217, 228-242, 277,
    289, 400, 430, 441
  Straw, The, 229
  Touch of the Poet, A, 286, 403, 409
  Welded, 230
O'Neill, James, 127, 278
Ooms, Casper, 359n
Opdycke, John B., 278
Orage, A. R., 200
Ordnance Department, 111-113, 344,
  357
Orsay, Leopold, 37-39, 202
Osborn, Paul, 435n
Othello (Shakespeare), 196, 331, 384,
  389
Our Town (Wilder), 314, 435
Outward Bound, 314

Pacific 1868, 380
Pagent, Robert, 392n
Pam, Max, 107
Pankhurst, Christabel, 72
Papa Is All (Greene), 335
Parade, 263
Paramount Pictures, 247
Paris, 38-39, 87-88
Parmalee, Maurice, 70
Parry, John, 29, 38, 40, 66, 172, 447
Pascal, Gabriel, 410-411, 418, 419, 420,
  423

Patch, Miss, 177, 295, 414, 420
Patent Applied For (Langner), 345-
  346
Patent Law Association of Chicago, 346
Patent System, 349-351
Patten, Richard Van, 395
Peg O' My Heart, 308
Pemberton, Brock, 263
Pemberton, Murdock, 93, 97
Perkins, Osgood, 301, 302
Peters, Charles Rollo, 118
Peters, Rollo, 102, 116, 118-121, 124,
  125, 297-298
Peterson, Verne, 447
Petitpas restaurant, 45-46
Philadelphia Story, The (Barry), 318-
  320
Pickering, Ruth, 69
Pickford, Mary, 74, 436
Pillars of Society (Ibsen), 298, 300-301
Pins and Needles, 263
Pinski, David, 127
Pirandello, Luigi, 155, 194, 207-208,
  216, 447
Pirate, The (Behrman), 337, 371
Pitoëff (French playwright), 154-155
Pittsburgh Playhouse, 445
Platt, Marc, 376n
Play's the Thing, The (Molnar), 153
Playwrights' Company, 257, 268, 327,
  328, 335, 337-338, 371
Plots and Playwrights (Massey), 101
Plutarch's Lives, 9
Poetica Erotica, 200
Poetry Magazine, 82, 86
Point Valaine (Coward), 257
Polan, Lou, 378n
Porgy (Heyward), 195, 217, 222, 226,
  248, 265, 371
Porgy and Bess, 169, 195, 226, 264n,
  265, 334-335, 371, 372, 440
Porter, Cole, 440
Porter, Russell, 348
Postal Telegraph Company, 259-260
Potter, Grace, 68-69, 105
Poussin, Nicolas, 26
Povah, Phyllis, 161
Power, Tyrone, 311
Power of Darkness, The (Tolstoy), 127
Powers, Tom, 214, 236, 290
Pratt, Caroline, 107
Press Cuttings (Shaw), 45
Princess Turandot (Gozzi), 306
Prohibition Era, 192-210
Provincetown Players, 67, 71, 99, 102,
  109-111, 117, 142, 229, 230, 297,
  439

Provincetown Playhouse, 67, 92
Prowse, Keith, 259
Pulitzer Prize, 166, 254, 324
Pursuit of Happiness, The, 294, 302-304
Pygmalion (Shaw), 215-216, 410
Pyne, Mary, 111

Quail, Antony, 438
Quincy, Massachusetts, 237, 239

Race with the Shadows, The (von Scholz), 163
Radio Corporation of America, 436
Rain (Randolph and Colton), 193
Rains, Claude, 214, 247, 253
Raitt, John, 390-391, 392n
Randolph, Clemence, 193
Random House, 72, 198
Rank, J. Arthur, 433, 434
Rape of Lucrece, The (Shakespeare), 21, 243
Raphael, Alice and Claire, 39, 44, 47, 302
Raquello, Edward, 328
Rathbone, Basil, 413
Rathenau, Kurt, 53, 57, 87
Rathenau, Walter, 53
Rattigan, Terence, 310, 380, 394, 427, 428
Rauh, Ida, 91-92, 95, 97, 99, 106
Ray, Sylvia, 187
Reader's Digest, 365
Reber, Neil, 108, 109
Red Cloak, The (Langner and Meyer), 99
Red Rust, 250
Redman, Joyce, 435
Reed, Florence, 393
Reed, John, 69, 70, 73, 93, 97
Reicher, Emmanuel, 58, 127
Reicher, Frank, 58
Reicher, Hedwig, 58
Reid, Whitelaw, 386
Reinhardt, Max, 57-58, 59, 171-172
Reinheimer, Howard, 383
Relapse, The, 437
Repertory System, 214-227, 243-244, 400
Reunion in Vienna (Sherwood), 253-254, 257
Rhondda Valley, South Wales, 5, 11
Rice, Elmer, 159, 193, 268, 440
Richman, Arthur, 159
Riegleman, Charles A., 428
Riggs, Lynn, 341, 368, 369
Riggs, Ralph, 376n

Right You Are If You Think You Are (Pirandello), 155, 194, 207, 216
Rise of Silas Lapham, The (Sabine), 126
Rivals, The (Sheridan), 334
Roache, Viola, 293
Roar China (Tretyakov), 248-249
Robbins, Leonard, 447
Roberts, Joan, 370, 376n
Robertson, Gladys, 209
Robeson, Paul, 196, 331, 384
Robinson, Edward G., 148n, 209, 214, 215n, 216, 244, 431
Robinson, Gladys, 431
Rochester American Opera Company, 225
Rodeo, 371
Rodgers, Richard, 154, 193, 205, 310, 322, 350, 368-371, 373, 375, 377, 379, 383, 390, 391, 392, 393, 422, 440
Roeder, Ralph, 92
Roege, Estelle, 105-107, 122, 147, 149, 172, 181, 183, 200, 203
Rogers, Edward S., 350
Rogers, Will, 284
Rolland, Romain, 244
Romains, Jules, 307
Romance, 314
Roosevelt, Franklin D., 261, 355-356
Roosevelt, Mrs. Franklin D., 377
Roosevelt and Hopkins (Sherwood), 355
Rose, Billy, 329
Rosebury, Lord, 10
Rosenberg, James N., 146
Rosing, Vladimir, 225
Ross, Harold, 160
Rostand, Edmond, 447
Royal, John, 435
Ruben, José, 101, 102
Ruskin, John, 26
Russian People, The (Simonov), 338-339
Ryder (Barnes), 110
Ruth, George Herman (Babe), 406
Rutherford, Margaret, 427

Sabine, Lillian, 126
Sacco and Vanzetti case, 186
St. James Theatre, London, 289
St. James Theatre, New York, 377, 393
Saint Joan (Shaw), 134, 174-183, 406, 411, 413, 418, 441
Sanderson, Julia, 210
Sanford, Erskine, 214
Sanger, Margaret, 79

Saqui and Lawrence, 3
Saroyan, William, 320-326, 401, 440
Saturday Evening Post, 29
Saturday Night Soap Company, The, 347n
Savo, Jimmy, 314
Savoir, Alfred, 253
Schenk, Joseph, 74
Scherman, Harry, 71
Schildkraut, Joseph, 154, 162-163
Schildkraut, Rudolph, 162
Schlosser, Herman, 31
Schmidt, Walter A., 350
Schnitzler, Arthur, 82, 447
Scholz, Wilhelm von, 163
School for Husbands, The, 5, 301, 302, 371
School for Scandal, The, 313
Schulgen, G. F. F., 362-363
Schwab, Charles, 87
Schwarzwald, Eugenie, 146-147
Scott, Howard, 70
Scott, Zachary, 313
Scotti, Antonio, 35
Sea-Gull (Chekhov), 100, 103, 171
Sea Island, Georgia, 281-282, 285
Seattle University Theatre, 445
Second Man, The (Behrman), 216, 219-220
Second Threshold (Barry), 389
Segal, Vivienne, 210
Seldes, Gilbert, 71
Seligsohn, Arnold, 353
Selwart, Tonio, 303
Sergava, Katherine, 376n
Seven Keys to Baldpate, The, 226
Shakespeare, William, 16, 20, 21, 22, 57-58, 76, 180, 196, 243, 257, 298, 320, 329-330, 331, 335, 384, 387, 389, 393, 415, 423, 427, 430, 432, 433, 434, 437, 438
Shakespeare Acting Company, 393
Shakespeare Festival Theatre, 449
Shakespeare Memorial Theatre, 437
Shannon, Effie, 131, 132
Sharaff, Irene, 352
Shaw, Charlotte (Mrs. George Bernard), 133-134, 139-140, 174-177, 180, 186, 189-190, 212-213, 289, 294-295
Shaw, George Bernard, 26, 45, 59, 82, 103, 123, 127, 128-129, 130-141, 142, 143, 146, 163-164, 174-191, 212-213, 221, 288-295, 394, 410-424, 430, 435, 443, 447
    Apple Cart, The, 184, 289-290

Arms and the Man, 213-214, 221, 222, 420
Back to Methuselah, 132-141, 174-175, 178, 292
Buoyant Billions, 416
Caesar and Cleopatra, 185
Candida, 184, 424
Devils' Disciple, The, 131, 419, 420, 421
Doctor's Dilemma, The, 134, 222, 424, 437
Fanny's First Play, 294
Geneva, 293-294
Getting Married, 131
Great Catherine, The, 435
Heartbreak House, 127-131, 184, 419
In the Beginning, 138
In the Days of Good King Charles, 413
Jitta's Atonement, 141, 185-186
Joan of Lorraine, 418
Major Barbara, 243
Man and Superman, 307, 414, 419
Millionairess, The, 294, 411, 423
Pygmalion, 215-216, 410
Quintessence of Ibsenism, 288
Saint Joan, 134, 174-183, 406, 411, 413, 418, 441
Too True to Be Good, 290, 293
Simpleton of the Unexpected Isles, The, 184, 256, 293
Tragedy of the Elderly Gentleman, The, 138-139
You Never Can Tell, 294, 420-421
Shaw, Irwin, 251
Shay, Frank, 71, 77
Sheffield, Justus, 71, 120, 124
Shepherd in the Distance (Hudson), 98
Sheridan, Richard Brinsley, 334
Sherman Anti-Trust law, 351
Sherwood, Robert, 142, 159, 160, 193, 253-254, 256, 264, 265-266, 268, 326-328, 355, 440, 441
Shields, Arthur, 407
Show Boat, 376
Shubert, Lee, 45, 100, 104, 141, 157, 185, 260-261, 305, 370
Shubert Theatre, 268, 319
Shumlin, Herman, 268
Sidney, Basil, 238
Sidney, Sylvia, 225
Sil-Vara, 222, 243
Silver Cord, The (Howard), 216, 218, 222
Silver Whistler, The (McEnroe), 447
Simon, Bob, 302

Simonov, Konstantin, 338, 340
Simonson, Lee, 102, 118, 120, 121, 125, 126, 132, 138, 162, 178, 210, 218, 248, 252, 263, 336-337
Simpleton of the Unexpected Isles, The (Shaw), 184, 256, 293
Sinclair, Bob, 336
Sinclair, Upton, 69
Sing Out, Sweet Land (Kerr), 386
Singer Building, 66, 73-74
Sirovitch, Dr. William, 349-350
Skin of Our Teeth, The (Wilder), 314
Skinner, Otis, 314
Skinner, Richard, 309
Sleeping Beauty, The, 8
Sloan, Alfred, 53
Sloan, John, 46
Sloan Kettering Cancer Foundation, 53
Smallens, Alexander, 265
Smart Set, 102
Smith, Duclie, 264n
Smith, Joseph, 348
Smith, Mark, 430n
Smith, Rex, 167
Smith, T. R., 197, 198, 199-200
Snow Goose, The (Gallico), 411
Sobol, Edward, 435n
Socialist Press Club, 45, 92, 93
Soldene, Emily, 35-36
Sondergaard, Gale, 243
Soudeykin, Sergei, 169, 265
South Pacific, 369
Soviet Russia, 130
Spaeth, Robert, 271-272
Spaeth, Sigmund, 297
Sparre, Fin, 358
Spencer, Mrs. Vivian, 370
Spoon River Anthology (Masters), 82
Squire, Ronald, 425, 426
Stage Door (Ferber and Kaufman), 435n
Stage Door Canteen, Washington, 331, 365
Stage Magazine, 21, 224
Stagehands' Union, 300-301
Stanislavsky, Constantin, 6, 57, 130, 167-171, 444, 449, 449n
Starbuck, Betty, 204
Stearns, Harold, 71, 192
Stebbins, Rowland, 302, 303
Steffens, Lincoln, 71
Stehli, Edgar, 214
Steinach, Dr. E., 134
Stern, Benjamin, 130-131
Stevens, Doris, 205
Stevens, Emily, 164
Stevens, Harold, 172

Stevens, Onslow, 307
Stevens, Langner, Parry and Rollinson, 172
Stevenson, Robert Louis, 10
Stockwell, Harry, 378n
Stoddard, Haila, 307
Straight, Mrs. Willard, 118
Strange Interlude (O'Neill), 217, 228-242, 277, 278, 289, 400, 430, 441
Strasberg, Lee, 250
Strathcona, Sir Donald, 39
Straw, The (O'Neill), 229
Streetcar Named Desire (Williams), 324, 332, 333, 393
Streets of New York, The (Boucicault), 297-298, 299-301
Strindberg, Johann August, 82, 288, 447
Strunsky, Anna, 69
Strunsky, Simeon, 69
Studebaker Theatre, Chicago, 221
Suffrage Parade, 47
Sulzberger, Arthur, 348
Summerville, Amelia, 121, 122
Suppressed Desires (Glaspell and Cook), 92, 103
Suzanna and the Elders (Marshall and Langner), 294, 307-308
Swan, Joseph, 370
Swan, The (Molnar), 153
Swansea, South Wales, 1-11
Swarthout, Gladys, 310
Swope, Herbert Bayard, 237
Szold, Bernadine, 55

Taming of the Shrew (Shakespeare), 21, 257, 264n, 327-328, 395
Tangerine (Langner), 209-210
Tanguay, Eva, 74
Tao House, 399, 400, 401
Tarkington, Booth, 394
Tate Galleries, 26
Taylor, George, 31-33, 37, 208
Taylor, Laurette, 308, 314
Tempest, The (Shakespeare), 196
Temple of Pallas-Athenae, The (Lewys), 276
Terry, Ellen, 19, 20, 22, 248-249, 330
Theatre Guild:
  Acting Company, 214-227, 243, 250, 251, 258, 316
  Alternating Repertory System, 214-227, 243-244, 400
  Board of Managers, 115, 120, 125, 158, 160-161, 170, 250-251, 268, 273-274, 320
  founding of, 115-129

Theatre Guild—*Continued*
    Guild Theatre, 190, 211-226, 268-269, 284, 291, 370, 371, 386
    policies, 116, 117-118
    Production committees, 158, 248, 273-274
    reorganization, 336-337
    school, 224-227
    subscription, 217, 223, 257, 261-262
Theatre Guild, The First Ten Years (Eaton), 103n, 227
Theatre Guild-American Theatre Society, 262, 448
Theatre Guild Magazine, The, 223-224
"Theatre Guild on the Air," 204, 429
Theatre Guild Quarterly, The, 223
Theatre Magazine, 223
Theatre Royal, 381, 393
There Shall Be No Night (Sherwood), 328-329
These Days (Clugston), 316
These Modern Women (Langner), 183
They Knew What They Wanted (Howard), 166, 387
Thomas, Senator, 361
Thompson, Daisy, 92
Thompson, Paul, 70
Throckmorton, Cleon, 297
"Ticket Code," 260
Tidings Brought to Mary, The (Claudel), 203
Tidman, Arthur, 23, 24, 26
Tietjens, Eunice, 82
Time of Your Life, The (Saroyan), 321-324, 326, 401
Times Square Theatre, 297
Tinlot, Gustav, 108
Tirpitz, Admiral von, 25
Tolstoy, Count Aleksei Nikolaevich, 59, 127
Tone, Franchot, 329
Too True to Be Good (Shaw), 290, 293
Topham, Frederick, 18, 19-20
Touch of the Poet, A (O'Neill), 286, 403, 409
Tovarich, 314
Tragedy of the Elderly Gentleman, The (Shaw), 138-139
Trammell, Niles, 435
Traubel, Horace, 69
Travers, Henry, 148n, 155, 214, 247
Treadwell, Sophie, 335
Treasure, The (Pinski), 127
Trebitsch (Austrian playwright), 185
Trifles (Glaspell), 103
Troubetzkoy, Prince Paul, 188-190
Tschappat, General, 359n

Tucker, Dudley, 92
Tucker, Elise, 38-39
Turgenev, Ivan, 245-246
Tuttle, Day, 309
Twelfth Night (Shakespeare), 22, 329-330, 331, 335
Twentieth Century Fox, 49
Twenty Thousand Leagues Under the Sea (Verne), 25
Two Blind Beggars and One Less Blind (Moeller), 97
Tyler, George, 330

Ulric, Lenore, 198
United Booking Office, 261
United Engineering Company, 344
United States Patent Office, 345, 351
United States Steel Corporation, 49-51, 429

Vajda, Ernest, 164
Valley Forge (Anderson), 263
Vandervell, C. A., 86-87
Van Druten, John, 428, 440
Van Patten, Richard, 395
Van Vechten, Carl, 160, 193, 195-197, 220-221, 290
van Volkenburg, Ellen, 82-83
Vanity Fair (magazine), 85, 237
Veblen, Thorsten, 158
Velie, Jay, 392n
Verne, Jules, 25
Versailles, Treaty of, 344-345
Victor, Eric, 372
Victoria, Queen, 6, 35-36
Victoria Regina, 329
Vie, Murvyn, 392n
Volksbühne Theater, 58, 127
Volpone, 222
Vonnegut, Marjorie, 102
Vorse, Mary Heaton, 70

Wade, Warren, 435
Waiting for Lefty (Odets), 263
Walker, June, 301, 302
Wallace, Henry, 365
Walling, William English, 69
Wanger, Walter, 124, 247
Waram, Percy, 243
Warner Brothers, 436
Washington Square Book Shop, 75, 199
Washington Square Players, 24, 44, 65, 67, 76-77, 90-104, 105, 109, 113, 115, 119, 228-229, 439, 441, 444
Wasserman, Jacob, 147
Waters, Ethel, 196
Watkins, Linda, 225

Watson, Betty Jane, 378n, 380n
Watson, Thomas J., 54
Way of the World, The (Congreve), 306
Wayne, David, 435
Webster, Margaret, 330, 332, 384
Weidman, Charles, 5, 302
Weinberger, Harry, 71
Welded (O'Neill), 230
Wells, H. G., 26
Welles, Orson, 269-273
Welsh, Mary, 407
Wenderroth, E. F., 172
Werfel, Franz, 147-148, 215, 384, 385, 386, 447
Wertheim, Maurice, 106, 122-123, 124, 158, 185, 212-213, 230, 233, 235, 248, 249, 337
Wertheimer, Herbert, 87
West, Rebecca, 197
West London Parliament, 31, 123
Westcott, Glenway, 55, 192
Westcross, South Wales, 7, 8
Western Union Telegraph Company, 259
Westley, Helen, 21, 72, 92, 93-94, 96, 114-116, 120, 121, 148n, 155, 162, 166, 196, 213, 214, 220-221, 241n, 253, 254, 257, 258, 263, 336-337
Westley, Jack, 93
Westport Country Playhouse, 173, 204, 251-252, 269, 294, 296-315, 423, 442, 447-448
What Every Woman Knows (Barrie), 311
What the Public Wants (Bennett), 144
White, Alfred E., 28, 29, 56, 172
White, Hervey, 107, 108
White, Miles, 371, 373
White, Walter, 196
White, William Wallace, 344
White, Langner, Stevens and Parry, 172
Whitman, Walt, 69
Whorf, Richard, 257, 327, 328
Whyte, Jeannette, 380
Whyte, Jerome, 371, 378, 380, 382
Wilde, Oscar, 70, 427, 428
Wilder, Thornton, 314, 435, 440
Wilkinson, Norman, 76
Willever, J. C., 259
Williams, Hope, 290
Williams, Lynn, 346n
Williams, Tennessee, 324, 331-333, 340

Wilson, John C., 309-310, 311, 312, 313, 314, 387, 388, 427
Wilson, Natasha, 309
Wilson, Woodrow, 344
Wiman, Dwight, 202, 302
Windheim, Marek, 380n
Windsor, Duke and Duchess of, 377
Windust, Bretaigne, 327
Wine of Choice (Behrman), 266-268
Wine Street Theatre, 5
Wings over Europe (Browne and Nichols), 83, 241, 243, 290, 429
Winnie the Pooh (Milne), 146
Winslow Boy, The (Rattigan), 427
Winter's Tale, The (Shakespeare), 21, 329-330, 393
Without Love (Barry), 336, 337
Wolfe, Elsie de, 202
Wolfe, Thomas, 158-159
Wolff, John, 432
Wong, Anna May, 306
Wood, Peggy, 424
Wood, Walter, 359n
Woodstock, New York, 107, 195
Woollcott, Alexander, 98, 157, 160, 164, 213, 220, 237, 266-267
Woolsey, Judge, 276
World's Illusion, The (Wasserman), 147
Would-be Gentleman (Molière), 314
Wright, Cuthbert, 76-77, 93
Wright, Frank Lloyd, 84
Wright, Orville, 343, 358
Wyatt, Jane, 301, 313
Wycherly, Margaret, 138
Wylie, Elinor, 197

Yeats, Jack, 45-46
Yeats, William Butler, 45
Yellow Jacket, The, 314
Yesterday's Magic, 370
Yost, Herbert, 148n
You Never Can Tell (Shaw), 294, 420-421
Young, Art, 71, 106
Young, Roland, 98, 99, 102
Young, Stark, 154
Yurka, Blanche, 148n

Zaharoff, Sir Basil, 30
Zeder, Frederick, 358
Zilboorg, Gregory, 161-162
Zweig, Stefan, 222, 273

The Mermaid

EDWIN L. HOWARD ARH.

Proposed Shakespeare Festival Theatre and Academy
Westport, Connecticut